BOTTOM LINE'S
MONEY SAVERS

LIVE LIKE A MILLIONAIRE ON JUST A LITTLE BIT OF MONEY

Bottom Line
Books

www.BottomLineSecrets.com

Contents

9 • SAVE ON HIGH-QUALITY HEALTH CARE

10 • HEALTH SECRETS AND MONEY SAVERS

11 • GET FIT FOR LESS

12 • TAX-SAVING STRATEGIES

13 • INVESTING: MONEY MAKERS, MONEY SAVERS

14 • MONEY SAVERS FOR YOUR RETIREMENT

15 • ESTATE PLANNING HELPERS

Preface

We are pleased that you've purchased our new book, *Bottom Line's Money Savers: Live Like a Millionaire on Just a Little Bit of Money*. We trust that you will find many helpful ideas and money-saving solutions for everyone in your family.

At Bottom Line Books and Bottom Line Publications, we aim to provide readers with the best information to help them gain greater wealth, better health, more wisdom, extra time and increased happiness.

When you choose a Bottom Line Book, you are turning to a stellar group of experts in fields that range from banking, investing, taxes, estate planning, insurance, real estate and health care to cars, computers, security, travel and self-improvement. Whether they specialize in the economy, consumer-health advocacy, or bargain travel, Bottom Line experts are the most knowledgeable and innovative people in the country.

How do we find these top-notch professionals? Over the past 28 years, our editors have built a network of literally thousands of expert sources. We regularly talk to our advisors affiliated with the premier financial institutions, law firms, universities and hospitals. Our sources include entrepreneurs, scientists, acclaimed authors, researchers, master craftspeople, nutritionists and chefs.

In *Bottom Line's Money Savers*, you will find the latest wisdom from many of these foremost experts contained in hundreds of carefully researched, up-to-date articles.

We are confident that the information in this volume can help you and your family enjoy a wealthier, wiser and healthier life.

The Editors
Bottom Line Books
Stamford, CT

1

Strategies for Super Savings

Penny-Pincher Shows You How to Slash Monthly Bills

People tell me that they cannot save enough money even when they cut back on luxuries. My solution? Cut recurring *base costs*. Most people can decrease so-called fixed costs by 10% and still live well. That means a family of four living on $90,000 a year should be able to save $9,000—or $750 a month. *Here's what you can do...*

SAVE ON CELL PHONE CHARGES

•**Contain cell phone costs with a prepaid phone.**

My favorite: Virgin Mobile (888-322-1122, *www.virginmobileusa.com*), which is popular in Europe. The phone can be very inexpensive after discounts and rebates at selected retail stores, such as Best Buy. You pay for minutes in advance and talk until your time runs out.

Calls cost 10 cents* per minute to/from other Virgin Mobile phone numbers and 20 cents* per minute to everyone else.

•**Lower your monthly rates.** Almost 40% of my listeners are unhappy with their cell phone service, mostly because it's too expensive.

To find the most economical plans in your area, compare prices at sites such as *www. getconnected.com...www.letstalk.com...www. myrateplan.com...*and *www.point.com.*

Important: Before signing a new contract, request a 30-day trial period for new phone service. Then rigorously test the service from key locations at peak use times.

SAVE ON ELECTRICITY

•**Ask your utility company about "time of day" energy programs.** You will be charged less for energy use during off-peak hours.

*All prices are subject to change.

Clark Howard, a self-made millionaire and host of *The Clark Howard Show*, an Atlanta-based consumer-advice radio show syndicated on 150 radio stations around the country. He is author of *Get Clark Smart*. Hyperion.

Example: Washington State residents pay 31 cents* per kilowatt-hour (kWh) between the hours of 7 am and 7 pm, but just four cents per kWh at all other times.

●**Inquire about any "power credit" programs.** These plans let the utility company control the amount of power used by your home's air-conditioning system. In return, you get a sign-up credit (typically $20) and save as much as $40 per month.

Example: In Georgia, the power company installs a switch on the outside of your home that connects to your central air-conditioning unit. At peak times (weekdays between noon and 7 pm), the power company controls your air conditioner and reduces the length of time it runs. You get a rebate of $2 each time it activates the switch. The change to your home's temperature is only a few degrees.

●**Ask your power company if it offers senior discounts** if you're age 50 or older and if it allows you to budget your payments with a preset monthly amount.

HALVE YOUR INTERNET SERVICE BILL

Get rid of your mainstream Internet service provider (ISP). At $20 or more per month, ISPs like EarthLink and MSN are up to four times as expensive as other ISPs.

Better: For $9.95 a month, *www.walmart.com* offers unlimited Internet access through NetZero (*www.netzero.com*).

REFINANCE YOUR MORTGAGE

It is not too late. Over the past several years, mortgage companies made a killing as so many Americans refinanced. Now the pool of people refinancing is smaller, so lenders have had to knock down their prices. The spread between the interest rates that mortgage lenders get and what they charge customers has decreased by one-half point. *It might pay to refinance if...*

●**You can shave at least one-half point off your current interest rate.**

●**You have an adjustable-rate mortgage.** Refinance to a fixed rate if you plan to be in

*All prices are subject to change.

the home for more than 18 months. Otherwise, the closing costs (generally $2,000 to $2,500) may outweigh savings. Check the rates at *www.bankrate.com* and *www.moving.com*.

Secret: Most airlines have formed marketing alliances with mortgage lenders. So, the higher your closing costs, the more miles you will get. Alliances generally aren't advertised—be sure to ask your credit card or mortgage company.

SAVE ON LONG-DISTANCE CALLS

Use your computer and/or calling cards. *My favorite computer-call offer now...*

●*www.net2phone.com* charges $24 per month* for unlimited calls from your PC to any phone in the US. Special software routes calls over the Internet and onto standard phone lines.

The minimum requirements: A broadband internet connection such as a cable modem, DSL or FIOS with a minimum speed of 150 kbps.

Other good calling-card offers...

●**Costco/Verizon card gives you 700 minutes for $19.99.** That is 2.86 cents per minute. Go to *www.costco.com* and click on "Services."

●**Sam's Club/AT&T card offers a 1000-minute card for $34.70**...or a seven-pack of 120-minute cards for $29.15, which charges 3.47 cents per minute for domestic calls. Go to *www.samsclub.com*. Search for "Prepaid Phone Cards."

●*www.callwave.com* is Internet answering-machine software that records incoming calls. It lets you use one phone line to surf the Internet and receive calls.

Cost: As little as $7.95 per month with a 30-day free trial.

FREE DIRECTORY ASSISTANCE

The phone company will typically charge $1 per request. Besides the phone book, the very same information is also free at *www.411.com*...*www.anywho.com*...*http://people.yahoo.com*...and *www.whitepages.com*. You can often get e-mail addresses and maps with driving directions at these sites.

*All prices are subject to change.

Single-Use Digital Cameras Aren't Worth the Money

In addition to the $15 to $20 purchase price, you pay nearly four times the cost for printing as for pictures taken with a regular digital camera and picture quality is poor. Single-use cameras have only two-megapixel resolution and uneven flash capability.

Consumer Reports, 101 Truman Ave., Yonkers, New York 10703.

Best Digital Video Camcorders for Your Money

Name-brand digital video camcorders are selling for as little as $350. These compact models come with such features as optical stabilization, in which the lens compensates for shaky hands…low-light capability…better color technology…and still-image resolution that is good enough to produce casual snapshots. Top choices include Sony DCR-HC42 Handycam and JVC GR-DF550US.

PCWorld.com, 501 Second St., San Francisco 94107.

Best Time to Buy Electronics

Retailers clear out inventory to make room for newly upgraded electronics equipment in January and June. Prices of older models typically fall by 10% or more.

Caution: Before buying, find out what new features are about to come to market. If they are ones you care about, purchasing an older model may not be a bargain after all.

Money, Time-Life Bldg., Rockefeller Center, New York City 10020.

How to Sell Unneeded Jewelry for the Best Prices

Nancy Stacy, who has spent 28 years in the jewelry business, first as a jewelry store owner in Morro Bay, California, and currently as a Master Gemologist Appraiser based in Walnut Creek, California. She is the owner of Contra Costa Gem Lab, a certified gem appraisal laboratory. *www.jewelry-appraisal.com.*

This may be a good time to sell old jewelry that you don't really wear anymore and that may be worth more in cash than in sentimental value. Gold recently traded at $735 an ounce—nearly double its price five years ago—and has been as high as $1,011 this year. Diamond prices have also soared.

Before you decide whether to sell a piece of jewelry, you need to know how much it's really worth. The best way to do that is to hire an independent appraiser who specializes in jewelry, ideally one accredited by the American Society of Appraisers. You can search for one on the group's Web site, *www.appraisers.org.*

Also check Pricescope.com, which includes diamond price comparisons and forums where previous clients of particular appraisers may have posted useful comments about them.

Appraisers charge $75 to $300 per hour, depending on their experience and region. An appraisal of a one-carat diamond ring might take 30 minutes. The appraiser should be able to provide a rough estimate of his/her charge before the appraisal. An appraisal might not be worthwhile if you are quite certain that the jewelry is not worth more than a few hundred dollars.

Helpful: Clean your jewelry before you bring it to the appraiser. Otherwise, the appraiser will likely have to clean it—at his/her hourly rate. Improper cleaning can damage jewelry, so refer to the jewelry cleaning instructions on my Web site, *www.jewelry-appraisal. com* (click "Jewelry Information").

Tell your appraiser that you intend to sell this jewelry. Request a written "quality assessment" that does not include an estimate of the value *and* a separate estimate of the jewelry's marketable cash value (the amount it would likely fetch if you sold it). Show the quality assessment to potential buyers without the value estimate. Many jewelry buyers assume that an appraiser's value estimate is an inflated retail or insurance value and so will offer much less.

Caution: Don't depend on free appraisals offered at jewelry stores or in urban jewelry districts. These appraisers might be unqualified or might quote lowball prices in hopes of buying your jewelry for less than it is worth. The reputation of the jewelry's designer…the quality of the workmanship…and the cut, clarity and color of the stones all might affect value dramatically in ways that an inexperienced appraiser might not understand.

WHERE TO SELL

Your appraiser should be able to recommend appropriate places to sell your jewelry. *Possibilities…*

●**Auction houses.** An auction house will give the seller about 70% to 80% of the winning bid and charge the *buyer* a 20% fee. This is a good way to sell higher-end jewelry. To find an auction house, visit *www.artfact.com.*

●**Consignment stores.** These often are the best places to sell used jewelry, but they do not pay until it sells, so they are not a great option if you need quick cash or don't want to take a chance that gold prices will drop. Expect a consignment store to claim a 40% to 60% commission.

●**eBay.** The Internet auction site is an effective, low-cost way to market used jewelry to a large number of potential buyers.

Downsides: Some bidders are thieves trying to steal your jewelry…and buyers might not trust your auctions unless you have a long track record on eBay. Consider hiring an eBay "trading assistant"—an independent eBay seller experienced in jewelry sales—to sell your items for you for a fee. (Visit *www.ebay tradingassistant.com.*)

●**Estate dealers.** Estate dealers buy jewelry and other items, often in large lots. In most regions, there are at least a few listed in the local phone book. Do not approach estate dealers until your jewelry has been appraised. An appraiser should be able to point you toward your area's estate dealers who are trustworthy.

HOW TO SELL "SCRAP"

If your gold jewelry does not carry the trademark of a high-end retailer or a designer whose work is respected and sought after by collectors…is not antique…does not contain gemstones…is in poor condition…or is prominently monogrammed, it likely is worth more melted down for its precious metal content than as jewelry. Call jewelry stores and ask if they buy scrap gold, and how much they pay. The scrap value minus 15% is generally a good deal.

How One Woman Saved $65 in Minutes

Marjory Abrams, publisher, newsletters, Boardroom Inc., 281 Tresser Blvd., Stamford, Connecticut 06901.

I f you think reviewing your bills is a thankless chore—think again. Recent errors a colleague caught on her phone bills…

●**Charges from her old long-distance provider** after she had switched ($42.88).

●**A $20 switching fee** that she wasn't supposed to pay.

●**A $2 charge for an international call option** that she didn't elect.

●**And…a federal excise surcharge tax** ($0.42) was charged twice.

Gary Schatsky, Esq., president of a financial advisory firm in New York City and Florida says not reviewing your bills is a missed opportunity. *Examples…*

Cell phones: People who consistently exceed the free-minute allotment on their wireless phone plans should ask their service providers if another plan would save them money. You may be able to change your plan retroactively—rescinding charges from the previous month. This once saved me $500.

Tax bills: If the IRS sends a notice that you underpaid taxes, penalties may be waived even if the assessment is valid. Ask your accountant.

Hospital bills: These are particularly error-ridden. Patients pay an estimated average of

$1,300 in overcharges per year, so always ask for an itemized statement.

Health insurance: If a claim is rejected by your health insurer, find out why. It may be a simple error. Fight any "no." If you expect a battle, consider consulting a professional.

Resource: Patient Advocate Foundation at 800-532-5274 or *www.patientadvocate.org*.

Credit card bills: Occasionally a vendor puts through a charge twice—and not necessarily in the same billing cycle. I once had a $704 charge posted in December and reposted in February. Compare receipts to monthly statements.

Magnificent Money Savers For Folks Over 50

Linda Bowman, Tucson–based professional bargain hunter. She is author of several books, including *Free Stuff & Good Deals for Folks Over 50, Free Stuff & Good Deals for Your Pet* and *Free Stuff & Good Deals on the Internet*. Santa Monica Press.

Do the words "senior discount" conjure an image of old folks lining up for the early bird special? Things have changed! Mature adults' opportunities to save are now so abundant that I wrote an entire book describing thousands of them—and had to update it only two years later.

Just look around. *You'll find freebies and discounts available almost everywhere…*

●**Museums.** By proclaiming your senior status, you'll save 50 cents* (off $3 admission) at the Paul Revere House in Boston (*www.paul reverehouse.org*)…$5 (off $10) at the Museum of Contemporary Art San Diego in La Jolla, CA (*www.mcasd.org*)…and $3 (off $18) at the Solomon R. Guggenheim Museum in New York City (*www.guggenheim.org*).

●**Sports.** Ask the public relations department of a local stadium, auditorium or arena (or the office of teams that play there) about individual or group senior discounts, year-round discount

*All prices are subject to change.

cards, special membership opportunities or senior citizen days.

Caveats: Many offers have restrictions.

Always carry your driver's license, passport, resident alien card, Medicare card or membership card in an over-50 group, such as AARP (formerly called the American Association of Retired Persons), as proof that you deserve a break despite your youthful appearance.

You must speak up. No one will say, "You look old enough." Would you want them to?

WHO'S A SENIOR?

"Senior citizen" once meant "Medicare recipient." Now, the lower limit of "senior" may be as young as age 50.

Some folks just passing 50 or 55 say they're embarrassed to request a discount. I ask them, "Do you want to save money or do you want to save face?"

I'm 56. My husband is 57. Thrift is a way of life for us. We seldom pay retail for anything. Although we're new to senior discounts, we try to remember to ask for them. And we celebrate our victories.

If you quail at the word "senior," consider this—AARP is the largest organization for seniors in the country. (*Membership cost:* $12.50*/year.) When I make a reservation for anything—plane, train, car, bus or hotel—I ask, "Do you have an AARP discount?" (I got a reduced price that way for a bed-and-breakfast in Sedona, AZ.) State your eligibility to join and you may not even have to be a member.

Failing that, I ask about discounts for automobile club members (i.e., AAA, *www.aaa.com*).

Note: AARP also lists best Web sites for people age 50 and older at *www.aarp.org/internet resources.*

LOOK FOR HIDDEN DISCOUNTS

Ferret out discounts everywhere. At a mall, visit the customer service kiosk and ask which of the stores are offering coupons or senior discounts. When you visit your hair salon, shoe repair shop, hardware store or dry cleaner, say, "I'm a senior. May I get 10% off my bill?"

If your request is declined, ask to speak to the owner and suggest creating such discounts.

*All prices are subject to change.

Mature adults reward providers of dependable service by returning again and again.

Resort and retirement areas in places such as Tucson, where I live, are swarming with age-50-plus visitors and residents. Attracting our business is good business.

Occasionally, I hear a radio spot advertising 5% off purchases by seniors at a chain of local grocery stores. Yet I've never seen such a sign in the store.

Some local taxi companies sell senior citizen discount coupons. Even your local gas station may have senior days.

Ask your state Office on Aging (listed in the blue pages of your phone book) for a membership card that will give you discounts at participating establishments.

In some areas of the country, companies that offer senior discounts display a special symbol on their ads in the Yellow Pages.

TRAVEL

Cruises, walking tours and other trips often have senior discounts…

●**Airlines.** Carriers offering senior fares—America West Airlines (age 65 and up), 800-428-4322 or *www.usairways.com/awa*, and Southwest Airlines (age 65 and up), 800-435-9792 or *www.southwest.com.*

●**Trains.** On some Amtrak trains (800-872-7245, *www.amtrak.com*), you'll get a 15% discount after you turn 62.

●**National Parks.** At 62, you can purchase an America the Beautiful-National Parks and Federal Recreational Land Pass for $10* at any National Park Service facility that charges an entrance fee. This lifetime pass to national parks, monuments, historic sites, recreation areas and wildlife refuges will also admit any accompanying passengers in a private vehicle, if the park has a per vehicle entrance fee. The pass will admit you, your spouse and your children, if the park charges a per person entrance fee.

Note: You must be a citizen or permanent resident of the US.

●**Hotels.** Hotel chains want your business. Many provide senior rates, but ask about other rates. A promotion that is available to the general public can cost less than the senior discount.

*All prices are subject to change.

●**International travel.** ElderTreks (800-741-7956, *www.eldertreks.com*), based in Toronto, will take small groups of people ages 50 and up on safaris to Antarctica, Europe and more. Your Man Tours in Inglewood, CA (800-922-9000, *www.ymtvacations.com*), is among the least expensive of the travel companies specializing in senior travel.

EDUCATION

For 30 years, the not-for-profit, Boston-based Elderhostel (800-454-5768, *www.elderhostel.org*) has offered low-cost, high-quality learning experiences. Last year, more than 170,000 people age 55 and over took part in programs throughout the US and in more than 90 other countries. Scholarships are available.

The North Carolina Center for Creative Retirement (828-251-6140, *www.unca.edu/ncccr*), established in 1988 by the University of North Carolina at Asheville, sponsors a College for Seniors, Creative Retirement Exploration Weekends and the Un-Retirement Option for those who are still working but are ready to plan their retirement.

Many colleges and universities will let seniors audit classes for nominal fees, sometimes with a meal plan. Campus housing is usually available only in the summer.

Age requirements vary: For example, a "senior" at the University of Vermont (800-639-3210, *www.learn.uvm.edu*) is 50-plus (and must also be a Vermont resident).

At some state schools, participants must be state residents. Schools allowing seniors from anywhere to audit courses free or at minimal cost include the Universities of Connecticut, Illinois and Massachusetts.

You Still Have Rights When You Buy "As Is"

Buying "as is" doesn't mean the buyer has no rights at all. "As is" clauses relate to quality, not to general class or description.

Example: If the buyer contracts to buy boxes of bolts as is, sight unseen, he or she won't be obligated if the boxes turn out to contain screws, not bolts.

Also, "as is" clauses don't override express warranties. They don't bar claims of fraud or misrepresentation. And they don't stop tort claims (personal injury actions if someone is injured by a defective product).

The late Dr. Russell Decker, professor emeritus of legal studies, Bowling Green State University, Bowling Green, OH.

Complain Your Way to Better Deals

Americans are not great defenders of their consumer rights. Two-thirds of the respondents in a major survey admitted to living with shoddy goods, incompetent services and broken promises. Only one-third of them had asked for redress.

People *should* complain. More than half of all consumer complaints result in some sort of satisfaction. (The psychological lift that comes with filing a protest is an added bonus.)

People don't complain because they think it won't do any good. *But there are effective ways to complain and get results…*

● **Have your facts straight before you act.** Be clear about dates, prices, payments and the exact nature of the problem.

● **Be specific about what you want done** —repair, replacement or refund.

● **Give reasonable deadlines for action you expect to be taken,** such as a week for store personnel to look into a problem. Deadlines move the action along.

● **Send copies of receipts.** Keep the originals for your records. File copies of all correspondence and notes (with dates) on any telephone dealings. Those records may be the pivotal factor if negotiations are prolonged or you must take your complaint elsewhere.

● **Be businesslike in your attitude** and project an expectation of a businesslike response.

● **Find out where you can go if the seller fails to make good,** and indicate your intention to follow through. Government agencies, such as a state attorney general's office, may need the very kind of evidence that your case provides to move against chronic offenders. Licensing boards or regulatory bodies are good bets for complaints against banks, insurance companies or professionals.

Additional recourse…

● **Consumer-action centers** sponsored by local newspapers and radio and television stations often get swift results.

● **Small-claims court.** If you can put a monetary value on your loss, you may get a judgment by suing in small-claims court. Collecting can be a problem (you must take the initiative yourself), but the law is on your side and the psychological benefits are enormous.

● **Trade associations** can be effective with their member organizations but not with outside companies.

Protect yourself before making large purchases or contracting for expensive services by dealing with reputable sellers. Companies that have been in business a long time have a vested interest in keeping their customers happy. Think about what recourse you will have if something does go wrong. A company with only a post office address, for example, will be impossible to trace.

Living the Good Life For Lots Less

Shel Horowitz, Northampton, Massachusetts–based author of the electronic book *The Penny-Pinching Hedonist,* available at the Frugal Fun Web site, *www.frugalfun.com.*

My wife and I travel, eat well and attend shows for a fraction of what others pay. *Our secrets…*

FRUGAL TRAVEL

● **Rent an apartment instead of staying in a hotel.** Furnished apartments can cost half as much. Since they have kitchens, you also save on meals. Type "furnished apartments" or "vacation rental apartments" and the name of your destination into an Internet search engine, such as *www.google.com*. Also check the "furnished apartments for rent" classified ads in the area's newspapers or through *www. onlinenewspapers.com.* Many large rental agencies will rent apartments for periods as short as one week.

● **Try Smartertravel.com.** It provides a free e-newsletter detailing last-minute bargains on hotels and airfare. It has listed great deals, such as $158 round-trip airfare from Chicago to Los Angeles and $119/night at The New York Helmsley Hotel.

● **Reserve a rental car far in advance for peak-season travel.** At some companies, you can lock in prices that are 25% to 50% below peak rates by calling at least one month before peak travel periods.

● **Visit US museums on free days.** Unlike most attractions, museums will typically waive admission fees one day a week. Inquire about free museum days at the local visitors bureau as soon as you arrive.

Example: Washington, DC's major museums are almost all free. In Chicago, at least one museum is free every weekday.

FRUGAL FUN AT HOME

● **Volunteer as an usher at concerts and plays.** Ushers will seat the audience before the show and after intermission, then help sweep up. You must arrive a little early and stay a bit late, but you are pretty much free to enjoy yourself during the performance. There often is an open seat. Promoters' names and phone numbers generally are listed on advertising posters. Call as far in advance as possible to ask if volunteer ushers are needed.

● **Take advantage of radio giveaways.** Put the station's number in your phone's memory so you can call quickly when a giveaway is announced. College stations provide the best odds since they have fewer listeners than commercial stations. I win tickets to at least five shows a year when I call stations regularly.

● **Go to the best restaurants in town**—for dessert and coffee. Even at high-end eateries, this shouldn't cost more than $10 or $15 per person. True, you won't experience everything the restaurant has to offer, but you'll get to linger and enjoy the ambience at very little cost.

Helpful: This is best done on weeknights and after 9 pm. Restaurants do not appreciate guests who arrive during peak hours and then spend little money.

● **Attend real estate showings at mansions.** You'll tour beautiful homes in the ritzy neighborhoods. Keep an eye out for high-end listings in local papers.

How to Get A Boat—Even a Yacht—On "Sale"

Nancy Dunnan, a financial adviser and author in New York City. Ms. Dunnan's latest book is titled *How to Invest $50–$5,000.* HarperCollins.

Just as with cars, a used boat is much cheaper—from 20% to 50% less than new. Also keep in mind that prices are lower in the cold weather, so try to buy before May.

Generally, but by no means always, the larger used boats are sold through yacht brokers (check with your local marina for names), while smaller boats are sold through the classifieds and "for sale" notices posted in marinas and marine-supply shops.

Compare all the prices you are quoted with those listed in the boating industry's two reliable guides, *BUC's Used Boat Price Guide* and *NADA's Marine Appraisal Guide.* Check your public library or local marina for copies or go to *www.buc.com* and *www.nadaguides.com.* NADA's site gives both the lowest retail price currently available and the average retail price …BUC's site lists some 15,000 boats for sale and provides the asking price but not the average retail price. So spend time browsing both.

Custom-Fitted Clothes at Off-the-Rack Prices

Custom-fitted clothing is available on-line for only a little more than off-the-rack clothes. Lands' End, at *www.landsend.com*, started the service, which now makes up 30% of its sales of jeans and chinos.

Robert Holloway, CEO of Archetype Solutions, developer of the software used by on-line retailers for custom-made clothing, Emeryville, California.

Discounts Just for The Military

The Veterans Advantage program offers veterans and those in the military, National Guard and Reserves—and their families—up to 70% off hotel rooms, 25% off car rentals, 25% off Airborne Express, 10% off Dell computers and 65% off prescription drugs. The program also offers 15% Everyday Savings on Amtrak plus discounts at theme parks, sporting events and more. Visit *www.veteransadvantage.com* or call 866-838-2774.

Forgotten Benefits For Veterans and Their Families

Attorney David Houppert, Esq., director of the veterans benefits program for Vietnam Veterans of America (VVA), a veterans' services organization in Silver Spring, Maryland. 800-882-1316. *www.vva.org*.

Although the military is required to tell active-duty personnel about veterans' benefits before they leave military service, the amount of information is massive and the application process often is complicated.

Result: Many veterans don't take full advantage of available benefits. In fact, an estimated half million veterans are not receiving the benefits to which they are entitled.

These benefits, which are administered by the US Department of Veterans Affairs (VA), are available to eligible veterans and their dependents—spouses, children—as well as their parents. *Here's how veterans can get the benefits that they're entitled to…*

●**Service-connected disability compensation.** These monthly, nontaxable payments are based on disability incurred during or aggravated by active military service. Generally, eligibility requires that the veteran's military service was honorable. There must be evidence of the onset of disease, injury or disability during service, a current medical diagnosis and, in most cases, a connection (called a "nexus") between military service and the current disability. (There are some disabilities for which the law presumes a nexus, such as exposure to radiation or toxic agents during service.) The monthly payment amount depends on the severity of the veteran's disability and current condition.

●**Nonservice-connected disability pension** is available when the veteran's service was honorable and included at least 90 days of active duty during a period of war, and the veteran is permanently and totally disabled as a result of a nonservice-related condition. Eligibility is subject to annual household income thresholds set by the VA.

●**Other VA benefits** offered to eligible veterans include vocational rehabilitation and employment training, educational assistance, special SBA loans and business assistance, home loan guaranties, life insurance and burial benefits.

Benefits for eligible family members include payments to veterans' natural children who have certain birth defects, educational assistance and survivor's benefits.

The VA also provides health care to eligible veterans and their dependents.

●**To learn more about veterans' benefits,** check the VA Veterans Benefits Administration Web site, *www.vba.va.gov*. Click on "Compensation & Pension" under "Benefits" to find the pamphlet *Federal Benefits for Veterans &*

Dependents, which lists all available VA benefits, helpful telephone numbers and Web sites and current payment rate tables. The VA site also lists veterans' benefits available from state governments. Or call 800-827-1000 to reach your nearest VA regional office.

Helpful: Because the claims adjudication process is so complex, many veterans' service organizations (Vietnam Veterans of America, Disabled American Veterans, Veterans of Foreign Wars, American Legion, Paralyzed Veterans of America, etc.) offer help free of charge.

Ask a qualified veterans service representative to assist you with your application and/or to help you appeal a denial of benefits. You can access veterans' service organizations' Web sites for information. For a list, go to *www.va.gov/vso*.

How to Cancel Your Cell Phone Plan or Internet Service

Some companies can make it difficult for customers to discontinue their cellular phone or Internet service.

To make sure your cancellation request is not ignored: Write down the date, time, name and ID number of the representative handling your call. Use the words "cancel" and "disconnect" in your request. If your bill is paid automatically from your bank account, direct your bank in writing to no longer allow withdrawals earmarked for the company. If you continue to receive bills, write to the company. If service still is not discontinued, write to your state attorney general and public utility commission, and send a copy to the company.

Also: If you paid by credit card, dispute the charge with your credit card company.

Michael Ostheimer, attorney at the Federal Trade Commission, Bureau of Consumer Protection, Washington, DC, *www.ftc.gov*.

Get Your Very Own 800 Number

An 800 number is not just for business. Personal 800 numbers are offered by many long-distance companies. Encourage kids away at college or other family to call you by letting them call toll-free on your personal 800 phone number. You can save money, too, with rates as low as 2.9 cents* per minute for interstate long-distance calls.

Bill Hardekopf, CEO, SaveOnPhone.com, a phone service comparison Web site, Birmingham, Alabama.

How to Save 60% or More On Your Phone Bill

Lawrence Harte, president of Althos, a communications technology consulting firm in Fuquay Varina, North Carolina. He is author of more than 50 books, including *Introduction to IP Telephony: Why and How Companies Are Upgrading Private Telephone Systems to Use VoIP Services.* Althos. For more information, go to *www.althosbooks.com*.

You can save 60% or more on traditional telephone service simply by placing your calls over the Internet.

Make calls from your computer—or from a regular telephone using an adapter through your high-speed Internet connection—to any phone in the world, even a cell phone.

BETTER WAY

While it has long been possible to make calls for free between Internet-connected computers, it has never been easy. Both parties had to be logged on to the Internet at the same time. The computer's "telephone number" was its Internet address.

By subscribing to an Internet telephone service provider (ITSP), neither party needs to be on the computer at all. Calls can be made from phone to phone, and sound quality is good.

You can use the Internet for local, long-distance and international calling. You can have more than one phone on the same line. Some

*All prices are subject to change.

ITSPs even allow you to use your existing telephone number.

SETTING UP YOUR SERVICE

●**Step 1.** *Choose an ITSP…*

My favorite ITSPs now: Vonage (*www.vonage.com*, 866-243-4357) and Deltathree (*www.iconnecthere.com*).

●**Step 2.** Decide how you want to make calls. *There are two ways…*

●Analog Telephone Adapters (ATAs) allow you to connect your existing telephone directly to your high-speed Internet connection.

You plug the paperback book–size adapter into a high-speed cable modem, DSL modem or data router, then plug the phone into the adapter.

Monthly charges for ITSP service using an ATA range from $15 to $35 for unlimited domestic service. International calls generally start at about three cents per minute.

●Internet telephones plug directly into a data jack so you don't need an ATA. You can purchase the phone from the ITSP. Prices generally range from $100 to $200, although the phones are available for as little as $39 with a prepaid service agreement.

SAVINGS

Here is the savings breakdown…

●**Per-minute charges.** Most ITSPs charge 1.5 cents to four cents per minute for domestic calls…three cents to 10 cents per minute for international calls. Others charge a monthly fee for unlimited calling.

There usually are no additional charges other than your standard Internet connection fees.

Traditional domestic long-distance charges are six cents to 10 cents per minute, and international phone calls are 10 cents to several dollars per minute.

●**Taxes.** Taxes can account for 25% or more of a typical telephone bill. In contrast, Internet telephone calls are not currently taxed.

OTHER ADVANTAGES

In addition to the cost savings, making telephone calls via the Internet gives you…

●**Features such as call waiting and caller ID for free.**

●**The ability to instantly add or remove telephone lines through a Web site,** a plus if you use the phone for business.

DISADVANTAGE

As with cordless phones, if you lose electricity, you won't have telephone service.

Self-defense: Keep your mobile telephone handy, just in case.

Easy Ways to Cut Your Phone Bill

Here are two ways that you can lower your phone bill…

●**Get rid of old,** wired home phones and replace with cell phones.

Advantages: Lower cost, especially for long-distance charges, which often are much lower for cellular service—and greater convenience, since phones can be carried from room to room or when traveling.

●**When you have a high-speed Internet connection,** such as by cable or DSL, phone service often is available through it at much lower than standard rates. Some companies, such as Verizon, provide free filters that keep the signal clear and offer a 30-day money-back trial period.

Bob Carlson, editor, *Bob Carlson's Retirement Watch*, Box 970, Oxon Hill, Maryland 20750.

Talk Your Way Into Great Deals on Everything

Sharon Dunn Greene, coauthor of *The Lower East Side Shopping Guide.* Brooklyn.

The biggest problem most shoppers have with bargaining is a feeling that nice people don't do it. Before you can negotiate, you have to get over this attitude.

Some ammunition…

●**Bargaining will not turn you into a social outcast.** All a shopkeeper sees when you walk in is dollar signs. If you are willing to spend, he or she will probably be willing to make a deal. He knows that everybody is trying to save money these days.

●**Bargaining is a business transaction.** You are not trying to cheat the merchant or get something for nothing. You are trying to agree on a fair price. You expect to negotiate for a house or a car—why not for a refrigerator or a winter coat?

●**You have a right to bargain,** particularly in small stores that don't discount.

Reasoning: Department stores, which won't bargain as a rule, mark up prices 100% to 150% to cover high overhead costs. Small stores should charge lower prices because their costs are less.

The savvy approach: Set yourself a price limit for a particular item before you approach the storekeeper. Be prepared to walk out if he/she doesn't meet your limit. (You can always change your mind later.) Make him believe you really won't buy unless he comes down.

Be discreet in your negotiations. If other customers can overhear your dickering, the shop owner will feel obliged to remain firm. Be respectful of the merchandise and the storekeeper. Don't manhandle the goods that you inspect. Address the salesperson in a polite, friendly manner. Assume that he will want to do his best for you because he is such a nice, helpful person.

Shop during off hours. You will have more luck if business is slow.

Look for unmarked merchandise. If there is no price tag, you are invited to bargain.

Tactics that work…

●**Negotiate with cash.** In a store that takes credit cards, request a discount for paying in cash. (Charging entails overhead costs that the store must absorb.)

●**Buy in quantity.** A customer who is committed to a number of purchases has more bargaining power. When everything is picked out, approach the owner and suggest a total price about 20% less than the actual total.

Variation: If you are buying more than one of an item, offer to pay full price on the first one if the owner will give you a break on the others.

Storekeeper's alternative: You spent $500 on clothing and asked for a better price. The owner said he couldn't charge you less, but he threw in a belt priced at $35 as a bonus.

●**Look for flawed merchandise.** This is the only acceptable bargaining point in department stores, but it can also save you money in small shops. If there's a spot, a split seam or a missing button, estimate what it would cost to have the garment fixed commercially and ask for a discount based on that figure.

Variations: You find a chipped hairdryer. When you ask for a discount, the manager says he will return it to the manufacturer and find an undamaged one for you.

Your reply: "Sell it to me for a little less and save yourself the trouble."

●**Adapt your haggling to the realities of the situation.** A true discount house has a low profit margin and depends on volume to make its money. Don't ask for more than 5% off in such a store. A boutique that charges what the traffic will bear has more leeway. Start by asking for 25% off, and dicker from there.

●**Buy at the end of the season,** when new stock is being put out. Offer to buy older goods—at a discount.

●**Neighborhood stores.** Push the local television or appliance dealer to give you a break so you can keep your service business in the community.

Secondhand Savvy

For great secondhand buys, look for out-of-the-way flea markets and antiques shops. Try estate sales—go early and avoid those open to dealers before the public. Visit clearance centers run by furniture-rental companies. Go to model homes in new subdivisions and ask when the furniture will go on sale. Try eBay.com…FurnitureFinders.com…and Office Furniture Warehouse of Pittsburgh, *www.my officefurniture.net.*

Good Housekeeping, 959 Eighth Ave., New York City 10019.

Save Up to an Hour a Day!

Barbara Myers, owner of The Time Manager, Newark, Ohio, which offers personal organizing assistance and workshops for several hundred clients in the Midwest. She has written 10 organizing guides, including "200 Ways to Save Time at the Office" (available at *www. ineedmoretime.com*).

Waiting for service eats up hours of our time every week. *Here is how you can save at least one hour a day...*

●**Have groceries brought to you** rather than going to get them. Some major supermarkets allow you to shop on-line and will deliver.

Examples: Stop & Shop and Giant, *www. peapod.com* (Chicago, East Coast)...Safeway, *www.safeway.com* (West Coast). Local markets may also offer delivery—ask your grocer.

●**Run errands when they're most convenient...**not when they become urgent. That way, you can avoid long lines.

●**Share errands with a close neighbor.** See if either of you can save the other a trip.

●**Buy in bulk to save time and money.** This works especially well for common items you often run out of, such as stamps, greeting cards, wrapping paper, soap, paper products, lightbulbs, etc.

DOCTOR/DENTIST APPOINTMENTS

●**Be the first appointment in the morning...**or the first one after lunch, when you are less likely to have to wait.

●**Make follow-up appointments before you leave**—even if your next visit isn't for six months. You'll have your pick of the schedule, and you won't waste any time calling for an appointment and negotiating the best opening.

●**Call before leaving for any appointment** to see if the doctor is running behind schedule.

SUPERMARKET

●**Shop on Tuesdays and Wednesdays.** Midmorning and late evening are best.

●**Turn the bar codes on items toward the cashier** as you are checking out.

RESTAURANTS

●**Make reservations.** It seems obvious, but those people standing in line didn't plan ahead.

●**Ask for the check at the same time you order your last item.** Pay the bill, and then sit as long as you want.

POST OFFICE

●**Order stamps,** shipping containers and more from the US Postal Service's Web site, *http://shop.usps.com*. Delivery is within three to five days for a $1* fee. Otherwise, midmorning or early afternoon in the middle of the week is when the post office is least crowded. Stamps also may be purchased at local drugstores, grocery stores and banks.

DELIVERIES AND REPAIRMEN

●**Bunch appointments.** It's unlikely that everyone will show up on time. Even if they do, it usually is manageable.

●**Turn waiting time into found time.** Keep a list of small tasks around the house that need to be done.

My favorites: Go through the medicine cabinet to toss out expired drugs...straighten up a room and clear out items that you no longer want.

MAKE THE MOST OF WAITING

Sometimes you have no choice but to wait in line or for an appointment. I always carry a small bundle of necessary tasks for those times. It includes bills to pay and my checkbook... thank-you cards to write...articles I never seem to get to read...as well as a mail-order catalog or two to browse through.

Cut Your Grocery Bills By a Whopping 75%

Susan Samtur, the author of *Cashing In at the Checkout* (Back in the Bronx Press) and editor of *Refundle Bundle*, a newsletter that reports on coupons and refunds, Box 140, Yonkers, NY 10710, *www.refundlebundle.com*.

If you clip coupons from the Sunday newspaper, your average savings per coupon is 81 cents. That's not bad—but if you look beyond the obvious places, your savings can be extraordinary. I use coupons to reduce my

*All prices are subject to change.

13

weekly spending for food and household items from $100 to less than $25. I often get staples such as toilet paper, spaghetti sauce and razor blades for free. *My best savings now…*

ON-LINE DISCOUNTS

On-line coupons have a greater average face value (97 cents per coupon) than store coupons and a longer average time until expiration (4.8 months versus three months). There are many discount resources, so it's very easy to be overwhelmed. Some require you to provide your name and e-mail address. To save time, bookmark a few Web sites that you'll use regularly.

●**Coupon clearinghouses.** These provide coupons from many manufacturers. Print and use them when you shop. When you have the time, visit several sites—one may offer bigger discounts than another for the same product. *Best sites…*

- *www.coolsavings.com*
- *www.homebasics.com*
- *www.refundsweepers.com*
- *www.smartsource.com*

●**Retail savings sites.** *Some of these sites feature savings at Old Navy, Eddie Bauer and Payless ShoeSource, among other stores…*

- *www.keycode.com*
- *www.bluefly.com*
- *www.couponparadise.com*
- *www.eversave.com*

●**Manufacturers' Web sites.** Look on the packages of favorite products for the manufacturer's Web sites. See if the sites offer promotions, coupons and/or rebates. *A few that are particularly generous…*

- *www.chickenofthesea.com*
- *www.clairol.com/brand/blonding/offers/trymefree.jsp. Example:* Full purchase price refund of up to $10.99 on any product from the Clairol Perfect Highlighting and Blonding Collection.
- *www.colgate.com*
- *www.cottonelle.com. Example:* $1.50 off the price of any two packages of Cottonelle Fresh Folded Wipes.

●**Discount codes for on-line shopping.** Stores depend on weekly sales, coupons and shopper's clubs to attract buyers. On-line merchants provide discounts using promotional codes. You type in the code when you go to the checkout page.

Recent example: www.barnesandnoble. com gave $5 off any purchase of $50 or more, plus free shipping on two or more items after I registered for its on-line newsletter. Since the purpose of a discount code is to attract buyers to on-line stores, you may find them on Web sites other than the ones where the coupons will be used.

Some sites with generous coupon codes and promotions…

- *www.couponmountain.com*
- *www.currentcodes.com*
- *www.dealcatcher.com*

●**Manufacturers' rebates.** Some retailers have taken all the hassle out of getting manufacturers' rebates. Simply register at their Web sites—for example, log on to *www.riteaid. com…www.walgreens.com…www.truevalue. com…*and *www.officemax.com.* When you make an eligible purchase at one of these stores, enter the transaction number listed on your receipt. The manufacturer will mail you a check in four to six weeks. These rebates can total more than $100 a month, so check back frequently.

●**Free products.** Check manufacturers' Web sites for free products. You'll also find lots of free products at *www.freebiemaniac.com.*

DOUBLE AND TRIPLE YOUR SAVINGS

I try to combine discounts from different sources. I'm able to get many products for free or close to it because I create "triple plays," combining savings from store sales, newspaper coupons and Web sites.

Example I: A 12-pack of Pepsi was advertised at my local supermarket for $2. A rebate sticker on the cans offered $10 back if I mailed in proofs of purchase for three 12-packs and three bags of Lay's potato chips. I purchased the three bags on sale for $5, less 75 cents off because I used three 25-cent coupons that I found on the Frito-Lay Web site. *Final cost for the soda and chips:* 25 cents—$10.25 minus the $10 rebate.

I love "double coupons." If I had made my purchases using double coupons at the supermarket, the soda and chips would have cost me nothing.

Example II: I could get two 96-tablet economy packages of Sudafed nasal decongestant at my neighborhood Eckerd drugstore for $7. I went to *www.eckerd.com* to get an additional $1 rebate. I also had a newspaper coupon for $1 off each package. *Final total:* $4—a saving of more than 40% off the sale price.

Pay-As-You-Go Plans

Joe Pawlikowski, senior editor at PrepaidReviews.com, a Web site that provides independent reviews of cell phones and prepaid cellular plans.

Standard cell-phone plans lock consumers into one to two-year service contracts that cost at least $40 per month. In contrast, there are "prepaid" or "pay-as-you-go" cellular plans that require no contract and can cost as little as $10 a month.

Unlike customers with standard plans, those with pay-as-you-go plans buy only the talk time they need. Unused minutes do not typically disappear at the end of each month, as they do with traditional calling plans. (Prepaid minutes can expire in a year or two, but most prepaid plans offer customers ways to prevent this from happening.)

Also, unlike most cellular plans, prepaid plans do not add taxes and fees above the expected charges…there are no penalties for going over a monthly minute allowance…and prepaid customers cannot be liable for thousands of dollars in charges if their phones are stolen and used without their knowledge.

Cost of cell phones: Expect to pay $20 to $40 for a typical cell phone, or more for a high-end model. You might be able to use a cell phone you already own, depending on which type of network it is designed for and whether the service provider that provided you with the phone has "unlocked" it for use with other providers.

Verizon and AT&T, the best-known names in cellular calling, offer unattractive prepaid deals,

charging as much as 25¢ per minute…or $2.99 per day plus per-minute charges for any day you use the phone. They prefer to steer customers into traditional contracts. *Better option…*

•**T-Mobile Pay As You Go** (800-866-2453, *www.t-mobile.com*). A package of 1,000 minutes costs $100—just 10¢ a minute and among the cheapest of any pay-as-you-go service.

Downsides: T-Mobile's prices are less attractive when minutes are purchased in smaller bundles—130 minutes cost $25, which is more than 19¢ per minute. Also, T-Mobile's coverage is excellent in some parts of the US but poor in others. Ask friends who have T-Mobile service to check signal strength in the places where you are likely to use your phone, or use the coverage map on the T-Mobile Web site.

Stock Up and Save at Warehouse Clubs

Phil Lempert, supermarket guru and food trends editor for NBC's *Today* show. He is also host of the syndicated Shopping Smart show on the WOR radio network and the author of four books, including *Being the Shopper.* Wiley. His Web site is *www.supermarketguru.com.*

Warehouse clubs such as BJ's Wholesale, Sam's Club and Costco Wholesale can really help you save a lot of money. In the past, they sold mainly bulk food and household goods in a no-frills environment. Recently, they have started offering everything from eyeglasses to insurance.

Be careful, though. Many items purchased at warehouse clubs cost more than those purchased at traditional stores. *Here, the best and worst deals…*

BIG SAVINGS

Your savings on these great club buys will more than cover the annual cost of membership—$45 at BJ's, $50 at Costco, $40 at Sam's…

•**Eyeglasses.** Many warehouse club locations now have on-site optical departments that turn out well-made eyeglasses for about 50% less than your local optician—a savings of $60 or more per pair. Some locations even offer eye exams. Contact lenses may be available as well. Prices are comparable to those at discount Web sites, but you don't pay for shipping.

●**Small,** disposable nonfood items. These products are perfect as bulk purchases because they don't go bad or take up much storage space. Expect to save up to 50% off of supermarket prices—sometimes more.

Among the best buys: Toothbrushes, razor blades, dental floss, soap, deodorant, garbage bags, sandwich bags, printer toner cartridges, contact lens supplies and batteries.

Example: One name-brand toothbrush might cost $3 in a supermarket. In a discount club, you'll pay perhaps $5 for a six-pack of the same brush, an annual savings of $13 per family member if you change toothbrushes every two months, as recommended by most dentists.

Caution: Batteries and contact lens supplies eventually go bad, so avoid buying more than you can use before their expiration dates. Do not store extra toothpaste and deodorant in the bathroom—they'll last longer if kept in a cool, dry place.

●**Alcoholic beverages.** Wine, beer and liquor at the warehouse clubs sell for 20% to 25% below prices in supermarkets and liquor stores. However, you might have to buy bigger bottles. You will find top brands as well as warehouse club brands.

Note: The selling of alcohol by warehouse clubs is prohibited in some states. Generally speaking, if the supermarkets in your state are allowed to sell alcohol, then warehouse clubs can as well.

●**Gasoline.** Many of the warehouse clubs now have their own on-site gas stations—with prices that typically are 10 to 20 cents per gallon lower than other stations in the region. If you drive 10,000 miles a year in a vehicle that gets 25 miles to the gallon, that 10- to 20-cent discount translates into $40 to $80 a year—as long as you don't have to go too far out of your way to get to the warehouse club.

●**Prepaid phone cards.** Warehouse clubs sell domestic long-distance phone cards for as little as three cents a minute. That is a better rate than you're likely to find on prepaid calling anywhere else.

Important: No matter where you purchase them, prepaid phone cards are a good deal only if you actually use them. Roughly 20% of all minutes purchased on prepaid phone cards are never used because the cards are lost or forgotten.

SHOP WITH CAUTION

Savings are possible at warehouse clubs on the following items, but shop carefully—you might find better prices elsewhere…

●**Consumer electronics.** Warehouse club prices on consumer electronics likely are below the regular prices at other major retailers. Warehouse clubs, however, may not stock a good selection of leading brand names…and special offers are common on consumer electronics elsewhere. You might find an even better deal during a sale at a national chain or on-line at such sites as Overstock.com and Buy.com.

●**Canned and frozen foods.** Even in a can, food doesn't stay fresh forever. Buying canned foods in bulk makes sense—but only if you'll consume it within a year. Bulk purchases of frozen foods are smart only if you have the freezer space—for example, if you have a second freezer in the basement.

●**Insurance.** Some warehouse clubs now offer auto and homeowner's insurance—but their prices may or may not beat quotes you can get elsewhere, so don't buy until you have shopped around. To compare insurance rates, check out these Web sites, *www.insure.com* or *www.insweb.com.*

●**Diet beverages.** These drinks start to lose their sweetness after three or four months. Don't buy in bulk unless you will drink it all before then.

Caution: If your warehouse club (or any store) keeps carbonated beverages outside in the summer, don't purchase these bottles or cans. Prolonged exposure to heat can rob soda of both sweetness and flavor. Similarly, don't store soda in a hot garage.

BAD DEALS

Not everything for sale at a warehouse club is a moneysaver…

●**Bulk perishable foods.** Warehouse club prices for perishable foods typically are no better than supermarket prices. Supermarket profit margins on food are so thin that it's tough for the warehouse clubs to do much better—and if food you purchase in bulk goes uneaten, you will lose money.

Examples: Spices aren't a wise bulk purchase—they start to lose their flavor in as little as two months, and many attract insects. The five-liter tins of olive oil that are sold at warehouse clubs are a good deal only if you can get through that much olive oil in a year. After that, it will begin to go rancid.

●**Premier memberships.** Some warehouse clubs try to sell special high-end memberships. For an extra charge each year, you can get additional savings and exclusive offers. These premier memberships don't make sense unless you're buying in quantity for a restaurant, business or large family.

SMART SHOPPING STRATEGIES

Other ways you can make warehouse shopping more advantageous…

●**Avoid the dolly.** All the warehouse clubs offer customers large dollies to wheel through the aisles. The size of these dollies makes even large purchases look small—until you get to the register. Stick to a shopping cart to keep purchases in perspective.

●**Use coupons selectively.** Some warehouse clubs accept coupons, but because so many food items are packaged in unusual sizes and quantities—and since warehouse clubs offer limited brands—you're better off using coupons at the supermarket for items that you buy regularly. Besides, unlike many supermarkets, warehouse clubs do not offer you double and triple coupon days.

Luxuries for Less— Clothing, Jewelry, Crystal and More

Sue Goldstein, creator of The Underground Shopper, a multimedia outlet that includes a Dallas-area call-in radio show on shopping and an Internet shopping site. *www. undergroundshopper.com.*

High-quality goods are available now at discounts on the Internet. *My favorite sites for luxury items…*

●**Designer clothing and accessories.** Save at least 50% on new and gently used designer items, including handbags, sunglasses, jeans, pants, tops, dresses, footwear and belts. Brands include Christian Dior, Fendi, Prada and Yves Saint Laurent.

Recent example: A black Versace velvet zip-top tote with organizer sold for $489.99. Similar ones retail at Versace Boutiques for $800 to $1,000. Rodeo Drive Resale, 888-697-3725, *www.rodeodriveresale.com.*

●**Gourmet coffees and teas.** Cavallini offers the same exotic blends used at five-star restaurants and resorts. 214-353-0328, *www. cavallinicoffee.com.*

●**Linens.** Bedsheet.com sells high-thread-count sheets for up to 70% off retail prices.

Recent example: A queen-sized supima cotton sheet set with a 1,000-thread count, which typically retails for $499.99, went for $199.99, plus $39.99 for two pillow cases. 800-965-5558, *www.bedsheet.com.*

●**Skin-care products.** This company sells skin-care and cosmetic products that usually are available only at spas and doctors' offices. Popular lines include Babor, Bare Escentuals, Blinc and Cellex-C. 800-709-1865, *www.spalook.com.*

●**Jewelry.** Order reproductions of jewelry worn by Hollywood starlets in legendary films.

Recent special: Vivien Leigh's Southern emerald earrings—synthetic green emerald earrings, each stone 1.03 carats, set in gold-plated sterling silver and surrounded by 10 cubic zirconia stones—for $60. 800-788-5600, *www. thehollywoodcollection.com.*

●**China,** crystal and flatware. Great prices on sterling silverware, stainless flatware, and silver home accessories, including such top brands as Lenox and Noritake. 800-426-3057, *www.silver superstore.com.*

How to Save on Big-Ticket Items

Always ask for discounts on big-ticket items, including appliances, electronics and high-end clothing. Research an item on-line so you know the fair price, then go to a local store and negotiate for at least 10% to 15% off that price. Don't *demand* a lower price—ask nicely if one is possible. This works best at stores where you shop regularly and know the salespeople and managers. Also, offer to pay cash in return for a discount.

At the very least, find out when an item will be going on sale. Be prepared to leave if you don't get the price you want. The manager may make an offer as you head for the door.

Gerri Detweiler, president, Ultimate Credit Solutions, Inc., Sarasota, Forida, *www.ultimatecredit.com*. She is author of *Reduce Debt, Reduce Stress*. Good Advice Press, 2009.

Department Store "Savings" Can Be Costly— Don't Get Caught

Gerri Detweiler, president, Ultimate Credit Solutions, Inc., Sarasota, Forida, *www.ultimatecredit.com*. She is author of *Reduce Debt, Reduce Stress*. Good Advice Press, 2009.

Beware of department store credit card offers that give you 20% off your first purchase. If you do not pay off your balance quickly, you'll end up spending far more than you save. Store credit cards carry an average interest rate of 19.8%—much higher than major credit cards, whose rates average 14%. If you make the minimum payment, the interest alone can cost you more than the original price of the item—even with your 20% savings.

Example: As a new cardholder, you save $500 on a $2,500 couch. By paying the minimum amount each month (around $40)—it will take you almost nine years to pay off your debt and cost you $2,260 in interest. Increase the monthly payment to $75, and you'll pay it off in three years but still fork over $657 in interest.

Best: Take advantage of the 20% savings, but pay off the entire amount immediately or transfer the balance to a low-interest major credit card before the introductory period expires.

Bartering—The Secret To Trading Your Way to Super Savings

Tom McDowell, executive director, National Association of Trade Exchanges, Mentor, Ohio.

The Internet has spawned electronic barter exchanges, making it easier than ever before to barter goods and services. If you're handy at making something people want or can offer a service, you can avoid running up credit card charges and spending cash, and you can obtain items at discount prices.

Example: A piece of jewelry costs you $25 to make but has a market price of $75. Through barter you can trade it for an item worth $75—in effect, paying only $25 for it.

One can barter services (babysitting, pet care, photography, writing, etc.) as well as goods. So barter can be a great resource for a small home-based or sideline business.

One can also barter excess personal belongings—such as the accumulated contents of an attic or garage—and perhaps get much better terms than from selling them in a lawn sale.

Barter is possible through local groups, national exchanges or among friends and associates.

To learn more about barter or to find a barter group located near you, visit the Web site of the National Association of Trade Exchanges, *www. nate.org*, or call the Association at 440-205-5378.

You can also find specialty barter exchanges on-line using a search engine. Enter the word "barter" and the name of the item you want to trade or acquire.

Caution: Bartering doesn't avoid income or sales taxes, which you still must pay.

Better Batteries for Less!

Save money on batteries with Panasonic's Oxyride models. They allow for faster shooting in digital cameras, faster flash recovery, faster battery-powered toys and brighter flashlights than high-end alkalines for the same price (about $5 for a four-pack) and they last up to twice as long. AA and AAA sizes. Available at major drugstores and discount retailers such as Target.

PC World, 501 Second St., San Francisco 94107.

Frugal Experts Reveal Little Tricks That Save Big Money

Sue Goldstein, creator of The Underground Shopper, a multimedia outlet that includes a Dallas-area call-in radio show on shopping and an Internet shopping site. *www. undergroundshopper.com.*

Deborah Taylor-Hough, the author of *Frugal Living for Dummies* (Wiley) and *A Simple Choice: A Practical Guide to Saving Your Time, Money and Sanity* (Champion). She publishes the free e-newsletter *Simple Times* from Olympia, Washington. Her site on the Web is *http://members.aol.com/ dsimple/times.html.*

Donna Watkins and her husband, Randal, who live in Palmyra, Virginia, and run the free on-line newsletter *The Frugal Life*, available at *www.thefrugallife.com*. Their moneysaving ideas were contributed by visitors to their Web site.

Economists insist that inflation is low, but you would never know it from looking at most people's energy bills or their children's college costs. *To find out how to save on these and other expenses, see below…*

UNDERGROUND SHOPPER
Sue Goldstein

●**Shop at Internet liquidators and consignment stores.** *I have found many bargains at discount stores, but prices often are even lower at their on-line counterparts…*

●Overstock.com (800-843-2446) and Smart Bargains.com (866-692-2742) are best for items like fine jewelry, electronics, designer accessories and more.

●Bluefly.com (877-258-3359) offers high-end designer clothes for men and women.

One recent example: Marc Jacobs red denim pants, $94.99—73% off the retail price of $355.

●Playitagainsports.com (800-433-2540) buys, sells and trades new and used sports gear and equipment, including treadmills, exercise bikes and elliptical machines.

●Dgse.com is a jewelry discounter that specializes in preowned Rolex watches that are substantially less than retail prices. Other pieces of jewelry are discounted by up to 50%.

●**Get the feel of a $1,500 mattress for less than $500.** Beddingtoppers.com (800-834-2473) offers durable foam mattress toppers that fit over your current mattress. They are made with the same memory foam used in higher-priced mattresses to hug the contours of your body.

Cost: Full size, up to $349…queen, as much as $399…king, up to $479. Shipping is free.

Extra-deep-pocket sheets are needed, but it should help your current mattress last longer.

●**Replace hardware on doors,** furniture and cabinets. It's a fast and cheap way to give your home a new look. Home stores have only limited selections.

Better: GoKnobs.com (888-465-6627) offers more than a half million choices at great prices.

●**Pamper yourself for less at the beauty schools.** A student hairdresser will cut your hair under their teacher's supervision for much less than salons charge. Facials, massages and spa pedicures are low-cost indulgences. Look in the *Yellow Pages* under "Beauty Schools."

●**Get low-cost blood tests at mobile clinics.** Offered through local health fairs, these mobile clinics have very low overhead, so the blood tests are inexpensive. They're great for people who don't have insurance or whose deductibles are higher than the cost of the test. Check your local newspaper listings.

●**Investigate discount drug programs.** Pharmaceutical firms will provide free drugs to anybody who qualifies, but there are more than 2,000 companies and each has a different program, criteria for acceptance and paperwork.

Prescription Assistance Specialized Services or PASS (800-727-7479 or *www.pass4rx.com*) handles the paperwork and communication among you, your doctor and the pharmaceutical companies. You don't have to be a senior citizen to participate. After paying an enrollment charge of $25, you pay only $30 per prescription for a 30-day supply. Some programs have an income ceiling of $19,000 for singles…$26,000 for couples. Others will waive the limit if a catastrophic illness has created a financial burden.

SIMPLE TIMES
Deborah Taylor-Hough

•**Double and triple your shopping discounts.** Print out coupons from these Web sites, and use them at your favorite on-line and traditional retail stores.

Favorites: *www.slickdeals.net* and *www.flamingoworld.com.*

Alternative: Visit rebate sites, such as *www.ebates.com* and *www.mypoints.com.* Click on their links to popular on-line retailers, such as Barnes & Noble, Nordstrom's and Target.

•**Encourage your college grad to work off student-loan debt.** Congress passed legislation that enables some federal agencies to repay as much as $10,000 in government student loans (up to $60,000 per employee) for each year a graduate is employed by the US federal government. Congressional employees and those in military service often are eligible, as are some college graduates who teach full-time in schools that serve low-income students and those who specialize in subjects that lack qualified teachers.

Information: 800-433-3243 or *www.finaid.org/loans/forgiveness.phtml.*

•**Slash food bills.** Textured Vegetable Protein (TVP) costs much less per serving than meat, is low in fat and has no cholesterol. TVP works best in spicy dishes—spaghetti sauce, soups, etc. It comes in dry form and must be reconstituted in boiling water. For more information on TVP and additional soy products, see *www.thesoydaily.com.* Available at health-food stores or at *www.healthyharvest.com.*

Helpful: Find recipes at *www.fatfree.com/recipes/meat-analogues.*

THE FRUGAL LIFE
Donna Watkins

•**Use half the amount of nuts that baking recipes require.** Some nuts sell for $8 or more a pound. If you toast them before adding them to recipes, the flavor intensifies, so it won't taste like you used less.

•**Make your old refrigerator much more energy efficient.** Spread a thin layer of petroleum jelly on the rubber gasket seals along the inside of the door. This prevents mildew and keeps in cold air. Avoid frequently opening and closing the refrigerator door, especially when the weather is warm.

•**Chop the cost of firewood.** Ask a local orchard if you can buy its pruned branches. They should dry by winter. For example, apple wood costs less than store-bought firewood and burns very well.

How Scowling Can Save You Money

Don't seem too happy when negotiating. You will probably not get as good a deal. People who scowl or seem about to get angry usually do better in negotiations because they are thought to be at or near their limit. Someone who is smiling is thought to be willing to be pushed a little more. So, do not hesitate to act indignant, for instance, when negotiating to buy a car. But avoid actually getting angry.

Donald Moine, PhD, business psychologist, Rolling Hills Estates, California, coauthor of *Ultimate Selling Power: How to Create and Enjoy a Multi-Million Dollar Sales Career.* Career Press.

Save $100 Just by Changing Lightbulbs

Chris Calwell, vice president of policy and research, Ecos Consulting, which specializes in energy-efficiency and pollution-prevention research, Durango, Colorado. *www.ecosconsulting.com.*

Compact fluorescent lightbulbs are now about equal in quality and similar in color output to incandescent bulbs. And they offer tremendous savings on home electric bills.

Compact fluorescent bulbs that screw into conventional sockets cost as little as $5 each—

less if bought in bulk. But a fluorescent's greater longevity and energy efficiency can save you $30 to $60 over the life of the bulb. Fluorescents last up to 10,000 hours, versus 750 hours for incandescents, and consume up to 75% less electricity.

About 20% of the average American household's annual electric bill—about $160—goes toward lighting. Switching a handful of a home's heavily used bulbs to fluorescents can save $100 or more a year.

Replace bulbs that get the most use…

- **Main kitchen light.**

- **Outdoor lights that are on from dusk until dawn.**

- **Living room,** family room or great room lights—wherever the family spends most evenings.

Halogen torchères are inefficient because they use a lot of electricity and direct light to the ceiling. Replace them with fluorescent torchères.

USING FLUORESCENT BULBS

It is a myth that fluorescent lights use so much energy starting up that it's more economical to leave them on. Turn off any bulb when leaving a room unless you will return within 15 minutes.

However, it is true that frequently turning a fluorescent light on and off will reduce its life span.

BUYING EFFICIENT BULBS

Select fluorescent bulbs by looking at the number of *lumens* on the package—not the number of watts. Lumens measure brightness. Fluorescents deliver much more light per watt of electricity.

Compact fluorescent bulbs are widely available in discount, hardware, home goods and lighting stores.

Helpful: Check the Energy Star Web site, *www.energystar.gov*, to find out if government or manufacturer rebates on fluorescent bulbs are available in your region.

The Only Shopping Web Sites You'll Ever Need

Joseph T. Sinclair, Vallejo, California–based author of several books about the Internet, including *eBay the Smart Way*. Amacom.

You can save a lot by buying second-hand items on-line, but not everyone wants to go through the hassle of bidding at auction sites such as eBay. *Here are two moneysaving options for buying used and new items on-line…*

GOOGLE PRODUCT SEARCH

The leading search engine Google now offers a shopping site (*www.google.com/products*). It does have paid ads, but they are posted only on the right side of the search results page. Item listings are free and submitted by individual merchants.

How it works: Type "digital copier" into Google, and it will produce a list of more than 200,000 Web sites, some selling copiers, most not. Type the same entry into Google Product Search, and you will see only links to digital copiers for sale by on-line merchants. Each listing displays price, make, model number and other important details. Most also include photos.

If you're looking for a specific model, type in the model number or name. Then you can click to sort the results by price. In seconds, you'll know the best deals available on-line. Most of the items listed on Google Product Search are new. Items are shipped by the merchants.

To search only for secondhand products, include the keywords "used"…"condition"… "refurbished"…or "preowned" to filter out the majority of the new goods.

Note: Froogle includes some sellers from eBay and Amazon.com.

For used items from Amazon.com, the shipping costs can be a few dollars more than the standard Amazon shipping costs. On eBay, the merchants determine shipping costs.

CRAIGSLIST

At most shopping Web sites, the heavier the item, the less likely you will save money after shipping costs. Craigslist (*www.craigslist.org*)

solves this problem by connecting buyers with sellers in their own region.

Best for: Secondhand furniture, appliances, exercise equipment, sporting goods, bikes and other large, heavy items.

Examples: Recently on Craigslist, you could find a $100 treadmill in Boston…a $60 solid teak desk in the San Francisco Bay area…and a $150 leather recliner and ottoman in New York City.

The service is available in more than 75 US cities and many international locations.

Another plus: The sellers are local, so you can see the items before you buy.

Craigslist's regional focus makes it a lot like newspaper classifieds, with one important twist—sellers don't pay for postings. With no classified ad expense, sellers generally offer attractive prices.

The Web site also is great for last-minute concert and sporting-event tickets. Sellers will offer steep discounts when a change in their plans prevents them from attending. This Web site also features help-wanted and personal ads as well as real estate listings.

Gateway to Internet Discounts

You can save money when shopping by going to a retailer's Web site through a portal instead of going to the site directly.

Retailers pay fees to Internet portals that direct customers to them. The portals pass part of these fees on to customers through discounts.

The typical discount is around 4%, and you can combine it with coupons and other bargain offers available to you. Portals work with many major retailers, including Lands' End, the Gap and Barnes & Noble.

Leading portals: Ebates.com, FatWallet. com, RebateShare.com.

Many more bargains: For a listing of more than 200 Web sites offering coupons and discounts on various products, visit the Yahoo! Web Directory at *www.yahoo.com*. Click on "Shopping," then click on "Deals," then on "Coupons."

Shrewder On-Line Shopping

Hillary Mendelsohn, founder of thepurplebook, LLC in Beverly Hills, California, *www.thepurplebook.com*. She is also the author of *thepurplebook: the definitive guide to exceptional on-line shopping*, Warner Books, which lists more than 1,700 on-line shopping sites in 20 different categories.

Shopping on-line takes you outside of the old, familiar stores and malls and brings a global bazaar right to your door. The variety of goods available on-line is breathtaking—with many items you will never see at the mall—and prices are often lower than you would pay elsewhere.

And yet, on-line shopping can be filled with many perils. You may be shopping with merchants you've never dealt with before (some of them half a world away), you don't get to see items before buying them and identity thieves could steal your most personal information.

Here's how you can be a savvy and safe on-line shopper…

FINDING WHAT'S BEST ON-LINE

While virtually every mass-market retailer sells on-line today, the beauty of the Internet is being able to find off-beat merchants selling hard-to-find treasures. Whatever you are into, from gourmet foods to sports memorabilia, it's available on-line. *Here's how to find it…*

●**Know how to search.** I love Google, but my favorite search engine for finding goods on-line is Dogpile (*www.dogpile.com*). Once you enter what you're looking for, Dogpile offers invaluable tips to help you refine your search. It also provides fewer results to wade through than most search engines. Once you decide to buy an item, such as a specific brand and style of shoes, go to BizRate.com (*www.bizrate.com*) to see which on-line merchant offers the best price. Take into account shipping prices when doing your comparison.

●**Look for contact information.** The hardest thing to find on-line is a telephone number that will let you make personal contact with the merchant—to ask questions and resolve disputes. I won't list a site in my book that doesn't have a listed phone number.

Hint: If a site doesn't have a listed phone number, sometimes you can find it by searching *http://yp.yahoo.com.*

●**Demand quick and easy shopping.** You should be able to complete the on-line transaction without a lot of wasted time and keystrokes. Avoid any site that requires you to enter tons of information (name, address, e-mail address, etc.) just to find out if an item is in stock.

●**Go with your gut.** If the site seems flimsy —without all the information you need to make your selection—skip it.

HOW TO HAGGLE

You will often pay less for an item on-line, since many sites don't charge sales tax and may offer free shipping. Mass-market retailers are doing more to encourage on-line shopping —including offering discounts. If you register with them, you can receive e-mail on their special offers, advance notification of sales plus coupons and discounts.

Even if a store doesn't specifically mention discounts to on-line shoppers, it may be possible to negotiate a better deal for yourself.

Most sites include a comments box on the order form. Use that box to ask for a lower price, or free shipping or gift wrapping.

Don't expect a biggie like Wal-Mart or L.L. Bean to bargain with you on-line. However, a smaller retailer may be willing to deal...especially if the item is one of a kind, such as a piece of handmade jewelry.

HOW TO SHOP SAFELY

While most identity theft does not take place on the Internet, you still want to exercise caution. *Here's how…*

●**Patronize sites that use a secure server.** This means that any information you enter online is encrypted before being transmitted. The standard for security is 128-bit encryption, and sites that offer it will usually display that information prominently.

Favor sites that display the VeriSign Secured Seal to indicate they use a secure server. The seal is in red, with a black checkmark.

●**Pay with your credit card**—rather than with a debit card. Your bank card number and often your PIN must be transmitted with a debit card transaction, making you vulnerable to hackers. Also, if there is a problem with the merchandise or the billing, or if the order was never shipped, you can withhold payment for the purchase from the credit card issuer. When you use a debit card, the money comes out of your bank account the instant you complete the transaction.

HOW TO TOUCH THE MERCHANDISE

The biggest problem with on-line shopping is that you can't hold the item in your hand and examine it for color, size, quality, etc.

Solution: Use sites that do the best job of illustrating and describing what you're buying.

If color is a factor, for example, you'll want to be shown all the colors in which the item is offered. With clothing, you'll want a chart of sizes, an explanation of how the items are sized and a guide to help you pick the size you'll need.

Important: Since there is always a certain amount of guesswork involved when shopping on-line, the merchant's return and exchange policies are critical. You must be able to return the item within a reasonable amount of time— at least 30 days—and get a full refund rather than just store credit against another purchase.

FOREIGN SHOPPING

You're not limited to the US when shopping on-line. You can purchase from merchants anywhere in the world. However, I do set a much higher standard for the international sites that I list in my book.

The site must be in English. It must offer a currency converter, showing the price of the item in both dollars and in the local currency. The site must also offer size conversion charts so you understand the difference between US sizes and European or British sizes.

Important: The cost of shipping must be reasonable, even if the item is coming from far away. If you're not careful, the cost of shipping can exceed the value of the item. The best international sites keep their shipping costs close to what it would cost to have the item shipped from a domestic supplier.

HOW TO RESOLVE COMPLAINTS

Most of the time, your on-line shopping will go without a hitch. Merchants have been selling on-line long enough to have ironed out the issues that made for trouble at the beginning.

Still, things can go wrong. Anticipate trouble by collecting all the documents you might need in case something does.

Save all records of your on-line order, including any e-mail the company sends you to confirm your purchase. Print the order page before you press the submit button. That will give you a copy of the order page just as you prepared it, with the color, size and shipping method that you selected.

If there's a complaint that can't be resolved with the merchant, or you think you've been a victim of fraud, complain to the Federal Trade Commission (FTC). This agency of the government polices on-line shopping.

Visit the FTC Web site at *www.ftc.gov* to see what your rights are, and for instructions on filing a complaint. "E-consumer.gov" is a special area of the FTC site that handles cross-border on-line shopping complaints.

Get a Discount On Virtually Everything On-Line

Before you shop on-line, search for promotional discounts for clothing, appliances, shoes, electronics, music and more. These discounts are applied during checkout if you include the proper code. Retailers put these codes on other sites as advertisements to lure you to their sites.

Best sources for promotional codes: *www. currentcodes.com…www.dealcatcher.com… www.dealhunting.com.*

Mary Hunt, editor of *Debt-Proof Living*, Box 2135, Paramount, California 90723, *www.debtproofliving.com.*

Pay Less for Internet Service

Get unlimited Internet access with NetZero through Wal-Mart for just $9.95 a month. Go to *www.walmart.com* and click on "See All Departments," then "Internet Service Provider."

Alternative: *www.cyberhotline.com* offers unlimited ad-free access for $14.95 a month.

Mary Hunt, editor of *Debt-Proof Living*, Box 2135, Paramount, California 90723, *www.debtproofliving.com.*

Compare Internet Service Providers

Compare Internet service provider prices in your area at *www.broadbandreports.com* or *www.findanisp.com.* A high-speed cable connection costs $40 to $60 a month. A digital subscriber line (DSL), which is slightly slower, costs $15 to $29. The slowest choice, dial-up service, averages less than $10 a month.

PC World, 501 Second St., San Francisco 94107.

Gambling for Bargains at Postal Service Auctions

A US Postal Service auction is an exciting combination of Las Vegas and a flea market—you gamble for bargains and come out a winner or loser, depending on the effectiveness of your strategy. In the meantime, you've had lots of fun, and you just may pick up the buy of a lifetime.

The Postal Service holds regular auctions of lost, damaged or undeliverable merchandise every two to four months in all major US cities. (The New York City Postal Service has an auction once a month.) Call the main post office in your city for time and date.

The merchandise that's available ranges from jeans and Oriental furniture to bottles of dishwashing detergent and microcomputers. In fact, anything that can be sent through the mail might turn up at a post office auction.

Items typically available: Stereo equipment, TVs, radios, dishes, pots and pans, tools, typewriters, clothing, books, coins.

HOW IT WORKS

●**Items are sold by lot.** Similar articles are often grouped together, such as a dozen jeans, four typewriters or three radios. The items must be purchased together.

Suggestion: Bring friends who might want to share a lot with you.

●**Lots are displayed the day before the auction.** Inspection is not permitted on the day of the sale, and viewing is all that's allowed. Lots are in compartments or bins that are covered with netting. Nothing (except clothing on hangers) can be handled or tested.

Suggestion: Many compartments are badly lighted, so bring a flashlight to get a good look.

●**All lots are listed by number on a print-out given out on the inspection day.** They are auctioned off by number, and each has a minimum acceptable bid listed next to it (never less than $10). But the minimum bid is no indication of how much the lot will sell for. Some go for 10 or more times the minimum bid listed.

●**All lots are sold "as is."** There is no guarantee of quality or quantity. Despite the disclaimer, the Postal Service is not trying to trick anyone into bidding high for damaged goods. It tries to mark items it recognizes as damaged.

Remember: All sales are final.

●**You must pay the day before the auction to obtain a paddle for bidding.** Each paddle has a number on it, which the auctioneer recognizes as your bidding number. To bid, hold up your paddle until the prices being called by the auctioneer exceed what you are willing to pay. The cost of the paddle will be refunded if you don't buy anything. Otherwise it is applied to the purchase price.

●**You must deposit 50% of the purchase price in cash or certified check** 30 minutes after buying a lot. It is desirable to bring several certified checks instead of one big one.

●**Merchandise must be picked up a day or two after the auction.** You must bring your own container.

The bidding at these auctions is extremely unpredictable and quirky. There is absolutely no way of knowing how much a lot will go for. Some lots are overbid, while others go for the minimum bid, often with no obvious relationship to actual value.

Example: At a recent auction, a set of inexpensive plastic dishes went for more than the retail price, while a much more valuable and lovely set of china dishes sold for less than the plastic ones.

Prices seem to depend on who is attending a particular auction and what they are in the market for.

Example: In furious bidding at the same auction, a number of dealers bid up a record-album lot to $750. But no one was interested in a number of lots of Reed & Barton silver-plated flatware, which went for the minimum bid of $5 per place setting.

BIDDING TIPS

●**Go through the list of lots carefully while looking at the merchandise** and write down your maximum bids. During the actual auction, bidding is confusingly fast, with prices rapidly increasing by $2 at a time as bidders drop out. Listen to the bidding carefully, and don't exceed your maximum.

●**Sit in the back of the room so you can see who is bidding against you.**

Why: If you're in the market for a particular item, you'll be aware of how many others are in the same market that day. Also, you can see people drop out of the bidding.

●**Take someone knowledgeable to the visual inspection,** especially if you're planning to bid on something like electronic equipment. Find out how much that particular piece is worth and calculate your top bid by including the cost of repair.

●**If you can't find someone who is knowledgeable,** stick to bidding on lots that you can see are in good shape.

Best bets: Dishes, cutlery, pots and pans, hand tools, furniture, clothing sold by the garment (much of the clothing is sold in huge bins and can't be inspected).

For more information and a list of upcoming auctions, go to *www.usps.com/auctions.*

Sneaky Supermarket Come-ons…How to Avoid Spending More At the Store

Phil Lempert, food editor for NBC's *Today* show. Based in Santa Monica, California, he is the author of many books, including *Being the Shopper: Understanding the Buyer's Choice.* Wiley. *www.supermarket guru.com.*

Food prices are soaring, and stores are pulling out all the stops to create the illusion of savings, value and good deals. *Here's how grocery stores get shoppers to overspend—and how to defend yourself…*

●**Buy one, get one free.** These offers make you feel that you are getting two items for "half price." But it isn't really half price if the cost is more than that of a similar item—and you're getting no bargain at all if you don't want or can't use more than one of a product.

Self-defense: Ask the manager whether you can buy one item for half the price of two. Stores don't advertise this alternative, but it often is allowed.

●**Limit four per person.** Scarcity exerts a powerful effect on shoppers. Any time you're restricted from buying, a hoarding mentality kicks in and you are likely to buy more than you need.

Problem: Excess items can spoil, sit in your cupboard for years or simply get thrown out.

Self-defense: Purchase only the amount that you reasonably need and can use, no matter how good the price.

●**Double discounts.** *Quick:* If you were given a choice of buying a $100 item at 50% off or buying the same item at 25% off with an additional 30% discount given at the register, which would you choose? Most consumers add the 25% and 30% and think that they are getting 55% off the product. In reality, they are paying $2.50 more.

Self-defense: Look at the fine print on the shelves to see if the store does "unit pricing" breakdowns for you (showing the final cost per ounce, pound, piece or whatever the unit is). Or better yet, bring a calculator to cut through the number games.

●**Country-of-origin labeling.** With the recent scare over tainted products from China, stores know that consumers will pay more for food they trust. I've seen supermarket signs promoting "Live Maine Lobsters" or "Washington State Apples" with fine print that reads, respectively, "Imported from Chile" and "Product of Mexico."

Self-defense: Don't trust store signs for foods' countries of origin. Check origin labels on the products.

For organic foods, which often are priced higher, look for proof of authenticity. To be 100% sure that the product is organic, the packaging should carry a stamp that reads, "OTCO" (which means it is certified by Oregon Tilth, a national nonprofit organic certification organization) or "USDA Organic."

●**Alluring end caps.** These are stand-alone display cases at the ends of aisles. On average, shoppers are 30% more likely to buy end-cap goods than those in the middle of an aisle. End caps seem to have good deals—some say, "Stock up now!" or "Great price!"—but half the time, they're not. In fact, these prime spots often are reserved for high-profit, so-called gourmet foods.

Self-defense: Buy from an end-cap only if it is truly a good deal. Be wary of freestanding (island) displays as well. They offer a different kind of impulse buy—expensive, "integrated" merchandise. For instance, an island display may group pricey strawberries, pastry shells and whipped cream together so that the customer thinks, *I'll make strawberry shortcake for dessert.*

●**Presliced produce.** Sliced foods can cost twice as much as whole foods.

Self-defense: Pay value-added prices for prepared meals only if they really save you significant time and effort.

Example: A ready-to-eat whole chicken may be worth twice as much to you as a raw one if it saves you an hour of so of preparing and roasting. I also am willing to pay more for packaged, combination salads because doing so saves me time and money. To prepare the same kind of salad myself, I would have to buy four different varieties of lettuce.

What Goes on Sale When— A Month-by-Month Guide To Smarter Shopping

If you're a serious shopper, you want to know when all the sales happen. *Here's a month-by-month schedule for dedicated bargain hunters...*

January: Appliances...Baby carriages... Books...Carpets and rugs...China and glassware...Christmas cards...Costume jewelry... Furniture...Furs...Lingerie...Men's overcoats... Pocketbooks...Preinventory sales...Shoes... Toys...White goods (sheets, towels, etc.).

February: Air conditioners...Art supplies... Bedding...Cars (used)...Curtains...Furniture... Glassware and china...Housewares...Lamps... Men's apparel...Consumer electronics...Silverware...Sportswear and equipment...Storm windows...Toys.

March: Boys' and girls' shoes...Garden supplies...Housewares...Ice skates...Infants' clothing...Laundry equipment...Luggage...Ski equipment.

April: Fabrics...Hosiery...Lingerie...Painting supplies...Women's shoes.

May: Handbags...Housecoats...Household linens...Jewelry...Luggage...Outdoor furniture ...Rugs...Shoes...Sportswear...Tires and auto accessories...TV sets.

June: Bedding...Boys' clothing...Fabrics... Floor coverings...Lingerie, sleepwear and hosiery...Men's clothing...Women's shoes.

July: Air conditioners and other appliances... Bathing suits...Children's clothes...Electronic equipment...Furniture...Handbags...Lingerie and sleepwear...Luggage...Men's shirts...Men's shoes...Rugs...Sportswear...Summer clothes... Summer sports equipment.

August: Back-to-school specials...Bathing suits...Carpeting...Cosmetics...Curtains and drapes...Electric fans and air conditioners... Furniture...Furs...Men's coats...Tires...White goods...Women's coats.

September: Bicycles...Cars (outgoing models) ...China and glassware...Fabrics...Fall fashions... Garden equipment...Hardware...Lamps...Paints.

October: Cars (outgoing models)...China and glassware...Fall/winter clothing...Fishing equipment...Furniture...Lingerie and hosiery... Major appliances...School supplies...Silver... Storewide clearances...Women's coats.

November: Blankets and quilts...Boys' suits and coats...Cars (used)...Lingerie...Major appliances...Men's suits and coats...Shoes... White goods...Winter clothing.

December: Blankets and quilts...Cars (used)... Children's clothes...Coats and hats...Men's furnishings...Resort and cruise wear...Shoes.

The Ultimate Cheapskate's Simple Ways to Save $8,000 a Year... His Secret—Going Green

Jeff Yeager, dubbed "The Ultimate Cheapskate," honed his "cheapskating" skills during 25 years of working with underfunded nonprofit agencies. He lives in Accokeek, Maryland, where he is pursuing his passion for writing and multimedia journalism. He is author of *The Ultimate Cheapskate's Road Map to True Riches.* Broadway. *www. ultimatecheapskate.com.*

A friend of mine once questioned my credentials as both a cheapskate and an environmentalist (I'm proudly both) when he discovered that I use disposable razors.

"What do you expect?" I said indignantly. "I hardly ever find the other kind in my neighbor's trash."

Okay, that's a joke. But what's not a joke is how much money you'll save by incorporating a few simple "green" practices into your life. Contrary to what many people think, living green—doing what's environmentally friendly— usually doesn't cost more. It's often the least expensive way to go. After all, the bottom line when it comes to conservation is consuming wisely—and that usually means spending less.

Here's how you can save more than $8,000 a year by going green…

● **Limit portions.** According to the US Department of Agriculture, roughly 25% of all edible food bought by Americans goes to waste. That is shameful in a world where billions of people are literally starving. Also, the raising, processing, packing, distribution, sale and waste disposal associated with the food we eat—and don't eat—creates a huge carbon footprint (a measure of the impact of our activities on the environment). The average US household spends more than $6,000 a year on food (groceries and meals out). If you eliminate waste by preparing smaller portions, eating leftovers and storing foods efficiently, you could save $1,500 a year.

● **Plant trees.** Trees improve air and water quality and increase the value of your home. According to the US Department of Energy, as few as three strategically planted trees in your yard can lower your heating and cooling costs. Trees can provide shade in the summer and block cold winds in the winter. Even if you spend $100 for each of those trees (that's only a few dollars a year when amortized over the life span of most trees), you will save as much as $250 a year when the trees mature.

● **Reduce your lawn.** A beautiful lawn typically requires water, as well as fertilizers, weed killers and pesticides. That can be costly for you and the environment. And if you hire a lawn service—the US lawn-care business is approximately a $12-billion-a-year industry—you're paying even more. Reduce your lawn space by half by planting a no-maintenance ground cover, such as pachysandra or creeping thyme, and trim half your lawn-care costs, say $500 if you are spending $1,000 a year now.

● **Be thrifty with clothes.** Only a small fraction of all clothing thrown away in the US is truly worn out, representing a tremendous waste of resources. Some clothing, including high-quality designer brands, finds its way into thrift shops and yard sales before it reaches the landfill. If you buy this gently used clothing, expect to save about 80% or more compared with the same items purchased new. With each US household spending an average of $2,000 annually on clothing, buying just half of your family's clothing at thrift stores allows you to save a fashionable $800.

● **Use fewer paper products.** The typical US household spends about $400 on paper products each year, with most of those products ultimately destined for recycling or a wastebasket. Make a pact to cut your paper use in half by using cloth napkins and towels instead of paper…and real plates and cups rather than disposable. Even after factoring in the cost of washing linens and dishes, you could save about $200 a year.

● **Become an energy-saving star.** As your household appliances need replacing, look for the Energy Star label when you are shopping for new ones. Energy Star is a US government program designed to help protect the environment—and save people money—by promoting energy-efficient products and practices (see *www.energystar.gov*). Energy Star–rated appliances are competitively priced and, when paired with other Energy Star recommendations (such as beefing up insulation and installing low-flow water fixtures), could save the typical household $400 a year.

● **Eat lower on the food chain.** In general, it takes more resources, generates more pollution and costs more money to eat foods high on the food chain, such as beef and poultry. It takes seven pounds of grain to add one pound of weight to cattle. The typical American diet–which includes more than 200 pounds of meat per year (an increase of 50 pounds since the 1960s)–is a far cry from the healthy diet recommended by the US Department of Agriculture's food pyramid (*www.mypyramid.gov*). If you eat more whole grains, fruits and vegetables, you and Mother Earth will be healthier and you'll likely save 20%, or about $1,200 , on your annual household food budget.

● **Drink tap water.** It takes 1.5 million barrels of oil every year to manufacture disposable plastic water bottles for the US market—that's enough to fuel 100,000 cars for a year. Also, if you drink only bottled water, you'll spend about $1,400 annually to get your recommended daily amount of H2O, as opposed to 49 cents for one year's supply of just-as-healthy tap water. Use the calculator at *www.newdream. org* to calculate your savings based on your actual consumption, but it's likely to be more than $1,000.

•**Stay close to home.** Each US household now generates an average of 10 vehicle trips per day. With the price of gas at closes to $4 a gallon, if you consolidate or skip just two or three of those daily trips, you'll save big money—and reduce pollution. According to AAA, it costs $9,369 a year (excluding loan payments) to keep the average car on the road. So after excluding fixed costs, such as insurance, finance charges, license and registration, a 25% reduction in use could mean a savings of $1,782.

•**Use your library.** You already own almost every book worth reading—your tax dollars were used to stock your public library. So instead of buying books, borrow them. You'll save trees and help reduce the publishing industry's War and Peace–size carbon footprint. Also borrow music CDs and movie DVDs. If you borrow one book a month instead of buying a hardcover for $25 and borrow two movies a month instead of spending $5 per movie at a video store, that's a total savings of $420 a year.

Helpful resource: To see how much more you can save by living green, use the Personal Emissions Calculator at *www.epa.gov/climate change/emis sions/ind_calculator.html.*

2

Better Ways to Save on Banking and Credit

Save Money on Managing Your Money

Regardless of the state of the economy, you do not want to pass up any opportunity to save money. Of the hundreds of ways to save, here are some of the best. Stop procrastinating. Put them to work for you now.

PERSONAL FINANCE

●**Banking.** Credit unions are a thrifty alternative to banks—they usually charge less for consumer loans and pay more interest on savings. Call local credit unions to inquire about membership or contact the Credit Union National Association (*www.creditunion.coop*, 800-358-5710) to find the address of your state association. Ask about the credit unions you may be eligible to join.

Important: Only join a credit union that has deposits that are insured by the National Credit Union Administration (NCUA), since this organization provides federal protection identical to the protection that the Federal Deposit Insurance Corporation (FDIC) provides banks.

Check money saver: Order checks directly from a printer (such as *www.checkworks.com*, *www.checksinthemail.com* or *www.checksun limited.com*) rather than purchasing them from your bank. These checks can be used at any bank.

Savings: Up to 50%.

●**Debt.** Reduce your debt to save money.

One way: Use money from savings accounts that pay low interest to pay off high-interest credit card debt.

Example: If you have a money market account paying 0.75% and credit card debt costing 14%, you're losing 13.25% in interest each year.

Lucy H. Hedrick, an expert on time and money management and the founder and president of Hedrick Communications, a publishing consulting firm located in Old Greenwich, Connecticut. She is author of *365 Ways to Save Money.* Hearst.

●**Credit cards.** Select the right type of card for your needs. Call around or visit *www. bankrate.com* to explore your choices. *What type of card you should look for…*

●If you carry a balance, opt for a low-rate credit card.

●If you pay off your balance each month, choose a no-fee card.

●If you spend a lot monthly, opt for special-offer cards. You can earn airline mileage, cash back or points toward merchandise.

Examples: Discover (877-347-2683, *www. discovercard.com*) gives a 5% cash back bonus, and Shell MasterCard (877-697-4355, *www.877 myshell.com*) lets you earn a 5% rebate on Shell gasoline and a 1% rebate on other purchases you make with the card.

●**Insurance.** Comparison shop for your insurance needs to find the lowest prices. Check other insurers or go to *www.insure.com* to get quotes from more than 200 leading insurers. *More cost-cutting ideas…*

●Cut car insurance 30% by increasing your deductible from $250 to $500.

●Cancel collision coverage on cars that are older than five years.

●Do not take the insurance coverage when renting a car—your own policy, and even major credit card companies to which the rental is charged, will cover any liability.

YOUR HOME

●**Mortgages.** You can save thousands of dollars in interest costs by accelerating your mortgage. *Options…*

●Pay additional principal with each payment.

●Pay one-half of the monthly amount due every two weeks. That adds up to one extra payment each year.

●If there are more than 15 years remaining on your mortgage, refinance using a 15-year loan. You'll pay more in the short run but save thousands overall.

●**Utilities.** Check to see if your utility company offers two-tier pricing. If so, run major appliances (washer, dryer, dishwasher) at off-peak times—weekends, holidays and weekdays between 10 pm and 10 am.

Purchase only energy-efficient appliances. They may cost you more up-front, but you'll save in operating costs over the life of the appliances. To check out energy ratings, look at the Energy Guide label on the appliance or go to the Web site *www.energyguide.com.*

●**Selling your home.** Market it yourself to save the usual 6% real estate commission. Make sure you have the time and ability to advertise and show your home to its best advantage.

If you can't, consider using a discount realtor. Help-U-Sell (909-693-5403, *www.helpu sell.com*) charges a flat fee that is payable at closing, the amount of which varies across the nation.

Savings: On a $200,000 home, you could pay as little as $6,000 (3%), rather than $12,000.

●**Moving.** Save on the cost of a move by…

●Moving on a weekday. Costs are 50% lower than on a weekend.

●Packing everything yourself, which saves at least 10%.

●Getting a binding estimate in writing before contracting with a mover. In about 25% of nonbinding estimates, the actual cost of the move exceeds the estimate. With a binding estimate, the price is guaranteed.

INVESTMENTS

●**Fixed income.** Buy the government instruments to save on purchase expenses and taxes. Savings bonds (Series EE and I) can be purchased from your bank or the US Treasury online at *www.savingsbonds.gov.* Interest is state tax free, while federal tax on interest can be deferred and may even be exempt if used to pay for higher education costs.

Treasury bonds and notes can be purchased directly from the Treasury on-line (*www.treasu rydirect.gov/indiv/myaccount/myaccount_lega cytd.htm*) or at a Federal Reserve bank. Here, too, there's no purchasing fee and interest is state-tax free.

●**Equities.** Save on investment costs by buying no-load mutual funds—the annual management fee is usually less than 1% and there are no sales fees to buy or to sell.

Buy stock through dividend reinvestment plans (DRIPs), which enable you to purchase stock directly from the company and reinvest dividends for more stock. There's usually only a small administrative charge for purchases. See *www.moneypaper.com.*

THE LAW

●**Power of attorney (POA).** Giving a POA to a spouse, adult child or friend can save you money should you become incapacitated. Your family can avoid the expense (court costs and attorneys' fees) of going to court to have someone appointed to manage your financial affairs.

●**Divorce.** Mediated divorces cost about 50% of what contested divorces cost.

Caution: Don't use mediation if you have questions about your spouse's honesty, if he/she is involved in criminal activity, is mentally incompetent or there is current physical abuse.

CARS

●**Pump your own gas.** Also, add oil and windshield fluid yourself. Buy oil and fluid by the case at an auto discount store. And, use a gas company credit card that offers a rebate on gas and other purchases.

●**Think twice before buying an extended-service contract.** It may merely duplicate the manufacturer's warranty. Check out the facts on auto-service contracts at the Federal Trade Commission Web site at *www.ftc.gov.* Click on "For Consumers," then "Automobiles."

COMPUTERS

Purchase a used computer (if it has a vendor warranty) or a refurbished one (which usually comes with a vendor warranty, although it may be a limited one). The best is a manufacturer-refurbished computer, one which has been restored to exact manufacturer specifications and comes with a manufacturer's warranty. Look for these at *www.gateway.com, www.dell.com* and *www.ubid.com.* Prices usually run about 25% below a comparable new computer.

TRAVEL

●**Travelers as young as 50 qualify for discounted rates** on hotels, cruises, airlines and car rentals if they are members of AARP (formerly called the American Association of Retired Persons). You do not have to be retired to join. Membership is $12.50* per year.

●**When booking a hotel room,** ask for a discount through AARP, military, business or any other discount plan available to you.

●**If you have the time,** volunteer to get off an overbooked flight—in exchange for cash or free round-trip tickets.

How to Slash Outrageous Bank Fees

Edward F. Mrkvicka, Jr., former chairman of a national bank and current president of Reliance Enterprises, Inc., a national financial consulting firm, 22115 O'Connell Rd., Marengo, Illinois 60152. He is author of *Your Bank Is Ripping You Off.* St. Martin's Griffin.

The key to bringing down many banking costs—and even boosting interest rates on savings—is developing a relationship with your local banker. No small bank will risk losing a large account because of a quibble over one-half of a percentage point in interest or a $25 monthly service fee. While Internet banks might charge less for checking, resolving problems can be a nightmare because you can't find out who is in charge or where records are kept.

Compare costs for services you need by calling at least three local banks.

Shortcut: Go to *www.bankrate.com* and click on "Checking & Savings."

To slash annoying banking costs…

OVERDRAFTS

The average fee for a bounced check is close to $30. Even if you have overdraft protection, you will be charged a fee plus interest. *Solutions…*

●**Ask the bank to refund the overdraft charge.** Many banks will oblige if you only make a mistake occasionally.

●**Avoid triggering overdraft.** Many charges result from debit cards as husbands and wives make purchases without telling each other. Use

*All prices are subject to change.

credit cards instead. Pay them off promptly to avoid interest charges.

●**Ask for "free" overdraft protection.** If you overdraw from your account, the bank will phone and give you a day—or more—to cover the shortfall at no charge.

Caution: Customers who frequently trigger overdrafts may lose this consideration.

MINIMUM BALANCE

This fee averages $6 to $11 per month if your account falls below the minimum for even one day. The average minimum required to avoid this fee is about $3,000 at traditional banks.

Solution: Choose an account with little or no minimum. Many banks offer truly free checking with no minimums for seniors and students.

INTEREST ON INSTALLMENT LOANS

If you take a three-year installment loan to buy a car, don't think that the interest costs will decline over time, as with a mortgage. In many cases, you will continue to pay interest on the initial amount throughout the loan's term.

Solution: Insist on a simple interest single-payment loan that will allow for monthly payments or a simple interest installment loan. Most banks make simple interest loans but don't necessarily volunteer this information.

Example: If you had a 48-month car loan for $10,000 at 10.25%, you would save $138.87 over the life of the loan with simple instead of traditional interest.

UNNECESSARY INSURANCE

When you take out a loan, bank officers will often try to sell you expensive *credit life and disability insurance*, which pays off the loan should you die or makes monthly payments should you become disabled. Some automatically write insurance into loan documents and don't discuss it with customers. Customers are afraid of disrupting the closing, so they don't question the extra charges.

Solution: Don't buy loan insurance from the bank. In the event of your death, it pays off only your loan balance. If you choose to protect a $10,000 four-year car loan, earmark $10,000 of your term life insurance policy for this purpose.

To compare term insurance rates, ask an independent agent or go to *www.insure.com* or to *www.term4sale.com.*

If unauthorized insurance is included in your loan documents, ask that it be removed before proceeding with the closing.

CASHIER'S CHECKS

Many banks charge $3 for cashier's checks.

Solution: Get a money order from the post office for about $1.

DELAYS IN CREDITING YOUR ACCOUNT

Many banks say they will not clear an out-of-state check for three business days. And, some checks take even longer. Since some banks are closed one weekday, if you deposit a check on the "wrong" day, your check might not clear for longer still.

Your bank receives payment for most checks from anywhere in the US within just 24 hours. Banks impose a waiting period and only count business days, not calendar days, so they can get free use of your money.

Solution: Ask for a brochure describing your bank's check-clearing policy. Direct deposits should clear immediately. If you need immediate access to cash, even from out of state, ask your banker to arrange it.

ATM FEES

Choose a bank that has no ATM fees. Locate other banks that don't charge ATM fees in case you are away from your branch's ATM. To find banks with no ATM fees, go to *www.bankrate.com* and click "Checking & Savings."

Get Bigger Rewards from Your Credit Card

To get the most that you can from reward credit cards…

●**Use only one.** You will generate bigger rewards by funneling spending to one card.

●**Don't carry a balance.** Rebate-card interest rates are 1% higher on average than rates on other types of credit cards.

●**Shop for the best deal.** In the past, rebate cards offered frequent-flier miles or cash. Today, rebates can be used for store discounts, gasoline, gift certificates, cars, even college savings.

●**Heavy card users** should consider one that offers a greater rebate when you reach a certain spending level.

Greg McBride, CFA, senior financial analyst at Bankrate.com, North Palm Beach, Florida.

More from Greg McBride...

Keeping Tabs on Your Credit Score

When shifting a balance to another credit card to obtain a lower interest rate, don't close the old credit card, says financial analyst Greg McBride. Closing it can reduce your credit score if it results in your having less available credit in relation to your debt.

Exception: If the debt arose from overspending, close out the old card to avoid the temptation that the larger credit limit may pose.

Maximize Credit Card Rewards

Use the same card all the time and charge everyday items, such as groceries, gasoline and on-line purchases to maximize your rewards. Find a card with the type of rebate that works best for you—some offer cash back, others give points redeemable for a variety of goods and services. Look for credit cards that have partnerships with more than one company. Always pay your bills in full every month—otherwise, finance charges will cost more than the rebate program gives you.

Curtis Arnold, founder and public relations director, CardRatings.com, which reviews and rates credit card offers, Little Rock, Arkansas.

Best Way to Deal with Credit Card Disputes

Web sites that tackle credit card disputes on your behalf charge hefty fees. Sites work on a contingency basis. If they succeed in getting a charge removed from your bill, you may have to pay as much as half the disputed charge.

Better: Handle the matter yourself. The federal Fair Credit Billing Act allows you to dispute a charge and withhold payment if the item you requested is different than what you received or if it is not delivered as agreed. You must submit your dispute in writing to the card issuer within 60 days from the mailing date of the statement on which the charge appeared. Include any documentation of your side of the story. If you phone in the dispute, follow up with written confirmation. Send your letter with return receipt requested to be sure the card issuer received it.

Gerri Detweiler, president, Ultimate Credit Solutions, Inc., Sarasota, Forida, *www.ultimatecredit.com.* She is author of *Reduce Debt, Reduce Stress.* Good Advice Press 2009.

Easy Way to Avoid Costly Late Fees

Some credit card issuers specify to the minute when payments are due. If you are five minutes late, you are charged a late fee.

Self-defense: Read your credit card statement to find the exact due date and time.

Daniel Ray, editor in chief, Bankrate.com, North Palm Beach, Florida.

Co-Signing a Loan Can Damage Your Credit Rating

If you co-sign a loan for someone who is late with the payments, your credit score will be affected and you may be liable for payments. The creditor can try to garnish your wages.

Self-defense: If you feel that you must co-sign—as parents often do for children who are borrowing for school or a home—insist that a copy of the bill be sent to you each month. Then you will know if payments are up-to-date and can take action if they are not, before your own credit is harmed.

Mark Kantrowitz, publisher, FinAid, on-line provider of financial-aid information, Cranberry Township, Pennsylvania. www.finaid.org,

Earn More Money... Pay Less Interest— How to Find a Credit Union

Patrick Keefe, vice president at the Credit Union National Association, Washington, DC, www.cuna.org.

Credit unions offer comprehensive banking services—credit cards, on-line bill paying and home-equity loans. Some even have securities brokerage subsidiaries.

Important: Credit unions pay higher rates on CDs and savings accounts than banks, and they charge less for mortgages and auto loans because of their not-for-profit status. Average rates are listed at *www.bankrate.com.*

CHOOSING THE RIGHT ONE

With more than 10,000 credit unions, practically anyone can find one that meets his/her needs. To compare, check with our organization, the Credit Union National Association (800-358-5710 or *www.creditunion.coop,* click

on "Locate a Credit Union"). *Here are some features to consider...*

●**Membership criteria.** Some credit unions are only open to residents of a particular city...employees of a corporation or government entity...members of a union, professional organization or fraternal association, including the Elks and Knights of Columbus. They also are open to members' relatives.

●**Array of services.** Credit unions provide everything from insurance to small-business loans of $80,000 or less—an amount too small for most banks to spend their time on. Others will only provide basic savings and checking accounts. If your credit union doesn't offer a service you need, call a member of the board of directors and request it. Or join more than one credit union.

●**Insured deposits.** Make sure that the credit union insures deposits by the National Credit Union Administration (NCUA).

●**Location.** If you prefer dealing with a teller, you'll need a credit union that has a nearby branch. If you do your banking using automated teller machines (ATMs) and the Internet, the location might not matter. For easy access, make sure that the credit union you choose is part of a bank ATM network.

Get Better Interest Rates Simply by Checking Your Credit Report

Steve Rhode, president and cofounder, Myvesta.org, a nonprofit financial-management organization in Rockville, Maryland, www.myvesta.org. Mr. Rhode is coauthor of The Ultimate Spending Plan Program Yearly Tracking Book. Debt Counselors of America.

Actively monitoring your credit report will ensure that you get the best possible rates and let you catch identity thieves in the act. But it's not so simple.

The major credit agencies may not all have the same information about you. If you have just one report, you won't get the whole picture.

GET YOUR CREDIT REPORTS

Check your credit reports for accuracy at least once every year. If they are incorrect, you might pay unnecessarily high rates or even be turned down for loans altogether.

Cost: $29.95* for a 3-in-1 Credit Report with a free credit score. But, under the *Fair and Accurate Credit Transactions Act of 2003* (FACT), you can receive one free credit report per year from each of the reporting agencies. Eligibility is based on a state rollout schedule set by federal law. See *www.annualcreditreport. com* for more information.

The three agencies: Equifax (800-685-1111, *www.equifax.com*)…Experian (888-397-3742, *www.experian.com*)…TransUnion (877-322-8228, *www.transunion.com*).

Easier: Obtain a consolidated report, which includes a credit score and data from any of the three reporting agencies or from my organization, *www.myvesta.org.*

ANALYZE YOUR CREDIT REPORT

Review your report, and immediately tell the credit provider and credit agency about any inaccuracies. It takes about two months for closed accounts to disappear from your credit history. You can get expedited service for a fee. *Look for…*

●**Active accounts you do not recognize,** such as credit cards or store charge accounts in places that you don't shop. Someone may have stolen your identity, or another person's charge accounts may have been included accidentally on your report. This frequently happens to people who have common surnames, such as Jones and Smith.

●**Inaccuracies,** such as debts listed as unpaid that were settled and payments listed as late that were made on time. These entries will remain on your record for seven years unless you correct them. Make sure late payments are not listed as uncollected debts.

Fixing mistakes: Ask the credit agency for a dispute form. The agency generally must investigate your concerns and then report back to you within 30 days.

*All prices are subject to change.

If the agency cannot verify the information that you questioned, it must delete it from your file and notify anyone who has requested your credit report within the past six months.

●**Old or unused charge accounts.** Too much credit can harm your rating even if most of the accounts are dormant.

What to do: Keep two or three of the oldest accounts open, and use them once in a while. Close the others.

Simple Ways To Cut Expenses And Save More

Bill and Mary Staton, founders of The Staton Institute, a financial education and counseling center in Charlotte, North Carolina, *www.billstaton.com.* They are authors of *Worry-Free Family Finances.* McGraw-Hill. Mr. Staton is also publisher of the weekly investment newsletter *E-Money Digest/Guided Portfolio Service.*

Now is a great time to get your financial house into good order, from expenses to investments. *Here are our three steps to help you relax and take the anxiety out of your finances…*

CUT NEEDLESS EXPENSES

People tend to forget about small purchases soon after they have made them, but these can add up fast. For example, a daily $3 cappuccino costs almost $1,100 over the course of a year. *Game plan…*

●**Jot down every purchase of more than $1 for seven days.** Exclude unavoidable costs, such as utility bills and mortgage payments. At the end of the week, tally the cost of the items you could have skipped without significantly impacting your quality of life. Most people will come up with between $50 and $100—that's $2,600 to $5,200 every year! *Some common money wasters…*

●Purchases made while shopping just for the fun of it—not for things you need.

●ATM cash-withdrawal fees of $1.50 to $3 at machines that are unaffiliated with your bank.

●Items bought because they were on sale, even though you didn't need them.

• Late-payment fees levied by credit card companies.

• Late-return fees from video rental stores and libraries.

• **Set a savings goal based on your seven-day waste estimate.** Have a fun use in mind for the money saved.

Example: If you waste about $50 a week, resolve to save $7 a day to fund a $2,500 vacation next summer.

Each week, put the money you would have wasted in a savings account or money market mutual fund specifically for this goal. Post a note on your refrigerator with the daily dollar amount you want to save so that you won't forget.

SHRINK BIG EXPENSES

Big expenses can't always be avoided, but they may be reduced. *Game plan...*

• **Eliminate credit card debt.** The average American family owes about $8,000 in credit card debt. Assuming a typical interest rate of 18%, that's almost $1,500 a year in interest charges alone.

Paying off credit card debt should be your top financial goal. If you can't pay it off immediately, transfer balances to the card with the lowest rate. Or apply for a new card that has attractive rates on balance transfers. To compare card offers, visit *www.bankrate.com*.

Important: Don't take out a home-equity loan to pay credit card debt. Today's low rates may be enticing, but the risk is too great. If you can't make the payments, you could lose your home. That can't happen if your only debts are to credit card issuers.

• **Buy less car than you can afford.** Vehicles are the biggest extravagance most families have. Yet all any car really needs to do is get you from one place to the next. You can get a perfectly nice, safe and reliable new sedan or minivan for about $20,000, not the $30,000 to $40,000 many people spend.

Examples: Honda Accord (starting at approximately $23,860)*...Toyota Camry ($21,075)...Dodge Caravan ($20,555).

Negotiating tool: Before buying a new car, look up the invoice price at *www.edmunds.com*. If you shop carefully, you can expect to pay that amount or less.

• **Be smart about big events.** The typical wedding now costs about $25,000. Parents don't like to scrimp on their child's big day, so they often borrow to finance a lavish celebration.

Better strategy: Set a limit. For example, tell your daughter that you're willing to spend up to $15,000 on her wedding. If she wants to spend more, she and her fiancé can pay the difference. If she wants to spend less, she can keep the remainder. Chances are that she will happily cut costs and pocket the difference. You will save money and give the newlyweds a head start on their nest egg.

INVEST INTELLIGENTLY

The easy strategy we teach is to invest only in shares of companies that have increased their dividends per share for at least 10 years in a row. We track all these companies in our annual directory, *America's Finest Companies*®. As reported in our directory, these companies have returned an average of 16.93% annually for the 10 years through March 31, 2005, versus 10.79% for the S&P 500 Index.

You can find a stock's dividend history in the *Value Line Investment Survey*, available at numerous libraries.

Sell a stock only when the company fails to keep increasing its dividend or if another stock with a steadily rising dividend is a better bargain based on its price-to-earnings ratio (P/E).

*All prices are subject to change.

Borrow Better...How to Get the Best Deal Now on Every Type of Loan

Greg McBride, CFA, a senior financial analyst for Bankrate.com, an on-line provider of interest rate information and financial advice based in North Palm Beach, Florida.

The ongoing credit crisis has made it more difficult to obtain loans, including mortgages, home-equity loans and even credit card and student loans.

But that doesn't mean it's a bad time to borrow if you qualify.

The Federal Reserve cut its benchmark interest rate from 5.25% to 2% in the past year, which helped lower rates on many types of loans. Also: The federal government's announcement that it would take over troubled mortgage giants Fannie Mae and Freddie Mac helped push down mortgage rates, at least temporarily.

To find the best deals today…

MORTGAGES

To get a rate anywhere near 6% on a 30-year mortgage with reasonable points and fees, you will need a credit score of at least 680 (preferably 720) out of 850…verifiable, stable income…and enough cash to make a down payment of at least 20%. Your interest rates will climb quickly as your credit score drifts below that level, and many lenders will not be interested in lending to you at all. Less-qualified borrowers should postpone their mortgage applications until requirements loosen up so that they can qualify for better rates.

Best values today: "Conforming" fixed-rate mortgages—those that are within current limits for Fannie and Freddie backing, which range up to $729,750, depending on location. Rates on adjustable-rate mortgages (ARMs) are nearly as high as those on 30-year fixed-rate mortgages at the moment, so it is wise to lock in today's relatively low fixed rates.

Rates on jumbo mortgages, those that exceed Fannie and Freddie limits, have been about 1.2 to 1.5 percentage points higher than conforming mortgage rates recently. If you require a jumbo mortgage to purchase a property, consider choosing cheaper property instead or make a larger down payment.

Where to shop: Shopping around among banks, credit unions and mortgage brokers has become even more crucial because rates vary greatly. Look at Web sites that compare mortgage rates, including my site, Bankrate.com.

Compare all loan costs, not just interest rates, before settling on an offer. Some lenders attempt to make loans appear attractive by charging low interest rates, but then tack on excessive fees and points.

Recent average rates for conforming loans: 5.99% for a 30-year fixed-rate mortgage and 5.68% for a 15-year fixed-rate mortgage. A 30% down payment can shave one-quarter to one-half percentage point off the rate.

HOME-EQUITY LOANS

Lenders have been cutting back credit limits and canceling some credit lines. But if you have at least a 20% equity stake in your home even after the value of your home has plunged in today's market, it is possible to obtain a second mortgage with an appealing rate. That means that the total amount of all loans secured by your home, including the home-equity loan or home-equity line of credit (HELOC), may not exceed 80% of the value of the property. If you have a HELOC and may need the money before long, consider drawing on the credit line now and letting the money sit in a bank account until you need it.

Best values today: HELOC interest rates, which are variable, were recently 5.4% (for $30,000 of credit) on average, well below the 7.9% average fixed rate for home-equity loans.

Where to shop: Same as for mortgages—see section on this page.

AUTO LOAN

Vehicle loans recently have been at the lowest rates in several years, helped by special financing offers from struggling auto manufacturers. Only car buyers with credit scores above 650 will be able to obtain the best rates, however. If you have poor credit, this is not a good time to finance a car.

If the dealer is offering a 0% rate, you will need a credit score of at least 680, and possibly 700, plus a 10% down payment in many cases. Determine your credit score in advance on *www.myfico.com*, and if it is too low, consider trying to improve it before you get a car loan.

Best values today: If you can afford the 36-month loan's higher monthly payments, lean toward a 36-month loan rather than a longer period. That way, you'll end up paying much less in total interest payments.

Where to shop: Local credit unions. Interest rates on new car loans often are more than half a percentage point lower at credit unions than at other types of lenders. Also, dealerships have more incentive to offer their best rates when they know that they must compete with another offer.

Examples of recent rates: 6.58% for a five-year new car loan…6.8% for a three-year new car loan…and 7.15% for a three-year used car loan.

CREDIT CARD LOANS

Credit card interest rates have fallen sharply in the past year, although credit card issuers such as American Express have slashed credit limits. If your credit score is above 620 and you have a card currently charging more than 15%, you should be able to obtain a lower rate for both balance transfers and new purchases.

Best values today: If you carry a significant balance and pay a high rate, switch to a card with low rates on balance transfers. This could include cards with ultra-low six- or 12-month introductory "teaser" rates, particularly if you expect to pay down your credit card debt in the near future. If you do not currently carry a balance on your cards but sometimes do, select a card with a low interest rate on new purchases. If you never carry a balance on your credit cards, select a rewards card or cash-back card.

Where to shop: Use Web sites that compare credit card features

STUDENT LOANS

It has become much more difficult to obtain student loans from private lenders in the past year, particularly if your credit score is below 650.

On the bright side, many government student loan programs recently have become more flexible and more appealing, with lower interest rates and higher borrowing limits in some cases. *Take full advantage of these programs before searching for private student loans…*

●**Stafford loans** provide undergraduates with up to $7,500 per year. Rates are capped at 6.8% with no credit check required.

●**Perkins loans** have rates capped at 5%. They are available only to students in extreme financial need and cannot exceed $4,000 per year.

●**PLUS loans** allow the parents of undergraduates to borrow up to the full cost of tuition with fixed interest rates capped at 8.5%. A credit check is required, but this credit check is more forgiving than those used by private lenders. See the US Department of Education Web site for more details (*www.studentaid.ed.gov*).

Where to shop: Fill out a Free Application for Federal Student Aid (FAFSA) form *(www.fafsa.ed.gov)*. Discuss grant programs and federal student loan programs with the college's financial aid office.

How Debt Can Make You Rich

David Bach, CEO and founder of FinishRich Inc., financial advisers and educators in New York City, *www.finishrich.com*. Mr. Bach is author of *Smart Couples Finish Rich*, *Smart Women Finish Rich* and *The Finish Rich Workbook* (all from Broadway).

Few people seem to be aware that there is a science to borrowing that will actually *build* wealth. Debt interest drains potential savings, but some purchases can yield big future returns. How does your debt load stack up? *Debt in the average US household…*

Mortgage balance: $69,277.

Mortgage payment: $669/month.

Car loan: $23,065.

Car payment: $412/month.

Credit card balance: $8,367.

This is an enormous debt load. The average American now spends a little more than 14% of his/her after-tax income to pay credit card bills and other debts. Some people pay a lot more, with mortgages alone taking up to 30% of their after-tax income.

MAXIMIZE "GOOD" DEBT

Good debt is money borrowed to buy an asset that appreciates in value. It allows you to build wealth over the long term. *Examples…*

●**Home mortgages.** Most homes appreciate in value, mortgage interest usually is tax deductible, *and* you get a place to live. The average net worth of a renter is $4,200…of a home owner, $132,000.

●**Education loans.** An advanced degree can help to increase your earning ability by as much as 80%. Up to $2,500 per year in interest on student loans is tax deductible in 2008 if you earn less than $55,000, or $115,000 if married ($60,000 or $120,000 respectively in 2009).

●**Business-improvement loans.** These are some of the best investments. They usually directly increase revenue.

●**Home-improvement loans.** These also are good debt just as long as you don't *over-improve* your house to the degree that your investment remains unrecoverable when you sell. Recoverable improvements are those that make your house more desirable, such as a new kitchen or bathroom. However, the cost of marble floors in a modest home might be hard to recover when you sell.

MINIMIZE "BAD" DEBT

Bad debt is money borrowed for items that don't contribute to your financial future. *Some examples…*

●**Auto loans.** Even if you get 0% financing, you still are taking on $20,000 or more in debt that could be used for an appreciating asset. In addition, just as soon as you drive off the car dealer's lot, your investment value declines by about 30%.

Better: If you drive less than 10,000 miles a year as part of your job, consider leasing a car and deducting the expense. Otherwise, buy a used car at a fraction of the cost of a new car. You still can deduct the cost of mileage accumulated for work.

●**Loans for vacations,** clothing, furnishings, appliances and entertainment.

●**Loans for weddings,** anniversary parties and other big celebrations. The average wedding now costs about $20,000 and can take 10 years to pay off.

CONTROL ALL DEBT

●**Record every cent you spend for one week.** I call it finding your "latte factor." If you spend $3.50 per day on a caffe latte, that same amount invested over 30 years at a 10% return would be a fortune—$242,916.

Helpful: A free worksheet on spending is available at *www.finishrich.com.* Just click on "The Latte Factor Calculator."

●**Keep debt payments under 15% of net income.** Anything higher almost always indicates future debt problems. It also makes lenders reluctant to give you loans.

To calculate your percentage of debt to income: Total all your monthly expenses. Subtract your mortgage payments or rent. Include credit card bills, personal loans, student loans, medical bills for services already rendered and car loans. Divide this figure by your monthly after-tax income—including salary, investment income, alimony and child support.

Example: If you have monthly after-tax income of $4,000 and debt payments of $580, your percentage of debt to income is $580 divided by $4,000, or 14.5%.

MANAGING WEALTH

●**Determine the real cost of a purchase before buying.** Real cost includes the interest you will pay. People get into big debt trouble because they fool themselves about real costs.

Example: A new computer is attractive at $499—but if you charge it and take two years to pay off the balance, it really costs closer to $600. Is the computer still worth the money?

Use the calculator in the "Credit Cards" section of *www.bankrate.com* to figure out the real cost of purchases.

●**Think of spending as a series of "either/or" choices.** Before you make any purchase, think about the trade-off—*If I buy this stereo, I can't go out to dinner for the next three months. Is the stereo worth it to me?*

●**Postpone buying anything that costs more than $100** until you think about it for 24 hours. This cuts down on impulse spending that you might regret later.

●**Automate your bill paying as much as possible.** Have your credit card payments and other debts automatically deducted from your checking account. Knowing that you'll have to pay off the balance in full each month might make you less likely to spend.

This practice also avoids interest penalties and puts an end to late fees, which now average about $30 per month.

Automatic payments can be made through most banks or through *www.paytrust.com* and *www.myezbills.com*.

•**Fund your dreams.** Set aside a portion of your after-tax income for vacations and treats. You are less likely to binge if you have something to look forward to.

BEWARE OF DEBT TRAPS

The average American's credit card debt is more than three times what it was in the early 1990s—and the average interest rate is 14%.

•**Avoid store credit cards.** It's easy to be lured by aggressive promotions. Many retailers give you 10% off your first purchase when you open a credit card account and offer special discount incentives to retain cardholders.

Best: Turn down these offers, no matter how much money you save. The only advantage is if you pay off your balance. Virtually all of my clients have good intentions, but sooner or later they slip. That's why store credit cards, which typically charge more than 20% interest, are such a lucrative business. Also, lenders look negatively at your credit report if you have a dozen cards with tens of thousands of dollars in available credit—even if you don't use it.

•**Be wary of "one year interest free" deals on furniture and electronics.** The fine print on some contracts stipulates that if you don't pay off your entire bill within a year, you're liable for 15% to 22% interest on the entire amount for the year.

Smart Money Strategies for Unmarried Couples

Steven J.J. Weisman, estate planning attorney in Cambridge, Massachusetts, and host of the nationally syndicated radio show "A Touch of Grey," which addresses financial issues for people over age 50. He is author of *A Guide to Elder Planning: Everything You Need to Know to Protect Yourself Legally & Financially.* Prentice Hall.

Living together out of wedlock is not just a trend among young people. The number of senior cohabiting couples has jumped by about 50% during the past decade, according to the US Census Bureau. Remaining single allows you to keep a former spouse's pension, military and Social Security benefits...keep your children's inheritance intact...and avoid liability if your partner has to spend down his/her assets to qualify for Medicaid.

But living together also deprives you of rights afforded to married couples.

Example: You and your partner buy a house. Shortly afterward, you break up. Since there is no law governing how you distribute the property in the event of a dispute, you may have to file a civil lawsuit to prove your financial contributions to the "partnership property."

If you live together without being married, here's how to protect yourself...

FINANCIAL RESPONSIBILITIES

If you didn't do it before you moved in together, put together an agreement that can be helpful in determining the rights and obligations of each partner during the relationship as well as if you break up. Decide how much you and your partner will contribute to the day-to-day costs for food, utilities, laundry, housing and the like. Typically, couples establish a joint household account to make bill-paying convenient but maintain separate bank accounts, credit cards, insurance and brokerage accounts.

Have a family law attorney draw up a "cohabitation agreement," especially if there is a significant discrepancy in wealth and/or income between you and your partner.

Reason: Not getting married doesn't prevent financial entanglement. For instance, if you have greater wealth and you and your partner break up, you could be sued for alimony-like support. *The agreement should address...*

●**Property you each owned** before you began living together, such as a home or an investment portfolio, as well as assets that you accumulated together.

●**How property should be divided if you split up.** What happens to the house if you break up? Will one of you have the right to stay in it and buy the other partner out...or will the house be sold and the proceeds divided?

Resource: Unmarried to Each Other, by Dorian Solot and Marshall Miller (Avalon).

JOINT PROPERTY

Never contribute money to the acquisition of, say, a house that is held solely in your partner's name. *Instead, you and your partner can jointly acquire the property as...*

●**Tenants in common.** This is convenient if one partner has more money to invest and wants to own a disproportionate percentage of the property or wants to bequeath his/her share to someone else—such as a child from a previous relationship—in his will. To establish a tenancy in common in real estate, the deed to the property should indicate each party's ownership percentage. For other assets, a contract, such as a domestic partnership agreement, can be used to establish each party's relative interests.

●**Joint tenants with rights of survivorship.** This means that you own equal shares in the property and the title automatically passes to the survivor upon one partner's death. This is best for unmarried couples who wish to avoid inheritance disputes—for instance, those who have ex-spouses and/or children from prior relationships but don't want the property to go to them, at least not right away.

Careful: Joint ownership can present tax problems for wealthy partners. Married spouses are able to pass unlimited amounts of money to each other free of estate tax while they're alive and after they die, but unmarried couples currently can pass along an estate of no more than $2 million before it is subject to federal estate tax. I have seen situations in which an unmarried partner had to sell a house in order to pay the taxes.

Alternative: Each partner purchases life insurance that can be used to cover the projected estate tax when either partner dies. (An agent and/or financial adviser can recommend how much to buy.)

Maintain careful records of each partner's contribution to the property. Estate taxes can be reduced if the surviving joint tenant can prove that he contributed to the purchase.

TAX BENEFITS

Unlike estate tax law, federal and state income tax laws favor unmarried couples. You and your partner are required to file separately, which means that you avoid the "marriage penalty"—the tax surcharge assessed on couples who jointly earn about $250,000 a year and up. Each of you also has more flexibility regarding deductions, allowing for greater tax savings than many married couples.

Example: If you jointly own a home but you have much more income than your partner, you could make the lion's share of the mortgage payments and charitable contributions and itemize deductions. Your partner, in turn, still would be able to take the standard deduction as a single filer.

Other advantages: You can claim your partner (and his/her minor children) as dependents and earn tax credits for them if you provide half of their total support and their annual taxable income doesn't exceed $3,500 each for 2008. (Nontaxable income such as gifts, welfare benefits and nontaxable Social Security benefits doesn't count.) Also, the IRS cannot attach a lien to your salary or personal assets if your nonspouse partner fails to pay his taxes.

Caution: Don't refer to your partner as your spouse. In some states, acting as if you were married makes you a "common law" husband and wife. If you are considered married by common law, you are married for federal income tax purposes.

Self-defense: Don't adopt your partner's last name, and don't refer to him as your spouse on public documents.

Ask a lawyer to draw up a...

●**Will.** Unless you designate your wishes in writing, your estate passes to your relatives in a manner specified by state law—which could be far from what you would want. (Your prized possessions could go to siblings with whom you haven't spoken in years.) A will gives you control and flexibility.

Example: You can leave your house to your children but stipulate that your partner may remain there rent-free for the rest of his life.

Note: In certain states, such as California, Hawaii and Vermont, registered domestic partners can inherit a portion of a deceased partner's property—but these laws carry extensive restrictions. I don't consider them a substitute for an inheritance plan.

●**Durable power of attorney.** This document gives your partner the authority to manage your legal and financial affairs on your behalf. Without one, your partner would have to go to state court and petition to be appointed your conservator if you became unable to act for yourself.

To find an attorney who specializes in estate planning for unmarried couples, go to *family. findlaw.com/marriage.* Also, *www.glad.org* (617-426-1350) and *www.lambdalegal.com* (212-809-8585) are geared toward same-sex couples but can suggest lawyers for any unmarried partners.

Beat the Wily Banks on Overdraft Fees

Jean Ann Fox, director of financial services for the Consumer Federation of America, a nonprofit consumer organization based in Washington, DC. *www.consumer fed.org.*

Penalties have soared for overdrawing money from your checking account. The average fee charged by the 10 largest US banks for withdrawing more money than is in an account is now $34.65. And such fees are per withdrawal. Example: Bank of America allows up to five overdraft fees per day, which could total $175 each day. Most banks also add "sustained overdraft fees" of as much as $8 per day if the overdrawn funds are not repaid within three to seven days. What can happen: Your bank takes longer than you expect to clear a check you deposited, and your account is overdrawn before the money becomes available. When the check finally clears, the bank claims the money for itself to pay the overdraft fees you unknowingly incurred. So you end up overdrawing even more money. *To avoid overdraft fees...*

●**Have your paycheck directly deposited into your checking account,** because direct deposits clear right away.

●**Sign up for true overdraft protection,** which links your checking to your savings account, credit card or line of credit to cover overages. There may be a fee each time, but it should be $5, not $30 or $35. Better yet, choose a bank that doesn't charge.

●**Ask whether your bank can provide E-mail or text-message warnings** when your checking account balance falls below a certain level.

Sneaky Fees Banks Charge on "FREE" Accounts

Legally, "free" means no minimum-balance requirements and no activity or maintenance fees, such as monthly service charges.

But banks quietly impose other fees—for using your debit card...closing your account before a certain period...even calling to inquire about your balance. For some accounts, you even may be charged for talking to a teller.

Self-defense: Before you open an account, ask for a list of fees. If your bank charges for debit card purchases, use the card only for ATM services at your bank's ATMs.

Ken McEldowney, executive director, Consumer Action, a national consumer education and advocacy organization in San Francisco, *www.consumer-action.org.*

Right Way to Make an Interest-Free Loan

Barbara Weltman, an attorney based in Millwood, New York, *www.barbaraweltman.com.* She is author of *J.K. Lasser's 1001 Deductions and Tax Breaks.* Wiley.

If you want to help a child, grandchild or other individual buy a home, pay college bills or meet other expenses, but don't want to risk giving your money away outright in case you need it later, an interest-free loan may fit the bill...

• **There are no adverse tax consequences to such loans**—as long as they do not exceed $10,000.

• **Loans larger than $10,000 but not exceeding $100,000 may result in "imputed interest"**—i.e., be treated for tax purposes as if they carried a market rate of interest. But imputed interest will exist only to the extent the recipient of the loan has investment income of over $1,000.

So, if loan proceeds are used for a purpose such as buying a home when the recipient has no investment income over $1,000, there will be no tax consequences, even for a loan that is as large as $100,000.

With an interest-free loan, you will retain the right to be repaid later, though if it turns out you don't need the money, you can later forgive all or part of the loan as a gift.

And in the meantime, you help the loan recipient with the 0% interest financing terms.

When interest-free loans exceed $100,000, you will have imputed interest, regardless of the borrower's investment income.

Technical rules apply, so consult an expert before acting.

Pay Your Bills For Free!

Free on-line bill paying is available at several bank sites—and they guarantee on-time payment or they will pay the late fee. Try Bank of America (*www.bofa.com*)...Chase (*www.chase.com*)...Citibank (*www.citibank. com*)...US Bancorp (*www.usbank.com*). On-line payments also are free at HSBC Bank USA (*www.hsbc.com*) but without an on-time payment guarantee.

Several other Web sites offer free on-line payment for customers under certain circumstances. Visit SunTrust (*www.suntrust.com*)... MyCheckFree (*www.mycheckfree.com*).

Money, Time-Life Bldg., Rockefeller Center, New York City 10020.

To Keep Interest Charges Low...

Your credit score determines the rate you'll be charged for a mortgage, car loan or on credit cards. *Major factors in scoring...*

• **Payment history.** Any late payments reduce your score.

• **Total debt.** A high debt load brings your score down.

• **Credit history.** The longer, the better.

• **Types of credit.** The more kinds you have, the better able to manage a loan you are considered to be.

• **New credit.** Applying for or receiving a lot of credit may reduce your score.

Jen Anthony, president, OnePay, a nonprofit debt management organization, Rockville, Maryland.

You Can Outwit Credit Card Companies—The Moves to Make Now…

Curtis Arnold, founder and CEO of US Citizens for Fair Credit Card Terms, Inc., which educates consumers about credit cards, based in Little Rock, Arkansas. Its Web site, CardRatings.com, features consumer reviews of credit cards. Arnold is author of *How You Can Profit from Credit Cards*. FT Press.

Hidden fees, high interest rates and penalties can make credit cards extremely expensive. *Tricks to help you cut costs and even come out ahead…*

SEEK 0% RATES

Credit card companies aggressively market introductory rates as low as 0% for the first six or 12 months. The interest rates then increase, sometimes dramatically. To win this game, shift your balance away from one introductory-rate card and onto another shortly before the low-rate period ends. Jumping from card to card can keep your rates low forever.

Watch for these low-intro-rate offers in the mail, or find them on-line at Bankrate.com or on my own site, CardRatings.com.

Caution: Don't enter any personal information on-line unless you are filling out an application on the card issuer's own site—and you see "https" in the Web browser address line, which indicates that the site is "secure."

To make intro-rate flipping work…

●**Choose cards with introductory periods of at least 12 months.** Switching cards more often is a headache. It could also hurt your credit rating because each time you apply for a new credit card, you trigger a credit inquiry, which could lower your credit score.

●**Avoid cards with high balance transfer fees.** There often is a fee to transfer a balance to a low-intro-rate card. It typically is worth paying this fee only when transferring a four-figure or larger balance, and only when the fee is capped at no more than $100.

Note: The "catch" in many of these offers is that there is *no* cap on the transfer fees.

Example: Many card companies charge a 3% balance transfer fee with no cap. Therefore, if you're moving a large amount of money, the transfer fee may negate the 0% introductory rate.

●**Follow the card's rules to the letter.** Your low introductory rate could turn into a much higher "default rate" if you are even a single day late with a payment. Set up automatic payments or pay your bill the day it arrives, to avoid problems.

There is some danger that you could get stuck with a big balance on a high-rate card if you cannot qualify for another low-rate introductory offer before your current one expires. If you prefer a simpler, lower-risk approach, apply for a card that offers a low fixed interest rate for the life of the transferred balance.

Example: Blue from American Express has a 4.99% fixed rate if the transfer is submitted at the time of application (800-223-2670, *www.americanexpress.com*).

DOUBLE UP

There's no rule saying that you can have only one credit card from a given card issuer. In fact, it may be to your advantage to have more than one.

If you receive a very appealing card offer from a credit card issuer with which you already have an account, go ahead and apply. If you are approved and are given a low credit limit on the second card, ask the card issuer to "reallocate" your credit limit from the card with less attractive terms to the one with more attractive terms. Reallocation is not an application for new credit—it's just a consolidation, so the card issuer often will do this without even performing an additional credit check. Some issuers won't grant a reallocation, so ask before you apply.

Example: You have a $10,000 credit limit on a Discover More Card (800-347-2683, *www.discovercard.com*) that charges a 17.99% interest rate, and you are approved for a $2,000 credit limit on a new Discover More Card with a 12-month introductory rate of 0%. Have most or all of your credit limit from the original card reallocated to the low-rate card.

Inexperienced customer service reps sometimes do not understand what customers mean by credit reallocation. If you have trouble, ask to speak with someone in the credit or balance-transfer department, and if that fails, ask to speak to a manager.

BUYER PROTECTION

Some cards provide buyers with various types of protection for purchases of items, but few cardholders take advantage…

●**Price protection.** Citi Diamond Preferred Card (800-456-4277, *www.citicards.com*) offers this guarantee for most non-Internet items. If you buy an item with the card, then see it advertised in print within 60 days for less than the amount you paid, you will get a refund of up to $250.

●**Purchase security.** If a covered item purchased with a card that provides this guarantee is accidentally damaged or stolen within 90 days, you are covered up to a certain dollar amount.

Example: Chase Visa cards cover up to $500 per occurrence (877-682-4273, *www.chase.com*).

●**Return protection.** If you try to return a covered item within 90 days and the store won't take it back, you can get a refund for the purchase price up to certain limits.

Example: American Express provides refunds up to $300 per item and up to $1,000 annually.

GET CASH BACK

With rewards cards, the credit card company pays you for your business.

There are many different types of rewards cards. Cash-back cards, which give you a cash rebate ranging from 1% to 5% of what you spend, provide the most useful reward and tend to be the easiest to use.

Examples: Blue Cash from American Express is a great cash-back card for big spenders, but the best rate—5% rebates for categories such as groceries and gasoline—does not kick in until you spend $6,500 each year. Chase Freedom Visa is a better choice for those who use their credit cards less frequently. It rebates 3% for each of three categories in which you spend the most in a given month and 1% on all other purchases.

To make cash-back cards work…

●**Do not carry a balance on these cards.** They usually have high interest rates.

●**Select a cash-back card that matches your spending habits.** Some provide more cash back on gas purchases, others at specific merchants.

●**Read the fine print to find out if the program caps your annual cash reward,** and stop using the card when you reach the cap.

●**Do not let the rewards encourage you to spend more than you otherwise would.**

Frequent-flier cards are less appealing. Today's crowded flights make rewards seats difficult to obtain.

Exception: A card that offers a large number of miles up-front just for signing up for the card (or soon thereafter) might be worth applying for. You may even be able to cancel the card as soon as you receive your miles and before any annual fees begin.

Example: Citi Gold/AAdvantage World MasterCard offers 15,000 miles on American Airlines if the cardholder spends just $750 in the first four months. It has no annual fee in the first year.

The Automatic Millionaire's Get-Rich Secret

David Bach, CEO and founder of FinishRich Inc., financial advisers and educators in New York City, *www.finishrich.com*. Mr. Bach is author of *Smart Couples Finish Rich, Smart Women Finish Rich* and *The Finish Rich Workbook* (all from Broadway).

Sticking to a budget means depriving yourself today for the sake of your future well-being. Few of us have the discipline that this requires—we dine at expensive restaurants …buy new cars every two or three years…and spend $3.50 for a cup of coffee. Result? Even people who have decent incomes live from paycheck to paycheck.

To save steadily, most people need to override human nature. How? By putting savings on autopilot. Arrange for a certain percentage of each paycheck to be tucked away. Doing so takes little discipline or effort. Many employers have automatic payroll-deduction plans for retirement accounts. You also can arrange for your bank or mutual fund firm to take money out of your bank account every month.

HOW MUCH TO SET ASIDE

Start out small. Save 1% of your salary. Soon, you can bump that up to 3%. Your goal should be to save at least 10%. Those with grander objectives should save 15% to 20%. You will be amazed by how little sacrifice is involved.

Say you now buy lunch at the office every day. By brown-bagging it (at a cost of $1 per day instead of $8), you can save $35 a week, or about $150 a month. If you earn a 7% annual return, that savings would increase to $73,791 in 20 years.

The best way to save is with a 401(k) or another tax-advantaged plan. If you save after-tax dollars, the federal government by itself takes about $3 of every $10 you earn. When you put $10 into a retirement plan, the entire sum goes to work and won't be taxed until withdrawal.

PAY DOWN YOUR MORTGAGE

Making regular mortgage payments is a form of forced savings.

To accelerate the process, see if your bank will allow you to pay off your mortgage early, perhaps by making one payment every two weeks instead of one a month. By following this system, you will make 26 half payments, or the equivalent of 13 monthly payments each year. You could pay off a 30-year mortgage in about 23 years.

Consider that a $250,000 30-year mortgage that has an interest rate of 8% will cost you $410,388 in interest. By paying biweekly, you will pay $119,000 less.

Shrewd Ways to Protect Your Assets from Creditors

Gideon Rothschild, Esq., CPA, partner in the law firm Moses & Singer LLP, 405 Lexington Ave., New York City 10174, *www.mosessinger.com.*

You do have a legal right to set up your affairs in a way that protects your property from unexpected claims—as long as you're not defrauding existing creditors.

New asset protection opportunities have recently arisen but there are also several unanswered questions to keep in mind.

DOMESTIC SELF-SETTLED TRUSTS

In a handful of states, you can put your own money in a trust for yourself and have those assets protected from creditors. In those states, you can set up a trust for yourself—known as a "self-settled trust"—manage the money, receive the income, have access to principal and block your creditors from laying claim to the assets in the trust.

A number of states, including Alaska, Delaware, Missouri, Nevada, Oklahoma, Rhode Island, South Dakota and Utah, permit residents to set up asset protection trusts.

Caution: There are no court decisions that indicate whether *nonresidents* can set up a self-settled trust in one of these states to gain asset protection. It may require US Supreme Court review to ultimately settle the issue.

Bottom line: There's no downside to a nonresident seeking asset protection in one of these states—other than the expense of setting up the trust. If a court permits creditors access to funds in the trust, the nonresident is no worse off than if the trust had not been set up in the first place. Also, there is the possibility that a court may uphold asset protection for nonresidents. Setting up such a trust creates a significant obstacle for any creditor, giving you negotiating leverage when settling a claim.

FOREIGN TRUSTS

Off-shore trusts (set up in another country) are also an effective way to protect assets from creditors. Foreign courts do not have to honor US court judgments.

Caution: Several US courts have imposed civil contempt orders against debtors whose foreign trusts were set up after claims were made against the debtors. In such cases, the debtor is ordered to pay the US judgment with funds in the foreign trust or face an undetermined amount of jail time. Whether or not this trend will continue remains to be seen.

WILLS AND LIVING TRUSTS

You have an opportunity to create asset protection for your family when making your estate plans. Parents will often set up trusts for their children to run until the children attain a certain age. However, it may be advisable to let assets remain in the trust indefinitely to protect against your children's future creditors or divorce claims.

Suggestion: Draft the terms of the trust to give an adult child maximum control over the funds without losing asset protection. This can be done by permitting the child to replace a trustee with someone who will cooperate with his/her wishes. The trustee can be permitted to purchase assets, such as a vacation house, which the child can then use and enjoy without exposure to creditor or divorce claims.

FLPS AND FLLCS

Family limited partnerships (FLPs) and family limited liability companies (FLLCs) can be used to provide a measure of asset protection. A creditor of a limited partner cannot obtain assets from the FLP. The creditor can only get a "charging order"—a right to any distributions made to the limited partner.

Result: Assets can then remain within the family, a creditor can only receive the distributions when and to the extent they are made.

Note: Where assets have been transferred to FLPs in an attempt to hinder or delay the claims of creditors, family limited partnerships do not protect assets from attachment by creditors.

529 TUITION PLANS

All states now allow college savings through tax-advantaged accounts known as 529 plans. Contribution limits and other rules for these plans vary by state. However, 529 plans may be the newest and best way to shelter funds from your creditors.

Funds contributed within a year of filing for bankruptcy have no protection—contributions between 365 days and 720 days before filing are protected up to $5,000. Funds are fully protected in the case of any bankruptcy filing more than two years after 529 contributions were made.

The limits of asset protection are high…

●**Contribution limits are substantial—** most plans have total (rather than annual) contribution limits, usually exceeding $100,000. Visit *www.savingforcollege.com* to find out about the contribution limits for each state. Or you could call the state education department for any state in which you are interested.

●**Contributors who set up plans for a beneficiary can avoid gift tax on contributions** in 2008 up to $60,000 ($120,000 if a contributor's spouse joins in the contribution) by averaging the gift over five years to take advantage of the $12,000 annual gift tax exclusion in 2008.

●**Contributors are not subject to any income limitations—**wealthy individuals can make contributions. And, they can even set up accounts for their own benefit (sometimes referred to as "solo 529 plans").

Assets enjoy deferral of tax on income until withdrawal *and* no tax on earnings if distributions are used for qualified education costs.

QUALIFIED RETIREMENT PLANS AND IRAs

Qualified retirement plans, including 401(k) accounts, are protected from the claims of creditors under federal law.

Exception: A state court can issue a qualified domestic relations order (QDRO), directing that payments from a plan be made to a former spouse, dependent or other person as "alternate payee."

IRA rollovers are fully protected in bankruptcy—money in traditional and Roth IRAs funded by contributions are protected up to $1 million.

How to Find a Good Credit Counselor

Nancy Dunnan, a financial adviser and author in New York City. Ms. Dunnan's latest book is titled *How to Invest $50–$5,000.* HarperCollins.

The credit counseling agencies can be extremely helpful, but be careful—the number of unscrupulous ones is on the rise. Before signing up, you should spend as much time researching the agencies as you would a new car.

Most agencies contact all of one's creditors to arrange a more comfortable repayment schedule. They also attempt to negotiate lower interest rates on your outstanding credit card balances. In turn, you make one monthly payment to the agency, which then parcels out the payments to your creditors.

Three steps you should take before signing on with an agency…

●**Find out about the fees.** Members of the National Foundation for Credit Counseling, or NFCC (an umbrella organization for counseling agencies) charge anywhere from nothing up to $75* for setting up a plan for debt management. Maintenance fees are an additional $10 to $25 per month. Members of the Association of Independent Consumer Credit Counseling Agencies charge maximums of $75 to set up a program and $50 per month for maintenance. Avoid any agencies that charge more.

Recommended: Get a quote for the setup and management fees in writing. If the agency says it can't do this, walk out the door.

●**Go to the agency in person.** Schedule an appointment with at least two agencies. You want to meet the credit counselor in person and see his/her credentials. Work only with a certified counselor. The NFCC (*www.nfcc.org,* 800 388-2227) will help you find ones in your area.

Useful: Many people find a support group that meets on a regular basis helpful. Contact Debtors Anonymous (*www.debtorsanonymous. org,* 781-453-2743) to find out if there is a support group near you.

●**Run a check.** See if any complaints have been filed regarding an individual agency at the Better Business Bureau (*www.bbb.org*).

Balancing act: Using a credit counseling service may have a negative impact on your credit rating. However, it's less damaging than when a bankruptcy shows up on your credit report.

Free Legal Help for Seniors

If you're age 60-plus, you should know about the not-for-profit Senior Legal Hotlines. Most of these are funded through the *Older Americans Act,* while several are supported by Legal Services Corporations or state bar funds.

The hotlines are staffed with attorneys who provide telephone advice and referrals for additional help.

*All prices are subject to change.

The hotlines are now available in California, Florida, Georgia, Hawaii, Iowa, Kansas, Kentucky, Maine, Maryland, Michigan, Mississippi, New Hampshire, New Mexico, Ohio, Pennsylvania, Puerto Rico, Tennessee, Texas, Washington State, Washington, DC, and West Virginia.

The legal advice is free except in Florida and Pennsylvania. For a list of hotline phone numbers, visit *www.seniorlaw.com/hotlines.htm.*

Make More Money

Donald B. Trone, president and founder of the Foundation for Fiduciary Studies, which operates in association with the University of Pittsburgh in Moon Township, Pennsylvania. He is coauthor of two manuals for the financial planning industry, *Procedural Prudence* (Veale & Associates) and *The Management of Investment Decisions* (McGraw-Hill).

Anyone can call himself/herself a financial adviser or consultant—a stockbroker, insurance agent, accountant, even a layperson who is good with numbers. In the past five years, the number of financial advisers has risen by almost 40% as consumers—hurt by the last bear market and intimidated by retirement planning—seek professional help.

Unfortunately, financial advisers aren't required as a general rule to act solely in your best interest—a standard known as "fiduciary responsibility."

Common: An adviser may not recommend the best mutual fund for you, but rather the best one for you that also pays him a commission.

Who you choose depends on your needs.

DECIDING WHAT YOU NEED

To find the right money coach…

●**If you need broad financial guidance—** such as help setting up a portfolio that you will mostly oversee yourself…a plan to pay for your children's educations…a retirement plan…estate planning and tax planning—go with a fee-only planner who has a certified financial planner (CFP) designation.

Fee-only advisers do not accept commissions. CFPs are required to pass a certification exam, have at least three years of financial-planning experience, adhere to a code of ethics, earn continuing education credits and pledge fiduciary responsibility.

Typical cost: One-time fee of $1,000 or more for a comprehensive plan.

Resource: Two associations can make referrals—The Financial Planning Association (800-322-4237, *www.fpanet.org*)…and the National Association of Personal Financial Advisors (800-366-2732, *www.napfa.org*).

●**If you want a professional to help manage your portfolio on an ongoing basis,** look for a chartered financial analyst (CFA). CFAs undergo rigorous training in stock and bond analysis, financial accounting and portfolio management. They are required to pass a certification exam, adhere to a code of ethics and pledge fiduciary responsibility.

Important: Never give an adviser full discretion over your portfolio, no matter how trustworthy he seems. You should receive at least a phone call or an E-mail when a trade is going to be made.

Typical cost: A fixed percentage of assets under management—0.5% to 2% annually for ongoing market advice and investment recommendations. For example, annual fees for an all-bond portfolio may average 0.5% of assets versus 1.5% for a mix of stocks and bonds.

Resource: For referrals to CFAs, go to *www.cfainstitute.org* or call 800-247-8132.

Alternatives…

●**Use a financial planner who charges hourly rates,** typically $100 to $300 per hour. For referrals, contact Garrett Planning Network (866-260-8400, *www.garrettplanning.com*), a network of planners who charge by the hour. Or get recommendations from your attorney or accountant.

●**Consider the new advisory services offered by large, no-load mutual fund companies.** They provide low-cost individualized portfolio advice by CFPs. For example, at Fidelity (800-343-3548, *www.fidelity.com*), counselors will manage a handpicked selection of Fidelity and non-Fidelity funds for clients who have at least $50,000 under management. Fees range from 0.25% of assets to 1.1%. Similar services are available from Vanguard (800-523-7731, *www.vanguard.com*) and T. Rowe Price (800-225-5132, *www.troweprice.com*).

SIZING UP CANDIDATES

●**Conduct a background check of prospective advisers and their firms.** You should work only with firms registered with the SEC. They are subject to government supervision.

Go to *www.sec.gov/index.htm*, click on "Check Out Brokers & Advisers" and on "Investment Adviser Public Disclosure." Search for the firm you want to investigate, and examine the firm's Form ADV. It contains information on the education and professional backgrounds of the firm's principals, types of clients, compensation, amount managed and disciplinary history.

You can find the same information through The Financial Industry Regulatory Authority (301-590-6500, *www.finra.org*). Any reputable adviser will make his ADV form available to you without your even having to ask.

●**Speak with at least two of the adviser's references.**

Questions to ask: Did the financial adviser educate you on complex financial issues? Did he carefully follow your directives? In particular, did he understand how aggressive/conservative a portfolio you wanted? Did he ever make mistakes or disappoint you? What did he do about it?

●**Once you are ready to hire a firm, get a written policy.** *It should include…*

●A promise that the adviser will act as your "fiduciary."

●List of potential conflicts of interest regarding product-based commissions and a reasonable explanation of how they are addressed.

●Explanation of the fee structure, what constitutes billable work and how fee disputes will be resolved—for instance, if the stock market drops and you make a quick call asking for advice. In this case, an adviser earning an asset-based annual fee should not charge for taking your call.

3

Great Insurance Money Savers

How to Survive Big Health Insurance Traps

New health insurance plan changes are cutting benefits and raising premiums for participants in each age bracket and income level. Many people are being left with limited or no coverage at all.

Any major life event—retirement, job change, divorce, the death of a spouse—puts you at risk of losing your insurance. It's not simply a problem for low-income families. Half of all Americans with health insurance fear that they won't be able to afford increases or that their benefits will be cut.

Top patient advocate Terre McFillen Hall tells how to avoid the traps. *Here are the most common crises and what you can do...*

PREEXISTING CONDITIONS

A 60-year-old Dallas woman had the opportunity to leave a company after 15 years to take a better job. She suffered from Parkinson's disease and was afraid that her new company's insurer would not provide coverage for her preexisting condition.

If the woman accepted the new position, she would have to honestly answer medical questions from her new insurer. Under the *Health Insurance Portability and Accountability Act of 1996* (HIPAA), however, she can't be denied the same insurance offered to all other employees because of her Parkinson's, nor can her new insurer charge her a higher premium.

Important: HIPAA doesn't guarantee that she will receive the same benefits as her old plan—her current doctor might not participate in the new insurer's plan, for example. Deductibles and claim limits can vary. She should examine the new policy before switching jobs. She also should look into getting a supplemental insurance policy.

Terre McFillen Hall, former executive director of The Center for Patient Advocacy, a nonprofit organization that lobbied members of Congress on patients' concerns and promoted fairness in the US health-care system, McLean, Virginia.

JOB CHANGE

A 48-year-old man from Alexandria, VA, quit his job in June and contracted to start a new one in September. He planned to spend the summer traveling but worried about the three-month gap in coverage. *There were two alternatives available to him...*

●**Consolidated Omnibus Budget Reconciliation Act (COBRA).** Under federal law, his old employer is required to extend coverage for him (and his family) for up to 18 months after he leaves.

Caution: He has up to 60 days after leaving his job to elect COBRA coverage, which then becomes retroactive for those 60 days. He will have to pay the premiums in full without any company contribution, plus a 2% administrative fee. COBRA applies only to businesses that have 20 or more employees.

Bonus: COBRA is particularly valuable for those who have a preexisting condition. They cannot be dropped, nor can the insurance company single them out for a rate increase should their care become increasingly expensive.

More information: Read *An Employee's Guide to Health Benefits Under COBRA*, free from the US Department of Labor. Call 866-444-3272 or visit *www.dol.gov/ebsa/pdf/cobra employee.pdf.*

●**Short-term medical insurance might be cheaper** if he is healthy. This usually provides coverage for two to six months and only for the major medical services—hospitalization, intensive care and services such as X-rays and laboratory tests.

Example: Less than $100 per month, with a $250 out-of-pocket maximum and a 20% co-payment up to $5,000. It doesn't cover preexisting conditions or pregnancies.

The cost/benefit of a plan depends on individual circumstances. COBRA, while more expensive, might be a better choice, depending on his family's needs, any preexisting conditions and anticipated medical treatments.

Companies to try: Assurant Health (800-553-7654, *www.assuranthealth.com*)...Golden Rule (800-444-8990, *www.goldenrule.com*).

UNINSURED ADULT CHILDREN

In San Francisco, the parents of a 22-year-old college graduate were worried. Their daughter worked as a temp and couldn't afford an individual health-care policy. Since she never got sick, she decided to go without insurance.

About one in three people between the ages of 18 and 24 has no health insurance, the highest proportion of any age group. A serious accident could wipe out this woman's savings, put her in debt for years and compel her parents to authorize her care if she should need hospitalization. This could then put them on the hook for her unpaid medical bills and wipe out their retirement savings. *Strategies...*

●**The parents should check their own policies first.** Some of the employer-sponsored plans allow dependent children of employees to be covered until age 23.

●**The daughter should get catastrophic major medical coverage at the very least.** If necessary, her parents can pay for the policy. Plans differ from state to state. Ask your doctor for recommendations.

Example: In California, for only $41 per month, a healthy person in his/her 20s can purchase a Blue Shield plan with a $2,400 deductible and a $6 million lifetime cap.*

SELF-EMPLOYED

A 50-year-old man from Philadelphia planned to start up his own business, but comprehensive coverage was beyond his reach without an employer sharing the cost. *Options...*

●**Managed-care policies,** such as HMOs, that require clients to use in-network physicians are the most affordable for individuals. More-expensive plans let you pick an out-of-network doctor. He can keep premiums down by electing high deductibles ($500 or more) but he should not skimp on prescription-drug coverage ($30 to $50 extra per month).

Reason: If he develops a condition that requires medication later on, he might not be able to get the coverage.

Example: The cholesterol-lowering drug *atorvastatin* (Lipitor) might cost $700 a year for an uninsured person, versus $100 a year in co-payments for an insured person.

*All prices are subject to change.

● **Use a health insurance broker to help find the best individual policy.** The National Association of Health Underwriters at 703-276-0220 or *www.nahu.org* can suggest member agents in your area. He should obtain quotes from several companies, including Digital Insurance at 888-470-2131 or *www.digitalinsurance.com* and eHealthInsurance Services at 800-977-8860 or *www.ehealthinsurance.com.*

● **Form his own small insurance group.** By forming a small company, he can get premiums that are 20% to 50% lower than individual policies.

Example: In New Jersey, just two people can qualify as a group as long as each works a minimum of 25 hours per week in his/her company and pays Social Security taxes.

● **Join a professional or trade association** or an alumni group that offers group coverage.

Examples: AARP (888-687-2277, *www.aarp.org*)…National Association for the Self-Employed (800-232-6273, *www.nase.org*)… United Service Association for Health Care (800-872-1187, *www.usahc.com*)…for US military members and their families, USAA (800-531-8722, *www.usaa.com*).

Finding Affordable Health Insurance

Jessica Waltman, vice president of policy and state affairs for the National Association of Health Underwriters, an insurance industry trade group, Arlington, Virginia. www.nahu.org.

If you don't have health insurance—because of a layoff or other job change, a divorce or a preexisting medical condition—don't give up. Efforts to expand health insurance coverage reportedly are becoming quite common. Illinois approved a plan to offer low-cost health insurance to children that began on July 1, 2006. As of July 1, 2007, Massachusetts mandates that everyone in the state carry health insurance, with employers with more than 10 employees required to contribute significantly to employee coverage (individuals who cannot

afford it can be covered by a state fund). On October 1, 2007, Vermont enacted a new state health insurance program to make coverage more affordable. Other proposals are being considered in other states.

Even under current law, it is possible to find coverage for you and your family, usually at a reasonable cost. *Options to consider if you need health coverage but are too young (under age 65) to qualify for Medicare…*

COBRA/STATE PLANS

For people who recently have lost group coverage, a smart choice may be to purchase a policy under COBRA, the temporary health benefits provision of the *Consolidated Omnibus Budget Reconciliation Act of 1986.* According to the rules, you can continue to be covered under your employer's insurance for up to 18 months at up to 102% of the former policy's costs, depending on your circumstances. This amount includes both the employee and employer's share, if your employer splits the expense with workers, as many do. (The extra 2% is for administrative costs.) COBRA usually is available only from companies that have at least 20 employees. (Your spouse and dependent children can be covered for up to 36 months.)

Paying the full tab can be a shock to someone who is accustomed to having an employer pick up most of the cost of insurance. However, while COBRA policies often are more expensive than those purchased privately on an individual basis, they usually have more comprehensive benefits.

What to do: Apply for COBRA through your former employer. For more information on COBRA, contact the US Department of Labor's Employee Benefits Security Administration, 866-444-3272, *www.dol.gov/ebsa.*

Helpful: Many states require smaller companies and others not bound by COBRA to offer some type of continuation of coverage to employees. For a database on health-care coverage options by state, go to *www.nahu.org/consumer/healthcare* or call 703-276-0220.

INDIVIDUAL POLICIES

Individual insurance is regulated on a state-by-state basis. You must buy a policy sold in your home state. Rules for individual health insurance outside a group plan vary from state to state, which affects pricing.

• **Medical underwriting.** In the vast majority of states, insurance costs are based on the applicant's health status. He/she will be assigned a rate class by the company and put into a pool with similar individuals who will be charged the same premium. Also, many states allow health insurers to issue *elimination riders* to people who have preexisting medical conditions. These riders allow you the option of picking a policy that covers all conditions or a less expensive policy that excludes certain preexisting conditions.

• **Pricing based on guaranteed issue/ community rating.** "Guaranteed issue" laws state that a health insurance company cannot reject you for coverage based on any preexisting medical condition. Community rating laws say that everyone in the same geographic area pays the same price for coverage, regardless of age or health. It may be easier for people with medical problems to obtain coverage in states with such laws, but there is a price involved.

Laws such as these make individual coverage in the state more expensive, on average, because insurers don't have the medical information to appropriately spread risk among the applicants. In these states, healthy young people are much less likely to purchase coverage. This makes coverage more expensive for everyone who does buy it.

Examples: * A healthy, 25-year-old man living in the New Jersey suburb of Haddonfield could pay $467.16 per month for a comprehensive individual policy with a $1,000 deductible. If he lived in Pennsylvania in the suburb of Wayne (20 miles away), he could buy the same policy for only $58.86 a month. A healthy, 60-year-old man in Wayne would pay $289.82 for that policy. A man of the same age living in Haddonfield would be charged the same $467.16 a month that the 25-year-old pays for the plan. These vast price differences are due to the community rating and guaranteed issue laws affecting individual insurance in New Jersey.

What to do: Purchase private coverage from an independent health insurance agent licensed

*Rates obtained by eHealthInsurance.com.

54

in your state. Use the agent locator at *www.nahu.org/consumer/findagent.cfm* or call 703-276-0220. You also can find quotes from Web sites such as *www.ehealthinsurance.com.*

HEALTH SAVINGS ACCOUNTS

For a tax-efficient way to pay for individual health insurance, consider a health savings account (HSA). You must select a policy with a high insurance deductible—in 2007 and 2008 at least $1,100 for individuals ($2,200 for families). Every year, you can make a tax-deductible contribution. You withdraw money from the account to cover out-of-pocket medical expenses. Those who attain age 55 by the end of the year can make an additional "catch-up" contribution in 2008 of $900. In 2008, the contribution limit increases to $2,900 for self-only coverage, or $5,800 for family coverage, with a $900 catch-up contribution. HSAs can be funded via a one-time contribution from an IRA. There is no contribution reduction for HSAs that start during the year.

For people who create HSAs but don't need to tap them, the accounts can function like individual retirement accounts. The money can be invested to grow tax-deferred. After age 65, you can withdraw the money for any reason, but you will have to pay income tax if it is used for nonqualified expenses.

COVERAGE FOR SERIOUS MEDICAL PROBLEMS

In most states, you can be turned down for individual coverage if you have a serious medical condition (e.g., HIV or cancer). Fortunately, most states have developed some way to provide hard-to-insure people with access to private individual health insurance coverage.

Thirty-three states provide high-risk pools. You can apply for high-risk pool coverage through an insurance agent or directly to the state. Coverage costs more than private coverage because all the people in the pool have serious medical problems, but rates are capped, generally between 125% and 200% of the average individual market premium. For instance, in a state where a healthy person pays $100 a month, someone of the same age in the risk pool might pay $150.

Twelve states use other means of providing hard-to-insure people with access to individual coverage (for instance, requiring coverage through a designated health insurance company of last resort). Five states—Arizona, Delaware, Georgia, Hawaii and Nevada—offer no individual coverage options for those who are hard to insure. For more information on insurance for those who can't get coverage privately, go to *www.nahu.org/consumer/healthcare*.

Health Plan Scams That Will Make You Sick

Hal Morris, veteran Las Vegas–based consumer affairs journalist who writes widely about scams, schemes and other rip-offs.

Con artists have latched on to health care as an easy way for them to make some quick money.

TOO GOOD TO BE TRUE

The scam: Unlicensed "health insurers" are promising lofty benefits, with premiums as much as 50% below prevailing rates.

Easy marks: Small-business owners as well as individuals seeking to bypass skyrocketing insurance coverage.

Those who fall for this scam discover that their premiums have disappeared and are left holding hefty unpaid medical bills. People seeking supplemental insurance to pay medical expenses not covered by Medicare are also victims of these scams.

Promoters of health insurance rip-offs often sway local insurance agents to market the plans. Those selling the coverage call themselves labor consultants or business agents.

While claims may be paid initially, the scammers then delay payments through a variety of excuses, leaving consumers and employers responsible for paying mounting bills.

MAIL-ORDER SCAM

Unscrupulous companies also pitch inappropriate coverage through the mail. The US Postal Inspection Service cites the case of a 93-year-old woman who, thinking she was purchasing a valuable health insurance policy, wound up with *maternity* insurance.

Postal officials urge recipients of deceptive or unsuitable health insurance promotions to bring them to the attention of the local postmaster or nearest postal inspector.

10 WARNING SIGNS

Red flags that mark a questionable health insurance plan…

1. Coverage is offered at rock-bottom rates. Be suspicious of a policy pitched as costing "only pennies a day."

2. References to "benefits" rather than insurance…"contributions" instead of premiums …"consultant fees" in place of commissions …sales and marketing materials that generally avoid use of the word "insurance."

3. Coverage typically is offered regardless of the state of an applicant's health—no medical examinations or even medical questionnaires are required.

4. Joining a "union" or "association" may be stipulated to obtain health coverage. Or payment of "dues" may be necessary prior to obtaining a policy.

5. With small employers, the agent pitches a deal tied in to the *Employee Retirement Income Security Act* (ERISA) or to a union. Legitimate ERISA or union plans are established by unions for their members or by employers for employees and are not sold by insurance agents.

Also appearing in the mix are plans that are offered exclusively through associations, guilds, trusts, unions or MEWA (Multiple Employer Welfare Arrangements). True MEWAs are designed to give the small employers access to low-cost health coverage on par with terms available to large firms.

6. Agent appears far too eager to sign you up for coverage.

7. Agent appears ill-informed on specifics, avoids sharing information and does not have precise responses to your questions.

8. Agent has no commission schedule and bases rates on ability to pay.

9. Agent doesn't have the name of the carrier underwriting the product—even as he/she markets the product as "fully insured," "fully funded" or "reinsured."

10. Name of so-called "insurer" may have a familiar ring to it—often it closely resembles the name of a legitimate organization. Also be on guard for names that suggest a connection with the federal government or Medicare.

HOW TO PROTECT YOURSELF

To establish that a health insurance plan is legitimate…

●**Carefully read all materials and Web sites of health insurance plans.** Verify that a genuine insurance company is involved and not one with a similar name. Also, call your state insurance department and check that the agent and product are state licensed.

Caution: Insurance scammers wrongly say federal law exempts state licensing. It doesn't.

●**Don't be influenced by glossy and well-illustrated marketing literature** or the high-pressure sales pitches, including mention of "it is your last chance" or "apply immediately." Verify information, and read the fine print.

●**Compare various insurance policies and costs.**

●**For small businesses,** seek references of employers enrolled with the provider. Ask the references about benefit payment history and claim turnaround time.

●**If you're suspicious of a plan,** contact your state insurance department about a firm's proposed coverage. Some states' Web sites make this task easy—type a name in a box on the screen.

●**Deal only with reputable agents.** Confirm via your state insurance department that the person offering the product is a licensed insurance agent with a proven reliability record. Insurance fleecers often use unlicensed agents to market their wares.

●**Be leery of a request to pay premiums in cash or a year in advance.**

●**Contact your state insurance department with any questions.** It is the very best resource for company/agent licensing requirements and available products. Also, if needed, consult with an accountant, attorney or other trusted adviser.

Suggestion: For the best route to state health insurance departments, visit the National Association of Insurance Commissioners' Web site at *www.naic.org/state_web_map.htm*, or call 866-470-6242.

Is Long-Term-Care Insurance Right for You?

Charles Mondin, director of the United Seniors Health Council, an educational program of the National Council on Aging aimed at helping seniors shop intelligently for health care, Washington, DC, *www.ncoa.org*. He is a contributor to *Planning for Long-Term Care.* McGraw-Hill.

Nursing home stays cost more than an average of $70,000 a year. In-home care averages more than $25 an hour. None of us knows what our needs will be, but we all face potentially tremendous costs.

Shop for a nursing home or nursing care now so that you won't be shocked if and when you must find a facility quickly. Facilities, level of care and prices vary widely.

There are several ways to come up with the money you will need. The sooner you address your future, the more options you will have to self-insure or buy long-term-care (LTC) insurance. Consult your financial adviser about the best choice for financial security.

YOUR NEST EGG

If you can pay nursing home costs out of your retirement savings, you probably do not need LTC insurance.

The main problem with self-insuring is that you don't know when—or even if—you actually will need the coverage, and there is no way to know how long you might need it.

The average stay in a nursing home is about one year. To be safe, assume that you might have to spend two years in a home.

General rule: If you can afford to cover at least two years for both you and your spouse, you should be adequately prepared.

If there is a family history of illness that might require a nursing home, LTC insurance probably is a good investment. But if you now have a chronic condition, you may not qualify.

The further ahead you think about LTC, the greater the possibilities you will have. If you're in your 40s or 50s, find out from an agent what LTC insurance would cost at your present age. Then see whether you can essentially self-insure less expensively by investing those premiums in an annuity to cover the cost of your care.

Annuities are available with a range of features, some providing guaranteed fixed income for life. Any financial planner should be able to do the comparisons for you.

YOUR HOME

Your home just may be your best financial resource to help pay for your care. Selling it would boost your nest egg and increase future income from investments. Consult several qualified real estate agents to learn its value.

Renting out your home is another alternative. You need a regular stream of income to pay for a nursing home—not a lump sum of cash.

A reverse mortgage allows you to tap your home's value while you continue to live in it. It provides you with income—in a lump sum or in regular payments over numerous years. The reverse mortgage loan is paid off upon your death—usually by selling the home.

Caution: It is possible to outlive the term of a reverse mortgage.

LTC INSURANCE

LTC is one of the most complicated types of insurance. Buy a policy at age 55, and you will probably pay less than $1,000 a year—but for 20 or 30 years.

Wait until age 75 to buy, and you'll pay up to $5,000 per year for a restrictive policy that might cover a nursing home stay but not home care and might not kick in until you've been in a nursing home for more than 90 days. A comprehensive policy for someone age 75 might run $7,000 a year. Wait even longer than age 75, and it becomes prohibitively expensive.

Ask your state's senior health insurance office for guidance. LTC terminology can be very confusing even to experienced insurance agents.

Example: Most companies provide "level premium" coverage. This doesn't mean that the premium is guaranteed to remain the same. It means that if you bought at age 60, your premium always will be what the company currently charges to insure any new 60-year-old policyholder—and that price can go up.

What to look for when you shop for LTC insurance…

Benefit period: Purchase coverage that lasts your lifetime, not a time period.

Benefit amount: Buy a policy that pays at least $100 a day and covers nursing home and in-home care. The benefit amount you need depends on the cost of nursing homes in the area in which you plan to live. The average nursing home now charges around $150 a day. However, more-expensive facilities can cost $200-plus a day. Be financially prepared to pay the difference.

Deductible/elimination period: The longer the elimination period—meaning the more of the nursing home stay you pay for before insurance kicks in—the less coverage will cost you. For most people, an elimination period of 60 to 90 days is the best value. You might save 10% on the premium that has a longer elimination period, but your expenses could eat up the savings. Also consider a rider that adjusts the benefit for inflation.

When you qualify for care: Be careful about how the insurer determines whether it will pay benefits. Policies that require a prior hospital stay or a physician to find you "ill" or "injured" can be too restrictive.

Less-restrictive policies require only that you need care because of a mental or physical impairment. You become eligible for the benefits if mental deterioration makes you a danger to yourself or to others, or if physical problems make it impossible for you to perform two or more activities of daily living (ADL)—such as eating, dressing, bathing, moving from bed to chair and using the toilet.

Since ADL definitions vary by insurance company, make sure you know how a company's policy defines them.

Note: Annuities and life insurance contracts can now offer a rider for long-term care coverage (called combination policies). Starting in 2010, distributions from such policies to pay long-term care expenses receive the same tax treatment as long-term care policies do now.

GOVERNMENT CARE

When your retirement income and assets are below levels set by your state, you may qualify for Medicaid to pay nursing home bills.

It is administered by each state, and the rules for coverage vary.

How to Protect Your Assets from Medicaid

Harry S. Margolis, JD, principal in the Boston law firm of Margolis & Associates. He is editor of *The Elder-Law Report*, a newsletter for attorneys...a fellow of the National Academy of Elder Law Attorneys...and president of ElderLawAnswers.com, a consumer-oriented Web site on elder law issues.

Almost no one believes that he/she ever will need Medicaid—the government health-care program for the poor.

Beware: More than half of long-term nursing home patients now rely on Medicaid. In fact, the government is pursuing some of these patients' estates to recover the money it paid to nursing homes on their behalf. Some states even have seized family homes after a patient's death.

SAFEGUARD YOUR MONEY

●**Buy long-term-care (LTC) insurance** to avoid the Medicaid problem. LTC insurance will pay enough of nursing home costs so that you are unlikely to need government assistance.

●**Give assets to your children or trusted friends.** To qualify for Medicaid, you must have almost no assets other than your home. Amounts vary by state, but individuals generally can have no more than about $2,000 in 2009 and their spouses no more than $104,400 in 2008 ($109,560 in 2009).

You also can qualify for Medicaid if you transfer your assets to your children or trusted friends at least five years before applying for the program. There is no tax when gifting up to $1 million over your lifetime.

If long-term nursing home care is likely to be in your future, keep only enough money to pay for three to five years of care before applying for Medicaid.

PROTECT YOUR HOME

●**Create a life estate deed with your lawyer.** It enables you to pass your house directly to your children while reserving the right to stay in it rent-free throughout your life. The house transfers to your children at your death. If you do go into a nursing home, your children can continue to care for the house or rent it out.

●**An irrevocable trust** allows you to transfer ownership of your house to a trust for your benefit. You can occupy it as long as necessary and specify to whom it should be given upon your death.

Both of these maneuvers constitute an asset transfer. A life estate deed makes you ineligible to receive Medicaid for up to three years. An irrevocable trust makes you ineligible for up to five years. Each has different tax consequences, so consult an attorney about which is best for you.

Important: Until recently, states usually did not seek recovery for their costs from homes that passed through joint ownership, trusts or life estate deeds. Some states now are seeking to recover patient Medicaid costs from these properties. Consult an attorney to learn about your state.

How You Can Save Up to 33% on Health Insurance

Alan Mittermaier, president, HealthMetrix Research, Inc., health-care research and consulting firm, Columbus, Ohio.

Married couples can save money on employer-provided health insurance by "blending" their coverage. If the two companies' plans offer comparable benefits, couples can cut premiums by up to one-third when each individual drops spousal coverage. If one plan is obviously superior, drop the weaker plan.

Caution: Drop your coverage only if there is no waiting period for preexisting conditions and your spouse's job looks secure. Don't blend coverage if either employer offers a "consumer-directed" health plan or similar medical savings account. In a typical consumer-directed health plan, employers put a fixed dollar amount in each employee's account annually. Employees then can spend those dollars as they want.

Important: Make sure the insurance package you settle on is strongest in the areas that are likely to be most important to you—prescription drugs, dental care, mental health, etc.

How to Fight Back When Your Health Insurer Says *No*

Rhonda D. Orin, Esq., managing partner in the Washington, DC, offices of the law firm of Anderson Kill & Olick, PC. She specializes in representing policyholders in insurance coverage disputes across the country. She is author of *Making Them Pay: How to Get the Most from Health Insurance and Managed Care.* Griffin.

A recent US Supreme Court decision against two participants in separate managed care plans in Texas underscores how difficult it has become to sue HMOs, PPOs and other health insurance companies. Therefore, it has become even more important to be a strong advocate for your own care.

PREVENTING PROBLEMS

Here is what to do to see that your insurer covers the treatments you need…

● **Get your doctor 100% behind you.** Your physician can be your strongest ally. In cases where treatment is not clear-cut, the insurer ultimately may defer to his/her recommendation. *If your doctor refuses to recommend a treatment that you think you need…*

● Ask him why, but be diplomatic. Tell him, "I want to take responsibility for my condition. Can you tell me what information you relied on to determine that I don't need this treatment?"

● Learn enough about your condition to ask intelligent questions. You might say, "Are you familiar with X (a reliable source that you trust), which recommends this protocol?"

Sources worth checking…

☐ MedlinePlus, from National Institutes of Health and US National Library of Medicine at *www.medlineplus.gov.*

☐ University of Iowa Hardin Library for the Health Sciences at *www.lib.uiowa.edu/hardinmd.*

☐ The Health Resource at 800-949-0090. For a fee, you can get medical research tailored to your specific problem.

If your doctor still isn't convinced, present him with a second doctor's opinion that supports the treatment. You may have to pay for the second opinion, depending on your insurance policy's rules.

● **Get a copy of your company's health plan** from your employer. Compare it to the shortened version that you received when you became eligible for coverage. If there are any discrepancies that pertain to your condition, notify your employer.

● **Check your state's mandatory benefits laws.** These regulations, which are not well-publicized, require health plans to cover specific illnesses and conditions. Call your state's department of insurance to see if your condition must be covered under state law. Contact information for state commissioners is available from the National Association of Insurance Commissioners (866-470-6242 or *www.naic.org/state_web_map.htm*).

Examples: Many states, including New York and California, require insurers to cover certain forms of infertility treatment. Maryland and some other states require coverage of gastric bypass surgery for morbidly obese patients.

If your insurer denies coverage even after you have reminded the representative of your state's mandate, forward the denial letter to your state insurance commissioner and ask for help.

Exception: Mandatory benefits laws may not apply to health plans that are fully funded, with claims paid by an insurance company, and do not apply to the government-run insurance programs, such as Medicare.

WINNING AN APPEAL

Most insurers require a written appeal within a certain number of days of the denial of treatment, and they in turn promise a decision within a certain number of days.

Caution: Don't drop your plan while negotiating—you have greater leverage if you are still a member. *To further boost your odds...*

●**Keep detailed records of the facts regarding your case**—not just insurance company correspondence and test results. Insurers often win because they maintain more detailed records than consumers do.

Also, keep notes of telephone conversations with insurance representatives. Include their names, titles, office locations and phone extensions. After every important conversation, send the person with whom you spoke a letter summarizing key discussion points. (If you can't get the representative's name, ask for his identification number.) In the letter, request that he write back if you misstated anything he said. If he doesn't object to doing this, it will strengthen your case.

●**Keep your cool.** Fighting an insurer can be extremely frustrating, but don't ever swear or use foul language on the phone or in a letter. That just allows the insurer to portray you as difficult and unreasonable.

●**Stick to the facts.** Insurers don't care how much you have suffered. They only want to know if their decision was correct based on an analysis of your medical records, other medical evidence and their internal policies.

Example: You're 48 years old and your doctor recommends a colonoscopy, but your HMO refuses to cover it, stating that the test is only for people over age 50. To get approval, you will need documentation—(a) a letter from your doctor telling why you need to have a colonoscopy (there is a family history of colon cancer)...(b) recent data from the American Cancer Society that directly support his opinion...(c) a statement from another physician saying that a colonoscopy is recommended.

●**Ask that your employer get involved.** Your company may have some leverage with the insurer, especially in disability insurance cases in which a condition affects your day-to-day abilities.

●**Follow the appeals procedure exactly.** Otherwise, an insurer may reject your appeal based on procedural grounds.

Most common: Failure to file required paperwork by deadlines.

●**Use as much of the insurer's own language as possible,** including terms from your plan documents. Always refer to the section number and the page where you found the citation.

●**If you lose your appeal, consider filing an external grievance.** All states will give you the legal right to be heard by an independent panel if your internal appeals are rejected. Call your state's department of insurance for details.

Alternatives: The state's department of insurance may investigate complaints. Send them the same material that you used for your appeal to your insurer. The agency will investigate within six months and order corrective action if necessary, including requiring the insurer to pay for all valid claims.

Your state attorney general also may be willing to open an investigation. You can obtain the contact information for your state attorneys general from the National Association of Attorneys General (202-326-6000, *www.naag. org/attorneys_general.php*).

Save Hundreds On Car Insurance

Most insurance companies will lower your premium by 5% when you drive less than 8,500 miles a year.

Other factors that can reduce your rates by 5% to 10%: Moving from an urban location to a rural area...reaching age 50...insuring your home and auto with the same company. Savings will vary, depending on your insurance company and home state.

Important: Notify your insurance company as soon as there are any changes involving your vehicle. This information affects your premium as well as your ability to collect on a claim.

Alejandra Soto, former communications manager, Insurance Information Institute, New York City, *www.iii.org*.

When to Change Car Insurance Companies

Consider switching car insurers if you are hit with a double-digit hike in price. Rates are rising significantly whether or not you have had accidents—but not all companies charge similar amounts to insure the same car.

To shop around: Use an independent agent —find one through the Independent Insurance Agents & Brokers of America (800-221-7917, *www.iiaa.org*)…go on-line to InsWeb.com for price quotes…contact one company that sells directly, such as Geico (800-861-8380, *www. geico.com*)…and try State Farm (800-782-8332, *www.statefarm.com*), which sells only through its own agents.

Jeanne Salvatore, an adjunct professor at Iona College in New Rochelle, New York, and Columbia University in New York City. She is senior vice president of public affairs at the Insurance Information Institute, an industry trade group, *www.iii.org*.

More from Jeanne Salvatore…

Drive Down Car Insurance Costs

For some quick ways to cut your auto insurance costs, take a look below…

●**Take the highest deductible you can afford.** A $1,000 deductible may reduce the cost of collision and comprehensive insurance by as much as 40%.

●**Drop collision and comprehensive coverage** when the value of a car is less than 10 times the premium.

●**Take every discount available.** Various insurers will provide discounts for low-mileage driving; for having an antitheft device, air bags, antilock brakes, daytime running lights; for having "good student" (sometimes defined as a B+ or better average) and college student away-from-home drivers and for carrying auto and homeowner's insurance with the same company.

You Can Save 25% on Home Insurance

Sharon Emek, a partner in CBS Coverage Group, Inc., an insurance agency in New York City which now represents more than three dozen insurance companies, *www. cbsinsurance.com*. A licensed insurance broker, she has 25 years of experience in the business.

The expense of homeowner's insurance is increasing again. *How to save 25% on home insurance costs…*

MAKE YOURSELF LESS OF A RISK

Your homeowner's premium depends on which "tier" your insurer puts you in. Your tier depends primarily on your claims history and credit score. Top-tier home owners can pay significantly less than those in the bottom tier.

Keep score: Few people know what their scores are or whether they are accurate. *To find out, order a copy of your credit report from each of the three national credit rating agencies…*

●**Equifax**, 800-685-1111, *www.equifax.com*.

●**Experian**, 888-397-3742, *www.experian. com*.

●**TransUnion**, 877-322-8228, *www.trans union.com*.

Under the *Fair and Accurate Credit Transactions Act of 2003* (FACT), you can receive one free credit report per year from each of the reporting agencies. Check each report for accuracy. You might find loans and/or credit cards listed for someone with a similar name.

To improve your credit score…

●**Pay off debt you don't need to carry.**

●**Close credit card accounts that you do not need.**

●**Correct errors,** such as a credit card you canceled or a bill that isn't yours.

Once you have improved your score, you or your agent can ask the insurer to reconsider your "credit insurance score"—derived from all your risk factors—and put you in a better tier.

To cut your premiums…

Since the primary purpose of insurance is to protect you from major losses, not to pay for relatively minor expenses, raise your deductible. Switching from a $250 deductible to a $1,000 deductible could save you as much as 25% on premiums. Then, if you suffer a loss anywhere near $1,000—even up to $1,500—cover it yourself instead of filing a claim.

The more claims you file and the bigger they are, the higher your premium. People with low credit scores tend to file more claims than those with high scores. File too many claims— more than one in any two-year period—and your insurer may not renew your coverage.

LOSS-PROOF YOUR HOUSE

Avoid common claims by maintaining your house properly…

●**Fix even minor roof leaks promptly,** and keep rain gutters clean.

●**Trim dead branches,** and remove dying trees before they fall and cause damage.

●**Install windstorm shutters** if you're in a high-wind area.

●**Improve drainage around the house,** and/or install an automatic sump pump if your basement tends to flood.

●**Check heating, electrical and plumbing systems,** and the roof every few years. It's best if a professional does this so problems are caught. Keep your chimney clean and unobstructed. The older your house is, the more important such maintenance becomes.

SHOP AROUND

Sticking with one insurer for the long haul might earn you a renewal discount of 5% or so on your premium. It also could get you more personal attention when you have a claim.

Still, don't just automatically renew year after year. Comparison shop among insurers at least every three years. The Internet makes it easy to get quotes from dozens of companies. Even if you normally buy your policy directly from an insurer, get several comparison quotes on exactly the same coverage from an independent agent.

You can buy homeowner's insurance online, but I don't advise this. There are so many variables that you probably need expert advice to get the right coverage.

Strategy: Use on-line quotes to get an idea of the price, but buy from an agent.

LOOK FOR TRUE REPLACEMENT COST

Buy a policy that pays the true replacement cost of any loss. Avoid the cash-value policies, which cost less but only pay the depreciated value of your loss. Insure only what might be damaged or destroyed. Don't insure land since it doesn't burn and can't be stolen.

Every insurance company will provide a cost-estimator worksheet to help you determine replacement cost. Some companies will send a representative to do a free on-site appraisal.

Don't overinsure by buying a market-value policy. Market value is what a buyer would pay for your home. In a hot market, that amount could exceed the cost of rebuilding the home. The opposite advice applies if you're in a fading neighborhood, where replacement cost might exceed market value.

STICK WITH QUALITY

A low premium won't be a bargain if the company is gone when you file a claim. Buy from a company with a rating of at least A minus from A.M. Best Co., *www.ambest.com.*

LOOK FOR DISCOUNTS

There's no haggling with insurers. Rates are set for groups who share attributes, not on a case-by-case basis. *But discounts are available…*

●**Alarm discount.** Up to 15% off if the home is protected by a comprehensive system (heat, smoke and burglar) linked to a central monitoring station. The insurer may insist on a system linked to the house wiring with a battery backup rather than one that uses only batteries.

●**High-value item discount.** You can save on the cost of coverage for "scheduled" items, such as high-end jewelry, if they are kept in a safe-deposit box at a bank rather than in a drawer at home. (A home safe is not likely to get you the discount.)

●**Multipolicy discount.** Many insurers discount if you buy multiple coverage from them, like auto, liability and homeowner's.

●**Other potential discounts.** *Nonsmoker,* when no members of a household smoke… *mature home owner,* for seniors or retirees… *renovation discount,* for upgrading old electrical, plumbing, heating or other systems.

KEEP YOUR POLICY UP-TO-DATE

Do an annual review to keep your coverage up-to-date. Add any costly new acquisitions—jewelry, paintings—to your policy, and inform your insurer about any significant remodeling.

Remember to reduce or eliminate coverage on items that aren't worth what they used to be. The costly projection TV you bought just a few years ago is worth far less today.

GAPS IN COVERAGE

Generally, homeowner's policies cover most common types of damage, including damage caused by fire, smoke, rain, lightning, wind, hail, snow, ice, theft, explosions, vehicles and the malfunction of electrical systems, plumbing, heating, air conditioning or appliances.

Damage from earthquakes or floods is not covered in standard policies. You need separate policies if you're in an area prone to flooding or earthquakes. For hurricanes, you may be covered for high winds but not for flood.

Trap: Thinking coverage for rain damage will automatically reimburse you, say, if your deck collapses, after a few days of downpours. The insurers might say this type of damage is the result of flood, not the rain itself.

Even if you don't live in a flood-prone area, consider flood insurance. Contact the Federal Emergency Management Agency (800-621-3362, *www.fema.gov/business/nfip*). Premiums vary widely, from a few hundred to a few thousand dollars a year, depending on the location of a house, its age and type of construction.

Finally, you need at least $1 million in personal liability coverage to protect assets from lawsuits. An "umbrella" policy will take over where liability coverage on your homeowner's and auto policies leaves off. The cost is about $150 a year per $1 million in coverage.

Does It Pay to Get Shipping Insurance?

Don't buy shipping insurance when sending a small gift through the US Postal Service. Though insurance costs only a few dollars, the Post Office rarely loses or damages items, so insurance is unnecessary on packages that are worth less than $100.

Eric Tyson, MBA, Weston, Connecticut–based financial counselor and syndicated columnist. He is author of Investing for Dummies. *Wiley.*

Life Insurance…Are You Wasting Your Money? Or Not Spending Enough?

Elizabeth S. Sevilla, CLU, ChFC, personal financial planner specializing in life insurance and tax senior manager, BDO Seidman, LLP, One Market-Spear Tower, San Francisco 94105.

Life insurance needs change with age. At a later stage in life, one may benefit from insurance in different ways than when young. *Here's what to know to keep your coverage meeting your needs…*

NEW USES

For young families, life insurance usually is used to assure that basic needs—such as paying a mortgage and providing for children—will be met should the family's wage earner die. *But later in life, when these original needs have passed—the mortgage is paid off, or nearly so, and children have grown up—your old insurance may become useful in new ways…*

●**New obligations.** Perhaps you have new mortgages (on a second home or investment property), your standard of living has increased to a level that requires extra protection or you have remarried and have obligations to a second family.

●**Bequests.** If you wish to leave funds to children or grandchildren, you may be reluctant to spend your savings on yourself—and your own quality of life may suffer as a result.

Strategy: Fund bequests with life insurance. This will free you to use your own assets as you wish while still providing for the younger generation.

A "second-to-die" policy that pays on the death of the survivor of a married couple can meet this purpose at low annual premium cost.

●**Charitable donations.** Insurance proceeds similarly can provide a bequest to charity without tying up any of your assets.

●**Estate tax liability.** Although there's much talk of the federal estate tax being repealed, this remains uncertain—and even if it is repealed, many states will maintain their own estate taxes.

Life insurance may be needed to protect valuable family assets (home, business, investments) from the tax authorities. State estate tax rules and exempt amounts vary, so check with a local expert.

●**Business.** If you are a key manager in your own family-owned business, insurance may be needed to protect the business from critical losses—such as if you had key knowledge or skills that generated certain income—in the event of your death. If you are an owner of a private business, insurance may be used to pay your survivors the value of your shares that are redeemed when you die. Typically, shares in a privately owned company are subject to a buy-back agreement so that ownership doesn't wind up with a stranger.

LETTING IT GO

On the other hand, your situation may have changed so much that your old insurance policy is no longer useful.

You simply may not need insurance any more. In this case, if you've used term insurance to date, you can just cancel the policy.

If you've used a policy that's built up cash value, you will want to make the most of this value. *Options...*

●**Surrender the policy** to the insurance company for its cash value.

Snag: The amount by which the cash value of the policy exceeds the premiums paid is taxable income—which is taxed at top ordinary income tax rates, not as tax-favored capital gains.

●**Donate the policy to charity.** If you intend to give cash or property to charity anyway, donating an unneeded insurance policy is likely a better idea. *Reasons...*

●If the charity keeps the policy until your death, you'll have provided them a bigger legacy than by donating cash or other property.

●You will avoid ever paying tax on your gain on the policy. In contrast, if you were to donate enough cash to the charity to get a deduction of the same size, you would face tax at ordinary rates when you cash in the insurance policy.

Opportunity: Donating a life insurance policy to charity is even better tax-wise than donating appreciated property (such as stock shares). In each case, taxable gain on the donated property is averted. But the gain on a life insurance policy is ordinary income, while that on stock or fund shares is tax-favored capital gain. So more tax is saved from a donation of insurance for gains of the same size.

●**Convert the policy to an annuity.** This provides an income stream over a set period of years or your lifetime. There is no immediate tax due, and the annuity continues to earn tax-deferred investment returns. Payments from the annuity will be partly taxable as ordinary income and partly a nontaxable return of investment.

Annuity options and rules are complex, so consult an expert.

NEW COVERAGE

If you find you need more or different coverage than in the past, you will need to look for a new insurance policy.

The good news is that the insurance market has become much more competitive in recent years, so you'll probably find lower premium costs and more options available (such as investment options for cash-value policies) than when you bought your old policy.

Opportunity: When you replace an old cash-value life insurance policy with a new one, you may not have to cash in the old policy and thus incur taxable gain. You can instead replace the old policy with the new one through a tax-free exchange that defers any taxable gain until the new, replacement policy is disposed of.

Requirements: The new policy must have the same owner and the same insured (or insureds) as the policy it replaces. (The new policy can be obtained from a different insurer than the old one.)

The details of the new policy will, of course, depend on its purpose and the need it meets.

Important: Insurance rules and related tax rules are complex. Have your insurance broker explain your options and give you a detailed financial analysis that compares your old and proposed new policy. The broker is required by law to do this, but in practice, the analysis may be neglected.

Collect a Higher Pension from Life Insurance

Retirees with a traditional defined-benefit plan usually have a choice of distribution options—"single life option" or "joint and survivor option." The first pays more per month, but only during your lifetime—your spouse gets nothing after you die. The second pays less but continues to pay as long as you or your spouse is alive. To maximize your pension, you can choose the single life option and buy life insurance with your spouse as the beneficiary. The earlier you buy it, the cheaper it is. You collect a higher pension for the rest of your life, some of which can be used to pay the insurance premium. The death benefit replaces your spouse's lost pension benefit if you die first. Be sure your policy is approved and in force before electing the single life option.

Byron Udell, JD, ChFC, CFP, founder/CEO, AccuQuote, consumer life insurance information service, Wheeling, Illinois. www.accuquote.com.

Slash Life Insurance Costs Big Time

Seymour Goldberg, Esq., CPA, Goldberg & Goldberg, PC, 100 Jericho Quadrangle, Jericho, New York 11753, www.goldbergira.com. One of the country's foremost authorities on IRA distributions, Mr. Goldberg is author of Practical Application of the Retirement Distribution Rules (IRG Publications) available at www.goldbergreports.com.

You can dramatically cut the after-tax cost of life insurance by owning it through a tax-favored qualified retirement plan—so that the premiums are paid with mostly tax-deductible rather than after-tax dollars…

TAX FACTS

Almost everybody needs life insurance during his/her working years—and people who own small businesses are likely to need it more than most.

Keys: The death benefit paid by a life insurance policy is tax free to the policy beneficiary—however, premiums paid for insurance are not tax deductible. So one must earn more than the premium amount to obtain enough after-tax dollars to pay it.

Example: If you're in the 35% tax bracket, you must earn $1,538 of income to obtain the after-tax dollars needed to pay every $1,000 of premium cost.

But many people don't realize that the Tax Code permits qualified retirement plans (generally company plans) to invest in life insurance. By purchasing insurance through a retirement plan, you get in effect a tax deduction for insurance premiums—because you deduct the plan contributions that are used to pay them.

If you are in a high tax bracket, this could reduce the after-tax premium cost by one-third or more after state and local taxes are considered. And the insurance death benefit remains tax free.

IRA LOOPHOLE

While the law allows qualified retirement plans to invest in life insurance, the terms of the plan itself must also allow it…

●**If you are an employee,** check the terms of your employer's retirement plan to see if it allows insurance purchases.

●**If you own your own business** and it doesn't have a qualified retirement plan that provides a life insurance investment option, you can either set up a new plan that has such an option or amend a current plan to give it one.

Legal note: The option to invest in life insurance must be available to all plan participants in a nondiscriminatory manner. And, life insurance should be among investments in the summary plan description distributed to employees. Do not amend a plan to become able to buy insurance for yourself while failing to tell employees about the option.

IRAs, unlike qualified retirement plans, cannot invest in life insurance. However, it is possible to use your IRA funds to buy insurance by transferring the funds to a business's qualified retirement plan.

IRA-to-qualified-plan rollovers have become much easier to make since the 2001 tax act. The use of IRA funds makes it possible to buy life insurance through a qualified plan that otherwise would lack the funds to do so.

Example: After 20 years as an employee at a big company, you then quit to start your own business and roll over your balance in the company's 401(k) retirement account to your own IRA.

You want to buy a million-dollar life insurance policy to protect your family. But the qualified retirement plan that you set up for the new business lacks the money to buy the insurance.

Provide it with the necessary money by rolling over your IRA into the new company's plan if permitted by the plan, and having the plan use that money to buy the insurance.

If you already own life insurance outside your retirement plan, paying after-tax dollars for it, it may be possible to transfer the policy to the retirement plan through tax-free exchange. The insurance would then be paid for with pretax dollars. This can be a much better option than canceling your existing insurance and buying a new policy through your plan.

For a Department of Labor opinion approving the sale of life insurance to a retirement plan for the policy's cash value, see Department of Labor Advisory Opinion 2002-12A, *www.dol.gov/ebsa/regs/aos/ao2002-12a.html.*

INCLUSION AMOUNT

The amount of an insurance policy's death benefit in excess of the policy's cash value remains tax free to the policy beneficiary of the retirement plan.

However, owning insurance through a retirement plan does not make the policy completely tax free.

Each year, a small amount is included in the policyholder's income that is attributable to the value of the policy, as determined by IRS Table 2001, published in IRS Notice 2001-10. However, the cost is much less than the savings obtained from holding the policy through the plan.

Example: For a 45-year-old person, each $1,000 of coverage will result in $1.53 being included in income. So $100,000 of coverage would create an annual maximum tax liability of $53.55—based on the top tax rate of 35%.

This small cost will be much less than the savings attained from the arrangement. Moreover, if you have a "rated" policy—so that you have to pay higher than average premiums—the amount included in income, "the inclusion amount," is a bargain because it is based on a "standard" IRS table.

In addition, the inclusion amount is recovered income tax free when the policy pays off, increasing the amount of the policy proceeds that are tax free.

This is because while the portion of the policy proceeds that are attributable to the policy's cash value are taxable, the amount that has already been taxed through the annual inclusion amount is tax free.

Example: An insurance policy offers a $100,000 benefit. When the insured dies, the policy's cash value is $6,000, and $4,000 was previously taxed to the insured through the annual inclusion amount. The amount that the beneficiary will receive tax free is $98,000—consisting of the $94,000 by which the benefit exceeds the policy's cash value plus the previously taxed amount of $4,000.

ESTATE TAX

The only drawback to owning life insurance through a retirement account is that the policy proceeds will be subject to estate tax. But that is only a problem if your estate is large enough to be subject to tax (currently more than $2 million)—and even so, estate tax probably can be prevented through a well-drafted overall estate plan.

However, you can avoid that problem. After you retire, you can transfer ownership of the insurance policy from the retirement plan to a life insurance trust or other individual, and if you live three years after doing so, the policy proceeds will escape estate tax as well.

Note: There are some income tax liabilities when you take the policy out of the plan.

Bottom line: Owning life insurance through a retirement plan can be a big cost saver.

Best: Talk to your insurance and retirement plan advisers.

Save Thousands by Giving Away Your Life Insurance Policy

Ralph C. Wileczec, CPA, CFP, vice president and senior private client adviser, Wilmington Trust, Wilmington, Delaware.

Give away your life insurance policy to save your heirs thousands of dollars in estate taxes. Life insurance proceeds (cash surrender value or death benefit) are considered part of your taxable estate—but if you don't own the policy, proceeds are not taxable. Giving the policy to your spouse is not usually a good idea—if he/she dies first, the proceeds become part of his estate and the problem remains. If you have adult children, give them the policy. You must report any policy value above $12,000 per recipient for gift tax purposes, since $12,000 per year is the most anyone can give anyone else tax-free in 2008, but the policy's eventual proceeds will not be taxed. (The tax-free amount for 2009 is $13,000.)

Caution: You cannot continue to pay policy premiums after making the transfer, but you can give the new owners up to the annual gift limit without any tax consequences—and they can use that money to pay premiums.

Sell Your Unwanted Life Insurance and Avoid Tax Traps

Lee Slavutin, MD, CLU, chairman of Stern Slavutin-2 Inc., an insurance and estate-planning firm, 530 Fifth Ave., New York City 10036, *www.sternslavutin.com.* Dr. Slavutin is author of *Guide to Life Insurance Strategies.* Practitioners.

Life insurance can protect your dependents in case of your premature death and provide liquidity to your estate. At some point, though, you may have accumulated sufficient liquid assets so that an existing life insurance policy is no longer necessary.

Strategy: Sell your life insurance policy to a third party. Even after you pay tax on the proceeds, the amount you receive could well exceed the proceeds from cashing in the policy or allowing it to lapse.

AN EVOLVING MARKET

Such transactions used to be called "viatical settlements," which involved policies sold by terminally ill individuals, often those with AIDS. However, recent medical advances have made it more difficult to forecast life expectancy for these patients, which makes it harder to set prices for such policies.

New look at old sellers: As a result, the focus today is on "senior life settlements," in which policies are bought from individuals who are not terminally ill but who have relatively short life expectancies. With cancer, heart attacks, diabetes, etc., longevity may be predicted within a range of years.

How it works: Generally, a number of insurance policies are combined into a single security, which is sold to investors. Thus, your life insurance won't be held by a single investor who will be motivated to speed your demise.

67

Key: A policy that you bought when you were younger and healthier will have premiums that are low in relation to the death benefit. If your health has worsened, buyers may be interested because those low premiums will make it cost effective for them to keep the policy in force.

As your health declines, the resale value of your life insurance rises.

Setting a price: The shorter the seller's life expectancy, the greater the purchase price as a percentage of the policy's face value.

Examples: Ann Thomas has a life expectancy between one and two years. A buyer might offer 60% of her policy's face value. That is, she might collect $300,000 up-front for a $500,000 life insurance policy because the investors hope to collect $500,000 in a relatively short time.

On the other hand, Harry Johnson, with a 10-year life expectancy, might be offered only $75,000 (15%) for his $500,000 policy.

Policy matters: You may be able to sell either a term or a permanent (cash-value) life insurance policy…

●**Term insurance.** As you grow older, your term insurance rates, if not fixed by your policy's provisions, might become so high that you're reluctant to keep it in force. If your term policy can be converted to a permanent life insurance policy, a buyer may be interested.

●**Permanent life.** These policies (whole life, universal life, variable life) are favored by buyers.

TAX TREATMENT

Viatical payments made to terminally ill individuals escape federal income tax. Some states also honor this tax exclusion.

Required: A physician has to certify that death is reasonably expected within 24 months. The payment must come from a "viatical settlement provider" that will report the amounts received by the insured individual to the IRS on Form 1099-LTC, *Long-Term Care and Accelerated Death Benefits.*

Senior lifetime settlements, which don't involve a terminal illness, don't enjoy tax exemption. Instead, the tax consequences will depend on the amount paid and the seller's cost basis in the policy.

The seller's basis in the policy generally will be the amount of premiums paid less any cash dividends received.

Example: Tom Smith, age 68, has been covered by a $2 million life insurance policy by his company. Smith, who has had a heart attack, is going to retire, so this coverage no longer is necessary.

Suppose a buyer, after looking at Smith's medical history and estimating his life expectancy, offers $300,000 for the policy. Smith's company had paid $300,000 in premiums and there have been no dividend payments, so the basis is $300,000.

Outcome: With a $300,000 basis and a $300,000 purchase price, no taxes will be due. If Smith's company had paid only $200,000 in premiums, taxes would be due on $100,000 of income.

Tax rates: What tax rates would apply to that income? That depends on the nature of the policy…

●**Permanent life insurance.** The difference between the basis and the cash value will be ordinary income, taxed up to 35%. Any excess qualifies for the bargain 15% rate on capital gains.

Example: Assume a basis of $200,000, cash value of $220,000, and a purchase price of $300,000. Of the $100,000 gain, $20,000 ($220,000 cash value minus the $200,000 basis) will be taxed as ordinary income while the remaining $80,000 would be a long-term capital gain.

●**Term life insurance.** Such policies have no cash value, so it's uncertain whether ordinary income or capital gains rates apply. You might take an aggressive position and report all the taxable income as a long-term capital gain.

POLICY PROCEDURES

Selling your insurance policy can make sense if you don't want to keep paying hefty premiums or if you would like more cash flow. *How to go about getting a good deal…*

●**Ask your insurance agent,** attorney, or accountant. If he/she isn't familiar with this market, and can't make a referral to an experienced professional, contact the Life Insurance Settlement Association (*www.lisassociation.org*, 407-894-3797) for a list of member companies.

●**Check references.** Before working with an unknown party, ask to be put in touch with some satisfied clients.

●**Check compensation.** Any fee or commission should be paid by the buyer, not by the seller.

●**Check the bids.** Always ask that bids be submitted on the stationery of the ultimate buyer, not an agent or broker, to make sure that you're seeing the actual offer from the purchaser.

●**Protect your privacy.** In some transactions, an unrelated third party is brought in to hold the buyer's funds in escrow. Then your insurance policy can be placed in escrow and the sale can be concluded.

Done properly, such a process can ensure that the money really is available and your identity is not revealed widely.

Life Insurance Loopholes

Edward Mendlowitz, CPA, partner, WithumSmith +Brown, 1 Spring St., New Brunswick, New Jersey 08901. He is author of *Estate Planning*. Practical Programs.

Smart insurance buyers can save a bundle in taxes, both in life and in the execution of their estates, if they look into the following strategies...

Loophole: **Life insurance proceeds are income tax free.** This is true even if only a few premium payments were made. However, life insurance premiums are not tax deductible.

●**Life insurance proceeds are partly or totally estate tax free if the policy (or part of it) is owned by the beneficiary,** not the insured.

Better: Use an irrevocable life insurance trust (ILIT) as the policy owner. If children or other individuals own the policy, it becomes available to an ex-spouse or unintended strangers in the event of divorce or a lawsuit against the child. The proceeds are estate tax free if you have no control over the policy.

Caution: Making your estate the beneficiary subjects the proceeds to tax.

●**Do not let your spouse own the policy.** A policy that's owned by the decedent or his/her spouse is taxed in the estate if both die simultaneously. Instead, use an ILIT as owner of the life insurance policy.

●**Do not name a former spouse as beneficiary.** If you do, the proceeds will be included in your estate because the policy will have been owned by the decedent.

Better: Set up an ILIT as owner in accordance with your divorce agreement.

Loophole: **So-called "Crummey letters" make annual gifts to a trust to pay for the life insurance premiums eligible for the annual gift tax exclusion.** (A Crummey letter notifies trust beneficiaries of their right to withdraw the amounts given to the trust.) If the beneficiaries do not waive their rights to their portion of the gift via a Crummey letter, the gift is subject to gift tax.

Loophole: **Policies purchased by an irrevocable life insurance trust are not subject to a "waiting period."** When existing policies are transferred to a trust, there is a three-year waiting period before proceeds are tax exempt.

Strategy: When policies are transferred to new trusts, the clock starts ticking. If the insured dies within three years, the proceeds are subject to estate taxes. Buy an inexpensive three-year term policy to cover estate taxes.

Loophole: **Use income from life insurance proceeds to pay an "allowance" to children's guardians if both parents die.** Establish the allowance provisions in the will or trust.

Loophole: **Avoid "transfer for value" taxation that applies when an owner sells the policy to the insured...**a partner of the insured...a partnership in which the insured is a partner...or a corporation in which the insured is an officer or shareholder.

Trap: When the policy is sold to any of the buyers listed, the excess of the proceeds over the premiums paid is taxable income to the recipient of the death benefit.

Loophole: **Write an "apportionment" clause into your will.** This designates that estate taxes attributable to inadvertently owned life insurance proceeds will be paid by the recipient, not the estate.

Loophole: **Employer-paid group term insurance premiums are tax free up to $50,000 of life insurance.** Premiums paid for policies over that amount are taxable at reduced rates determined by IRS tables.

Loophole: **Whole life insurance creates a tax-free buildup of cash value that offsets premiums in later years.** When paid as part of the life insurance proceeds, it is not taxed ...nor when borrowed from the policy...when withdrawn, it is tax free to the extent of total premiums paid.

Loophole: **Match insurance to your coverage needs using the tax deferral features of life insurance.** Universal life insurance provides flexibility to modify the face amount or premium when personal circumstances change. Variable life combines life insurance with a tax-deferred or sheltered investment fund.

Benefits: The insured "owns" the investment part of the policy, including the investment risk. When the insured dies, the proceeds are income tax free. Also, the insured can borrow against the cash value.

Outright distributions are subject to income tax to the extent that they exceed total premiums paid. They are not subject to penalty for distributions made before age 59½—variable annuity distributions are.

Loophole: **Payments made under a life insurance policy to a terminally ill insured are income tax free, like a "death" benefit.**

Loophole: **Fund shareholder and partnership buy-sell agreements with life insurance.** When the death benefits are received, the recipient pays no income tax. The proceeds are then used to purchase the deceased owner's shares tax free. Be aware that you cannot deduct premium payments, and C corporations may be liable for alternative minimum tax.

Loophole: **Fund cross-purchase agreements with life insurance.** When a buy-sell agreement is funded with life insurance, the entity uses the proceeds to acquire shares. With a cross-purchase arrangement, the remaining owners receive the death benefits and then use them to buy the shares. This way, they get a tax-favored stepped-up basis for the shares.

4

Best Ways to Buy or Sell a Home

14 Ways to Sell Your Home Faster

Don't ever underestimate the power of a good first impression. A home that is attractive from the road can sell in as little as half the time, making it less likely that you'll have to reduce the asking price.

LANDSCAPE

1. Edge lawns and flowerbeds. A sharp edge gives a well-maintained look. Conversely, grass or weeds sprouting up from cracks in paths and driveways implies neglect.

2. Add color. Plant flowers to make the front of a house come alive, particularly if the home itself is white or a dark color.

3. Patch cracks in walkways and sidewalks, even if the sidewalk is the town's responsibility. If tree roots have shattered a section, consider rerouting the sidewalk around the tree. Also, sweep all walks.

4. Trim overgrown trees and shrubs. Remove dead or dying plants.

HOUSE FACADE

5. Polish the doorknob. If the main entryway's doorknob or knocker is showing signs of age, it's worth spending $150 or so for the set to replace it.

6. Remove potted plants, statues and decorations from the front stoop. They make it look cluttered and smaller.

7. Use similar drapes in front windows. Most home owners select drapes and blinds for the way they look inside the home—but different colors and shapes in the front windows make a home look unbalanced.

8. Replace broken and missing shingles. Just a few bad shingles give the impression of roof problems—a major turnoff for potential buyers.

Jim Fite, president of the Dallas-based Century 21 Judge Fite Company, one of the largest Century 21 affiliates in the world, with more than $800 million in annual sales and 600 associates, *www.century21judgefite.com.*

OTHER DETAILS

9. Remove weathered basketball hoops. Only keep them up if they look new and have nets.

10. Match your mailbox to your home. A cutesy mailbox is appropriate if you have a cutesy home. A $500,000 home shouldn't have a $10 mailbox.

11. Take down a dilapidated backyard fence, particularly if it can be seen from the street or driveway.

12. Remove any of your decorative items that could be considered clutter. Walkway lights and garden fountains are fine. Garden gnomes, out-of-season Christmas lights and other ornamentation should be packed away.

13. Keep garage doors closed. Even tidy garage interiors just do not look as neat as closed garage doors. Garbage cans, rakes, bikes, etc. should be stored inside.

14. Maintain the *For Sale* sign. A post that is leaning or in need of painting implies your home has been on the market for a long time. That suggests problems.

Smartest Ways to Increase Your Home's Value

David Gershon, CEO of Empowerment Institute, which works with local governments to form and promote active neighborhood improvement programs, Woodstock, New York, *www.empowermentinstitute.net*. Mr. Gershon is author of *The Livable Neighborhood: About Making Life Better on the Street Where You Live*. Empowerment Institute.

How do you increase the value of your home, beautify your neighborhood and get to know your neighbors? Start a street association.

My own organization has helped thousands of community groups to deal with noise, traffic, crime and pollution—and have fun doing it.

ORGANIZE

The best way to get people involved is by going door-to-door. Chat about neighborhood issues, then invite neighbors to your first meeting. Once you get together, a frank discussion of the neighborhood's needs and the residents'

abilities will help the group decide where the focus should be.

Inspiration is the key to success. Prepare for the meeting with lists of problems and possible solutions. Then let the group brainstorm its own creative ideas. Don't force your own agenda.

Common problems and possible solutions to bring up…

TRAFFIC

Speeding vehicles are a problem everywhere.

Actions: Have all the members of your neighborhood association display signs in their yards reading *30 Is Legal, but Neighbors Drive 25* or *Thanks for Not Speeding*.

Neighbors can take turns holding up these signs throughout rush hour. Remember to wave and smile at all the drivers as they pass by—especially since you will know some of them.

Ask the police to set up radar-activated electronic signs that display the speed of passing cars. Or request that they set up speed traps periodically.

Request speed bumps, stop signs or other remedies from your area's traffic department.

CRIME

Don't wait for police to improve security.

Actions: Ask police and political leaders to set up a block watch or a community-oriented policing services (COPS) program. These organize residents into a watchful presence that helps police prevent trouble. This can range from simply learning how to watch for suspicious activity throughout your neighborhood to actually walking the streets as part of a neighborhood patrol.

Example: In one Philadelphia community, the neighborhood watch met to discuss techniques for getting rid of the drug dealers. Some of those same drug dealers also attended to see what they were up against. When they realized the community was getting organized, the drug dealers left the area.

Meet regularly with a police liaison to discuss other problems and what can be done to solve them.

Important: Don't institute such efforts without the proper training—you could endanger yourself and your neighbors.

If your town has no such programs, contact the National Crime Prevention Council (202-466-6272, *www.ncpc.org*) for help.

BEAUTIFICATION

You don't have to let an eyesore go unchallenged. *Possible solutions…*

Actions: Planting trees on the public land along your street can increase property values by 15%. Designate a landscape committee and have its members list the streets that could be improved by planting trees. Contact your local parks department about recommendations for trees to plant, and ask for permission to put them in. When no such program or department exists, ask for government permission to plant trees and get planting advice from a nursery.

Important: Be sure to appoint group members to care for newly planted trees during the first year.

Make the most of what your neighborhood has. Expose and landscape rock outcroppings. Paint old-fashioned streetlights and bridges. Such special touches can make your neighborhood *the* place to own a home. If you're lucky enough to have wetlands or a stream, schedule a clean-up day. Ask for help from your local government's department of parks, solid waste or environmental protection. The reward is a beautiful spot.

BETTER LIVING

Street and neighborhood associations make life much more fun, healthful and cheaper, too. *Additional ideas to discuss at your meeting…*

● **Walking and jogging clubs** motivate members to exercise together.

● **Baby-sitting and day-care collectives** let parents trade certificates, each of which represents one hour of babysitting/child care.

● **Food cooperatives** are organized by people who buy in bulk at lower prices. Some of these groups contract with local farmers to get fresh vegetables.

Information: National Agricultural Library at *www.nal.usda.gov.*

Best Home-Buying Deals

On average, houses at auctions will sell for 90% to 110% of what they would bring through traditional methods, but bargains can be found. The best deals are at *absolute* auctions, where the opening price is set by the bidders, and the seller must accept the high bid. To learn more about auctions, search the National Association of Realtors' Web site at *www.realtor.org*, using the keyword "auction." Inspect the house and the neighborhood before bidding. Also, set a maximum bid.

Dorothy Nicklus, broker and auctioneer and owner of 24/7 Auctioneer, Guttenberg, New Jersey, *www.247auctioneer.com.*

 # House-Hunting Help

Chase Magnuson, president, National Real Estate Foundation, Carlsbad, California, *www.nationalrealestatefoundation.org.*

When shopping for a house, there are three ways that will increase your success…

● **Get preapproved**—not just prequalified—for a mortgage so that you won't need a financing contingency clause in your contract.

● **Drive through neighborhoods you like** to find for-sale signs.

● **Ask neighbors to let you know of houses that come on the market.**

To find homes being sold by the owner: Subscribe to "for sale by owner" scouting services, such as Landvoice, 888-678-0905, *www.landvoice.com*, $39.99/month…or find "for sale by owner" sites on the Internet. If possible, provide the seller with a letter from your bank indicating that funds are available for 10% of the home's purchase price. Make an offer within 24 hours of seeing a house.

Home-Buying Basics

When looking for a home, the watchword is patience. You won't know exactly what you want, nor will you have a good feel for what is available at a given price, until you have seen a lot of properties.

Also: Use a buyer's real estate agent that represents *you* in the sale. A traditional broker can be helpful, too—but they work for *sellers*. A broker's job is to get the seller the highest price, so beware how much you reveal to him/her. Look for a broker who is willing to spend time finding the best house for you, rather than one looking to close a quick sale.

Jean Chatzky, the financial editor for *Today* on NBC and editor-at-large for *Money* magazine. She is also the author of *Pay It Down!* Portfolio. Her Internet site is *www.jeanchatzky.com.*

A Plus for Seniors

The new housing law benefits seniors ages 62 or older. *The Housing and Economic Recovery Act of 2008* raises the maximum amount for a reverse mortgage to $417,000 to $625,500—up from the previous limit of $200,160 to $362,790, depending on where a borrower lives. The new, higher limit applies nationwide rather than by county. Also, reverse mortgages—which do not have to be repaid until the borrower moves permanently, sells or dies—now will cost less.

Most important: Origination fees may not exceed 2% of the initial $200,000 borrowed and 1% of the remaining balance, to a maximum fee of $6,000. This cap is subject to future inflation adjustment.

Kiplinger.com.

Three Ways to Find Real Estate Bargains

Below is some good advice on how to find values in today's overvalued real estate market…

●**Decode newspaper classifieds.** Motivated sellers use such phrases as *mortgage assumption*—you can avoid the down payment by taking over the seller's mortgage…*will finance*—you borrow from the seller…*investor liquidation* and *estate sale*—the seller needs a quick deal.

●**Ask for leads.** Leave your contact information with store owners, letter carriers, home owners who are holding garage sales, personnel professionals at local corporations, insurance agents and members of the clergy. Tell them that you buy residential real estate, and offer $100 for a lead on any property that you ultimately purchase.

●**Check on-line listings.**

●The National Real Estate Investors Association has links to local networks of investors and brokers. 888-762-7342, *www.nationalreia.com.*

●BuyBankHomes.com and Realtor.com link to properties around the country listed on the Multiple Listing Service (MLS), the same database real estate agents use.

How to Find the Best Agent for Selling Your Home

Adriane G. Berg, Lebanon, New Jersey–based attorney, speaker, stockbroker, host of a personal finance radio show on the Business Talk Radio Network and author of *How Not to Go Broke at 102! Achieving Everlasting Wealth.* Wiley. For more information, go to *www.wealth102.com.*

Choose a real estate agent who specializes in selling your kind of house. Most people assume that multiple listing services, which share data about available properties, have leveled the playing field among all real estate agents.

Reality: A listing agent who understands your neighborhood can increase your selling price by thousands.

Example: A New Jersey couple in their 60s owned an 11-room Victorian home. It was architecturally stunning but lacked central air conditioning and was costly to heat. The first broker advertised the house as "Large Victorian. Needs Work." The best offer was $500,000 and only if the couple was willing to renovate it first. A second broker marketed it to buyers of historic homes.

The house sold for $680,000—no renovations required.

Don't Pay Referral Fees to Arrange a Reverse Mortgage

Larry Swedroe, director of research, Buckingham Asset Management, St. Louis. *www.bamservices.com.*

The Department of Housing and Urban Development (*www.hud.gov/groups/seniors.cfm*) provides lenders' names at no cost. These lenders do not charge for application or approval.

Caution: Reverse mortgages usually are tax-free, but they may affect eligibility for need-based public benefits, such as Medicaid.

More information: With a reverse mortgage, you get money from the lender every month or a lump sum, a credit line or a combination of these options. The reverse mortgage is paid from the proceeds of the sale of the house after you move or die. The amount you can borrow depends on your age and other factors. Loan costs can be high and may not be amortized if you move within five years—these mortgages are best if you plan to stay in your home long term.

Don't Forget to Get Your Permit

Home-remodeling permits are the home owner's responsibility—not the contractor's. Although contractors may promise to file the appropriate paperwork with the city, not all do.

Important: If the correct permits are not obtained, the home owner may have to have work redone when he/she wants to sell the property. Contact your town's building department to find out what permits are required.

Greg McBride, CFA, senior financial analyst, BankRate.com, North Palm Beach, Florida.

When Lending Money Is a Great Deal for You!

Keith Gumbinger, vice president, HSH Associates, publisher of mortgage and consumer loan information, Pompton Plains, New Jersey. *www.hsh.com.*

Lending to a family member so that he/she can buy a home can be beneficial for you both. You're likely to receive higher interest than from an income-producing investment, and the loan is secured by real estate. Your relative won't have to go through a mortgage qualification process and will get a lower interest rate than from a bank. He also can save up to 30% on closing costs. As with a bank loan, he can take a tax deduction for mortgage interest.

Important: You must charge a minimum interest rate set by the IRS. If you don't, you could be taxed as if you received the required amount or be subject to gift tax. To find the rate, go to *www.irs.gov* and search for the term "Applicable Federal Rate."

Helpful: For a one-time charge of $649, Virgin Money (800-805-2472, *www.virginmoney us.com*) will draw up mortgage documents and legally record the mortgage. For $249 a year, it will service the loan and allow the borrower to manage his account on-line.

Six Ways to Lower Your Property Tax Bill

Nancy Dunnan, a financial adviser and author in New York City. Ms. Dunnan's latest book is titled *How to Invest $50–$5,000*. HarperCollins.

You have the right to protest a property tax bill. But do the footwork, or hire a specialist—a property tax consultant or attorney (most charge on a contingency basis). *If you do it yourself…*

●**Call your local tax assessor's office to find out about the appeals deadline.** It is typically 30 to 120 days after property tax bills are mailed out.

●**Check your written assessment for any errors**—look at square footage and number of bedrooms and bathrooms, etc.

●**At the tax assessor's office,** compare your assessment against at least five comparable homes of the same age and size in your neighborhood that have lower tax bills.

●**Take photographs of comparable houses as backup.**

●**Attend someone else's hearing** in order to familiarize yourself with the procedure and officials involved.

●**Ask for an informal meeting** with the tax assessor. If your request for a meeting is denied, then be sure to follow your town's procedures for a formal hearing.

Also: Check out *How to Fight Property Taxes,* available from the National Taxpayers Union at *www.ntu.org* or 703-683-5700.

Cost: $6.95 (price subject to change).

Shrewd Ways to Use Your Home as a Tax Shelter

Diane Kennedy, CPA, a tax strategist for more than 20 years, and founder of D. Kennedy & Associates located in Phoenix. She is also coauthor of several books, including *Real Estate Loopholes: Secrets of Successful Real Estate Investing* (Warner Books) and author of *Loopholes of the Rich* (Wiley). Her web site is *www.taxloopholes.com.*

From a tax perspective, there's never been a better time to own a home. *Below are four loopholes to take advantage of…*

SHORT-TERM OWNERSHIP

The home-sale exclusion is one of the mosts generous tax breaks in the Internal Revenue Code. Starting in 2008, married couples and widow(er)s (within two years of the death of their spouse) can avoid tax on up to $500,000 in capital gains ($250,000 for a single person). This break can be used over and over.

To get it, you have to have owned the home and used it as your principal residence for at least two of the five years before the sale. Most people, however, don't realize how easy it is to use the exclusion even if you do not meet this two-year test.

Loophole: **If you needed to move out of a house before the two years were up because of an "unforeseen circumstance,"** you still can get a partial tax break. Unforeseen circumstances are defined very liberally. They include, for example, natural disasters, a change in your employment or becoming self-employed, divorce or legal separation and multiple births from the same pregnancy.

How it works: Say you are promoted—or even demoted—at work. This is considered a change in employment, so you can sell your house and take a partial tax break even if you don't satisfy the two-year test. The same is true if you start, change or discontinue a business.

Example: You would like to move from the appreciated property in which you have lived for less than two years. Before selling, you start a simple home-based business. Assuming that you sell the house after living in it for one year, you would get half of the maximum tax break because one year is half of two. You and your spouse could exclude up to $250,000 (half of $500,000) of any gain on the sale. And, a single filer could exclude up to $125,000 (half of $250,000).

HOME-OFFICE DEDUCTION

Some people don't deduct depreciation for a home office because they think it will cause them to owe tax on the gain allocated to the office when they sell the home. But, this is not the case.

Loophole: **As long as the home office is part of your house—and not a separate structure—you will get the full principal-residence capital gains exclusion.**

How it works: If you have taken a depreciation deduction for the office portion of your residence, you need to "recapture" the depreciation when you sell the home.

Example: If you have taken $10,000 of depreciation and are in the 25% bracket, you would owe $2,500 in tax—25% of $10,000—when you sell the home. You can keep whatever is left of the $500,000 or $250,000 exclusion on gains.

Paying less tax now (by depreciating) is worth more than the cost of recapturing depreciation later. For rules on depreciation, see IRS Publication 946, *How to Depreciate Property,* available by contacting 800-829-3676, *www.irs.gov.*

ASSET PROTECTION

In these litigious times, it's very easy to imagine someone tripping on your driveway and suing you, putting your home and other assets then at risk.

Strategy: To protect your home from creditors, transfer it to a single-member limited liability company (LLC). This isn't necessary if you live in states with "unlimited homestead protection"—where equity is protected—such as Texas and Florida, and you've lived there for more than two years.

Loophole: **Home owners who make such transfers still will be entitled to the mortgage interest deduction and capital gains exclusion.** There can be only one owner, perhaps you and your spouse holding the title as joint tenants. You don't need to file an additional business tax return for the LLC.

DIVIDE AND CONQUER

You may be able to sell part of your property at a profit and still get the benefit of the capital gains exclusion.

For example, your home sits on 40 acres. A developer buys 39 acres, from which you make a $300,000 profit. Then, a year later, you sell the house and the remaining acre for an additional $150,000 profit.

Loophole: **According to the Treasury Department, you are allowed to take the full $500,000 or $250,000 capital gains exclusion on the combined gain if you complete the "split sale" within two years.**

In the example above, the total $450,000 gain ($300,000 plus $150,000) would be tax free, provided the house was sold within two years of the prior sale of the land and all other conditions were met.

Deductible Home Improvements

A hurdle to deducting medical expenses is that only those in excess of 7.5% of your adjusted gross income (AGI) are deductible.

But costly home improvements made for medical purposes may get you over the hurdle.

Examples: Modified bathrooms, widened doors and stairways, elevators, wheelchair ramps, air-conditioning and even swimming pools all may qualify as deductible medical expenses.

Rules: The improvements must be primarily for a medical purpose and are deductible up to the extent their cost exceeds any increase in the home's value. (Or deductible without regard to value if the improvement is made to accommodate a disability condition.)

But if a home improvement gets you over the 7.5%-of-AGI threshold, all your other medical costs in addition to it—such as for prescription drugs—become deductible, too.

Connie Lorz, EA, past president of the California Society of Enrolled Agents, Sacramento.

Vacation-Home Tax Loopholes

Bob Trinz, senior tax analyst at Thomson/RIA, which provides tax information and software to tax professionals. He edits several RIA publications, including *Federal Taxes Weekly Alert.*

There's no place like home under the tax code. If you own a home—even a vacation home—and rent it out each year, you can claim all kinds of tax breaks. *Here's a rundown...*

●**If you rent out your home for 14 days or fewer per year,** the income is tax free. This might be especially lucrative if your home is near the site of a major sporting event or in a resort area. If you go over the 14-day mark, all the rental income must be reported.

Caution: You won't be able to claim rental-related tax deductions, such as cleaning and advertising.

If you own a business or professional practice, those 14 tax-free days can include days your vacation home is rented to your company for an executive meeting or employee picnic. This won't work for sole proprietors.

As long as you charge a fair rental price, your company can take a deduction while you enjoy the tax-free income. Be sure to consult your company's tax adviser before employing this strategy.

If you rent out your vacation home for more than 14 days a year, it may be taxed in one of two ways...

●**As rental property.** Your second home is considered rental property if you personally use it for no more than 14 days and rent it out for more than 14 days...or you use it for more than 14 days but this use represents no more than 10% of the number of rental days.

Example: You use your vacation home for 30 days a year and rent it out for 335 days. Your personal use is less than 10% of your rental days, so your vacation home is considered rental property.

Drawback: If your vacation home is treated as rental property, you might lose some mortgage interest deductions.

If you have a loss on the rental, you might be able to deduct it right away. Losses of up to $25,000 can be deducted each year if your adjusted gross income (AGI) is $100,000 or below. For AGIs above $100,000, the maximum deductible loss gradually declines. It disappears when AGI reaches $150,000.

If these losses can't be deducted right away, they can be deducted when you sell your vacation home. Rules are complex, so consult your tax adviser.

●**As a residence.** In the above example, if you had rented the home for only 329 days, your personal use would have accounted for more than 10% of the rental period, so the home would be taxed as a residence. This means that you probably would be able to deduct your mortgage interest and property taxes.

Drawbacks: You will be taxed on rental income, although expenses such as utilities and insurance can be used to offset it. No rental losses can be deducted, even when you sell your home.

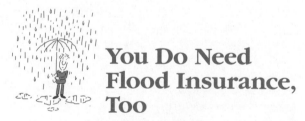

You Do Need Flood Insurance, Too

Jeanne Salvatore, an adjunct professor at Iona College in New Rochelle, New York, and Columbia University in New York City. She is senior vice president of public affairs at the Insurance Information Institute, an industry trade group, *www.iii.org.*

As residents of the Gulf Coast learned—in a tragic way—homeowner's insurance does not cover flood damage.*

*As defined by the federal government's National Flood Insurance Program (NFIP), a flood is an inundation of dry land caused by overflow of inland or tidal waters, unusual and rapid accumulation or runoff of surface waters from any source, mudflow or collapse of land along the shore of a lake as a result of erosion caused by water exceeding anticipated cyclical levels.

Trap: Even if your house is above sea level and seemingly out of harm's way, you can be a flood victim. According to the Federal Emergency Management Agency (FEMA), about 25% of all flood claims come from outside high-flood-risk areas…

●**Floods and flash floods occur in all 50 states.**

●**Reservoirs,** lakes, ponds, rivers and even small streams overflow.

●**Accumulated snow melts too rapidly.**

●**New land development changes natural runoff paths.**

Damaging floods aren't always signaled by water rushing through the streets. A single inch of water can cause costly damage to your home.

BUYING FLOOD INSURANCE

Federal law requires you to carry flood insurance as a condition of obtaining a mortgage if you live in a designated high-risk flood zone. This is defined by FEMA as a 100-year flood plain (meaning the area has a 1% chance of flooding in any given year). About 10% of the US falls into this category.

You can ascertain your flood zone by checking flood insurance rate maps for your area, which can be obtained at the FEMA Map Service Center (*www.msc.fema.gov*). On-line access is $2.50 per map…paper copies, which can be purchased at the Web site, are $4 each, or call 800-358-9616.

These maps reflect the risk of flooding of your home. Knowing this risk helps you decide how much flood coverage you should buy and what preventive steps you can take at your home before a flood occurs.

Even if you don't carry a mortgage, you should still have flood insurance. If you're a renter, for example, your landlord is responsible for the home's structure but not for your belongings.

Note: You can purchase flood insurance for your personal property to complement an existing renter's insurance policy.

Government-subsidized flood insurance policies can be obtained from licensed insurance agents and brokers. Policies are made available through the National Flood Insurance Program (NFIP) only if your community participates.

Ask your insurer or go to the NFIP Community Status Book Web site at *www.fema.gov/fema/ csb.shtm*. Policies are sold and administered through roughly 90 participating insurance companies. Contact your insurance agent for details or visit the NFIP Web site at *www. floodsmart.gov* or call 888-379-9531 for a list of participating companies.

Government-sponsored flood insurance is very affordable, although the higher the area's flood risk, the higher the premium. With NFIP you can cover your house for losses ranging from $20,000 up to a maximum of $250,000. You can cover the contents of your house for losses ranging from $8,000 up to a maximum of $100,000. The average premium for $100,000 of building coverage in a high-risk area is $400 a year, and as little as $112 annually for $20,000 of building and $8,000 of content insurance for low-risk areas.

If you live in an area where real estate prices are higher than the maximum coverage, you may be able to buy supplemental coverage from a private insurer. Speak to your insurance agent about coverage and costs.

Important: Don't delay obtaining a flood insurance policy—there is a 30-day waiting period before coverage begins.

BEFORE THE FLOOD

To protect yourself against flood damage, take the following precautions right now…

●**Take photos of important possessions and store them away from danger.** The pictures will be of help in case you file a flood insurance claim.

●**Store important documents and irreplaceable items where they are unlikely to be damaged** in a flood. Basements are not a good choice.

●**Have a licensed electrician raise electrical components,** such as switches and circuit breakers, above your home's projected flood elevation. This is the height floodwater will likely reach in your home, determined from your local flood elevation map.

●**Have a licensed plumber install backflow valves** or plugs to prevent floodwaters from entering your drains, toilets and other sewer connections.

Important: If your home is in danger of being flooded and you have a federal flood insurance policy, you may obtain reimbursement for certain damage-prevention costs…

●**Rental for storage space and sump pumps.**

●**Use sandbags and lumber to erect a barricade.**

Buying or Selling a Home? How to Get A Much Better Deal

Blanche Evans, editor of *Realty Times*, the Internet's most visited independent real estate news service, Dallas. She is author of *Bubbles, Booms, and Busts: Make Money in Any Real Estate Market.* McGraw-Hill. Last year, she was named one of the "25 Most Influential People in Real Estate" by *Realtor Magazine. www.realtytimes.com.*

Over the past decade, real estate tools on the Internet have morphed from novelty to near necessity. The Web simplifies the search for home-related information. It provides mortgage rates…estimated home values and selling prices…local demographics, crime statistics and cost-of-living data…school ratings…descriptions of activities and amenities, such as restaurants…and detailed interactive maps, satellite images and "virtual tours" of homes—all without leaving your desk. Most sites are free.

For sellers, there are sites where you can list your home yourself, thereby reducing or eliminating real estate agent commissions.

Strategies for using the Web to help you buy or sell a home…

BUYING A HOME

●**Determine your price range.** There are millions of homes listed on the Web. Instead of wasting time wading through listings for homes you can't afford, go to *www.bankrate.com* or *www.mortgagecalc.com* for calculators that help you figure out what you can afford.

●**Sort through listings.** Until a few years ago, only real estate agents had access to lists of homes from the giant information-sharing Multiple Listing Service (MLS). Now you can access many of those listings yourself, although some details, such as the original listing price and commission rates, may be available only to real estate agents.

Start with *www.realtor.com*, which has three million listings, along with prices—far more than any other site.

Next, move on to the local real estate agent Web sites. You often can find these through Realtor.com. Local sites often have more accurate and up-to-date information about homes than national sites.

●**Compare prices.** Get tax records, sales histories and prices of "comparables"—homes in the area that are similar to the one you're interested in—at *www.zillow.com*. It offers maps showing prices in neighborhoods, plus loads of historical charts and graphs displaying how a particular home's value has risen or fallen in the past 30 days or since its last sale.

Another site, *www.homegain.com*, combines several services—letting you estimate home values, get prequalified for a mortgage, view listings, compare real estate agents and commission rates, and even find a moving company.

Caution: Estimated home values vary on different sites and are not based on appraisals. Property and pricing details can be inaccurate. Double-check details with agents and area home owners.

●**Compare features.** Using satellite imagery, *www.trulia.com* has teamed up with Google Earth to let you "fly" down to treetop level to look at available properties in near 3-D. Yahoo's real estate site—*realestate.yahoo.com* —and *www.bestplaces.net* let you research a neighborhood for schools, recreational facilities, crime statistics…even how many Starbucks coffee shops there are.

If you are willing to pay a fee to get more detailed information than is available on free sites, consider *www.neighborhoodscout.com*, which provides school district ratings and crime rates, as well as how much median home values have changed. Subscription plans range from one month ($29.99) to six months ($89.94).

●**Consider a newly built home.** Amid the plunge in new-home sales, builders are slashing prices by as much as 20% and offering other incentives. Homes available from three of the biggest US home builders are listed at *www. beazerhomes.com…www.kbhome.com…*and *www.tollbrothers.com.*

Aggregator sites: Newly built homes around the US are listed at *www.american homeguides.com…www.inest.com…*and *www. newhomeguide.com.* Inest.com offers rebates of 1% of the purchase price for homes bought based on their listings.

●**Compare mortgage rates** from more than 70 mortgage lenders at *www.e-loan.com* (800-533-5333) for help. At *www.priceline.com,* name the mortgage terms you want, then see whether such a loan is available. At *www. hsh.com,* compare mortgage rates and find names of lenders by state. Also try *www.mort gage.com…www.quickenloans.com…*and *www. bankrate.com* for similar information.

●**Get preapproved for a loan.** Buyers with strong credit can get loan preapproval from an on-line lender, print out the preapproval notice and carry it with them while looking at houses.

SELLING A HOME

●**List your home.** If you're willing to list and show your home yourself, you can save thousands of dollars in real estate agent commissions with the Internet.

At *www.owners.com,* you can choose from several listing packages. The basic one is free and allows you to write a description of unlimited length and run it on the site with five photos for seven days. You can upgrade products and services starting at $2.95. For $377, Owners. com will list your home on your local MLS for six months. If a broker brings you a home buyer in response to your listings, you can negotiate a commission rate—which usually is up to 3%—but you won't have to pay a seller's agent, saving you up to 3%. If a home buyer responds to your Web listing directly, there is no commission.

●**Set your dream price.** Even if you don't necessarily expect to sell your home, on *www. zillow.com* you can post a "Make Me Move" price that is so high it might convince you to change your mind if someone offers that price.

Caution: Even though the Internet can be a powerful selling tool, a real estate agent may bring more potential buyers to your house…help you avoid mistakes, such as overpricing your home…stage a successful open house…help

you negotiate a better price…and even help coordinate your work with a real estate attorney.

What to Do If You Inherit a House

David Schechner, real estate attorney and principal, Schechner & Targan, West Orange, New Jersey.

In many cases, it is a mistake to rent out an inherited house unless you want to own investment property. Typically, the income doesn't compensate for the cost and aggravation. It's best to sell it and find other investments.

Exceptions: You plan to live in the house in the near future or you can get a hefty rent.

To decide whether you want to rent or sell, determine…

●**The extent to which taxes and other costs offset rental income.**

●**Cost of cosmetic improvements and repairs** to comply with building codes.

●**Cost and hassle of complying with various laws**—health, safety and tenants' rights.

Also check in your state to see if you can remove a tenant without cause at the end of his/her lease. In many states, you can't unless you sell the property.

Important: See a lawyer about lease terms …make sure your insurance liability coverage is adequate.

Pros and Cons of Home Loans and Margin Loans

Jerry Lerman, CPA, managing director for RSM McGladrey, 1185 Avenue of the Americas, New York City 10036.

Borrowing against a home provides some handsome tax benefits. And borrowing against a securities portfolio can provide even greater tax breaks.

HOME LOANS

Under the mortgage interest rules, you can fully deduct the interest on home-acquisition loans for a first and second residence up to a total of $1 million.

To qualify as a home-acquisition loan, the money must be used to buy, build or improve your first or second home and the debt must be secured by the same residence.

Trap: Debt secured by a primary residence to buy a second home doesn't pass the second test, so the interest isn't deductible, up to the $1 million limit.

Note: If you refinance your home acquisition debt with a larger mortgage, only the amount of the original mortgage that is refinanced qualifies as home-acquisition debt.

What happens to debt secured by a home that is not home-acquisition debt? It's considered "home-equity debt."

Lower limit: You are allowed to deduct the interest on no more than $100,000 worth of home-equity debt.

Loophole: Even though less interest is deductible, you can take the deduction, no matter how the money is spent.

Example: Using a line of credit secured by your home, you borrow $150,000 to pay personal bills. Your total interest comes to $9,000 the first year.

Interest on the first $100,000 of home-equity debt ($6,000) is deductible but interest on the excess $50,000 ($3,000) is not deductible.

Loophole: You can decide to treat home-equity debt as debt not secured by your home. In some cases, this results in a larger deduction.

Example 1: If you borrow $150,000 on a home-equity line of credit and $50,000 of that is used for business-related expenses, then you can elect to treat that $50,000 as trade or business debt, which may be deductible.

Example 2: In another situation, you borrow $150,000 to purchase a second home. You can elect to have the excess $50,000 treated as investment-related debt, stating that you're holding the second home for investment.

In that case, all the interest on the excess $50,000 may be investment interest, which is deductible up to the amount of your net investment income.

Your net investment income will come from dividends and interest. You can count net capital gains, too, if that would work to your advantage, knowing that you may lose the benefit of the lower 15% long-term capital gains rate.

MARGIN LOANS

As you can see from the list below, borrowing against your home poses some problems...

1. Home-acquisition debt can be used only for buying, building or improving a home.

2. Home-equity debt is limited to the equity you have in your home.

3. Only $100,000 of home-equity debt provides deductible interest.

Strategy: Instead of borrowing against your home, borrow against your securities portfolio. Most brokerage firms extend so-called margin loans. *Ground rules...*

● **"Purpose" loans** are used for purchasing other securities (other than tax-free investments). In general, you can borrow up to 50% of the value of your collateral with purpose loans (90% for government securities such as T-bills).

Example: With $500,000 worth of stocks, bonds and funds in your portfolio, you might borrow $250,000 to buy other securities. You now hold $750,000 worth of securities, securing your $250,000 loan.

● **"Nonpurpose" loans** can be used for anything else, other than buying securities.

● **Interest rates.** You'll pay less for a margin loan than you would for credit card debt or a personal loan from a bank.

Example: For margin loans, your brokerage firm might charge one point over the prime lending rate. If the prime rate is 4%, you would pay 5% on margin loans.

Tax treatment: Purpose loans produce investment interest, which is deductible up to the amount of net investment income. Interest on loans used to buy tax-free investments like municipal bonds is not deductible.

Nonpurpose loans generally produce nondeductible personal interest. However, if the borrowed money is used in your trade or business, the interest may be deductible.

SPREADING THE RISK

Borrowing against your securities may make sense when you have a large position of one highly appreciated stock.

Let's say that you own $1 million worth of ABC Co. stock, purchased many years ago for $50,000.

Trap: If you sell the shares, you'll have a $950,000 capital gain and could owe nearly $200,000 in tax ($142,500 in federal, plus any state taxes).

If you hold the shares, though, an Enron-like disaster could wipe out a great deal of your net worth.

Strategy: Borrow against your ABC shares, and use the proceeds to invest in a diversified portfolio. The interest will be deductible, up to the amount of your net investment income, and you will reduce your exposure to a single stock.

Savvy maneuvering can cut your exposure to your large stock position and your tax bill.

For example, you borrow $1 million against your ABC shares and invest $100,000 in each of 10 different stocks. Some of your new holdings go up, others go down.

Suppose you sell the losing positions and take losses that total $150,000. You also sell enough of your ABC shares to take a $150,000 gain.

Your losses offset your gains so no taxes are due. All sales proceeds can be invested in other securities, further diversifying your portfolio.

Risk: This strategy still leaves you exposed to a steep drop in the price of ABC shares.

However, stock brokerage firms offer sophisticated techniques for limiting your losses. Often, this will involve the purchase and sale of listed stock options.

Caution: If you create too much protection for your appreciated shares, you may be subject to "constructive sale" rules that trigger gain recognition, for tax purposes. (If your options are structured in such a way as to eliminate virtually all of your risk, you have made a sale for tax purposes.)

Once you have the downside protected (limiting your risk of losses), you can then borrow against the resulting position. Your interest payments will be deductible against your net investment income.

MARGIN LOAN RISK

Margin loans pose risks. If the value of the securities used as collateral decreases, you will then face a margin call. You'll have to come up with additional cash or securities to back the loan, or some collateral will be sold.

A forced sale of appreciated collateral, in turn, will trigger a capital gains tax.

Strategy: Keep your borrowing to only 20% to 30% of the value of the collateral to reduce your exposure to margin calls. At most firms, a drop of 28% will trigger a margin call. You'll still be able to enjoy tax and investment benefits.

Real Estate Values vs. Homeowner's Insurance

Douglas Liptak, CPA, CFP, head of insurance operations at SignatureFD, a wealth management firm in Atlanta.

Real estate values and homeowner's insurance values do not necessarily correlate. The decrease in the value of your home (and many others) is probably due to the housing crisis, to growing supply and weak demand for houses.

Homeowner's insurance premiums, on the other hand, are based on the concept of "insurance to value." That means insurance companies set homeowner's premiums according to the estimated cost of rebuilding a home from scratch if there is a total loss.

Thus, premiums take into account not only the cost of building materials, but also debris removal and labor.

In recent years, raw material costs have increased exponentially. The higher costs have been attributed to increased demand resulting from catastrophes (such as hurricanes) as well as from the continued growth of developing countries.

Fuel, which is used to transport building materials, is also considered in setting insurance premiums. Even though prices have come down lately, they're still very high.

Therefore, even though the resale value of your home may be decreasing, your insurance premium is increasing to keep up with the higher costs of rebuilding or repairing a home.

Mortgage-backed Securities

Nancy Dunnan is a New York City–based financial and travel adviser and author or coauthor of 25 books, including *How to Invest $50–$5,000*. HarperCollins.

Mortgage-backed securities are also called pass-through securities because mortgage payments (interest and principal) made by borrowers are "passed through" to investors. They are essentially packages of loans, assembled and sold to investors.

How they work: When home buyers take out mortgages from banks or lending companies, these "primary" lenders can then sell those mortgages to governmental, quasi-governmental or private entities. These mortgages are then bundled into securities for sale to hedge funds, mutual funds, insurance companies, pension funds and the public.

Note: The actual mortgages are not sold. Instead, bond-like securities are issued. These are debt obligations with claims tied to the interest and principal paid by the mortgage borrowers.

The most commonly known entities that bundle mortgages into securities and then sell them are the Federal National Mortgage Association (Fannie Mae) and the Federal Home Loan Mortgage Corporation (Freddie Mac). Also, there are others, including brokerage firms, that participate in this process—purchasing mortgages from primary lenders and using monthly payments to pay investors who buy shares.

The current problem stems from securities filled with subprime mortgages—home loans

made to consumers with poor credit histories and who, when faced with trouble, such as rising interest rates or job loss, are likely to default on loan payments.

More information: US Securities and Exchange Commission (888-732-6585, *www.sec.gov/answers/mortgagesecurities.htm*)…Fannie Mae (800-732-6643, *www.fanniemae.com*)…Freddie Mac (703-903-2000, *www.freddiemac.com*).

Top Home-Buying Mistakes

Steve McLinden, real estate adviser, Bankrate.com, North Palm Beach, Florida, a provider of interest rate information and personal finance news, articles and commentary.

If you are over age 50, buying a home, and planning to live in it a long time, don't make these common mistakes…

●**Failing to check community offerings.** Don't move to a community just for its looks, low local taxes or cost of living. See if the community offers entertainment, adult education, sports and recreation opportunities, a senior-friendly community center and high-quality health facilities.

Idea: Take vacations in the community to learn what it is like before moving there.

●**Buying a home with too many stairs.** Seek a level, single-floor layout in the home you buy.

Also: Look for nonslip floors and senior-friendly bathrooms. It will be more expensive to remodel a house to add these things later.

●**Overlooking future transportation needs.** Will you be able to get around via public transportation if and when you can't drive or choose not to?

●**Being too far away from family.** In later years, personal contact with siblings, children and grandchildren may be very important to you. Don't move too far away from them.

Defer Taxes on Real Estate Sales

Eva Rosenberg, MBA, EA, enrolled agent and founder of the award-winning Web site *www.TaxMama.com*, Box 280549, Northridge, California 91328. Her on-line columns frequently cover real estate tax law, including tenants-in-common exchanges. She is author of *Small Business Taxes Made Easy*. McGraw-Hill.

The long-running real estate boom has enticed many investors to buy rental properties. Most invest in relatively small properties—rental houses, modest apartment buildings, etc. By the time they factor in the cost of hiring a property manager or devoting their own time to operational details, many decide it's more lucrative and convenient to sell these properties and reinvest the proceeds in income-producing securities.

Trap: Doing so triggers capital gains tax.

With older properties in which the mortgage has been refinanced several times, the tax may be higher than the cash proceeds. (The depreciated basis will be low, increasing the taxable gain, while repayment of a large mortgage will cut down on cash to the seller.)

IN THE DEPTHS OF DEBT

The above problem may be most severe for investors who have refinanced highly appreciated property.

Example: Joe Jones bought a professional office building in his hometown many years ago for $100,000. The building is now appraised at around $1 million.

Over the years, Joe has refinanced the building a few times as it went up in value. The mortgage has increased to $800,000.

Now Joe wants to sell the building so he won't have to deal with management responsibilities any longer.

Assuming that Joe has fully depreciated the building and nets $950,000 from the sale after expenses, he would have an $850,000 long-term gain. This gain would be taxed at the maximum long-term capital gains rate of 15%. The $100,000 worth of depreciation recapture would be taxed at 25%. *Total tax:* $152,500.

(Many states and even some cities would tax this income, too, which would add to Joe's obligation.)

If Joe pocketed $950,000 from the sale and owed at least $152,500 in tax, his after-tax profit would be less than $800,000.

Even if he hadn't refinanced the investment property this heavily, a sale still would likely generate a sizable tax bill.

Joe's solution: Use a like-kind exchange with ownership shared by other investors.

To qualify for an IRS safe harbor in this type of transaction, replacement property must be identified within 45 days of selling the old property. The new property must be acquired within 180 days of the sale.

Since swapping one small property for another probably won't reduce Joe's management commitments substantially, he structured the exchange so that ownership is by *tenants-in-common* (TIC).

Instead of exchanging his property for another comparably valued one, he swapped for an interest in a larger property—a piece of a major office building or a regional mall, for example.

IRS guidelines allow up to 35 investors to hold TIC interests in such properties.

As owner of a TIC interest, Joe shares in the property's operating profits, pro rata. As one of 20 equal owners, for example, he would get 5% of any cash distributed to the owners.

At the same time, his fortunes aren't locked in to those of the co-owners. If Joe decides to sell (and pay the deferred tax bill of $152,500, plus tax on any current profits), he is allowed to dispose of his interest, even if his co-owners prefer to hold on to the building. If Joe wants to sell his interest, it's up to him to find a buyer. The sponsor of the deal may be able to help him find a buyer.

How such an investment would save Joe money: Joe could sell his apartment building, receive $950,000, and pay off his $800,000 mortgage. The $150,000 net proceeds would be held by an unrelated third party, such as a real estate attorney or a trustee known as an accommodator. Recapture tax as well as capital gains tax would be deferred.

Then Joe could seek to invest his $150,000 in a TIC interest, which also has a mortgage, so

85

the total purchase price of the property (among all investors) is at least $950,001.

(This is a hypothetical example. Some TIC programs have minimums of $250,000 or more.)

The same 45- and 180-day time constraints apply to a TIC exchange, as described earlier.

HOW TO FIND TIC DEALS

TIC deals around the country are constantly being offered for sale.

Why is it easier to evaluate a TIC deal within 45 days than to locate your own replacement property? *Two reasons...*

●**Organized TIC deals already have been selected and analyzed by the sponsors.** Prospective investors can read the reports—and scrutinize the backgrounds of the people putting together the offering—rather than viewing properties themselves.

●**You may designate several potential TIC deals before the 45 days end.** You will have time to evaluate them more carefully and choose the right one before your 180 days run out.

If the time limits are met, and you receive neither cash nor debt relief from the exchange, it's likely that no taxes will be due.

Note: You may need to add your own funds to cover the selling costs in order to avoid paying taxes on what would otherwise be considered "boot."

Boot is any cash or debt relief you receive, or when the buyer's funds are used to pay your sales costs. The IRS regards that as if you had received the money and used it to pay the commissions and fees yourself.

Caution: The tax advantages of TIC exchanges are not assured. Like-kind exchanges of real estate properties are tax deferred under Section 1031 of the Tax Code. However, no ruling states that properties can be exchanged for TIC interests.

Positive signs: The IRS has not come out with a ruling *prohibiting* TIC exchanges. Considering that an estimated $3 billion worth of TIC exchanges were done last year, it's likely that the IRS would have announced any opposition by now.

In addition, the IRS has issued Revenue Procedure 2002-22, outlining the conditions that a TIC exchange must meet in order to be submitted to the IRS for a private ruling. (Doing so is not practical because of the time constraints, but Revenue Procedure 2002-22 indicates that the IRS will approve a TIC exchange if it's done according to regular like-kind exchange rules.)

Strategy: Make sure that you exchange property for property. A major risk in organized deals is that the IRS will say that you've exchanged property for a security, which would not be a like-kind exchange. If you are offered a TIC interest by people who have securities licenses rather than real estate licenses, seek legal advice on whether a tax-deferred exchange will be approved.

To locate TIC sponsors and accommodators: Visit the Web sites of the Tenant-in-Common Association (*www.ticassoc.org*), a group of TIC attorneys, lenders, sponsors, and intermediaries...or of Omni Brokerage, Inc. (*www.omni1031corp.com*) or CreaapHarbor LLC (*www.capharbor.com*), investment firms active in bringing together buyers and sellers via TIC exchanges.

Home-Selling Security

Avoid closing delays by getting a "ready to close title guarantee." This title protection service from National Homestead (*www. nationalhomestead.com*) uncovers mortgage errors, tax liens, fraudulently recorded documents and other kinds of problems. It can take up to 60 days to clear a problem. If a problem is missed, National Homestead indemnifies the customer, ensuring that the sale will go through. Sellers can avoid legal fees, lost sales and delays with this service.

Cost: $295, paid by the seller.

Note: Title insurance covers only title defects that occur before you buy the home.

David Schechner, real estate attorney and principal, Schechner & Targan, West Orange, New Jersey.

When Relocating... Sell First, Buy Later

Rent a furnished apartment, and put your belongings in storage. This gives you time to hold out for a better price on the old house and shop for a new one.

● **Research the new area.** Talk to local residents, and check out neighborhoods. Visit *www.schooltree.org* for details about public schools nationwide.

● **Use a national bank,** so you don't have to close old accounts and open new ones.

● **Get change-of-address forms** in on time so you can stay up-to-date on bills.

● **Sign up for a cell-phone plan** with unlimited in-network calling so that family members who must stay behind to take care of unfinished business can be in contact without incurring high phone bills.

Money, Time-Life Bldg., Rockefeller Center, New York City 10020.

Real Estate Buying and Selling Basics

Follow the steps below in order to save time and money.

● **Get preapproved for a mortgage.** Prequalification letters are meaningless.

● **Negotiate the mortgage origination fee** with your lender—and the commission with your real estate agent.

● **Use the Internet** to look for homes—magazines and other sources go out-of-date quickly.

● **If a buyer wants to back out** after a contract is signed, let him. It is too costly for the seller to sue to force a closing.

● **Comparable-property listings** are only a starting point for valuing a home. Upgrades and location also must be factored in.

Rhonda Duffy, CEO and broker, Duffy Realty, Atlanta. www.duffyrealtyofatlanta.com.

New Law Makes Reverse Mortgages More Attractive

Tyler Kraemer, Esq., a Colorado Springs–based attorney specializing in real estate, finance and estate planning. He is coauthor of The Complete Guide to Reverse Mortgages. Adams Media.

The ice-cold real estate market makes this a poor time to sell a house, and suddenly cautious lenders are making home-equity loans more difficult to obtain. Reverse mortgages are a third way for older home owners in need of cash to access the equity tied up in their homes. (Reverse mortgages typically are available to home owners age 62 and older.)

When a home owner takes out a reverse mortgage, he/she essentially converts a portion of his home equity into cash. The home owner can receive cash in a lump sum, monthly payments, a line of credit or some combination. When the home is sold, the loan must be repaid. Any remaining equity goes to the borrower or his heirs.

During the home owner's lifetime, no payments are due unless he moves out. Plus, no income verification is necessary to qualify for a reverse mortgage.

The catch: The biggest complaint with reverse mortgages has always been that they are expensive. Historically, up-front fees could run 5% to 6% of the home's value, and all major reverse mortgage programs have adjustable interest rates, so rates can go higher.

What's new: The federal *Housing and Economic Recovery Act of 2008*, signed into law in July, includes provisions that make Home Equity Conversion Mortgages (HECMs), by far the most common type of reverse mortgage, a bit more attractive...

● **Loan origination fees on HECM reverse mortgages are now capped at 2% of the first $200,000 of the home's value,** and 1% of the remainder, with an overall cap of $6,000. This cap could save borrowers perhaps $1,000 to $2,000 compared with previous fee schedules.

●**The potential size of HECM reverse mortgages is increased.** In the past, home owners could borrow no more than $363,790, and often the amounts were lower still, depending on home values in the region. The new law creates a national limit of $417,000, but this can rise to as much as $625,000 in certain high-value regions.

●**Reverse mortgage lenders are barred from engaging in certain questionable sales practices.**

Example: Reverse mortgage lenders are prohibited from requiring the purchase of annuities and certain other financial products in connection with reverse mortgages—a strategy that rarely works in the home owner's favor.

Caution: Even with the new laws, reverse mortgages are a pricey way to obtain money. A home owner should consider all other options before getting a reverse mortgage.

Timing: The new rules on reverse mortgages became effective on enactment, but the new loan limits will not go into effect until December 31, 2008, when prior legislation expires.

5

Around-the-House Money Savers

How to "Clean Up" from Cleaning Up Your House

It pays—quite literally—to look through your house periodically and either sell or give away possessions that you no longer need or want.

Some of these items may be far more valuable than you might expect them to be. Postcards, fountain pens, photographs and everyday dishes are just some of the often-overlooked objects for which the collectors seem to have an endless fascination.

Before selling any of your possessions: Consider whether it is an heirloom that might best be kept in the family. If so, choose a family member who will cherish it and pass it on when the time comes.

When you give a valued possession to a relative, make sure that he/she understands its importance to your family history as well as its monetary value.

APPRAISALS COME FIRST

If you decide to sell an item, get an appraisal to establish the item's age, authenticity and monetary value. The first and most important rule of selling your possessions is never to sell anything before you know what it is worth.

Appraising 20 items will take a professional appraiser about two hours. The charge ($100 to $350 per hour) can almost always be recouped by being able to sell items for more than you might otherwise have thought they were worth.

To locate an appraiser: Ask for referrals from the trust department of your bank, your attorney or your homeowner's insurance agent. Ask the prospective appraisers to let you speak with several of their previous clients, and reject any who won't.

If an appraiser offers to buy any of the items he's pricing, thank him for his time, and then look for another appraiser. Tell the person you

---

Joe L. Rosson, an antiques columnist and cohost, with Helaine Fendelman, of *Treasures in Your Attic* on PBS TV and coauthor of *Price It Yourself*. HarperCollins. Mr. Rosson lives in Knoxville, Tennessee.

choose that you want the items appraised for their "fair market value." That's the amount you may reasonably expect to receive.

It's never a good idea to take your possessions to an antiques shop or mall to obtain an appraisal. Often, proprietors aren't appraisers, and their goal may be to buy your items rather than to give you useful information. Once your possessions have been appraised, consider the options for selling them at maximum profit.

AUCTIONS

If the fair market value of any of your possessions is more than $1,500, the international auction houses, such as Sotheby's (800-813-5968, *www.sothebys.com*) and Christie's (212-492-5485, *www.christies.com*), can provide you with a better chance of selling them for their estimated value—and sometimes much more.

Reason: International auction houses attract a large number of serious buyers who have serious money.

The drawback is that the auction house may believe your item isn't something it can sell, and its fees can be significant. You might also have to wait six months before your item actually comes up for sale.

Best strategy: Send the auction house a picture and description of an item, say that you're *considering consigning it for sale* and ask for an estimate of what it would bring. Estimates are free, and if they are in error, it's usually on the low side.

Caution: Don't ask an international auction house for an appraisal unless you have large quantities of fine things and are willing to pay big bucks.

Alternatives…

●**Local auction houses.** They can be an efficient route for selling a large number of objects that are not valuable enough for international auction houses.

Most local auction houses will pick up your goods (sometimes for a charge that may be a small percentage of sales), sell them and give you 65% to 75% of the proceeds.

Be aware that local auctioneers are seldom experts in art or antiques and need all the information you can provide. In addition, hometown auctions are not effective for selling

items worth less than $25 because these are often lumped together in box lots.

Visit your local auction houses to find out which has the largest audience and most spirited bidding. Choose the one that is most businesslike and seems to be getting the best prices.

●**Internet sales.** If you are Internet-savvy, eBay and other on-line auction services can be an easy way to sell possessions because they reach millions of potential buyers. Fees average about 6% of the sales price, much lower than at traditional auction houses.

On the Internet, however, you will compete against a large number of sellers with similar objects. As a result, your items may be lost in the vast number of items being offered for sale and may not get a satisfactory bid.

OUTDOOR MARKETS

You can usually rent space at a flea market or an outdoor antiques show for less than $100 a day. It can be a way of selling your possessions and also having fun.

Keep in mind that flea market shoppers are bargain hunters. Outdoor antiques shows, on the other hand, will draw serious, knowledgeable collectors, often with deep pockets.

YARD SALES

If you are selling what some people might call junk, yard sales can be a quick way of disposing of it at a small profit.

The disadvantages are that no object is likely to bring more than $50 (and usually less) and that you could miss more profitable opportunities at local auction houses.

When having a yard sale, post a sign saying, "All merchandise sold as is. All sales final."

Also check local rules, which often restrict or even prohibit outdoor neighborhood sales.

CHARITIES

If you have any possessions that are difficult to sell, giving them to charity is a great way to help an organization and reduce your taxes at the same time.

Caution: To satisfy the IRS, keep a copy of the appraisal and a picture of any item given to charity. And, of course, consult your tax adviser.

Make Life Easier—Organize Your Home

Julie Morgenstern, founder of Julie Morgenstern Enterprises, whose clients include the New York City mayor's office, Time Warner and the Miami Heat basketball team, *www.juliemorgenstern.com.* She is author of *Organizing from the Inside Out.* Henry Holt.

The next time you're about to put off the task of tossing out old possessions, consider the advantages of…

●**More space to enjoy your home.** An uncluttered house or apartment is easier to keep clean and easier to entertain in and just more pleasant to be in.

●**Better organization.** Hunting for objects takes time and causes anxiety, especially when the object is important, such as a document or treasured gift. Organizing and finding items are easier when you have fewer of them.

●**Bringing joy to friends and relatives and even strangers in need.** More people than you realize may want the possessions you no longer need.

●**Lower taxes.** By giving unwanted objects to a charity, you may be eligible for an income tax deduction.

●**Profits.** When you sort through your possessions, you occasionally find items that are surprisingly valuable.

OVERCOMING HURDLES

Despite the big benefits of throwing out your unneeded possessions, many of us shrink from the task.

The biggest obstacle is the guilt that many people feel when they discard objects that came from a beloved relative. Guilt can also be strong in individuals who inherited a Depression-era mentality of saving every item that might possibly be of use in the future.

Guilt can nearly always be overcome by giving unneeded items to other family members who will treasure them or to people who can genuinely use them. An old picture frame, for example, may be useless to you but treasured by a relative who knew that it came from a great-grandparent.

Don't think just of your relatives but also of friends and children of friends. A neighbor's child, for instance, could be in college, where he/she might be able to use the old couch that's been taking up space in your basement.

Fear is the other big hurdle that often prevents people from throwing out unneeded possessions. Fear typically affects those who feel more secure when they're surrounded by a trove of familiar objects.

Overcome fear by concentrating on what the effort will allow you to do—all the benefits mentioned above.

Many families hesitate to throw away objects for fear that they might be valuable. If that's the case in your home, settle the issue by getting them appraised. Once you find out what the actual value is, you can make an informed decision about keeping the item or selling it.

Professional appraisers usually charge $100 to $350 per hour and can evaluate about 10 items in an hour. To locate an appraiser, check your bank, attorney or insurance agent.

GETTING THE JOB DONE

●**Step 1.** Go through your house room by room. Examine each possession.

Ask yourself: *Do I use this object? Do I love it?* If you don't answer *yes* to either question, it's time to discard the item.

●**Step 2.** Put a tag on each item you want to discard. Use tags of different colors to indicate the specific way you intend to dispose of the object in question.

Example: A red tag for items to be thrown away, green for charities, blue for gifts, etc.

●**Step 3.** Begin disposing of items. Cart them to the trash, contact people you want to give them to or ask charities to take the items away.

If the job looks too daunting—or if you get bogged down once you start—ask for help from a friend or relative, or hire someone to assist. Many high school students, for example, would be eager for the $5 an hour you might pay them.

Caution: Before disposing of any object, examine it thoroughly. You may occasionally find money, jewelry or other valuables that have long been forgotten in pockets of clothing, drawers of furniture and even pages of books.

For charitable donations, IRS rules are tricky, so give to a well-known organization or consult with your accountant or tax preparer to make sure a charity is qualified, as well as for rules about receipts and other documentation.

OFF-SITE STORAGE

For most people, renting a long-term storage unit is rarely worth the $100 a month that even a small space is likely to cost. But there are exceptions.

Example: Individuals with small apartments who inherit a houseful of items for which they have no room.

People in doubt about throwing away a large number of possessions are another exception. For them, it can make sense to put the objects in a storage facility for a limited time, such as three months.

If they don't need any of the items during that time, it will then be much easier to get rid of them.

KEEP CLUTTER AWAY

To prevent yourself from accumulating unwanted possessions in the future…

●**As mentioned earlier,** periodically look at items in your house and then ask yourself the two basic questions, *Do I use this object? Do I love it?* Unless you answer *yes* to either one, dispose of the object immediately.

●**Each time you make a purchase,** look for an item to throw away. All too often, when we buy a new jacket, blouse or pair of shoes, we miss the opportunity to dispose of an old one we haven't worn for years.

There's an even greater opportunity to get rid of household furnishings, such as table lamps, whenever we buy a new one.

More from Julie Morgenstern…

Where to Send Your Stuff

Lighten the task of getting rid of clutter by contacting…

●**A charity that picks up donated goods.** Check out Goodwill Industries (800-741-0186,

www.goodwill.org) or check the Salvation Army (*www.salvationarmyusa.org*, look in your local directory for a telephone number).

●**An organization that finds nonprofit organizations in your area** that are looking for the specific goods you want to donate. In most instances, the nonprofit will then collect the items.

Two of the best known: Excess Access (415-242-6041, *www.excessaccess.com*) and Inkindex (*www.inkindex.com*).

●**A removal service such as 1-800-GOT-JUNK?** (800-468-5865, *www.1800gotjunk.com*). The company's rates are generally low, but vary from area to area.

Look Here for Household Tips, Hints and Helpers

Useful tips and tidbits on more than 1,200 subjects are available free at *www.tipking.com*. The site suggests olive oil to get paint off hands, vinegar to brighten laundry and much more. Search by topic—new ideas are posted daily. You can even add your own useful information and advice.

Katie Weeks, freelance writer, *Home*, 1633 Broadway, New York City 10019.

Nine Trouble Spots to Look for Before Buying An Older Home

Weldon Sikes, founder, American Association of Home Inspectors Inc., Lubbock, Texas, *www.aahionline.com*.

Older homes often are better built than new homes, but they also are likely to have particular problems due to their advanced age.

Common problems in older homes, according to a survey by the American Association of Home Inspectors…

●**Inadequate surface drainage,** such as deficient grading, that can lead water to penetrate basements.

●**Inadequate wiring for today's needs** or that has been unsafely installed over the years —a real safety hazard.

●**Roof damage** caused by old or damaged shingles or inadequate drainage.

●**Heating systems with inadequate or malfunctioning controls** or with blocked or unsafe exhaust.

●**Inadequate overall maintenance** leading to crumbling masonry, makeshift wiring, broken fixtures, etc.—older homes need more maintenance than new ones.

●**Damage to structural components,** including the foundation walls, floor joists and door headers.

●**Plumbing problems** due to old or incompatible piping materials, and faulty fixtures and waste lines.

●**Inadequate caulking on windows,** doors and wall surfaces, which allows water and air to penetrate.

●**Poor ventilation** due to the "oversealing" of a home to save energy. Making a home excessively airtight can cause excessive interior moisture, which rots joists, beams and rafters.

Self-defense: When thinking about the purchase of an older home, have it professionally inspected to identify these and other potential costly problems.

Wood Flooring— Why It's Worth Every Penny

Wood floors cost more than carpet but last longer. Plus, they cost much less than stone or tile and are easier on the feet. Wood also softens a room's acoustics and is easy to clean if protected with a polyurethane finish.

Home, 1633 Broadway, New York City 10019.

Surprising Uses For Vinegar

Vinegar can be used in many different situations. *Here is a list of four to get you started…*

●**To eliminate odors in a freshly painted room**—place one to two bowls of vinegar in the middle of a well-ventilated room until the odor is gone.

●**To remove soap and hard-water buildup on chrome fixtures**—place tissues over stained areas and pour full-strength vinegar on them…let sit for five minutes, then remove and rinse.

●**To give homemade bread a flaky crust**—brush vinegar on top before baking.

●**To relieve itching caused by insect bites**—soak a cloth in vinegar and place on the affected area.

Good Housekeeping, 959 Eighth Ave., New York City 10019.

Make Your Own All-Purpose Cleaners— Naturally

All-purpose surface cleaner—mix one quart of hot water…one teaspoon of vegetable oil-based soap or oil-based detergent, such as Seventh Generation…one teaspoon of borax… and two tablespoons of white vinegar. Scouring paste—mix baking soda with enough liquid soap to form a paste. Window cleaner—mix one-quarter cup of white vinegar with one quart of warm water.

Prevention, 33 E. Minor St., Emmaus, Pennsylvania 18098.

If It's Broke—Fix It... Small Appliance Money Savers

Try fixing small appliances before throwing them out. The Gourmet Depot (800-424-6783, *www.thegourmetdepotco.com*) sells replacement parts for many kitchen appliances and personal-care tools, such as electric shavers.

Examples: Sunbeam coffeemaker glass carafe, $13.95...jar base, Hamilton Beach blender, $3.95.

23 Ways to Keep Heating Bills from Crushing You

Asa Aarons, consumer advocate and founder of Just AskAsa.com, a consumer-focused Web site. His reports are also featured on television, including on NBC's *Today* show. Aarons has won national recognition for reports on consumer strategies to save money on fuel, utilities and taxes.

Winter is sure to be hard on your pocketbook. *Here are three reasons why that is and many ways to help offset the cost...*

●**Heating oil.** According to the National Energy Assistance Directors' Association, the national average cost to heat a home with oil this winter will be $2,388. That's up about 23% from last winter.

●**Natural gas.** Even though prices have dropped in recent weeks, consumers can expect to pay more this winter.

Example: Utility companies in New Jersey have asked state regulators to approve a 20% hike in rates to cover costs that have nearly doubled since January.

●**Electricity.** Costs are soaring for electricity, too.

Example: Con Edison in New York received approval for a 22% hike in electric rates to cover its higher production costs.

To reduce your heating costs, take immediate action...

NO-COST WAYS

1. Wear a sweater during the day and use an extra blanket at night. Then you can set the thermostat at 68°F during the day (or lower, depending on your constitution) and 60°F at night—a proven way to save hundreds of dollars.

2. Don't set the thermostat higher than the desired temperature to speed up heating. The house will *not* warm up any faster—instead, you will overshoot your desired temperature, and you may well forget to turn the thermostat back down.

KEEP HEAT INSIDE

3. Close external leaks. Mail chutes and the spot around the clothes dryer vent are key culprits for heat loss. Ducts running through attics, crawl spaces, garages and basements are another common source of leaks.

What to do: Seal duct joints with mastic paste (reinforced duct sealant), metal-backed tape or an aerosol sealant. Regular duct tape should not be used because it cannot withstand temperature extremes. Ductwork is usually hard to get at, so sealing is best left to a professional.

4. Inspect your house for hidden openings. After dark, with all of the inside lights off, have a friend stand outside and shine a high-powered flashlight around the exterior while you remain inside. Any light coming through walls that you see inside translates to heat leaks that should be sealed.

5. Use incense to help you test for drafts. First, turn off exhaust fans and make sure that windows are closed. Then move about the house holding the incense. If the smoke drifts sideways, it could indicate a leak.

6. Lock windows and sliding doors. This gives the panels their tightest possible seal.

7. Add sealant to the glazing putty in your windows if it is dry and cracked. Also seal any visible cracks around the windows between the sash (the movable part) and the frame with weather stripping or cloth.

8. Close storm windows properly. If you don't have storm windows, put plastic film made for insulating windows on the inside. This acts as an interior storm window.

Cost: About $10 for two three-foot-by-five-foot sheets, available at hardware or building-supply stores.

9. Stop heat loss from under exterior doorways. Place a draft blocker across the bottom of the doorway. For a more permanent solution, attach weather stripping to the bottom of the door.

10. Check the location of your thermostat. A drafty window or an exterior door near your thermostat can turn your heating system on unnecessarily.

Best: Put your thermostat on an inside wall away from a window or door.

11. Close vents/registers/baseboard heating/radiators in unused rooms. But make sure to keep the rooms warm enough to prevent water pipes that might run through adjacent walls from freezing.

12. Keep your damper closed when not using the fireplace. An open damper allows about 8% of your heat to escape up the chimney.

13. Cover through-the-wall and window air conditioners for the winter. Close the vents and put an insulated cover, available at hardware or building-supply stores for about $25, on the air conditioners to complete the seal.

14. Buy a programmable thermostat. Set your heat to ramp down at night and up in the morning...down again before you leave the house...and up a half hour before you come home, so when you arrive, the chill will be out of the house.

15. Buy heating oil in the late summer or early fall. The price of home heating oil is usually lowest in the off season.

USE NATURE

16. Heat with wood. Buy a wood-burning stove and seasoned firewood by the cord, or buy a pellet stove and use wood pellets. Wood pellets are more economical than firewood. They are also less trouble, since a hopper lets the fuel down into the stove as needed—rather than continually feeding the stove yourself.

17. Consider solar. A federal tax credit for installing solar water heaters and solar panels is in effect through 2016. The tax credit is 30% of the cost of the system, not including the cost of installation.

18. Use the warmth delivered by sunlight. Remove unnecessary tree branches and other barriers to give your home more exposure to the sun. Open shades, blinds and drapes to let sunlight—and solar warmth—in.

OTHER MONEY SAVERS

19. Consider portable electric heaters. New federal regulations require all portable heaters manufactured after July 2008 to include enhanced energy saving features. So, it may be less expensive to use a small space heater than cranking up the furnace if you only want to heat one room or supplement inadequate heating in a specific area. Be sure to keep all doors to the room closed for maximum efficiency.

20. Add a furnace humidifier. This increases your perception of warmth—68°F with moisture can feel warmer than 72°F without it. A humidifier can be added to any type of heating system.

21. Change or clean furnace filters every few months, no matter what kind of heating system you have. Running your furnace at peak efficiency will save you money.

GET PROFESSIONAL HELP

22. Get a free "energy audit" from your utility company, which evaluates the efficiency of your home's heating and cooling systems in addition to assessing how you can save energy. Get an energy audit by a home energy rater if your utility company doesn't perform this service. A home energy rating will also give you an idea of the energy efficiency of your home and help you make informed choices about which improvements are likely to have the most effect.

You can find a home energy rater at Residential Energy Services Network (*www.natresnet. org*). You could also use a Building Performance Institute Inc. (*www.bpi.org*) accredited contractor to do an energy audit. Cost for these services is about $250 to $1,000 (depending on your location), but potential savings may make the expense worthwhile.

23. Have your heating system serviced annually. This includes a thorough cleaning of the blower (and nozzle if it uses oil), and making any necessary adjustments. The furnace's combustion efficiency should be tested to calculate how completely the fuel is burned and how much of the heat is traSnsferred into your home.

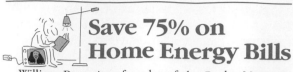

Save 75% on Home Energy Bills

William Browning, founder of the Rocky Mountain Institute's Green Development Services, a consulting group that helps to engineer energy efficiency. The White House and the Sydney 2000 Olympic Village have been among its clients. He has coauthored two books, including *A Primer on Sustainable Building*. Rocky Mountain Institute.

Americans could be saving a full three-quarters of the $150 billion they spend on energy each year.

Best ways to save money without spending a fortune...

●**Upgrade to modern super windows.** Super windows, filled with argon or krypton gas and covered with a special film, are up to 12 times more efficient than regular windows. Yet they still look like normal glass.

These windows, which are widely available, buffer noise and prevent ultraviolet light from fading carpets, upholstery, drapes and artwork. They also cut down on drafts caused by ordinary windows.

Example: A window rated R-7 or better—meaning that the window has seven times the insulating value of a single pane of glass—will gain more heat in the winter than it loses, even when it faces north in Buffalo.

Specialists can suggest windows with properties that are appropriate for your climate. Look in your *Yellow Pages* under "Windows."

Cost: 15% to 50% more than the standard double-pane windows. However, they can pay for themselves in less than a decade, and some utility companies offer rebates.

Average price for a standard-sized super window: $150.

●**Install heat barriers.** In hotter climates, a radiant barrier placed above the attic insulation can decrease cooling costs by up to 15%. This plastic film has an aluminum coating on one side that reflects heat from the sun and can save up to $30 a year.

Cost: 10 cents to 45 cents per square foot installed. A heat barrier pays for itself in as little as 10 years in average Sun Belt homes, but it is rarely cost-effective in the north.

●**Repair the heating/cooling systems.** Air escaping from ducts can reduce heating, ventilation and air-conditioning (HVAC) efficiency by up to 20%. Sealing the seams can save $260 of a typical household's annual $1,300 energy bill.

Hire an HVAC contractor to seal your ducts for $500 to $900. Or do it yourself if the ducts are accessible in the attic or crawl space. Check your ducts every 10 years. Use mastic, a high-strength adhesive that is applied with a trowel or brush.

Cost: $10 to $15 per gallon. A typical house might require five gallons. Mastic is available at home-improvement stores and heating-supply wholesalers.

Beware: Duct tape, despite its name, does not effectively seal ducts. Over time, it dries out and loses its seal.

Helpful: Replacing your HVAC system's filter every six months can increase efficiency—saving up to $20 a year.

●**Repair caulking and weather stripping.** Every year, about $13 billion worth of energy escapes through holes and cracks in heated and air-conditioned US homes. A one-eighth-inch gap under a door is the equivalent of a two-inch-square hole in a wall.

Plugging the air leaks around windows and doors reduces heating/cooling bills by as much as 30%—or up to $400 a year on the average home. The job should take less than 10 minutes per door or window. Check for new leaks every five years.

Cost: Less than $5 per window and $10 per door in materials.

●**Block conduits.** As part of your weatherization project, install rubber gaskets behind electrical outlets to prevent hot and cold air from escaping.

Cost: Less than $1 per gasket, available in home-improvement and hardware stores.

●**Fill insulation gaps.** As homes age, insulation settles and sags, creating gaps behind walls and in attics. You can locate these gaps with infrared cameras, often loaned out by utility companies. Some utilities also will perform a free energy audit for you.

Cans of expanding foam insulation are available for about $5 each and pay for themselves in just a few months. If you can't reach the problem area easily, call a professional. Sometimes he/she has to inject insulating foam inside your walls.

●**Insulate your water heater.** This saves about $40 a year if you have an electric water heater…$15 a year for a gas one.

Cost: About $20 for a tank wrap. Call your energy provider for details.

BUILDING IN ENERGY EFFICIENCY

More energy-saving opportunities are cost effective when you build or buy a house…

●**Select a smart design.** The shape and orientation of your house can cut heating/cooling costs by 30%.

In the cold regions, the longest sides of the home should run east-west to increase exposure to the sun in the south. Buildings in hot climates should be long and run perpendicular to the prevailing winds to increase ventilation.

●**Build with generous insulation.** I suggest twice the insulation factor that is required by code. One way to do this is by using structural insulated panels (SIPs). The panels consist of a layer of insulation that's sandwiched between two layers of strand board. They can save 40% to 60% in heating/cooling costs.

Homes built with SIP walls are sturdier than most timber-frame houses. The energy savings can pay for the additional 10% in construction costs within 10 years—less in extreme climates. In addition, the initial cost can be offset because you will need a much smaller furnace.

●**Don't be impressed by the phrase "built to code."** Code is only the minimum standard allowed by law. If a builder says a home's insulation "meets code," he/she is saying that if it was any worse, it would be illegal.

Instead, ask how the house compares with federal Energy Star guidelines or if there is a state energy rating system. Click on "Home Energy Analysis" under "Home Improvement" at *www.energystar.gov* to compare your house with the Energy Star criteria.

●**Look for Energy Star**–certified homes to save 30% on energy. This government energy program evaluates the energy efficiency of appliances and will certify houses when builders or developers request the service. Such homes use about 30% less energy, a savings of about $400 a year in an average house. They don't cost any more than typical houses, but they use insulation, insulated windows, architectural layout and other techniques to achieve the savings.

Bonus: Reduced mortgage rates and fees are available from some lenders for these homes. For more information, click on the "Find Local Homebuilders" section of Energy Star's Web site, *www.energystar.gov.*

●**Consider your commute.** Even the most energy-efficient home won't reduce your total energy bill if it's miles from your work, favorite stores and entertainment. Money saved on electricity and heating will be spent on gasoline.

Example: If a couple adds 25 miles each way to both of their daily commutes, they add approximately $3,600 to their yearly gasoline bill, assuming their vehicles get 25 miles per gallon and gasoline costs $3.50 per gallon. That is more than the average family spends on home energy in a year.

Best: Live near your job and in a town that is conducive to walking.

Important: There are federal tax credits for making certain energy-saving improvements such as insulating your home for 2009.

10 Ways to Keep Your Home Dry

Bill Keith, who was a remodeling contractor for 25 years in St. John, Indiana. He now is host of *The Home Tips Show* on Chicago-area PBS-TV and radio stations.

Moisture can be a home owner's greatest enemy. When problems aren't addressed quickly, the cost of repairs can reach well into the thousands. The resulting mold and mildew can cause health problems, too. *Common trouble spots in the home…*

ATTICS

There are three major causes of attic moisture…

●**Leaky roof.** Leaks often occur where the roof meets chimneys, vents, skylights and other openings. Roofs also may leak when leaves and branches collect on top of or in gutters. This debris forms dams that prevent rainwater from flowing freely. When the water pools and backs up under the shingles, it seeps through the roof and into the attic.

●**Ice dams** can cause wet attics in winter and spring. These dams form when heat escaping from the interior of the house melts ice and snow on the roof. The resulting cold water rolls down the inclined roof until it reaches the eaves, where it refreezes. This ice can back up under the shingles or cause water to pool and get under the shingles. Either way, water can work its way through the roof and into the attic.

Solution: Increase the thickness of your home's attic insulation. The proper amount of insulation for most regions is between R-38 and R-49, which translates to 12 to 20 inches of fiberglass.

●**Poor air circulation.** If your attic doesn't vent the air when it's hot out, it can turn into a sweatbox. Poorly installed insulation is the most common culprit. Home owners add insulation to trim energy bills without realizing that they must leave three- or four-inch-wide gaps in the insulation at the eaves to permit air flow.

Solution: Cut two- to three-foot lengths of drainspout or use Styrofoam baffles, available in home-improvement stores, to keep air channels open.

It is best to insert the baffles before installing insulation, but if necessary, you can force them into place between or alongside existing pieces of insulation. Free airflow must be possible through at least every second rafter pocket (that is, through at least half of the eaves).

Adding or adjusting insulation isn't technically difficult, but it's easier and safer to have a handyman install it for you. For more information, consult "Ceilings and Attics Fact Sheet," from the US Department of Energy (available at *www.eere.energy.gov.* In the search box, insert "celings and attics"...the first result is the one that you want.

Arrange to have a checkup by a roofing professional every two or three years so that leaks don't develop in the first place. These checkups cost $75 to $150, or more if you have a large, multipitched or difficult-to-reach roof.

Caution: Falls from ladders result in many injuries. To be safe, hire a roofing professional for repairs and a gutter-cleaning service for maintenance.

INSIDE THE HOME

If your home's interior humidity is above 65%, mold and/or mildew problems are likely to develop. You can monitor moisture with a humidistat, available from a home-improvement store for less than $50. *Common causes of humidity problems...*

●**Showering or cooking in poorly ventilated areas.** Bathroom fans should be on while you are showering and for at least five minutes after, or you can open windows to provide necessary ventilation. Stove ventilating fans should run while cooking and for at least five minutes after. Don't use them longer—you'll be throwing away expensively heated (or cooled) air.

If humidity problems persist in a bathroom, you might need a more powerful exhaust vent, for $30 and up plus the cost of installation.

If the persistent humidity problem isn't tied to a specific bathroom, a dehumidifier placed in the utility room (where your furnace and water heater are kept) might be the solution.

Cost: About $200 for a high-quality Energy Star model. Set it to come on whenever humidity climbs above 50%.

●**Leaky pipes** are the second major source of in-home moisture problems. They are most common in bathrooms, kitchens and laundry rooms—but water pipes can be located behind any wall.

A leaky pipe can be tricky to find because the problem is more likely to be slow seepage than a large, obvious drip. If the leak is in an out-of-the-way spot, the first sign might be a mildewy smell that won't go away no matter how well you clean. You also might see swelling or a chalky discoloration around the base of bathroom or kitchen cabinets that sit directly on the subfloor. Tile floors often hide the worst water damage, but wood cabinetry that is in direct contact with a wood subfloor can wick the moisture upward until the problem is visible.

To find a leaky pipe: Head down to your basement, and shine a flashlight up at the flooring beneath the trouble area to see if there's discoloration. Feel all the exposed water pipes in the vicinity of the musty odor to see if any are moist. If you suspect the leak is hidden behind a wall, use a moisture meter, which registers the moisture content of the wood or drywall next to it. These are available at hardware stores for as little as $80.

Expect to spend several hundred dollars to replace a leaky pipe, plus several hundred more for drywall repair if the plumber has to cut through your wall to reach the problem. Cutting through tile, of course, can cost even more—but leaks must be fixed.

●**Shut-off valves** for toilets and sinks are a common source of leaks. Replacement valves are available at home-improvement stores for about $4 each and are easy to install with a pair of large wrenches—just remember to shut off your home's water first.

●**Toilets.** If your toilet rocks back and forth, gently tighten the bolts that hold it down.

Caution: If you make it too tight, you could crack the ceramic bowl. If the toilet still rocks, the floor underneath might be uneven. Plastic shims, available at home-improvement stores for less than $1 apiece, might solve the problem. Stick a shim or two between the toilet and the floor in front or in back as needed until it no longer rocks. Then trim the shim so that it doesn't extend beyond the edge of the toilet. Seal with mildew-resistant caulking, available for a few dollars a tube at hardware stores. This prevents moisture from getting in and keeps the shim from showing.

If the toilet leaks but doesn't rock, the wax ring, a gasket between the base of the toilet and the floor, might need to be replaced.

Cost: About $5.

BASEMENT

Many sealants claim to provide moisture-proof barriers for basement walls, but they rarely work well.

If a hill or slope near your property is funneling water down into your basement, try one of these strategies…

●**Extend gutter downspouts.** Extend them further from the home to prevent water from seeping inside.

●**Install a French drain.** Dig an 18- to 24-inch-deep trench at least four feet away from the house on the uphill side. Line the trench with plastic draintile. These perforated plastic tubes (sold in 50- to 100-foot-long rolls) are placed in French drains as well as alongside a home's foundation and covered with gravel. Position the draintile to steer water away from your house. Plant flowers on both sides of the trench to improve its appearance. If you would prefer not to do the digging, a professional excavator should be able to do the job for perhaps $200 to $400.

●**Replace the original draintile** around your home's foundation. Persistent leaks might mean that this draintile needs to be dug up and replaced. A professional excavator typically charges $3,000 to $5,000 to do this—the tile itself is cheap, but labor costs are considerable.

You also might have to replace any landscaping that needs to be pulled up in the process. If the exterior of your home is extensively landscaped and your basement is unfinished, it might be more practical to have the new draintile installed below the *interior* perimeter of your basement. An excavator accomplishes this by digging a trench just inside your foundation walls. Costs are comparable to putting the trench outside, only without the landscaping issues.

Helpful: If you're having a new home built, remind the contractor to include draintiles around both the outside and inside perimeter of the home. For an extra $100 to $200, you'll have a great insurance policy against future basement moisture.

●**Use a sump pump.** These devices remove accumulations of water from the lowest point in a drainage system, typically the basement. If your home is built on a hill, your draintile might use gravity to divert water away from the home. Otherwise, the draintile will be angled to bring the water to a sump pump—ideally one with a battery backup in case the power fails in a storm. Sump pumps cost around $80…battery backup systems, around $200. Expect to pay a plumber about $200 to install the pump.

A Lien Can Be Placed Against Your Home

With each payment, insist on an affidavit from the subcontractors and materialman's certificates from suppliers, and require an affidavit at the end of the project stating that the contractor has paid them all in full.

Consumer Reports Money Adviser, 101 Truman Ave., Yonkers, New York 10703.

Ways to Prevent Frozen Pipes During Power Outages

Keep the fireplace lit and the flue open…open cabinets under sinks to allow warm air to circulate around pipes…slightly open all faucets to permit a stream of water…close doors to rooms that don't contain pipes—such as bedrooms—and that won't be used during the emergency. If there is a severe risk that the temperature will remain below 32°F for an extended period, fill 10 five-gallon buckets with water for emergencies.

Tim Carter, former custom remodeler and home builder, Cincinnati, and author of the syndicated column "Ask the Builder." *www.askthebuilder.com.*

Money to Burn— Updating Your Fireplace

Replacing the mantel for a few hundred dollars can renew a fireplace. A total makeover—replacing mantel, hearth and masonry surrounding the firebox—can cost several thousand dollars.

Also consider: A gas insert, which can be started by remote control.

Cost: $400 to $1,800, plus installation.

Bill Keith, who was a remodeling contractor for 25 years in St. John, Indiana. He now is host of *The Home Tips Show* on Chicago-area PBS-TV and radio stations.

Cheaper Ways to Heat Your Home

Don Vandervort is founder of HomeTips.com. A home-improvement expert based in Glendale, California, he has written more than 30 books on home improvement, including Home Magazine's *How Your House Works*. Ballantine. He appeared as segment host on HGTV's *The Fix. www.hometips.com.*

Toni Boyd is assistant director of the Geo-Heat Center, a research organization funded by US Department of Energy grants at the campus of Oregon Institute of Technology in Klamath Falls, Oregon. The Geo-Heat Center provides technical assistance and information about geothermal power to consultants, developers and the public. *http://geoheat.oit.edu.*

Bills for heating oil, natural gas and electricity are expected to reach record highs thiss winter. Home owners are searching for different ways to heat their homes. *Here are two alternatives that are rapidly growing in popularity…*

PELLET STOVES

A pellet stove is a type of woodstove that burns small pellets made of compressed sawdust or other wood waste. It can be an effective way to trim winter heating expenses.

Pellets typically cost $200 to $300 per ton, and most home owners burn between one and three tons per year, depending on the size of the stove and usage. That's significantly cheaper than heating with oil, gas or electricity at today's prices. Still, pellet stoves are not appropriate for every home. *Drawbacks…*

●**Pellet stoves heat from one central point and do a poor job of warming distant rooms.** Only if your home is small or has an open layout will a pellet stove supply most—though likely not all—of your heating needs. Pellet stoves require more attention than furnaces. Home owners must manually add pellets and clean out ashes usually once each day.

●**The sudden surge in pellet stove popularity means that you might not be able to get the stove you want by the start of winter.** There even could be winter pellet shortages or pellet price increases.

●**Installing a pellet stove might increase your homeowner's insurance rates or void your policy.** Speak with your insurer before buying a stove.

PELLET STOVES vs. WOODSTOVES

Is a pellet stove a better choice for you than a conventional woodstove?

Lean toward a pellet stove if…

• **You want to stretch your heating dollar as far as possible.** Wood prices vary regionally but usually are higher than pellet prices.

• **You don't want to fuss with your heating system more than necessary**. Log-burning stoves require more time and attention than pellet-burning ones because you must add logs more frequently.

• **Your chimney or flue would require an expensive insert or upgrade to serve a conventional woodstove.** Pellet stoves are much less likely to require this. Most pellet stoves are vented through a special vent pipe that penetrates the roof, and some high-efficiency models are designed to be vented directly through a wall.

• **You have asthma or other lung disease.** Pellet stoves usually burn much cleaner than conventional woodstoves.

Lean toward a conventional woodstove if…

• **Your home is on a large wooded property.** Why pay for pellets if you can harvest your own logs for free?

• **Your region experiences frequent power failures, and you don't have a backup generator.** Pellet stoves require electricity for ignition and for operating the feed mechanism and blower. Conventional woodstoves do not require electricity.

• **A nice-looking fire is important to you.** Conventional log fires tend to be more aesthetically pleasing than pellet stove fires, which are very small. Some pellet stoves do have realistic artificial logs.

• **There is no source of reasonably priced pellets near your home.** Having pellets shipped to you will greatly increase their cost.

BUYING A PELLET STOVE

Most pellet stoves cost between $1,500 and $4,500, depending on heating capacity. Installation typically adds $300 or $400 to this price—more if the local labor rates are high or the installation is complex.

Stick with respected pellet stove brands. *These include…*

Harman (717-362-9080, *www.harmanstoves. com*).

Quadra-Fire (509-684-3745, *www.quadrafire. com*).

St. Croix (402-728-5255, *www.stcroixheat.com*).

Whitfield, made by Lennox Hearth Products (800-953-6669, *www.lennoxhearthproducts.com*).

I recommend buying the service plan if one is offered by your stove dealer. These complex machines do occasionally require service.

You will have to choose between a top-fed and a bottom-fed pellet stove. Top-fed models usually are a bit easier to operate, but they often require pricey high-grade pellets to run properly. Bottom-fed models usually run on standard-grade pellets.

Ask the stove dealer to demonstrate the stove's ash-removal procedure before you buy. Select another stove if removing the ash seems complex or messy. Also, ask the dealer to help you choose a stove of appropriate size for the space you want to heat.

For more information on pellet stoves, go to my site, *www.hometips.com/pellet_stoves.html.*

GEOTHERMAL…HEAT FROM THE EARTH

Geothermal heat pumps (GHPs) have been around for more than half a century. They now are receiving widespread attention as home owners search for alternatives to the high cost of burning oil or gas.

GHPs, also known as geoexchange systems, use liquid-filled pipes to shift heat from the ground or groundwater into the home. The earth just a few feet down maintains its temperature surprisingly well all year, ensuring that GHPs have a reliable source of heat even during the coldest winter days.

This process can be reversed in the summer, with GHPs transferring heat into the ground, thus cooling the home. GHPs also can supply hot water (supplementary water heating might be necessary depending on your system's capacity and your family's hot-water needs)…heat a swimming pool…or even melt snow off a driveway.

SAVINGS AND COSTS

The main benefit of GHPs is their energy efficiency. Savings vary greatly, but home owners usually can cut their heating costs by at least 25% and sometimes by as much as 75% or more. The larger the home, the more you will save. Savings on cooling and water heating are possible as well, though likely to be less substantial.

101

The main drawback of GHPs is their high up-front cost. An extensive piping system must be buried on the property, in addition to the cost of the heat pump itself. Expect to spend $12,000 to $14,000, installed, for a "three-ton" GHP system capable of heating a typical 1,800-square-foot home. Thus, it is best to install a geothermal system when you're building a home, but it can be retrofitted. Depending on your location and energy prices, a geothermal system can pay for itself in three-to-eight years. Payback will be fastest in regions where combined heating and cooling bills are highest.

Helpful: If there is groundwater not too far below your property or a deep pond or lake, it might be possible to have a GHP system installed for as little as $10,000. Contractors sometimes can take advantage of water to construct a GHP system that does not require an extensive network of pipes.

If your home has air ducts but they were not designed for use with a central air conditioner, they might not be large enough for a GHP system. Upgrading the ducts would add thousands to your costs. The system can be used with baseboard heating if it is designed for a geothermal system. Most existing baseboards are not adequate, because they require higher water temperatures.

If pending federal legislation is approved, it would extend tax credits of up to $4,000 through the end of 2014 to home owners who install ground-source heat pumps. For more information on incentives for geothermal and other heating systems, go to the Web site of the Database of State Incentives for Renewables & Efficiency (*http//dsireusa.org*).

Tricks to Keep Burglars Away from Your Home

Walter T. Shaw, one of the most notorious jewel thieves of the past half-century. Based in Fort Lauderdale, Florida, he is author of *A License to Steal,* an account of his career as a jewel thief and his father's career as a tele-communications inventor. Omega. A movie based on the book is slated to go into production later this year. *www. alicense2steal.com.*

A man's home might be his castle, but few homes have moats and battlements. If a burglar wants to break in, he probably can—and in these tough economic times, a burglar is more likely to do so.

Fortunately, most burglars are lazy and fearful. They target the homes that look like they will be the easiest to rob with the lowest risk of capture. Your home does not need to be impregnable—it simply needs to be less appealing to burglars than others in your neighborhood.

How to reduce the odds that your home will be targeted—or send the would-be burglar running if it is...

•**Keep your garage door closed** as much as possible. Leaving the garage door open when you go out tells all who pass that there's no car inside and it is likely that no one is at home.

Open garages also provide convenient cover for burglars. They can simply walk or drive into the garage, shut the door behind them, then force open the door connecting the garage to the home without worry that they will be seen.

Regularly leaving your garage door open when you are home and there is a car parked in the garage is a bad idea, too. A burglar might figure out that your garage door tends to be closed only when no one is home.

Of course, if you have expensive bikes or yard equipment in your open garage, you're inviting burglars to walk right in and take them.

•**Stay out of the obits.** The newspaper obituary page offers burglars a handy guide to which homes are going to be vacant when. Burglars simply wait until the time and date listed for a funeral or memorial service, then break into the homes of the local residents mentioned among the relatives of the deceased.

If you provide an obituary for a family member to a local paper, either do not list survivors or do not mention when the memorial service will be held. Instead, provide a contact phone number for those who wish to attend.

•**Post a "Beware of Dog" sign.** Dogs bark and bite, which makes them effective burglar deterrents. Even if you do not own a dog, a sign warning that you do could encourage a burglar to target a different home. You also could attach a dog's chain to a stake in your yard to add to the illusion.

If you buy a dog to scare off burglars, favor a small, "yippy" dog over a big one. Most little dogs bark incessantly when strangers approach their homes. Big dogs might bark a few times, but unless they are trained as guard dogs, they're less likely to keep it up.

●**Post a "video surveillance" or "you are being videotaped" sign** on the front gate or elsewhere around your home. Burglars fear being photographed even more than they fear alarm systems. They have time to flee if an alarm sounds, but there might not be much they can do once their image is caught on tape.

Putting up inexpensive, fake video cameras in conspicuous locations around your home improves the illusion. Fake cameras are available in home stores or on Web sites, such as Amazon. com, for $10 to $20 apiece, sometimes less.

●**Remove thick hedges and privacy fences.** Burglars love to break into homes with doors or windows that are not visible from the road and from neighboring homes. They can take their time breaking into these homes without fear that they will be seen.

If a high hedge or fence around your home provides potential cover for burglars, replace the hedge with plants no taller than knee-height…and replace the fence with a lower fence, a chain-link fence or a wood fence that has spaces between the slats.

●**Don't let mail or newspapers pile up when you are on vacation.** This makes it easy for burglars to see that the home is vacant. Unfortunately, stopping delivery informs newspaper deliverymen and other strangers that you will be away. It is better to ask a trusted neighbor to collect your mail and newspapers for you.

●**Also, be sure to have someone mow your lawn in the summer** or shovel your walk if it snows in the winter.

●**Use lights and radios to make it seem that someone is home.** Homes that are completely dark before bedtime are obvious targets for burglars. Timers, available for a few dollars at home stores and hardware stores, are a reasonably effective solution.

Also, leave a radio on and tuned to a talk station when you're away so that anyone who approaches the home will think someone is inside.

●**Install motion-activated floodlights on every side of your home,** not just over the driveway and front door. Bright lights scare away most burglars.

Housekeeping Expert Reveals Five Favorite Secrets

Try these helpful cleaning tips from a housekeeping expert…

●**Use a fabric softener sheet** to clean TV and CRT computer screens.

●**Set a hair dryer on cool,** and use it to blow dust off of lampshades and plants.

●**Damp-mop wood floors coated with polyurethane**—don't wax or use ammonia.

●**Put a drop of cologne on a lightbulb** when the light is off. When you turn the light on, it will scent the room.

●**A weak solution of white vinegar and water** cleans food preparation areas.

Tom McNulty, a writer based in Eden Prairie, Minnesota, and author of *Clean Like a Man: Housekeeping for Men (and the Women Who Love Them)*. Three Rivers.

Home Improvements That Pay Up to 93%

Home improvements that recoup the most when you sell…

A complete kitchen makeover returns 80%, while a more moderate updating can recover 75%…changing an attic into a bedroom suite returns 93%…turning a basement into a room for socializing brings back 79%…adding a full bathroom returns 84%.

Statistics from a Cost vs. Value Report from *Remodeling*, a renovation trade publication, Washington, DC.

Conserve Water... Save Money

Save $200 a year by conserving water. *Just follow these suggestions and you will be saving in no time...*

•**Stop leaks**—check your home's water heater, fix leaky faucets and water-supply tubing, and check outdoor systems, such as sprinklers, for leaks.

•**Replace toilets that are more than 10 years old**—high-efficiency low-flow models, which cost about $300, save 25 gallons per day.

•**Buy an energy-efficient washing machine**—"Energy Star" models use 50% less water. For more water-saving tips, visit *www.h2ouse.org.*

Karl Kurka, assistant director, California Urban Water Conservation Council, Sacramento, California.

When It Pays to Fix an Appliance...and When It's Time to Buy a New One

Dan O'Neill, founder of Appliance411.com, a home appliance information Web site. He has 15 years of experience in the appliance-service industry in Ontario, Canada, and has been assisting US and Canadian consumers through his Web site since 1997.

A basic appliance repair that might have cost $50 or $60 in the early 1990s now is likely to run $100 or more, including parts and labor. (Repairmen typically charge $50 or more just to diagnose a problem.) That's a lot of money considering that many new appliances cost only $300 to $400.

When does it pay to repair an appliance? In general, if a repair costs less than half as much as buying a new appliance of equal quality, it's worthwhile—but there are exceptions.

Here's a guide to deciding whether to fix household appliances, plus some repairs you can easily do yourself...

REFRIGERATORS

If your fridge is more than 10 years old, you're probably better off replacing it than repairing it. Refrigerators can be expensive to repair, since key components such as the compressor—the heart of the refrigeration system—are enclosed in sealed systems and require special tools to service. What's more, a new fridge with a favorable Energy Star rating will save at least $40 a year in electricity, compared with a refrigerator from the early 1990s—you will save more than $100 a year if your old fridge dates to the 1970s.

If a fridge is less than 10 years old, repairing it can make sense, especially if it is a high-end model. Compared with other appliances, fridge problems are tricky to diagnose. *Common problems...*

•**Leaking.** If the area under the fridge is wet, there might be a clog in the drain tube. If water is on the inside roof of the refrigerator portion of a freezer-on-top model, the leak might be from the freezer drain tube.

Repair cost: $80 to $100.*

•**Stops running or stops cooling.** Any number of components can cause these problems, including broken thermostats, defrost timers, compressors and condenser fan motors. Or it could be as simple as a faulty wire.

Repair cost: $100 and up, depending on the problem.

Do-it-yourself repair: If your refrigerator still cools but not very well, unplug it and thoroughly clean the dust and dirt from the condenser coils with a bottle brush. This should improve the appliance's heat-transfer ability and could solve the cooling problem. You might need to remove the grill or move the fridge to get at the coils from the back. Home owners also might be able to unclog drain tubes and solve some refrigerator leaks. It depends on how easy it is to reach the fridge's drain tube—at least some disassembly of the appliance will probably be required.

WASHING MACHINES

Any repair that can be done for $100 or less is worth doing unless the washer has had

*Repair costs are estimates. Actual costs will vary based on skilled labor rates in your region and the cost of parts for your specific model.

repeated problems or is showing signs of rust on its internal parts—rust suggests that water is getting into places it isn't meant to be, meaning that the washer might not have many years left. *Common problems...*

●**Fails to drain or drains slowly.** This might mean that the pump has failed or the drain line is clogged. Repair cost: $100 to have a new pump installed or $80 to unclog the drain lines.

●**The motor is working, but the tub doesn't spin.** The problem might be a broken or worn belt. (If your washer uses multiple belts, the "drive" belt connecting the motor to the tub is the likely culprit.)

Repair cost: Less than $100. (All modern Whirlpool and most modern Kenmore washers use plastic motor couplings instead of belts, but they, too, should cost less than $100 to replace.)

●**The motor is broken.** The cost of the repair will vary. Ask for an estimate before you commit to the job.

●**The electronics system fails.** If the system fails on a computerized washer, it may be time for a new one. A repair could cost hundreds of dollars. If the washer is high-end and only a few years old, it might be worth the expense.

Do-it-yourself repair: If water is leaking, it could be a hose. Try tightening the connection or replacing broken pieces of hose. If the hose still leaks, a pro often can fix it for less than $100.

DRYERS

It's usually wise to repair broken dryers. Most fixes are inexpensive, and there's no reason that the repaired dryer can't keep running for many years. My dryer was made in 1969, and it's still going strong. Newer dryers don't do a much better job drying than older ones, and they're not much more energy efficient. In fact, many dryers made 20 years ago are more solidly built than today's models. *Common problems...*

●**The motor fails.**

Repair cost: $200. True, you can get a new low-end dryer for a little more than that, but it might be worth $200 to repair a higher-end unit—one that has more than two heat settings

and the ability to sense electronically when clothes are dry.

●**The dryer is operating,** but clothes remain cold and damp. The heating element may need to be replaced.

Repair cost: $150—higher if it's difficult for the repairman to get to the part.

Do-it-yourself repair: If your dryer is drying very slowly, the problem might be a clogged dryer vent. If the vent hose isn't hidden in your wall, you should be able to clear it yourself by disconnecting the hose and removing anything that has built up inside.

DISHWASHERS

It's often worth repairing a broken dishwasher if it is a mid-range to high-end model that is less than 10 years old. *Common problems...*

●**Drainage.** The cause could be simply a clogged internal or external hose, or it could be something major, such as a broken pump or motor.

Repair cost: $80 to clear a clog or replace a belt...$100 to $300 to correct a simple malfunction—prices vary by model. It's worth calling a serviceman for an estimate unless it's a low-end dishwasher.

●**Leaks.** These can be caused by failed seals or overfoaming due to excessive use of a rinse agent.

Do-it-yourself repair: Before you call a repairman, check the rubber seal around the interior perimeter of the door for signs of deterioration or displacement. If you find deterioration, you can replace the seal yourself. The new one should just slide or clip in. Also, try reducing your rinse agent use, particularly if your region has soft water. If leaks still occur, a broken pump might be the problem.

Repair cost: $15 to $100 for a new door seal. Add another $80 if you hire a pro to install it. The cost of replacing the pump varies with the cost of the part.

Caution: Fix any leak quickly to prevent damage to the motor. If the pump and the motor must be replaced, it may be time for a new dishwasher unless the current one is newish and high-end.

6

World's Best Vacation Deals

Free (or Almost Free) Lodging Around The World

Why should you pay even the lowest rates for hotel rooms when you can find lodgings that are absolutely free, or almost free?

Join a "hospitality exchange," and you will be able to stay in other people's homes in the US and abroad. In return, you agree to host visitors in your home at your convenience.

Bonus: This is a great way to make new friends, and many hosts are happy to act as local guides.

Exchange clubs differ in purpose. Some clubs were formed to promote peace and friendship among peoples of the world, while others are strictly about cheap lodging.

Some charge yearly membership fees. Most provide on-line directories of their members and leave the visit arrangements up to you. In many instances, it is recommended that you request lodgings for no more than a few nights.

HOSPITALITY EXCHANGE

This association of "friendly, travel-loving people" publishes two directories per year full of listings of members who want to stay in one another's homes. You make your own contacts and plan your visit at a time that is convenient for both parties.

Membership cost: $20* a year, $35 for two years.

Information: 301-854-0388, *www.hospex.net.*

AFFORDABLE TRAVEL CLUB

This exchange club is limited to travelers over age 40. You receive an annual directory from which you choose your hosts and others choose you. Visitors pay hosts $15 for a single room

*All prices are subject to change.

Joan Rattner Heilman, an award-winning travel writer based in New York State. She is the author of *Unbelievably Good Deals and Great Adventures That You Absolutely Can't Get Unless You're Over 50.* McGraw-Hill.

or $20 for a double per night and $10 for each additional person. The club also offers house-sitting and pet-sitting services where club members move into your house while you are on vacation and enjoy a visit to your neighborhood in exchange for caring for your house or pets.

Membership cost: $65-80* a year.

Information: 253-858-2172, *www.affordable travelclub.net.*

GLOBALFREELOADERS.COM

Everything is free in this cooperative network of people willing to accommodate travelers, from membership to your home stay. In return, you must host other travelers whenever convenient. Although most members are Australian, American, British or Canadian, there are about 12,000 members in more than 130 countries.

Cost: Free.

Information: *www.globalfreeloaders.com.*

EVERGREEN BED & BREAKFAST CLUB

This club is exclusively for travelers over age 50. You pay $10 for a single room or $15 for a double for each overnight stay, including breakfast. Choose host families from the club's directory, and arrange your visit directly with them. A quarterly newsletter keeps you up-to-date.

Membership cost: $60 a year for singles, $75 for couples.

Information: 800-962-2392, *www.evergreen club.com.*

SERVAS

Servas, the world's oldest free hospitality exchange, was formed more than 50 years ago to promote friendship and peace among people throughout the world. Working through mutually arranged visits, it enables hosts and visitors "to share their lives, interests and concerns regarding social issues."

More than 15,000 hosts in 125 countries welcome other members in their homes for a night or two without charge. It is open to travelers of all ages, who must provide two letters of reference and be interviewed for acceptance.

*All prices are subject to change.

Cost: $50* per adult a year for travel within the US only, $85 for US plus international travel.

Information: 707-825-1714, *www.usservas.org.*

LESBIAN AND GAY HOSPITALITY EXCHANGE INTERNATIONAL

This network of approximately 500 people around the world offers hospitality to other members at no charge beyond the membership fee. Established as a way to make the world a friendlier place for its members, LGHEI issues an annual directory from which to choose potential hosts for two-night stays.

Membership cost: $40.

Information: *www.lghei.org* or LGHEI, c/o J. Wiley, Smetana Str. 28, Berlin, Germany. 011-49-30-691-95-37.

WOMEN WELCOME WOMEN WORLD WIDE

This club was formed to foster international understanding and friendship among women from many cultures. Women Welcome Women World Wide (5W) now has approximately 3,000 members in 70 countries.

In addition to providing a listing of all members with descriptions of themselves and their homes, it also schedules conferences and gatherings that are announced in its three newsletters each year. Partners, family and friends are allowed to accompany members on visits, although they may not join the club.

Membership cost: $67 a year.

Information: 011-44-1494-465441, *www. womenwelcomewomen.org.uk.*

*All prices are subject to change.

More from Joan Rattner Heilman...

Vacation Surprises in American Cities

If you are looking for lots of charm and unique ambience, forget all the big tourist towns. Save your money by sneaking away to these overlooked smaller cities.

PROVIDENCE, RHODE ISLAND

The billion-dollar revitalization program has recently transformed Providence, RI, from an old industrial backwater to one of the liveliest, most colorful Eastern cities. Although it has been thoroughly modernized, Providence retains the feel of colonial America because so much of its original architecture has been preserved and restored to its former glory.

The Performing Arts Center, renovated railroad station, State House, gigantic convention center, upscale Providence Place Mall and six major hotels are all clustered conveniently in or around downtown along the riverfront called Waterplace Park. A stunning gathering place and home to summer concerts, street performers, gondolas, restaurants and shops, it is famous for WaterFire, which is an installation of 100 bonfires lit in the river every night from May through November.

Cross the Venetian-style bridges spanning the rivers and walk to Benefit Street, where you'll find the largest single collection of restored colonial homes in America. The walking tour through the neighborhood is a must. Also not to be missed are the many museums, such as the Rhode Island School of Design Museum and the John Brown House, the home of the founder of Brown University. For a look at a traditional Ivy League campus, walk around the grounds of Brown University.

This city is easy to see by riverboat, walking or bus tour, or the hop-on-and-off trolley buses. And as you go, be sure to look at the outdoor sculptures decorating the downtown area, even on the light poles.

Information: Providence Warwick Convention and Visitors Bureau (800-233-1636, *www.go providence.com*).

INDEPENDENCE, MISSOURI

Independence, a charming Midwestern city laden with Victorian mansions on leafy tree-lined streets, is best known as the hometown of President Harry S. Truman. The biggest attractions in town are the Truman Historic Home and the Truman Presidential Museum and Library, open to the public year-round, and the new Truman Walking Trail, 43 sidewalk plaques that guide visitors along the same route the president strolled every day after his retirement.

The National Frontier Trails Museum (open year-round), also in the historic downtown area, explains the city's history from the Lewis and Clark expedition (1804–1806) to its role as the starting point for Western expansion in the mid-1800s. Among the original buildings are the 1827 Log Courthouse, once the only courthouse between the Missouri River and the Pacific Ocean, and the Pioneer Spring Cabin, a typical frontier home. Also open to the public are the limestone cells in the 1859 jail once occupied by Confederate Civil War guerrillas and famous outlaws, like Frank James and Cole Younger, who both rode with the Jesse James gang.

Not to be overlooked in Independence is the Mormon Visitors Center. The Center commemorates Joseph Smith, founder of the Mormon Church, who proclaimed Independence to be the City of Zion and the site of the second coming before he left for the West.

Information: City of Independence Tourism (800-748-7323, *www.visitindependence.com*).

PORTLAND, OREGON

Portland, a sophisticated city with a relaxed atmosphere, is loaded with cultural institutions and events. Its most popular gathering place is Pioneer Courthouse Square, an art-filled plaza in the heart of town with an amphitheater, a waterfall fountain and a 25-foot sculpture that forecasts the weather.

An eminently walkable city, Portland is home to a handful of theatrical companies, a symphony orchestra and an opera company, as well as 239 parks and gardens. Two of the biggest and most popular parks are Forest Park, the largest urban wilderness in an American city, filled with forested walking trails, and Washington Park, where visitors flock to the many attractions, including the International Rose Test Garden with more than 500 varieties of roses, the Oregon Zoo and the Hoyt Arboretum. Across town is The Grotto, a 62-acre forested religious sanctuary that also includes the Botanical Gardens.

Making your way through the historic Old Town District, known for all its cast-iron architecture, take time to stop in at any of the many microbreweries and hip coffeehouses. Plan to see the Portland Saturday Market, the nation's largest open-air market, open during weekends from March through December 24. It's known for the crafts and jewelry made by local artisans, its food court and street performers.

To see Portland from the water, cruise the Willamette River on the *Portland Spirit*, a sleek, modern-looking yacht that runs year-round. Food is available on board.

Information: Portland Oregon Visitors Association (877-678-5263, *www.travelportland.com*).

CLEVELAND, OHIO

Cleveland is another former industrial town that has transformed itself into a major cultural center. It boasts one of the largest performing arts centers in the nation outside of New York, with five restored 1920s theaters that are home to the renowned Cleveland Opera, the Ohio Ballet, the Great Lakes Theater Festival and traveling Broadway shows.

Some of Cleveland's newest attractions can be found along the shores of Lake Erie—the Rock and Roll Hall of Fame, the Great Lakes Science Center and the Cleveland Browns Stadium. And stretching out along the banks of the Cuyahoga River, which meanders through town, is the Flats, the entertainment and warehouse district that's chock-full of restaurants and nightclubs.

About four miles east of downtown is University Circle, the country's largest concentration of cultural arts and medical and educational institutions (more than 50 of them) within one square mile. The sites include the Cleveland Botanical Garden, the Museum of Art, the HealthSpace Museum, Severance Hall, which is home to the world-renowned Cleveland Orchestra, and the Cleveland Botanical Garden, which re-creates a Costa Rican rain forest and a Madagascan desert under a glass roof.

Cleveland is also where you'll find Case Western Reserve University, with its flamboyant Peter B. Lewis Building designed by the architect Frank Gehry. His buildings—the Guggenheim Museum in Bilbao, Spain, concert hall at Bard College in New York State and the Walt Disney Concert Hall in Los Angeles—have thrilled people around the world.

Information: Convention & Visitors Bureau of Greater Cleveland (800-321-1001, *www.positivelycleveland.com*).

ST. AUGUSTINE, FLORIDA

America's oldest city, St. Augustine, FL, was founded in 1565. It boasts Spanish colonial and revival architecture found nowhere else in the country, splendid gardens, beautiful beaches and good birding.

Walk along the narrow tree-lined streets of the historic district, with its early 18th-century houses and massive 19th-century Spanish revival hotels. Visit the Fountain of Youth Archaeological Park (Ponce de Leon may have found the legendary fountain here when he discovered Florida in 1513) and be sure to take a sip.

And, don't miss the Castillo de San Marcos, an imposing fortress which overlooks the Atlantic Ocean, the Spanish Quarter Museum, the St. Augustine Alligator Farm, the only place in the world with every species of crocodilians on display, and the lighthouse and museum, with 219 steps to climb for a panoramic view of Matanzas Bay and the Atlantic Ocean.

Don't miss the free guided tour of the Ponce de Leon Hotel, a lavish Spanish revival structure built by the millionaire developer Henry Flagler at the end of the 19th century. The hotel, with its Tiffany stained glass, gold-leafed Maynard murals and electricity done by Thomas Edison, is now the home of Flagler College.

Information: St. Augustine, Ponte Vedra & the Beaches Visitors and Convention Bureau (800-653-2489, *www.getaway4florida.com*).

Also from Joan Rattner Heilman...

The Key to Traveling With Pets

An increasing number of lodgings—from low-cost motel chains to luxury hotels—now welcome pets in guest rooms. Some even offer amenities like special pillows, bowls and gourmet menus.

Facilities have opened up in many cities to provide daytime or overnight care for your pet while you are doing the town. There are even doggy country clubs, complete with swimming pools, gourmet biscuits and massages.

FINDING A HOTEL

At least one-third of all locations of the largest lodging chains, which include Super 8, Howard Johnson, Holiday Inn and Travelodge, give the nod to pets. All the La Quintas will welcome them if they are under a certain size. And so do many inns, bed-and-breakfast establishments and, surprisingly, even luxury hotels, like the Four Seasons in Atlanta and the Hotel Monaco in Chicago.

For listings of thousands of hotels, motels, bed-and-breakfasts and inns that accept pets, go on-line to such Web sites as *www.petsonthego. com*, *www.petswelcome.com* or *www.takeyour pet.com* and search for the area or city where you would like to stay. These sites also dispense other helpful information about leaving home with a pet and even include periodic e-letters.

Guidebooks are another route to finding a welcoming destination. *Pets on the Go!* by Dawn and Robert Habgood (Dawbert) describes appropriate lodgings throughout the US along with information about the surrounding areas. The new edition of *AAA's Traveling With Your Pet—The AAA PetBook* also lists thousands of hotels that accommodate pets along with their owners. Both the publications include advice for making the trip more enjoyable for everyone.

If you prefer to stay at a specific hotel or lodging chain, call and ask about its pet policy or check its Web site. For example, Holiday Inn's Web site at *www.holiday-inn.com*, enables you to look up the pet policy at any of its locations worldwide.

RESTRICTIONS

Sometimes there are restrictions on the type of creatures that may share your room. Many motels or hotels allow only dogs and/or cats.

Often there is a limitation on the size of these guests. Some do specify, for example, that dogs and cats may weigh no more than 15 pounds. La Quinta takes them up to 50 pounds.

Some lodgings do insist that the animal be housebroken and that you take your dog with you on a leash when you leave your room. At least one specifies no barking. Cats are usually no problem when it comes to noise.

LUXURY HOTELS

There is an amazing number of upscale hotels around the country that are so eager for visits from you and your pet that they offer special amenities just for them. *Examples...*

●**Loews Hotels.** Its "Loews Loves Pets" program, available at most Loews hotels in the US and Canada, offers a complimentary bag of pet treats and a toy, specialized bedding for dogs and cats, place mats with food and water bowls, a room service menu that includes a variety of dishes such as grilled chicken or lamb for dogs, liver or salmon for cats.

More information: Call 800-235-6397 or visit *www.loewshotels.com*.

●**Four Seasons.** Goodies offered at the Four Seasons Hotel in Atlanta include a ceramic pet bowl, a dog biscuit made by the pastry chef, room service featuring both chopped steak and grilled chicken breast, and a newsletter, *The Pampered Pooch*, that tells you such things as the best places in town to walk your dog.

More information: Call 800-332-3442 or visit *www.fourseasons.com*.

●**Fairmont.** Four-legged guests at the Fairmont Scottsdale Princess in Arizona can get the "Paws on Board" package—a welcome biscuit, special bowl, a pet room with soft beds, toys, gourmet food and more.

More information: Call 800-257-7544 or visit *www.fairmont.com*.

●**Kimpton.** Most of the Kimpton Boutique Hotels are well-known for pampering their pet guests. For example, the Hotel Monaco Chicago has its "Furry Friends Package" in which dogs get a special bed, a bowl and a doggy bone. Cats receive a disposable litter box and bowl and a special kitty treat. Both get a souvenir bandanna. Upon request, the hotel also provides a complimentary goldfish companion during your stay.

More information: Call 866-610-0081 or visit *www.monaco-chicago.com.*

IT'S A GREAT LIFE

•**Biscuits & Bath** in New York City provides day care for your pooch, a lap pool for refreshing swims, indoor grassy running fields, birthday parties and Sunday brunches for both of you at four locations.

More information: Call 212-419-2500 or visit *www.biscuitsandbath.com.*

•**America Dog & Cat Hotel** offers free time to hit the casinos for travelers who take pets to Las Vegas. Sign up for day care or overnight stays in private pet suites with color TVs, super-soft beds and an enclosed yard. Other amenities include bubble baths and limousine transfers.

More information: Call 702-795-3647 or visit *www.doghotel.net.*

•**Paradise Ranch** in Sun Valley, California, is a bed-and-breakfast for canine guests only, with full-sized furnished bedrooms and real beds, play yards with waterfalls and wading pools. For dogs staying overnight accustomed to sleeping with their owners, a human "bed buddy" is provided for an extra fee.

More information: Call 818-768-8708 or visit *www.paradiseranch.net.*

ODDS AND ENDS

•**Take a pet to Britain.** Dogs and cats can now travel to the UK from the US without undergoing six months' quarantine. They must, however, meet certain criteria set up by the UK Pet Travel Scheme, such as vaccination against rabies, treatment for tapeworms and an ID microchip. Continental Airlines now operates services for pets from Newark, Houston and Cleveland to London.

More information: Visit *www.britainusa. com.*

•**Finding a pet-sitter.** If you would rather leave your pet home when you travel, consider finding a professional and certified "in-home pet-sitter."

More information: Contact the National Association of Professional Pet Sitters at 856-439-0324 or visit *www.petsitters.org.*

Little-Known Way to Get a Great Deal on a Vacation

Booking your vacation through a wholesale club such as Costco or BJ's can cost less than buying it on-line or through a travel agent. Selection is limited, so don't join a membership club just to book a trip. If you already belong, consider booking through the club. Some hotel packages were 50% less expensive at wholesale clubs than on-line.

National Geographic Traveler, 1145 17 St. NW, Washington, DC 20036.

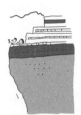 # Luxury Cruises for As Little as $80/Day

Susan Tanzman, who is frequently named one of the top 200 travel agents in the US by *Travel Agent* magazine. She is president of Martin's Travel & Tours, 3415 Sepulveda Blvd., Los Angeles 90034.

Today's growing number of cruise lines, ships, itineraries, onboard activities and pricing systems make it easier than ever to pick a cruise that's fun and affordable.

By knowing the ropes, you can spend as little as $80 a day per person for an inside cabin for two, $150 a day for a cabin with a sea view or $400 to $500 for a luxury cabin or suite.

You can cruise on a ship that has 3,000 other passengers or on a craft with only a few hundred. If you have already been on the familiar Caribbean routes, consider a cruise to Quebec City on Celebrity Cruises, the California wine country on American Safari Cruises or Monte Carlo on Sea-Dream Yacht Club.

111

Internet discounters and cruise lines themselves frequently offer cut-rate prices, but it's often wiser to book through a travel agent, unless you're already familiar with the cruise lines and their ports of call.

Reason: Knowledgeable travel agents can give you the information that cruise companies might be reluctant to share or that Internet sites don't have.

BOOKING SMART

Tell the travel agent exactly why you want to go on a cruise—to visit interesting ports, take part in onboard activities or just to lounge on deck and enjoy the ocean.

Once the agent suggests several cruises, ask…

●**How large is the vessel?** The number of passengers often determines the atmosphere of a cruise.

If you're one of 3,000 passengers, you'll have the opportunity to meet lots of people and participate in a wide variety of onboard activities.

But it's usually best to choose a much smaller vessel if you're looking for a romantic cruise where you can dine, dance and stroll the deck with someone you love.

Rule of thumb: Whenever there are more than 1,200 passengers, the multiple seatings will likely make meals less relaxed.

●**Who are the other passengers?** Cruise lines cater to different types of passengers. Crystal Cruises, for instance, attracts many passengers over the age of 50. Many cruises cater to parents traveling with their adult children. Others have activities for kids traveling with their parents or grandparents.

●**What activities does the cruise offer?** Activities usually include gambling, swimming, exercise classes, dancing, nightclub entertainment, non-gambling games and lectures on a wide range of subjects.

Examples: History, sea lore and wildlife.

●**What's the cabin size?** Ignore pictures of cabins in brochures and on the Web that make accommodations appear larger than they actually are.

Important: Ask for the actual dimensions and ask about portholes.

SAVING MONEY

Myth: To get a bargain price, you must book a cruise a few days before the ship sales.

Reality: Whenever a cruise isn't fully booked as quickly as the company anticipates, it routinely discounts the fare, even if the departure date is months away.

Here's how to get the best value for your money when looking for a cruise…

●**Don't book cruises when school is out.** Discounts are seldom available at these peak periods, and airfares to the port of departure are also higher.

Moreover, cruises at high seasons are rarely as much fun as they are at other times.

Example: Crowded ships and overworked staffs are the norm for most European cruises in July and August and for many Caribbean cruises in early January.

●**Book your own transportation to the port of departure.** All lines will provide air or transfer services to passengers of their cruise line. In many cases, allowing your travel agent to make these transportation reservations can provide you with tremendous savings in the cost of these services.

●**Ask about the price of shore excursions.** Some excursions are well worth the $40 to $200 that they typically cost, but others are a waste of money. In many port cities, for instance, you can walk or take an inexpensive taxi to the most interesting areas.

●**Ask about group rates.** Some lines have group rates for organizations or a certain number of people that are much lower than individual fares. Others offer discounts on the amount of money that group members spend on board.

●**Find out what's included in the price.** Some cruise lines include beverages, games and entertainment in their prices—others don't.

●**If you plan to drink alcoholic beverages on a cruise,** consider bringing some of your own or buying a bottle at your first port. Also pack some soft drink mixes, especially if you travel with children who might charge several sodas a day to your bill.

Bringing drinks of your own can mean a big savings because most cruise lines charge high prices for them.

Example: A couple who enjoys several soft drinks during the day and a cocktail or two in the evening can easily spend $300 to $400 on beverages on a week-long cruise.

STAYING HEALTHY

The cruise ships occasionally report incidents where a large number of passengers become ill, often with stomach problems. Though there are no complete statistics available, it's very doubtful that you are more likely to become ill on a cruise ship than at any restaurant. *Recommended…*

● **Purchase travel insurance just in case.** It should cover medical expenses, including evacuation if needed. Most policies also cover travel delays and loss of luggage.

Typical price: $20 to $30 a day.

● **If you are concerned about tobacco smoke,** choose a cruise that limits smoking to certain areas of the ship.

SEASICKNESS

Don't necessarily give up on a cruise because you're vulnerable to seasickness. *To reduce the chance of becoming ill…*

● **Book cruises on large vessels,** which are less susceptible to the movements that cause seasickness.

● **Don't sail at a time of year when waters may be rough.**

Example: November in the Caribbean waters. The travel agents who book cruises are usually very knowledgeable on the subject.

● **Ask your doctor to prescribe a medication for motion sickness.**

Save Money by Swapping…

Swap homes with someone from another country, and eliminate lodging costs from your travel budget.

Added benefit: You can live like the locals during your stay.

Home-exchange Web sites: Digsville.com, HomeExchange.com, Homelink.org.uk, Intervacus.com, Exchangehomesoia.com, Sabbatical Homes.com, HomeAroundtheWorld.com and SeniorsHomeExchange.com.

Annual membership fees: $45 to $125.

Cruise Line Rip-Off

Many cruise companies now automatically add a charge of $40 to $120 for trip insurance unless you specifically state that you do not want it.

Best: If you do want trip insurance, you can probably get it for a better price elsewhere. Ask your travel agent.

Arthur Frommer's Budget Travel, 530 Seventh Ave., New York City 10018.

Luxury Cruises for Less

Eagle Travel is one of a select group of travel companies that receive special discounts on luxury cruises for their clients.

Recent example: A 10-day cruise in the Mexican Riviera, $1,749 per person with $200 in shipboard credit and a shore event in Puerto Vallarta.

Information: 800-326-7172, *www.eagletravel inc.com.*

Sue Goldstein, author of more than 70 books on bargain shopping and host of a Dallas-area call-in radio show on bargain shopping. *www.undergroundshopper.com.*

On-Line Travel Auctions

On-line auctions for travel can get you very good deals—if you do some research first. Don't assume that the retail value listed at auction sites is accurate—it may reflect high-season or full-fare rates. Check sites with firm prices, such as *www.bestfares.com...www.travelocity. com...*and *www.expedia.com*, then set a bidding limit before visiting an auction site.

Caution: Auction-site packages often don't provide specific dates. You must make reservations after winning the auction—on a space-available basis. If you're not flexible about travel dates, you may be unable to use the trip.

Best travel auction sites: *www.luxurylink. com...www.skyauction.com.*

Tom Parsons, editor, BestFares.com, 1301 S. Bowen Rd., Arlington, Texas 76013.

Free Parking At the Airport

Overnight parking at the airport is getting more and more expensive. As an alternative, several hotel chains have park/fly packages. If you spend the night before your flight at a hotel that offers this package, you can then leave your car in the hotel's well-lit, guarded parking lot—for free. Most include a shuttle to/ from the terminal, coffee (sometimes breakfast) and a morning newspaper.

The typical package includes up to seven nights' parking. However, you may be able to negotiate a low (but not a free) parking rate for longer stays.

Among the chains providing this deal are Hampton Inn (800-426-7866, *www.hampton inn.com*)...Radisson (800-333-3333, *www. radisson.com*)...and Red Roof Inns (800-733-7663, *www.redroof.com*).

Nancy Dunnan, editor and publisher of *TravelSmart,* Dobbs Ferry, New York, *www.travelsmartnewsletter.com.*

More from Nancy Dunnan...

Fly Through Check-In Lines At the Airport...

Send your luggage ahead to avoid the long check-in lines at the airport and at baggage claim. Luggagefree charges only $1.65* to $4.40 per pound for shipping anywhere in the continental US. The cost is $3.50 per pound to Hawaii and Alaska; $6.50 to $7.75 per pound for international shipments. There is a minimum charge for all locations and a charge for pick up of your luggage. Luggagefree supplies all shipping labels, wraps your bags in heavy plastic, tracks them and lets you know when they arrive. Bags are automatically insured for up to $1,000—additional coverage is available.

Information: 800-361-6871, *www.luggage free.com.*

*All prices are subject to change.

Also from Nancy Dunnan...

Your Rights in an Airport Search

Before you go through airport security, be sure you know your rights...

•**If selected to be patted down,** you may ask to have it done out of view of other passengers and by a screener of the same gender.

•**You may ask to be examined by hand** instead of by X-ray machine.

•**If you take injectable medicines,** you may carry syringes that have a professionally printed label.

•**If you have a pacemaker,** you may request a pat-down inspection instead of walking through a metal detector.

•**You may request a pat-down** if you do not want to go through the metal detector for religious or cultural reasons.

More information: On-line at Transportation Security Administration's Web site *www. tsa.gov,* click on "For Travelers."

Nancy Dunnan tells how to...

Get the Best Seat on the Plane

To find the best airline seat check *www.seat guru.com.* Select the airline you're flying and the type of plane, and the site will tell you which seats are the roomiest and quietest. All seats are color coded for "poor," "be aware" and "good."

How to Get a Refund on Your Airfare

If the airfare drops on a scheduled flight, you may be able to get a refund for the difference. But, it depends on the airline. Airlines usually will refund the difference if you find a lower fare for which you still qualify—on the same airline, for the same flight.

Example: If your current ticket requires 14-day advance purchase and the cost drops 15 days before your departure.

Some airlines charge fees of $50 to $100 to change your flight. Some will post a refund to your credit card...others will give you only a voucher for future air travel—usually good for one year.

Randy Petersen, publisher, *InsideFlyer*, 1930 Frequent Flyer Point, Colorado Springs 80915, *www.insideflyer.com.*

Upgrading Your Frequent-Flier Program...

When switching to a new carrier's frequent-flier program, you may be able to get elite status without accumulating the required miles. Show the airline your elite-level travel patterns on your current carrier and which of the new carrier's routes you expect to use.

Helpful: Contact the vice president or manager of the carrier's frequent-flier program, and explain how much you will be flying in the future. Request a specific level. Once enrolled, you must fly enough to maintain the status.

Bob Jones, consumer specialist for OneTravel.com, a value-oriented travel Web site, East Greenville, Pennsylvania.

Get a "Free Day Trip" on Your Airline

On trips to distant locations, consider planning a several-hour layover en route. This can provide a low-cost vacation dividend.

Example: Whenever you are flying from the US to Europe or beyond, you can schedule your flights to create a long layover—as long as it is no more than 24 hours—in Paris or London. The airline may even provide food vouchers for meals during the layover. The result is a free day in Paris or London.

Arthur Frommer's Budget Travel, 530 Seventh Ave., New York City 10018.

Rent Cars Away from the Airport for Big Savings

One of the big national car-rental companies recently quoted a price of $68/day for a car rented at the San Diego airport...or $42 for the same car rented downtown.

More: Getting into town from the airport is easier and less costly than ever in many major cities—using public transportation, airport shuttles or even taxis at some in-city airports.

Family Fun, 114 Fifth Ave., New York City 10011.

Savvy Rental-Car Strategies

Nancy Dunnan, editor and publisher of *TravelSmart*, Dobbs Ferry, New York, *www.travelsmartnewsletter.com.*

Use *www.travelocity.com* to determine the "going rate" for a rental car in the area to which you will be traveling. Check the total price, including taxes and fees, and the gas tank policy. If traveling within the next week, check *www.lastminutetravel.com.* You might be able to get a larger car at the price you would pay for a compact. Using the prices you found on the previous sites, bid a lower price for a rental car at *www.priceline. com.* If your rental-car bid is accepted, your credit card will be charged immediately.

If you still can't find the deal you want, check *www.rentalcars.com,* which tracks deals on rental-car company Web sites. And, don't overlook individual rental agency Web sites. Most post last-minute specials that toll-free operators may not know about. Many rental-car companies also offer additional discounts to members of such groups as AAA or AARP as well as teachers, government employees and military personnel.

More Rental-Car Savings

If you are picking up and returning a rental car to the same location, bid for car rentals at *www.priceline.com* and *www.hotwire.com.* They only cover same-city rentals and may get you much lower rates than rental companies offer by phone or on-line.

Strategy: Find the best rate companies offer. Then start with a much lower bid for a full-size car. If it is not accepted, go down one size and up slightly on the bid...or try again 72 hours later, when these bidding sites allow rebids.

Jens Jurgen, Box 833, Amityville, New York 11701.

Keeping Your Home Safe While You Travel

Before you go away on a vacation...remove first-floor window air conditioners, and lock windows before leaving...consider installing security bars (with interior quick release, in case of fire), especially on ground-level windows that are not easily seen from the street, such as those in the basement or the back of

the house...and finally don't leave garage-door remotes in cars left at home in the driveway.

Jean O'Neil, director of research and evaluation for the National Crime Prevention Council, Arlington, VA, *www. ncpc.org.*

Safety Tips for Solo Travelers

Nadine Nardi Davidson, travel consultant, Travel Store, Inc., Los Angeles, and author of several books, including *Travel with Others Without Wishing They'd Stayed Home.* Prince.

Traveling alone can be adventurous and fun, but at the same time solo travelers need to take important safety precautions like the following...

●**Leave a copy of your itinerary with a friend** or relative back home, so you can be tracked down.

●**Read guidebooks and carry maps of the cities you plan to visit,** so you don't get completely lost.

●**Check in with the US consulate.** Ask about trouble spots.

●**Only stay in hotels or motels with interior hallways.** Take the same precautions in a foreign city that you take at home.

●**Don't walk down dark alleys** or in dimly lit streets at night.

●**Latch the chain-lock** when you're in your hotel room.

●**Don't wear expensive jewelry** or carry expensive luggage, particularly when in a Third World country.

●**Carry your money**—and passport—in a money belt or pouch that you wear under your clothes.

●**Take public transportation only in daylight,** so you can see where you're going and assess the area for safety.

When sightseeing, keep an eye on the time and make sure you have a safe way—a taxi, for instance—to get back to your hotel.

Spontaneous Savings—
Five Ways to Travel Cheap

Erik Torkells, editor, *Arthur Frommer's Budget Travel*, 530 Seventh Ave., New York City 10018, *www.budgettravel. msnbc.com.*

The Internet makes it easier than ever before to get last-minute travel bargains. Airlines and other travel firms now routinely offer their unsold inventory at a discount at the last minute on-line, while travel Web sites collect this information and make it available to consumers.

How to use the Internet to get the best deals...

•**Subscribe to free e-newsletters.** Many airlines and travel packagers announce sales to those who subscribe to their newsletters. And many travel Web sites collect bargain information and distribute it by e-mail to their subscribers.

•**Have Web sites watch for deals for you.** Travelocity.com will automatically send you e-mail notification when airfares in the price range you specify for the flights you want become available. Other sites, such as Orbitz. com, alert you to special prices.

•**Check airlines' Web sites.** The airlines' very best bargains often are offered only on their own sites.

•**Underbid on Priceline.** After finding the best travel bargain you can, bid 20% less to get the same thing through Priceline.com. You'll be surprised how often you succeed.

•**Target Saturday and mid-week trips.** Fewer people travel on these days, so flights are less full—and are more prone to being discounted.

Short Trip Tips

Best for booking short trips of three days or fewer are airline Web sites, which often post last-minute special deals...or a knowledgeable travel agent. Using bid-for-travel options at such sites as Priceline.com or Hotwire.com may mean inconvenient departure times and long layovers, which you don't find out about until you accept the offer. This could mean you leave late on the first day and return early on the third—effectively cutting a three-day trip to one day.

Jens Jurgen, Box 833, Amityville, New York 11701.

Broadway at Bargain Prices

Lower-cost seats for Broadway shows are available through specialty Web sites. BroadwayBox.com posts discount codes to dozens of shows and offers e-mail alerts when more shows become available. TheaterMania. com and HitShowClub.com offer free memberships and work directly with the shows themselves to offer reduced-price tickets. Entertainment-Link.com charges $39 for six months of access to reduced ticket prices and lists the specials at TKTS reduced-price ticket booths in Manhattan.

But: No discount site can be counted on for reduced-price tickets to major hit shows.

The Wall Street Journal.

Be Your Own Travel Agent

If you travel frequently, save money by becoming your own travel agent. You don't have to perform the traditional duties of a travel agent. Simply make travel arrangements—reservations for flights, car rentals, hotels, cruises, etc.—on-line through your own Web site linked to that of Global Travel International (GTI).

Cost: $49.95/month. You, your friends, family and business associates can book travel through that site.

Example: You are retired and travel frequently with friends, for whom you make travel arrangements through GTI. Through these referrals, you receive discounts, depending on volume. If you use the site only for personal travel, you still will be eligible for travel agent rates for more than 12,000 hotels and cruise and vacation packages.

Information: 800-951-5977, *www.global travel.com.*

Deep Discounts Through Charter Flights

Find charter flights on-line through companies that sell seats on charter planes—often at deep discounts if you buy within two weeks of departure. Try SunTrips (*www.sun trips.com*) and Vacation Express (*www.vaca tionexpress.com*). Destinations and departure dates are limited. Other charter Web sites allow bookings only by travel agents. For the widest choice of charter flights, you must use a travel agent—there is no central listing of charter departures on the Web.

Arthur Frommer's Budget Travel, 530 Seventh Ave., New York City 10018.

Save Hundreds on Round-Trip Airfares

Flying into and out of smaller secondary airports can shave hundreds of dollars off round-trip airfares.

Other benefits: Shorter security line waits, lower parking fees and probably closer proximity to your home.

Downside: You most likely will have to fly on discount airlines, which may have fewer flights and planes and may not be listed on big travel sites, such as Orbitz and Travelocity.

The Wall Street Journal.

Inside Information on Airfares and Upgrades

ExpertFlyer.com and FlyerTalk.com can give you information about airfares and upgrades. Using fare codes that explain restrictions, travelers can search for special offers, frequent-flier award seats and upgrades that do not appear on the popular travel sites Travelocity, Expedia and Orbitz. ExpertFlyer.com's premium service is offered for $9.99/month.* FlyerTalk.com is a travelers' message board that you can search to find code information. Flights can't be booked through these sites, but travelers can use the code information to get the best deals through other Web sites or travel agents.

The Wall Street Journal.

Incredible Deals on Unclaimed Baggage

The Unclaimed Baggage Center purchases luggage and packages that are left on airlines. Items are then sold at deep discounts on-line at *www.unclaimedbaggage.com* and at the

*All prices are subject to change.

store in Scottsboro, Alabama. The merchandise can include cameras, clothing, electronics, jewelry and sporting goods.

How to Be Your Own Tour Guide

Joan Rattner Heilman, an award-winning travel writer based in New York State. She is author of *Unbelievably Good Deals and Great Adventures That You Absolutely Can't Get Unless You're Over 50.* McGraw-Hill.

There is a good compromise between traveling on your own and going on a group tour with a bunch of total strangers— think about giving self-guided touring a try.

Long popular in Europe, you'll save a bundle of money and get a customized trip. You choose your own travel dates, itinerary, level of lodging and companions.

You move along at your own pace, by yourself or with friends or family, stopping wherever you please and getting a taste of the local culture. You follow a carefully planned route with advice on what to see and do along the way and the assurance of emergency support ready to help you out if you need it.

Nightly accommodations and, often, meals, are prearranged, so you don't have to be concerned about logistics. And—a major plus—on land trips, your luggage is transported to your next lodgings, getting there before you do. *Some of the best self-guided tours...*

WALKING COASTAL NORMANDY

Averaging eight to 10 miles of walking a day, this seven-night self-guided tour along the coast of Normandy starts out at Caen, the historic town that is home to the World War II Peace Memorial and a château that was built by William the Conqueror.

You make your way on foot along the coast, retracing the movements of troops during the invasion of Normandy and visiting all the key beachheads, batteries, bunkers and memorials, lodging in charming country inns or family-run hotels. Among other overnight stops in this rural region, you spend one night in Bayeux, the first French town liberated in 1944.

Your luggage goes on ahead. Daily breakfast and dinner are included, along with transfers, maps and a guidebook. Most of the terrain you cover is flat with a few short climbs. You can choose any departure date from May through September.

Cost: About $1,149* per person, double occupancy, not including airfare.

Information: Discover France, 800-960-2221, *www.discoverfrance.com.*

BIKING INN TO INN IN VERMONT

Spin your wheels at a leisurely pace around southern Vermont's rolling hills, charming villages, streams and lakes, arriving at a quaint country inn at the end of each day to spend the night, dinner and breakfast included.

You may customize the trip to suit yourself, choosing inns according to the distance you want to cover each day. One six-night itinerary with about 25 miles per day of easy to moderate biking begins in the arty village of Brandon and takes you around Lake Dunmore and into Middlebury.

Then, you explore the countryside as you ride into Vergennes, Vermont's smallest city, go south along Lake Champlain, pass through apple country and take the ferry from Larabee's Point for a visit to Fort Ticonderoga, then back to Brandon. Detailed route maps show you the way.

Cost: Varies according to room and season.

Information: Country Inns Along the Trail, 800-838-3301, *www.inntoinn.com.*

SAILING ON THE CHESAPEAKE BAY

Pick up your own 34-foot power catamaran in Annapolis, Maryland, and skipper it yourself—even if you are only a rookie boater—for a week on Chesapeake Bay's peaceful waters. You will get an introductory briefing, waterway guides with navigation maps and a captain's manual. Twenty-four-hour emergency assistance is just a phone call away.

Then, you're on your own to motor wherever you like along the Chesapeake's many miles of shoreline, harbors, rivers and coves. Stop at historic towns, eat meals aboard or in

*All prices are subject to change.

the local restaurants. You sleep on your boat, which will feature two double cabins, with a shared bath and shower, a living area and a fully equipped galley for cooking.

Cost: About $3,200* per week per boat plus fuel.

Information: Crown Blue Line at Sunsail, 888-350-3568, *www.sunsail.com.*

HIKING IN IRELAND

Enjoy this self-guided hike on Ireland's famous Dingle Way. A walking route follows old tracks, mountain trails and green roads, passing through villages and farmlands. You trek about 10 to 15 miles a day, following detailed route descriptions and maps.

Guesthouses along the way are already booked for you, your luggage is transferred and all you have to do is walk and enjoy the views. Your tour starts and finishes at the village of Camp on the north side of the Dingle Peninsula and takes you along minor country roads, assisted by yellow markers and road signs. If the weather is bad or you don't want to walk so many miles on a given day, you can take a van to your next inn for an additional charge.

Cost: Seven nights, $775; 9 nights, $905.

Information: Hidden Trails, 888-987-2457, *www.hiddentrails.com.*

CYCLING IN CALIFORNIA'S WINE COUNTRY

On this adventure, you pedal through towering redwoods, along winding rivers and past geysers, vineyards and wine chateaus in the famous Napa and Sonoma Valleys north of San Francisco.

Included are your accommodations, breakfasts, one dinner, luggage transfers, your bicycle and a ride back to your starting point at the trendy town of St. Helena. You cover an average of 30 miles (four to five hours) a day, with options for more mileage or rest days. Overnights include St. Helena…Calistoga, known for its thermal spas and mud baths…and Healdsburg, surrounded by vineyards.

Cost: About $2,200 for six days/five nights, depending on the level of accommodations and day of departure.

*All prices are subject to change.

Information: Randonnée Self-Guided Vacations, 800-242-1825, *www.randonneetours. com.*

BARGING ON THE ERIE CANAL

Navigate your own traditional European-style canal boat (with two to six passengers) through dozens of locks on upstate New York's historic Erie Canal. You get a quick course on skippering and needn't be an experienced boatperson, especially since you can't go any faster than about six mph.

Pass through the newly restored waterway, stopping anywhere you please along the route for the night, a meal, a bike ride, a hike or a visit to a historic town.

Each boat has sleeping cabins, a kitchen and bathrooms, plus a small outside deck. Choose from two departure locations, one near Syracuse and the other near Rochester. You're on your own for all meals, which can be cooked aboard or taken on shore.

Cost: $2,300* to $2,975 per week, depending on size of the boat. The price includes fuel and tolls.

Information: Mid-Lakes Navigation Co., 800-545-4318, *www.midlakesnav.com.*

DRIVING THROUGH THE CANADIAN ROCKIES

Hop into your rental car for a six-night driving tour that starts in Vancouver, British Columbia, and winds up in Calgary, Alberta. This self-guided tour will take you through some of the most breathtaking sights of western Canada and the Rocky Mountains.

After your first night on the waterfront in downtown Vancouver, you drive to the Lac le Jeune resort in Kamloops, stopping at Minter Gardens in Chilliwack. Ride the Hell's Gate airtram in the Fraser Canyon.

Then it's on to Jasper in the Rockies, where you get a Snocoach ride on the Columbia ice fields, followed by Lake Louise and Banff before driving to Calgary.

You may customize your trip yourself, choosing your own route, your own level of accommodations and the length of time on the road, with the costs adjusted accordingly.

*All prices are subject to change.

Cost: About $1,650* per person, but prices vary depending on the level of accommodations you choose.

Information: Canadian Mountain Experience, 888-867-5448, *www.canadianmountain.com.*

More from Joan Rattner Heilman...

Hit the Rails for an Amazing Vacation Close to Home

Take an upscale train trip and you can travel in style through the most spectacular scenery in North America. Lounging in a comfortable seat or eating a good meal in the dining car while watching the world go by is undoubtedly the most relaxing way to travel. *Here are some of the best train trips on this continent today...*

ROCKY MOUNTAINEER

The Rocky Mountaineer's famous two-day, all-daylight sightseeing rail journey takes you through the Canadian Rockies, providing stunning views of snow-covered mountain peaks, dense forests, canyons and glaciers. Its luxury GoldLeaf Service features a bilevel dome coach with an observation platform on the upper level and a dining lounge below. The less expensive RedLeaf Service carries passengers in coaches with huge picture windows.

With onboard commentary along the way, the train leaves from beautiful, cosmopolitan Vancouver on Canada's west coast and ends in Banff or Calgary in Alberta, stopping overnight at a hotel in Kamloops, British Columbia. A second route ends in Jasper, Alberta.

Your meals are included in the price. You eat breakfast and lunch onboard and dinner on land. The trip can be extended into multiday vacations with land stays and sightseeing in Victoria, Lake Louise and Jasper.

Cost: For the six-day trip—$2,059* to $2,969 per person, double occupancy, depending on the season, for GoldLeaf service. For RedLeaf service it is $1,459 to $2,129 per person, double occupancy, depending on season and level of overnight accommodations. Operates April

*All prices are subject to change.

through October, with the peak season in the warmer months.

Information: Rocky Mountaineer Vacations 888-867-5448, *www.rockymountaineer.com.*

COPPER CANYON, MEXICO

Located in Mexico's Sierra Madre Mountains, Copper Canyon is four times the size of the Grand Canyon and is one of North America's most thrilling sights. An excellent way to see it in all its glory is on this eight-day all-inclusive roundtrip adventure by Caravan Tours. You'll spend your nights in hotels along the way.

After one night in El Paso, Texas, you then go by motorcoach into Mexico to travel through rangeland, desert and apple country and stay the next night in the small lumber town Creel, the highest stop of the tour.

Here you board a private first-class railroad coach that winds past waterfalls, cliffs and tropical farmlands on your way to the colonial town of El Fuerte. There, you'll stay for two nights and go on a river float trip and a walking tour. The train continues its journey, passing through 86 tunnels, crossing 38 bridges and climbing almost 8,000 feet before reaching the village of Barrancas in the heart of Copper Canyon and where you'll check in to a picturesque lodge for the night.

The next day, you will travel back along the same route through the canyon, with a stop in Chihuahua before returning to El Paso.

Cost: $995* to $1,195 per person, double occupancy. Trips are scheduled year-round.

Information: Caravan Tours, 800-227-2826, *www.caravantours.com.*

THE SKEENA

Perhaps the least known of the great North American rail trips is aboard VIA Rail Canada's Skeena. The 725-mile, two-day daylight journey in the Canadian Northwest starts out at Jasper, Alberta, climbs the Rocky Mountains, rolls along the Skeena River valley and finally winds down to the Pacific, ending at Prince Rupert, British Columbia, a small city located on a deep fjord on the Inside Passage.

Totem Deluxe Class passengers have exclusive use of a vista-dome observation lounge car and meals (included in the cost) served at

*All prices are subject to change.

their seats. The economy-class passengers can watch the beautiful scenery through panoramic windows and purchase their meals onboard to eat at their seats.

The Skeena stops overnight in Prince George, where passengers lodge in accommodations of their choice (price not included, and you must make your own reservations), then set forth in the morning for Prince Rupert, a historic fishing and cannery town. The Skeena runs four times a week from May through October and may be taken in either direction.

Cost: Approximately $649* (US) per person in Totem Deluxe…from $293 (US) in Comfort.

Information: VIA Rail Canada, 888-842-7245, *www.viarail.ca.*

QUEBEC TO NOVA SCOTIA

VIA Rail Canada's Ocean Service travels overnight in either direction between Montreal and Halifax, some 800 miles to the east, stopping at Moncton along the way. The line made its inaugural run in 1904 and has been operating ever since then.

Departing from Montreal (or vice versa from Halifax), the train follows the south shore of the St. Lawrence River, crossing the province of New Brunswick. Halifax is the cosmopolitan capital city of Nova Scotia.

Dubbed "a rolling bed & breakfast," Easterly Class on the Ocean features double bedrooms, private washrooms, continental breakfast and big picture windows to watch the towns and rolling countryside go by. Lounge cars are available for cocktails and socializing, while the dining cars serve the traditional Canadian cuisine. Those who are planning a stay in Nova Scotia in June through October can connect with Via Rail's day-touring train between Sydney, located on Cape Breton Island, and Halifax.

Cost: For the basic overnight journey in peak season, June through October, from approximately $292* (US) per person, double occupancy. November through May, $161 (US).

Information: VIA Rail Canada, 888-842-7245, *www.viarail.ca.*

*All prices are subject to change.

Also from Joan Rattner Heilman…

Best Travel Companies for Folks 50+

Many travel companies cater to the fast-growing 50-plus crowd, travelers who gravitate toward tours with people their own age who have similar likes and cultural interests. They also desire comfortable quarters and unhurried itineraries.

Among the top companies that make it their business to give older travelers what they're looking for…

●**Elderhostel.** For people age 55 or older and their travel mates of any age. Elderhostel's affordable one- to four-week programs—which number in the thousands—are hosted by educational and cultural institutions in all 50 states and 90 countries. 800-454-5768, *www.elderhostel.org.*

Examples: Exploring desert culture in and around Palm Springs, California…or a cruise around Australia's Great Barrier Reef to Sydney and Melbourne.

●**50plus Expeditions** specializes in adventure travel all over the world, from visiting Ecuador's rain forests to cycling alongside the Danube in Austria. Small-group tours are escorted by local guides. 866-318-5050, *www.50plusexpeditions.com.*

●**Grand Circle Travel** offers international vacations exclusively for people age 50 or over. They include classic escorted tours…extended stays in such destinations as Costa del Sol and Sicily…European river cruises…and a variety of ocean cruises with land-based stays in ports of call. 800-959-0405, *www.gct.com.*

●**Overseas Adventure Travel** combines creature comforts and unique accommodations with unusual destinations that include Peru, Morocco and Botswana. These trips are rated from "easy" to "demanding." Groups are limited to 16 participants over age 50. 800-493-6824, *www.oattravel.com.*

●**Senior Tours Canada.** This is Canada's largest operator of fully escorted tours. It takes tourists age 50 and older on leisurely, "worry-free" vacations worldwide. The trips range from traditional tours to resort vacations and cruises. Destinations include Scotland and Northern

California as well as a cruise through the Panama Canal. 800-268-3492, *www.seniortours.ca.*

Best Time to Book a Seat

Best time to book most airline seats—around midnight eastern time any day of the week. That is when most airlines update availabilities. If you are looking for weekend specials, check airline sites late Thursday night or just after midnight. Most airlines release weekend specials late on Thursday night.

Assen Vassilev, cofounder and CEO, Lessno.com, a discount flight and hotel Web site.

Fill Up Before You Return Your Rental Car

Car-rental companies are charging as much as $8 a gallon to refill the gas tank if you don't do it yourself before returning the car. The biggest companies charge the most—but even smaller firms charge about $6 a gallon. Enterprise typically charges the least but still significantly more than prices at the pump.

Self-defense: Always refuel a rental car before returning it.

Survey of eight car-rental companies at 10 airports by *USA Today.*

On-Time Travel

To arrive on time, fly on a Saturday. That's the day on which flights are least likely to be late. Fridays are the worst days for late arrivals. Thursdays are second-worst.

Also helpful: Travel in September, the month with the best on-time record...always fly nonstop...consider nearby alternative airports instead of larger, busier ones.

Condé Nast Traveler, 4 Times Square, New York City 10036.

Relax When You Travel

Day spas at airports can make travel a little more relaxing—offering facials, full-body hot-stone massages and other services.

Examples: D-parture Spa at Newark and Orlando airports has a "Weary Traveler" treatment that includes a pedicure, 10-minute foot rub and (based on availability) napping privileges. Oasis Day Spa at Terminal 6 of JFK Airport in New York has a 15-minute "Jet Set Facial" that includes gentle cleansing and hydration. XpresSpa in San Francisco, Pittsburgh, JFK and Philadelphia offers a "Stress and Tension Eliminator" with head, face, neck and shoulder massage.

Cooking Light, Box 1748, Birmingham, Alabama 35201.

How to Pick A Reliable Tour Company

Nancy Dunnan, editor and publisher of *TravelSmart,* Dobbs Ferry, New York, *www.travelsmartnewsletter.com.*

No matter where you choose to go, there are three steps you can take to safeguard your travel dollars...

● **You get protection against a travel company's failure if the company is a member of the US Tour Operators Association.** These firms must post a $1 million bond to be used solely for reimbursing consumers in case of loss due to bankruptcy or failure to refund deposits within 120 days of a trip cancellation. For a members list, call 212-599-6599 or visit *www. ustoa.com.* (The Association also has several free brochures on travel planning and safety.)

● **Check with a travel agent.** Agents who have been in business for a number of years are familiar with the reliable and not-so-reliable tour operators. Keep in mind, however, that not all tour companies work with agents.

● **Don't book your trip on-line** unless the company has an old-fashioned postal address, will send written literature that you can study and evaluate, and informs you in writing of its refund policy.

More from Nancy Dunnan...

Five Wonderful Travel Web Sites

For great travel bargains and helpful information, check out these Web sites...

●*www.seatguru.com* maps the best and worst seats, by type of jet, on 27 US and international air carriers.

●*www.icruise.com* offers low cruise prices and live Webcams on ships to show you what facilities look like.

●*www.farealert.net* will track down pricing errors, including mistyped flight or hotel rates, and e-mail them to subscribers.

●*www.travelzoo.com* posts deeply discounted resort and spa stays in the "Lodging Specials" section. Discounts change regularly and are for stays within the next few weeks.

●*www.luxurylink.com* sells discount resort vacations.

How to Get the Lowest Travel Rates On-Line

Jens Jurgen, Box 833, Amityville, New York 11701.

The travel Web site that offers the lowest fares on a particular route varies from day to day—sometimes from hour to hour.

To get the best deal: Check prices at the major sites—*www.expedia.com, www.orbitz. com* and *www.travelocity.com*—and the sites of individual airlines, especially low-fare carriers, such as JetBlue or Southwest or, for intra-Europe flights only, Ryanair.com. PC users can access SideStep (*www.sidestep.com*), a free software-based search engine that gathers information about low airfares and hotel and car-rental rates from hundreds of Web sites.

Other options: Bid for tickets, hotel rooms and car rentals at *www.priceline.com*...search

for low fares at *www.hotwire.com*. These sites provide exact itineraries or hotel names only after your price is accepted, and travelers don't earn frequent-flier mileage.

Important: Always compare total prices—including taxes and all fees. Most independent travel sites also charge a $5 to $6 booking fee.

Newest site: Travelaxe.com, which is similar to Sidestep.com. It searches multiple hotel-booking sites simultaneously.

Favorite Money-Saving Travel Web Sites

Pauline Frommer, executive editor on-line for *Arthur Frommer's Budget Travel*, New York City. Her column titled "The Savings Sleuth" has appeared on the MSNBC Web site at *www.msnbc.msn.com*.

Use these helpful search engines to scour the Internet for the best travel bargains available...

●**Mobissimo Travel Search.** This new service looks beyond US Web sites and searches the world for great deals. *www.mobissimo.com*.

●**Cheapflights.** Compare flight schedules and prices. *www.cheapflights.com*.

●**Kayak.com.** This easy-to-use site is from the cofounders of Orbitz, Travelocity and Expedia. It searches more than 60 travel sites for great deals.

For cruise seekers: Dealing with a cruise discounter rather than a cruise line directly can get you 25% to 50% off the price. Offerings vary, so check with several discounters. *Favorites...*

●**CruiseCompete,** 800-797-4635 or *www. cruisecompete.com*.

●**CruisesOnly,** 800-278-4737 or *www.cruises only.com*.

●**GalaxSea Cruises of San Diego,** 800-923-7245 or *www.galaxsea.com*.

Save Up to 75% More on Hotel Rooms

First research hotel room rates and deals at travel sites, such as *www.orbitz.com…www. travelocity.com…www.travelweb.com…www. hotwire.com…*and *www.hotels.com.* Also check with the hotel directly, then bid for a room at *www.priceline.com.* You often can get a room for 30% to 75% less than the lowest price at other sites, especially for late bookings.

Helpful: Access *www.biddingfortravel.com* before making a bid. Successful bidders post their results at this site—giving you guidelines for your bids.

Jens Jurgen, Box 833, Amityville, New York 11701.

Ten Secrets That Hotels Don't Want You to Know

Peter Greenberg, travel editor for NBC's *Today* show as well as chief correspondent with the Discovery network's Travel Channel. He is also author of *Hotel Secrets from the Travel Detective.* Random House. *www.peter greenberg.com.*

You want a hotel to be your home away from home, but many aspects of hotel pricing and policy are really anything but homey. *Here's what you need to know…*

GETTING A ROOM

•**You can get the best rate by calling the hotel's local number,** not the 800 number, which usually links callers to an off-site centralized call center. Instead of asking for the reservations desk, ask to speak with the manager on duty, the general manager or the director of sales. These people have the authority to negotiate room rates.

It's often possible to beat a hotel's best advertised price by 20%, particularly if you call just a few days before your visit. First, shop around for the best deal on a third-party Internet travel site, such as Expedia.com or Hotels. com. Don't take the deal—just jot it down.

Then call the hotel and explain to a manager or director that you know these Web sites mark up room prices by 20% to 40%. Tell the manager you would like to split the difference—say you'll pay 20% below the price you found on-line. Unless the hotel is filled to capacity, the manager is likely to take you up on your offer.

•**Everything is negotiable.** Think parking is overpriced? If the lot looks half empty, offer less than the daily rate. Planning to make a lot of phone calls? Some hotels offer a per-day flat fee for long-distance in the US and local calling —usually about $9.95—but you must ask for it.

•**Rooms are available even when a hotel has no vacancies.** In any large hotel, a few rooms usually are listed as "out of order" at any given time. The problem might be something as simple as a stain on the carpet or a chair that has been sent out for repairs. If you're desperate for a last-minute room in a hotel that claims to have none available, tell the manager you are willing to take an out-of-order room that has only a minor problem. You might even be able to negotiate a better rate, since the room would otherwise sit empty.

•**"Guaranteed" rooms really aren't guaranteed.** When you make a hotel reservation, you often are asked to "guarantee" your room with a credit card—but there's still a chance that the hotel will give away your room if you arrive late. Providing a credit card number improves the odds that your room will be held—but it still pays to call to confirm that you're coming if you won't arrive until after 9 pm.

SAFEGUARDING VALUABLES

•**A thief takes one credit card,** not your entire wallet. It's no secret that crime is common in hotels. The new twist is that some hotel thieves now take just one credit card when they find an unguarded wallet in a room—and leave everything else untouched. Frequently, a victim doesn't notice the card is missing until the credit line is maxed out.

Travel only with the credit cards that you really need, and check your wallet carefully if you accidentally leave it unattended.

•**Your bags aren't safe with the bellhop.** Even in elite hotels, luggage can be stolen right off the luggage carts in the lobby. Though these bags theoretically are in the possession of the bellhop, the hotel assumes no legal responsibility for the loss.

If your bag is going to sit for more than a few minutes, ask that it be placed in a secure room. Keep valuable items in the hotel safe.

Helpful: High-end luggage might impress fellow travelers, but it also impresses thieves. The cheaper or uglier your luggage looks, the greater the odds that a thief will target someone else.

●**It pays to tip the housekeeper every day.** Exchange a few pleasant words with the housekeeper if you see him/her—and leave a $2 or $3 tip each day. You'll receive better service—housekeepers are the most overworked, underpaid and underappreciated people in the hotel, so any gesture will be appreciated.

Knowing the housekeeper also reduces the chances that your room will be burglarized. Dishonest housekeepers are less likely to target guests they have met. If a burglar enters your room while it is being cleaned and pretends to be you—a common ruse—the housekeeper will be able to spot the impostor.

MORE INSIDER SECRETS

●**Hotel rooms are infested with germs.** Certain items in hotel rooms never get cleaned. The biggest trouble spots include the TV remote control, telephone and clock/radio. Travel with a package of antibacterial wipes, and be sure to clean these items when you arrive.

Also, while reputable hotels provide fresh linens, bedspreads might be cleaned only once every few months. Remove them from the beds as soon as you check in. Ask for clean blankets as soon as you arrive.

●**Lost-and-found is a great resource for cell-phone users.** If you have a cell phone, odds are that someday you'll forget to bring your recharging cord or lose it in transit. If you're staying at a hotel, there's no need to buy a replacement. Recharging cords are the number-one item left behind in hotel rooms. Most hotels are willing to lend cords from their lost-and-found—but guests rarely ask.

●**Not all concierges are really concierges.** A true concierge is the most connected person around town. He can obtain tickets to sold-out events…reservations to popular restaurants…

prescriptions filled in the middle of the night… even a new heel on a shoe by 8 am. (A tip of $10 to $20 usually is appropriate—more if the concierge really worked miracles.) But not all hotels that advertise "concierge service" truly provide it. Many simply assign a regular hotel employee the role each shift.

An elite concierge wears a gold key on his lapel. It's the emblem of Les Clefs d'Or— French emblem for "Keys of Gold"—a prestigious international concierge organization.

More from Peter Greenberg…

The Registered Traveler

The Registered Traveler program is not the best way to avoid airport hassles, warns travel expert Peter Greenberg. The government's program, which costs about $100 annually, is intended to speed prescreened travelers through airport security. However, it is up and running at only about 20 airports. Also, while the lines for registered travelers might be shorter than the regular security lines, registered travelers still may be subject to thorough searches.

More reliable ways to avoid airport hassles: Print out boarding passes beforehand, and take only carry-on luggage.

Best-Rate Guarantee From Hotels

Hotel chains are offering best-rate guarantees when you reserve rooms on their Web sites. If you find the same room for a better rate on another site within 24 hours, the chain may offer you an additional 10% off the lowest rate or even a free night's stay. Rules vary by hotel chain, and are subject to change.

Participating hotels: Clarion, Comfort Inn, Courtyard, Crowne Plaza, Days Inn, Doubletree, Econo Lodge, Fairfield Inn, Hilton, Holiday Inn, Hyatt, Marriott, Ramada, Sheraton, Super 8 Motels, Westin and Wyndham.

USA Today, 7950 Jones Branch Dr., McClean, Virginia 22108.

For a More Comfortable Hotel Stay...

When registering for a hotel room, ask for something specific, such as a room with a view or one closer to the elevator, etc. This eliminates the chance that you will get stuck with an undesirable room. If you have stayed at the hotel previously, mention that when you check in. Also, never settle for an unacceptable room—instead, call the front desk and ask for a reassignment.

If you are planning to stay a week or more, write to the hotel manager personally at least one week ahead of time and ask for a "space-available" upgrade, a price break or extras, such as restaurant credits, free shoe shines or free high-speed Internet access. And, at check-in, ask to meet the manager to say hello.

Chris McGinnis, travel correspondent for CNN Headline News in Atlanta, and author of *The Unofficial Business Traveler's Pocket Guide*. McGraw-Hill.

To Keep Jewelry Safe While Traveling

Pack it in your carry-on bag, not in checked luggage. Airlines are not responsible for loss or theft of jewelry. Use containers that fasten tightly—a purse-sized organizer or plastic bags that zip closed. Never put jewelry in plastic bins that go through security. Put it in a purse or briefcase and close it. In hotels, the front-desk safe is the most secure place. If a safe is not available at the front desk, hide jewelry in a bag, inside another bag, hanging inside a dress or in a suit pocket. Write down your hiding place, and keep the notation with you. Do not use the in-room safe, and do not leave valuables visible in your room. Never take anything on a trip that cannot be replaced. Leave antiques and family heirlooms at home.

Susan Eisen, certified gemologist and jewelry appraiser in El Paso, Texas, and author of *Crazy About Jewelry! The Expert Guide to Buying, Selling and Caring for Your Jewelry*. Full Circle International.

Safest Floors in Any Hotel

The safest floors to stay on in a hotel are the third through sixth. Burglars most often target rooms on the first and second floors due to ease of entry and exit (through windows, doors to patios and pools, etc.). You are also better off on these floors in case of fire. Above the sixth floor you'll have a long walk down and firefighting equipment may have a hard time getting up.

John Fannin, founder, SafePlace Corp., 2 Righter Parkway, Wilmington, Delaware 19803, *www.safeplace.com.*

Find Great Travel Bargains On-Line in Five Simple Steps

Sandy Berger, author of *Sandy Berger's Great Age Guide to On-line Travel*. Que. She is president of Pinehurst, North Carolina–based Computer Living Corp., a computer consulting company, and has been a guest on hundreds of radio and TV shows. Her Web site, Compu-KISS, provides tutorials and lifestyle technology information for baby boomers and seniors, *www.compu-kiss.com.*

Shopping on-line for airline tickets, hotel rooms and rental cars could save you hundreds of dollars on your next vacation. The challenge is knowing where to find the best deals. Dozens of new travel Web sites appear each year, all of them claiming to offer big savings, but no one has time to try them all. *Here's the smart way to find on-line travel bargains...*

Step 1: Go to the source.

The special bargain prices offered directly by airlines, hotel chains and car rental chains on their company Web sites often are lower than the prices available through third-party travel sites.

Type the name of an airline, hotel chain or car rental company into a search engine to locate its Web site, then look for a tab labeled "Special Fares," "Special Deals," "Special Offers" or something similar. Most of these sites also let you sign up for E-mail notification of future bargain rates, which is a great way to keep posted on travel deals.

Example: On Continental Airlines' Web site, click "Deals & Offers," then click "continental.com Specials" for last-minute bargain fares, or "Special Offers" for ongoing promotional rates. (Continental is particularly likely to offer bargain fares to or from Houston, Cleveland and Newark, New Jersey, where the airline operates hubs.)

Such special deals are most appropriate for travelers who can be flexible about when and where they go, not those who need to reach a specific destination on a specific date.

If you do not have time to check every major airline or hotel chain site, at least check the sites of the airlines that have the most flights out of your local airport and the large hotel chains that you like the most. Note: Try the same kind of search on car rental sites.

Cruise lines also feature attractive last-minute deals on their Web sites in the weeks prior to departure. Before accepting one of these deals, however, consider that unless you live in or near the cruise's city of departure, you will have to buy airline tickets as well. If last-minute airfare to the cruise's departure port (and back from its destination port) is expensive, your last-minute cruise bargain might not be so cheap after all.

Step 2: Try the "big three" Internet travel services.

Expedia.com, Orbitz.com and Travelocity. com are the largest, most comprehensive travel Web sites. (While not one of the top three, Kayak.com, which searches multiple other travel sites, is worth trying, too.) You can use these sites to search for the best rates on a specific travel itinerary or scan their lists of last-minute specials. Though these sites are very similar in many ways, it is worth trying all of them. They frequently turn up different rates and different deals for the same itinerary.

Expedia, Orbitz and Travelocity tend to offer their very best deals less than one week in advance of the travel date—but only if airlines, hotels and rental car companies happen to have excess inventory. When demand is strong, last-minute prices can be extremely high. If you have a specific destination and date of travel in mind, it is best to search these sites two months or more in advance. During holidays: If you can be flexible, you might be able to snap up last-minute bargains by looking just before the date you hope to leave. Otherwise, shop far in advance.

Consider searching these sites for package deals that bundle airfare, hotel and rental car—or two of the three—together. Expedia, Orbitz and Travelocity sometimes offer very attractive deals to those who buy two or three of these things at once, particularly when they are traveling to a popular vacation destination such as Orlando, Las Vegas or San Francisco. (Also search for airfare, hotel and rental car individually, to make sure that the package really is a good deal.)

Note: The prices quoted by travel Web sites can change rapidly. If one rate is substantially better than any other rate that you have found, wrap up your rate comparison quickly and take the deal before it disappears.

Step 3: Search bargain-hunter travel site Hotwire.com if you are planning a last-minute trip.

Hotwire works with airlines, hotels, automobile rental agencies and cruise lines to sell remaining inventory in the week or two before the travel date. Markdowns of 50% or more are common.

Example: The site sometimes offers rental cars for less than $10 per day.

Other bargain-hunter travel sites worth a look include Cheapflights.com and LastMinute Travel.com.

Step 4: Vet your hotel on-line.

Hotel "bargains" are not truly bargains if the hotel is not a nice place to stay. Unfortunately, it sometimes is difficult to judge the quality of a hotel before you arrive. Ratings found in printed travel guides are often inaccurate or out of date.

Solution: Visit Web sites TripAdvisor.com and VirtualTourist.com to read hotel reviews from other travelers before reserving a room on-line.

Do not let just one or two extremely positive or negative reviews sway you excessively—these reviews might have been posted by a biased source, such as the hotel's management or a disgruntled ex-employee. Pay most attention to the latest reviews, because older reviews could include out-of-date information.

Step 5: See if Priceline.com can beat the best deal that you have located.

Priceline.com lets users make an offer, then either accepts or rejects their bids.

Once you have located the best price that you can find on airline tickets or a rental car from the Web sites mentioned above, bid perhaps 20% less on Priceline.com. If your bid is rejected, accept the best offer that you have found elsewhere.

Helpful: The Web site BidonTravel.com offers more strategies for smart Priceline bidding.

Priceline.com is best used for airline tickets and rental cars, not hotel rooms. The Web site does not tell you which company is accepting your bid until after you have completed the transaction. That usually is not a problem with airline tickets and car rentals—it doesn't make much difference whether Hertz or Avis rents you a car—but it can make a big difference with hotel rooms. When you bid on a hotel stay at Priceline, you gamble that the hotel that accepts your offer is somewhere that you would want to stay—not a worthwhile gamble, in my view.

Note: You have limited control over what you get. For example, you can't choose flight times, and while you can choose the size of a rental car, you can't choose the model.

CLOSING THE DEAL

Use a credit card to pay travel Web sites. Credit cards provide a measure of consumer protection that debit cards and other forms of payment do not—if unexpected fees or charges are tacked on to your bill, you can contest them through the card issuer.

How to Complain To the Airlines

Peter Greenberg, known as the "Travel Detective," is travel editor for NBC's *Today* show and editor of the travel Web site PeterGreenberg.com. His latest book is *The Complete Travel Detective Bible*. Rodale.

Your flight was canceled…the airline lost your luggage…or you got hit with an undisclosed extra fee.

Complaints about airlines have risen to record levels—most airlines receive hundreds of complaint letters every day.

As a travel writer who travels more than 400,000 air miles a year, I have learned what works and what doesn't when it comes to getting airline complaints resolved.

HOW TO INCREASE YOUR ODDS…

●**Be your own devil's advocate.** Ask yourself whether your complaint is justified. Did you really arrive at the airport in sufficient time to make your plane and check your bags? Was your plane delayed because of airline incompetence…or weather, over which the airline had no control? Did the airline really fail to disclose important information to you…or did you simply fail to read all the fare rules ahead of time? If you can't honestly say that your complaint is justified, don't waste your time complaining.

●**Deal with the situation quickly.** As soon as a problem occurs, seek out the airline official with the highest seniority at your location. My never-fail rule: Never take a "no" from someone who is not empowered to give you a "yes." Always ask to speak to the supervisor. When you speak with him/her, calmly explain your problem and ask for his help in solving it.

●**Write a letter.** If talking with a supervisor fails to get you an immediate solution to your problem, then it's letter-writing time. Send your letter certified mail, return receipt requested, to the chairman of the airline.

Always send a copy to the Consumer Affairs Office at Aviation Consumer Protection Division, C-75, US Department of Transportation, 1200 New Jersey Ave. SE, Washington, DC 20590.

●**Be a good reporter.** Writing a letter that simply expresses your displeasure with an airline or an individual incident isn't enough. It's the details that you include that often can make the difference. Include specific dates, flight numbers and times. It's also important to get first and last names of the airline representatives with whom you interacted and, if appropriate, the names of any witnesses. Keep the letter short, and stick to the facts.

●**Be nice.** Let the airline know that you intend to fly on its planes again and that you hope things will be better next time. If you're a frequent-flier, be sure to include your account number—it stands to reason that the more you fly a particular airline, the more the airline wants to keep you happy.

●**Never say the word "never."** Threatening never to fly the airline again sends the message to that airline that it has already lost you as a customer, therefore it has no incentive to be nice to you.

●**Don't send originals.** Send photo-copies, but make sure that you send everything that has a bearing on your complaint—boarding passes, ticket receipts, purchase receipts for lost items and, where appropriate, photos.

●**Understand the rules.** For example, if an airline lost your bag, you can't claim damages for lost jewelry, furs and negotiable financial documents (or cash). Each airline has a specific list of excluded items. If the airline lost your bag for more than 24 hours, there's a reasonable expectation (if you're not at your home airport) that you would need to buy some replacement clothes. But purchasing a $2,000 designer suit as "replacement" clothing won't get you a reimbursement check for that amount from the airlines. Keep in mind that airlines have limited liability and compensate for lost items in luggage at their depreciated value, not what it would cost to buy them new.

●**Ask for what you want—but be realistic.** If your plane was delayed, that probably doesn't qualify you for a first- class seat to Hong Kong.

●**Don't be surprised if the airline doesn't send you a check,** but instead offers you vouchers for your "inconvenience," usually dollar-value coupons that are good for discounts on a future flight on that airline. Read these vouchers carefully. Many have restrictions and expiration dates.

●**Write again.** If you don't hear back after three weeks or you get a form letter that doesn't address your complaint, write to the chairman again—and again copy the Department of Transportation. As before, enclose copies of your tickets, boarding passes and any other written or photographic evidence you have to support your claim.

Last resort: Go to small-claims court. This is a lot easier than it might seem. You don't need to hire a lawyer, and many states have increased the claim limits for filing cases in small-claims court (some states have increased the limit to $10,000 or more). Keep in mind that an airline ticket is a contract for service and that your argument probably will need to center around the airline's failure to live up to that contract.

Smart Travel Preparation

Before going on a trip, prepare medical histories for yourself and everyone traveling with you. Keep one copy with your passport and other valuable documents...one in your suitcase...and one at home in a place where it can be easily located. Include doctors' names and their contact information...health insurance information, including policy numbers and the 24-hour contact numbers...type of blood...any chronic health conditions...all known allergies to foods and medicines...eyeglass prescriptions ...and the name of a family member or close friend to contact in an emergency.

Susan Foster, packing expert, Portland, Oregon, and author of *Smart Packing for Today's Traveler*. Smart Travel.

Get Paid to Travel

Cruise ship lines hire numerous seniors and retirees as photographers, casino staff, doctors, nurses, counselors, exercise trainers and more. Accommodations are austere compared with those of paying passengers—but you get paid to travel and meet people from all around the world.

Useful: To learn more and/or file a job application on-line, visit *www.cruiseshipjob.com*, the Web site of the New World Cruise Ship Employment Agency.

7

Spare Time Money Savers

Professional Bargain Hunter's Favorite Freebies, Bargains And Discounts

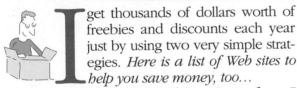

I get thousands of dollars worth of freebies and discounts each year just by using two very simple strategies. *Here is a list of Web sites to help you save money, too...*

●**I always ask about bargains when I shop.** Few are actively advertised.

●**I visit "freebie" Web sites weekly...**

●*www.thefreesite.com*
●*www.mycoupons.com*

EXPERT ADVICE

●**Free medication information** on proper drug use, side effects, precautions and more from the American Society of Health-System Pharmacists. *www.safemedication.com*

●**Expert advice on anything.** Hundreds of topics and experts to answer any question. *www.askanexpert.com*

TRAVEL

●**Use frequent-flier miles** in addition to cash to buy merchandise on-line from major sellers, such as Amazon...KB Toys...The Sharper Image...Lands' End...etc. *www.points.com.*

●**Free golf.** Free greens fees...or up to 50% off at 3,400 golf courses in North America by joining Golf Card International.

Membership: $65/year. 800-321-8269...*www.golfcard.com*

●**Bargain cruises.** Book a week before a cruise sails, and save up to 75% off list prices. Last Minute Travel, 800-442-0568, *www.lastminutetravel.com*...Moment's Notice Travel, 888-241-3366, *www.moments-notice.com*

●**Free international accommodations.** If you like to travel and meet people from different countries and cultures, this organization, founded by a group of world travelers,

Linda Bowman, Tucson–based professional bargain hunter. She is author of several books, including *Free Stuff & Good Deals for Folks Over 50, Free Stuff & Good Deals for Your Pet* and *Free Stuff & Good Deals on the Internet.* Santa Monica Press.

131

provides addresses of people who are offering free accommodations if you agree to host another traveler. *www.stay4free.com*

●**Save on admission to national parks.** Annual Passes are sold at any National Park entrance area…888-GO-PARKS (467-2757)… *www.nationalparks.org*

Cost: $80/year for unlimited entry to parks and sites.

KIDS

●**Blogs and photos of favorite baseball players.** Plus Fan Forum to discuss baseball issues…e-mail players…check team Web sites for schedules and player information, etc. *www.mlb.com*

●**On-line arcade games.** *www.freearcade. com*

●**Arts and crafts,** activities, puzzles, games and card designs for kids. *www.crayola.com*

●**Back-to-school projects.** Decorative switch plate cover…spirally snake…cardboard castle and more. *www.elmers.com*

●**Homework help.** School librarians offer free on-line research tips to students in kindergarten through high school. American Library Association, *www.ala.org*, search for "Homework help."

HELP FOR SENIORS

●**Free or low-cost legal advice.** Provided by nonprofit legal services programs, questions are answered for people over age 60. Some organizations also provide free services, such as reviewing documents that you fax to them. *www.seniorlaw.com*

●**Fast-food discounts.** Arby's, Denny's, Pizza Hut, Sizzler and other chains offer discounts at participating franchises to seniors (age varies according to chain).

Typical: 10% to 20% off the price of a meal plus a free beverage or a reduced-price senior menu.

●**Expert advice for seniors on health and lifestyle issues,** discussion forums, special offers, freebies and more. Contact *www. seniorsite.com* for advice on caregiving for seniors, Medicare, retirement, health, relationships, travel, etc.

●**Bus, train and rental car discounts.** Greyhound Line's discount for travelers age 65 and older gives members 5% off passenger tickets. 800-231-2222…*www.greyhound. com*. Amtrak offers a 15% discount for travelers age 62 and older. 800-USA-RAIL (872-7245)… *www.amtrak.com*. Alamo knocks about 15% (amount varies according to location) off car rentals for AARP drivers age 55 and older. 800-GO-ALAMO (462-5266)…*www.alamo.com*

●**Free or low-cost college courses.** Seniors can audit classes at scores of US educational institutions. Inquire at local universities. *Examples…*

●Boston University. $80 per course for students age 58 and older. 617-353-9852…*www. bu.edu/evergreen*

●University of Illinois. $15 per course. 217-333-1462 or 877-455-2687…*www.continuinged. uiuc.edu*

●University of North Carolina. Courses are $20. 919-962-3000…*www.fridaycenter.unc.edu*

PETS

●**Farm animals (goats, sheep, hens).** Farm Sanctuary, 607-583-2225 (East Coast) or 530-865-4617 (West Coast)…*www.farmsanctuary.org*

●**Discounted pet products.** Free coupons available at *www.couponsurfer.com* (click on "Pet Food & Supplies").

●**Free dog food.** Get three cans of pet food with purchase of Regal Dog Food, and other gifts when you join the Very Important Pet Club…as well as special incentives with each purchase. Regal Pet Foods, 800-638-7006… *www.regalpetfoods.com*

●**Free classified ads for pets of all types,** *www.pet-expo.com*. Free classified ads for those buying or selling a horse, *www.thehorsemarket.com*

How to Get Top Dollar for Your Collectibles

The late Ralph and Terry Kovel, Cleveland-based authors of 90 books on antiques, including *Kovels' Antiques and Collectibles Price List 2008*. Random House Reference.

The prices you'll receive for collectibles depend on what, where and how you sell. The more you know about the value of what you're selling, the more successful you'll be.

VALUING THE UNKNOWN

If you come into collectibles, say by inheritance, *never* throw anything out before finding out what it's worth. We've heard countless stories of people jettisoning stacks of magazines from the 1930s and 1940s or old costume jewelry in the belief that they couldn't be worth much. They find out later that the items were worth hundreds of dollars or more.

To learn the value of a collectible, ask a knowledgeable friend who collects what you have. Or use general on-line price guides—such as *www.kovels.com*, which lists prices for more than 450,000 collectibles and antiques. Also look for specialized price guides at your local library for specific collectibles, such as Lladró, Hummel and Walt Disney ("Disneyana").

Collectors clubs and forums also allow you to see information about prices. The portal to these on-line sites is *www.collectorsresources.com.*

Note on appraisals: We don't generally recommend using a professional appraiser. They're costly—as high as $350 per hour—and a houseful of Grandma's things could take days to go through. Besides, 90% of the items are probably worth less than $100.

But, if you suspect that you have something valuable, it may be worth the cost. Contact the International Society of Appraisers (*www.isa appraisers.org* or 312-224-2567) or the American Society of Appraisers (*www.appraisers.org* or 800-272-8258).

WHERE TO SELL

- **Garage or lawn sale.** Withhold items with higher values that can fetch more at auction. Price the rest to sell quickly. This is the best way to go if you have little time and lots of cheap stuff to sell.

- **Home sale.** If you're disposing of the contents of a home, use the house itself to sell the furnishings.

- **Antiques stores.** Dealers may buy your lot in total. But expect to receive no more than 50% of the listed value. Only if a piece is in mint condition and exceptional will they pay slightly more.

- **Consignment shops.** You collect what's received, minus the commission that is charged by the shop. Get a receipt with a description that includes any blemishes for every item you consign so you can keep track of what's sold and reclaim unsold items.

- **Auction houses.** Valuable items—$10,000 and up—often fetch the best prices through live auctions. Call a local auctioneer, or send photos and details, such as measurements, to major auction houses.

Examples: Sotheby's (*www.sothebys.com* or 541-312-5682) or Christie's (*www.christies. com* or 212-492-5485). Both have dozens of specialist departments running the gamut from ancient art to watches. International auction houses such as these will find the right venue for your collectible—for instance, a silver sale in London or a rare book sale in Amsterdam.

Important: Get a copy of the auctioneer's business terms so that you'll know what commissions and fees you'll have to pay if your item is sold. Also set a reserve (the minimum price you're willing to accept) on each piece.

- **Internet auctions.** There are two kinds of Internet auctions. In one, you sell items yourself at a site that just provides a place for you to list them. The heavyweights for this kind of auction are eBay (*www.ebay.com*) and Amazon.com Auctions (*www.auctions.amazon. com*). Where a live auction may attract several hundred potential buyers, on-line sites draw thousands. All sites make you register and pay both a listing fee and a selling fee on successful auctions.

Note: Only about 30% or less of the items listed actually sell.

Alternative: Internet auction sites that function the same as large auction houses at an actual physical location—they even have catalogs available ahead of the auction date. Bidding may take place just on the Internet, or on the Internet at the same time as people bid at a physical location. These auction sites are good for certain collectibles, such as sports memorabilia, stamps, coins and toys. Go to *www.vendio.com* to find sites that specialize in your collectibles category. There are additional specialized sites, such as *www.mastronet.com*, for sports memorabilia, and *www.bertoiaauctions.com*, for toys and dolls.

●**Collectibles magazines.** You can place an ad in specialized magazines and antiques newspapers. This is a low-cost way to sell your collectibles and, hopefully, get top dollar—you're marketing directly to interested buyers. Make your ad short and to the point. Be sure that it honestly represents the item.

Examples: Antique Trader (*www.antique trader.com* or 888-457-2873) has national coverage and lists shows…Maine Antique Digest (*www.maineantiquedigest.com* or 877-237-6623) gives a lot of interesting gossipy detail… and AntiqueWeek (*www.antiqueweek.com* or 800-876-5133) reports on what has happened and what's ahead.

Important: Receive payment before you ship. Shipping is your responsibility. Insure your item when you ship it. United Parcel Service (UPS) offers some insurance, but you may need more.

Note: When insuring through the postal service, we have found that it's difficult to collect from them if something happens to the package.

●**Internet classifieds.** Like collectibles magazines and newspapers, this venue lets you list for free or a small charge. TIAS.com (*www.tias.com*), an on-line antique mall with more than 1,000 dealers, has 275,000 readers of its on-line collectibles newsletter.

●**Swap shows.** Rent a table at your local collectibles "trade and swap" show—you'll find listings in your local newspaper, on the Internet or through your chamber of commerce. This venue requires some time and preparation, but you can make lasting contacts with dealers and collectors. Price everything before you set up.

Important: Know the lowest you'll go on each item.

SHARE WITH UNCLE SAM

Don't ignore income tax on collectibles. As long as you've held an item for more than one year (or inherited it), gain is taxed at up to 28%. Collectibles gains don't qualify for the 15% capital gains rate.

Strategy: If you inherit something you plan to sell, do so sooner rather than later. (Your basis for figuring gain is its value at the time of the person's death.) If the value declines, you'll have a loss that you can't deduct. There's no loss allowed for tax purposes on the sale of personal items.

Smart Fund-Raisers For Your Club, Society Or Church

Andy Robinson, fund-raising consultant in Plainfield, Vermont, and author of *Selling Social Change (Without Selling Out)*. Wiley & Sons.

Scott Pansky, partner, Allison & Partners, Los Angeles–based marketing firm that works with nonprofits.

Valerie Reuther, Coupeville, Washington–based trainer of professional fund-raisers.

Fund-raising has become very difficult in recent years. Here are four offbeat-but-effective techniques that may work for your next fund-raiser.

FROM ANDY ROBINSON

●**Send invitations to an event that isn't going to happen.** Explain that there will be no dull speeches, rubber chicken or blistering walks. If they just send in their $50 "entry fee," they can stay home with their families.

Example: The Community Food Bank in Tucson sponsors an annual "Full Sun, No Run" charity marathon. Participants receive T-shirts that read *I didn't run.*

●**Collect stuff, not money.** Ask members to donate items for a yard sale. Post flyers and place classified ads in papers—many will run ads for free. See if the town will donate a location, such as a park.

FROM SCOTT PANSKY

● **Trade publicity for goods and services.** Contact the PR department of a local company that can help you.

Examples: A nursery could provide supplies for your garden club in exchange for being the club's sponsor. Or a sporting-goods chain could let your runner's club distribute membership forms in its stores. Dole Foods donated food to a walkathon for the United Autism Alliance. Dole's name was on T-shirts and brochures.

FROM VALERIE REUTHER

● **Throw small parties,** not huge events. Ask group members to host dine-around dinners in their homes. Bring the parties to a central place for dessert and coffee. Attendance is better at intimate parties than at large, formal dinners—and there are no catering costs.

All of these ideas work well as annual programs—and the planning will become easier. Good luck!

Find Out What Your Collectibles Are Worth On-Line

Malcolm Katt, owner, Millwood Gallery, specializing in militaria and other collectibles, Millwood, New York, and an eBay PowerSeller since 1998.

Thanks to the success of the on-line auction site eBay, which holds hundreds of collectibles auctions every hour, collectors who previously relied on guidebooks to determine collectible values now use real-time on-line prices for greater accuracy. eBay auctions have redefined "scarcity"—many collectibles once thought to be rare are quite common, and prices are reduced due to the increased supply. Rely on "field-based" values (prices that buyers actually are paying). To check the recent price history of a collectible,

go to *www.ebay.com* and click on "Advanced Search," then "Completed Listings Only." If you insure your collectibles, stay current with eBay prices and periodically adjust coverage based on the market value of your collection.

Wine for Less

Opt for a bag-in-a-box "cask" (wine is packaged in plastic bags in a cardboard box) or wine in paperboard containers. Taste tests suggest quality is as good as traditionally bottled versions—and prices are much lower.

Example: Some high-quality three-liter cask Australian Shiraz sells for about $14, more than 40% less than the same amount of wine packaged in standard 750-milliliter bottles.

Other pluses: Corkscrews aren't needed, and leftovers remain fresh longer.

BusinessWeek, 1221 Avenue of the Americas, New York City 10020.

Fine Dining for Far Less

On-line discounts are available for 1,100 upscale restaurants in the US. Most are in California, Florida, Illinois and New York. Book an off-peak table through *www.dinnerbroker. com* and save up to 30%—applied before your bill is handed to you. At *www.restaurant.com,* you can buy gift certificates at half price. And, if you dine out often, you can earn points toward dining "cheques" for every reservation you book at *www.opentable.com.*

Kiplinger's Personal Finance, 1729 H St. NW, Washington, DC 20006.

Get Free Government Newsletters by E-Mail

Government newsletters on a wide range of subjects are available on the Internet.

Examples: Health and medicine, business, travel, housing, safety and consumer protection, military affairs, Social Security and much more.

Requested newsletters will be sent directly to your e-mail address. For a complete list of what is available, log on to the government's Internet portal, USA.gov, at *www.usa.gov* and scroll down to "Reference and General Government." "Free E-Newsletters" is under the heading "Publications."

Who Needs Satellite Radio When You Can Listen On-Line?

Thousands of radio stations worldwide transmit programs on-line—and there are many "Internet only" stations as well. Listen to anything from Antarctica's A NET playing the blues, at *www.anetstation.com*, to the morning news from the Vatican at *www.vatican.va* (just enter "radio" in the search box). Leading radio portals such as *www.radio-locator.com* search through thousands of stations to find what you're looking for by location, broadcast format or station name.

Never Check E-Mail in the Morning...and Other Surprising Time-Savers

Julie Morgenstern, founder of Julie Morgenstern Enterprises, LLC, a time-management and corporate-productivity consultancy, New York City.

She is author of *Never Check E-Mail in the Morning and Other Unexpected Strategies for Making Your Work Life Work.* Fireside. *www.juliemorgenstern.com*

You work hard but can't seem to get everything done. There are just too many responsibilities, interruptions and demands. *Rather than working longer, you need to learn to use your time better—and*

sometimes that means doing things that seem counterintuitive...

●**Shorten your workday.** If 10 hours isn't enough, try nine-and-a-half. Losing 30 minutes of work time each day makes you organize your time better. No longer will you tolerate interruptions...make personal phone calls from the office...or chat around the water cooler. Your pace will pick up, your focus will sharpen, and you'll soon find that you're getting more done despite the shorter workday.

Bonus: You have freed up two-and-a-half hours for yourself each week.

This works just as well outside the workplace. Allot fewer hours for chores and projects, and you're more likely to buckle down and get them done.

●**Take a break.** Hard workers often feel that they don't have time to take a break. Recharging your batteries isn't wasted time—it keeps you running. Escape from your workday life for at least 30 minutes each day or a few hours each week. Use this escape time to do whatever it is that most effectively transports you away mentally from your daily responsibilities. That might be reading a novel, exercising at the gym or listening to classical music. These escapes keep your mind sharp and your energy level high.

If you just can't find the time, add the escape more formally to your schedule. If your escape is exercise, plan a game of tennis or golf with a friend—the friend will be counting on you, so it will be tough for you to back out. If your escape is music, buy season tickets to the local symphony—you're more likely to attend if you already have purchased the tickets.

●**Don't look at e-mail first thing.** Instead, use the morning to focus on your most important tasks. Most people's minds are sharpest in the morning, and completing important responsibilities before lunch creates a sense of relief and accomplishment that can carry you through the afternoon.

Helpful: When you reply to an e-mail, try to fit your entire response in the subject line. Some people waste hours each day crafting long responses when short ones are all that's needed.

●**Avoid the urge to multitask.** When many things need to get done, it's tempting to try to do them all at once. But multitasking isn't the secret to productivity—it's a sure way to be inefficient.

According to a study published in *Journal of Experimental Psychology*, it takes the brain four times longer to recognize and process each item it is working on when multitasking than when it is focused on a single job. Other studies have found that work quality suffers when we try to multitask.

To get many things done, either in the office or at home, do just one thing at a time. If another obligation crops up or an unrelated idea pops into your head, pause from your current task only long enough to jot it down in your planner (not on a scrap of paper, which could get lost).

●**Be your own boss.** Even if you are an employee with a company, think of yourself as an independent entrepreneur working *with* your company, not as a hired hand working for it. We all are self-employed, in a manner of speaking. We work for the sole proprietorships that are our careers. There's a productivity advantage to be had by keeping this in mind—independent contractors know that they must continue to deliver results every day to retain their clients, while employees sometimes allow themselves more slack and act as if their employers owe them something.

●**Cut people off.** Learn to put off interrupters without causing offense. When someone needs you, say, "How much time do you need? If it's more than a few seconds, let's schedule it for later so I can give you my full attention." The time will be more convenient for you, and the person may solve his/her own problem in the meantime.

Greet callers with, "What can I do for you?" rather than "How are you?"—the latter might be taken as an invitation to chat.

●**Don't do chores when big deadlines loom.** Faced with a big, important task and several small, easy, but less vital chores, many people start by tackling the chores. Knocking these off provides a sense that progress has been made, and it clears the tables to focus

on the big responsibility—but it's still a poor strategy.

Always tackle the most important job first, though it might be the most difficult and time consuming. In the corporate world, the most important task usually is the one that will generate or save the most money for the company. If you put off this crucial task, unforeseen complications or new assignments might prevent you from getting the important tasks done at all.

How to Play the Slots and Win Big

Victor H. Royer, a gambling industry consultant in Las Vegas who has worked for some of the leading casinos and slot machine manufacturers. He is author of 18 books on casino gambling, including *Powerful Profits from Slots*. Kensington.

Until the mid-1980s, slot machines truly were one-armed bandits with the house having an advantage of 20% or more.

Since then, casinos have come to rely on slot machine players for most of their revenues. This has created competition among casinos and dramatically sweetened the odds for the players.

Here's how to maximize your chances of winning when playing the slots…

WHERE TO PLAY

●**Visit Vegas.** Slot machines in Las Vegas offer the best odds in the country, giving the house an advantage of just 2% to 4%. Only an expert blackjack player has better odds in a casino. But beware—slot machines in bars or other noncasino locations generally offer terrible odds.

Slots in Reno and in the tribal casinos of the East Coast are not quite as advantageous as those in Las Vegas, but they're still better than those in Atlantic City, where house advantages of 6% to 8% are common. Riverboat and tribal casinos of the Midwest generally offer the worst odds, with house advantages of as much as 10%.

●**Look for high-profile "slot islands."** Casinos want gamblers to see people winning. In most casinos, slot islands—clusters of four to six slot machines (sometimes on slightly raised platforms)—are placed where the aisles intersect. These machines often offer the best chance of a jackpot.

Also try slot machines located near the main casino cage, where winnings are collected.

●**Avoid slot machines near table games.** Casinos don't want the noise of slot machine payouts to disturb the people playing black-jack or craps.

Also skip slot machines located near buffet lines. Casinos know that people standing in line will play the slots out of boredom even without frequent payoffs.

PICK THE RIGHT MACHINE

●**Choose $1 slots.** Quarter slot machines typically have much lower payback rates than $1 machines. The $5 or $10 slots offer even better odds, but most recreational gamblers would go through their money too fast to make these machines enjoyable.

●**Choose three-reel machines.** These tend to have slightly better odds.

●**Look for "double-up" or "triple-up" machines.** These offer two or three times the usual payout as well as marginally better odds.

My favorite slots: All reel and video slots from IGT, including Double Diamond, Triple Diamond, Triple Lucky 7s and Triple Double Dollars.

●**Don't invest too much in "progressive" slots.** These machines—which offer a shot at huge jackpots that build up over time, some-times into the millions of dollars—will typically have poor odds. They exist for the same reason that lotteries exist—people like to dream big.

MORE STRATEGIES

●**Bet the most coins per pull that a machine allows.** The majority of slot machines offer a better percentage of return when more coins are played.

Example: The highest jackpot on a $1 machine might be $800 if a single $1 coin is played. However, if two $1 coins are played simultaneously, the jackpot becomes $2,000—

that is a 150% increase in return for a 100% increase in your investment.

●**Play after the crowds.** Most slot machine players visit the casinos between the hours of 5 pm and 11 pm. If you play just after all the crowds leave, the slot machines are likely to be full of their money. That's when you will have a better chance of finding a machine that will produce a winning jackpot.

●**Switch machines if you have several "almost" jackpots.** If a machine comes close to a jackpot several times—say, all three sev-ens are visible but not in the payout line—that does not mean it is about to pay off. My expe-rience suggests it is less likely to hit the jackpot anytime soon.

Play Your Cards Right for More Casino Fun—for Less

Jerry Patterson, a gambling instructor and author of several books on gaming, including *Casino Gambling: A Winner's Guide to Blackjack, Craps, Roulette, Baccarat, and Casino Poker.* Penguin. His Internet site is *www.casinogamblingedge.com.* To get the free report "The 10 Casino Gambling Decisions That Lead to Winning Ses-sions," e-mail Jerry Patterson at *jpe21@aol.com* or send in a self-addressed, stamped, business-sized envelope to Jerry Patterson Enterprises, Inc., Box 236, Gardnerville, Nevada 89410 or call 800-257-7130.

Fast-paced games, mysterious rules and big crowds make a casino intimidating. However, if you play your cards right, casinos can be great places to find excitement, see new sights and socialize. With a bit of luck, you might actually win some money. With just a little research, you can plan a fun-filled trip at a big savings.

FIND THE BEST

Large casinos are generally the most accom-modating for first-time visitors and casual gam-blers, frequently called "recreational players" in casino jargon. Big casinos are more likely to have the services that recreational players like, including free game instructions, first-class entertainment and gourmet dining.

Many also have sports facilities, and some—such as Borgata in Atlantic City and Mohegan Sun in Connecticut—provide health spas. Non-smoking sections, once unheard of, are now common in many US casinos.

For casual casino visitors, it's wise to go during peak hours—afternoons and evenings.

Tables are crowded and games are usually slower. That means there are more opportunities to socialize with other players and fewer chances to lose money. Off-peak hours are usually favored by serious, high-stake gamblers who may dislike amateurs at the table.

Ask the host at casinos you are considering visiting how much money you have to spend to receive complimentary meals, entertainment or a hotel room.

Note: Nearly all gambling resorts ban cameras from the casino itself, and most of them frown on cell phones.

To find casinos, ask a travel agent, look in the *Yellow Pages* or search an Internet casino directory. StatesCasinos at *www.statescasinos.com* is a good place to start.

Before visiting, call the casino or visit its Web site to check for specials on bus fares, entertainment, rooms and meals. Rooms are usually in the $175 to $300/night range, but specials can cut rates in half.

Example: The classy New York-New York Hotel & Casino in Las Vegas recently had a $69-a-night special. More economical rates can be found at the smaller hotel casinos.

Nightclubs are pricey, often more than $200 a person for dinner and a floor show. But entertainment can be lavish. Do you remember Steve Lawrence and Eydie Gorme? They still appear at casinos, including a recent engagement at the Silver Legacy Resort Casino in Reno, Nevada.

To save money, ask a casino employee or taxi driver where to find less expensive nightclubs. Many cities with casinos are also near historic or natural landmarks, such as Hoover Dam, which is near Las Vegas and the boardwalk in Atlantic City.

GO FOR COMPS

A few decades ago, only high rollers could expect casinos to give them free rooms and meals. Today, thanks to competition among casinos, anyone who spends a couple hundred dollars is likely to get a complimentary buffet meal. If your gambling bankroll is $1,000 to $2,000, you may be eligible for a free room or nightclub show.

Look for the counters where the players are signing up for comp cards, or the casino hosts' area or offices to find out where to sign up for a player's card. This looks like a credit card and keeps track of your play.

Each time you play, ask the employee in charge of the game to "mark" your card. At slot machines, you insert the card in a special slot where it's marked electronically.

LEARN FIRST, THEN PLAY

Many large casinos offer free lessons in the popular games, especially craps and blackjack. Even if you've played these games before, it pays to take lessons, which typically last about an hour. Instruction is helpful because rules are complex and game etiquette even trickier.

Examples: There are specific signals to tell the dealer how you want to play a blackjack hand…although not necessary, it's customary to tip the dealer 2% to 5% of your winnings. If you lose, there's no obligation to tip.

GAIN AN EDGE

Watching a game before you play is a good way to see whether the table is running hot or cold. It's best to choose a table with winning players. To get an idea of whether they are winning or losing, note the players' chips on the table and whether they seem happy or sad.

Also important to know: At blackjack, no shuffle is completely random, meaning that it can favor either the house or knowledgeable players.

At roulette, croupiers often operate the wheel in a way that favors some numbers over others.

Noticing these anomalies is only one way that players can gain an advantage. By studying blackjack, craps or roulette, you also can gain an edge over the casino. It's best to avoid those bets heavily weighted in favor of the house—such as the bets in the center of the layout at the craps table, the insurance bet at blackjack and betting on the inside numbers at

139

roulette. Play the "even money" outside bets, such as red or black, instead.

While learning the basics of blackjack or craps may take less than an hour, learning the finer points can require many months.

One of the most effective ways to learn is through up-to-date books on blackjack, craps and other casino games.

For more information about casinos, gambling books and gambling tips, I recommend the *American Casino Guide, 2009* (Casino Vacations), by Steve Bourie. This guide contains a wealth of information, such as listings of all US casinos by state, and $1,000 in valuable casino coupons, including discounts on rooms, food, rental cars and lots of freebies. The book also has articles and tips by noted gambling authors.

LIMIT YOUR LOSSES

Unless you spend time studying and then become a disciplined player, expect to lose a little at a casino. *To keep losses low…*

●**Avoid the new games that casinos are touting.** The odds are very long against winning. Examples include Spanish 21, Three Card Poker and Let It Ride.

●**Set spending limits.** Most people can have fun with $100 a day. If you can't keep to a limit, don't raise it. Ask a friend to hold your ATM and credit cards. If you still can't resist breaking your budget, don't go to casinos.

●**Check the minimum bets before you start playing.** At blackjack, for instance, minimums can vary between $5 and $100. By betting at low-minimum tables, you can stretch out your budget.

●**If you have a friend with you who is good at playing,** ask him/her to critique your play. If you are interested in additional ideas and instruction on how to beat the casinos, you can start by reading my report "The 10 Casino Gambling Decisions That Lead to Winning Sessions."

Five Questions that Guarantee You'll Get the Most for Your Money

Dorothy Leeds, New York City–based motivational speaker and communications consultant to many Fortune 500 companies. *www.dorothyleeds.com.* She is author of *The 7 Powers of Questions.* Perigee.

Shoppers can get more for their money simply by knowing what to ask. *Best questions…*

●**May I speak to the manager?** Whatever you want—a better deal, a return that stretches the rules, free gift wrapping—the odds are better if you ask the person in charge. A sales associate is bound by store policy. A manager can bend the rules.

●**What can you do for big spenders?** Recently, I spent a lot of money in a clothing store. Before I made my purchases, I asked what the store would do for me if I bought everything I had selected. They threw in $100 worth of free merchandise.

Helpful: Be polite, not demanding, when you ask for extras. You're more likely to get what you want.

●**Can you show me something else?** The more time a salesperson spends with you, the more anxious he/she is to make the sale—particularly if a commission is involved. If you have the time to linger over a decision, it might just land you a better deal.

●**Will this item go on sale soon?** Was it on sale recently? If a store will soon mark down an item—or if it had been reduced and is now back to regular price—there is a good chance you can get the sale price now.

●**What new features will the next generation of this product include?** When will it arrive? Certain products, such as electronics and computer goods, are constantly being updated. Ask the salesperson if the item in the store is likely to be replaced by a new model soon.

Secrets of Becoming a Late Bloomer—It's Never Too Late to Reinvent Yourself...

Connie Goldman, a former host of National Public Radio's All Things Considered and the author of several books, including *Secrets of Becoming a Late Bloomer.* Hazelden. She lives in Hudson, Wisonsin.

We generally think of late bloomers as people who were not successful until late in their lives. In fact, most late bloomers had fulfilling careers before taking their lives in new directions. Groucho Marx, for instance, was a famous movie actor whose career had ground to a halt when, at age 60, he began hosting a new type of TV show. When Winston Churchill was around the same age, many thought that he was washed up as a politician. Soon afterward, he became prime minister of Great Britain. And even Grandma Moses—who was nearly 80 when she began creating her now-famous paintings—had been long known among her friends as an expert embroiderer.

Most late bloomers, of course, never make headlines, though they also move forward in new and fulfilling ways...

●**Natalie was age 67 when she joined the Peace Corps,** learned Spanish and became a schoolteacher in Peru.

●**Martha was 71 when she used her experience in stamp collecting** to start a successful mail-order business.

●**Robert, an attorney, was 65 when he began caring for his ailing wife and mother-in-law.** After attending to those obligations, he started a new career as a teacher at a local college. Now 80, Robert is still teaching.

OVERCOMING HURDLES

As we grow older, most of us become so wrapped up in old routines that we don't consider striking out in new directions.

Trap: Many of us spend our later years moping around because we never fulfilled the biggest dreams of our youths, such as skippering a sailboat around the world or becoming a professional ballet dancer.

Better: Keep in touch with your dreams, but make them more realistic. Instead of ruminating about sailing around the world, for instance, think now about buying a small sailboat and taking less ambitious trips. Or, if you aspired to be a ballet dancer in your youth, now consider volunteering at the local ballet company. What's important is that the activity you choose is personally rewarding.

STRATEGIES THAT WORK

Each late bloomer moves forward in his/her own way, and the first step is often difficult. *Strategies...*

●**Keep a journal for a week or two.** Write down your daily activities as well as the goals that you would like to pursue. Keeping a journal of this type is an easy way to spot the activities that are now unnecessary, usually because they've been part of your routine for many years.

Example: Socializing regularly with friends whose company you no longer truly enjoy.

Written words are powerful. Once we see our goals written down, we're far more likely to take them seriously.

●**Discuss your goals with others.** Many older people have struck out in new directions, and how they did it can be both instructive and inspiring. Some friends are likely to encourage you, but others may point out drawbacks that you hadn't thought about.

By talking with a friend who went back to school late in life, you may discover that the process is easier than you imagined. Someone else, on the other hand, may point out that starting a consulting business may take far more time than you thought.

●**Exploit your creativity.** History shows that becoming a late bloomer nearly always involves using creativity that may have been neglected for many years. There's creativity in everyone, whether it's in managing a company, coaching a sports team, inventing new recipes or even arranging flowers. If you have any doubts about your creativity, jot down in your journal what you most enjoy doing. What you'll see is a list of ways to be creative.

Some late bloomers make use of their neglected creativity to start a new and profitable career. Many more use their creativity to help friends and/or family members. Regardless of which path you choose, using your creativity leads to more enjoyment in life and the building of self-confidence.

●**Learn something new.** Take a course in a subject that's always interested you—a foreign language, painting or computer programming, for instance. Classes at local colleges and adult education centers can also be great places to make new friends. Don't feel obliged, however, to finish a course you don't like.

Going on trips and joining book clubs can also be enjoyable ways to increase your knowledge. Or you can ask friends to teach you something that you always wanted to learn.

Learning also has an advantage that's not always appreciated—it makes you more open to new experiences.

●**Laugh more often.** No one knows why humor helps us deal with problems, but it usually does. And when you strike out in new directions, problems will almost certainly occur. You might, for example, sign up for the wrong course at a local college. By laughing about the mistake, you won't let it discourage you from enrolling later in the right course. In fact, laughing at your mistakes is a well-known way to build self-confidence.

●**Give it a try.** Early in life, changing directions can be risky. That's because we're on a career path and may also have family obligations. Later in life, the risk is usually lower. Take advantage of the opportunity. If you say, "I can't do that," you'll never really know if you could.

In fact, nearly all late bloomers have one thing in common —their willingness to take a chance. If you have any doubts, look at the originality of a Grandma Moses painting or read one of Churchill's defiant wartime speeches.

Think Up Your Own Reality TV Show

You may be paid for your idea—and have a chance to help make it happen. The new

Web site TalpaCreative.com is soliciting reality-show ideas from the public. It is free to join the site, but you must explain why you want to participate—and agree to certain rules and restrictions regarding ownership of your ideas. The site, cofounded by reality-show producer John de Mol, plans to buy the rights to promising concepts and develop them—with help from the originators.

Times Machine

Browse 70 years of *The New York Times*, from the first issue on September 18, 1851, through December 30, 1922. Read accounts of Lincoln's assassination, the sinking of the Titanic, the end of World War I and more. Flip through virtual editions of the pages, and click on and read any article of interest for free.

http://times machine.nytimes.com .

Fun at the Races—Easy Rules to Boost Your Odds

Andrew Beyer, horse racing columnist for *The Washington Post*, creator of the *Daily Racing Form's* Beyer Speed Figures and author of several books on handicapping, including *Beyer on Speed.* Houghton Mifflin.

A day at the races can provide the excitement and conviviality that are missing today in many other pastimes. And winning can make the experience even more fun.

Although only the experts who analyze races for hours a day can expect to win consistently, casual racegoers can increase their chances by following a few simple rules…

SET LIMITS

Put a ceiling on how much you'll bet during any one day at the track. A useful rule is to risk what you would be prepared to spend on dinner for two at a fine, but affordable, restaurant. For many people, that would be about $100.

USE RELIABLE DATA

The vast majority of race fans rely on the *Daily Racing Form* for information on horses, tracks, jockeys, trainers and other factors that influence the outcome of races. The publication is on sale at most large newsstands for about $5.

Information: 800-306-3676, *www.drf.com.*

It takes a while to learn how to read and interpret the data, but casual racegoers can benefit from these two statistics…

• **Beyer Speed Figures.** These are comparative numbers based on the performance of each horse in every race it has entered, as adjusted for the particular speed of the tracks on which it has run.

Examples: The Kentucky Derby winner might have a Beyer Speed Figure of 120, while a habitual also-ran at minor racetracks could have a figure of 30.

In general, horses with higher speed numbers will beat those with lower figures. Though a horse with a speed figure of 97 won't always beat one with a figure of 96, a horse that has a figure of 105 will nearly always finish ahead of a horse rated at 75.

• **The trainer's record.** Statistically, the record of a trainer is much more important than that of a jockey. The *Daily Racing Form* makes it easy to compare trainers' records.

Strategy: Bet only on horses whose trainers have a winning record above 20%. Avoid betting on horses with a trainer whose winning percentage is in single digits.

Note: Even experienced bettors occasionally ignore trainer records.

Example: In the 2002 Kentucky Derby, War Emblem had one of the country's top trainers as well as the highest Beyer Speed Figure, but when he won, he paid odds of 20 to 1.

Helpful: If you don't see a clear choice after looking at the speed number and other information, don't bet, or don't bet heavily.

AIM HIGH

Strive for one or two big wins for the day rather than trying to limit your losses with a series of small bets. You can do that either by betting a large portion of your $100 on one race or by playing the exacta or another type of combination bet where the payoff is big.

The logic: It's more fun to aim for a big payoff. In the long run, your chances of winning, say, $200 on one combination bet are just as good as the odds of winning that much by making small, "safe" bets on each race.

Typical combination bets…

• **Exacta.** Picking the winner as well as the second-place finisher in a single race.

• **Trifecta.** Picking the first three finishers in a single race.

• **Superfecta.** Picking the first four finishers in a single race.

• **Daily double.** Picking the winners of two designated races—usually the first two.

• **Pick three.** Picking the winners of three designated races.

• **Pick four.** Picking the winners of four designated races.

LEAVE EMOTIONS AT HOME

Basing bets on your emotions is a sure way to lose.

Example: If you lose a bet in an excruciating photo finish, you may feel the urge to bet the next race heavily in a desperate effort to recoup. Resist that temptation.

If you've won several races in a row, you might become overconfident and start to bet rashly. Resist that temptation, too.

Helpful: Whenever you're tempted to let emotions replace discipline, skip a couple of races. Go to the lounge and relax.

If you maintain betting discipline, racetracks can be a bargain. The general admission at most racetracks is about $3, clubhouse figures a little higher. Today's best tracks also have excellent restaurants and elegant lounges where you can watch simulcasts of the races.

Mr. Beyer's favorite tracks…

• **Belmont Park,** Elmont, NY, 516-488-6000, *www.nyra.com/index_belmont.html*

• **Del Mar Thoroughbred Club,** Del Mar, CA, 858-755-1141, *www.delmarracing.com*

• **Gulfstream Park,** Hallandale Beach, FL, 800-771-8873 or 954-454-7000, *www.gulfstream park.com*

●**Santa Anita Park,** Arcadia, CA, 626-574-7223, *www.santaanita.com.* For information on special luncheons for seniors that are held several times a year, call 626-574-6400.

●**Saratoga Race Course,** Saratoga Springs, NY, 718-641-4700 or 518-584-6200, *www.nyra.com/index_saratoga.html*

Sports News Anytime, Anywhere

John Skilton, president of SkilTech, Inc., which designs and maintains Web sites for more than 25 professional sports teams and leagues, Elkton, Maryland, *www.skiltech.com.*

Want to check a score and can't wait for tomorrow's paper? Want to confirm a rumor about a coach leaving your favorite team? Or maybe you are just curious about who holds the record for the most blocked shots in the NBA? (See below for the answer.) *Free, fascinating sports news and trivia await you on the Web...*

FOOTBALL

●**College news, scores and standings for every level,** from Division I-A through Division III. Includes a complete NCAA football rule book and record book. *www.ncaafootball.com*

●**Division III college football.** You can follow teams that don't get much coverage in the media. Links to Internet audio broadcasts of many games. *www.d3football.com*

●**The National Football League's official site offers statistics,** schedules and links to team sites. *www.nfl.com*

●**NFL news, stats and schedules.** See what your team might look like next year with the mock draft at the Pro Football News Network Web site. *www.profootballnews.net*

BASKETBALL

●**College and pro news for men's and women's teams,** plus a basketball record book that has *the answer* to the question asked above—Elmore Smith holds the record for the most blocked shots in an NBA game (17 on October 28, 1973). *www.basketball.com*

●**College basketball coaches,** such as Arizona head coach Lute Olson, check in with their own sports columns. *www.collegeinsider.com*

●**Division III basketball.** A great way to keep tabs on these college basketball teams. *www.d3hoops.com*

●**Basketball news about every level,** from the high school level through the NBA and WNBA. *www.insidehoops.com*

●**Business side of basketball.** Interesting articles and news. Check which teams owe others draft picks from past trades or own the rights to other teams' future picks. *www.realgm.com*

HOCKEY

●**Historical hockey stats.** The Internet's largest repository of hockey data. *http://hockeydb.com*

Example: Mark Messier passed Gordie Howe for the National Hockey League's (NHL) most-games-played record.

●**The NHL's official site has scores,** schedules and links to team sites. *www.nhl.com*

BASEBALL

●**Official site of Major League Baseball.** Find season statistics and links to team sites. *www.mlb.com*

●**On-line photos of hundreds of major- and minor-league ballparks.** A great way to select interesting parks to visit on vacation. *www.digitalballparks.com*

GENERAL

●**CBS Sportsline.** Sports coverage from the CBS TV network. *www.sportsline.com*

●**ESPN.** One of the largest sports sites. *www.espn.com*

●**Our Sports Central.** Minor-league sports articles and links. *www.oursportscentral.com*

●**Pro Sports Daily.** News and rumors about big-league baseball, football and basketball. *www.prosportsdaily.com*

Newsgroups—The Most Overlooked Resource On the Internet

Patricia Robison, president, Computing Independence, Box 2031, New York City 10011. She is a technology security specialist and gives seminars on business continuity and disaster recovery.

Internet newsgroups provide two-way conversations with people around the world on nearly every subject that you can imagine—investments, science, vacation spots, consumer products, hobbies, sports, politics and more.

You can use newsgroups to make lots of new friends who share your interests, to research just about any subject you can think of or simply read them for fun.

Newsgroups were created many years before there was a World Wide Web, but many Web users don't even know they exist.

HOW THEY WORK

Each newsgroup acts as a discussion group on a particular subject. There are more than 20,000 newsgroups.

People post messages and others post replies. Anyone can participate or simply observe. Many people include their e-mail addresses in their messages so that they can be reached privately.

The simplest introduction to newsgroups is through the Google Web-based newsreader. Go to *http://groups.google.com*. On the page that comes up, you will see a directory of newsgroups. You can look through it to find a group that may be of interest to you, or enter a subject in the search box to have Google find related newsgroups.

To learn how to participate, click on "Groups Help" for the simple instructions.

Bonus: Google also has an archive of past newsgroup postings dating back to 1981—so that you can locate everything anyone has ever posted on a subject of interest to you, among more than 800 million messages.

TYPES OF NEWSGROUPS

Most groups are open, so anyone can post anything in them. Some are "moderated," so that any off-topic or offensive messages are blocked or deleted.

Examples: The newsgroup *misc.taxes* is open and the scene of much vociferous debate about tax politics. The newsgroup *misc.taxes. moderated* accepts only questions about the tax law that are discussed by tax professionals—although anyone can submit a question.

Other newsgroups to try…

● **alt.folklore.urban**—for discussion of urban legends.

● **rec.boats.cruising**—for advice on boating.

● **rec.gardens**—for gardeners.

● **sci.military.moderated**—for discussion of current military affairs.

● **soc.retirement**—for talk regarding retiree issues.

● **talk.politics.misc**—for unrestrained political discussion.

Remember, in unmoderated groups, anyone can say anything. Therefore, if the group follows a controversial subject—such as politics—comments may get heated. Also, information may be unreliable.

But most newsgroups have a cadre of regular, expert members who are well informed. By "lurking"—watching the group for a while—you can learn more about who they are and whose opinion to value.

The Secret to Making Better Decisions

Dan Ariely, PhD, the James B. Duke Professor of Behavioral Economics at Duke University, Durham, North Carolina, and a visiting professor at Massachusetts Institute of Technology (MIT), Cambridge. He is author of *Predictably Irrational: The Hidden Forces That Shape Our Decisions.* HarperCollins. *www.predictablyirrational.com.*

We all like to think that we make smart decisions, but according to behavioral economist Dan Ariely, PhD, our choices often defy logic and rationality. Ariely's research has shown that even when we assume we are acting in our best interests, our reasoning abilities are influenced by our expectations and emotions.

By becoming more aware of these tendencies, we can make decisions that serve us better. *We asked Ariely for some common examples of irrational decision-making and how to choose more intelligently...*

●**We splurge on a lavish meal but clip coupons to save 25 cents on a can of soup.**

When deciding how much to spend on something, we often think in relative terms.

Example: In surveys, when asked whether they would walk five blocks to save $7 on a $15 pen, most people say yes. But they say they would not walk that distance to save $7 on a $1,500 suit. The $7 represents nearly 50% of $15 and less than one-half of 1% of $1,500, so we perceive the 50% savings as more valuable. But the outlay of time is the same, so rationally, the total purchase price should not make a difference.

Similarly, a 25-cent savings seems dramatic when we are purchasing a low-priced item, such as a $1.50 can of soup. We may spend lots of time clipping coupons, even though the savings are small and there are many more satisfying things that we could be doing with our time.

Rational response: Instead of comparing the amount of savings on a product or service to its total price, ask yourself what else you could buy for the amount saved. This question gives you a point of comparison that has nothing to do with percentages.

Example: "Seven dollars would buy me three cups of coffee. Is the time spent walking five blocks worth three cups of coffee?"

Also consider "opportunity cost," which is a way economists acknowledge the value of time. Ask yourself, What else could I be doing with this time if I were not clipping coupons?

●**We are attracted to what's "free," even if it really costs us more in the long run.**

The word "free" engages the emotions. "Free" offers create such intense excitement that we often don't bother to consider the potential downside.

Example: You are choosing between two credit cards. One credit card has a $100 annual fee and charges 8% interest. The other card is free—it has no annual fee—but the interest rate is 11%. Most people choose the free card, but the higher interest rate ends up costing them far more than $100 a year. (Of course, if you pay off the balance every month, the no-annual-fee card makes sense, but most credit card holders carry a revolving balance.)

Even giveaways, such as free samples at conference booths, have their downside. When we take home free things that we don't need, we then must deal with clutter, find a place to store the items or take time to dispose of them. Free samples of a medication may get us started on an expensive drug when a cheaper one might work just as well or better.

Rational response: When considering a free offer, ask yourself, What is the hidden cost?

●**A 50-cent aspirin makes a headache go away, but a one-cent aspirin doesn't.**

Our expectations have an enormous influence over our physical experiences. When a person takes a pain reliever, merely expecting the medication to work causes the body to secrete opioids, powerful chemicals that act much like morphine. The ingredients in the drug also help to relieve pain, but even a placebo pill causes the release of these morphinelike chemicals in response to the belief that pain relief is on the way.

Our expectations also affect our perception of quality. When comparing similar products at different prices, we typically assume that the higher-priced product is better—even if the ingredients in both products are exactly the same, as with aspirin.

Rational response: Make your unconscious expectations conscious. Instead of automatically reaching for a higher-priced product, ask, "Why is product A more expensive than product B? Are the ingredients different...or am I paying more for marketing, branding and packaging?" If the products are virtually the same, choose the lower-priced one and say to yourself, I am confident that this product will help me.

●**A money-back guarantee convinces us to buy something that we may not need.**

Owning something changes our beliefs about it almost immediately. Once you become an owner, you place greater value on whatever you bought.

Example: In a department store, an attractive coffee table catches your eye. You are not sure whether you actually need a new coffee table or how it will look in your home, but it comes with a 30-day money-back guarantee. You tell yourself that you will try it out and return it if you don't like it.

When you get the table home, you move other furniture to make room for it, put magazines on it and reposition the rug around it. Now it feels like your coffee table, making it more precious to you—and harder to return.

Rational response: Acknowledge this tendency to get attached quickly to things you own. Be skeptical any time you think, I'm just taking it home to try. Instead, say, The likelihood of my returning this purchase is very low. Do I still want it?

Tips for Tipping

Peggy Post, great-granddaughter-in-law of etiquette pioneer Emily Post. She is a director and spokesperson for the Emily Post Institute in Burlington, Vermont, and author of *Emily Post's Etiquette, 17th Edition*. HarperCollins. Her Web site is *www.emilypost.com.*

During the holidays, it's customary to thank those service providers who help you throughout the year, often with a tip. Accompany the cash with a handwritten note that expresses your appreciation. Let the provider know how pleased you are with what he/she does for you. If you tip regularly at the time of service, you may forgo a holiday tip or cut back on the amount below. If you need to economize this year, select the two or three people whose services are especially appreciated and give to them. A small gift or baked goods with a note of thanks are appropriate substitutes.

Here, guidelines on what to give…

•**Babysitter, regular.** One evening's pay, plus a small gift from your child.

•**Barber.** Cost of one haircut, plus possibly a small gift.

•**Beauty salon staff.** $10 to $60 each, giving the most to those who provide the most for you, plus possibly a small gift.

•**Child's teacher.** Gift certificate for a coffee shop or bookstore…book…picture frame…fruit basket or gourmet food item…or joint gift with other parents and children—not cash. Check the school's policy.

•**Day-care providers.** $25 to $70 each, plus a small gift from your child. If you use only one or two providers, consider a higher amount.

•**Dog walker.** One week's pay.

•**Garage attendants.** $10 to $30 each, to be distributed by the manager.

•**Housekeeper/cleaner.** One day's pay.

•**Letter carrier.** Postal regulations allow carriers to accept gifts worth up to $20, but not cash.

•**Massage therapist.** Cost of one session.

•**Nanny.** One week's to one month's salary, based on tenure and local custom, plus a small gift from your child.

•**Newspaper carrier.** $10 to $30.

•**Nurse, private.** Gift, not cash.

•**Nursing home employees.** Gift, not cash.

•**Package deliverer.** Small gift if you receive deliveries regularly (most delivery companies prohibit the acceptance of cash gifts).

•**Personal trainer.** Cost of one session.

•**Pool cleaner.** Cost of one cleaning.

•**Residential building personnel…**
  •Superintendent. $20 to $80.
  •Doorman. $10 to $80.
  •Elevator operator. $15 to $40.
  •Handyman. $15 to $40.

•**Trash/recycling collectors.** $10 to $20 each.

•**Yard/garden worker.** $20 to $50.

Simple Secrets for a Successful Dinner Party

Dinner parties need not be complicated. *Follow these simple strategies for an evening your guests will remember...*

●**Have interesting music playing when guests arrive,** such as *Café Atlantico* by Cesaria Evora or *Avalon* by Roxy Music.

●**Collect everything needed for drinks,** and set it out on a table in the living room, so that everyone can help themselves.

●**Make sure your menu is simple enough** so that you can enjoy the party yourself.

●**Serve dinner in the kitchen** to make guests feel like family.

●**Let guests help out if they want to**—it makes them feel like part of a team.

Ina Garten, Southport, Connecticut–based cookbook author and host of the Barefoot Contessa *TV series on the Food Network. Her most recent book is* Barefoot Contessa at Home. *And she is author of* Barefoot in Paris: Easy French Food You Can Make at Home. *Both from Clarkson Potter.*

When Fun Is Tax Deductible

Sandy Botkin, Esq., CPA, CEO of the Tax Reduction Institute, 13200 Executive Park Terrace, Germantown, Maryland 20874, www.taxreductioninstitute.com. *He is a former IRS attorney as well as a senior tax law specialist and author of the best-selling* Lower Your Taxes Big Time! *McGraw-Hill.*

What's even better than spending lots of wonderful weekends and evenings out on the town? Legitimately deducting the expenses from your business taxes. You can do this if you have your own business—even if it is only a sideline...and it should not increase your risk of an audit.

MEALS AND ENTERTAINMENT

You can deduct *half* the cost of meals and other entertainment that has a business purpose. There is no limit on the amount that can be deducted, and receipts are not necessary for expenses of $75 or less.

IRS requirements...

●**A business purpose.** It could be as simple as soliciting business from a prospect. Depending on your particular industry, *anybody* could be a prospect.

●**Surroundings conducive to discussing business.** The IRS will not believe you talked business at the theater or while playing golf. You must set aside some time to talk undisturbed within 24 hours of incurring your expense. Even a telephone conversation will do.

Example: You take business prospects out for dinner, then to a play and for drinks afterward. You don't have to mention business during the fun, just as long as you discuss it at some other point within 24 hours.

●**Adequate records.** These need to include who was entertained...when...where...the specific business purpose of the entertainment...its cost...and a receipt (if the cost was more than $75). Record the amount in a business diary or ledger on the same day.

Caution: All five items must be recorded in a "timely" manner—near the date on which the entertainment occurs—in order for the deduction to be allowed.

HOME ENTERTAINMENT

Expenses incurred when entertaining at your home are among the most overlooked deductions. The IRS considers your home conducive to business...and costs often are less than the $75 minimum for receipts.

Regulations don't require you to spend a specific amount of time discussing business, so it is easy to qualify everyone attending an event as a business guest.

Example: You invite a guest and his/her spouse to your home for a dinner party, during which you have a one-minute discussion with the guest about obtaining referrals for your business. This lets you deduct half the cost of entertaining both the guest and his spouse. You can repeat the process with other guests.

Larger parties can make it difficult to discuss business with every guest and record each conversation in your diary.

Better: Demonstrate a business purpose for the party by announcing it in the invitation and having some form of display showing a business intent or discussion.

Example: Celebrate your business's anniversary, and put up a business-related display. For proof, take pictures of it with all the guests milling around. Also save the invitation.

FOLLOW THE RULES

●**Spouses and guests.** If your business guest brings his spouse or another guest, you also can bring a spouse or guest and then deduct half the costs for all four people.

●**Season tickets.** When you purchase season tickets to sporting or cultural events, you must deduct each event separately.

Example: You have season tickets to eight football games per year. If you invite business guests six times, you can deduct half the cost of the tickets to those six games only.

●**"Dutch treat" meals and those you buy for yourself.** If you split the cost of a business meal with another person or pay for your own meal, you can deduct half your expense to the extent that it exceeds your average meal cost.

Useful: My experience is that IRS auditors typically determine average meal costs by using a "50%/30%/20% rule." Total your food receipts for one month, and the IRS will deem 50% of the total to be for dinner...30% for lunch...and 20% for breakfast.

Example: If your food bills average $140 per week, $70 would be for dinner. The average cost over seven days would be $10 per dinner. Under the "Dutch treat" rule, your business dinners would be deductible to the extent that their costs exceed $10. Thus, if you and a business associate spend $200 on a fancy business dinner and split the cost, you could deduct half of $90.

SPECIAL 100% DEDUCTIONS

You can deduct the full cost of some business expenses...

●**Entertaining employees.** If you host an event to entertain your employees, you must invite an entire group or department—not just your friends.

Example: You own a small business. You invite all of your employees and their spouses for a night on the town as a business celebration. You can then deduct 100% of these costs for everyone.

●**Sales promotions.** You can deduct the cost of food and beverages provided *during* a presentation at your home, office or an off-site location—not afterward.

GIFTS

●**Business gifts of up to $25 per recipient annually.** There is no limit to the size of a gift and no dollar limit to the deduction if you give your gift to a company or department without naming a specific person.

THE PIG RULE

All of these deductions are subject to what CPAs call the *pig rule*—the deduction amounts must be reasonable.

Example: A doctor who deducted $35,000 for meals said that he "ate only for business reasons." He lost all of those deductions.

Earn $10/Hour or More With a Metal Detector

Dick Stout, founder and former president of Federation of Metal Detector and Archaeological Clubs, Inc., McClellandtown, Pennsylvania. He is author of several books on metal detecting, including *The New Metal Detecting...The Hobby.* White's Electronics.

Have you ever wondered if those people scanning the ground with metal detectors find anything valuable? Take it from me, a longtime "detectorist," we do. I have unearthed Civil War uniform buttons and cannon balls...gold and diamond rings appraised for as much as $1,500...and, while visiting Europe, Roman coins more than 2,000 years old. It's not unusual for an experienced user to find more than $10 in coins per hour at the beach the Monday after a sunny summer weekend.

However, metal detecting is a bit like fishing—one day you get dozens of hits, the next day nothing at all. It takes patience and is worth doing only if you enjoy the search and are looking for a hobby that gets you outside on nice days. It's also a way to further an interest in coin collecting or local history.

BUYING A METAL DETECTOR

There are metal detectors on the market for as little as $50, but these bargain-basement models don't work well. A decent entry-level metal detector costs $200 to $400 and will find a dime as far down as eight inches and a quarter down to 12 inches. *Reliable brands include…*

- **Fisher**, 915-225-0333, *www.fisherlab.com*
- **Garrett**, 800-527-4011, *www.garrett.com*
- **Minelab**, 702-891-8809, *www.minelab.com*
- **Tesoro**, 928-541-1522, *www.tesoro.com*
- **White's Electronics**, 800-547-6911, *www.whiteselectronics.com*

You'll also need a good set of headphones. Get the type that completely covers your ears so you don't miss faint signals.

Cost: $20 to $50.

Dealers often rent metal detectors for about $20 a day. If you're not certain that metal detecting is for you, rent before you buy.

When you select a detector, lighter is better. Every pound counts when you're carrying it around for hours.

Your metal detector should let you switch between an "all-metal" setting and a "discriminate" setting. Use the all-metal setting to search wide areas, then switch to discriminate when you get a hit to weed out the garbage. The discriminate setting is adjustable—you'll want to set it so that it's sensitive enough to react to a pull tab from a soda can. If a detector skips over pull tabs, it also might skip over gold rings.

Some metal detectors have ID meters that tell you what you have found—but these identification systems are right only about two-thirds of the time.

SEARCH STRATEGIES

Where to search depends on what you hope to find. If you're looking for modern objects, such as coins and jewelry, search soon after the crowds have departed—at the beach the

Monday after a nice weekend or on a fairground the day after a concert.

Bring along a garden trowel with serrated edges for grassy areas and a sieve for the beach.

If you're looking for old coins or other historical items, read about the region's history to learn where buildings once stood and people gathered.

The best time to search is the day after a heavy rain, because metal detectors can "see" farther down into moist earth than dry.

Decorating for Next to Nothing

You want your home to look better than it does, but spending thousands of dollars to hire a decorator and buying new furniture is out of the question. What can you do?

Professional room arrangers create a new look using the furniture and accessories you already possess. They typically charge $100 per hour…$300 to $500 per room.

We asked six interior arrangers to share their favorite decorating tricks…

ARRANGING FURNITURE

- **Find the room's natural focal point.** Most rooms have an architectural feature that draws the eye—often a window or fireplace. Arrange furniture around that feature. If you add an additional focal point, such as a TV, position it near the architectural focal point.

- **Separate "heavy" furniture.** If a room contains a dark armoire and a dark-colored couch, place them on opposite sides of the room. Left together, they can make a space feel unbalanced.

Joanne Hans, owner, A Perfect Placement, an interior-arrangement firm in Mechanicville, New York, *www.aperfectplacement.com*.

- **Turn an oversized room into two or more activity areas.** If a room is so large that you can't have a comfortable conversation sitting at opposite ends, turn a corner into its own cozy space with two chairs and a table arranged for private conversation.

Sarah Susanka, Raleigh, North Carolina–based author of *Not So Big Solutions for Your Home*. Taunton. Her Web site is *www.notsobighouse.com*.

●**Pull the sofa away from the wall.** Then put a table behind it to create depth and interest. The table should be just a bit shorter than the couch and 12 inches deep. Because the table will be hidden behind the sofa—and perhaps covered with a cloth—even a cheap table will do. Sears and JC Penney have them for about $100. Top them with plants, books and framed photos. If the table is not hidden, put a basket with a fern underneath.

Gina March, owner of the St. Louis–based interior rearrangement firm *It's Your Stuff! Professional Home Styling*.

●**Borrow from the dining room if you don't have enough seating in the living room.** Many dining-room sets come with two armchairs that sit unused. It's perfectly acceptable to put these chairs elsewhere in the house. Borrow from other rooms, too. A nightstand can become an end or hall table. A bathroom mirror can be used in the hall.

Wendy Dilda, instructor, Realty Enhancements in Rancho Santa Margarita, California, *www.realtyenhance ment.com*.

●**Never position furniture so you have to walk around it to enter a room.** It makes the room uninviting.

Chayse Dacoda, a featured designer on TLC's room-makeover series *While You Were Out*. She runs Dacoda Design in Los Angeles, California and New York City, *www.dacodadesign.com*.

RUGS

●**Put an angled area rug in a small room.** Small rooms can be a decorating challenge because they often leave few options—you might have no choice but to push all of the furniture up against the walls. To add interest, place an area rug at an angle to the dimensions of the room. Area rugs can be placed on wall-to-wall carpeting as well as on wood or tile floors.

Judy Alto, owner, Interior Expressions, in Annapolis, Maryland.

WINDOWS

●**Buy curtain rods that are up to three feet wider than the windows.** Hang curtains that cover the extra inches on each side. This makes a room look grander. Hang the curtain rod higher than the top of the window—this makes the ceiling appear higher, too.

Chayse Dacoda, a featured designer on TLC's room-makeover series *While You Were Out*. She runs Dacoda Design in Los Angeles, California and New York City, *www.dacodadesign.com*.

Our Favorite Penny-Pinching Secrets

Clark Howard, a self-made millionaire and host of *The Clark Howard Show*, an Atlanta-based consumer-advice radio show syndicated on 150 radio stations around the country. He is author of *Get Clark Smart*. Hyperion.

Mary Hunt, editor, *Debt-Proof Living*, Box 2135, Paramount, California 90723, *www.debtproofliving.com*.

Ellie Kay, founder of *Ellie Kay & Company LLC*, 3053 Rancho Vista Blvd., Palmdale, California 93551. She is author of *How to Save Money Every Day*. Bethany House. *www.elliekay.com*.

Whenever there are tough economic times, the country's leading penny-pinchers find new ways to be thrifty. *Here are their favorite bargains and deals...*

●**Ask your local store to honor product prices you find on the Web.** Print out the Web page, and ask the store's manager to give you the same price. You will get the item right away and won't have to pay shipping costs.

This tactic is most effective with certain items that cost more than $100, such as expensive electronics.

Great site for comparison shopping: www. coolsavings.com

●**Repair appliances yourself.** When an off-warranty appliance breaks, servicing it can be more expensive than replacing it. Many home-appliance manufacturers provide over-the-phone repair instructions. *You can also order replacement parts through the following hotlines...*

●General Electric, 877-959-8688

●Whirlpool/KitchenAid, 888-222-8608

●Maytag, 877-232-6771

●**Make perishables last longer.**

●After opening a bottle of soda, gently squeeze the sides, forcing the soda to the top before putting on the cap. This pushes out air so soda stays carbonated longer.

●Keep bread in the freezer, and use frozen bread to make sandwiches. By lunchtime, the bread will be defrosted.

●**Find up-to-the-minute entertainment listings,** events and Web deals. *Check out…*

- *www.wsoctv.com*
- *www.kirotv.com/seattleinsider*
- *http://neworleans.cox.net*

●**Buy replacement pieces for old board games.** If you are missing a few strategic LEGO pieces, Monopoly game money or Scrabble tiles, you can buy new pieces very inexpensively.

Example: A complete new set of Scrabble tiles (Hasbro) can be ordered for $6.50. The game retails for at least $12.99.

Resources…

- Hasbro, 800-327-8264 or *www.hasbro.com.*
- LEGO, 800-422-5346 or *www.lego.com.*
- Milton Bradley, 800-327-8264 or *www.hasbro.com.*
- Parker Brothers, 800-327-8264 or *www.hasbro.com.*
- Playskool, 800-327-8264 or *www.hasbro.com.*

●**Save on furniture.** Ordering custom-built furniture from a local craftsman can cost 30% less than buying from a furniture store. Check the *Yellow Pages* under "Furniture Designers" or "Custom Builders."

Before you call, decide on the furniture style…how many pieces you want…type of wood…whether you want a natural, painted or varnished finish…and your price range. Ask to see samples of the craftsman's work…and get references from other customers.

Alternative: The display furniture in model homes can often be purchased from local home builders.

Caution: Model-home furniture may be smaller than average. For example, the designers might put a double bed in the master bedroom, instead of a queen-size one, so the room looks larger. A dining room set may have two or four chairs, instead of six.

●**Take advantage of Internet coupon sites.** Coupons can be used for on-line purchases or they can be printed out for in-store use. *Favorite sites…*

- *www.coupons.com*
- *www.smartsource.com*
- *www.valpak.com*
- *www.valuepage.com*

●**Join institutions that offer reciprocal memberships.** The zoo in Alamogordo, New Mexico, for example, charges $25 a year for a family membership. This also entitles members to visit hundreds of zoos, aquariums and wildlife parks across the country for a fraction of the usual entrance fees. One day at a zoo in New York City can save your family more than the cost of an annual membership.

Check reciprocal benefit policies of local museums. Most list a Web page in the *Yellow Pages*, so you can check membership policies on-line. *Other resources…*

- American Zoo and Aquarium Association, *www.aza.org.*
- For reciprocal museum memberships to science museums, *www.astc.org.*

No-Name Product = Savings

Save on electronics by choosing a no-name product instead of a name-brand one.

Example: With DVD players, there is little difference between a $35 one and one that sells for $200. Big price differentials for the same product also are common for cameras and TVs. For information on buying electronics, go to CNet.com and click on "Compare Prices."

Money, Time-Life Bldg., Rockefeller Center, New York City 10020.

Bargain Prices on Designer Clothing

Designer clothing at bargain prices can be found at The $15 Store (*15dollarstore.*

com). It sells quality children's, junior and junior plus-sized apparel...shoes, outerwear and accessories—including hats, sunglasses, jewelry, belts and purses. Most items are $15. Brands include XOXO, Bongo and Lulu.

Recent bargain: Romeo & Juliet Couture beaded tank, which retails for $108, sold for $15. Free shipping for orders of $100 or more.

Sue Goldstein, creator of The Underground Shopper, a multimedia outlet that includes a Dallas-area call-in radio show on shopping and an Internet shopping site. *www.undergroundshopper.com.*

Stop Smoking for Free

On-line stop-smoking programs provide round-the-clock help for people trying to kick the habit. Smokeclinic.com has a free step-by-step program and offers free electronic gift certificates. QuitNet.com provides an active chat community with expert advice, a directory of local support programs and self-assessment tools among other benefits at no cost. The American Lung Association offers a quit-smoking action plan through its Freedom From Smoking Online cessation clinic (*www.ffsonline.org*).

8

Saving Money on Your Car

11 Ways to Pump Up Your Gas Savings

High gasoline prices make it more important than ever to save on fuel. Most people do know to avoid higher octane fuel than their cars require and to keep their cars tuned up and tires inflated. *Other money saving ideas that you might not have thought of...*

●**Check the gauge.** Be aware of the amount of gas in your tank. When the tank is half full, start looking for a gas station. This gives you time to comparison shop. Avoid interstate and highway gas stations—gas on a busy highway costs 10 to 15 cents more per gallon than the same brand and grade in less-trafficked areas. Buying self-service gas saves 10 cents or more per gallon. Compare prices on-line at *www.gas pricewatch.com* and *www.gasbuddy.com.*

●**Buy big-box gas.** Some wholesale clubs sell discounted gas at member-only pumps. Their gas averages about 12 cents a gallon less than gas at regular stations. Try BJ's (*www.bjs.com*).

●**Get a gas card.** Major gas companies offer a 1%* to 6% discount if you use their MasterCard or Visa when buying their brand of gas. Sunoco and Exxon-Mobil both have cards and rebate programs. The BP Visa Card, for example, has no annual fee and gives a 5% rebate on gasoline (*www.bp.com*, 888-312-7427).

The Visa card cosponsored by AAA gives 5% back on all purchases at the pump, regardless of brand (no annual fee, 800-551-0839, *www. aaa.com*). Pay your bill in full each month so interest costs don't wipe out the savings.

●**Don't let your car idle.** If you're going to be at a standstill for more than a minute, turn off the engine. Idling consumes up to one gallon of gas per hour. It also wastes more gas than restarting the engine.

*All prices are subject to change.

Nancy Dunnan, editor and publisher of *TravelSmart* at *www.travelsmartnewsletter.com.* She also is a financial adviser and the author of numerous books, including *How to Invest $50–$5,000.* HarperCollins.

●**Map unfamiliar routes in advance,** so you won't get lost and waste gas.

●**Drive strategically.** Combine errands to avoid shorter trips. Use cruise control—it cuts down on gas as well as speeding tickets. Avoid roads that have a long string of traffic lights. Don't slam on the brakes or accelerate rapidly —this lowers gas mileage by 33% at highway speeds and by 5% around town.

●**Buy gas early in the morning or late in the evening** when it is cool outside to reduce the amount of evaporation.

●**Take alternative forms of transportation.** Use public transportation, or even walk or bike. Get a scooter—Vespas and other scooters get 40 miles per gallon (mpg) to 60 mpg. Consider a diesel-powered car—they have 20% to 40% better fuel economy than gas cars. Look into a gas-electric hybrid.

●**Park in a shady spot in hot weather** so you don't need to blast the air-conditioning as soon as you get back in your car. Air-conditioning reduces fuel economy dramatically.

●**Keep the windows closed.** When traveling on highways on long trips, open windows can create air drag and reduce your mileage by as much as 10%.

●**When renting a car, choose the model that gets the best gas mileage.** Most Hondas, Toyotas and Hyundais as well as the Pontiac Vibe and Dodge Neon get 29 mpg or more in highway traffic.

To compare fuel economy among cars: *www.fueleconomy.gov.*

Driving Mistakes You Don't Know You're Making

John Kennedy, executive director of defensive driving courses at the National Safety Council, 1121 Spring Lake Dr., Itasca, Illinois 60143, *www.nsc.org.*

Driving mistakes can be very costly. A serious collision can end your life, but even a minor one can wipe out your savings unless you're well insured.

Serious road crashes are common in the US, causing some 2.4 million disabling injuries and 44,700 deaths a year. Many of these crashes are the result of poor driving habits. These errors are hard to spot because they're often the result of physical changes that occur gradually over many years. In some cases—visual acuity, for instance—even a slight change can create serious risks.

Even worse: When you catch yourself making one kind of mistake, you may be distracted from noticing your other driving errors. People with hearing problems, for example, may concentrate so hard on listening to road sounds that they neglect to look for hazards at intersections.

Costly driving mistakes that are easy to overlook…

●**Putting up with daytime glare.** As we grow older, we may have difficulty with bright light, which often causes a glare that's a serious risk on the road.

Self-defense: If adjusting your car's sun visor doesn't work, try wearing lightly tinted sunglasses when you drive. And of course, talk with your eye doctor, who may recommend medical procedures, such as cataract surgery, if needed.

●**Putting up with nighttime glare.** Glare is more common at night. If you experience it, the best solution is simply not to drive when it's dark. Also, people who are susceptible to daytime glare are often distracted at night by their dashboard lights.

Self-defense: When you drive at night, try dimming the dashboard lights. When oncoming traffic approaches, avoid looking directly at the bright headlights and instead glance toward the right side of the road.

●**Driving after dark** if your nighttime vision isn't as good as it used to be.

Self-defense: When you visit your eye doctor, ask about your nighttime vision. If the doctor finds a problem that can't be corrected, restrict your nighttime driving.

●**Failing to compensate for loss of peripheral vision.** Peripheral vision loss can result from many medical conditions, including high blood pressure and migraine headaches.

Self-defense: Have your eye doctor check your peripheral vision at least once a year.

If you've lost peripheral vision, ask your doctor if the amount is enough to warrant giving up driving. If you've lost only a small amount, you may be able to compensate by turning your head very, very slightly from time to time as you drive.

●**Overlooking drug effects.** Since medication is intended to make us feel better mentally or physically, it's often difficult to anticipate problems it may cause.

In fact, prescription drugs can interact with each other and with over-the-counter (OTC) medication in ways that aren't always predictable, causing drowsiness, disorientation and other conditions that impair your driving ability.

Warning: If you drive while impaired from a drug interaction, you can be charged with "driving under the influence" just as you would if you had been drinking alcohol. The charge can result in a hefty fine, increased insurance premiums, possible loss of your driver's license—and even jail.

Self-defense: Give each doctor who prescribes drugs for you a list of other medications you're taking, including OTC drugs and herbal supplements. Ask the physician to check on possible interactions, and before taking a new OTC medication, check again with your doctors.

●**Turning up the radio while you drive.** Many of us enjoy listening to music or keeping up with the news, but a car radio can be dangerously distracting.

Self-defense: If you have the radio on, keep the volume just high enough so you can hear it.

Smart move: Whether the radio is on or not, keep a window open just a crack so you're more aware of outside sounds, especially horns and sirens.

●**Keeping your foot on the accelerator when there's a chance you'll soon need to use the brakes.**

Self-defense: Put your foot over the brake pedal every time you take it off the accelerator—you'll be able to stop a fraction of a second faster, often a lifesaving margin.

Also helpful in improving reaction time: Regular physical exercise (with the approval of your physician). Also, when on the road, taking frequent breaks when on a long driving trip—at least once every couple of hours.

●**Not showing caution when approaching intersections.**

Self-defense: Even when there's little traffic, drive defensively by slowing down at intersections, where a high percentage of collisions occur. Scan ahead to anticipate problems, such as a car that runs a red light from either your right or left. If there's a particularly treacherous intersection on your route, consider taking another road.

ON TOP OF YOUR GAME

Driving well—like playing a sport well— is a skill that takes continual practice. AARP, the American Automobile Association and the National Safety Council are three nationwide organizations that offer low-cost refresher driving courses—both on-line and in the classroom.

Courses from the three groups vary from state to state but usually take six to eight hours and cost less than $65. All courses emphasize defensive driving, including techniques for judging distance and making evasive maneuvers.

Added benefit: Most insurance companies reduce premiums for liability and collision coverage—typically by 10%—for drivers who complete a refresher course. *To find a course in your area, contact your state motor vehicle bureau or...*

●**American Automobile Association** (407-444-7000, *www.aaa.com*).

●**AARP** (888-227-7669 and 800-350-7025, *www.aarp.org/families/driver_safety*).

●**National Safety Council** (630-285-1121, *www.nsc.org*).

Fix a Scratch or Chip on Your Car for Less

Eric Peters, Washington, DC–based automotive columnist and author of *Automotive Atrocities! The Cars We Love to Hate*. Motorbooks International. *www.ericpeters.com*.

If you have scratches on your car, beware. Bare steel is susceptible to rust. Even a small area showing the primer coat will corrode quickly. This can result in a big repair bill.

Fixing a small scratch or chip is easy. All you need is a tube of touch-up paint in the correct factory pigment as well as several cardboard matches. The parts counter at your car dealer or an auto-parts store can sell you the right color for your model.

Cost: About $6. A body shop would charge you about $60 to do the job.

When the scratch is bigger than a pencil eraser or metal is dented, take your car to a body shop for professional attention.

To repair the smaller chips—one-quarter-inch or less…

●**Clean and dry the area** using regular car-wash soap and water.

●**Thoroughly mix the touch-up paint.**

●**Work a small drop of paint onto the spot** using the ragged edge of a paper match. (The applicator brush that comes with some paint is hard to control.)

●**Dab on just enough paint to cover the damaged area.** Don't paint outside the edge of the chip or scratch. Use paint sparingly.

●**Allow the first coat to dry for several hours,** then dab on a second coat. Two light coats are better than one thick coat.

●**Let the car sit overnight.**

●**Use polishing compound to blend the repaired area** with the surrounding paint. My favorite products for this are Turtle Wax and Meguiars Dual Action Cleaner Polish.

Cost: Less than $19.

●**Finish the job by waxing the entire car.** When this is done right, the repaired area should be very hard to distinguish.

More from Eric Peters…

Get Top Dollar for Your Used Car

It takes some savvy planning to get the most for your old car and to get it quickly. Do it right, and you'll be several hundred dollars richer. *Eight steps to getting more for your car with the least hassle…*

●**Find out the fair market price.** Check out the Kelley Blue Book at *www.kbb.com* or the National Automobile Dealers Association at *www.nada.org.* Guides are available in libraries and bookstores.

You can save time by selling to a used-car dealer or a gas station. Expect to be offered as much as 10% below what you could get if you sold it on your own. If you want to keep that money or the offers are too low, then sell the car yourself.

●**Set your price.** Decide on the price you want, and pad it by 10% so you can negotiate with people who want to haggle.

●**Prepare the car.** Clean the vehicle inside and out. This can increase your selling price by up to 15%. Fix problems—especially those that affect safety. Most people won't buy cars with existing problems. Weigh the cost of a repair against your expected return. If the cost is high, disclose the problem and discount the price.

Caution: If you knowingly sell a car with a safety problem but don't disclose it, you can be sued.

Cars in poor mechanical shape and worth less than $1,000 are good candidates to sell for scrap or to give to charity for a tax deduction.

Get a new state inspection sticker to show that the car meets requirements. Some states insist on an updated emissions certificate before new tags/registration can be issued.

●**Advertise.** Put an ad in your local newspaper's auto section.

Include: The make, model, year, mileage, options (air conditioning, automatic transmission, sunroof, etc.), color, an honest description of condition, your telephone number and times to call. If the vehicle is in poor shape, has faded paint or needs work, mention it. People will find out when they visit, so don't waste your time or theirs.

●*Showing the car.* Talk up your car's best points, show repair records and cite the used-car guide valuations if a prospect makes you an offer that's too low.

Always accompany a prospective buyer on a test drive. Do not be hesitant about refusing this courtesy if you have any doubts about the individual—people have been carjacked during test drives. If you agree to a test drive, ask to see his/her driver's license and proof of insurance. If something were to happen, your insurance company might demand proof that you confirmed the test driver was trustworthy. Jot down the information, and leave it behind.

Caution: Don't permit anyone under age 18 to drive your car without a parent or guardian present. People under 18 rarely have their own insurance. If he has an accident, you could be held responsible for the damage and any injuries. Furthermore, as a minor, he cannot enter into contracts or sign any legal documents, such as a car title. A parent or guardian must sign on his behalf.

●**Preparing paperwork.** Draw up a bill of sale yourself listing the sale price, the car's year, make, model and vehicle identification number (VIN). The VIN is on the car's title and also on the left side of the dashboard near the windshield. Date the document and state that the vehicle is sold "as is" to ensure that an unforeseen problem does not come back to haunt you. Print your name and the buyer's name. Each of you sign the agreement and keep a copy.

Example: Sold one (YEAR, MAKE, MODEL), VIN (XYZPDQ), with (XX,XXX) miles, to (PRINT BUYER'S NAME) for the amount of $X,XXX. Vehicle is sold "as is." Signed, (SELLER) (BUYER) (DATE).

●**Transfer title.** On the car title, there is a box in which the owner must sign before the buyer can go to the department of motor vehicles and have a new title issued in his name. Don't sign the bill of sale or the title until you are paid in full. Accept only cash or a certified check or money order.

Beware: The new owner's plates must be on the vehicle when it leaves your home. You don't want to receive his parking or speeding tickets. Acquiring new tags is the responsibility of the buyer.

●**Notify the department of motor vehicles and your insurance company of the sale.** Most departments of motor vehicles have Web sites that explain how to do this. Go to a search engine, such as *www.google.com*, and search under the keywords "DMV" and your state. Call or write your insurance company after the vehicle has changed hands.

How to Be Sure a Used Car Hasn't Been In a Serious Accident

Many used cars are rebuilt after they have been "totaled." Your best bet is to have a qualified and trusted mechanic examine the car thoroughly and check out its history with Auto-Check at *www.autocheck.com* and/or CarFax at *www.carfax.com.*

AutoCheck charges $12.99* for a basic report, while CarFax charges $29.99. You'll need the car's vehicle identification number (located on the dashboard or doorpost of the car). The report will indicate if the preowned car was in a flood, hailstorm, accident or fire…if it was stolen, salvaged, rebuilt or used as a rental car, taxi or police car…and if it's had an odometer rollback.

Money Saver: As we go to press, CarFax offers a free record report (a list of how many records there are on a specific vehicle) and free Lemon Check.

Nancy Dunnan, editor and publisher of *TravelSmart* at *www.travelsmartnewsletter.com.* She also is a financial adviser and the author of numerous books, including *How to Invest $50–$5,000.* HarperCollins.

More from Nancy Dunnan…

Legally Get Out of a Car Lease

To get out of a car lease, try using one of the "early termination services." They will not only try to match you with someone interested in taking over your lease, they will also walk you through the procedure. Either you or the buyer will have to pay a fee, but that is something you can negotiate.

Two services: LeaseTrader (800-770-0207, *www.leasetrader.com*) and Swapalease (866-792-7669, *www.swapalease.com*).

Shrewd Reasons a New Car Is Better Than a Used One

Here are three sound reasons to purchase a new vehicle instead of a used one…

●**The interest rate on a bank loan for a new car is lower than that for a used car.**

●**The average new-car buyer now spends approximately $23,200** and keeps the car for

*All prices are subject to change.

eight years, while the average used-car buyer spends $11,000 and keeps the car for three to four years. So over time, the cost for new and used cars is almost the same.

●**Used cars cost more to repair.**

Ashly Knapp, CEO, AutoAdvisor.com, a nationwide consumer auto-consulting service, Seattle.

How to Get a Great Deal on a New Car

To get the best deal on a new car, price the exact car you want at the manufacturer's Web site. Also price the car at *www.kbb.com…www. autoadvisor.com…*and *www.edmunds.com.* Check with three local dealers for availability and their best price. Then go to the manufacturer's Web site and enter the zip codes of areas within a 1,000-mile radius—a weekend of driving—to get dealer names and phone numbers. Make an offer to local dealers…car-buying services, which you can locate using any Internet search engine…and dealers in the other cities. Typically, local dealers will try to match your best price.

Steer Clear of Scams When Buying a Car

Bernard Brown, a Kansas City, Missouri, attorney as well as cofounder of the National Association of Consumer Advocates, located at 1730 Rhode Island Ave. NW, Washington, DC 20036. *www.naca.net.*

Car scams are increasing, not just with sales of used vehicles but also new vehicles. While it may be possible to sue if you're the victim of a scam, lawsuits are expensive and lengthy. *It's much wiser to avoid scams at the outset…*

THE YO-YO SCAM

Typical scenario: The dealer asks the buyer of a new or used car for, say, a $1,500 or $2,000 down payment and mentions that interest will be 5%.

The salesperson spreads a handful of documents on a desk and asks the buyer to sign in several places. Among these papers is a document that says the buyer's purchase isn't final until all financing is confirmed by the lending company with which the dealer does business.

Often, the buyer is so eager to close the deal that he/she doesn't read each form carefully. Moreover, unscrupulous dealers try to rush customers and handle documents with what they call a "five-finger fold" to cover up the contents.

The buyer drives off the car lot with his purchase, but then a week or two later, the dealer telephones to say that the financing didn't go through. The car dealer asks for an additional $2,000 on the down payment and says the interest rate will now be 9%.

If the buyer objects, the dealer points out that he signed an agreement saying that the purchase wasn't final until financing was confirmed. Car dealers may also apply pressure by saying the buyer's trade-in has already been sold (which is usually untrue). The buyer sees little choice and then reluctantly agrees to the new terms.

Protection: After you tell a salesperson that you will purchase a car at the offered price, refuse to sign an agreement that makes the sale contingent on financing, and insist that the car dealer arrange for the financing while you wait. Never sign over your title until the financing is confirmed.

Most dealers will agree to these terms. Stay away from any that won't. But even if a dealer agrees, study everything you sign to make sure that there is no language that makes the sale contingent on financing.

Yo-yo scams exist because auto dealers make a large part of their profit by selling loan agreements to large, nationwide finance companies.

Example: An auto dealer may get a 5% loan approved by a finance company but then charge the customer 9%. The dealer pockets the difference.

Such transactions themselves *may* be legal, but few customers are aware of this practice. Yo-yo scams, however, are illegal because they involve deceiving customers.

DISGUISED PROBLEMS

Many unscrupulous car dealers are experts at covering up evidence that a car has been in a wreck. A vehicle that was structurally damaged can be unsafe, and cars involved in collisions may not last as long as others.

Similarly, unethical dealers often try to hide high mileage by rolling back the odometer. Or they conceal flood damage or a vehicle's use as a delivery vehicle by sprucing up the car.

Protection: Ask the dealer to let you take a used car to a body shop, which can spot signs of a wreck, and to a mechanic who can check out the vehicle for other problems.

Many body shops and mechanics will not charge for inspecting the car because they hope to get your business later. Even if they do charge, the fee is usually less than $50.

Don't conduct business with any automobile dealer that won't let you have a used car inspected. Insist on inspection even at large national chains or if the vehicle is still under the manufacturer's warranty.

It's been my experience that most auto information services, such as on-line search services, are often not reliable for checking on whether a car has been wrecked, which is why it's especially important to have a car checked by a body shop and a mechanic before you buy it.

Reasons: You may be dealing with an honest salesperson at an unethical dealership, and evidence of a wreck can invalidate a manufacturer's warranty.

If you discover evidence that the car has suffered minor damage, negotiate the price down if the repair shop believes it's safe to drive. Otherwise, take your business to another dealer.

When shopping for a late-model used car, it's nearly always best to buy a vehicle with only one previous owner whom you can ask about any wrecks or problems that may have occurred. However, less-than-straightforward dealers often conceal a car's ownership history.

Protection: Refuse to buy a car unless the dealer lets you speak with the previous owner. That might seem like an excessive precaution, but it really isn't. If the dealer refuses to let you contact the previous owner, there is a good chance he's trying to cover up a problem.

Some dealers claim that privacy laws prevent them from disclosing owners' names, but this is untrue. In fact, after you buy a car, you'll see the previous owner's name on the title.

OVERPRICED FINANCING

While not engaging in anything illegal, many dealers charge high interest rates, often taking advantage of a buyer's eagerness to drive off the lot with a newly acquired vehicle.

To find cheaper financing: Check with your bank or credit union for the going rate on automobile loans. If the auto dealer charges more, tell him that you'll buy the car but only at whatever you discover to be the going rate. Most dealers will quickly agree for fear of losing the sale. Alternatively, tell the dealer that you'll handle the financing through your bank or other lending institution.

Smart negotiation tactics: When you first speak with a salesperson, never say that you intend to pay cash or finance the vehicle yourself. If you do, the dealership may quote a high sticker price to make up for its lost profit on financing.

It's also wise to stay away from any service contract that a dealer might offer. Evidence shows that the cost of these contracts is usually greater than the amount that will likely be paid out to the owners.

If you're concerned about future repair bills, shop for a car that's still under the manufacturer's warranty.

PHONY ADS

Today, a growing number of unethical dealers disguise their identities by placing classified ads in newspapers and local magazines.

This practice, known as "curbstoning," is often used to sell cars that have been in accidents or that have other problems. Curbstoners rely on unwary buyers who are more trusting of individuals than of dealerships.

Protection: Insist on seeing the title, which will tell you whether an individual or dealership owns the car. Don't do business with a dealership that disguises itself as an individual. The car may well have problems.

Five Reasons to Splurge on a New Car

Eric Peters, Washington, DC–based automotive columnist and author of *Automotive Atrocities! The Cars We Love to Hate.* MotorBooks International.

From a strictly financial standpoint, it pays for most people to buy used cars. *But five engineering improvements might make it worthwhile for you to consider a new model...*

●**Safer brakes.** Today, even many economy cars have four-wheel disc brakes, and antilock brake systems are becoming common. *Brake Assist*—a new feature that further reduces stopping distances during emergency braking—also is being featured in family vehicles from Toyota, Volvo and others. Brake Assist automatically applies full pressure to the system during an emergency stop if the driver fails to depress the brake pedal fully. This slows the car more quickly.

●**Intelligent navigation systems.** The latest in-car satellite navigation systems can direct you around traffic jams and help you find the best route to your destination. Real-time data about traffic conditions is uploaded into the system automatically every few minutes via the car's onboard satellite radio hookup. That data is compared against your planned route in the global positioning satellite (GPS) navigation computer. If there's a bottleneck ahead, an alternate route is displayed. Cadillac CTS and Acura RL offer this technology on some models. Intelligent GPS should filter down to less expensive models soon.

●**Bodies that don't rust—and paint jobs that last.** Today's vehicles are so well-protected against rust by multiple coats of protective undercoating and chip-resistant primers that body rot is becoming a rare sight.

●**Engines that don't pollute.** At least 95% of the combustion by-products of any 2008 model-year car is just harmless water vapor and carbon dioxide. And, several models from Ford, General Motors, Honda, Toyota and Volvo qualify as ultra-low emissions vehicles (ULEVs), with virtually no harmful emissions.

●**Improved gas mileage.** Even the worst-offender two-ton V8 sport-utility vehicle can get mileage per gallon (mpg) in the middle-teens when on the highway. And American drivers no longer have to squeeze themselves into microsized subcompacts to get 30 mpg.

Vastly improved fuel economy with little difference in size, power or performance can be credited to electronic fuel injection and the widespread use of overdrive transmissions. Both reduce engine operating speeds (and thus fuel consumption) once a vehicle has reached road speed. Seven-speed automatics (BMW and Mercedes-Benz) and continuously variable transmissions (CVTs) hold the promise of even bigger mileage improvements. CVTs deliver the fuel economy of a manual transmission with all the ease of an automatic.

Better Deals on New Cars

Ken and Daria Dolan are authors of five books on personal finance, including *Don't Mess with My Money.* Currency Doubleday. They are frequent guests on national television news programs, including NBC's *Today* show. They were money editors on *CBS This Morning* and *CBS News Saturday Morning* for four years and hosted their own show on CNBC. *www.dolans.com.*

The holiday season is the perfect time of year to give yourself a gift—a new car at a great price. Reason? It is crunch time for dealers who want to make their sales quotas not just for the month but for the whole year. This puts them in the mood to move cars off the lots—even if it means selling them cheaper than they would like.

Here are the steps to gaining control of the entire car-buying process so that you can get a better deal...

●**Decide between a 2008 and 2009 model.** Dealers want to clear old models off their lots to make way for new ones, so automakers will offer plenty of rebates and low-interest financing on 2008 models.

Example: In 2005, Ford announced a no-haggle "Keep It Simple" promotion, which ran until January 3, 2006. It combined rebates and reduced prices for most of its 2005 and 2006 Ford, Lincoln and Mercury models. The 2005 Ford Expedition SUV was selling for $26,285, versus its retail price of $36,325. Ford also offered, for the first time, incentives on gasoline-electric hybrid vehicles. GM and Chrysler also have launched similar year-end promotions.

Many people hesitate to buy a 2008 model late in the year because of concerns about resale value—buyers will see the car as a year older than it actually is. But savings on 2008 models versus comparable 2009 models can range from a few hundred to a few thousand dollars or more.

If you plan to keep the car longer than five years, the difference in resale value between a 2008 and a 2009 of similar condition will be minimal. If you plan to keep your new car for fewer than five years, buy a 2009 model.

●**Check financing options before you go car shopping.** If you think that you will need financing, compare rates on car loans at *www.bankrate.com* or get quotes from local lending institutions. Their rates generally are one to two percentage points below those offered by car dealers. If your credit score is 650 or higher (out of 850), you should ask for the lowest available interest rate, whether you decide to finance with the dealer or a local lender. If your score is below 650, be prepared to pay at least one or two percentage points more.

Request a free copy of your credit report at *www.annualcreditreport.com*, or call 877-322-8228. You can purchase a copy of your credit score here or through one of the credit reporting agencies, usually for $15 or less.

●**When considering a specific car,** check the white label on the driver's-side door or doorjamb—it shows the month and year in which the car was manufactured. In most cases, the older the car is, the more anxious the dealer will be to sell it. In fact, you can save money by looking for "slow sellers"—models whose national "days' supply" (a projection of how long the current on-hand inventory will last) exceeds 60 days. You can find this figure in *Automotive News*, a trade publication available at major newsstands and in large public libraries. Or you can subscribe for $155 per year (52 issues). 888-446-1422, *www.autonews.com*.

●**Drive a hard bargain.** Salespeople know that most new-car buyers walk into dealerships unprepared to negotiate one of their biggest purchases ever.

Smart strategy: Instead of negotiating *down* from the sticker price, negotiate *up* from the dealer's invoice price (what the car costs the dealer).

Some dealers might sell you a car *below* invoice price. How is this possible? Some invoice prices quoted in car-pricing guides are above the actual

cost to the dealer because they include holdbacks (a portion of manufacturer's suggested retail price or invoice price repaid to the dealer after the sale) and dealer rebates from the manufacturer. However, if the invoice price includes regional marketing fees—which increase the dealer's cost—you may have less negotiating room. For pricing information, go to *www.edmunds.com* or check *New Car Buying Guide 2008* (Consumer Reports), available at libraries and bookstores.

Other sources: *www.carsdirect.com, www.autousa.com* and *www.invoicedealers.com*.

●**Don't be a "turnover"**—a customer who is passed along to another salesperson because the first one couldn't get you to sign a contract. A more aggressive salesperson will then try to close the sale. To better control the process, keep negotiating with the salesperson you started with—or go to another dealership.

●**Don't trust a dealership to give you a fair trade-in price for your old car.** To get the best price, do your best to sell your car to a private party. Check out prices that thousands of other sellers are asking for different cars at *www.kbb.com* and *www.autotrader.com*.

●**Don't give your Social Security number to a salesperson.** He/she often will use that information to check a shopper's credit history. Unnecessary credit checks can hurt your credit score.

●**Hand over your driver's license only when you go for a test drive,** and then only for it to be photocopied. Write on the copy, in bold letters, *Credit Checks Not Authorized!* The Federal Trade Commission forbids unauthorized credit checks. By doing this, you have made it clear that you won't allow one. Your credit rating is none of the dealer's business unless you decide to discuss financing.

Important: Don't let anyone from the dealership hold on to the original license. You can't make a quick exit without your license in hand.

●**Explore dealer financing only after you have settled on a price.** Don't be suckered by the question "How much of a monthly payment can you afford?" Many times, the salesperson is trying to divert your attention from the actual price of the car. By manipulating the loan terms, he can get you the monthly payment you ask for and still get the highest overall price for himself.

Nor should you fall prey to "If you spread out the payments over 72 months (or more), you'll be able to afford this beauty." If you can't afford to pay off the car in 36 or 48 months, it's probably beyond your budget. Find a less expensive car.

Important: If you don't need financing, don't sit down with the "F&I" (finance and insurance) person. One of his/her jobs is to sell you expensive—and often unnecessary—add-ons, such as undercoating, an overpriced extended warranty, a security system or paint sealant.

●**Put your deposit on a credit card.** Don't use cash or a check. If something goes wrong between contract and delivery, it might be hard to get back your cash or check. With a credit card deposit, you can get the card issuer in your corner in the event of a dispute.

●**Never forget the ultimate weapon—** every salesperson's greatest fear—your ability to vote with your feet by walking out of the showroom. Don't be afraid to use it!

Car Loan Savings

Save hundreds to thousands of dollars by refinancing your car loan. These loans are available at rates as low as 6%.* The better your credit, the lower your rate. Your only cost is a recording fee, usually $15 or less, to register the name of the new lender. Car loans are available through most AAA Clubs at *www.aaa.com,* as well as credit unions, banks and the on-line lenders, such as Capital One Auto Finance at *www.capitaloneautofinance.com* and E-Loan, Inc. at *www.eloan.com.* Lenders typically will not refinance loans for less than $7,500.

Barbara Wilson, product manager for financial services, Automobile Club of Southern California in Los Angeles at *www.aaa-calif.com.*

*All rates are subject to change.

Slippery Sales Tricks at Quick-Oil-Change Garages

Don't buy more service than you need at a quick-oil-change garage. Some offer low prices for a basic oil change, then try to get you to pay more for additional work.

Examples: $40 for an engine flush or oil flush, which is rarely necessary…$60 for a fuel-injection-system cleaning, which is not needed routinely and is best done by a certified auto mechanic…unneeded coolant and transmission-fluid changes.

If a salesperson suggests any of these services, say you will have your mechanic look into it.

Geoff Sundstrom, director of public relations, AAA, Heathrow, Florida.

New-Car Trap

Assuming that the car you are picking up is in perfect condition is a trap you don't want to fall for. If you fail to spot damage before driving off the lot, the dealer might be unwilling to fix it for free.

What to do: Inspect the car for dents, scratches, etc. Make sure that all requested options are in the vehicle. Test features—sound system…air conditioning…power windows, etc. Ask that problems be acknowledged in writing and then repaired.

Most dealers will provide a free loaner until your car is ready.

Eric Peters, Washington, DC–based automotive columnist and author of *Automotive Atrocities! The Cars We Love to Hate.* MotorBooks International.

Buying a "Preowned" Car Is Smarter than Ever

Major quality improvements in the auto industry result in many brands of cars now running well for 100,000 miles or more. But a car's market value falls sharply after its first purchase. So buying a used car that has been well maintained can give near-new quality at a big cost saving. Opportunities abound because the auto-leasing programs of recent years are flooding the market with such cars—many of which can be purchased with warranties.

Best: Buy a car 18 to 36 months old, since depreciation in value slows significantly after that. Savings on a two-year-old car may be $10,000 or more on many cars.

John Nielsen, director, automotive repair and buying, AAA, Heathrow, Florida.

The Best Preowned Vehicles

The best preowned vehicles are those certified by the manufacturer—not a used-car dealer, which can define "certified" any way it wants. Manufacturers certify only the best used vehicles and often provide an extended two-year warranty. Vehicles that do not meet the manufacturers' standards are sold to used-car wholesalers.

Before buying a certified vehicle: Check the window sticker to make sure that the certification is from the manufacturer.

Manufacturers that offer the best certification programs: Honda/Acura…Toyota/Lexus…Volvo…VW.

Eric Peters, Washington, DC–based automotive columnist and author of *Automotive Atrocities! The Cars We Love to Hate.* MotorBooks International.

Pothole Protection

Don't hit the brakes for an unavoidable pothole. Just take your foot off the gas and let your car's shock absorbers and suspension handle the impact. Hitting the brakes lowers the frame of the car toward the ground so that the underside becomes more likely to hit—and get damaged.

TravelSmart, www.travelsmartnewsletter.com.

Warranty Tips

You can have your car serviced anywhere without voiding the manufacturer's warranty. You also can use any brand-name, quality parts—original manufacturer parts are not required. Just be sure to have the vehicle serviced at recommended intervals, and keep careful records. Read the fine print on service requirements carefully to stay in compliance.

Example: Your normal driving pattern may fall into what the manufacturer calls "severe service," requiring more frequent checkups.

C.J. Tolson, editor, MotorWatch, Box 123, Butler, Maryland 21023, *www.motorwatch.org.*

Amazing! Gasoline Quality Varies from Station to Station

Not all gas stations sell the same quality gasoline. They use different additives and have different alcohol content.

Best: Choose a few stations, and fill up at each a few times. Keep track of your miles per gallon, and then frequent the station where your vehicle gets the best mileage. If you see a delivery truck at the station, wait at least one day before filling up—refilling the station's tanks can stir up sediment in the storage tanks, which can plug your fuel filter. Don't let the gas level go below one-quarter of a tank so your fuel pump doesn't run dry and fail. Look for on-line gas specials in your area at *www.gasbuddy.com*.

David Solomon, certified master auto technician and chairman, MotorWatch, consumer automotive membership organization, Box 123, Butler, Maryland 21023, *www.motorwatch.org*.

Buying a Car? Avoid These Gas-Guzzling Options

Eric Peters, Washington, DC–based automotive columnist and author of *Automotive Atrocities! The Cars We Love to Hate*. Motorbooks International. *www.ericpeters.com*.

With gas around $4 a gallon, here are some gas-guzzling options that you might want to avoid in your next vehicle…

●**All-wheel drive (AWD).** This feature has become very popular, but unless you routinely have to drive in heavy snow or on unplowed roads, a regular front-wheel-drive car or even one with rear-wheel drive might be a better choice.

AWD typically adds 100 pounds or more to the weight of a vehicle, and it increases the load on the engine—which means it takes more power (and burns more fuel) to propel the car. All else being equal, the gas mileage of an AWD-equipped vehicle usually will be two to three miles per gallon lower than that of the same vehicle without AWD. Also, AWD costs more and potential repair costs are higher because the vehicle has more components.

●**Smaller engine.** When there's a choice between a four-cylinder and a V-6 (or between a V-6 and a V-8), many people assume that the larger engine will be the thirstier one. This may be true in the government's mileage tests, which are meant to simulate "typical" driving at various speeds and under various conditions, but it isn't necessarily true in real-world use.

Test-drive the vehicle with both the smaller and larger engine under conditions similar to what you will put it through on a regular basis. If you live in a hilly region, for example, you may find yourself having to floor the gas pedal with the smaller engine just to maintain speed on hills, thus using more gas.

Also, over the long term, the life of a small engine that you are constantly pushing to its limits is apt to be shorter than the life of a larger engine that isn't being challenged in this way.

●**Manual transmission.** In years past, it was generally true that, all else being equal, a car equipped with a manual transmission used much less gas than the same car with an automatic transmission.

But today's automatic transmissions are far more efficient than those of the past. They also routinely have as many as six or even seven forward speeds, which maximizes fuel economy.

Also, while a manual transmission might offer a slight theoretical edge over an automatic, in the real world, many drivers can't drive their manual-equipped cars as efficiently as a modern automatic can drive itself.

If you do drive a stick shift: To maximize gas mileage, try to engage the clutch and shift gears smoothly at optimal speeds, which are usually listed in the owner's manual. Many people "ride" the clutch—failing to shift smoothly—which cuts down on efficiency and wears down the transmission.

●**Aggressive "sport" or "off-road" tires.** The wider your tires—or the more "knobby" the tread for 4x4 trucks and SUVs—the higher the vehicle's rolling resistance, which improves traction but reduces fuel economy. These tires cost more to replace than standard, all-season tires and wear faster than standard tires because of their softer, special-purpose compounds.

Surprising AAA Discounts That Can Save You Thousands a Year

In addition to cheaper rates on most major hotels and discounts on vacation attractions, American Automobile Association (AAA) members can obtain discounts that average 35% on generic drugs and 15% on brand-name drugs at eight out of 10 pharmacies.

Other discounts: 10% off from Payless Shoe-Source…30% off glasses at LensCrafters…6% off most Dell computers.

On-line-only discounts: 5% off books, DVDs, CDs, and more at Barnes & Noble (*www. aaa.com/barnesandnoble*)…20% off of flowers through *www.ftd.com/aaa.*

Find additional discounts, including those tailored to your own local area, by logging on to *www.aaa.com/save.*

Average annual AAA membership fee: $60.

Gail Acebes, director of partnership programs, AAA, Heathrow, Florida.

Gas-Buying Tip

A sudden drop in gas mileage could be due to alcohol in the gas you buy. Automotive technicians are reporting that even brand-name gas can contain up to 20% alcohol. Alcohol content will cause a 10% to 15% reduction in gas mileage.

Self-defense: Try different brands. Calculate miles per gallon (mpg), and use the brand that gives the highest mpg.

David Solomon, certified master auto technician and chairman, MotorWatch, consumer automotive membership organization, Box 123, Butler, Maryland 21023, *www. motorwatch.org.*

Car-Repair Shops to Avoid

A void car-repair shops that don't have computers to evaluate and monitor cars. More cars are being powered by computers. In order to keep up, garages need to have PCs that are fully integrated with all operations. When considering a new garage, start with small jobs, such as an oil change. If that goes well, bring more of your business to the garage and become a regular customer. That will get you

better treatment than unfamiliar customers when you have problems or emergencies.

John Nielsen, director, automotive repair and buying services, AAA, Heathrow, Florida.

Less Driving

D riving less because of high fuel costs could save you an average of 5% to 15% on auto insurance rates, which are based in part on how much you drive. Call your insurance company and explain how many fewer miles you're driving, especially if you no longer drive to work. Ask for a lower rate to reflect your new circumstances.

J. Robert Hunter, director of insurance, Consumer Federation of America, Washington, DC.

How to Get the Best Prices for Tires

I f you know what tires you want, go to the Web sites such as *www.tirerack.com* or *www.tires.com* to find a low price for tires delivered to a garage near you. But before placing your order, phone local garages and give them a chance to meet the on-line price. Even if they do not, they may give you free mounting and balancing or other services that could more than make up the price difference.

Jennifer Stockburger, auto and tire test engineer, *Consumer Reports*, 101 Truman Ave., Yonkers, New York 10703.

Sour Deals—When a New Car Is Considered A Lemon

I f your car must be returned repeatedly to the dealer for the same repair and the dealer is unable to fix it satisfactorily, it may be a lemon.

Specific laws vary by state. Generally, defects must show up within 12 to 24 months or 12,000 to 24,000 miles from the time of purchase. State lemon laws allowing you to return the car for a full refund or a replacement apply only if the defect is repeatedly unfixable. Dealers usually have one or two chances to fix a serious safety problem, such as defective brakes or steering…and three or four chances to fix any other serious problem, such as engine failure or violent shaking. If you disagree with the manufacturer's proposed settlement—say you want a refund, not a new car—you may need to go through arbitration. Just because a vehicle has multiple defects requiring frequent service doesn't mean that it will legally be considered a lemon. Find out about your state's lemon law at *www.lemon lawamerica.com.*

James Turner, executive director, HALT, organization for legal reform, Washington, DC. *www.halt.org.*

Smart Windshield Care

Clean grit and tar from wiper blades regularly. Abrasive grit scratches windshield glass, and tar causes streaks. Grit and tar also make wiper edges wear more quickly, so there is less of a blade to clean the windshield.

Best cleaner: A paper towel or rag soaked with windshield solvent or rubbing alcohol.

Lift the blade away from the windshield and then gently rub the towel or rag along the length of the blade several times.

Do this at least once every season—more often if possible.

David Solomon, certified master auto technician and chairman, MotorWatch, consumer automotive membership organization, Box 123, Butler, Maryland 21023, *www. motorwatch.org.*

Never Use Your Debit Card to Buy Gas

Wrongdoers have invented a way to hijack card information when a credit or debit card is used to buy gasoline at a pump. The information is electronically stored in the machine until the hacker returns to the gas station and collects the information.

Safety: Use only credit cards at gas pumps.

Why: Credit cards offer much better protection, with credit card companies generally removing disputed charges right away. Debit cards take money right out of your bank account, and it can be much more difficult to get that money back.

Luci Duni, director of consumer education, TrueCredit, San Luis Obispo, California, *www.truecredit.com.*

If Your Car Breaks Down In a City Far from Home

Do not take it to where the tow truck operator or a cab driver recommends—you'll be at that shop's mercy.

Better: Call the best hotel in town. Ask the concierge there for a recommendation for a tow company. It is part of the concierge's job to protect the hotel's reputation by giving out only good advice, so you can expect to get it.

David Solomon, certified master auto mechanic, *MotorWatch*, Box 123, Butler, Maryland 21023.

Get Best Car Rental Rates Through "Blind" Bidding

At travel sites where you pay for the "best deal" without knowing what car rental company is giving it to you, you'll probably get the best bargain.

Examples: Priceline.com and Hotwire. com. Usually, if you get the rental you want, it doesn't matter who gives it to you. So look for the best price rather than the "brand name."

Alternative: Check out local rental companies.

Travel and Leisure, 1120 Ave. of the Americas, New York City 10036.

Proven Ways to Make Your Car Last 300,000 Miles

David Solomon is a certified master auto mechanic and chairman of MotorWatch, an automotive safety watchdog organization, and editor of *MotorWatch*, Box 123, Butler, Maryland 21023. *www.motorwatch.com.*

Some drivers appear to have great luck keeping their vehicles trouble free for many years—even decades. Others don't even make it past 60,000 miles without major problems. The longevity of your vehicle can depend on what type you own, but driving and maintenance habits also are crucial. A few proven techniques—some easy, some more complex but worth the effort—can help keep your vehicle running beyond the 300,000-mile mark.

DRIVING TECHNIQUES

●**Coast as much as possible.** Plan your approach to red lights, stop signs and turns long before you reach them. Don't accelerate unnecessarily and then step on the brake at the last moment—that wears down brakes quickly.

●**Accelerate slowly.** Avoid jackrabbit starts. Flooring the gas pedal when the engine is cold is a major reason for blown head gaskets, which are expensive to fix. Drive as though you have an egg between your foot and the gas pedal. Reserve rapid acceleration for emergency situations.

●**Allow the engine to get hot.** To help flush contaminants, such as fuel and moisture, from the motor oil, drive at highway speeds for 30 minutes at least once a month.

●**Delay heating or cooling.** To prevent adding an extra load on the engine, allow it to run for a minute so that it is lubricated before you turn on the windshield defroster or air conditioner.

●**Run the air conditioner or windshield defroster** at least once a month (even in cooler weather) for about a minute to circulate oil through the heating and cooling system. Otherwise, oil may settle in the compressor, causing the system to stop operating.

●**Use the parking brake.** If you don't use it at least once a week while parked—even if you're not parked on an incline—the parking brake can freeze up and fail to release.

●**Wind down turbocharged engines.** The engine should be allowed to idle a few minutes before you shut it down. This allows the turbo to stop spinning while it is still being lubricated with motor oil. (Don't close the garage door until the engine is off.)

●**Avoid two-footed driving.** Using the left foot to brake can lead to unconscious riding of the brakes, which wears them out and confuses the engine control computer, possibly leading to stalling, surging and high emissions.

●**With manual transmissions, use the brakes and not the gears to slow down**— brakes are cheaper to replace than the transmission. For most manual transmission vehicles, aim to operate the engine between 2,000 and 3,000 revolutions per minute (RPM) to avoid overworking or over-revving the engine. Don't keep the clutch pedal pressed any more than necessary. Keep your hand off the gear shift when driving to avoid excess strain on the transmission. Don't necessarily park in gear—if another car bumps into yours while yours is in gear, the transmission could be damaged.

Exception: Park in gear is for extra traction on inclines.

●**With automatic transmissions,** shift into park when idling for extended periods to allow the transmission to cool down. Don't idle for long periods in neutral, because some bearings are not lubricated in neutral.

FUEL CHOICES

Try to use a gas additive with every fill-up because modern gasoline doesn't contain enough detergents to keep the fuel system clean. Avoid additives that contain methanol, methyl, alcohol, xylene, toluene or acetone—these can damage the fuel system hoses and pump.

Best: Redline SI-1 or Chevron Techron (usually $7 to $9 per bottle).

Use the octane called for in the vehicle's owner's manual. Putting premium fuel in an engine designed for regular, or vice versa, won't deliver better mileage, and it can cause a buildup of carbon in the combustion chambers, which hurts driving performance.

Don't let the fuel level drop below one-quarter tank. A low tank promotes condensation, which can damage the fuel pump.

Don't fill the tank to the top of the filler neck. Topping off after the gas hose clicks can damage the evaporative emission canister, which will cause the "check engine" light to come on. Repairs could cost more than $500.

ROUTINE MAINTENANCE

Determine the normal life expectancy for major parts so that you can replace them before they fail.

Example: Most people never think to replace their radiator, but a radiator should be changed every 10 years or 150,000 miles—or sooner, depending on your driving conditions.. A list of the normal life expectancies for most parts is posted at *www.motorwatch.com* (click on "Automotive Bible," "Service Charts," then "Depart Parts Chart").

Rotate tires every 7,500 miles to extend tire life and improve gas mileage. (Some vehicles have tires that cannot be swapped from front to back or side to side.) It's also a good opportunity for your technician to check the vehicle for potential problems, such as leaks or parts that are about to fail.

Have the battery tested annually at a shop that uses a "conductance" tester, which can predict battery life. When the battery wears out, replace it with an Absorbent Glass Mat (AGM) battery, which lasts at least twice as long as an ordinary battery, offers more cranking power, recharges faster and increases starter and alternator life. AGM batteries are sealed and don't vent explosive gases or cause corrosion of the cables or nearby electrical components, as conventional batteries do.

Examples of AGM batteries: Optima, Odyssey (prices start at $130).

If the battery can be opened up, you can top off the electrolye fluid (use distilled water only for this).

Clean the throttle body and fuel injectors every 30,000 miles—unless a gas additive is used regularly.

Change spark plugs every 60,000 miles. Replace plug wires, if applicable, every 100,000 to 120,000 miles.

OTHER HELPFUL STEPS

Keep only a few keys on the ignition key ring. The extra weight from a fistful of keys will wear out the ignition switch prematurely in some vehicles.

Use a car cover if you don't garage your vehicle. It reduces environmental damage to the paint and sun damage to the interior.

Best: Covers ranging from $80 to $400 available at *www.auto chic.com* (800-351-0605).

Use a windshield sunshade or dashboard cover to preserve the dash vinyl when parked in the sun.

Are Your New Tires Old?

Tire age is a new safety concern. Tire life can be affected by exposure to sunlight, ozone, ambient heat and nearness to engine exhaust compounds. Tire compounds contain antiaging chemicals that are active only when the tire is in use—lack of use actually speeds up aging.

Caution: Tire dates, which appear on or inside the sidewall, are difficult to decode. Tire dealers may sell unsuspecting consumers tires that are at the end of their life spans. Ask the tire dealer to decode the expiration date. Avoid tires that are more than a few years old, especially for an infrequently used vehicle, recreational vehicle, trailer or spare.

C.J. Tolson, editor, MotorWatch, Box 123, Butler, Maryland 21023, *www.motorwatch.org.*

Insist that Others Wear Seat Belts for Their Safety and Yours

In a car crash, unbelted passengers can become human projectiles and are a danger to other passengers—including those who are wearing seat belts.

Recent study: Belted passengers are 20% more likely to be killed in a crash when there is an unbelted person in the car.

Peter Cummings, MD, MPH, professor of epidemiology, University of Washington, Seattle.

Automotive Rip-Offs

David Solomon, certified master auto technician and chairman, MotorWatch, a consumer automotive membership organization, Box 123, Butler, Maryland 21023, *www. motorwatch.org.*

C ar owners constantly need to be on the lookout for rip-offs—from an auto-repair shop selling unnecessary services to the cheap knockoffs passed off as quality products. *Here are today's most common traps…*

•**Air-conditioning (A/C) system sealers** temporarily plug up leaks but ultimately create clogs, leading to compressor failure. Once a do-it-yourself sealer is used, all the A/C parts must be replaced. If you suspect a leak, have your mechanic check your A/C system.

•**Cheap A/C refrigerants** can be found for about one-tenth the price of proper refrigerants, but they can cause serious damage to hoses, seals and O-rings. Once the damage is done from a do-it-yourself kit, you will have to pay for repairs as well as the removal and disposal of the cheap refrigerant. When your mechanic is changing your refrigerant, ask what type is being used—vehicles manufactured in the last decade require R-134a—and beware of any deal that seems too good to be true.

•**Engine oil system flushing** supposedly gets rid of contaminated oil. In fact, it's unnecessary because flushing doesn't even reach the dirty parts. It also can leave behind solvents that will accelerate engine wear. Just have your oil drained and replaced according to your car's maintenance manual.

•**Fake air bags** leave you and your passengers without air bag protection. Some fakes are sophisticated enough to activate the dashboard air bag light, giving the appearance that bags are functional even if none are present. When air bags are replaced, ask for documentation showing the source of the air bag module and components. They all should come from the car's manufacturer, not a third party.

•**Odometer fraud** has reached epic proportions. Before purchasing a used car, always run a car background check to make sure that the odometer was not tampered with. Go to *www. autocheck.com* or *www.carfax.com.*

Cost: $12.99–$19.99.* Or ask a reputable dealer to run a check for you.

*All prices are subject to change.

Save Money When Your Car Overheats

T o cool an overheating engine shut off the air conditioner, and avoid riding the brake in traffic. Race the engine to increase coolant circulation and dissipate heat. Turn on the heater to draw heat away from the engine. If overheating continues, shut off the engine and open the hood. If necessary, bring the car to a service station.

Car & Travel, 1415 Kellum Place, Garden City, New York 11530. 11 issues. Free to members of AAA.

Don't Buy a New Car Model

T here typically are far more problems with reliability during the first year of a new or completely redesigned car model than there are for older models or later years of new models.

Best: Wait at least one year, preferably two, to buy a new or redesigned model. When searching for used cars, buy models that were in production for at least two years when they were new.

To research a model: *www.edmunds.com.*

Consumer Reports, 101 Truman Ave., Yonkers, New York 10703.

Test-Drive *Before* You Buy a Car

Do you want to test-drive a new car without the salesperson in the car? Convince him/her that you are a serious buyer. Explain why you like that specific car and what competing models you're considering. Be prepared to show your driver's license, explain where you work and give your phone number. If the dealership limits test-drives to a specific route with a salesperson in the car, take that drive—then, after returning, explain that you like the car and would like to drive it again alone. If considering an expensive or exotic car, visit the dealership first and expect to return another day for a test-drive.

Consensus of car salespeople and dealership managers, reported in *Car and Driver.*

9

Save on High-Quality Health Care

Be a Savvy Medical Consumer and Get the Best Care

For more than 30 years, I have been helping consumers to help themselves when dealing with the maze that is the American health-care system. If there is one thing I have learned, it is that the savviest medical consumer generally gets the best care.

But being savvy is not always so easy. Although many medical providers work hard to keep their patients informed, others fall short. For example, very few doctors advise men who are scheduled to have a prostate-specific antigen (PSA) test that they should not ejaculate during the four days prior to the test. It has been standard medical knowledge for more than a decade that this can lead to a false-positive PSA test result. Studies also show that up to half the time, pharmacies are not distributing literature about the drug being dispensed, even though this is required by law. And most patients report getting little or no information about how to care for their condition when they are discharged from a hospital, even though they should be receiving it.

Here's some advice…

●**Speak up.** Whether you are dealing with a doctor, hospital or pharmacy, ask questions. Remember, you are the customer. You need to make the decisions. And you have the right to an answer. If it's not your style to ask questions—or you're too sick—then bring along a family member or a friend who can speak for you. Courts throughout the country have upheld your right to have someone of your choice with you in an examining room or at the hospital.

●**Be your own medical researcher.** Several years ago, a prestigious medical center

Charles B. Inlander, a consumer advocate and health-care consultant based in Fogelsville, Pennsylvania. He was founding president of People's Medical Society, a consumer health advocacy group. He is the author of more than 20 books, including Take This Book to the Hospital with You. *St. Martin's.*

told a Midwestern couple that their son had an inoperable growth on his brain and had just a few months to live. When the family called me to find out what they could do, I advised them to get on the phone, the Internet and into the library to learn as much as possible about their son's condition. Within a few days, they discovered a surgeon in New York City who routinely operated on children with this condition. They took the boy to see him and within a week the growth had been removed. That young man has been healthy ever since. Web sites, such as *www.webmd.com* or *www. healthcentral.com*, are good resources. Reference books published by the American Medical Association, Harvard Medical School or the Mayo Clinic are also helpful to own.

●**Take nothing for granted.** As intelligent as your physician may be, he/she cannot know everything. That's why it's so important to obtain second or even third opinions for a serious diagnosis or invasive treatment. Studies show that up to 20% of all diagnostic second opinions do not confirm the first opinion.

Serving as your own health-care advocate requires effort, but it always pays.

Rx for Soaring Hospital Bills

There are a variety of things you can do to keep hospital bills down. While in the hospital, keep a notebook by your bed. Ask a friend or relative to jot down the names of doctors who treat you, along with medications and services you receive. Be sure to ask for an itemized bill. This will make it easier to find mistakes.

If you can't pay your bill: Negotiate with the hospital—many will agree to an interest-free payment plan. Don't overpromise—offer to pay what you realistically can afford, not what you think the hospital expects. If you can't honor your commitment, you could end up dealing with a collection agency.

Jim Tehan, credit expert, Myvesta.org, nonprofit financial-management organization, Rockville, Maryland.

Save a Bundle on Health-Care Costs

Charles B. Inlander, a consumer advocate and health-care consultant based in Fogelsville, Pennsylvania. He was founding president of People's Medical Society, a consumer health advocacy group. He is the author of more than 20 books, including *Take This Book to the Hospital with You.* St. Martin's.

There's good news and bad news about health-care costs. The bad news is that, according to the federal government, health-care costs are expected to rise by an average of more than 7% this year. That's double the rate of inflation! So what's the good news? *Right now, you can save a bundle on your out-of-pocket health-care costs, which total an average of $1,200 per person each year, if you...*

●**Shop for the right insurance.** Chances are you are paying far too much for health insurance. For example, most employers now offer more than one plan, including new types of insurance called "consumer-driven plans." These plans have high copayments and deductibles ($500 to $1,000) but low premiums (25% to 30% lower than standard plans). This type of insurance also allows you to build up a cash reserve during years when you use few medical services. That money can then be carried over in later years to pay copayments and other out-of-pocket costs, such as for drugs not covered under your plan or even cosmetic surgery. Younger people and/or people who are generally healthy benefit most.

Medicare beneficiaries also can save big on their supplemental health insurance (Medigap). These are the insurance policies that you buy to pay for medical services not covered under Medicare. The federal government allows companies to sell 10 different Medigap plans, labeled A through J. The plans differ by the benefits they offer (for example, different drug coverage, more mental-health services, etc.), but all Plan A policies are exactly the same, no matter who they're sold by. The same is true for all Plan B policies, Plan C policies, etc. What is not the same is the price! Companies can charge whatever they want for each policy. By shopping around (your state's insurance department has a list of approved Medigap issuers), you can cut 30% or more from your premiums (a savings of about $300 to $500).

●**Cut your drug costs.** Everyone has heard that it's a good idea to ask if there is a generic available when your doctor is about to write a prescription. But few people realize just how much money they can save. Generics can be up to 70% cheaper than the brand-name version (and require lower copays if you have drug coverage). And studies show that they are just as effective. If a generic is not available, ask your doctor to prescribe an older brand-name drug. For most people, these drugs work just fine but are up to 50% less expensive than newer brand-name drugs.

●**Do not use a specialist for primary care.** There are three types of primary-care physicians for adults—general practitioners, family practitioners and internists. Each is trained to treat all aspects of your health, not just a particular condition or part of your body. These doctors almost always charge a lot less than a non-primary care specialist, such as a cardiologist or gynecologist. On top of that, studies show that primary care doctors are generally far more experienced and effective at treating common ailments, such as minor ear, eye or skin infections, and colds and flu. In other words, you get better care at a lower cost.

More from Charles Inlander...

Your Medical Records And Your Rights

Medical records at your doctor's office are about you, but they don't belong to you. They belong to the doctor.

You have a right to see the records and get copies, but the doctor can charge you for the copies and the time it takes someone in the office to make them.

Some states restrict what doctors can charge to a certain amount per page.

Also from Charles Inlander...

The Pros and Cons of "Off-Shore" Medicine

In years past, "medical tourism" referred mainly to the practice of bringing people from foreign countries to the US for high-quality medical care. In recent years, the term has assumed a new definition, as US citizens leave the country for more affordable surgery and other treatments. Hundreds of thousands of Americans are seeking foreign medical care each year, and this trend is expected to grow as US insurance companies consider covering "off-shore" medicine. *But before you jump on a plane, here are some important points to consider...*

●**Is it safe?** Americans have long assumed that foreign medical care is more dangerous than that offered here at home. But high-quality medical care can be found in many places throughout the world. The Joint Commission on the Accreditation of Healthcare Organizations, the private group that accredits hospitals in the US, has an international branch (*www.jointcommissioninternational. org*) that accredits foreign hospitals. If you are thinking about going abroad for medical care, make sure that the facility you are considering has been accredited by the joint commission. Also, check on the training of the doctors who would be caring for you. Look for physicians who were educated at US medical schools and completed a residency in their area of specialty at a US hospital. This is not a guarantee that you will receive high-quality care, but it does give you some reassurance because it is easier to check the reputation of medical schools and residency programs in the US.

●**Will I really save money?** MedSolution (*www.medsolution.com*), a Canadian medical-tourism firm, recently released these cost comparisons: Hip replacement—$40,000 in North America, $15,000 in France and $5,800 in India...coronary angioplasty—$35,000 in North America, $18,400 in France and $3,700 in India. Many people going abroad for face-lifts and other cosmetic procedures are paying 30% to 50% of US prices.

●**Do I have all the facts?** It's usually best to use a medical-tourism firm. To find one, search the term "medical tourism" on the Internet and/or consult the informational Web site *www.medicaltourismguide.org*. The firm you select will ask for your medical records to review, and you will then be matched with a doctor and hospital. These firms handle all the details, including travel and hotel arrangements. But make sure you get references for the firm (check for complaints with the Better Business Bureau or the attorney general's office in the firm's home state) as well as the hospital and doctors they recommend to you (ask the firm for contact information for patients treated at these medical facilities).

Buyer beware: If something goes wrong with your overseas medical care, emergency treatment will be provided (your insurance probably won't cover the cost, though). Also, you have no legal recourse in the US against the overseas provider. Each country has its own malpractice laws. Most are not as protective as those in the US. Very few foreign hospitals or doctors will be of much help to you once you return to the US. Make sure that you have a doctor here who is ready to provide follow-up care.

Also from Charles Inlander...

Ouch! Over 90% of Hospital Bills Have Errors

In 1982, when our daughter was born, I discovered that our $3,000 hospital bill contained $1,000 worth of errors. After weeks of my making calls and threats, my insurer received a refund. But, sadly, not much has changed when it comes to medical billing. Several studies have found that more than 90% of all hospital bills have errors in them, as do a large percentage of physicians' bills.

Many people who discover errors let them go because insurance companies, Medicare or Medicaid pay most medical bills. That's a costly mistake. If you pay a copayment or deductible, your out-of-pocket costs are higher if there is an error. Plus, unfixed billing errors contribute to higher insurance premiums the next year.

Here is how to make sure your medical bills are accurate...

●**Insist on itemized bills.** Many hospitals, clinics and medical practices send out bills that lump services into broad categories, such as "pharmacy" or "medical equipment." That's not good enough. You should receive an itemized bill listing each specific charge. Look for questionable items, such as the same medication given more than two or three times a day or charges for doctors you neither saw nor authorized. Don't be afraid to challenge anything that looks wrong. Ask the billing office to show you a written order from the doctor or the nurse's record of the service or care.

●**Keep a log.** It's often hard to remember exactly what happened at a doctor's visit or a hospital stay. That's why it is a good idea to keep a written log of the services you received. Jot down who treated you and what service was administered. A woman once showed me a bill that claimed blood was drawn from her six times on each of the eight days she was hospitalized. She knew blood was only taken once a day because she wrote everything down. She knocked more than $1,800 off her bill!

●**Use your doctor as an ally.** If you see something fishy on the bill, call your doctor. A friend of mine did this when he was charged for a series of outpatient lab tests that he didn't remember receiving. His doctor looked into it and found that his lab tests had been mixed up with another patient's at the lab's billing office.

●**Take action.** If you discover a questionable charge, call the hospital or the office where the error occurred. If you are not satisfied with their response or they are taking too long, call your insurance company and ask for the "fraud division." You'll get faster service and attention. If they do not act, contact your state's attorney general's office and ask them to intervene. If you are covered under Medicare, call 1-800-MEDICARE (633-4227) to report the problem. The federal government has become extremely aggressive in recent years about billing errors.

With more than $1.3 trillion being spent on medical care each year, billing errors are bound to occur. But the numbers can be drastically reduced if we all carefully review and report the errors we find.

Medical Myths That Can Wreck Your Health

Nancy Snyderman, MD, chief medical editor for *NBC News.* She is a head and neck cancer surgeon and associate clinical professor in the department of otolaryngology/head and neck surgery at the University of Pennsylvania, Philadelphia. Dr. Snyderman is cofounder of LLuminari, a communications network of health experts, *www.bewell.com,* and author of *Medical Myths That Can Kill You.* Crown.

Americans know more about health issues than ever, yet certain medical myths persist.

Examples: You can't really catch a cold by going outside without a coat in the winter (colds are caused by exposure to a virus)...you don't have to drink eight glasses of water each day to remain healthy (the best guide is to drink when you're thirsty—you'll need to drink more if you're mowing the lawn on a hot summer day than if you're sitting quietly indoors)...and stress does not cause ulcers (ulcers are usually caused by the Helicobacter pylori bacteria).

Most medical myths are relatively harmless, but a few endanger the health of those who subscribe to them. Even medical professionals might believe these myths, which could put their patients at risk. *Five of the most widespread and dangerous myths...*

Myth 1: Vaccinations are only for kids. American adults rarely receive vaccinations, except perhaps a flu shot and a tetanus booster. Some vaccines for pneumonia and meningitis are very appropriate for older people—and Zostavax, a shingles vaccine, is specifically designed for those age 60 and older.

Vaccinations you may need...

●**Shingles vaccination.** Ninety percent of today's adults had chicken pox as a child. And while this gives them lifetime immunity to chicken pox, it does not protect against shingles (both shingles and chicken pox are caused by the same virus).

Note: Since people may not know or remember whether they had chicken pox, the vaccination is usually given anyway.

●**Tetanus booster.** Get a tetanus booster every eight to 10 years.

●**Pneumonia (pneumococcal) vaccination.** Get this if you have never had one...or if you had one more than five years ago and were under age 65.

●**Meningitis vaccination.** Get this if you have not already had one.

●**Polio vaccination.** This is given on an as-needed basis, even if you were immunized as a child, particularly before traveling to a Third World country.

Important: Some adult vaccinations, including the shingles vaccine and tetanus boosters, usually are covered by health insurance. Others often are not, so discuss coverage with your insurer.

Myth 2: Annual checkups are unnecessary. The US Preventive Services Task Force, an expert panel set up by the US Public Health Service, argued in 1995 that annual checkups are not cost-effective because they only rarely reveal serious diseases. This has encouraged many Americans to stop scheduling checkups.

The task force failed to consider that annual checkups do more than catch major diseases. *They also...*

●**Establish a relationship between patient and doctor.** Patients who feel comfortable with a primary care physician are more likely to seek timely care for future health concerns.

●**Give patients a chance to receive treatment for nagging problems that they otherwise would have endured.**

●**Provide doctors with an opportunity to discuss fitness and lifestyle issues with patients.** Many cases of cancer, heart disease and stroke could be avoided if patients simply followed the exercise, diet and lifestyle advice offered by doctors during routine physical exams.

The Congressional task force was correct about one point—annual health exams are most effective when they are targeted to a patient's specific health risks based on his/her lifestyle and family history. So, if a parent had heart disease or cancer, especially at an early age, discuss with your doctor whether you should be tested more vigilantly than standard recommendations.

Myth 3: My heart is fine as long as my cholesterol reading is below 200 milligrams per deciliter (mg/dl). Your total cholesterol reading is relatively unimportant. Your level of one particular type of cholesterol, called low-density lipoprotein (LDL), is a much better indicator of heart disease risk. If your LDL level is below 130, your risk for heart disease is likely to be low. However, if you suffer from high blood pressure, obesity, a family history of heart disease or other heart disease risk factors, your LDL reading might have to be below 100 or even lower to be considered safe.

Helpful: If you have trouble lowering your LDL cholesterol, don't drink unfiltered coffee, such as espresso, cappuccino, Turkish coffee and coffee brewed in French press coffeemakers—they contain naturally occurring oils called terpines that can increase LDL cholesterol levels.

Other heart disease myths...

●**Many patients focus on the wrong component of their blood pressure reading.** For those over age 50, a systolic, or upper, blood pressure number above 140 is a much better indicator of cardiovascular disease risk than is a high diastolic, or lower, blood pressure reading. The diastolic number was once thought to be more important, and the misconception persists.

●**Carrying a little extra weight is not necessarily an indication of elevated heart disease risk.** If your excess fat is mostly around your hips, it probably has little effect on your heart. If the fat is primarily around your midsection, however, your odds of heart disease (and diabetes) are greatly increased.

Myth 4: My doctor will identify cancer before I ever could. Certain types of cancer, including skin cancer, testicular cancer and breast cancer, are usually first spotted by patients. Waiting for your next doctor's exam to turn up suspicious spots or lumps could greatly decrease the odds of a successful outcome if you do have one of these forms of cancer.

A second common cancer belief—that cancer is almost always a death sentence—is also a myth. There are many types of cancer,

and medical science has made tremendous progress in treating some of them, such as Hodgkin's lymphoma and acute lymphocytic leukemia.

Progress has also been made with many forms of cancer that still have distressingly high fatality rates. Where patients once died in months, they might now live for years.

Myth 5: A natural product is a safe product. Many people assume that the natural supplements sold in health-food stores are great for their health. But because natural supplements are exempt from government safety and effectiveness testing, it is difficult to know which ones are good for us and which are bad for us.

Example: The naturally occurring compounds ephedra and tryptophan have been found in "natural" over-the-counter products—but they have proven to be unsafe.

We can't even be certain that natural supplements contain the ingredients and dosages that they claim. Further, what is safe for one person can be dangerous for someone else.

This doesn't mean that all natural products should be avoided, just that natural supplements should be purchased only from trustworthy stores and upon the advice of a knowledgeable alternative health practitioner.

Give your doctor a list of any natural supplements that you are considering taking—there might be basic health risks, or the supplement might interact poorly with your prescription medications.

How to Get Dental Care for Less Money

Jordan Braverman, MPH, former director of legislative and health policy analysis at Georgetown University's Health Policy Center, Washington, DC. He is author of several books on health-care policy and financing, including *Your Money & Your Health.* Prometheus.

D ental care is rarely covered by Medicare... few retirees have dental insurance...and those who have dental insurance often find that their coverage is very limited.

Dental bills average around $677 per year for the typical senior, and a major procedure, such as a root canal or a dental implant, can push that tab into four or even five figures.

Exception: Medicare usually will pay dental bills if they are related to a medical incident that requires a hospital stay, such as jaw reconstruction following a car accident.

Some resources that could help you dramatically reduce your dental bills or even provide dental care for free…

HEALTH INSURANCE

Insurance can help pay dental bills. *Options to consider…*

•**Dental insurance.** If you have access to subsidized group dental insurance through an employer or former employer, it likely is worth having. If not, the case for dental insurance is less compelling.

Dental insurance typically features copayments as high as 50%…annual benefit caps in the low four figures…often long waiting periods before expensive procedures are covered…and usually only 80% coverage if your dentist is out of network. Dental insurance premiums for seniors are about $430 per year for individual plans. That's a steep price for such limited coverage, but not necessarily an awful deal if you have reason to believe that you will require significant dental work within a few years, perhaps because your dentist has warned you that a major procedure cannot be put off too much longer.

If you do decide to sign up for dental insurance, consider the policies offered through AARP. Rates on AARP dental policies often are a bit lower than what comparable individual dental coverage would cost elsewhere.

More information: Visit *www3.deltadental ins.com/aarp/.*

If you do have dental insurance, confirm that your dentist will accept it before agreeing to any procedure. Work with him/her to get the most out of the insurance if he does.

Example: If the dental work you require is not an emergency and significantly exceeds your coverage's annual benefits cap, ask your dentist if the work—and the bill—could be spread out over two or more plan years.

•**Private health insurance.** If you do not have dental insurance but have private health insurance in addition to Medicare, this health insurance could include some basic dental benefits. Read the plan literature or call the insurance company's customer service department to find out.

•**Medical flexible spending accounts (FSAs).** FSAs can substantially trim the effective cost of dental care by allowing patients to pay for health-care bills—including dental bills—with pretax dollars. Unfortunately for retirees, FSAs are available only to employees whose employers offer FSAs as part of their benefits packages.

HAGGLING

Dentists' bills often are negotiable—but only if you discuss costs before having the dental work done. Ask if you can get a senior discount or a cash discount if you pay in cash. Either of these appeals could net you savings of 5% to 10%.

Call other dentists' offices to ask their prices for the procedure. If you find a better rate, tell your dentist that you are on a tight budget and ask if he can match the lower price.

Get a second opinion before agreeing to any major procedure. There's a chance that your dentist could be recommending an expensive procedure that is not necessary. Have your dental files, including the most recent test results and X-rays, forwarded to the dentist who will provide this second opinion so that you do not have to pay to have these repeated. You will have to pay for the second opinion, but the cost of a simple office visit is so much lower than the cost of an elaborate dental procedure that it can be a smart investment if there is any chance that the original dentist was wrong.

IF YOU HAVE A LIMITED INCOME

You probably can get dental care even if your financial resources are very limited…

•**Medicaid.** Medicaid is available only to those with low incomes and limited assets. Eligibility rules and program benefits vary by state. In most states, Medicaid provides at least basic dental care for those living near or below the poverty line.

To find out if you qualify, contact your state's Medicaid Office. (Visit *www.benefits.gov,* select Medicaid/Medicare from the Benefits Quick Search menu, then choose your home state. Or call 800-333-4636 for a contact phone number for your state's Medicaid office.)

Helpful: Nursing homes are legally required to arrange for dental care for residents who use Medicaid to pay for their stays. That typically means that they must either bring a dentist to the nursing home or transport the resident to a dentist's office to receive care.

●**Local and state dental associations.** Many have programs that provide dental services for free or reduced rates to those in financial need. Services are provided by dentists who volunteer their time. Eligibility requirements vary.

State and local dental associations can be found on the Web site of the American Dental Association (ADA)—at *www.ada.org,* select "Dental Organizations" off the menu, then check both the "Constituent (State) Directory" and the "Component (Local) Directory" to find relevant associations. Or call the ADA at 312-440-2500 and ask for your state dental association's phone number.

Example: The Connecticut Dental Association sponsors an annual "Mission of Mercy" program that provides free cleanings, extractions and fillings on a first-come, first-served basis. Unlike most programs of this sort, Connecticut's Mission of Mercy does not require proof of limited income. The next event is scheduled for April 17 and 18, 2009, in New Haven. See the Connecticut Dental Association's Web site for more information (*www.csda.com/ctmom/ctmom4.html*).

●**Public or nonprofit dental clinics.** Available in many regions, these typically charge very low rates, perhaps linked to the patients' ability to pay. In some cases, treatment is free.

Your area Agency on Aging should be able to direct you to any dental clinics in your region and might know of other local low-cost dental options for seniors. (Call the US Administration on Aging's Eldercare Locator, 800-677-1116, or use the Locator on the Web at *www.eldercare.gov* to find your local Agency

on Aging if you cannot locate it in your phone book.) Your local or state dental association also might know of area clinics.

MONEY-SAVING OPTIONS

If you are too well off to qualify for low-income dental programs, consider these options…

●**Local dental colleges.** Performed for perhaps half the usual cost, the work is done by dental students under the supervision of qualified instructors. The quality of the dental care tends to be good…however, a dental school might not provide a full range of dental services.

The American Dental Education Association Web site can help you find dental schools in your region. (At *www.adea.org,* click "About ADEA" then "Who We Are," and "Predoctoral Dental Education Programs.") Typing "dental schools" and the name of your state into Google.com also can help you find any schools in your region.

●**Retail dental centers.** Usually located in shopping malls, they typically charge 10% to 20% less than traditional dentists' offices.

How to Keep Your Medical Information Private

John Featherman, personal privacy consultant and president of Featherman.com in Philadelphia.

Charles B. Inlander, a consumer advocate and healthcare consultant based in Fogelsville, Pennsylvania. He was founding president of People's Medical Society, a consumer health advocacy group. He is the author of more than 20 books, including *Take This Book to the Hospital with You.* St. Martin's.

The medical privacy form is the long-awaited result of the *Health Insurance Portability and Accountability Act of 1996* (HIPAA), intended to protect privacy, not take it away (*www.hhs.gov/ocr/hipaa*).

Below, Charles Inlander gives some examples of medical privacy problems…

●**Drug companies** obtaining patients' names for marketing purposes.

•**Insurers** telling employers about employees' health problems.

•**Embarrassing messages** concerning diagnoses or other confidential matters left on patients' answering machines.

•**Medical information** given to the media without the patient's consent.

•**Names of organ donors** released to the organ recipients without their consent.

The rules went into effect on April 14, 2003. Now most health-care providers, health insurers and others who have access to your records are required to send you an explanation of how they use and disclose your medical information. Small health plans (those with annual receipts of no more than $5 million) had an extra year to comply.

Released information is limited to the minimum amount needed for the purpose of the disclosure. For example, physicians may send an insurer information about injuries from an accident—not the patient's entire medical file.

Advice from John Featherman…

Never sign blanket waivers and review privacy notices before receiving services. You can change them to limit information released to the specific date, doctor and condition. Patients have the right to ask for even more privacy restrictions. *Some examples…*

•**Requesting that all mail from the doctor** be sent to your address of choice.

•**If you are hospitalized,** requesting that your name, general condition, etc. not be included in the patient directory.

•**Seeing a copy of your file** before it is sent to a third party. Make sure it contains only relevant information.

A health-care provider does not have to agree to your add-on requests—but it must abide by any agreement that it makes with you.

Other newly mandated rights…

•**You may inspect and copy your medical records**—and request corrections to errors that you find. You can't demand them.

•**You may request a listing of what medical information has been sent out about you**—and to whom.

Lest you feel too safe, Mr. Featherman explains that many entities are exempt from the rules—law-enforcement agencies, life insurance companies, auto insurers whose plans include health benefits, workers' compensation providers, agencies that deliver Social Security and welfare benefits, Internet self-help sites, cholesterol screeners at shopping centers or in other public places.

How Medicare "D" Pays for Your Drugs

Judith Stein, Esq., executive director, Center for Medicare Advocacy, Willimantic, Connecticut, a nonprofit organization providing information and guidance on Medicare, *www.medicareadvocacy.org.*

The Medicare Part D pays for drug bills until costs reach $2,700 in 2009 (above your annual deductible and copayments).

Then you pay 100% of the bills between $2,700 and $6,153.75 (the "coverage gap"). After drug costs top $6,153.75, your drug plan resumes coverage—you continue to make copayments.

Example: Assume your monthly drug bills total $600 and Part D plan requires a $295 annual deductible and a 25% copayment for each prescription. In addition, your monthly premium for Part D is $50. *How the numbers work out for you if you have coverage for all of 2009…*

Your total out-of-pocket costs for 2009 are $4,128.75—the $295 deductible, plus [$2,700-$295] x 25%, plus the donut hole of $6,153.75-$2,700.

Should your drug costs increase in the future, your proportional savings will ramp up quickly–because all the excess will be covered at 75%.

Mail Order—Your Medicine Money Saver

Buying medicines by mail can save you money. Many insurers and employers are requiring it for long-term-use drugs.

Reason: Mail-order pharmacies have lower overhead costs than neighborhood ones, so prices are cheaper.

Also: Mail-order pharmacies allow a three-month order, so consumers often can save two copayments by making one copayment for a three-month supply.

Plans usually allow antibiotics and emergency supplies of medicine to be picked up at local drugstores.

Charles B. Inlander, a consumer advocate and health-care consultant based in Fogelsville, Pennsylvania. He was founding president of People's Medical Society, a consumer health advocacy group. He is the author of more than 20 books, including *Take This Book to the Hospital with You.* St. Martin's.

Personalized Report Cuts Prescription Costs For Folks 55+

If you're age 55 or older, you can now get a personalized report on programs you qualify for that can help you reduce your prescription drug costs. The National Council on the Aging has created a new Web site that will provide the report directly to you.

How it works: You just enter your personal information and more than 1,200 programs in all 50 states are searched through to find benefits that you qualify for. More than 1,450 brand-name and generic medications are included. Visit *www.benefitscheckup.org.*

The Very Best On-Line Pharmacies

Nancy Dunnan, editor and publisher of *TravelSmart* at *www.travelsmartnewsletter.com.* She also is a financial adviser and the author of numerous books, including *How to Invest $50–$5,000.* HarperCollins.

To find out if a Web-based pharmacy is legitimate, begin by asking your health insurer who it has made arrangements with. Many major insurance companies have set up discount plans with on-line or mail-order pharmacies.

If you do not receive prescription benefits, check the on-line pharmacies with the National Association of Boards of Pharmacy (*www.nabp.net*) to find out if the site is a licensed one. On the home page, go to the "Internet Pharmacy" button and take time to read the helpful consumer tips.

Name recognition is another factor. Large companies, such as Drugstore.com (*www.drugstore.com*) and Walgreens (*www.walgreens.com*), not only are legitimate, they often provide some of the lowest prices within the US.

Finally, don't overlook your neighborhood drugstore. Due to the intense pressure from on-line and mail-order competitors, some not only have reduced their prices but also will deliver for free.

Low-Cost Doctor Care

Jim Miller, an advocate for senior citizens, writes "Savvy Senior," a weekly information column syndicated in more than 400 newspapers nationwide. Based in Norman, Oklahoma, he offers a free senior newswire service. To sign up, go to *www.savvysenior.org.*

There are a variety of programs and services that provide free or low-cost medical care…

●**Health centers.** Federally funded by the Health Resources and Services Administration (HRSA), these health centers provide low-cost health and dental care. You pay what you can afford based on your income. 888-275-4772, *http://findahealthcenter.hrsa.gov.*

●**Hill-Burton facilities.** There are more than 200 Hill-Burton health-care facilities around the country that offer free or reduced-cost health care. Eligibility standards vary by facility, but most require your income to be at or below two times the US poverty guideline (see *http://aspe.hhs.gov/poverty/08poverty.shtml*). 800-638-0742 (800-492-0359 for Maryland residents), *www.hrsa.gov/hillburton.*

●**Free clinics.** Nationwide, there are about 1,000 privately funded, non-profit, community-based clinics that provide care to those in need at little or no cost. To locate a clinic in your area, call your local hospital or go to *www.freemedicalcamps.com*.

●**Indian Health Service (IHS).** An agency within the Department of Health and Human Services, IHS provides free medical care to approximately 1.5 million American Indians and Alaska Natives. *www.ihs.gov*.

●**Remote Area Medical.** A nonprofit, all-volunteer, charitable organization that provides free health, dental and eye care to uninsured or underinsured people in remote areas of Kentucky, Tennessee, and Virginia. *www.ramusa.org*.

EYE CARE

●**EyeCare America.** This program, coordinated by the American Academy of Ophthalmology, provides a medical eye exam and up to one year of treatment at no out-of-pocket expense for seniors and diabetics. 800-222-3937, *www.eyecareamerica.org*.

●**Mission Cataract USA** provides free cataract surgery to people of all ages who don't have Medicare, Medicaid or private insurance and have no other means to pay. 800-343-7265, *www.missioncataractusa.org*.

●**Vision USA.** Coordinated by the American Optometric Association (AOA), Vision USA provides free eye-care services to uninsured and low-income workers and their families who have no other means of obtaining care. 800-766-4466, *www.aoa.org*.

●**New Eyes for the Needy.** A not-for-profit eyeglass program that accepts donations of used prescription eyeglasses and distributes them to people in need. 973-376-4903, *www.neweyesfortheneedy.org*.

●**Lions Club.** Your local Lions Club can help you find free or discounted eye-care and eyeglasses programs, including the Give the Gift of Sight program (*www.givethegiftofsight.org*), along with other local services. Call 800-747-4448 to get the number of your state Lions Club office, which can refer you to your community representative, or go to *www.lionsclubs.org*.

Medical Mistakes— It's Enough to Make You Sick

Charles B. Inlander, a consumer advocate and health-care consultant based in Fogelsville, Pennsylvania. He was founding president of People's Medical Society, a consumer health advocacy group. He is the author of more than 20 books, including *Take This Book to the Hospital with You*. St. Martin's.

While doctors are facing a crisis surrounding the soaring cost of medical malpractice insurance, we medical consumers are facing a crisis of our own. The number of medical errors is on the rise, and despite a great deal of talk among medical experts, little progress has been made in reversing that trend.

Although most people think of medical errors as occurring in hospitals, they're just as common *outside* this setting. About four out of every 250 prescriptions filled at local pharmacies contain a mistake. That comes to 52 million erroneously filled prescriptions per year! Non–hospital-affiliated surgical centers are also a hotbed of errors and are rarely inspected by state governments or accrediting organizations.

I've always advised the importance of getting second opinions and carefully checking out your doctor and hospital. *Additional advice to help you…*

●**Check your medications.** About 20% of all hospitalizations are related to pharmacy errors or reactions to medication. When your doctor prescribes a pill, ask him/her to give you a sample or show you a picture from a book such as the *Physicians' Desk Reference*. Check out markings, size and color. If you get a sample, take it with you to the pharmacy and compare it with the drug that you are dispensed. Anytime you fill or refill a prescription, ask the pharmacist (not the pharmacy tech) to review the product and usage with you. Ask him to check the medication again and to explain the best way to use it and any warnings. He is required by law to do so if you ask.

●**Make sure your doctor communicates.** Studies show the number-one reason malpractice suits are filed is that the physician fails to communicate the risks and options associated with a treatment and his experience performing it. Several years ago, I assisted a woman whose surgeon had recommended a specific treatment for cancer. When she started to ask questions, he said, "I'm an expert at this. I'm telling you what you need." She acquiesced and did not question him further. The procedure not only was unsuccessful, but also caused her serious internal injury. She later found out the doctor had never performed the surgery before but had not told her. Afterward, she sued him and won. If your doctor dodges your questions or seems in a hurry to get out of the examining room, beat him to the door.

●**Use hospital-affiliated outpatient surgical centers.** While there is still a chance for error, the physicians at such surgical centers must have privileges at the hospital with which the center is affiliated, and personnel are usually hospital employees. Hospitals typically enforce stricter standards for their staffs than nonaffiliated centers. These centers are also accredited by the same agency that accredits hospitals.

By doing your homework and asking the right questions, you can greatly reduce your chances of being affected by a medical error.

Save 65% or More on Prescription Drugs

Marshel D. Davis, assistant professor, health sciences department, University of Arkansas–Little Rock, *www.ualr. edu.* His PALS workshop for upperclassmen is among the most popular courses in the health sciences department.

A 49-year-old woman with arthritis cut her medication bills from about $400 a month to $250...an 80-year-old man with high blood pressure, diabetes and heart disease reduced his monthly drug expenses from $250 to $63...and a 72-year-old woman with a breathing problem lowered her bills from $400 a month to $40.

Anyone can save as much as 30% on prescription drugs—more if he/she is older than

65—just by following the lessons learned by my students. Their cost-cutting discoveries—a class project—led to the creation of the hugely successful Prescription Assistance Line for Seniors (PALS) hotline. It helps hundreds of Arkansas residents each month.

Here is their money-saving advice, gleaned during months of interviews with doctors, hospital officials, health-care workers, drug companies and patients...

BUY IN BULK

Buying prescription drugs in bulk makes sense for people who take medications for chronic or long-term conditions. Doctors almost always are willing to write prescriptions for larger quantities unless they believe a patient might misuse a drug.

Example: One drugstore charges $10.99 for a one-month supply (30 100-milligram tablets) of atenolol, often prescribed for high blood pressure. A one-year supply (360 tablets) of the same strength costs $54.49.

Savings: $77.39.

The savings is even more dramatic for people who take expensive drugs.

Example: Not long ago, PALS was contacted by a middle-aged man who took two tablets a day of a popular arthritis drug. He had been paying $242 for 100 tablets. PALS advised him to buy 300 at a time for $369.

Savings: $869/year.

GENERIC DRUGS

Physicians often continue to prescribe brand-name drugs long after generics have appeared on the market. Nevertheless, when asked, most physicians will prescribe generics. Patients can save 10% to 20% over brand-name drugs. And in many cases, savings are even more substantial.

Example: One hundred 150-mg tablets of the ulcer drug Zantac cost about $195. The same amount of *ranitidine*, the generic equivalent, costs $15.

Even if your doctor doesn't prescribe generics, ask your pharmacist. Most states permit him/her to substitute the generic version of a brand-name drug.

To find out if there's a generic equivalent of a drug, call your doctor or pharmacist or search the Food and Drug Administration's Orange Book at *www.fda.gov/cder/ob/default.htm.*

If your prescription is available only as a brand name, ask your doctor if he/she can prescribe a similar, less expensive drug instead.

FREE SAMPLES

Most physicians receive a constant supply of samples—especially of new drugs—from pharmaceutical companies.

If your doctor doesn't have free samples of your medication, he might be able to get some by asking the manufacturer. Ask your doctor.

Example: One man who contacted PALS was able to save more than $350 last year because he asked his doctor for samples of an expensive arthritis drug. Patients may be able to get six months' worth of free samples in one visit.

DRUG DISCOUNT CARDS

Some pharmaceutical companies offer free cards that entitle people with low incomes to substantial discounts on up to 200 drugs purchased at pharmacies.

The companies may require copies of IRS forms and/or bank statements as proof of income. Some require people to use specific pharmacies. *Major drug discount cards...*

●**Together Rx Access**—a program sponsored by Abbott Labs, AstraZeneca, Aventis, Bristol-Myers Squibb, GlaxoSmithKline, Janssen, Ortho-McNeil, Novartis and others.

Savings: 25% to 40% on more than 275 brand-name prescription drugs.

Income ceiling: $30,000 individuals/$40,000 family of two. 800-444-4106 or *www.togetherrx access.com.*

Free cards without income ceilings: Caremark RxSavings Plus, 800-552-8159, *www. caremark.com,* which offers savings of 20%... Nations-Health, 800-298-1554, *www.nations health.com,* which offers savings of 25%.

PRESCRIPTION ASSISTANCE

Several drug companies provide cards that guarantee up to a year's supply of free drugs to low-income consumers who qualify. Research cards from organizations that manufacture the drugs you take. Annual income limitations typically are around $20,000 for a single person, $25,000 for a couple. Most programs are available only to Medicare patients or people with disabilities. *Major prescription assistance programs include...*

●**Bristol-Myers Squibb Patient Assistance,** 800-736-0003, *www.bmspaf.org.*

●**Bridges to Access,** from GlaxoSmithKline, 866-728-4368, *http://bridgestoaccess.gsk.com.*

●**Novartis Patient Assistance Program,** 800-277-2254, *www.pharma.us.novartis.com/ novartis/pap/pap.jsp.*

Information on patient assistance programs (PAPs) is available from the Partnership for Prescription Assistance (PPA), on the Web at *www. pparx.org* or by phone at 888-477-2669.

PILL SPLITTING

You might be able to cut drug prices in half simply by splitting pills. A 100-milligram (mg) tablet often costs the same as a 50-mg tablet of the same medication. Ask your doctor or pharmacist if large dosages are cheaper per milligram. Make sure your pill is safe to split—not all of them are.

To ensure that you get the right dosage, use a mechanical pill-splitting device, sold at pharmacies for about $10.

Important: Medicare beneficiaries can save money on prescription drug costs under Medicare Part D, which went into effect on January 1, 2006. For details visit *www.medicare.gov.*

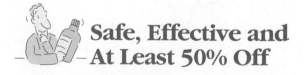

Safe, Effective and At Least 50% Off

Use AB-rated generics. They work as well as brand-name drugs, are just as safe and cost at least 50% less.

Secret: Ask your pharmacist which drugs have the AB rating—it does not appear on the label.

Generic-drug manufacturers get AB ratings after submitting equivalency tests to the US Food and Drug Administration. The rating means the drug gets into the body at the same rate as the brand-name drug. Inactive ingredients may differ but don't affect the drugs' quality or safety. In rare cases, someone may have a reaction to an inactive ingredient in a generic—but that also could happen with a brand-name drug.

Susan Proulx, PharmD, president, Med-ERRS (Medical Error Recognition and Revision Strategies), a subsidiary of the Institute for Safe Medication Practices, Horsham Valley, PA, *www.med-errs.com.*

Seven Ways to Save on Health Care

Scott Bellin, vice president, Thesco Benefits, LLC, *www.thesco.com.*

It costs a lot less to stay healthy than to get well. And health insurers are making wellness more affordable by covering wellness programs beyond routine doctor visits. *Benefits include…*

●**Discounts on memberships** to selected fitness clubs, or partial reimbursement.

For example: $50 to $100 back for every six-month period during which you visit the gym 60 times (two or three times a week). That's like getting paid to stay fit.

●**Discounts on quit-smoking programs.**

●**Discounts on supplements and OTC drugs.**

●**Discounts on vision care,** eyeglasses and contact lenses at specified optical chain stores.

●**Alternative-medicine treatments.** A growing number of insurers cover these under regular programs and require only a copayment. Others give discounts on acupuncture, massage therapy, naturopathic medicine, yoga, etc.

●**24-hour health information hotlines,** staffed by registered nurses.

●**Customized support for chronic conditions,** heart disease, diabetes, etc.—including educational material and testing reminders.

To learn what your insurer offers, contact your company's benefits administrator and visit your insurer's Web site regularly for updates.

Faster Treatment In the ER

For faster emergency treatment, call 911 so that you arrive by ambulance or other emergency medical vehicle, rather than by car.

Recent study: Patients with chest pain who drove to emergency rooms arrived sooner than those who waited for emergency medical services (EMS). But the EMS group received initial treatment 26 minutes earlier than those using private transportation.

Reason: EMS workers start treatment as soon as they get to the patient.

Mohamud Daya, MD, associate professor of emergency medicine, Oregon Health & Science University, Portland.

How to Pick A Healthy Hospital

Some on-line hospital rating sites have limited coverage…rely on unofficial information…or don't adjust ratings for the severity of cases treated at each hospital.

Choosing a hospital requires research. Call and ask how many times a year the hospital has performed the procedure that you need. Compare three or four hospitals within 100 miles of your home. Both your doctor and the hospital should have performed the procedure often— higher volume tends to improve outcomes.

How to Choose the Right Assisted-Living Facility

Robert M. Freedman, Esq., founder and fellow of the National Academy of Elder Law Attorneys. He is a partner in the New York City elder-law firm of Freedman, Fish & Grimaldi, LLP, *www.ffglaw.com.*

Assisted-living facilities are the fastest-growing segment of the senior housing market, with more than 800,000 residents in approximately 35,000 facilities across the US. They offer greater independence for residents and lower prices than nursing homes, plus a degree of support not available in retirement communities.

Assisted living is popular with seniors age 80 and older who still are in relatively good health and value their independence but are no longer able to live completely on their own because they can't drive, have trouble walking, etc.

WHAT ASSISTED LIVING OFFERS

Typically, residents live in one-bedroom or studio apartments, though larger accommodations often are available. Each unit comes with a private bath and kitchenette, but many residents eat two or three meals each day in a communal dining room.

Most assisted-living facilities schedule social activities and outings. There might be a shuttle bus to the mall. There even might be a pool and tennis courts on the premises.

While these facilities don't provide the full medical support of a nursing home, most of the rooms are equipped with emergency buttons, so residents can call for help. Some facilities do check in on residents at intervals.

Assisted-living facilities usually offer access to aides for residents who require daily assistance, such as help with bathing, dressing or using the toilet.

WHAT TO LOOK FOR

In most states, assisted-living facilities are minimally regulated, with no governmental oversight. *To find the right facility, consider...*

●**Services.** Does the facility offer the support needed?

●**Terms of commitment.** Most facilities will permit the residents to sign up on a month-to-month basis.

●**Social atmosphere.** Talk with a few residents. Are they friendly and of a similar age and energy level?

●**Food quality.** Sample at least two meals.

●**Attractiveness of the rooms.** Is it a pleasant place to live?

●**Activities.** Do the residents seem bored or happy and active?

COST

Room, board and the basic services at an assisted-living facility cost anywhere from $1,800 to $3,500 per month. If you need help with daily living, expect to pay an hourly rate comparable to prevailing rates for home care in the region. That can add up to a few thousand dollars extra per month.

Most residents pay for assisted-living facilities out-of-pocket, but the following may help...

●**Long-term-care insurance policies written in the past five or six years** may include some coverage for assisted living. With an older policy, if the only other alternative is a nursing home and you can show that assisted living is cheaper, the insurance company might pay for the expense.

●**Medicaid might be available to seniors who have limited resources.** Check with your state's Medicaid department for details. A list of state Medicaid Web sites is available at *http://cms.hhs.gov/medicaid/stateplans/.*

●**Tax deductions.** The portion of the cost of assisted living attributable to health care is tax deductible, though the part attributable to housing costs is not. Ask the assisted-living facility to provide a cost breakdown for you.

RESOURCES

●**Assisted Living Federation of America,** 703-894-1805, *www.alfa.org.*

●**The National Center for Assisted Living,** 202-842-4444, *www.ncal.org.*

10 Ways to Protect Your Patients' Rights

Natalie J. Kaplan, a former hospital legal consultant, now in private practice in New York City.

P eople who are asked to sign medical consent forms are often in the worst possible psychological shape to make a decision about anything. Serious illness is a terrible shock. It brings out the part of human nature that wants to abdicate responsibility and put fate in the hands of an omnipotent being—in this case, the doctor. It's important to understand before you get sick what your rights as a patient are and what medical consent actually means.

The law in this country guarantees the patient an informed consent. That means the patient must be thoroughly informed in advance about all significant aspects of the proposed treatment. Consent is necessary in all nonemergency situations in which there are invasive procedures or treatments involving risks. This includes not only surgery but also more minor procedures such as invasive diagnostic tests or injections of any substance that may have negative side effects.

Making a decision about treatment of a serious illness is traumatic. *Things you should do to be sure your decision is the right one…*

●**Some hospitals provide patient representatives.** Ask for one to sit in on the informed-consent procedure.

●**Write down all your questions in advance.** Take notes or use a tape recorder for the answers.

●**Ask the doctor for recommended reading about your illness and its treatment.**

●**Get second (or third) opinions.**

●**Take a friend or relative with you.** Someone who is uninvolved will be cool-headed enough to get more information.

●**Don't agree to anything just to get it over with.** Listen closely to the alternatives and also the risks.

The essence of informed consent is what takes place between the patient and the doctor. A consent form signed by the patient does not in itself constitute informed consent. The form is simply evidence collected by doctors and hospitals as protection in case of an eventual lawsuit. In all states the patient has the right to an explanation and must understand the procedure, and in some states the informed consent must be obtained by the doctor performing the procedure.

Example: The risks of anesthesia must be explained by the anesthesiologist. The explanation must be in simple language the patient can understand. *Basics…*

●**Consent for a medical procedure on a child or an unconscious adult can be given over the telephone,** but hospitals and doctors will want it confirmed in writing.

●**Consent can be revoked at any time prior to the procedure.** Medical consents are not legally binding prior to the procedure, and you don't give up any rights to change your mind when you sign a form.

●**Consent must be to a specific procedure.** A general consent form is not evidence of consent for those specific procedures that require that specific information be imparted to the patient to make him or her "informed."

Recommended: Sign general consent forms for basic hospital care. After you're admitted, it's still the hospital's and doctor's responsibility to explain any specific procedures in order to obtain consent that's informed.

●**Consent is not necessary for an emergency procedure** where the patient is incompetent or unconscious and no authorized person can be located to consent.

Emergency: This is any procedure that is medically necessary to treat a condition dangerous to life or health.

Get Your Money's Worth from a Medical Checkup

Leo Galland, MD, director, Foundation for Integrated Medicine, which promotes a comprehensive approach to health care, New York City. His latest book is *The Fat Resistance Diet.* Broadway. *www.fatresistancediet.com.* Dr. Galland is a recipient of the Linus Pauling award.

The managed-care revolution has drastically reduced the amount of time doctors spend with patients. During the typical office visit, your doctor barely has time to investigate troublesome symptoms and check your weight…pulse…heartbeat…blood pressure, etc. That's not enough.

A thorough exam should also address your overall physical and emotional well-being…

diet…lifestyle…and any "silent" symptoms that can increase your risk for health problems.

Most doctors take a medical history, listing current health issues…prescribed medications…allergies, etc. This information is critical.

Helpful: When writing down your concerns, give your doctor any additional information that he/she may fail to include in the medical history.

●**How's your diet?**

●**Are you taking any herbal or dietary supplements?**

●**Do you get enough sleep?**

●**Are you physically active?**

●**Are you experiencing sexual problems?**

Also mention if you smoke, how much alcohol you drink and whether you're having difficulty in your personal relationships. Try to keep the list to one page.

THE PHYSICAL

To save time, doctors often take shortcuts during the physical. This can affect not only your current diagnosis and treatment—but also your future health. *Here are the steps most commonly omitted…*

●**Blood Pressure.** This vital sign is typically checked in one arm while the patient is sitting. For a more accurate reading, blood pressure should be tested in *both* arms, preferably while you're lying down.

If blood pressure differs by 15% or more between arms, there may be blockages in the large blood vessels.

Important: If you're taking blood pressure medication—or if you get dizzy when you change positions—your doctor should check your blood pressure immediately after you stand up. If the pressure drops by more than 10%, a change in dosage of blood pressure medication may be needed.

●**Eyes.** Most of us go to an ophthalmologist or optometrist. But if you don't see an eye specialist regularly and you're age 40 or older, your internist or family practitioner should measure the pressure on your eyeballs to test for glaucoma and look for lack of lens clarity —an early sign of cataracts.

Bonus: A careful eye exam can also reveal blood vessel narrowing or small hemorrhages on the retina—indicators of vascular conditions that increase your heart disease risk.

●**Hamstrings.** Few doctors test these muscles at the back of the thighs to identify potential back problems. To do so, the doctor should ask you to lie on your back and lift each leg to a 90° angle.

If you can't perform the lift, you may need a stretching program to relax the hamstrings.

●**Lymph Nodes.** The lymph nodes in your neck are typically checked, but doctors should also check those in the groin and under arms. Swollen lymph nodes may signal infection. It is possible that lumps could indicate cancer.

●**Pulse Points.** Your doctor probably checks the pulse in your neck and/or groin—but may skip your feet. If pulse strength differs in these three areas, it can be a sign of peripheral arterial disease.

●**Skin.** Many doctors ignore the skin altogether, assuming that it should be examined by a dermatologist. Not true. The skin should also be checked during a general medical checkup.

To examine your skin, your doctor should ask you to disrobe so he can look for moles on all parts of your body, even your scalp and the bottoms of your feet.

If you have moles larger than one-half inch—or if your moles have gotten larger, darkened or changed their shape—you should get a referral to a dermatologist for a melanoma screening.

●**Thyroid.** This butterfly-shaped gland at the base of the neck is often missed during the lymph node exam. By palpating the thyroid, your doctor can screen for thyroid cancer.

FOR WOMEN ONLY

●**Breast and Reproductive Organs.** Most doctors check the breasts for suspicious lumps, but few doctors show women how to perform monthly exams at home.

Helpful: When performing a self-exam, move all eight fingers, minus the thumbs, up and down instead of in a circle. That way, you'll cover the entire breast.

If you don't see your gynecologist on a regular basis, your doctor should also perform rectal and vaginal exams. These exams should be performed simultaneously—it makes it easier to identify suspicious masses.

FOR MEN ONLY

●**Testicles and Rectum.** When examining men age 40 or older, most doctors perform a digital rectal exam to screen for prostate cancer. However, they often fail to perform a testicular exam to check for testicular cancer. Your doctor should also teach you how to do a testicular self-exam.

Beginning at age 50—earlier if there's a family history of prostate cancer—every man should have a prostate-specific antigen (PSA) blood test performed every three years...or more often if abnormalities are found.

LABORATORY TESTS

Routine blood tests include cholesterol levels...liver and kidney function...blood glucose levels...and a white blood cell count. But we now know that other blood tests can be important if a patient shows signs of certain conditions. *These tests include:*

●**C-reactive protein.** Elevated levels of this inflammation marker can indicate heart disease risk.

●**Homocysteine.** Elevated levels of this amino acid are linked to heart disease and stroke.

Helpful: The B vitamin folate, taken at 200 mcg to 400 mcg daily, reduces homocysteine levels.

●**Iron.** Elevated levels of this mineral cause iron overload (a condition known as hemochromatosis).

●**Lipoprotein (a).** Elevated levels of this blood protein increase the risk for blood clots.

●**Magnesium.** Low levels of this mineral can cause fatigue, generalized pain and/or muscle spasms.

●**Zinc.** A deficiency of this immune-strengthening mineral can lead to frequent infection.

How to Cut Costs of Chronic Conditions Like Heart Disease, Cancer, Diabetes and More

David Nganele, PhD, president of DMN Healthcare Solutions, a health-education company based in New York City. He is founder of Harmony Health Communications, where he developed award-winning disease-management programs in cooperation with doctors, drug companies and community groups. He is author of several books, including *The Best Healthcare for Less.* John Wiley & Sons.

A chronic disease can be financially devastating even for someone who has health insurance. Benefit limits often are reached before the condition is under control.

People without insurance may be forced to borrow money or sell assets when faced with such conditions as recurring cancers, heart disease, depression and diabetes.

Making lifestyle changes—quitting smoking, improving your diet and exercising—can reduce the need for medication for many conditions. In addition, sufferers can eliminate some costs entirely by understanding how hospitals, drug companies and doctors do business. *Most effective cost-saving strategies...*

AT-HOME CARE

●**Become an expert.** Learning all you can about your illness may help you discover lower-cost treatments and aspects of the condition that even your doctor may not know about. You'll also benefit psychologically from putting yourself in charge instead of relying solely on your doctor.

●**Contact associations specializing in your condition.** They can help you to locate low-cost treatment centers and suggest ways to prevent your condition from worsening.

Example: Adding supplemental chromium, magnesium and vanadium to your diet may help with diabetes.

Associations for several common illnesses...

●American Cancer Society, 800-227-2345, *www.cancer.org.*

• American Diabetes Association, 800-342-2383, *www.diabetes.org.*

• American Heart Association, 800-242-8721, *www.americanheart.org.*

• American Kidney Fund, 800-638-8299, *www.kidneyfund.org.*

• Depression and Bipolar Support Alliance, 800-826-3632, *www.dbsalliance.org.*

If you're unsure of the appropriate organization, contact the American Medical Association for a referral (800-621-8335, *www.ama-assn. org*).

• **Investigate alternative treatments,** such as acupuncture and biofeedback. Many now are covered by insurance. Even if they're not, they may cost less and be more effective than conventional treatments. For information, contact the federal government's National Center for Complementary and Alternative Medicine at 888-644-6226, *www.nccam.nih.gov.*

• **Buy drugs in large quantities to save on copayments.** Most insurers charge a copayment for each prescription, regardless of the drug's cost. Copayments today can be as high as $50.

Ask your doctor to write 90-day prescriptions, instead of 30-day. You will reduce your copayment by two-thirds.

Example: If you take eight prescription medicines—not unusual for someone with a chronic condition—and have a $30 copayment, your cost will fall by $1,920, or two-thirds—from $2,880 (8 x $30 x 12) to $960 (8 x $30 x 4).

If your insurance company won't allow more than a 30-day supply of a drug from a local pharmacy, ask your health insurer if it uses a mail-order drug service. They typically supply 90-day quantities. Most insurers prefer that you order by mail because it holds down their costs.

• **Ask your doctors for free samples.** Pharmaceutical companies give away billions of dollars worth of samples for doctors to pass on to patients. Don't be embarrassed to ask. If your doctor doesn't have samples, ask him to prescribe generic drugs. For all but a very small percentage of patients, generics are just as effective as brand-name drugs. If you do have insurance, you may have a smaller copayment with generic drugs.

Example: A patient who suffers from depression and doesn't have drug coverage typically pays about $687 for 90 tablets of Prozac in 40-milligram (mg) strength. The generic equivalent represents a saving of 30% or more.

• **Take part in a clinical trial.** Each year, thousands of people with chronic ailments receive free treatment by taking part in trials designed to assess new drugs and procedures. The drug industry or National Institutes of Health (800-411-1222, *www.nih.gov*) coordinates most of these trials.

Important: Participants are given a consent form explaining the trial. Read it, and ask questions before signing.

Some trials are *open*—all the participants are given the medicine being tested and are informed about the results of the trial at each stage.

Other trials are *double-blind*—some participants are given the treatment while others receive a placebo. This prevents test results from being skewed by psychological factors. Patients—and often the doctors who administer the drug—aren't told who has received the drug and who has received the placebo.

Despite the risk that you won't receive any treatment, don't rule out a double-blind trial. If you take part in one, you have about a 50-50 chance of receiving cutting-edge medication.

Even if you get the placebo, doctors typically take you out of the trial if your condition worsens, so you can resume treatment on your own.

HOSPITAL-BASED CARE

• **When you are hospitalized, put your primary-care physician in charge.** Doctors who are unfamiliar with your health history might recommend costly, unnecessary procedures.

Primary physicians, as a rule, recommend fewer procedures than other doctors at a hospital. Your primary doctor already is familiar with your condition and may have tried a variety of treatments for you in the past.

You might even ask your primary physician to help check your hospital bill for inaccuracies. As a patient with a chronic illness, you need to be vigilant about not reaching insurance policy limits sooner than necessary.

● **Consider treatment at a teaching or government-run hospital or clinic.** These institutions usually charge patients according to their ability to pay. They can make sense for people with limited incomes, especially those who lack insurance or have passed their insurance limit.

Information: Health Resources and Services Administration, 800-400-2742, *www.hrsa.gov.*

● **Negotiate with the hospital and other providers.** Pay what you can now, and work out a payment plan for the rest. Or ask for a fee reduction. A hospital or doctor nearly always will compromise because reducing the bill may be cheaper than paying a collection agency or not collecting at all.

● **Get the opinion of more than one doctor before any procedure.** Second opinions increase your chance of finding less expensive—and perhaps more effective—treatment.

Example: Cancer treatments vary greatly in cost and outcome. Since few doctors are experts in all procedures, it's best to weigh the options with different specialists.

Many chronic disease sufferers don't get more than one opinion because they think that their insurance will not pay for a second opinion. In fact, most policies will pay for two or three consultations as long as the doctors are in the insurer's network of approved physicians.

Latest Medicare Scam—Old Bills

Nora Johnson, a medical billing auditor with Medical Billing Advocates of America, a nationwide network of independent medical billing advocates, Caldwell, West Virginia. *www.billadvocates.com.*

Recently, bill-collection agencies have been contacting some seniors saying that Medicare claims from years past have been denied, and these individuals must pay up. Some agencies have legitimately purchased lists of unpaid debts from hospitals—but others might be scams. Under no circumstances should you immediately pay any such bill.

Better: Send a certified letter to the collection agency stating that you're disputing the bill and that you want to see a copy of the Medicare denial. By law, you are entitled to receive this.

Many collection agencies will give up at this point, but if you are sent a copy of the Medicare form, try to determine the reason for the denial. Medicare claims often are denied because of coding mistakes or missed deadlines—these things are the fault of the hospital or health-care provider. If that's the case, contact the billing department at the hospital or the health-care provider, explain that the fault was theirs and ask to be sent a new bill showing a balance of zero.

Helpful: Medicare forms are difficult to interpret. If you can't figure out the reason for the denial, contact Medicare at 800-633-4227.

Even if the Medicare claim denial wasn't the hospital's fault, you can be billed only if the hospital can prove you signed an "Advanced Beneficiary Notice" form when you received treatment, establishing that you knew the procedure might not be covered.

Also, you might not have to pay the bill if the statute of limitations on debt collections has expired. That could be from three to eight years, depending on your state. Check with the office of your state's attorney general or at *www.fair-debt-collection.com.*

Don't make even a small partial payment to the collection agency without confirming the charge is legitimate—doing so can reset the statute-of-limitations clock on the rest of the bill.

10

Health Secrets and Money Savers

How to Pay *Much* Less for Medical Care

Most people never think about negotiating fees with a doctor or other health-care provider. Negotiating is something we do with a car dealer or at a flea market. But the truth is, doctors and hospitals negotiate fees with insurance companies and the government all the time. So why not with you? If you have health insurance, you can save by negotiating such health-care fees as copayments. If you are uninsured or need a medical treatment that is not covered by your insurance, you can save even more. *How to negotiate fees for health care and medical products...*

●**Don't be afraid to ask.** Most doctors are willing to lower their fees for people with limited budgets who may not have health insurance (or only very basic coverage). But you must initiate the negotiation.

My advice: If the quoted fee is more than you can pay, ask if some other payment arrangement, such as paying in monthly installments, can be made or if the fee can be lowered.

What you might say: "What is the fee for this treatment/service? Unfortunately, I can't afford that. Can we negotiate?" If you have been treated by the health-care provider for many years, mention your loyal patronage.

●**Talk to the right person.** In a recent report published in *U.S. News & World Report*, a hospital's chief financial officer (CFO) noted that it is common for hospitals to reduce charges by 30% for needy or uninsured patients who contact the CFO directly. He noted that most hospitals give large health insurers discounts of 60% or more, so deals with individual patients are still profitable to the facility.

Charles B. Inlander, a consumer advocate and health-care consultant based in Fogelsville, Pennsylvania. He was founding president of People's Medical Society, a consumer health advocacy group. He is the author of more than 20 books, including *Take This Book to the Hospital with You.* St. Martin's.

My advice: Always negotiate with a decision-maker. For fee reductions at a hospital, before you receive surgery or any other treatment, call the hospital and ask the operator to connect you to the office of the CFO or the assistant CFO—one of them must sign off on all of the hospital's financial negotiations. At a doctor's office, talk directly to the doctor about lower fees—not the nurse, office manager or receptionist.

What you might say to a doctor or hospital CFO: "What does Medicare pay you for the service or treatment I am going to get? Will you accept the same payment from me?"

● **Request a discount on medical products.** Several years ago, I took a friend to a hearing-aid shop, and we negotiated 40% off the lowest quoted price. Since most stores that sell hearing aids, wheelchairs and other types of durable medical equipment are privately owned, and typically mark up products by 50% to 100%, you usually can strike a good bargain with the owner.

My advice: Shop around before negotiating and don't forget to check prices on the Internet. Then start by offering 20% less than the best price you found elsewhere. Offer to pay in cash rather than by credit card or check—this saves the merchant a processing fee.

The worst that can happen if you try to negotiate a medical fee is that your request will be turned down. But chances are you'll save a tidy sum with little effort on your part.

Get Your Drugs at 50% Off—or Even Free

Edward Jardini, MD, a family physician at Twin Cities Community Hospital in Templeton, California, where he has served as chair of the pharmacy and therapeutics committee. He is the author of *How to Save on Prescription Drugs: 20 Cost-Saving Methods.* Celestial Arts. *www.howtosaveondrugs.com.*

Anyone who regularly takes prescription medication knows how pricey drugs can be.

Fortunately, there are places where you can buy your drugs for less—or even get them for free. The key is knowing where to look.

Important: Although most low-cost drug programs have income eligibility requirements, do not assume that you won't be accepted into a program just because your income is officially too high. Many programs will consider applications on a case-by-case basis.

Best resources for finding low-cost or free medications…

DRUG DISCOUNT NETWORKS

Some groups connect patients to public and private assistance programs that provide discounted or free drugs to eligible patients. *These include…*

Partnership for Prescription Assistance (888-477-2669, *www.pparx.org*). This collaborative network of professional medical organizations, including the American Academy of Family Physicians, and private groups links patients with more than 475 public and private patient assistance programs that offer more than 2,500 drugs at reduced cost or no charge. Income qualifications vary by state.

Together Rx Program (800-444-4106, *www.togetherrxaccess.com*). Backed by a consortium of pharmaceutical companies, this program provides a 15% to 40% discount on more than 300 brand-name and generic prescription drugs. The program targets people who don't have prescription drug coverage with annual incomes of $30,000 or less for individuals…$40,000 for a family of two…and up to $70,000 for a family of five.

PHARMACEUTICAL PATIENT-ASSISTANCE PROGRAMS

Major pharmaceutical companies have their own patient-assistance programs that offer many—though not all—drugs at a discount, or even for free, to people who cannot afford them. Eligibility requirements vary—even families earning up to $70,000 a year can qualify. Some companies evaluate applications on a case-by-case basis.

To obtain a free copy of Directory of Prescription Drug Patient Assistance Programs, call the Partnership for Prescription Assistance at 800-762-4636. To determine the manufacturer of a particular drug, ask your pharmacist or go to *www.PDRhealth.com/drugs/drugs-index.aspx. Among the pharmaceutical companies with programs…*

Abbott Patient Assistance Program (800-222-6885, *www.abbott.com*). Click on "Global Citizenship."

AstraZeneca's AZ & Me Prescription Savings Program (800-292-6363, *www.astrazeneca us.com*).

GlaxoSmithKline (888-825-5249, us.gsk.com). Click on "A Helping Hand" for a list of all GSK drug-assistance programs.

Lilly Cares Patient Assistance Program (Eli Lilly) (800-545-6962, *www.lillycares.com*).

Merck Patient Assistance Program (800-727-5400, *www.merck.com/merckhelps/patientas sistance/home.html*).

Novartis Patient Assistance Foundation (800-277-2254, *www.pharma.us.novartis.com*).

Pfizer Connection to Care (866-776-3700, *www.pfizerhelpfulanswers.com*).

Roche Labs Patient Assistant Foundation (877-757-6243, *www.rocheusa.com/programs/ patientassist.asp*).

Schering-Plough Cares (800-656-9485, *www. schering-plough.com*). Click on "Consumer Health Care," then "Patient Assistance and Support Programs."

Wyeth Pharmaceutical Patient Assistance Program (800-568-9938, *www.wyeth.com*).

Some pharmaceutical companies also offer coupons that can be printed from their Web sites, as well as discount card programs offering savings on some products. Check the drug manufacturer's Web site for details.

Cheap, Handy Pain Remedy

Charles H. Hennekens, MD, DrPH, professor of medicine, epidemiology and public health at University of Miami (Florida) School of Medicine. He is a leading expert on low-dose aspirin for the treatment and prevention of cardiovascular disease and was the founding principal investigator for the Harvard-based Physicians' Health Study and Women's Health Study.

Aspirin is one of the best treatments for fever, headache and other aches and pains. It also is the safest and least expensive drug for preventing heart attack—

and it can greatly increase survival in those who have just had a heart attack.

Recent research suggests that aspirin may have other important uses as well. It prevents colon cancer and may prevent breast cancer. It may even slow the progression of Alzheimer's disease.

Important: Don't take aspirin for more than two weeks—and don't exceed the recommended dosage on the label—without consulting your doctor. Regular use can cause intestinal upset or bleeding, although these side effects are rare at the low doses required for prevention of chronic diseases.

Here, a look at the latest findings…

HEART ATTACK PREVENTION

Most heart attacks occur when a clot in a coronary artery prevents blood from reaching the heart. Aspirin blocks the effects of thromboxane A2, a substance that initiates clotting. The Physicians' Health Study (PHS), a landmark study that followed 22,071 men age 40 and older, showed that aspirin reduced the risk of a first heart attack by 44%.

New finding: It is now believed that inflammation in the arteries may be just as important as blood clots in causing heart attacks. In the PHS, patients with the highest levels of C-reactive protein, a marker of inflammation, had a 52% drop in heart attack risk when taking aspirin.

The aspirin dose currently recommended to reduce clotting is too low to have a significant effect on inflammation. Studies are under way to determine if higher doses of aspirin would be beneficial.

Who should consider aspirin: Anyone who has a history of heart problems or greater-than-10% risk of having a heart attack within the next decade based on a standardized scoring method developed by the Framingham Heart Study. (Ask your doctor to calculate your risk, or go to *www. framinghamheartstudy.org* and click on "Risk Score Profiles.") Those at risk include many men over age 40 and women over age 50—especially those who smoke or have high cholesterol or high blood pressure. There would be 100,000 fewer first heart attacks each year if patients in these groups took aspirin regularly.

Dose: Up to 325 milligrams (mg)—one adult aspirin—daily. A dose as low as 81 mg (one baby aspirin) daily can be effective.

New warning #1: If you have a history of heart problems, don't stop taking aspirin without talking to your cardiologist. Patients routinely are advised to stop taking aspirin before surgery or other invasive procedures, such as colonoscopy, tooth extraction and biopsy, to reduce the risk of bleeding.

Recent study: More than 4% of 1,236 heart patients who stopped taking aspirin had coronary "events," such as heart attack, within one week.

New warning #2: Take aspirin at least two hours before other nonsteroidal anti-inflammatory drugs (NSAIDs). Data from the PHS found that men who regularly took aspirin and other NSAIDs, such as ibuprofen and naproxen, had no reduction in heart attack risk. That's because NSAIDs can inhibit aspirin's heart-protecting effects.

DURING A HEART ATTACK

In a study of more than 17,000 heart attack patients, those given aspirin during a heart attack had a 23% lower death rate during the first 35 days as well as significant decreases in subsequent heart attack and stroke.

Taking aspirin inhibits the activity of blood platelets, responsible for clotting, within 10 to 15 minutes.

The clot-dissolving drug streptokinase, routinely given after heart attacks, decreases the death rate by 25% but causes hemorrhagic stroke (bleeding in the brain) in about three of every 1,000 patients. It also has to be given within six hours of a heart attack to be effective. Aspirin has a much longer "therapeutic window"—24 hours after the onset of heart attack symptoms.

Dose: 325 mg at the first sign of symptoms, such as chest pain or pressure, shortness of breath, lightheadedness or pain that spreads to the shoulder, neck or arms. Be sure to tell emergency personnel that you have taken aspirin.

Important: If the tablet is coated, crush it before taking it to hasten absorption. If the person having a heart attack is unconscious, put a noncoated 325-mg aspirin under his/her tongue.

MIGRAINE

Migraine sufferers have a 20% to 30% decrease in attacks when they take aspirin every other day. Platelets contain histamine, a chemical that triggers spasms in brain blood vessels, causing pain. Aspirin makes platelets less "sticky" and inhibits the release of histamine.

New finding: Aspirin is as effective as sumatriptan (Imitrex), a prescription migraine drug. A study of migraine patients showed that those who took high doses of aspirin at the onset of symptoms had a better response and fewer side effects than those taking intravenous Imitrex.

Dose: 81- to 325-mg aspirin daily or every other day for prevention…at least 1,000 mg for an acute attack.

ARTHRITIS

Aspirin inhibits the synthesis of prostaglandins, chemicals that cause inflammation and pain. It's the best NSAID for any condition that involves inflammation, such as arthritis. If arthritis pain is managed with other medication, low-dose aspirin therapy also should be considered to reduce risk of cardiovascular disease. Patients with rheumatoid arthritis have a higher risk of cardiovascular disease.

Dose: Two 325-mg tablets six times daily… or two 500-mg tablets four times a day for treatment and prevention.

COLON CANCER

Aspirin reduces risk of colorectal cancer. Researchers looked at more than 1,100 people diagnosed with colon cancer. Those given aspirin had a lower incidence of recurring polyps, and their risk of advanced lesions declined by more than 40%.

Aspirin is thought to block two enzymes, cyclooxygenase 1 and 2, inhibiting the growth of cancer cells and their ability to establish a blood supply.

Dose: 81-mg aspirin daily if you have a family history of colorectal cancer or other risk factors, such as polyps.

MORE RESEARCH NEEDED

●**Breast cancer.** Women who take aspirin seven or more times a week are 26% less likely to get the most common form of breast cancer. Between 60% and 70% of breast cancer cases are estrogen receptor–positive, meaning the presence of estrogen causes tumors to grow. It's thought that aspirin blocks an enzyme used in estrogen production.

Even though women taking aspirin for other conditions may gain protection against breast cancer, the research is too preliminary to recommend aspirin solely for this purpose.

●**Alzheimer's disease.** Alzheimer's patients who take aspirin regularly perform better on language, memory and other cognitive tests. Aspirin reduces brain inflammation and improves circulation—but it's still not clear if it slows the progression of the disease.

●**Gum disease.** Studies suggest that aspirin may reduce the risk of periodontal disease, probably due to its anti-inflammatory and anti-platelet effects. If you have gum disease, ask your dentist if aspirin might be effective for you.

Diabetes Fighter in Your Kitchen

Four to five cups of caffeinated coffee a day can cut diabetes risk by 30%. Drinking more has no added benefit. Decaffeinated coffee has only a slight effect. Tea has none. Other caffeinated beverages, such as cola, were not studied.

Caution: Additional study is required before researchers can recommend coffee to protect against diabetes.

Frank B. Hu, MD, PhD, associate professor of nutrition and epidemiology at Harvard School of Public Health, Boston, and the leader of a study of more than 100,000 people, presented at a meeting of the American Diabetes Association.

Seven Simple Skin-Saver Secrets

Nicholas Lowe, MD, clinical professor of dermatology, UCLA School of Medicine, and senior lecturer in dermatology, University College, London, England. He is coauthor of *Skin Secrets—The Medical Facts Versus the Beauty Fiction.* Collins & Brown.

Antiaging creams for your skin are virtually becoming a reality, as the fine line between cosmetics and skin medications continues to blur. Here are ways to keep your skin young and supple, whether you're male or female, and no matter what your age.

●**Apply full-spectrum sunscreen every morning.** While some skin types are more prone to wrinkles than others, the way your skin ages has less to do with your genes than with the amount of sunlight your skin is exposed to.

Up to 80% of skin damage is ascribed to the ultraviolet rays of the sun—both ultraviolet B (UVB) rays, which are the primary cause of sunburn and skin cancer, and ultraviolet A (UVA) rays, which are largely responsible for the damage that is associated with aging.

Unlike UVB rays, UVA rays can penetrate your skin even on cloudy days. That's why the most important way to keep your skin young is to apply full-spectrum sunscreen (which absorbs both UVA and UVB rays) of SPF-15 or higher every morning.

Women should apply it right after bathing, then let the sunscreen dry before putting on makeup. Men should apply right after bathing and shaving.

This sunscreen rule holds even if you don't plan to be outdoors for very long.

Reason: Sun damage can occur even while you're driving your car—UV rays go right through your windshield.

Breakthrough: It's never too late to start this regimen. Researchers have found that by protecting your skin this way on a daily basis, you can actually begin to reverse sun damage that has already occurred.

●**Apply topical antioxidant cream.** Most skin damage is caused by the toxic effect of free radicals—rogue molecules created during the natural cell oxidation process. These molecules are missing a crucial electron, and so they try to grab an electron from wherever they can, often tearing apart healthy cells in the process. When skin is exposed to sunlight or some other toxin, such as secondhand cigarette smoke, the production of free radicals accelerates.

To fight off these vicious free radicals, your body comes equipped with its own all-natural antioxidants, which have extra electrons that can be given up to neutralize the rogue molecules. You can get added protection by taking supplements of the antioxidant vitamins A, C and E (be sure to consult your doctor for the dosages that are right for you). However, while a daily multivitamin pill provides antioxidant protection to much of your body, unfortunately only about 1% of dietary vitamins make it through to your skin.

Better solution: Apply a topical antioxidant cream to your skin about 10 minutes before your sunscreen.

Example: SkinCeuticals Topical Vitamin-C Skin Firming Cream.

● **Try using a retinoid cream.** I advise my patients not to waste their money on the expensive skin creams now sold in better department stores. They do not provide any special benefits to their skin. On the other hand, the topical retinoid *tretinoin* (a vitamin A derivative)—available by prescription under the brand names Retin-A, Renova and Avita—can reverse many signs of sun damage, including finely crisscrossing lines, areas of whitish pebbling, spider veins in the cheeks and rough, dull, uneven or yellowish skin tone. It can also generate new collagen, a fibrous tissue protein, making the dermis (the layer beneath your epidermis, or outer skin) plumper and firmer.

I recommend using either a 0.05% formulation of tretinoin or an even milder cream containing 0.025%. Apply the cream either every other night or every third night. It should be applied to your face and any other body parts you're concerned about, preferably about 30 minutes after washing. Within four to six months, you'll start to see significant improvement in your fine wrinkles, along with a clearer, smoother skin surface and a generally brighter, rosier complexion.

Tretinoin is best used at night—because it's degraded by sunlight and it makes your skin more sensitive to ultraviolet light.

Warning: Tretinoin can be irritating to the skin, although after two to six weeks, your skin should develop resistance to the worst signs of irritation, such as becoming red, flaky or itchy.

● **To moisturize your face, use a glycolic acid cream.** A cream containing glycolic acid in the range of 5%—such as NeoStrata Ultra Moisturizing Face Cream—will moisturize and protect your skin and will also help reverse the drying effects of retinoid creams. Glycolic acid stimulates the synthesis of new skin tissue and inhibits the effect of free radicals. I recommend applying one of these skin moisturizers every morning, and—if you're also applying a tretinoin cream—again in the evening, on those nights when you're not using the tretinoin. Follow the same rule of applying it to a clean face about 30 minutes after washing.

Note: If your doctor prescribes a stronger glycolic acid cream, he/she will probably recommend using it only at night.

● **Use as few different makeup products as possible**—to minimize your chances of developing contact dermatitis, a skin condition marked by inflammation, redness, itching or broken skin. This condition, sometimes called allergic dermatitis, is actually caused by chemical irritation, rather than an allergic reaction. The more chemicals your skin is exposed to, the greater chance irritation will occur.

● **Drink alcohol in moderation.** Heavy consumption of alcohol (more than one drink a day for women, or one or two drinks a day for men) dilates the blood vessels, leading to spider veins in your cheeks. It can also exacerbate rosacea—a skin condition marked by flushing, lumpiness, red lines and a swollen, red nose.

● **Avoid cigarette smoke.** Smoking cigarettes will cause widespread free-radical damage to your skin, causing it to age prematurely. The act of smoking also causes fine lines to develop around the lips. As previously noted in this article, however, even exposure to someone else's cigarette smoke will accelerate the activity of toxic free radicals in your skin, leading to skin damage.

Smile! Here's the Secret To Cleaner Dentures

Microwaving dentures kills 70% more microorganisms than soaking them in denture-cleansing solutions alone.

What to do: Ask your dentist if your dentures are safe to microwave. They should not contain any metal, porcelain or soft liners. Once you have received your dentist's consent, place dentures in a microwave-safe container at least twice as tall as the dentures. Fill the container with enough water to completely cover up your dentures and to allow two inches between the water and the top of the container. Add one denture-cleansing tablet and let it dissolve. Place a paper towel over the container. Microwave on high for two minutes. Let dentures cool. Rinse and wear. Microwaving three times weekly is enough for most healthy people.

R. Thomas Glass, DDS, PhD, professor of forensic sciences, pathology and dental medicine, Oklahoma State University Center for Health Sciences, Tulsa.

Best Brush to Buy

To take better care of your teeth, use a toothbrush labeled *extra soft, ultra soft* or *sensitive*. If you can't find one at a grocery store or drugstore, ask your dentist for one.

Best: Brush twice a day, and floss once a day. Limit brushing time to two minutes, and have your dentist or hygienist show you how much pressure to apply—most people brush too hard, harming teeth and gums instead of just cleaning them.

Alan Winter, DDS, a periodontist in private practice, New York City.

Fight Cavities While You Sleep

To fight cavities while you're sleeping, use your finger or toothbrush to rub a dab of fluoride toothpaste along the gumline before bed. Overnight, teeth will absorb the enamel-strengthening fluoride.

Luke Matranga, DDS, associate professor of general dentistry, Creighton University School of Dentistry, Omaha.

Safest Ways to Kill Deadly Germs

Kimberly M. Thompson, ScD, associate professor of risk analysis and decision science at Harvard University School of Public Health in Boston. She is the coauthor of *Overkill—How Our Nation's Abuse of Antibiotics and Other Germ Killers Is Hurting Your Health and What You Can Do About It.* Rodale.

Infectious diseases that end up in the headlines, such as severe acute respiratory syndrome (SARS), pose very little risk to most Americans. You're far more likely to get sick from the microbes that are already living in your own home.

Examples: A kitchen sponge can harbor 7 billion organisms…and a "clean" cutting board might have 62,000 bacteria per square inch.

The Centers for Disease Control and Prevention estimate that food-borne microbes *alone* cause 76 million illnesses a year. We can't even begin to estimate how many people get sick, or die, from bacteria and viruses in the home.

Many families automatically reach for antibacterial products or heavy-duty cleaners. *But don't overdo it.* Antibacterial products can weaken your resistance to harmful bacteria, which may ultimately increase your risk of getting sick.

Smart idea: Use an antibacterial soap after handling raw meat—probably the most common source of household infection—or if anyone in your home is sick or has a compromised immune system due to chronic illness.

Otherwise, plain soap and water are fine for hand-washing, and homemade natural cleaners can be just as effective as cleaning products that contain harmful chemicals.

KITCHEN

The sink is the most germ-ridden space in the house—and often contains more fecal matter (from washing meats) and *E. coli* bacteria than the average toilet.

Rinse the sink with hot water after every use. Clean it twice a week with a scouring powder, such as Ajax or Comet. Disinfect it weekly with a mild bleach solution—one tablespoon of bleach mixed with one cup of hot water. *Also…*

●**Replace sponges once or twice a month,** and run them through the dishwasher each time you use it. Sponges are the perfect breeding ground for harmful germs.

•**Stock up on dishtowels...**and change them every other day to prevent germs from passing among members of the family. Washing them in hot water and running them through the dryer will kill bacteria and viruses.

•**Use separate cutting boards for meats, poultry and seafood**—and scrub them with dish detergent, such as Joy or Dawn, and hot water after each use. Clean all plastic cutting boards in the dishwasher.

BATHROOM

Even if you wear gloves when cleaning the toilet or bathtub, it is a good idea to wash your hands afterward. This eliminates bacteria from water that may get on your hands as you take off the gloves. *Also...*

•**Clean the bathtub at least once weekly** with scouring powder or a solution made with one-half cup of bleach and one gallon of water.

•**Sweep the bathroom floor at least once weekly** and clean with a basic cleaner, such as Lysol, or a solution made with one gallon of hot water...two tablespoons of borax...one teaspoon of dish detergent...and five drops each of patchouli and lavender essential oils. These oils contain effective natural disinfectants.

•**Wipe the bathroom sink and counters after every use.** Once a week, use a disinfectant made with one-quarter cup distilled white vinegar and one-half teaspoon of dish detergent in two cups of warm water. The bathroom sink is a bacterial hot spot because germs on your hands can spread to faucets.

•**Disinfect the toilet bowl, seat and outer surfaces weekly** with a commercial cleaner or with a solution made with one-half cup of baking soda...one-half cup of borax...one-quarter cup of distilled white vinegar...one teaspoon of dish detergent...three drops of sweet orange essential oil...and two drops of patchouli essential oil. Let it soak for an hour, scrub, then flush. Wipe and disinfect the handle daily because it's frequently touched by unwashed hands.

•**Close the toilet lid when you flush.** During flushing, bacteria disperse into the air and can land on any surface that's within six feet—including toothbrushes.

WASHING MACHINE

If there are young children in your household, every time you wash dirty underwear, millions of fecal bacteria are deposited on the inner surfaces of the washing machine—and can spread to the next load. Every few weeks, disinfect the machine by running it empty, using hot water and adding one-half cup of bleach.

TELEPHONES

Many bacterial illnesses are transmitted just by touching the telephone and then touching your eyes, nose or mouth. Wipe all phone surfaces every two weeks with a cotton ball that's moistened with rubbing alcohol or spray with a natural antibacterial.

To make: Combine one tablespoon of borax ...one cup of hot water...one cup of distilled white vinegar...one-half teaspoon of dish detergent...one-half teaspoon of sweet orange essential oil...and one-quarter teaspoon each of rosemary and lavender essential oils.

DOORKNOBS

Disinfect them at least once a month with some rubbing alcohol or the natural antibacterial spray described above. Wipe them off daily when someone in your family is sick with a cold or flu. Doorknobs are great locations for bacteria to be transferred from the hands of a sick person to other members of the family.

Other spots to disinfect frequently: Refrigerator handles, light switches and banisters.

Amazing Cornmeal Cure for Foot and Nail Fungus

Howard Garrett, known as "The Dirt Doctor," *www. dirtdoctor.com*. He has devoted his career to educating the public about organic gardening. Mr. Garrett hosts the Texas radio show *The Natural Way* on WBAP. He is also author of *The Dirt Doctor's Guide to Organic Gardening.* University of Texas.

Ed Dillard was listening to my regional radio talk show on gardening and heard a caller ask how to get rid of fungus on roses. I answered, "Use cornmeal."

For 27 years, Dillard had been plagued by toenail fungus. He had thick, ugly yellow nails and wondered if cornmeal would work.

Dillard soaked his feet for one hour in cornmeal and warm water. There was no change in his nails. But about a month later, he noticed healthy pink nail tissue at the base of his big toenail, though he had soaked only one time. He repeated the cornmeal soak weekly and about a year later, he was fungus-free.

He called me and told of his success on the air. Since then, I have heard from thousands of people who have used cornmeal to treat nail fungus, athlete's foot, ringworm and other fungal problems. Some physicians speculate that the microorganisms in cornmeal, activated by warm water, literally eat the microscopic fungi.

Cornmeal Rx: Put one inch of cornmeal, yellow or white, in a pan, and add just enough warm, not hot, water to cover it. Let this sit for 30 minutes. Then add enough warm water to cover up your feet. Soak for at least one hour once per week until the fungus is gone. For other fungal problems that require soaking in a bath, add two cups of cornmeal to the water.

The Real Sting in Cut Care

Common wound cleaners can do more harm than good. *Mercurochrome* and *merthiolate* contain mercury, which is toxic. Rubbing alcohol damages and dries out skin and hydrogen peroxide and iodine damage the skin and slow healing. Betadine in a concentration of 1% or less is safe for cleaning wounds, but it could cause iodine poisoning if used on large open wounds. Antibiotic ointments may help prevent infection in minor wounds, but they can cause skin irritation and allergic reactions.

What to do: Clean the wound under cool running water, or swab it with a clean, wet cloth. Use soap on the surrounding skin—not on the wound itself. Apply an adhesive bandage to keep the wound clean and moist to reduce scarring. Don't pick at scabs—these are the body's natural bandages.

UC Berkeley Wellness Letter, 632 Broadway, New York City 10012.

Save on Medicines— All-Natural Remedies

Mark A. Stengler, ND, naturopathic physician in private practice, La Jolla, California…adjunct associate clinical professor at the National College of Natural Medicine, Portland, Oregon…author of many books, including *The Natural Physician's Healing Therapies* and coauthor of *Prescription for Natural Cures* (both from Bottom Line Books)…and author of the *Bottom Line/Natural Healing* newsletter.

The big advantages of most conventional drugs are that they work quickly and are standardized for predictable effects.

However, herbs, vitamins, minerals and other supplements can offer a safer approach because they are less likely to trigger side effects. Be patient—they may take as long as six to eight weeks to work.

Important: Never start a new treatment before consulting your doctor, especially if you currently are taking medication.

Here are six common health problems and the best natural treatments for each…

HYPERTENSION

About 50 million Americans have high blood pressure, the leading cause of stroke and cardiovascular disease. Conventional drugs work, but they often cause fatigue, dizziness and sexual problems.

Patients who have Stage 1 hypertension—a systolic (top) number of 140 to 159 and a diastolic (bottom) number of 90 to 99—frequently can achieve normal blood pressure with a low-sodium diet, exercise and weight loss. *These natural treatments also help…*

●**Hawthorn.** *300 milligrams (mg) three times daily.** This herb dilates arteries, reducing blood pressure. It also is a mild diuretic that reduces blood volume. Most patients who take

*Recommended dosages are for people who weigh 150 to 200 pounds. Adjust the dosage up or down according to your weight. Consult your doctor for more details.

hawthorn have a drop in blood pressure of 10 to 15 points over eight weeks. Once blood pressure is down, you may be able to reduce the dosage or stop taking the herb altogether. Ask your doctor.

●**Magnesium.** *250 mg twice daily.* You can take this with hawthorn to relax artery walls and increase blood flow.

INSOMNIA

Side effects of over-the-counter (OTC) insomnia drugs include daytime drowsiness and side effects of prescription drugs include drowsiness as well as a high risk of addiction. Try out these natural treatments. Take each separately for two nights before making a decision about which works best for you.

●**Valerian.** *300 to 500 mg (or 60 drops of tincture) taken 30 to 60 minutes before bedtime and/or if you awaken during the night.* This herb appears to increase brain levels of *serotonin,* a neurotransmitter that's relaxing. It's also thought to increase the amount of the neurotransmitter *gamma-aminobutyric acid* (GABA), which has a calming effect on the brain. Valerian is just as effective as the sleep drug *oxazepam* (Serax) but does not cause the "hangover" effect.

●**5-hydroxytryptophan (5-HTP).** *100 to 200 mg taken 30 to 60 minutes before bedtime and/or if you awaken during the night.* Levels of this amino acid, which helps elevate brain levels of serotonin, often are lower in people with insomnia.

●**Melatonin.** *0.3 mg taken 30 to 60 minutes before bedtime.* Levels of this sleep hormone rise during the hours of darkness—but many adults, especially those age 65 and older, have insufficient levels to achieve restful sleep.

SEASONAL ALLERGIES

It is best to avoid pollen as much as possible—by keeping windows closed and running an air purifier in the bedroom...staying inside during peak pollen times (usually mornings and evenings)...and washing bedding regularly. *The following natural treatments can be taken together and can prevent allergies...*

●**Nettle leaf.** *600 mg three times daily.* This herbal antihistamine is effective for mild to moderate allergies and causes none of the drowsiness of some antihistamines.

Helpful: After using nettle leaf for up to two weeks, cut the dose in half. The lower dose will be effective once the initial loads of histamine are reduced.

●**Quercetin.** *1,000 mg three times daily.* It belongs to a class of water-soluble plant pigments called *flavonoids.* Quercetin strengthens the immune system and inhibits the release of histamine in people with allergies.

PROSTATE ENLARGEMENT

About half of men age 50 and older suffer from benign prostatic hypertrophy, an enlargement of the prostate gland that can interfere with urination. The prescription drug *finasteride* (Proscar) will shrink this gland but may cause impotence. The following natural treatments don't bring on this side effect. *I often advise my patients to take all three for maximum effectiveness...*

●**Saw palmetto.** *320 mg daily.* This herb inhibits an enzyme that converts *testosterone* to *dihydrotestosterone,* the form of the hormone that fuels prostate growth.

●**Nettle root (not leaf).** *240 mg daily.* It reduces the hormonal stimulation of the prostate in a different way than saw palmetto and often is used in conjunction with saw palmetto.

●**Zinc.** *90 mg daily for two months, then 50 mg daily as a maintenance dose.* Also, take 3 mg to 5 mg of copper daily. Long-term supplementation with zinc depletes copper from the body.

OSTEOARTHRITIS

This is the leading cause of joint pain and stiffness. Conventional treatments (aspirin, *ibuprofen,* etc.) reduce symptoms but often cause stomach bleeding. The following natural treatments don't have this side effect. *They can be taken together...*

●**Glucosamine.** *1,500 to 2,500 mg daily.* Found naturally in the body, glucosamine promotes new cartilage growth and reduces inflammation. A four-week German study of patients with osteoarthritis of the knee reported that ibuprofen resulted in faster pain relief—but glucosamine supplements brought comparable pain relief after two weeks and were much less likely to cause side effects.

After a few months, you may be able to cut back to 500 mg daily. If you discontinue glucosamine completely, benefits wear off after a few months.

●**SAMe.** *400 to 800 mg daily.* Pronounced "Sammy," this chemical compound (*S-adenosylmethionine*) is found in all living cells. It promotes flexibility of joint cartilage and cartilage repair. One German study of 20,641 patients found that 71% of those who took SAMe supplements for eight weeks reported good or very good results.

MENOPAUSAL DISCOMFORT

Hot flashes and night sweats are caused by declines in progesterone and estrogen. Conventional hormone replacement therapy reduces discomfort but may increase risk of heart disease, cancer and other ailments. *Natural treatments without these risks (use one or both)…*

●**Black cohosh.** *80 mg daily for mild to moderate discomfort…*160 mg daily for severe symptoms. This herb inhibits the release of *luteinizing hormone* (LH) by the pituitary gland. Elevated levels of LH after menopause contribute to hot flashes, night sweats and other symptoms.

●**Natural progesterone.** *20 mg of cream (about one-quarter teaspoon) twice daily.* Natural progesterone, derived from wild yams, is as effective as synthetic forms but less likely to cause side effects, such as water retention and weight gain. Apply the cream to breasts, forearms or cheeks for maximum absorption.

Important: Use only natural progesterone under a doctor's care. Blood levels have to be monitored very carefully, generally every six to 12 months.

Injuries—When to Use Hot…When to Use Cold

First-aid rules for injuries can be a bit confusing. *Here is the lowdown…*

●**Cold reduces inflammation.** Apply cold to acute injuries, such as a newly sprained ankle or a pulled muscle.

●**Heat improves circulation.** It's best for chronic pain, such as from tight muscles or a sore back.

●**Alternate heat and cold** if you have soft-tissue damage and/or stretched ligaments, such as an ankle sprain. Heat aids in restoring range of motion. Apply cold for 20 minutes per hour as desired for the first 24 hours. The next day, use warmth for 20 minutes per hour as desired.

Caution: Don't apply cold for more than 24 hours or warmth for more than 72 hours. If inflammation continues beyond 72 hours, see a doctor.

Richard O'Brien, MD, spokesman for the American College of Emergency Physicians. *www.acep.org.* He is clinical instructor at Temple University School of Medicine and an emergency physician at Moses Taylor Hospital, both in Scranton, Pennsylvania.

Drugstore Reading Glasses May Do the Trick

Drugstore reading glasses work well for people who need the same correction in both eyes. These inexpensive glasses make up for the lost ability to change focus while doing close work. In addition, there is a bonus effect of mild magnification. These glasses are not appropriate if you need different corrections in each eye or have astigmatism. Even if you wear drugstore glasses, you should see an eye doctor every two years—every year after age 60—to be checked for vision changes and eye diseases.

Donald Schwartz, MD, spokesman, American Academy of Ophthalmology, San Francisco.

Boost Immunity with Tea

People who consumed five cups of black tea a day for one week had five times more germ-fighting proteins in their blood than they did before they started to drink tea.

Theory: The immune-boosting capacity of black tea is derived from *L-theanine*, an amino acid that is found in black tea as well as other nonherbal teas.

Good news: Regularly drinking just two cups a day may confer many of the same benefits.

Because tea can reduce absorption of iron, people with iron-deficiency anemia should be sure to limit their intake of tea.

Jack Bukowski, MD, PhD, assistant clinical professor of medicine, Harvard Medical School and Brigham and Women's Hospital, both in Boston.

Duct Tape Really Can Cure Warts

Placing duct tape (or other tape) over warts to get rid of them is not just an old wives' tale. A recent study found that placing tape over warts is more effective at eliminating them than standard medical therapy.

The study: Participants who had warts on fingers, palms, heels or soles of the feet were divided into two groups. One group put tape on warts for six days, then soaked the warts and scraped them with emery boards, waited 12 hours and reapplied the tape, repeating the process. The other group had their warts frozen off by a doctor, which is standard therapy.

Result: After just two months, 85% of those using the tape had gotten rid of their warts, versus only 60% of those who had received the standard freezing treatment.

Dean R. Focht III, MD, fellow, division of gastroenterology, hepatology and nutrition, Cincinnati Children's Hospital Medical Center, Ohio.

"Senior" Vitamins Not Worth the Cost

Special "senior" formula vitamins offer little more than regular multivitamin/mineral supplements—even for those age 65 or older. These formulas, including Centrum Silver and Geritol Extend, may provide more of the B vitamins but hardly any additional amounts of other important vitamins and minerals, such as vitamin E and calcium. Seniors require more nutritional supplementation because of their decreased ability to absorb nutrients and their generally less nutritious diets. However, basic all-purpose multivitamins should be sufficient. They're less expensive, too.

Michael Hirt, MD, founder and medical director, Center for Integrative Medicine, Tarzana, California. *www.drhirt.com.*

Surprising Disease Fighter

Hot cocoa fights disease better than wine or tea. One cup of hot cocoa contains about 611 milligrams (mg) of *phenols* and 564 mg of *flavonoids*, two powerful antioxidants that protect against cancer and heart disease. By comparison, a glass of red wine has 340 mg and 163 mg, respectively, of these compounds, while green tea has 165 mg and 47 mg...and black tea has only 124 mg and 34 mg.

Bonus: Although chocolate also is very rich in antioxidants, it is high in saturated fat. The equivalent amount of cocoa contains less than 1 gram (g) of saturated fat.

Chang Y. Lee, PhD, professor and chairman, food science and technology, Cornell University, Geneva, New York.

Dip into Honey for a Longer Life

Honey may help prevent heart disease and cancer. It is as rich in antioxidants as some fruits and vegetables. The darker the color, the higher the antioxidant level. Buckwheat honey has the highest levels. Clover honey—the most commonly available type—has two to three times less but still is a good antioxidant source. Use honey instead of sugar in cereal, tea, etc.

Nicki Engeseth, PhD, associate professor of food chemistry at the University of Illinois in Urbana, and leader of a study of honey's effect on human blood, published in the *Journal of Agricultural and Food Chemistry.*

Apples Really Do Keep The Doctor Away

In a recent finding, incidence of lung cancer was reduced by 60%...asthma by 20%...and death from heart disease by 20% in people who ate one apple a day.

Theory: Apples are rich in the bioflavonoid *quercetin*, which helps block the accumulation of free radicals in the body. The cell damage caused by free radicals contributes to the development of these diseases.

Self-defense: Eat one small apple a day for this benefit.

Other quercetin-rich foods: Onions, cabbage, blackberries and cranberries.

Paul Knekt, PhD, epidemiologist for the National Public Health Institute in Helsinki, Finland. His study was published in *The American Journal of Clinical Nutrition.*

Vinegar Boosts Insulin Sensitivity Up to 40%

In a recent study, healthy patients and patients with a prediabetic condition known as insulin resistance drank a vinegar drink (⅛ cup of vinegar, diluted with ¼ cup of water and sweetened with saccharine) or a placebo drink before a high-carbohydrate meal. The vinegar

treatment improved insulin sensitivity by up to 40% in both groups.

Theory: Vinegar inhibits the breakdown of carbohydrates, thereby decreasing the blood glucose spikes that occur in people who have diabetes.

If you are diabetic or insulin resistant: Talk to your doctor about drinking diluted vinegar before meals.

Carol S. Johnston, PhD, professor of nutrition, Arizona State University East, Mesa.

Save Money on Acne Creams

Over-the-counter acne creams are just as effective for mild to moderate acne as prescription oral antibiotics.

Bonus: Use of topical creams—such as Clearasil and Oxyderm—does not lead to antibiotic resistance.

Hywel C. Williams, PhD, professor of dermatology, University of Nottingham, England, and leader of a study comparing commonly used acne treatments, published in *The Lancet.*

Nuts Lower Your Risk for Diabetes

Eating a handful of nuts or peanuts or one tablespoon of peanut butter five times a week protects against adult-onset (type-2) diabetes. These foods are high in unsaturated fat, fiber and magnesium, which helps improve insulin sensitivity and glucose metabolism and lower cholesterol levels. Read food labels carefully, and use these foods as only one part of a well-balanced diet.

Rui Jiang, MD, research fellow, department of nutrition, Harvard School of Public Health, Boston, and leader of a cohort study of the Nurses' Health Study, published in *The Journal of the American Medical Association.*

Easy Ways to Ward Off Winter Colds and Flu... And Boost Your Immunity

Robert Rountree, MD, director of Boulder Wellcare, a family practice in Colorado. He is also a member of the adjunct faculty at the Institute for Functional Medicine, Gig Harbor, Washington. He has been researching immunity for more than 20 years and is a coauthor of *Immunotics: A Revolutionary Way to Fight Infection, Beat Chronic Illness, and Stay Well.* Putnam.

Some people are laid low by every ailment making the rounds, while others will sail through the winter with nary a sniffle. The strength of your immune system is the critical factor. This army of cells and chemicals guards your intestinal tract and mucous membranes and patrols your bloodstream.

Overwork, stress and insufficient sleep can sap the vitality of these disease fighters. Regular exercise is known to improve immune function. But above all, your defending troops must be well fed to stay strong.

FEEDING YOUR IMMUNE SYSTEM

The number-one cause of immune weakness is *micronutrient starvation*, a shortage of vitamins, minerals and protective plant-based substances called *phytochemicals*.

These micronutrients are abundant in fruits and vegetables, but only about 25% of Americans consume the five daily servings recommended by the National Institutes of Health.

To maximize your intake of the key micronutrients, eat for color. Choose deep-colored fruits and vegetables whenever you can. These are filled with natural disease-fighting phytochemicals, such as carotenoids and flavonoids.

Best fruits in order: Blueberries, blackberries, strawberries, raspberries, plums, oranges, red grapes, cherries, kiwis, pink grapefruit.

Best vegetables in order: Kale, spinach, brussels sprouts, alfalfa sprouts, broccoli florets, beets, red bell peppers, onions, corn, eggplant.

Choose organically grown fruits and vegetables. Preliminary research suggests that organic produce may have more phytochemicals than conventionally grown plant foods.

If you choose to use nonorganic fruits and vegetables, scrub them all thoroughly with a cleanser, such as Fit Fruit & Vegetable Wash, to help remove pesticide residues.

In addition to upping your intake of fruits and vegetables, eat fish at least twice a week. Fish contains omega-3 fatty acids, a type of polyunsaturated fat that boosts health and protects against some cancers.

I recommend wild salmon because it has very little mercury. Avoid large fish that are high in mercury, such as swordfish, shark, king mackerel and tilefish. Canned tuna is better than fresh because it comes from smaller fish.

If you don't like fish, you can take fish oil or flaxseed oil supplements. Be sure to follow instructions on the label.

Foods to avoid: Sugar-filled candies, cakes, cookies, jams and refined carbohydrates, such as white bread and pasta. These elevate blood sugar and interfere with the enzymes and cells of the immune system.

Foods that are heavy in saturated fat (such as red meat and whole-milk products) and trans fats (margarine and many commercially prepared desserts) weaken cell membranes and sabotage immune function.

SUPERCHARGERS

Everyone should take a daily multivitamin/mineral supplement that includes vitamin C, 2,000 milligrams (mg)...vitamin E in the form of tocopherol complex, 200 to 400 international units (IU)*...magnesium, 200 to 300 mg...as well as selenium, 100 to 200 micrograms (mcg). If you're still getting sick, you may need to boost your immune system with additional supplements. This is particularly important if you are under stress, work in a school or hospital or travel extensively—all of which will put you at high risk of infection. *You can take all of the following every day if you wish...*

•**NAC,** short for *N-acetyl-cysteine,* a type of amino acid. It boosts levels of *glutathione,* a keystone of the body's armor against the toxic free radicals. It thins mucus, making

---

*Due to the possible interactions between vitamin E and a variety of drugs and supplements as well as other safety considerations, be sure to consult your doctor before taking vitamin E.

the respiratory system less prone to infection. NAC is protective against colds, flu and sore throats.

Dose: 500 to 600 mg/day.

●**Grape seed extract,** which is rich in concentrated *proanthrocyanidins*, highly potent forms of the health-boosting bioflavonoids that are found in berries, citrus fruits and onions. These fortify the body against infection, help soothe inflammation, stimulate germ-fighting natural killer cells and increase the production of *interleukin-2*, a messenger chemical that activates other immune cells.

Dose: 150 to 300 mg/day.

●**Astragalus.** For thousands of years, traditional Chinese medicine has used this herb to strengthen the body's *we'i ch'i* ("defensive energy"). It is a general immune-system tonic that also can help fight a cold or flu if you're already sick. It stimulates the activity of *macrophages*, which swallow bacteria and viruses whole, and other disease-fighting cells.

Dose: 1,000 to 2,000 mg/day.

●**Probiotics.** The lower intestinal tract is host to colonies of bacteria, mostly friendly species that keep destructive germs in check by crowding them out, stimulating production and activity of white blood cells and producing natural germicidal substances. Poor diet and exposure to antibiotics (including those that have entered the food chain in chicken and beef) can deplete the body of its micro helpers.

Dose: 10 to 20 billion organisms of *L. acidophilus* daily in capsule or powder form. Follow package labels.

●**Green tea.** It is particularly helpful in the digestive tract, where it kills harmful bacteria. The antioxidants in green tea are more powerful immune boosters than vitamin C or E.

Dose: Two cups daily, or 1,000 mg of extract.

AN IMMUNE-FRIENDLY LIFESTYLE

●**Sufficient rest.** Sleep deprivation robs your body of the downtime it needs for self-repair. A single sleepless night markedly lowers immune activity. If you have trouble sleeping, try taking at bedtime L-theanine (100 to 400 mg)…or valerian (200 to 800 mg)…or melato-

nin (1 to 5 mg). If you are pregnant or taking medication, check with your physician.

●**Moderate exercise.** Physical activity invigorates your immune system, but exercising to exhaustion creates damaging stress. Don't try to make up for a whole week of inactivity on the weekend.

●**Home hygiene.** Drink only filtered water, and use unbleached paper goods and nontoxic cleaning supplies.

●**Workplace protection.** Run an ionizer/air purifier next to your desk. Don't use the pens, keyboards or phones of coworkers who are often sick. Be wary of bathroom doorknobs—push the door open with your arm or grasp the knob with a paper towel.

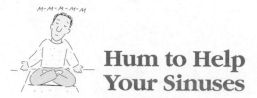

Hum to Help Your Sinuses

Humming can help relieve sinus infections. In a recent study, nitric oxide, a gas that is lethal to bacteria, increased 15-fold in the nose during humming. An increase in nitric oxide indicates improved sinus air exchange, whereby fresh air enters the sinuses and replaces "old air." Poor ventilation of the sinuses is a risk factor for sinus infections.

Self-defense: To ventilate sinuses, hum for one minute every one to two hours.

Jon O. Lundberg, MD, PhD, associate professor of physiology and pharmacology at the Karolinska Institute, Stockholm, Sweden.

Arthritis Food Cures

Isadore Rosenfeld, MD, Rossi Distinguished Professor of Clinical Medicine at Weill Medical College of Cornell University in New York City. He is also the author of nine books, including *Doctor, What Should I Eat?* (Warner) and *Dr. Isadore Rosenfeld's Breakthrough Health* (Rodale).

Both osteoarthritis and rheumatoid arthritis cause painful inflammation that usually becomes worse with age. But the proper food choices can help reduce this pain—without the side effects caused by some painkillers.

Best food: Fatty fish (salmon, mackerel, sardines, etc.). The omega-3 fatty acids in fish counter the effects of *prostaglandins*, chemicals that promote inflammation. Eat three or more fish meals weekly. If you are pregnant, ask your doctor whether you should eat fish.

Also helpful: Brazil nuts. They contain selenium, a trace mineral that may reduce arthritis symptoms. One Brazil nut supplies the recommended daily intake of 70 micrograms (mcg).

Approximately 20% of all osteoarthritis and rheumatoid arthritis cases are linked to food allergies. Common offenders include soy, coffee, eggs, milk, corn, wheat, potatoes, beef, pork and shellfish (especially shrimp).

I advise patients with severe arthritis to stop eating these problem foods, one at a time, to see if symptoms improve.

Foods that Trigger Hay Fever

Some foods and herbs contain proteins similar to those found in ragweed pollen and can cause allergy symptoms ranging from mild (itching, sneezing) to severe (asthma, sudden blood pressure drop).

Foods and herbs to avoid: Bananas, cantaloupes, cucumbers, honeydew, watermelon, zucchini, chamomile and echinacea.

Helpful: Avoid these items if they make your mouth tingle or itch when you eat them.

If you're allergic, these foods and herbs also may trigger hives, watery eyes, a metallic taste or itchy palate (roof of the mouth).

Leonard J. Bielory, MD, director, Asthma and Allergy Research Center, University of Medicine and Dentistry of New Jersey, New Jersey Medical School, Newark.

Why Sex Is Good For Your Health

Beverly Whipple, PhD, RN, a certified sex educator, counselor, researcher and professor emerita at Rutgers University–Newark. She is a coauthor of the international best seller *The G-Spot and Other Recent Discoveries About Human Sexuality* (Dell) and *Safe Encounters: How Women Can Say Yes to Pleasure and No to Unsafe Sex* (Pocket). She was a consultant for the report "The Health Benefits of Sexual Expression" for the Planned Parenthood Federation of America, Inc.

Was it good for you? Scientists now have a definitive answer to that classic post-sex query. The answer is *yes—very good for you.*

A recent review of dozens of studies shows that sexual expression is good for the heart… the immune system…and the reproductive system. Plus it helps to control pain, stress and depression.

An active sex life may even extend your life. A Welsh study of more than 900 men ages 45 to 59 showed that those who averaged two or more orgasms per week had half the risk of dying during the 10-year period of the study, compared with those who had orgasms less than once a month.

How does sexual expression work to benefit the body and mind? Doctors worldwide are searching for answers, but one biological fact stands out—sex triggers the release of many powerful chemicals.

BENEFITS

●**Longevity.** In addition to the Welsh study, a study of 252 men and women in North Carolina showed that frequency of intercourse was a significant predictor of longevity for men.

In a Swedish study of 392 older men and women, married men who stopped having sex before the age of 70 were more likely to die by age 75 than married men who continued to be sexually active (for women, there was no association between frequency of sexual intercourse and mortality).

●**Heart disease.** In the Welsh study, men who had orgasms less than once a month had twice the rate of fatal heart attacks, compared with men who had orgasms two or more times a week.

Possible explanation: The hormone DHEA is released with orgasm. Research on middle-aged men suggests that the lower the level of DHEA in the blood, the higher the risk of heart disease.

●**Breast cancer.** In a French study of 146 women ages 25 to 45 who had never had children, those who had sexual intercourse less than once a month had a higher risk for breast cancer than those who had sex more often.

Possible explanation: Sexual arousal and orgasm lead to increased levels of the sex hormone oxytocin, which may help prevent breast cancer.

●**Immunity.** Two psychology professors at Wilkes University in Pennsylvania measured levels of *immunoglobulin A* (IgA) in 112 subjects. This immune factor is essential in defeating viruses. Subjects who had sexual intercourse once or twice a week had IgA levels that were 30% higher than those who didn't have sex.

●**Reproductive system.** A woman's reproductive health is directly affected by her sex life. A study of more than 2,000 women found that sexual activity and orgasm during menstruation may protect against endometriosis. In this disease, cells of the uterine lining, or endometrium, grow in some other part of the pelvic area, such as the ovaries, cervix or bladder, and can prevent pregnancy.

Studies also show that regular intimate sexual activity with a partner enhances fertility by regulating menstrual patterns.

In addition, sex can help prevent premature births. A 2001 study of 1,853 pregnant women showed that those who had some type of sexual activity after 24 weeks of pregnancy— sexual intercourse with orgasm, sexual intercourse without orgasm and/or orgasm without sexual intercourse—were somewhat less likely to deliver prematurely.

Before this study, it was theorized that sexual activity between 29 and 36 weeks increased the risk of early delivery. (Always check with your doctor about when or if sex should be avoided during pregnancy.)

●**Pain.** Many medical reports show that sex relieves pain, including back pain, menstrual cramps, arthritis and migraine.

Example: In one study, stimulation of the female lab rats caused the pelvic nerve to release *vasoactive intestinal peptide* (VIP). When injected into animals, VIP has a pain-blocking power stronger than morphine.

●**Insomnia.** A psychologist who surveyed 1,866 US women found that 32% had masturbated in the past three months to help get to sleep more easily.

Possible explanation: The hormones released may act as a natural sedative.

●**Emotional health.** Studies show that sexual satisfaction is a strong predictor of higher quality of life.

Examples: A Canadian study of 75 men between the ages of 18 and 27 showed that men who were not sexually active had the highest risk for depression. In one American study, the women who masturbated indicated a higher level of self-esteem than women who did not.

Studies also show that sexual activity and orgasm reduce stress, which may be related to the release of oxytocin.

BETTER SEX

To improve your sex life, avoid these behaviors, which can interfere with the enjoyment of sexual expression…

●**Not communicating with your partner.** Don't expect your partner to figure out what you enjoy on his/her own. Tell or show your lover what you like. He'll enjoy it more, too.

●**Being goal-oriented.** If you are focused solely on achieving orgasm, sexual expression is like a staircase. Each step leads to the next, and you don't stop to enjoy where you are— every look and caress.

If you are pleasure-oriented, sexual expression is like a circle. Any activity on the circle— holding hands, cuddling, kissing—is an end in itself and doesn't have to lead to anything else. In pleasure-oriented sensuality and sexuality, you and your partner enjoy every moment and reap the health benefits.

My Natural Cures For Sore Throat

Jamison Starbuck, ND, a naturopathic physician in family practice and a lecturer at the University of Montana, both in Missoula. She is past president of the American Association of Naturopathic Physicians and a contributing editor to *The Alternative Advisor: The Complete Guide to Natural Therapies and Alternative Treatments*. Time Life.

On the final ascending mile of a recent backpacking trip in the Grand Canyon, I developed a sore throat. Many people assume that antibiotics are the cure for sore throat, but that's usually not the case. A virus is most often to blame. Allergy, dry or smoky air, or overuse of the vocal cords also can cause sore throat. Less frequently, a sore throat can be due to a bacterium known as "strep." The only way to diagnose strep is with a throat culture. If the test is positive, antibiotics usually are needed.

Natural medicines offer great relief for the majority of sore throats. If you use these remedies promptly, at the first sign of throat distress, you may well save yourself a visit to your doctor and lost days of work or play. A natural cure for sore throat may seem time-consuming, but it usually takes care of the problem within 24 hours, as it did in my case.

● **Gargle.** My favorite gargle is freshly made chamomile tea (cooled to tolerance). Use one teabag per four ounces of water, steeped for six minutes. Chamomile has anti-inflammatory effects and will reduce sore throat pain. Gargle for 60 seconds and then spit out. Repeat as needed for pain. To boost the antiseptic properties of your gargle, add one teaspoon of hydrogen peroxide to each four-ounce chamomile gargle.

● **Drink tea.** Demulcent herbs moisten and reduce irritation in mucous membranes. The best choices for sore throat are licorice root, slippery elm, marshmallow root and fenugreek. You can buy these herbs individually in bulk and make a tea using two teaspoons of any combination of the herbs per six ounces of water. Or buy a sore throat formula in teabags. My favorite is "Throat Coat" by Traditional

Medicinals, available in many health-food stores. Do your best to drink six ounces of tea every two waking hours until your symptoms are gone.

● **Try hydrotherapy.** To hasten healing, use hydration and a heating compress. At the first sign of a sore throat, hydrate by having an eight-ounce glass of water every waking hour. Use a heating compress twice a day. Cover a hot, moist towel with a dry towel and let it cool slightly so you don't burn yourself. Wrap it around your entire neck and leave it in place for five minutes. Remove the hot towel, and immediately wrap your neck with a towel doused in cold tap water, covered with a dry towel. Leave the cold wrap in place for 20 minutes if you can. Alternating the hot and cold stimulates circulation in the inflamed tissues of the throat, allowing the throat to heal.

● **Take immune-boosting tinctures.** I recommend a combination of equal amounts of the herbs echinacea, *Oregon grape root* (Mahonia aquifolium), *wild indigo* (Baptisia tinctoria) and *myrrh* (Commiphora).

Typical dose: One-quarter teaspoon of the tincture in four ounces of water every four hours until your throat feels better.

If you don't notice improvement within a day or two—or find you are getting worse—see your doctor for an exam and throat culture.

Supplements May Relieve Allergies and Asthma Better than Drugs

Richard Firshein, DO, director of the Firshein Center for Comprehensive Medicine, which specializes in treating allergies and asthma, New York City. A sufferer of asthma himself, he's also the author of *The Nutraceutical Revolution* (Riverhead) and *Reversing Asthma* (Warner).

Millions of Americans suffer from asthma and allergies, frequently triggered by such airborne substances as mold, dust mites or pollen. The immune system identifies these normally harmless substances as dangerous and releases inflammatory chemicals that trigger sneezing, wheezing and congestion as well as other symptoms.

The drugs used for these conditions—antihistamines, inhaled steroids, etc.—curtail symptoms but frequently cause side effects such as fatigue or anxiety.

Better approach: Studies have shown that many over-the-counter supplements act as natural antihistamines/anti-inflammatories that can reduce or prevent allergy or asthma flare-ups —without side effects. My patients who use nutritional supplements often are able to stop taking asthma and allergy drugs or significantly reduce the dosages. You can take one or all of the supplements below daily, but always check with your doctor first.

QUERCETIN

Quercetin is a member of a class of nutrients known as bioflavonoids. It is a powerful anti-inflammatory that helps to prevent the lungs, nasal passages and eyes from swelling after allergen exposure. It also inhibits the release of *histamine*, a chemical that triggers allergy and asthma flare-ups.

What I recommend to my patients: 300 milligrams (mg) twice daily. If your symptoms are severe, increase the amount to 1,000 mg twice daily until symptoms abate. Then switch back to a maintenance dose of 300 mg twice daily. Quercetin works better for prevention than short-term treatment. It usually takes several weeks to become effective.

VITAMIN C

This potent antioxidant has a mild antihistamine effect.

What I recommend to my patients: 500 to 1,000 mg each day. Vitamin C may cause diarrhea in some people. Divide the daily amount into two doses to reduce the risk of this side effect. Also, patients with a history of kidney stones should talk to their doctors before taking vitamin C supplements.

NETTLES

A traditional herbal remedy for allergies, nettles inhibit the body's production of inflammatory prostaglandins. In one study of 69 allergy patients, 57% had significant improvement in symptoms after taking nettles. Nettles work quickly, often within hours, and can be taken during flare-ups.

What I recommend to my patients: 300 to 600 mg daily.

MAGNESIUM

This mineral is a natural bronchodilator that relaxes muscles in the airways and promotes better breathing. Supplementation with magnesium may be especially helpful if you're taking corticosteroids or other asthma drugs—they tend to decrease the amount of magnesium in the body.

What I recommend to my patients: 200 to 600 mg daily.

ALLERGY TESTS

Your doctor may recommend skin or blood tests to determine if your allergies are caused by dust mites, mold, pollen, etc. Once you know what you're allergic to, you can take steps to minimize exposure.

Example: If you're allergic to dust mites, you can buy mattress and pillow casings that are impervious to allergens…and use a vacuum that has a high-efficiency particulate air (HEPA) filter.

Natural Acne Remedies

Here is a list of four natural remedies to help with acne problems…

●**Oregon grape root fights bacteria and inflammation.** It can be applied topically or taken as a tincture.

●**Echinacea can stimulate healing** when taken internally and kill bacteria when used externally.

●**Tea tree oil is a topical anti-inflammatory and antimicrobial that can reduce the number of lesions**—but some people are allergic to it.

●**Oregano oil is a strong antimicrobial** that can be used topically, but it has a strong smell.

Best: Use these remedies under the supervision of an experienced practitioner.

Alan M. Dattner, MD, holistic dermatologist, New Rochelle, New York. *www.holisticdermatology.com.*

Natural Relief for Nagging Coughs

Jamison Starbuck, ND, a naturopathic physician in family practice and a lecturer at the University of Montana, both in Missoula. She is past president of the American Association of Naturopathic Physicians and a contributing editor to *The Alternative Advisor: The Complete Guide to Natural Therapies and Alternative Treatments.* Time Life.

Cough tops my list of bothersome medical complaints. A cough is annoying, not only to the sufferer but also to everyone within earshot.

Acute coughs are most often the result of a viral upper respiratory illness. Allergy, asthma, environmental irritants and sinusitis also can cause cough. In most cases, we cough because our body is trying to heal itself by getting rid of mucus or other irritants in the respiratory tract. Unfortunately, the effort isn't always successful—acute coughs can last for three to six weeks, long after other viral symptoms, such as runny nose and sore throat, have disappeared. If you have a cough that has lasted longer than six weeks—or three to four days if accompanied by pain, fever or other symptoms—see your doctor for a physical exam. Such coughing can indicate serious illness, such as emphysema, lung cancer, tuberculosis or pneumonia. If your cough is not due to a life-threatening condition, natural remedies can provide substantial relief.

Coughs generally are worse when your mucous membranes and the air around you are dry. You can begin to ease your cough by drinking enough fluids (at least eight 8-ounce glasses of water daily) and by using a humidifier in your home or office.

To soothe your respiratory tract and make expectoration of mucus more effective, try a cough "elixir" that contains honey and the herbs *elecampane* (Inula helenium), *marshmallow root* (Althaea officinalis), *mullein* (Verbascum thapsus) and *wild cherry bark* (Prunus serotina). Most natural-food stores carry a cough formula that contains these ingredients.

Good product: Old Indian Wild Cherry Bark Syrup by Planetary Formulas. Follow the manufacturer's recommended dose.

If your cough still persists, you might want to try one of the following homeopathic remedies…

● **Rumex.** Use when cough causes a tickling sensation in the back of the throat. This type of cough is usually dry, worsens while talking and prevents sleep.

● **Spongia.** Use when cough sounds croupy (like a seal's bark) and causes a dry throat. This type of cough improves after the sufferer consumes warm foods or beverages. It may be accompanied by shallow breathing or panting.

● **Phosphorus.** Use when cough is accompanied by hoarseness, sore throat pain and/or tightness and weight in the chest. This type of cough often worsens when the sufferer goes from warm to cold temperatures.

Purchase 30C potency pellets of the remedy that most closely matches your symptoms. Take two pellets, dissolved under the tongue, two times per day for up to three days. If you have selected the right remedy, your cough should improve within that time. You can then discontinue the treatment.

Let the Sun Shine In

Surgery patients in sunny rooms had drug costs 21% lower than those of equally ill patients in darker rooms.

Possible reason: People feel less pain when they are in a better mood, and sunlight seems to improve mood.

Bruce Rabin, MD, PhD, medical director of the Healthy Lifestyle Program at the University of Pittsburgh, and leader of a study of 89 spinal-fusion patients, published in *Psychiatric Medicine.*

Super-Healing Herbs— They Ease Colds, Block Strokes, Boost Memory And More

Mark Blumenthal, founder and executive director of the American Botanical Council (ABC), *www.herbalgram. org*, an Austin, Texas-based independent, nonprofit organization dedicated to disseminating reliable information about herbs and medicinal plants. He is senior editor of the English translation of *The Complete German Commission E Monographs—Therapeutic Guide to Herbal Medicines* (Integrative Medicine Communications), a clinical guide on the safety and efficacy of herbal medicines, and senior editor of *The ABC Clinical Guide to Herbs.* ABC.

It was headline news when *The New England Journal of Medicine* published a study that cast doubt on the effectiveness of echinacea. The message to the countless consumers spending more than $300 million annually on the purported cold-fighting herb? *Save your money.*

University of Virginia School of Medicine researchers had found echinacea to be no more effective than a placebo at combating cold and flu symptoms. But don't clear out your herbal medicine chest just yet.

What went largely unreported was that study participants received only 900 mg of echinacea daily—less than one-third of the dose recommended by the World Health Organization for combating upper-respiratory infections. That's akin to expecting one-third of a dose of aspirin to relieve a headache.

What's the other side of the story? Dozens of clinical studies point to echinacea's effectiveness, including an August 2004 Canadian trial in which volunteers who took echinacea at the onset of colds experienced 23% milder, shorter symptoms, such as sore throat, stuffy nose, chills and headache, than those taking a placebo—a benefit that researchers linked to a marked increase in circulating white blood cells and other cells of the immune system.

More work is needed to identify the optimal echinacea species (supplements are commonly derived from *E. purpurea, E. pallida* or *E. augustifolia*) and the most potent plant parts (roots, stems, leaves or flowers).

Meanwhile, best results have been achieved by taking 3,000 mg daily of an echinacea product that combines one of the above-mentioned species and parts at the first sign of cold or flu until symptoms resolve.

Caution: If you're allergic to ragweed, avoid echinacea supplements derived from stems, leaves or flowers—they may contain pollen and trigger a reaction. Use an echinacea root supplement.

Five other herbs with scientific evidence on their side…

GARLIC

What it does: Helps prevent and possibly reverse arterial plaque buildup (atherosclerosis), a major risk factor for heart attack and stroke…reduces risk for stomach and colorectal cancers…and acts as a blood thinner to reduce the risk for blood clots.

Scientific evidence: In a recent German study, 152 patients with advanced atherosclerosis who took 900 mg daily of garlic powder for four years experienced a 3% decrease in existing arterial plaques in their neck (carotid) and thigh (femoral) arteries. Those taking a placebo experienced more than a 15% increase in arterial plaques.

Potential side effects: Bad breath and indigestion. Because garlic has a blood-thinning effect, it should not be used if you take aspirin regularly or an anticoagulant drug, such as *warfarin* (Coumadin). To minimize bleeding risk, ask your doctor about discontinuing garlic supplements at least one week before undergoing elective surgery.

Typical dose: One clove of fresh, minced garlic daily, or 200 mg to 300 mg of standardized garlic powder, taken in pill or tablet form, three times daily.

GINKGO

What it does: Improves memory and concentration in people with early-stage senile dementia or Alzheimer's disease, as well as in healthy adults, by increasing blood flow to the brain. May also relieve tinnitus (ringing in the ears), vertigo and altitude sickness, as well as vascular problems such as intermittent claudication, a painful calf condition caused by decreased circulation to the legs.

Scientific evidence: An overwhelming majority of ginkgo trials have shown positive results. At least 33 randomized, controlled trials have shown this herb to enhance mental functioning or slow cognitive deterioration in older patients with dementia, while another 13 controlled studies have shown ginkgo to boost memory and cognitive performance in healthy adults.

Potential side effects: Stomach upset, headache, rash and/or dizziness. Like garlic, ginkgo should not be taken with aspirin or a prescription blood thinner such as warfarin. The herb was previously believed to increase the effects of monoamine oxidase inhibitor (MAOI) antidepressants, such as *phenelzine* (Nardil), but this has been refuted.

Typical dose: 120 mg daily. Nearly all positive ginkgo trials have used one of three formulations that are produced in Germany and sold in health-food stores in the US under the brand names Ginkoba by Pharmaton Natural Health Products...Ginkgold by Nature's Way... and Ginkai by Abkit Inc.

MILK THISTLE

What it does: Because of its strong anti-oxidant activity, milk thistle detoxifies the liver and may help regenerate liver cells. It may be appropriate for patients with alcohol-related liver damage or infectious or drug-induced hepatitis, as well as anyone who is regularly exposed to industrial pollutants.

Scientific evidence: At least 19 out of 21 clinical studies (a total of 2,200 people out of 2,400) have shown milk thistle to protect the liver against invasive toxins and possibly even stimulate the generation of new liver cells.

Potential side effect: Loose stools.

Typical dose: Take 140 mg of milk thistle three times daily.

SAW PALMETTO

What it does: Relieves the symptoms of benign prostatic hyperplasia (BPH), a noncancerous swelling of the prostate gland, which causes frequent and/or weak urination and is common in men over age 50.

Scientific evidence: In nearly two dozen clinical trials, saw palmetto has proven almost equal to prescription drugs, such as *finasteride* (Proscar) and *terazosin* (Hytrin), for relieving the symptoms of BPH. Unlike prescription prostate medications, which can cause side effects, including diminished libido, saw palmetto causes only minor adverse effects. Saw palmetto does not inhibit the production of prostate-specific antigen (PSA), a protein that, when elevated, serves as an early warning for prostate cancer. (Conventional BPH drugs suppress PSA, complicating prostate cancer screening.)

Potential side effects: Stomach upset or nausea if taken on an empty stomach.

Typical dose: 320 mg daily. It requires four to six weeks to take effect.

VALERIAN

What it does: The root combats insomnia and acts as a mild sedative to relieve anxiety or restlessness.

Scientific evidence: All of the nearly 30 clinical studies to date have shown the herb to be effective against insomnia and anxiety. In a recent German trial, taking 600 mg of valerian root extract daily proved as effective as the prescription tranquilizer *oxazepam* (Serax) for improving sleep quality, but with fewer side effects. Unlike prescription sleep aids, valerian isn't habit-forming, won't leave you feeling groggy the next morning and doesn't diminish alertness, reaction time or concentration.

Potential side effects: None known. It is best to avoid combining valerian with conventional sedatives, such as *diazepam* (Valium), since the herb may exacerbate the drug's sedating effects.

Typical dose: 2 g to 3 g of the dried crushed root, infused as a tea...or 400 mg to 800 mg in supplement form, taken one-half hour before bedtime.

Life-Saving, Money Saving Natural Flu Therapies

Jamison Starbuck, ND, a naturopathic physician in family practice and a lecturer at the University of Montana, both in Missoula. She is past president of the American Association of Naturopathic Physicians and a contributing editor to *The Alternative Advisor: The Complete Guide to Natural Therapies and Alternative Treatments.* Time Life.

During the worst flu pandemic in history, the 1918 Spanish flu, naturopathic treatments—including hygiene, nutrition and homeopathy—saved more lives than conventional medicine.

To create your own naturopathic flu defense, follow these steps*…

●**Be vigilant about hand-washing and hydration.** The flu virus enters your body via your respiratory tract, typically when you inhale infected droplets from a sick person's sneeze or cough. Try to keep your distance from people who are sneezing and coughing. The virus also can be transmitted if you touch an infected droplet or mucus from a sick person and then rub your eyes, nose or mouth. If the virus can attach itself to the walls of your nose, throat and/or lungs, it will stay there and multiply. Hand-washing before eating and after visiting any public place will lessen your exposure. Adequate hydration (½ ounce of water per pound of body weight daily) keeps your mucous membranes moist, which makes it more difficult for viruses to attach.

●**Boost your immunity.** Research shows that eating fruits, vegetables and grains boosts your immunity, while a diet rich in sugar, fats and salt increases your risk of getting sick. During flu season, also take these potent, immune-boosting nutrients: B-complex (find a supplement that contains at least 50 mg of vitamin B-6 and 800 micrograms of folic acid)…2,000 mg of vitamin C…and 2,000 mg of fish oil.

Caution: Do not take fish oil if you take *warfarin* (Coumadin) or another blood thinner.

*To learn more natural flu-prevention strategies, read the book *Flu: Alternative Treatments and Prevention* by Randall Neustaedter, OMD. North Atlantic.

●**Use a homeopathic remedy.** Several homeopathic flu-prevention remedies, such as Mucococcinum, Oscillococcinum and Influenzinum 200C, are available at health-food stores or through holistic practitioners. At the beginning of flu season, take one dose per the label instructions under the tongue once a week for three weeks. Then continue with one dose once every three weeks for the rest of the winter.

In my 17 years of practice, I have seen individually prescribed homeopathic remedies successfully treat the flu. If you do get the flu, to find a practitioner trained in homeopathy in your area, go to the National Center for Homeopathy Web site, *www.homeopathic.org.* Or consult the American Association of Naturopathic Physicians, 866-538-2267, *www.naturopathic.org.*

●**Do not be afraid.** Fear causes stress, which lowers immunity. Speak to your doctor about your flu risk. Natural therapy is effective for most healthy people. A flu shot and/or the antiviral drug *oseltamivir* (Tamiflu) may be recommended for older adults and people with compromised immunity.

Inexpensive Folk Remedies Really Work

Earl Mindell, PhD, RPh, an authority on nutrition, drugs, vitamins and herbal remedies. He is also the author of *Natural Remedies for 101 Ailments* (Basic Health) and *Earl Mindell's Vitamin Bible for the 21st Century* (Warner).

Physicians often dismiss folk remedies as quaint, not effective or potentially unsafe. That's a mistake.

Research has now found that some traditional remedies work as well—or even better—than drugs. What's more, most of these traditional treatments are safer than drugs because they rarely cause side effects or interact with other medical treatments.

Best folk cures*…

*Check with your doctor before trying these remedies. Herbs can be dangerous for some people, including pregnant or breast-feeding women.

COLDS

There is good reason that mothers have long advocated chicken soup as an effective cold remedy. Studies have confirmed that chicken soup increases the activity of antiviral immune cells and at the same time reduces throat and sinus inflammation.

What to do: Eat a bowl of chicken soup twice daily at the first sign of a cold.

Helpful: Add a pinch of cayenne to chicken soup. *Capsaicin*, the chemical that makes cayenne and other peppers taste hot, reduces congestion as effectively as over-the-counter (OTC) medications.

HEADACHES

Most headaches are caused by muscle tension and/or emotional stress. Millions of Americans cannot take aspirin or other painkillers because of drug interactions or side effects, such as stomach irritation.

What to do: Using your thumb and forefinger, squeeze the area between your upper lip and nose for five seconds. Repeat as needed. This technique helps to block the nerve signals and will significantly decrease headache pain in many sufferers.

INSOMNIA

Sleeping pills can be addictive and are notorious for side effects, such as dizziness, depression and headaches.

What to do: Drink a cup of valerian tea at bedtime. Valerian root, available in tea bags at health food stores, contains *valepotriates* and other sleep-inducing compounds. A traditional remedy for anxiety as well as sleeplessness, it's now recommended by Commission E, the European equivalent of the FDA.

Chamomile, hops and lavender teas will also help you rest, but they are not as potent.

NAUSEA

Ginger is the best treatment for all forms of nausea, including motion and morning sickness. The active ingredients, *gingerols*, are more effective than OTC antinausea drugs.

What to do: Each day you have nausea, drink two to three cups of ginger ale that contains natural ginger. This variety is available at health-food stores. The ginger-flavored ingredients in commercial brands of ginger ale won't have the same effect.

As an alternative, make ginger tea. To prepare, chop about one tablespoon of fresh gingerroot and steep it in hot water for about 10 minutes. Drink one to three cups daily.

SORE THROAT

Most people have heard that gargling with warm saltwater reduces sore throat pain. However, few prepare and use the mixture properly.

What to do: Add three teaspoons of table salt to one cup of warm water and stir. Gargle with a full one-cup mixture at least two to three times daily. Viruses, which cause colds, cannot survive in a high-salt environment.

TOOTHACHE

Conventional treatments for toothache range from OTC products, such as Orajel, to powerful prescription painkillers. But one of the best treatments is a generations-old folk remedy.

What to do: Dip a toothpick in oil of clove, available at health-food stores and some pharmacies, and apply it to the sore area. The pain will disappear almost instantly. Reapply as necessary. If pain persists for more than a few days, see your dentist.

Stay Out of the Doctor's Office

Thomas Rogers, ND, naturopathic physician in private practice at Whidbey Island Naturopathic, Oak Harbor, Washington, *www.whidbeynaturopathic.com*, and adjunct faculty member who teaches medical procedures and orthopedics at Bastyr University, Kenmore, Washington.

You don't need a doctor for headaches and heartburn and other minor health problems. Most ailments can be treated easily with remedies made from common household items or naturopathic products available at pharmacies and health-food stores.

Caution: Any symptoms that seem unusual… come on suddenly…or don't go away within one week always should be checked by a physician. Also, if you are taking any medications, check with your doctor before taking any additional remedies.

Conditions you can treat yourself…

TENSION HEADACHE

A tension headache usually is triggered by physical or emotional stress. Aspirin and other nonsteroidal anti-inflammatory drugs may help, but they frequently cause stomach upset and, if overused, may trigger rebound headaches.

Remedies: Put a few drops of lavender oil on your index fingers, and rub it on your temples and the muscles at the back of your neck. Lavender penetrates the skin to slow activity in the limbic system, the part of the brain connected with emotions.

You also can try a combination supplement that contains *bromelain* (a pineapple enzyme) and *curcumin* (found in the spice turmeric). This combination suppresses the production of *prostaglandins*, pain-causing chemicals. Follow label directions.

HEARTBURN

This occurs when stomach acids surge into the esophagus.

Remedies: Add one-half teaspoon of baking soda to one cup of warm water and drink it. This mixture neutralizes acid. Or take capsules that contain *deglycyrrhizinated licorice* (DGL). Follow label directions. Licorice creates a gel-like barrier that protects the esophagus from stomach acid. Another option is a supplement called *Robert's Formula*, which contains such soothing herbs as marshmallow and slippery elm (do not use this remedy during pregnancy and lactation).

FLATULENCE

Gas is produced when bacteria in the colon ferment carbohydrates that aren't digested. The resulting buildup of hydrogen, methane and other gases causes discomfort and sometimes embarrassment.

Remedy: Have a cup of fennel tea, available in tea-bag form. Or pour eight ounces of boiling water over one-half teaspoon of crushed fennel seeds. Cover the cup, and let steep for 15 minutes. Drink the tea as often as needed.

SINUSITIS

Sinusitis is an infection of the sinus cavities behind the facial bones around the nose and eyes. It can cause difficulty breathing as well as facial tenderness and headaches.

Remedy: Add one-half teaspoon of salt to eight ounces of warm water. Cup some of the solution in your palm (wash your hands first), and sniff it deeply into each nostril. Or you can use a commercially prepared saline spray. Do this up to three times a day to reduce swelling of the sinus lining, promote better drainage and inhibit growth of harmful organisms.

Avoid milk, cheese and other dairy foods during sinusitis flare-ups. Dairy triggers the production of excess mucus.

COUGH

A cough results when nerves in the respiratory tract are irritated by a cold, flu or other type of illness.

Remedies: For a wet cough (one that produces phlegm)—boil water in a pot. Turn off the heat, and add three drops of eucalyptus oil. Lean over the pot with a towel draped over your head, and inhale the steam. This helps open nasal and bronchial passages and expel phlegm. Do this twice a day.

For a dry cough—make up a tea from wild cherry bark. Just measure one teaspoon of dried chopped cherry bark into an eight-ounce cup, and pour boiling water over the bark. Cover up the cup, and let the bark steep for 15 minutes. Drink one cup three times a day.

PULLED MUSCLE

Soreness usually means that you have overexerted a muscle, causing microscopic tears.

Remedies: Right after the injury occurs, wrap ice in a towel or T-shirt and apply to the area for up to 20 minutes. Repeat every few hours. If possible, elevate the area above the level of your heart.

In addition, you can place three 30C pellets of homeopathic *Arnica* under your tongue every 15 minutes for one to two hours to reduce pain and inflammation.

Also take 500 to 750 milligrams (mg) of magnesium citrate daily until the pain subsides. To prevent diarrhea from the magnesium, divide the dose into several smaller ones and take them throughout the day.

SWIMMER'S EAR

This infection of the outer part of the ear usually is caused by fungi that thrive in moist environments.

Remedies: Warm one-half of an onion in a microwave for about 10 to 20 seconds and hold it very close to, but not touching, the affected ear for a minute or two. Warm onion releases sulfur-based gases that inhibit fungi, bacteria and viruses and ease pain. You can reheat and reuse the onion several times. Or moisten a cotton swab with citrus-seed extract, and apply it to the outer part of the ear and ear canal. Citrus kills fungi and bacteria.

To prevent the infection from recurring, just swab the outer part of the ear with rubbing alcohol after swimming or bathing. This makes it harder for fungi to survive.

INGROWN NAIL

This irritation where the nail enters the skin is painful and slow to heal but rarely serious.

Remedy: To ease pain and inflammation, mix one-half teaspoon of bentonite clay with one-half teaspoon of goldenseal powder and enough witch hazel to make a paste. Apply it to the nail bed, and cover with a warm wash-cloth for 15 minutes. Do this twice a day until the area heals.

Natural Ways To Boost Your Immunity

Mark A. Stengler, ND, naturopathic physician in private practice, La Jolla, California…adjunct associate clinical professor at the National College of Natural Medicine, Portland, Oregon…author of many books, including *The Natural Physician's Healing Therapies* and coauthor of *Prescription for Natural Cures* (both from Bottom Line Books)…and author of the *Bottom Line/Natural Healing* newsletter.

Y ou *can* boost your immunity. With the right preparation, quick intervention and a lineup of powerful, natural virus fighters, there's a good chance that you can enjoy fall and winter without a cold or flu. This is especially important as we face the prospect of a deadly avian flu pandemic.

KNOW YOUR ENEMY

Colds and flu are both caused by viruses. They are spread through the air by coughs and sneezes and through contact with contaminated objects, such as a doorknob or a hand that has been used to cover a cough.

Flu viruses are a lot more powerful than typical cold viruses. Cold symptoms are mainly confined to the head, neck and chest. Flu causes more generalized symptoms—fever, body aches, nausea, cramping, vomiting and severe fatigue. Flu also can develop into bronchitis. In the worst cases, it can lead to pneumonia and other severe respiratory diseases that are sometimes fatal, especially in the elderly or others with weakened immune systems.

START WITH PREVENTION

•**Avoid spending time around people who already are sick,** particularly if they're coughing or sneezing. If you live with someone who is sick, sleep in separate rooms. Wash your hands frequently during cold-and-flu season, and don't share towels—assign one to each family member or use paper towels. Keep your hands away from your face, especially your nose, mouth and eyes.

•**Take a multivitamin/mineral supplement** that provides a base of nutrients to support a healthy immune system. A formula that I recommend in my practice as a preventive against viral infections is Wellness Formula by Source Naturals (to find a retailer near you, call 800-815-2333 or go to *www.sourcenaturals. com*). It contains vitamins A and C, which are involved in the formation of antibodies…the minerals zinc and selenium…and immune-supportive herbs, such as garlic, echinacea and astragalus, which increase the activity of virus-fighting white blood cells. The dosage used to prevent infection is two capsules daily during cold-and-flu season, taken in conjunction with your year-round multisupplement.

•**Reduce exposure to toxins.** You are more vulnerable to viral infection when your body is "distracted" by having to deal with toxins that can damage or suppress the immune system.

Toxins aren't necessarily exotic—they could include sugar and alcohol consumed to excess, fast food and other unhealthy food laced with artificial preservatives and/or pesticides. Toxins also include small but significant amounts of metals—mercury, arsenic and lead—that you can get from food, water and air pollution.

It is even more vital to eat healthfully during cold-and-flu season. Go easy on holiday sweets and other treats, and you will be less likely to get sick.

Many people cut back their exercise regimens in winter months—a big mistake because exercise strengthens your immune system. Also consider sitting in a dry sauna once or twice a week for 20 to 30 minutes…or a wet sauna for 10 to 15 minutes. Saunas increase sweating, which excretes toxins. Be sure to check with your doctor first if you have diabetes or heart disease.

●**Be positive.** Toxic emotions can have a negative impact on your immune system. Anger, anxiety, resentment, loneliness and other chronic emotional difficulties trigger the release of hormones that suppress immune function. Seek support to overcome these problems if they linger.

RELY ON NATURE'S VIRUS KILLERS

If you start to come down with a cold or the flu, eat lightly so that your body can focus on healing. For the first 24 hours, consume filtered water, broths and soups with lots of garlic, onions and spices, such as turmeric and cayenne, which relieve congestion, promote circulation and have a natural anti-inflammatory effect. Herbal teas (especially ginger, cinnamon and peppermint) and steamed vegetables also are good choices. When you're feeling better, move toward a more normal diet.

I have found several supplements to be effective for treating colds and flu. Consider taking these when people around you are sick or when you first feel symptoms. You can use one or any combination until you feel better. These are safe for children when given in dosages of one-quarter to one-half of what I recommend for adults. The bigger the child, the higher the dose.

●**Lomatium dissectum** is a plant once used by Native Americans to fight Spanish flu. Preliminary research shows that lomatium has the ability to prevent viruses from replicating and to stimulate white blood cell activity. With colds and flu, I often see improvement within 24 hours. In my experience, the only side effect has been an allergic reaction in the form of a measles-like rash in a small percentage of users. This rash disappears a few days after lomatium is discontinued.

Eclectic Institute makes a potent product called Lomatium-Osha (800-332-4372, *www. eclecticherb.com*), which soothes the respiratory tract. This product is 50% alcohol, so take only the dosage recommended on the label. For children, add one-quarter to one-half of the adult dosage to hot water and let it sit for five minutes so that the alcohol evaporates. Women who are pregnant or nursing should not use lomatium.

●**Elderberry** can stimulate the immune system, enhance white blood cell activity and inhibit viral replication. Flu patients have reported significant improvement within 48 hours of taking elderberry. It also helps with colds. The elderberry used in research studies is Sambucol Black Elderberry Extract from Nature's Way (to find a retailer, call 800-962-8873 or go to *www.naturesway.com*). Adults should take two teaspoons four times daily…children, one teaspoon four times daily.

●**Echinacea.** Contrary to recent media reports, extracts from this plant can be effective for treating colds and flu. Echinacea makes the body's own immune cells more efficient in attacking viruses. The key is using a product that has been processed to contain a high level of active constituents. Two potent, well-researched products are Echinamide Alcohol-Free Liquid Extract, Natural Berry Flavor, and Echinamide Anti-V Formula Softgels, both from Natural Factors (to find a retailer, call 800-322-8704 or go to *www. naturalfactors.com*).

If you feel a cold or the flu coming on, take 20 drops of liquid extract or two capsules every two waking hours for 24 hours, then cut back to every three waking hours until the illness has passed.

The same company makes a liquid preparation called Anti-V Formula, which contains

Echinamide, lomatium and other virus fighters. It is the most aggressive product for colds and flu from the Natural Factors line and can be used instead of the other supplements. Take 1.5 ml every two waking hours for the first 48 hours and then every three waking hours until the illness is gone.

●**N-acetylcysteine (NAC).** This nutrient thins the mucus that comes with colds and the flu. In addition to making you feel better, NAC helps to prevent sinus and more serious chest infections. It increases levels of the powerful antioxidant *glutathione* in the body, which, in turn, improves immune function. NAC is available at any health-food store and many pharmacies. If you tend to get the flu every year, take 600 mg twice daily when you are around people who have the flu or if you start feeling sick yourself.

●**Vitamin C** fights viral infections. Start with 5,000 mg daily in divided doses. If loose stools occur, cut back to 3,000 mg (or less).

HOMEOPATHIC REMEDIES

Homeopathy is based on the idea that "like cures like"—substances that cause certain symptoms in a healthy person can cure those same symptoms in someone who is sick. *For the flu, I recommend the following homeopathic treatments…*

●**Homeopathic influcnzinum.** Made from active flu strains, this stimulates the body's own defense system to resist infection. It can be used for prevention or treatment of flu and has no side effects.

Take two 30C-potency pellets twice daily for two weeks at the beginning of flu season (in early November). Take two pellets four times daily when exposed to flu sufferers or if you start to have symptoms. It is available from health-food stores and The Vitamin Shoppe (866-293-3367, *www.vitaminshoppe.com*).

●**Oscillococcinum** is another great homeopathic remedy for flu, which is also available from The Vitamin Shoppe, health-food stores and pharmacies or by calling 800-672-4556 or visiting *www.oscillo.com*. It can be taken at the first sign of flu and is the number-one–selling homeopathic flu remedy in the US.

Natural Ways to Warm Up Cold Fingers and Toes

Jamison Starbuck, ND, a naturopathic physician in family practice and a lecturer at the University of Montana, both in Missoula. She is a past president of the American Association of Naturopathic Physicians and a contributing editor to *The Alternative Advisor: The Complete Guide to Natural Therapies and Alternative Treatments.* Time Life.

Cold extremities are not always just about the weather. Whenever a patient of mine complains of cold hands and feet, I consider whether it could be related to poor thyroid function, anemia or Raynaud's disease (a condition in which small arteries, usually in the fingers or toes, constrict in response to exposure to cold). Cold extremities are a primary symptom of all these conditions. Cold hands and feet can also be a secondary symptom of other conditions that affect circulation. These include rheumatoid arthritis, lupus, arterial disease and high blood pressure.

If you have chronically cold hands and feet, see your doctor. Ask for a screening physical and get blood tests—a complete blood count (CBC), as well as a thyroid profile, lipid panel and C-reactive protein test—to determine if your symptoms may bc caused by anemia, a thyroid disorder or heart disease.

If your physician finds no physical cause for your problem, here's my advice…

●**Bundle up!** This seems obvious, but you'd be amazed at how many of my patients who complain of cold hands and feet fail to wear proper clothing in cold weather. When you are outdoors, wear thick, lined wool mittens (not gloves), wool socks and insulated shoes or boots. Carry your dress shoes or athletic shoes and socks in a bag, and put them on only after you have arrived inside a heated building. In addition, wear a scarf and a hat.

●**Eat warm food.** In the coldest months, choose soups, stews, roasts and hot cereal over salads, sandwiches and cold cereal. Cooked food already has begun to be broken down, requiring less work than cold food to digest.

This leaves your body with more energy to keep you warm.

- **Drink tea.** Although all hot beverages are temporarily warming, caffeine and other components of coffee constrict blood vessels, which promotes cold extremities. Green and black teas contain flavonoids, which promote blood vessel health and support good circulation.

- **Take supplements.** In addition to a multivitamin, be sure to get 50 milligrams (mg) of B-6 as well as 300 mg of magnesium. Vitamin B-6 promotes blood vessel health. And, magnesium helps prevent muscle spasms and encourages blood flow to hands and feet.

- **Keep moving.** Regular aerobic exercise is one of the best cures for poor circulation and cold extremities. Be sure to hydrate by drinking room temperature or warm water.

- **Use cayenne pepper.** Cayenne slightly irritates the skin, bringing blood to the area of the body it touches. To warm your feet, sprinkle one-half teaspoon of ground cayenne into each of your socks. You can experiment with the amount to see if you need more or less. If you have diabetes, do not use cayenne pepper for this purpose.

Lemon Balm Boosts Memory

In one recent study, participants who took standardized word- and picture-recall tests scored significantly better several hours after taking a 1,600-milligram (mg) capsule of dried lemon balm leaf than when they were given a placebo.

Theory: The herb binds to brain chemical receptors, enhancing their ability to send and receive information.

What to do: Add three teaspoons (or three tea bags) of dried lemon balm to two cups of boiling water. Steep for five minutes and then strain, Drink daily. Or take a 1,600-mg supplement daily.

David Kennedy, PhD, professor of psychobiology and psychology at Northumbria University, Newcastle upon Tyne, England.

Tomatoes Fight Heart Disease, Too

Lycopene, the phytonutrient that gives tomatoes their red color, has been shown to fight malignancies of the prostate, lungs and stomach.

New finding: Women who had the highest levels of lycopene in their blood were only half as likely to develop cardiovascular disease as those with the lowest levels.

Theory: Lycopene prevents LDL "bad" cholesterol from being oxidized and deposited in arterial plaques.

Although this study focused on women, researchers believe these findings also may hold true for men.

Helpful: Add to your diet a serving per day of lycopene-containing foods, such as one-half cup of tomato sauce, one-half pink grapefruit or one cup of watermelon.

Howard D. Sesso, ScD, assistant professor of medicine, Harvard Medical School, Boston.

Thrifty Way to Lower Stroke Risk

Getting more fruit in your diet will help you prevent stroke.

Recent finding: People who ate almost one pound of fruit a day (the equivalent of about five standard-sized apples or pears) had a 40% lower risk for ischemic stroke, which occurs when a clot blocks an artery, than those who ate one-third of a pound of fruit a day.

Theory: The antioxidants, minerals and fiber found in fruit help prevent stroke by fighting common risk factors, such as elevated blood pressure and cholesterol.

Soren Paaske Johnsen, PhD, associate professor of clinical epidemiology, Aarhus University Hospital, Denmark.

Powerful Ways to Stop Cancer Now

Patrick Quillin, PhD, RD, clinical nutritionist located in San Diego, *www.nutritioncancer.com*, and previous vice president of nutrition for the Cancer Treatment Centers of America. He is the author of 15 books, including the best-seller *Beating Cancer with Nutrition*. Nutrition Times. He edited the textbook *Adjuvant Nutrition in Cancer Treatment* and organized three international symposiums on that topic.

Every year, more than 1.4 million Americans are diagnosed with cancer. Nearly half of all Americans eventually will get the disease—and about 25% of them will die from it. But there is a powerful way to reduce your risk of getting cancer.

Specific nutrients and foods can help prevent or correct cellular, hormonal and other imbalances that may lead to cancer. The supplements that are mentioned here are available at health-food stores and some supermarkets.

FISH OIL

The most common nutritional deficiency in Americans is low *eicosapentaenoic acid* (EPA). It is one of the omega-3 fatty acids found in the oil of fatty fish, such as salmon and tuna. A healthy diet will have a 1:1 ratio of omega-3 to omega-6 fatty acids (found in vegetable oils). The typical American diet has a 1:16 ratio.

EPA helps prevent cancer by improving cell membrane dynamics—the ability of each cell to receive hormones and signals from other cells while also absorbing essential nutrients and expelling waste products. EPA also increases immune function and lowers levels of hormones that contribute to breast and other cancers, such as estradiol.

What I recommend to my patients: One tablespoon of fish oil daily. For capsules, follow dosage recommendations on labels. Carlson Laboratories, Dr. Sears, Nordic Naturals and the Pharmax brands are reliable. Take it in the middle of a meal to avoid "fishy" belching or reflux.

CLA

Another fat that helps prevent cancer is *conjugated linoleic acid* (CLA), found in the meat and milk of grass-eating animals, such as cattle,

deer, sheep and goats. CLA helps build healthy cell membranes, permitting the cells to absorb nutrients, process hormones and expel waste. It's hard to find CLA-rich foods in the markets because most livestock in America are fed grain, not grass.

What I recommend to my patients: Three grams (g) of CLA a day. You can get that from an eight-ounce serving of grass-fed beef. Look for such brands as Lasater Grasslands Beef, available at most specialty food stores. On days when you don't eat grass-fed red meat, you can take a CLA supplement—three 1-g soft-gel capsules a day.

VITAMIN D

People who live in Boston have, on average, double the risk for breast, colon and prostate cancers, compared with residents of San Diego. Why? Many scientists think it's because Bostonians, like other northerners, don't get enough vitamin D, which is produced whenever skin is exposed to sun.

Vitamin D is one of the most powerful anti-cancer nutrients. It facilitates the absorption of calcium, a mineral that not only builds strong bones but also is critical for "telegraphing" messages between cells. Poor cell-to-cell communication can contribute to cancer. Studies show that levels of vitamin D in fortified foods rarely equal the claims made on the labels. There is a debate as to whether synthetic vitamin D—the kind found in supplements—provides the same cancer protection as the naturally produced vitamin D.

What I recommend to my patients: During the summer, get 15 minutes a day of the midday sunshine with no sunscreen (without burning) on the face and bare arms. The body stockpiles vitamin D in the liver, so you're set for the rest of the year.

VITAMIN C

In a report published in the *American Journal of Clinical Nutrition*, 33 of 46 studies showed that vitamin C protects against cancer. Cancer feeds on blood sugar (glucose)—and lowering chronically high blood sugar is crucial to preventing cancer. When you get enough vitamin C, you cut in half the amount of blood sugar that enters cells.

What I recommend to my patients: 500 to 1,000 milligrams (mg) of vitamin C a day, in three divided doses, taken with meals. Cancer patients may need higher doses, which usually are given intravenously.

Other ways to normalize blood sugar levels include regular exercise, weight loss and a diet that emphasizes lean meats, beans, nuts and produce. Five daily servings of fruits and vegetables nets you 300 mg of vitamin C.

SELENIUM

During the four-year Nutritional Prevention of Cancer Trial, scientists gave 1,312 participants either 200 micrograms (mcg) of the trace mineral selenium or a placebo. The results showed that selenium lowered the risk of prostate cancer by 63%, colon cancer by 58% and lung cancer by 46%.

Selenium can strengthen the immune system, help to repair DNA damage and protect cells against toxins.

What I recommend to my patients: 200 mcg of selenium a day. Look for *selenomethionine*—selenium bound in yeast—because it is absorbed the best. A particularly good food source is Brazil nuts (just four nuts will provide 200 mcg).

Caution: More is not better. Selenium supplements in doses of 2,000 mcg or higher can be toxic.

GREEN TEA

Literally hundreds of studies have now proven that green tea and its various extracts can prevent and, in some experiments, reverse cancer. These extracts work by different mechanisms, among them *apoptosis* or "programmed cell death." In other words, green tea orders cancer cells to commit suicide.

What I recommend to my patients: Drink three eight-ounce cups of green tea a day. If you don't like the taste, take supplements of green tea extract, available in capsules. Be sure to follow the dosage recommendation that's on the label.

KILLER CONSTIPATION

Chronic constipation creates toxemia in the colon. Cancer-causing chemicals from the environment are ingested but not expelled quickly. Normally friendly food-digesting bacteria then produce toxins that end up in the bloodstream.

What I recommend to my patients: To ensure a daily bowel movement, get plenty of high-fiber foods…drink 64 ounces of filtered or bottled water a day…and exercise regularly. Prune juice and figs often relieve constipation. Or try a gentle herbal laxative, such as *psyllium* (Metamucil), following the dosage recommendation on the label.

Cinnamon… The New "Statin"?

Cinnamon may work almost as well as statin drugs to control cholesterol and triglycerides. It was found to be equally effective in a recent study of people with type 2 diabetes—and may also work for healthy people. Cinnamon contains a substance that seems to help the body utilize insulin more efficiently. The study indicated that one-half teaspoon per day was enough—but speak with your doctor before stopping any prescribed medication.

Richard Anderson, PhD, research chemist at the USDA Beltsville Human Nutrition Research Center, Maryland.

An Orange a Day Keeps Cancer Away

Daily consumption of citrus fruits, such as oranges, reduces risk of mouth, larynx and stomach cancer by up to 50%.

Reason: Citrus fruits contain high levels of antioxidants, which strengthen the body's immune system.

Another benefit: One serving of citrus fruit as part of the recommended five daily servings of fruits and vegetables can reduce stroke risk by 19%.

Katrine Baghurst, PhD, the program manager and researcher for the Commonwealth Scientific and Industrial Research Organization in Adelaide, Australia, and leader of a study of a meta-analysis of 500 papers, published in Horticulture Australia.

A Single Slice Helps Prevent Cancer

Researchers who recently tracked 8,000 Italians report that those who ate pizza one or more times a week were 59% less likely to get cancer of the esophagus and 26% less likely to develop colon cancer than the participants who did not eat pizza.

Reason: Tomatoes and olive oil have been shown to reduce the risk for various cancers.

International Journal of Cancer, Heidelberg, Germany.

Natural Relief For Migraines

Available in pharmacies as well as in health-food stores, coenzyme Q10 (coQ10) has long been used to treat high blood pressure, heart disease, cancer and Parkinson's disease.

Recent study: Migraine sufferers who took 100 milligrams (mg) of liquid coQ10 three times a day for three months averaged 3.2 migraines per month versus 4.4 migraines per month before the study. Those who received a placebo reported no change.

Seymour Diamond, MD, founder and director, Diamond Headache Clinic, Chicago, *www.diamondheadache.com*.

Natural Remedies for Chronic Skin Problems

Mark A. Stengler, ND, naturopathic physician in private practice, La Jolla, California…adjunct associate clinical professor at the National College of Natural Medicine, Portland, Oregon…author of many books, including *The Natural Physician's Healing Therapies* and coauthor of *Prescription for Natural Cures* (both from Bottom Line Books)…and author of the *Bottom Line/Natural Healing* newsletter.

Chronic skin problems, such as eczema, psoriasis and acne, are some of the most common reasons people visit dermatologists. Conventional topical treatments (ointments and lotions) are helpful, but many people find they work only temporarily.

The majority of chronic skin problems need to be addressed internally as well as externally because they often are the result of internal problems related to digestion, detoxification and liver function.

Several natural remedies are effective, and they rarely have side effects. Allow four weeks for improvement of chronic skin problems… one to two days for acute flare-ups. For each condition, you can use all the remedies recommended. Unless otherwise noted, they prevent as well as treat the condition. All are available in drugstores and/or health-food stores.

Important: Never start a new treatment without consulting your doctor, especially if you are taking any medications or are pregnant.

ECZEMA

●**EPA (*eicosapentaenoic acid*).** This long-chain fatty acid in the omega-3 family has potent anti-inflammatory properties. The highest concentrations are found in fish and fish oils, but EPA also is prevalent in other foods, such as flaxseed and walnuts.

It is hard to get enough EPA from fish and/or walnuts, so I suggest that adults take fish oil in a dosage containing 1.8 grams (g) of EPA daily or two tablespoons of flaxseed oil daily, whichever you prefer.

●**Evening primrose oil.** This contains a different essential fatty acid known as *gamma linolenic acid* (GLA), which helps reduce skin inflammation. Take 2,000 milligrams (mg) of primrose oil daily.

●**Probiotics.** These good bacteria prevent food sensitivities that often are connected with eczema. Friendly bacteria are found in yogurt (look for products with live cultures, such as Horizon Organic and Stonyfield Farm). Good bacteria also are in sauerkraut, kefir (a cultured milk product, like yogurt), miso and cottage cheese. It's hard to get enough from food, so I suggest a supplement. Take four billion organisms (usually one to two capsules) daily between meals.

●**Sulphur.** This homeopathic remedy will soothe skin and relieve itching. It is particularly helpful if eczema is worse after bathing and in warm environments. For acute flare-ups, take two pellets of a 30C potency twice daily for one week. Then stop taking this remedy, unless the symptoms return.

●**Chamomile (*Matricaria chamomilla*).** Chamomile contains a group of phytonutrients that have strong anti-inflammatory properties. Apply a cream to the affected areas two to three times daily until symptoms disappear.

●**Oatmeal baths soothe itchy skin.** Tie up one-quarter cup of oats in cheesecloth or a leg from nylons, and let water from the tap run over it before you soak in the bath. Oatmeal also can be purchased as a powder and added to your bath. Pat, don't rub, yourself dry.

PSORIASIS

●**Fish oil.** Take 5 g twice a day. It will significantly reduce the itching, scaling and redness of psoriasis lesions.

●**Dandelion root (*Taraxacum officinale*).** This supports liver detoxification, which improves psoriasis. Take 300 mg of the capsule form three times daily with meals.

●**Aloe vera.** One study showed that a 0.5% aloe vera cream used for four weeks significantly relieved psoriasis lesions. Apply aloe vera cream twice daily.

ACNE

●**Zinc.** One double-blind study found that taking 30 mg of zinc for three months was an effective treatment for acne for almost one-third of patients. Adults should take 45 mg of zinc twice daily with meals for three months and then reduce the dosage to 30 mg daily for long-term supplementation. To maintain mineral balance, take zinc in conjunction with copper at a dose of 3 to 5 mg once a day.

●**Burdock root (*Arctium lappa*).** This herb treats many of the causes of acne, including hormonal imbalance, inefficient liver activity and skin bacteria. You can take 300 mg of the capsule form, 30 drops of tincture or one cup of tea three times daily.

●**Fish oil.** Take supplements or flaxseed oil in the dosages recommended for eczema.

●**Tea tree oil gels or creams.** Tea tree oil is an antiseptic and an anti-inflammatory. Apply topically once daily.

WOUNDS/BURNS

●**Aloe vera.** Apply this topically twice a day until the burn or wound is healed. Look for a product that contains a high concentration (80% or higher) of aloe.

●**Calendula officinalis.** This soothing herb is an antiseptic. Apply it as a gel or cream twice a day.

●**Vitamin C.** Take 1,000 mg twice daily to promote wound healing. For quicker healing, take 400 international units (IU) of vitamin E* and 30 mg of zinc daily as well.

Beer Builds Better Bones

Dietary silicon, found in whole grains and their products (such as beer), decreases bone loss *and* promotes bone formation. Beer is an especially good source because it is readily absorbed. Other sources of silicon include oat bran, barley and rice.

Warning: More than two drinks per day for men or one for women is considered harmful.

Ravin Jugdaohsingh, PhD, senior research fellow, gastrointestinal laboratory, Rayne Institute, St. Thomas's Hospital, London.

Now Hear This— You Can Protect Your Ears

Michael D. Seidman, MD, director of the division of otologic/neurotologic surgery, department of otolaryngology–head and neck surgery, Henry Ford Health System in West Bloomfield, Michigan. He also is director of the Otolaryngology Research Laboratory, a codirector of the Tinnitus Center, medical chair of the Center for Integrative Medicine for the Henry Ford Health System and founder of Body Language Vitamin Company, *www.bodylanguagevitamin.com.*

About 28 million Americans have trouble hearing. The most common cause is the general wear and tear on the ears

*Due to the possible interactions between vitamin E and various drugs and supplements as well as other safety considerations, be sure to talk to your doctor before taking vitamin E.

as you age. This is triggered by the gradual weakening and eventual death of hair cells in the inner ear or degeneration of the auditory nerve, or both. *To protect your hearing…*

BLOCK SOUND

Sound is measured in decibels (dB). A whisper is 15 dB…normal conversation, 50 to 60…a rock concert or jet engine, 120…a gunshot or firecracker, 140. If you have to raise your voice to be heard, you're listening to an 85-dB sound or higher.

Sounds above 85 dB can permanently damage ears by destroying the hair cells of the inner ear. This includes sounds you might not think are dangerous, such as a blow-dryer (85 to 90 dB) or loud music in an exercise class (110 dB).

I suggest carrying earplugs with you. They reduce sound by 18 to 22 dB. Use them when flying, on a hunting trip, mowing the lawn, riding a snowmobile and blow-drying your hair. Spongy, compressible plugs or waxlike plugs, available at most drugstores, do a good job.

TAKE NUTRITIONAL SUPPLEMENTS

These antioxidants, available at drug and/or health-food stores, may help fight hearing loss by reducing cell-damaging free radicals. As always, check with your doctor before starting any supplement.

●**N-acetylcysteine (NAC).** NAC is a biochemical precursor to *glutathione*, an antioxidant shown in numerous studies to reduce hearing loss in animals exposed to loud noise. A federally funded experiment with humans now is in progress. In the study, 600 marines at Camp Pendleton in California are undergoing rifle training—which typically reduces hearing in about 10% of trainees—while taking a supplement that contains NAC. I suggest 500 milligrams (mg) of NAC two or three times a day.

●**Alpha-lipoic acid and acetyl-L-carnitine.** Scientists studied three groups of aging rats for six weeks. Group 1 received alpha-lipoic acid. Group 2 got acetyl-L-carnitine. Group 3 didn't get any supplements. Before and after the supplementation, the rats' hearing loss was tested. Group 3 had an "expected age-associated deterioration" in hearing of three to seven dB. But Groups 1 and 2 had an "actual improvement in hearing" at varying frequencies—a great result.

I suggest taking 150 mg of alpha-lipoic acid daily and 600 mg of acetyl-L-carnitine daily.

●**Other antioxidants and supplements that are scientifically proven to help protect hearing** include vitamin C (500 to 800 mg daily), which improves hearing of low frequencies…vitamin E* (200 to 600 international units [IU] daily), which improves hearing of high frequencies…and lecithin (500 to 750 mg daily), which resulted in 75% improvement in hearing in lab animals, compared with a placebo.

IMPROVE HEALTH

Like every organ, ears need good circulation for optimal function. People who have a high total cholesterol and LDL and/or excess weight may have a reduced blood supply to the inner ear, which can cause hearing loss. *To improve your circulation…*

●**Eat a diet rich in fruits and vegetables** and low in saturated fat.

●**Exercise regularly**—at least 30 minutes of aerobic exercise four times a week.

●**Don't smoke.**

●**Maintain an appropriate weight.**

●**Drink lots of water**—eight eight-ounce glasses a day.

If these lifestyle measures are not effective, your doctor may recommend statin drugs to lower cholesterol.

A WORD ON HEARING AIDS

If you feel that you might need a hearing aid, see an audiologist. Ask your doctor for a recommendation.

An audiologist can determine the type of hearing aid that is best for your problem and properly fit it to your ear. *Also…*

●**Don't hunt for "bargains."** Good hearing aids range from $600 to $3,000, depending on the type. They usually are not covered by insurance or are partially covered at best.

●**Buy two.** If you have hearing loss in both ears, wear two aids.

●**Give your hearing aid a chance.** At first, most people don't like how a hearing aid feels.

*Due to the possible interactions between vitamin E and various drugs and supplements as well as other safety considerations, be sure to talk to your doctor before taking vitamin E.

Break yours in. Wear it for two hours the first day, then three, then four, etc.

HOW'S YOUR HEARING?

If you answer *yes* to one or more of the following questions, consult an audiologist…

●**Do I frequently ask people to repeat themselves?**

●**Have I been turning up the TV?**

●**Do I know that people are speaking** but often can't tell what they're saying?

●**To hear better, do I turn an ear** in the direction of the person speaking?

●**Do I find it difficult to hear children's or women's voices?**

●**Do I have trouble hearing words that contain S, F, Sh, Ch, H or soft C sounds** (all of which have higher frequencies than other sounds)?

Curry May Fight Alzheimer's

The ingredient that gives curry its distinctive color, curcumin, is filled with potent antioxidants called phenols that may also have anti-inflammatory properties. Curcumin triggers the production of an enzyme that protects against the oxidative diseases—possibly including Alzheimer's. Further research is needed to determine whether curcumin will boost health in humans. For now, consider eating Indian food once a week or adding a teaspoon or two of curry to vegetables and meat dishes you make at home.

Nader G. Abraham, PhD, professor of pharmacology, New York Medical College, Valhalla, New York.

Disease Fighters from the Grocery Store

Steven Pratt, MD, an assistant clinical professor of ophthalmology at the University of California, San Diego, and senior staff ophthalmologist at Scripps Memorial Hospital in La Jolla, California. He is coauthor of SuperFoods Rx: Fourteen Foods That Will Change Your Life. William Morrow.

Most health-conscious eaters will try to do their very best to follow the basic dietary recommendations, such as eating seven to nine daily servings of fruits and vegetables. Unfortunately, these guidelines really do not tell us which foods will provide the maximum nutritional value.

Now: Researchers have targeted a handful of specific superfoods that contain phytonutrients (disease-fighting plant-based chemicals), vitamins, minerals and healthful fatty acids. These nutrients act as powerful antioxidants (to fight heart disease, cancer, even the aging process)…anti-inflammatories (to reduce inflammation that can lead to heart disease, eye disease and cancer)…and immune system boosters (to help in warding off infection).

This is not to say that these foods are the *only* ones worth eating. Each has "healthful cousins" that are nearly as beneficial.

Example: Any vegetable in the cabbage family (brussels sprouts, cauliflower, bok choy) offers some of the same benefits as broccoli. But broccoli combines the greatest number of healthful nutrients.

THE TOP THREE

When it comes to nutritional value, three foods qualify as the best of the best…

●**Blueberries contain more antioxidants than any other fruit.** Besides plentiful quantities of vitamins C and E, blueberries contain such phytonutrients as anthocyanins (which give the fruit its distinctive color) and ellagic acid. These phytonutrients work synergistically —that is, the unique combination of nutrients maximizes the benefits of each.

Research shows that blueberries have anti-inflammatory effects, improve mental performance and also reduce the rates of urinary-tract infection.

Healthful cousins: Red grapes, cranberries, blackberries, cherries, raspberries, boysenberries, strawberries.

Goal: One to two cups fresh or frozen daily.

●**Salmon is an excellent source for the omega-3 fatty acids,** which control inflammation and keep cell membranes healthy. It's also rich in vitamin D, selenium and protein.

Increasing your intake of the omega-3s will reduce your risk for coronary artery disease, cancer and age-related macular degeneration. Omega-3s also have been shown to lower high blood pressure and ease symptoms of arthritis and lupus.

Important: Much of the salmon available today is raised on fish farms, where it is exposed to high levels of contaminants, such as PCBs. Whether fresh, canned or frozen, buy only salmon that is specifically marked *wild Alaskan.*

Healthful cousins: Halibut, sardines, herring, sea bass and trout, which are all low in mercury. Canned albacore tuna is rich in omega-3s, but it's best to limit consumption to one can per week because of possible mercury content.

Goal: Three ounces of fish, two to four times per week.

●**Spinach is rich in the antioxidants lutein and beta-carotene…**the minerals calcium, iron, magnesium and zinc…and omega-3 fatty acids. It's also a good source of betaine, a fat-derived compound that fights elevated homocysteine, a cardiovascular risk factor. A number of studies now link spinach consumption with lower rates of colon, lung, stomach, ovarian, prostate and breast cancers. It also appears to protect against cataracts and age-related macular degeneration.

Healthful cousins: Kale, collards, Swiss chard, mustard greens, romaine lettuce.

Goal: Two cups raw or one cup steamed every day.

HIGH IN THE HIERARCHY

●**Oats are the nutritional powerhouse of whole grains.** They are a rich source of fiber, including beta-glucans, which help to protect against heart disease…and minerals, including magnesium, potassium, zinc, copper, manganese and selenium, all of which lower the risk for high blood pressure, diabetes, cancer and heart disease.

Healthful cousins: Wheat germ, flaxseed, whole wheat, barley, buckwheat, millet and amaranth.

Goal: Five to seven daily servings (one serving equals one slice…one-half cup cooked…three-quarters to one cup dry).

●**Pumpkin is rich in healthful carotenoids.** It is also the best source of the combination of alpha-carotene (twice as much as carrots) and beta-carotene—which work optimally as a team.

Carotenoid-rich foods (not the supplements) have been shown to reduce the risk for lung, colon, breast and skin cancers. Canned 100% pure pumpkin is just as nutritious as fresh.

Healthful cousins: Carrots, sweet potatoes, butternut squash.

Goal: One-half cup most days.

●**Tomatoes are a cornucopia of carotenoids**—alpha-carotene and beta-carotene, lycopene, lutein, phytoene and phytofluene.

All are beneficial, but lycopene does deserve special mention. It's been linked to reduced rates of cancer (particularly prostate malignancies). When joined with lutein, lycopene also fights age-related macular degeneration.

Important: Although uncooked tomatoes have higher levels of other carotenoids, the lycopene in cooked tomatoes is most readily absorbed by the body.

Healthful cousins: Try watermelon or pink grapefruit.

Goal: One daily serving of processed tomatoes (one-half cup sauce) or healthful cousins (one watermelon wedge…one-half pink grapefruit), and multiple servings of fresh tomatoes each week.

●**Walnuts contain omega-3 fatty acids,** vitamin E, potassium, protein, fiber and cholesterol-lowering compounds known as plant sterols.

Studies suggest that eating a handful of nuts (about one ounce) five times a week lowers the risk for heart attack by up to 50%.

Caution: Because nuts are high in calories, do not overindulge.

Healthful cousins: Almonds, pistachios, sesame seeds, pecans.

Goal: One ounce, five times a week.

OTHER SUPERFOODS

To round out the list above, try to incorporate oranges...soy...tea (black or green)...raw or cooked broccoli...yogurt (with live cultures)...skinless turkey...and/or beans (pinto, navy, lima, chickpeas) in your diet on all or most days of the week.

The "Soda" that Relieves Indigestion

More than 60% of people who drank a glass of carbonated water daily experienced a reduction in bloating, nausea, belching, pain and other symptoms of indigestion and constipation, according to a recent two-week study.

Theory: Carbonated water will stimulate the proximal (or upper part) of the stomach, which promotes more efficient digestion. Carbonated water may also increase the efficiency of gallbladder emptying.

If you suffer from indigestion and constipation: Ask your doctor if adding carbonated water to other treatment strategies, such as a high-fiber diet, may be beneficial.

Rosario Cuomo, MD, assistant professor of clinical and experimental medicine, University of Naples "Federico II," Naples, Italy.

Cranberries Fight Prostate Cancer

In new research, disease-fighting flavonoids found in cranberries destroyed human prostate cancer cells in laboratory experiments.

Theory: Flavonoids interfere with the signals that tell cancer cells to proliferate.

More research is under way to confirm these findings. In the meantime, eat homemade cranberry sauce, snack on whole dried cranberries (sold in supermarkets) and/or drink 100% cranberry juice.

Peter J. Ferguson, PhD, research associate, London Regional Cancer Program, London, Ontario, Canada.

Natural Sex Boosters

Ray Sahelian, MD, a board-certified family-practice physician and nutritional consultant in private practice in Marina del Rey, California. He is the author of *Natural Sex Boosters* (Square One) and *Mind-Boosting Secrets* (Bottom Line Books, *www.bottomlinesecrets.com*).

The drug *sildenafil* (Viagra), introduced in 1998, revolutionized the treatment of sexual dysfunction. However, it and related drugs, such as *vardenafil* (Levitra) and *tadalafil* (Cialis), have significant limitations.

Although these impotence medications work well at promoting blood flow to the penis, they have little or no effect on libido or sexual sensation in men—or in women.

These drugs also have potentially serious side effects, such as vision problems, and some doctors believe that they may be dangerous for men with cardiac conditions, such as irregular heart rhythms, history of heart attack or heart failure.

However, sex-boosting herbs have been used successfully for hundreds of years in Brazil, China, India and parts of Africa.

The following supplements, available at most health-food stores, can improve virtually all aspects of sexual performance, including increased desire, improved genital blood flow in men and women, and stronger erections in men.*

Start by choosing one herb that seems to best fit your needs. After one to two weeks, you can combine it with another supplement to enhance the effect. Or simply use a formula that combines these herbs.

Important: When combining herbs, cut the recommended dose of each in half to avoid potential side effects, such as restlessness.

*Check with your doctor before taking any of these products.

HORNY GOAT WEED

This herb increases energy and libido in both men and women...and may produce firmer erections in men.

Horny goat weed reportedly got its name when a Chinese herder noticed that his goats became more sexually active after eating the plant. It's thought to influence levels of *dopamine* and other neurotransmitters that affect libido and mood. It also contains flavonoids, plant chemicals that dilate blood vessels and promote erections.

Scientific evidence: A study conducted in Beijing on 34 patients receiving dialysis for renal failure found that horny goat weed enhanced sexual activity in the patients taking it.

Typical dose: 500 mg to 2,000 mg daily. Start with 500 mg and increase, if needed. Side effects include restlessness and insomnia.

MUIRA PUAMA

This herb increases libido...orgasm intensity...and skin and genital sensitivity in men and women.

The bark and roots of this Amazon tree, sometimes known as "potency wood," increase sexual desire and sexual fantasies in men and women, and also facilitate a woman's ability to have an orgasm. It appears to work by promoting blood flow to the genitals in men and women.

Scientific evidence: A clinical study of 262 men, conducted at the Institute of Sexology in Paris, found that taking muira puama for two weeks improved libido in 62% of those studied.

Typical dose: 500 mg to 1,000 mg in capsule form three consecutive days each week.

Important: Muira puama should be taken in the morning. That's because it can cause insomnia when taken in the afternoon or at night. Muira puama may cause restlessness in some people during the daytime.

TRIBULUS

This herb increases energy and libido in both men and women...and improves erections in men.

This common roadside weed contains *protodioscin*, a chemical compound that is thought to increase production of the sex hormone testosterone in both men and women. It also dilates blood vessels in the penis, promoting firmer erections.

Scientific evidence: An animal study conducted at the National University Hospital in Singapore showed that rats that were given tribulus for eight weeks were found to experience firmer erections.

Typical dose: 500 mg to 1,000 mg daily. Take tribulus for one week, then stop for one week, and so on. This minimizes the risk for potential side effects, such as restlessness and increased body temperature.

ASHWAGANDHA

This herb increases mood and sexual desire and function in men and women. It can improve sex drive in both sexes by acting as a relaxant, and it also assists men in maintaining an erection.

Ashwagandha produces a calming effect by mimicking the action of GABA, a neurotransmitter in the brain that promotes relaxation. It also boosts nitric oxide production. Nitric oxide is known to enhance penile erection and vaginal sensitivity by increasing engorgement of the genital organs through blood vessel dilation.

Scientific evidence: A laboratory study conducted at the University of Texas Health Science Center found that ashwagandha inhibits the number of nerve cells that fire in the brain, much like the neurotransmitter GABA, resulting in an antianxiety and mood-enhancing effect.

Typical dose: 300 mg to 500 mg one to two times daily.

Important: For better absorption, take ashwagandha on an empty stomach.

Caution: Ashwagandha may cause drowsiness in some individuals. Do not drive after taking this herb.

Better Way to Heal Irritable Bowel Syndrome

When individuals who have irritable bowel syndrome (IBS)—a disorder of the large intestine characterized by abdominal pain and changes in bowel habits and stool frequency—took up to 640 milligrams (mg) of artichoke leaf extract a day, symptoms were reduced in more than 25% of people.

Theory: Artichoke leaf extract stimulates the liver to produce bile, which helps the body to process fats and reduce bloating...acts like a natural laxative...and may promote the growth of healthful bacteria in the colon.

If you have IBS: Try one teaspoon of liquid extract mixed with a glass of water three times a day or take a 320-mg standardized extract capsule twice a day.

Caution: If you have gallstones or biliary tract disease or are allergic to artichokes, do not take artichoke leaf extract.

Rafe Bundy, PhD, research fellow, School of Food Biosciences, University of Reading, England.

"Shore Way" to Block Breast Cancer—Seaweed

Japanese women get less breast cancer than Americans, possibly because about 10% of their diet consists of kelp, a form of seaweed. In laboratory studies, animals given kelp had lower levels of *estradiol*, a hormone associated with breast cancer. Kelp can be purchased at specialty grocery stores. Don't take kelp supplements—they're too high in iodine.

Journal of Nutrition, 9650 Rockville Pike, Bethesda, Maryland 20814.

Common Spice Eases Knee Pain

In a recent study, participants who took two 500-milligram (mg) tablets of *gingerol*, the component that gives ginger its bite, twice a day for three months experienced the same reduction in inflammation as when they took aspirin for three months.

Caution: Ginger can thin blood, so consult your doctor before trying.

Prevention, 33 E. Minor St., Emmaus, Pennsylvania 18098.

Improve Your Mood With Flower Power

Jamison Starbuck, ND, a naturopathic physician in family practice and a lecturer at the University of Montana, both in Missoula. She is past president of the American Association of Naturopathic Physicians and a contributing editor to *The Alternative Advisor: The Complete Guide to Natural Therapies and Alternative Treatments.* Time Life.

If stress or difficult emotions have got you down, flower essence remedies may be the solution. Most of us experience negative emotions from time to time—irritability, gloom, anger, self-reproach or a sense of inadequacy. They can be especially troublesome if you're facing a temporary, acute situation. You may be fearful of flying or public speaking. Or maybe you are having marital trouble or a good friend has just died.*

Flower essences are dilute, springwater extractions of the flowers of nonpoisonous trees, shrubs and plants. They are gentle, non-habit-forming and can be used alone or in conjunction with other medications. They cost only about $7 to $10 for a two-month supply. Adults and children can safely use these remedies.

Flower essences were developed in the 1930s by Edward Bach, MD, a London-based physician, bacteriologist, researcher and homeopath. Dr. Bach originally developed 12 remedies. There now are 38 Bach flower essences. I have prescribed Bach flower remedies for 15 years and, even though some patients are initially skeptical, I find that these essences work well for emotional problems and stressful times. *Each remedy, available in health-food stores, is used to correct a specific negative emotion...*

●**Tension.** Vervain is used to treat insomnia and restlessness in people who are perfectionists and inclined to tackle too many tasks at once.

*If you experience severe depression, disabling panic attacks or suicidal thoughts, seek immediate medical attention. You may require prescription medication.

•**Resentment.** Willow is used to treat stress that has caused irritability, dissatisfaction, grumbling and a loss of one's sense of humor.

•**Anxiety for others.** Red chestnut helps people who fear that something bad will happen to another.

•**Self-reproach.** Pine treats people who are overly conscientious, blame themselves for all mistakes and are prone to overwork.

To begin using flower essences, find the words to describe the emotions you are experiencing in response to a stressful situation. With the help of a naturopathic physician or *The Bach Flower Remedies* by Edward Bach, MD, and F.J. Wheeler, MD (available at most libraries), determine which Bach flower remedy most accurately matches your emotions. You can combine up to four remedies. Take four drops on the tongue up to six times a day, at least 15 minutes before or after consuming food or beverages. Use the remedy for up to one month or until your emotional issue is resolved. If symptoms have not improved after one month, consult your healthcare professional.

Naturopathic physicians learn to use Bach flower remedies in naturopathic medical school. In addition, the Dr. Edward Bach Centre in Mount Vernon, England, as well as various organizations in the US offer training courses for lay practitioners. If you're interested in consulting a lay practitioner, ask for a recommendation from your local health-food store.

11

Get Fit for Less

The Secret to Improving Your Workouts—Eating The Right Foods at the Right Times Maximizes Your Exercise Performance

You already know that a regular exercise routine—ideally, at least 30 minutes of vigorous activity daily—is among the smartest steps you can take to protect your health.

What you may not know: Consuming the right foods and fluids is one of the best ways to improve your exercise performance.

If your body is not properly fueled—regardless of the type, frequency or intensity of physical activity—your energy levels are more likely to wane, your muscles will be more susceptible to fatigue and soreness, and you'll find it harder to maintain your desired weight. *My secrets...*

1. Remember to drink enough fluids before exercise. Research shows that about half of people who work out in the morning are dehydrated when they begin to exercise.

Why is fluid consumption so important? When you're dehydrated, your heart must pump harder to get blood to your muscles. Being dehydrated also impairs your ability to perspire and cool yourself.

Advice: Drink one cup of water or a sports drink, such as Gatorade, before your workout and another during your workout. If your workout is vigorous or lasts more than 60 minutes, you may need to consume more fluids.

Also remember to drink fluids throughout the day. You don't have to limit yourself to water. Milk, tea, coffee, fruit juice and carbonated beverages also count toward your daily fluid intake.

Heidi Skolnik, CDN, a certified dietitian nutritionist and director of sports nutrition for the Women's Sports Medical Center at the Hospital for Special Surgery in New York City. A regular contributor to NBC's *Today Show*, she also is a sports nutrition consultant to the New York Giants football team and the School of American Ballet.

Caution: Your risk for dehydration is increased if you take a diuretic drug, have diabetes or are an older adult—the body's thirst center functions less efficiently with age.

2. Don't exercise on an empty stomach. When you don't eat for several hours—including the time when you're sleeping—your blood sugar levels decline. This can leave you with less energy for physical activity and at risk for injury.

The quickest solution is to consume carbohydrates, which are your body's primary energy source. Carbohydrates are found mainly in starchy foods, such as grains, breads and vegetables, as well as in fruit, milk and yogurt.

Advice: If you're exercising before breakfast, first have half a banana or a slice of toast. If you're exercising just before lunch, eat a healthful mid-morning snack—and a mid- to late-afternoon snack if your workout is before dinner. It's okay to eat the snack right before your workout.

3. Eat a balanced breakfast. Eating a good breakfast helps get your metabolism going—and may help you consume fewer calories during the rest of the day.

Advice: Choose whole-grain foods (such as oatmeal or whole-grain cereal or toast) to fuel your muscles…a serving of dairy (yogurt, low-fat milk or cheese) or another protein (such as eggs or Canadian bacon) to promote muscle repair…and fruit (such as a mango, berries or melon) for vitamins and disease-fighting phytonutrients.

4. Fill in your nutritional "gaps" with lunch. Like breakfast, your midday meal should include healthful carbohydrates and protein.

Advice: At lunch, get some of the nutrients you may not have included in your breakfast. For example, if you ate fruit in the morning, eat vegetables at lunch. If your breakfast included a dairy product as your protein source, eat lean meat or fish at lunch.

Example of a healthful lunch: A salad with grilled chicken, legumes, peppers, broccoli and an olive oil–based dressing.

5. Eat an evening meal. If you exercise late in the afternoon or after work, don't skip your evening meal. You may wake up the next morning with a "deficit" that can lead you to overeat.

Advice: Strive for a balance of unprocessed carbohydrates (such as brown rice or vegetables) lean protein (such as fish or poultry) and a little healthful fat (such as nuts or olive oil).

Example: A shrimp and vegetable stir-fry served over one-quarter cup of brown rice.

Simple Way to Improve Your Workout

For better results, vary your workout. If you usually use a particular machine at the gym, use a different one of the same type. If you exercise at home, do it at a different time of day, or face your equipment in a different direction. If you do a series of activities, change the order in which you do them. If you usually work out at the same pace, change your speed—this can actually work different muscles in certain exercises, such as weight lifting.

Cooking Light, Box 1748, Birmingham, Alabama 35201.

Weight-Loss Secret

Yogurt helps you lose weight while protecting muscle.

Recent study: Overweight people who ate three servings of yogurt daily for 12 weeks lost 22% more weight, 61% more body fat and 81% more abdominal fat than people who ate a similar number of calories but no dairy products.

Michael Zemel, PhD, professor of nutrition and medicine and director of the Nutrition Institute, University of Tennessee, Knoxville. He is coauthor of *The Calcium Key: The Revolutionary Diet Discovery That Will Help You Lose Weight Faster.* Wiley.

How to Stick To an Exercise Program

Doug Levine, founder of Crunch, a chain of health clubs with locations in New York City, Los Angeles and other major US cities. He also is founder of PUSH, an interactive on-line fitness program, based in Miami, Florida, *www.push.net.*

Less than one-third of people who start an exercise program stick with it through the first year. *Secrets to staying on track...*

VARY YOUR WORKOUT

People tend to follow the same exercise routine and may overwork certain muscle groups.

Instead, try to work different muscles on different days.

Example: Run on a treadmill on Mondays...exercise your chest and back muscles on Wednesdays...work legs and arms on Fridays.

Do the same for out-of-gym workouts. Alternate bike rides with fast walks. Go to the pool now and then.

MAKE HOBBIES ATHLETIC

Everyone should have at least one athletic hobby, such as golf, tennis, walking, skiing, bicycling, dancing, bowling or swimming. Even gardening counts if you do it vigorously enough. You're more likely to stick with activities that are fun, regardless of the health benefits.

GET A WORKOUT PARTNER

Having someone to talk to makes the time go faster and the exercise more fun. Some health clubs have programs that pair members for regular workouts. Or ask around at work or in your neighborhood to find someone who enjoys the same activities that you do.

CHOOSE A PROGRAM-PACKED CLUB

If you plan to join a health club, select one that offers classes of interest to you. Many health clubs offer aerobics, yoga, kickboxing, spinning and tai chi classes—and that's just the beginning.

Classes also are a great way to try new things, meet new people and stay motivated.

COMPETE

You don't have to be an elite athlete to get a thrill out of competition. Plus, knowing that you'll be competing motivates you to work out.

Just about every community has a variety of athletic events for people of all ages and fitness levels—5K walks and runs, kayak races, volleyball tournaments, etc. Newspapers, health clubs and YMCAs usually have listings of upcoming events.

GET A TRAINER

The average health club has at least 60 aerobic and weight-lifting machines. New members often don't know how to use the machines and may stop going because they don't feel confident. Ask a trainer at the club to show you how to use the equipment.

You also may want to hire a personal trainer. The average rate is about $55 an hour.

If you would like a trainer to help you at home, ask for referrals at a local health club.

Yoga Can Help Keep Weight Off

Yoga can help keep weight off even though it does not burn many calories

Overweight people in their 50s who regularly practiced yoga lost about five pounds over 10 years, while people of similar ages who did not practice yoga gained more than 13 pounds.

Possible reason: Yoga may help people stay more attuned to their bodies and eating habits—making it easier to avoid habits such as eating when stressed or bored.

Alan Kristal, DrPH, associate head, Fred Hutchinson Cancer Research Center, Seattle.

Get Fit Without Costly Gym Fees

High-quality exercise facilities often are available at lower cost than fancy health clubs.

Examples: Large hotels often have fitness centers and let people who work or live in the area use them during off-peak hours at reasonable fees—but you have to ask, they don't advertise it...many religious centers and churches have fitness centers...YMCAs, YWCAs and similar organizations have fine facilities at reasonable prices...employers often make discounted health club memberships available as a benefit, and health insurance may cover part of the cost of membership.

Also: The "great outdoors" can be the best health facility of all—and it's free!

Mary Hunt, editor, *Debt-Proof Living*, Box 2135, Paramount, California 90723, *www.debtproofliving.com.*

Avoid Germs at the Gym

With many people using the same equipment day after day, you'll want to protect yourself from germs at the gym. Wipe down machines before and after use. Use disinfectant spray if the gym supplies it or carry moist towelettes in your gym bag. Also, wash hands thoroughly before going home, especially if you have been using dumbbells and holding bike handlebars.

Shirley Archer, MA, health and wellness educator and fitness expert, Stanford University School of Medicine, Palo Alto, California. She is the author of *The Everything Weight Training Book.* Adams Media.

Easy Exercises You Can Do Anytime, Anywhere

Joan Price, a Sebastopol, California-based dance and fitness instructor who specializes in helping beginning exercisers. She is author of *The Anytime, Anywhere Exercise Book—300+ Quick and Easy Exercises You Can Do Whenever You Want!* Adams Media.

We all know we should exercise on a regular basis—but only about one in every five Americans actually gets a 30- to 60-minute workout most days of the week. Even these committed exercisers often run into trouble when their schedule is disrupted by work, travel or family responsibilities.

The solution? Stop thinking of fitness as a separate undertaking and instead, start taking advantage of all the exercise opportunities that crop up during the course of your day-to-day activities.

In addition to keeping up with your regular schedule of cardiovascular exercise, here are eight strengthening and stretching exercises you can perform without missing a beat in your daily routine...

ABDOMINAL ALERT

This simple movement will give you an abdominal workout *and* improve your posture.

What to do: From a sitting position, sit up tall and pull your abdominal muscles in, lifting your chest and rib cage as you exhale. Hold for four to six seconds, then release slowly as you inhale. Repeat eight to 12 times.

Perform this: While driving, watching television or sitting at your desk.

Helpful: If you perform this exercise while driving, adjust your rearview mirror so you can see out of it only when you're in the "sitting tall" position. This will remind you to maintain this posture.

BACK STRETCH

If you spend long hours sitting in a chair, a back stretch provides welcome relief.

What to do: Stand about arm's length behind a chair, with your hands resting on the top of the backrest. Keeping your head upright, bend forward from the hips, lowering your upper body and pushing your buttocks away from the chair until you feel a stretch in your mid and upper back. Hold for 10 to 60 seconds. If your chair has rollers, increase the stretch by pushing it forward slightly as you lower yourself.

Perform this: While standing at your desk or watching TV.

CALF STRENGTHENER

Here's a good way to strengthen your lower legs, back and abdomen.

235

What to do: Stand on a telephone book (the bigger the better) with your toes facing the book's spine and your heels hanging over the edge opposite the spine. For better stability, this exercise can also be done standing on a step while holding a railing or on a curb while holding a signpost for balance.

Keeping your back straight, push up onto the balls of your feet while counting for two seconds, hold for another two seconds, then count for four seconds as you lower yourself back down. To help stay balanced, tighten up your abdominals and buttocks.

Keep doing for two minutes or until your calves tire, whichever comes first.

Perform this: While waiting for a bus or watching TV.

OUTER THIGH LIFT

This exercise strengthens and tones up your outer thighs while standing.

What to do: While standing on a step or on a curb, bend your left leg just slightly at the knee and slowly lift your right leg out to the side, keeping your knee facing forward and your foot flexed. Do this eight to 12 times, then switch legs and repeat.

BUN SQUEEZE

Here is an efficient way to tone up your buttocks whenever you're standing.

What to do: Squeeze the buttock muscles in both cheeks as tightly as you can, then hold the contraction for two seconds. Release for two seconds. Repeat eight to 12 times.

Perform this: While in line at the store.

NECK ROLL

A good neck stretch helps relieve neck and shoulder tension.

What to do: Let your head fall gently to the left side, until your ear is close to your left shoulder. Return to the upright position. Repeat the same movement on the right side. Continue alternating left and right four to six times.

Next, slowly roll your head from one shoulder down toward your chest, then back up to the opposite shoulder. Repeat in the opposite direction. Perform the full movement four times.

Do *not* tilt your head back. This can compress the neck and spine and may cause dizziness by impinging blood flow.

Perform this: While sitting at a desk, talking on the phone or taking a shower. In the shower, stand with your back facing the showerhead so the water hits your neck and shoulders.

JUNK-MAIL CRUMPLE

Believe it or not, crumpling up junk mail is a great way to strengthen your forearms and relieve wrist tension from typing or writing.

What to do: Open an envelope, pull out the letter and hold it in one hand. Starting at one corner, crumple the letter into your palm, bit by bit, until it forms a tight ball. Squeeze the ball a few times, then throw away.

Perform this: While opening your mail.

Exercise illustrations by Shawn Banner.

Simple Exercise Relieves Back Pain

Ninety percent of people who complain of an aching lower back get relief with a simple exercise called a standing backward bend.

What to do: Stand with your feet shoulder-width apart and tighten your buttocks. Place your hands on your buttocks and then stretch backward as far as you comfortably can. Slowly return to an upright position. Repeat 10 times, trying to bend back a little farther each time. Perform every two hours throughout the day. Frequency can be decreased as pain subsides.

See your doctor if pain worsens, wakes you up at night or if you feel numbness in your hands or feet.

Peggy W. Brill, board-certified clinical specialist in orthopedic physical therapy with a private practice in New York City. She is also the author of *Instant Relief—Tell Me Where It Hurts and I'll Tell You What to Do*. Bantam.

Get Big Health Benefits From Just a Little Exercise

Steven Blair, PED, former president and CEO, Cooper Institute for Aerobics Research, Dallas.

Health experts no longer believe that you have to "break a sweat" to improve your health through exercise.

Numerous studies now indicate that people who merely walk, rather than jog or run, significantly reduce risk of heart attack, diabetes and other chronic illnesses.

Key: The primary determinant of the health benefit obtained from exercise is the total dose of the exercise, not its intensity. For instance, burning 1,000 calories per week through exercise will produce about the same health benefit whether you do it through 20 minutes of intense exercise three days a week or 30 minutes of moderate exercise five to seven days a week. The 30 minutes don't have to be in one session—they can be incurred, say, 10 minutes at a time at different times during the day.

More good news: When you start exercising after being sedentary, the largest health benefits occur right away. And, moving from moderate to strenuous exercise will further improve your health by only a lesser amount.

The 10-Minute Workout

Ten minutes of jumping rope equals 30 minutes of running at a pace of more than five miles an hour.

To be sure the rope is the right length: Stand on its center with feet together. Hold the rope against your sides—the handles should come within a few inches of your armpits.

Before jumping, warm up with 20 arm circles. While exercising, jump high enough for the rope to clear your feet.

Dan Robey, marketing and communications consultant, Miami, and author of *The Power of Positive Habits.* Abritt.

Exercise Boosts Brain Function

Loss of cognitive ability late in life is only partly genetic. Regular exercise can offset it. In two studies, highly fit and aerobically trained people showed higher levels of activity in parts of the brain related to cognitive performance—and much greater preservation of brain tissue.

Stanley J. Colcombe, PhD, Beckman Institute Fellow, Beckman Institute for Advanced Science and Technology, University of Illinois at Urbana-Champaign.

Almonds for Weight Loss

In one finding, people who ate a moderate amount of almonds, three ounces a day, lost more weight than those on high-carbohydrate diets who ate the same number of calories.

Theory: The fat in almonds may not be completely absorbed by the body.

Try a handful of almonds between meals to satisfy hunger and stop unhealthy snacking.

Michelle Wien, DrPH, RD, department of diabetes, endocrinology and metabolism at the City of Hope National Medical Center in Duarte, California, and leader of a study of 65 overweight and obese adults, published in the *International Journal of Obesity.*

Drink Tea to Lose Weight

A recent study of more than 1,100 people found that those who drank tea at least once a week for more than 10 years had 20% less total body fat and 2% less abdominal fat than those who drank none. The study took into account lifestyle factors, including age, physical activity and food intake. Results applied to black, green and oolong tea.

Theory: Tea may increase metabolic rate while lowering absorption of sugars and fat-producing molecules.

Chih-Hsing Wu, MD, associate professor at the Obesity Research Center, department of family medicine, National Chang Kung University Medical College, Tainau, Taiwan, and the leader of a study of more than 1,100 people, reported in *Obesity Research*.

Lose an Extra Five Pounds With this Drink

Drinking water increases your body's metabolic rate—causing it to burn extra calories—partly because it must heat the water to body temperature. Though modest, this effect is real.

Estimate: A person who increases his/her water consumption by 1.5 liters per day for a year would burn an extra 17,400 calories for a weight loss of about five pounds.

Also: Water has no calories, so if you drink it as a substitute for calorie-laden drinks (such as soft drinks), it will help you lose weight by reducing caloric intake.

Michael Boschmann, MD, Franz-Volhard Clinical Research Center, Berlin, Germany, reported in *WebMD*.

The Calcium Diet—Lose Weight Faster with this Vital Mineral

Michael Zemel, PhD, professor of nutrition and medicine and director of the Nutrition Institute, University of Tennessee, Knoxville. He is coauthor of *The Calcium Key: The Revolutionary Diet Discovery That Will Help You Lose Weight Faster*. Wiley.

Why now are two out of every three Americans so overweight? Certainly we are eating more and exercising less. But there is another cause—a lack of the mineral calcium in our diets.

If you are among the Americans getting the lowest average level of calcium—which is 255 milligrams (mg) per day—you are 84% more likely to be overweight than if you are among those people getting the highest average level of calcium—1,346 mg per day—according to a recent examination of statistics from the federal government's Health and Nutrition Examination Survey.

Simply by getting adequate calcium in our diets, as many as four out of five of us could lose the extra weight.

CALCIUM AND YOUR FAT CELLS

Calcium does far more than just keep your skeleton strong. Without enough calcium circulating in your bloodstream, your heart wouldn't beat, your blood wouldn't clot, your hormones wouldn't regulate your metabolism and your nerves wouldn't transmit signals.

If calcium levels fall—if you eat a diet low in calcium, for example—the body releases more of the hormone *calcitriol*. Calcitriol increases absorption of calcium in the intestines, so you get the most calcium possible from food.

In addition, it increases reabsorption through the kidneys, so that you lose as little calcium as possible through excretion.

Calcitriol also controls how fat cells work. When you get too little calcium and more calcitriol is released, your fat cells make and store more fat, causing weight gain.

MORE PROOF

In a study we conducted at the University of Tennessee, overweight people were put on one of three eating plans for six months.

●**Group 1** ate a diet that was 500 calories below maintenance level—the level at which you neither gain nor lose weight—and had no more than one serving of dairy a day for a total of 400 to 500 mg of dietary calcium.

●**Group 2** ate the same calorie-restricted diet but took an 800-mg calcium supplement for a total of 1,200 to 1,300 mg of calcium.

●**Group 3** also ate the calorie-restricted diet but included three servings of low-fat dairy a day, bringing their total calcium intake to 1,200 to 1,300 mg.

Results: Group 1 lost 6% of total weight… Group 2 lost 7.5%…and Group 3—the low-fat dairy group—lost 11%. Group 3 also lost more body fat than the other groups, particularly around the waist area. This is an important finding because a slimmer waist is associated with a lower risk of heart disease, stroke, diabetes and cancer.

This means that adding three servings of low-fat dairy to your diet can…

● **Increase the amount of weight you lose by 70%.**

● **Increase the amount of body fat you lose by 64%.**

● **Help you lose 47% more fat** from around your belly.

Other studies have replicated these findings as well. In a 10-year study of 3,000 people ages 18 to 30, researchers at Harvard University discovered that people who ate three servings of dairy a day had a 60% lower risk of being overweight than those who consumed less calcium.

FOOD VERSUS SUPPLEMENTS

Studies show that calcium from dairy foods is more effective for weight loss than supplements. Why? Food is a complex mixture of known and unknown components. There is a cooperation among the components that can't be reproduced in a nutritional supplement.

Dairy contains calcium and a host of other biologically active components, including the amino acid *leucine*. Recent research reveals that leucine may increase the ability of muscle to use fat.

WHAT TO DO

To lose an average of one pound per week, you need to cut calorie intake and increase calorie burning by about 500 calories per day, or 3,500 calories per week. To boost the loss to 1.5 to two pounds, you need three or four servings of dairy a day, for a total of 1,200 to 1,600 mg of calcium. The easiest way to get that is with three servings of no-fat (skim) or low-fat milk (eight ounces per serving), yogurt (eight ounces) or cheese (1.5 ounces or two ounces processed).

Strategy: Have milk before a meal. Studies show that getting a liquid form of dairy before eating helps you feel full sooner at that meal and eat less at the next meal.

If lactose intolerant, try yogurt with live cultures or cheese (it has very little lactose) or take a lactose supplement when consuming dairy.

To cut 3,500 calories a week: One brisk, hour-long walk will burn about 250 calories. If you do that four times a week, you still need to cut 2,500 calories per week, or about 350 calories a day. Look for one or even two high-calorie items that you can eliminate from your daily diet.

Examples: A 12-ounce cola has 150 calories…two tablespoons of full-fat salad dressing, 150…a glazed doughnut, 250…a four-ounce bagel, 300.

Just eliminating these items will help you to lose weight, but boosting calcium will help you lose more.

Great Web Sites for Losers!

Anne M. Fletcher, RD, weight-loss expert in southern Minnesota and author of *Thin for Life*. Houghton Mifflin.

There are now numerous Web sites on the Internet for dieters and those concerned about good nutrition. *Here are some of the ones I recommend…*

● **www.thedietchannel.com** has more than 600 links to sites with dietary and nutritional information.

● **www.dietitian.com** is a question-and-answer site on dozens of topics, such as diets and vitamins.

● **www.foodfit.com** has weight calculators, menu planners and e-mail newsletters.

Spicy Foods Curb The Appetite

In one recent study, people who ate a sauce containing *capsaicin*—the compound that makes hot peppers spicy—consumed an average of 200 fewer calories over the next three hours than those who didn't eat the sauce.

Theory: Spicy foods are more satisfying, so there's less desire to eat more.

If you are trying to lose weight: In addition to cutting back on calories and fat and getting regular exercise, consider eating more spicy foods. For recipes containing hot peppers, go to Pepper Fool at *www.pepperfool.com*.

Angelo Tremblay, PhD, director, Institute of Nutraceuticals and Functional Foods, Laval University, Ste-Foy, Canada.

Talking and Walking May Hurt Your Back

Talking during your walking workout can be dangerous.

Reason: Talking causes short periods of reduced abdominal muscle activity that leaves the spine temporarily more susceptible to injury.

Theory: The same muscles are used for both breathing and control of your back. If you walk and talk at the same time—causing you to inhale rapidly and exhale slowly—the central nervous system is faced with competing demands.

Self-defense: Walk—or jog—silently.

Paul Hodges, MD, professor of physiotherapy, University of Queensland, Brisbane, Australia.

Secret to Burning More Calories

Just 30 minutes of strength training with weight machines will burn off more calories (about 240) than walking for 30 minutes (about 200). And weight lifting boosts metabolism by 25% for an hour after exercise, burning even more calories.

Helpful: Perform 30 minutes of weight training three times a week in addition to at least 30 minutes of aerobic exercise daily.

Wayne Westcott, PhD, exercise physiologist for South Shore YMCA, Quincy, Massachusetts.

Cheap Running Shoes Are Just as Good as $80 Pairs

A recent study of persons who buy running shoes found that while most people willingly pay high prices for them, the buyers of expensive shoes suffer just as many injuries as those of cheap shoes. More than 70% of buyers spent more than $80 for their running shoes—but there was no significant difference in the incidence of injury between those who paid $20 for shoes and those who paid $120.

Conclusion: Proper fit and comfort are what's important in a running shoe, not price.

Nancy Kadel, MD, associate professor, Department of Orthopaedic Surgery, University of California, San Francisco Medical Center.

Take the Stairs

Stair climbing is a "weight-bearing" exercise that builds bone mass and helps prevent the onset of osteoporosis.

Key: Like muscle, bone just gets denser and stronger as a result of being put to work.

The bone-building exercises include jogging, walking, dancing and racquet sports. Resistance training with weights and machines is excellent because it builds both bone and muscle mass.

Contrast: Biking and swimming aren't good bone-building exercises.

Lynn Chard-Petrinjak, communications manager for the National Osteoporosis Foundation, Washington, DC, *www.nof.org*.

Choosing a Gym Doesn't Have to Be a Workout

Michael F. Roizen, MD, chief wellness officer, The Cleveland Clinic. He is author of *RealAge* and *The RealAge Makeover* (both from Harper). He is founder of RealAge.com.

Joining a health club can be a great investment—or a boondoggle. Only one-third of people who join a gym work out more than 100 days a year. *Here's what you need to do before you join…*

●**Try it out.** Most clubs will let you work out free at least once before joining. Use the free session to test the equipment as well as the atmosphere.

●**Determine your workout needs.** Some people like being pampered in an upscale gym. Others are happy in a concrete room with just a treadmill and free weights.

●**Ask about classes.** Does the schedule work with yours? Is there an extra charge, or are the classes included with membership?

●**Make sure someone will be there to answer questions.** Good gyms have trainers available who will teach you to use the equipment properly. There should be no charge for this service.

●**Find a place that's close.** Most people will continue with their workouts only if the club is within 12 miles of their home or office.

10,000 Steps to A Better Life

Robert N. Butler, MD, president, International Longevity Center, New York City. He is former chairman of the department of geriatrics and adult development, Mount Sinai Medical Center, New York City, the first department of geriatrics in an American medical school. He won the Pulitzer Prize for *Why Survive? Being Old in America.* Johns Hopkins University Press.

When I lived in Washington, DC, in the 1960s, I began participating in one of the most effective and enjoyable forms of exercise I know. Early each morning, a friend and I met for a fast, invigorating walk. I didn't have to take lessons or join a gym, and it was a great way to start the day. Those early morning walks were the beginning of a valuable lifelong habit.

MIRACULOUS BENEFITS

Walking for exercise has a long tradition. Thomas Jefferson, who lived to be 83 at a time when average life expectancy was about 40, walked four miles every day. He wrote that the purpose of walking was to "relax the mind."

Now we know that walking briskly for 30 to 60 minutes each day also can help people live longer, healthier lives. Fast walking burns about the same amount of calories per mile as running, and it doesn't pound the joints. It builds endurance, enhances muscle tone and flexibility and strengthens bones. It also helps prevent heart disease, hypertension and diabetes.

In a study of Harvard graduates, the Mayo Clinic discovered that men who burned 2,000 or more calories a week by walking lived an average of one to two years longer than those who burned fewer than 500 calories a week walking.

GETTING STARTED

The only equipment a walker needs is a comfortable pair of canvas or leather shoes designed specifically for walking.

I've found it helpful to do simple stretching exercises before and after a walk.

Example: I raise my left leg on a tabletop, pointing my toes toward the ceiling. I hold the position for a minute. Then I repeat the stretch with my right leg. If a table is too high, use a chair or sofa.

Some people prefer to walk on a treadmill. Or you may choose to take advantage of day-to-day opportunities to increase your walking.

Examples: Walking up flights of stairs instead of riding the escalator or elevator…parking far away from store entrances…or even walking to the store.

The rule of thumb when you're walking is to break a sweat. Aim to reach your target heart rate (THR).

To determine THR: Subtract your age from 220. Multiply by 0.8 (80%).

10,000 STEPS

Jefferson shipped from Paris to his home in Virginia a cumbersome device that accurately counted every step he took. Today, we have a more portable version known as a pedometer, which can be clipped to a belt or waistband to count the number of steps taken. In fact, "steps per day" has become a standard unit of exercise measurement. Studies here and in Japan show that the average person needs to take at least 10,000 steps per day—what you would do in a strenuous 30-minute workout—to get maximum health benefits. At the International Longevity Center, we sell a pedometer (212-288-1468, *www.ilcusa.org*). Pedometers also are available at sporting-goods stores.

WALKING GROUPS

In recent years, hundreds of walking clubs have sprung up nationwide. You can find them by going on-line and typing "walking clubs" into a search engine.

Example: American Volkssport Association has 350 walking clubs. Go to *www.ava.org* or call 800-830-9255.

Since my return to New York City in 1982, I have walked with a group of early risers on weekends. (During the week, I walk on my own.) We get together around 7:30 am, take a brisk turn around a six-mile trail in Central Park and then enjoy a leisurely, healthy breakfast. Old friends and new get to meet and support each other's efforts to stay healthy. I credit my walking buddies with helping me reach my goal of 10,000 steps a day.

Low-Cost Ways To Keep You Fit

Reduce your risk of premature illness. If you recognize how your mind and body interact to create health or become vulnerable to disease, you can build a lifestyle to help protect yourself from health crises.

●**Purify your drinking water.** Consider purifying your drinking water. Drinking water is a major source of environmental toxins.

Experts say that more than one million Americans drink water that contains significant levels of cancer-causing chemicals, such as arsenic, radon and chlorine by-products. Similarly, the US Centers for Disease Control and Prevention report that millions of Americans become sick from waterborne microorganisms every year.

●**Take your vitamins.** Think about taking daily vitamin supplements. Some experts believe that vitamins may improve healing and wound repair, decrease heart disease and reduce the body's ability to produce free radicals (negatively charged ions that cause tissue damage and promote cancer). Check with your doctor to be sure which supplements are appropriate for you.

●**Exercise.** Try to exercise at least five days a week. The key is to find a way to use your body that is sensible and not traumatic.

Any type of exercise that raises your heart rate is beneficial. You may wish to start with a brisk 10-minute walk, working your way up to 45 minutes.

But if you already have an exercise routine that gives you a workout, there's no need to change.

●**Sweat for success.** Consider taking a weekly sauna or steam bath. In addition to its ability to cool the body, sweating is one of the most important self-healing mechanisms because it allows the body to rid itself of unwanted or excess minerals and toxins.

Sweat in dry heat (sauna) or wet heat (steam), or a combination of the two. If you don't belong to a gym, try steaming in an enclosed shower for 15 to 20 minutes. Be sure to drink plenty of water before you enter the sauna or steam room, and drink enough afterward to replace lost fluids.

●**Eat right.** Think about getting potentially unhealthy foods out of your refrigerator and pantry. Certain foods are suspected of inhibiting your body's ability to heal itself. They include polyunsaturated oils (safflower, corn, sunflower), artificially hardened fats (vegetable shortening, margarine), artificial sweeteners (aspartame, NutraSweet, saccharin) and artificial colorings.

Experts believe that polyunsaturated oils oxidize rapidly when exposed to air. Oxidized fats can damage DNA, promote cancer development and speed aging and degenerative changes in body tissues. Use olive oil in moderation instead.

Consider adding fruits and vegetables to your diet, especially cruciferous vegetables (broccoli, cabbage), dark-colored fruits (red grapes, blueberries) and cooked greens (Swiss chard, kale, collards). In addition to their high fiber and vitamin/mineral content, cruciferous vegetables and dark-colored fruits have been shown to have significant anticancer properties.

Try to eat more whole grains and soy products. Data show that a diet rich in fiber can enhance digestion, reduce the risk of colon cancer, help lower cholesterol and slow the absorption of sugar into the bloodstream. Whole-wheat bread, brown rice and buckwheat are particularly beneficial.

The addition of soy products not only increases your overall fiber intake, but also provides a form of protein that is lower in saturated fat than animal products.

THE ART OF BREATHING

Focusing attention on your breathing can enhance your ability to relax and promote your body's good health and self-healing. Breathing exercises may help make your visit to the doctor's office something to smile about.

Here are some breathing exercises that experts suggest…

●**Inhalation breath observation.** Sit in a comfortable position with your back straight and eyes closed. Focus attention on your breathing, noting the point where you inhale. For noticeable results, do this for five minutes each morning.

●**Exhalation breath observation.** Sit in a comfortable position with your back straight and eyes closed. Focus on your breathing, but concentrate on when you exhale instead of when you inhale.

●**Relaxing breath.** Sit in a comfortable position with your back straight and eyes closed. Touch the tip of your tongue to the inner surface of your front teeth and then slide it upward slightly to rest on the ridge between the teeth and the roof of your mouth.

Keeping it there, inhale through your nose for four seconds. Hold your breath for seven seconds. Exhale through your mouth. Repeat four times. This can be done in the morning or evening.

●**Stimulating breath.** Sit in a comfortable position with your back straight and eyes closed. Touch the tip of your tongue to the inner surface of your front teeth and then slide it upward slightly to rest on the ridge between your teeth and the roof of your mouth.

Breathe in and out rapidly through your nose, keeping your mouth closed slightly. Your breathing should be audible. Try this exercise for 15 seconds, and then increase the time by 10 seconds each time until you can do it for up to one minute. This exercise is best practiced in the morning.

Start Walking for Your Exercise—It's Free!

Walking is a great way to exercise for free. While a leisurely stroll has only minimal health benefits, studies show that moderate to brisk walking at a three- to five-miles-per-hour pace can significantly improve your fitness level.

STRETCH BEFORE AND AFTER YOU WALK

To avoid any injuries that would increase your medical expenses, it's important to stretch before and after you walk.

At the start and finish of your workout, spend two minutes stretching your calf muscles, the hamstrings in the back of your thighs, the quadriceps in the front of the thighs, the inner thigh muscles and the lower back.

Be careful not to overstretch, particularly when muscles are not warmed up. Stretch to the point of gentle tension in the muscles.

MALL WALKING IS
WEATHER-FRIENDLY WALKING

You can walk in a mall for free and be protected from unpredictable weather. Many shopping centers open early so people can walk there in the mornings. Also, you don't have to worry about potholes or oncoming traffic. Mall walking is a great activity for beginners who want to walk at a relaxed, moderate pace.

Health-Club Money Savers

To save money when joining a health club, don't join an expensive club that offers more equipment or activity options than you will ever use. For example, if you want to lift weights or take an exercise class, a health club with a sauna or pool may be an unnecessary additional cost.

Also, before you join, ask about new member perks, such as a free session with a personal trainer.

And, if you may need to take a long-term break for travel or other reasons, find out if the club can freeze your membership and start it up again on your return. Then you won't have to pay for the time you're not using it.

JUDGING WHETHER A CLUB
IS WORTH YOUR MONEY

One of the best ways to choose a quality health club that's worth your money is to thoroughly inspect its facilities. Good health clubs will be equipped with certain features, such as:

●**Trainers and instructors who are certified by agencies** like the American College of Sports Medicine (317-637-9200, *www.acsm.org*) or the Aerobics and Fitness Association of America (877-968-7263, *www.afaa.com*).

●**Orientation sessions for new members.**

●**Staff members who monitor the exercise areas.**

●**Classes at several levels of skill.**

●**Clean and updated equipment and locker rooms.**

●**Safety and club rules clearly posted.**

If you are still unsure whether to join after you thoroughly inspect a club's facilities, you may want to check with your state or local consumer protection agency or the Better Business Bureau to find out if any negative reports have been filed against the club, and what they were about.

BEFORE YOU COMMIT

Before making a commitment to an annual membership, consider whether you're investing your money in the right place. Here are some tips on how to safeguard your money:

●**Consider trying out a club before you join.**

●**Visit the club on the day that you would want to work out.** Notice if the club is too crowded, and if the equipment or class you want is accessible.

●**Think about joining a health club that offers several free visits** or a short, low-cost trial membership.

●**Try to arrange paying for your membership on a monthly basis,** or join a club that offers a 90-day trial membership.

●**Try to negotiate your membership fees.** You may be able to join the club at a price that is lower than the initial offer.

●**Always check out the club's refund policy before you sign up.** You don't want to find out after you join that your satisfaction is not guaranteed for more than one or two weeks.

HEALTH CLUBS TO CHECK OUT

Many health clubs are individually run and owned, but there are a few chains that have facilities nationwide.

Here are some nationwide chain facilities you may want to check out:

●**Gold's Gym** (800-457-5375, *www.goldsgym.com*)

●**World Gym** (310-827-7705, *www.worldgym.com*)

●**Bally Total Fitness** (800-515-CLUB (2582), *www.ballyfitness.com*)

Some chains, such as Bally Total Fitness, offer a two-week guest pass, and others have newsletters with free health and fitness information. Your best option may be to join a club that offers the perks that suit your own interests and fitness goals.

●**How to find them.** To find health clubs near you, look in your *Yellow Pages* under "Fitness Clubs" or "Health Clubs." Once you find some that are conveniently located, you can then do some inspecting and make some cost comparisons.

●**Consider the YMCA/YMHA.** Many YMCA/YMHAs across the country offer low-cost, quality health and fitness programs.

If you are interested in swimming, running or walking around a track, or joining a low-key exercise class, you may want to opt for joining a YMCA/YMHA program. Joining a Y will give you the opportunity to make a small investment for a fitness program before you invest a lot more money in a private health club. Some are at least as good as private clubs. And many Ys have senior health programs that enable people over 50 to work out with their peers.

Stress Free!

A great way to reduce stress, pain, anger and anxiety (for free) is to turn inward and meditate.

There are many ways to meditate and many thoughts on how to do it. But most experts agree that, no matter what your reason or method, spending 10 to 20 minutes (twice a day, every day) relaxing your mind may help you lead a healthier and happier life. Try this simple technique:

●**Choose a word,** sound, prayer or phrase on which to focus.

●**Sit in a quiet, comfortable place.**

●**Close your eyes** and begin to breathe slowly and deeply while relaxing your muscles.

●**Repeat your focus word,** prayer or phrase silently to yourself as you exhale.

●**As your mind starts drifting, acknowledge it**—and return to your repetition.

The Amazing No-Sweat Exercise Plan

Harvey B. Simon, MD, associate professor of medicine at Harvard Medical School and a founding member of the Harvard Cardiovascular Health Center, both in Boston. Dr. Simon is the author of five previous books on health and fitness. His latest is *The No Sweat Exercise Plan.* McGraw-Hill.

For the past two decades, as "no pain, no gain" has reigned as a fitness mantra, most experts have told us that physical activity won't significantly improve our health unless we perform intense aerobic exercise.

Now, it turns out that this was only half the story. Intense exercise that makes you perspire does reduce your risk for heart disease, diabetes, some types of cancer and other serious illnesses. But, until recently, it wasn't clear that moderate and gentle exercise—everything from sex to yard work—also can help guard against serious illness.

RESEARCHERS IDENTIFY BENEFITS

A study published in the *American Journal of Medicine* followed 110 healthy but sedentary men, ages 48 to 64. One group went about their normal routines without adding any exercise. The second group performed their normal routines but also played 18 holes of golf (and walked the course) two to three times a week. By the end of the 20-week study, the golfers lost weight, reduced their waist sizes and improved their cholesterol levels. The nongolfers experienced no changes.

Since then, more than 22 studies, involving about 320,000 people, have examined how moderate exercise affects cardiovascular health and longevity. The results are stunning. Moderate physical activity can decrease the risks for heart disease (by 18% to 84%)…stroke (by 21% to 34%)…diabetes (by 16% to 50%)…colon malignancies (by 30% to 40%)…and dementia (by 15% to 50%).

How did the experts miss all these benefits? In assessing a fitness program's efficacy, most researchers have traditionally only measured aerobic capacity—that is, how much oxygen your lungs can hold and how efficiently you use it. To improve that particular measure of fitness, known as "maximum volume of oxygen," or VO_2 max, you do need to work out hard.

But when researchers began investigating measures of good health based on everyday activities, they found that even small doses of moderate exercise really do add up. Health benefits can be obtained by climbing 55 flights of stairs per week or even by gardening for one hour per week. The point is to just get moving.

HOW TO MEASURE EXERTION

With all this evidence confirming the benefits of moderate exercise, I felt that a system was needed to measure the value of various everyday physical activities. That's why I created cardiometabolic exercise (CME) points, which assign values to physical activities based on the degree of exertion that's required to perform them.

You can significantly improve your health by accruing a total of 150 CME points per day (or about 1,000 CME points per week). Even if you're a couch potato, you can work up to the target level of about 1,000 points a week over the course of nine weeks. Gradually building up to your target level helps prevent injury.

Important: If weight loss is your goal, you may need to work harder or longer, doubling the target number of CME points to approximately 2,000 per week.

Caution: Before starting a new exercise program, consult your doctor. If you have heart disease or are at risk (due to family history, high blood pressure, etc.), you should have a stress test. For this test, you will receive an electrocardiogram (ECG), a painless procedure that measures electrical impulses flowing through the heart, during exercise.

For healthy people, a simple 12-minute self-test devised by Kenneth H. Cooper, MD, a renowned fitness expert, can help assess your level of fitness.

What to do: See how far you can go by walking, jogging or running for 12 minutes. To measure the distance accurately, do this on a track or use a pedometer. If you are out of shape, do not push yourself too hard. Your fitness level is considered poor to fair if you cover less than ¾ of a mile...good if you can cover ¾ to one mile...very good for 1 to 1¼ miles...and excellent for more than 1¼ miles. Take your rating into account when choosing activities for your exercise program.

CREATING A PROGRAM

For people who use everyday physical activity as the core of their exercise program, it's a good idea to add some strength exercise, such as weight training...some flexibility exercises, such as yoga or stretching...and balance exercises, such as tai chi or even standing on one foot while brushing your teeth. Strength training improves muscle mass and bone density. Flexibility exercises help prevent injury and reduce stress. Balance exercises help protect you from falls.

Over the nine-week period, aim to work up to 15 to 20 minutes of strength training two to three times a week...flexibility exercises for 10 to 15 minutes three to four times a week...and balance exercises for five minutes three to four times a week.

12

Tax-Saving Strategies

Tax-Saving Moves that Could Save You a Bundle

Do not miss out on these very smart tax-planning moves for the last few months of the year. *By taking these actions, you could save a lot of money…*

●**Review capital gains and losses.** Managing long-term and short-term gains is now even more important with the top tax rate on long-term gains for securities at no more than 15% through 2010, while short-term gains are still taxed at as much as 35%.

At year-end, you want to be able to offset any short-term losses against the highly taxed short-term gains—not against long-term gains that otherwise would be tax favored.

If it's close to year-end, and your investments for the year to date have produced net short-term losses and net long-term gains, you might want to realize some extra short-term gains before year-end to offset the short-term losses.

Short-term gains that otherwise would be taxed at high rates can be taken tax free when offset by the short-term losses, while preserving your tax-favored net long-term gains.

Best: Review your entire investment portfolio well before year-end, so you can make last-minute moves to net out gains and losses in the optimum manner.

If you have gains on investments that you've held for almost a year, don't forget the tax savings that will come from holding them for more than a full year. Don't sell them too soon.

●**Make gifts to family members.** The tax rate in 2008 and 2009 for both dividends and capital gains is zero for persons in the 10% or 15% tax bracket or zero—which covers income up to $65,100 ($67,500 in 2009) on a joint tax return or $32,550 ($33,550 in 2009) on a single return in 2008. This makes the opportunity to

Sidney Kess, attorney and CPA, 10 Rockefeller Plaza, New York City 10020, coauthor/consulting editor of *Financial and Estate Planning* and coauthor of *1040 Preparation and Planning Guide*. (Both are from CCH.) Over the years, he has taught tax law to more than 710,000 tax professionals.

save taxes by shifting investment income to family members in these low tax brackets greater than ever before.

Caution: Children under age 24 who are full-time students and who do not provide more than half of their own support through earned income are subject to the kiddie tax. This means they pay the same capital gains rate as their parents and cannot benefit from the zero tax rate.

● A family business run as a regular "C" corporation holds accumulated earnings. If you make gifts of stock in it to low-bracket family members, you can then distribute its accumulated earnings to them through dividends taxed at 0% in 2008 and 2009. This does not apply to children who are subject to the kiddie tax.

Gifting money can also serve to reduce your taxable estate.

Opportunity: The annual gift tax exclusion lets you make as many gifts as you wish of up to $13,000 per recipient, free of gift tax. The limit is $26,000 when gifts are made jointly with a spouse. But gifts must be completed by December 31, 2009, to use the exclusion for 2009.

Example: If you don't make gifts by the end of 2009, then the chance that you and your spouse have to make a $26,000 tax-free gift to each of your children, or other recipients, will be lost for the year.

● **Hire children before year-end.** If you have your own business, even if it is only a sideline, you can hire your young children or grandchildren to give them tax-free or low-tax income for the year. Your business can deduct the salaries at its higher tax rate.

Children can receive up to $5,700 of earned income tax free, and up to $33,950 owing no more than a 15% tax on a single tax return in 2009.

Bonus: The earned income can enable the child to make a Roth IRA contribution of up to $5,000 for 2009. Investment returns on these funds can compound for many years and then be withdrawn by the child tax free—which gives the child a great head start on financial security.

In addition, once a child has the qualifying earned income, you can make a gift to the

child of the funds used to make the Roth contribution.

Strategy: If your children don't have earned income yet this year, try to get them some by year-end—from someone else if not you. Even a small amount contributed to a child's Roth IRA can compound into big benefits in future years.

● **Time marriage and divorce around year-end.** The new tax law significantly reduces the "marriage penalty" by giving married couples a standard deduction and 15% tax bracket equal to two times the amounts for singles.

Planning: Being married now is more likely to save taxes for a couple when one spouse has little or no income. Because marital status at the end of the year determines tax treatment for the full year, people who are planning to marry or divorce around the turn of the year may want to marry before year-end and divorce after year-end.

● **Use increased retirement plan contribution limits.** The maximum contributions to tax-favored retirement plans generally increased in 2008. Persons over age 50 can make "catch-up" contributions to 401(k)s, IRAs and other kinds of retirement accounts.

Make the most of the higher contribution limits. Check that you've maximized contributions, and plan to make contributions early in the year whenever possible. The sooner funds are put into a tax-favored account, the more time they will have to earn returns.

● **Beware of state taxes and the alternative minimum tax (AMT).** Be alert to the fact that many states have not adjusted their tax laws to conform with the changes in the federal law. Therefore, steps that take advantage of the federal law changes could very well result in an increased state tax bill.

Plus, the federal AMT may pose increased risk to those who take advantage of the federal law changes in ways that increase state taxes.

Example: A large federal tax deduction for state and local taxes is one of the common triggers of the AMT, which you pay if it is higher than your regular tax. So persons who take advantage of the lower federal tax rate on long-term capital gains by taking a lot of them, and who incur increased state taxes on the gains they take, may find themselves facing the federal AMT as a result.

Safety: Be sure to consider state taxes and the AMT when you plan your best tax strategies for the rest of the year.

Last-Minute Tax Savers

Be sure to take advantage of these last-minute tax-saving strategies before the year comes to a close...

●**Charge deductible expenses on your credit card before year-end.** You can deduct the expense this year, even if you don't pay the charge off until a later year.

Examples: Medical bills, charitable contributions, business supplies.

Note: This rule applies only with general-use charge cards like Visa, MasterCard, etc., not with store cards.

●**Make charitable contributions**—and get acknowledgments of them. Last-minute donations can reap charity deductions—but remember, you now need an acknowledgment from the charity or a bank record for a gift of any amount.

●**Exhaust flexible spending accounts (FSAs).** If you have a medical or dependent-care FSA at work, spend all your contributions to it by year-end (if your plan does not have a grace period extending for 2½ months into the following year). If not spent by December 31, the remaining money is forfeited.

Note: You can make a one-time transfer of the balance in an FSA to a health savings account (HSA) up to the lesser of the balance on the date of transfer.

Some possibilities: See your physician, purchase prescription drugs, eyeglasses or other medical items.

●**Adjust paycheck withholding.** If you've underpaid or overpaid your taxes so far, you can balance your payments for the year by changing withholding on your last paycheck. *If you've...*

●Overpaid, reduce withholding to get your refund in advance through an increased paycheck.

●Underpaid, increase withholding to avoid an underpayment penalty.

Save Big on Taxes

Larry Torella, CPA, tax partner at Eisner LLP, 750 Third Ave., New York City 10017. He is author of Eisner's annual year-end tax-planning guide.

You can save tens of thousands of dollars on taxes with these year-end strategies. But watch out—the new tax rules also increase the chance that you will be hit hard with alternative minimum tax (AMT).* *Seven dos and don'ts...*

●**Don't prepay property taxes or state and local income tax**—at least not until you check with your tax adviser. Many Americans who pay estimated income tax make their January tax payments before December 31 in order to deduct the payment one year sooner.

Trap: Tax law changes in the past few years are likely to reduce your regular tax more than what you would owe under AMT. If you prepay taxes, you will further reduce your regular tax relative to AMT. Prepaying could result in your owing AMT because state tax payments can't be deducted from AMT.

●**Don't accelerate deductions**—for the same reason as above. Again, check with your tax adviser. Unreimbursed medical expenses, such as eyeglasses and certain medical procedures, can be deducted if the total exceeds 7.5% of your adjusted gross income (AGI) for the year. Don't make next year's expenditures early to meet that threshold until you check with your adviser about your AMT exposure.

The same goes for miscellaneous deductions—for tax preparation, unreimbursed employee

*AMT is a tax that an increasing number of Americans must pay instead of regular tax. You must calculate your tax both ways and then pay whichever amount is higher. Especially vulnerable are people with many dependents, high state income tax or high miscellaneous deductions.

business expenses and investment expenses, such as publications and software. These can be deducted for regular tax purposes if the total exceeds 2% of your AGI.

●**Sock away more for retirement.** Contribution limits for 401(k) plans now are $16,500 for 2009—$22,000 for those age 50 or older in 2009.

Caution: 401(k) contributions are deductible for purposes of regular tax and AMT. Nevertheless, consult a tax adviser to make sure contributions don't make you subject to AMT.

●**Make gifts.** You can save even more by giving appreciated stocks or fund shares instead of cash. Recipients who qualify for the zero capital gains tax rate in 2009—single taxpayers age 18 or older with taxable income of up to $33,550 in 2009…or married taxpayers having taxable income of up to $67,900 in 2009—would benefit most from gifts of appreciated property that they can then sell.

Opportunity: You can remove thousands of dollars from your taxable estate. You and your spouse can give $26,000 a year as a couple to each recipient, including charities, without having to pay gift tax.

●**Buy a sport-utility vehicle (SUV) or a truck** if you need a sizable car for your business—even if it is a sideline business.

You can deduct up to $133,000 for 2009 for any business that purchases no more than $530,000 of equipment in 2009. Business cars don't qualify for the full expensing deduction, but SUVs that weigh more than 6,000 pounds, but not more than 14,000 pounds have a $25,000 cap on the expensing amount.

For any expensing deduction, the equipment must be in use by December 31. It does not matter if you make the payments this year or next year.

●**Use losses to offset capital gains.** Losses that exceed your gains can be deducted against income—up to $3,000 a year.

Example: In early December, you determine that you have net long-term capital gains of $10,000. You owe $1,500 to the IRS (15% capital gains tax). The tax is higher for any short-term gains.

Take $13,000 worth of losses by December 31. Now you will have a $3,000 net capital loss ($13,000 – $10,000) for the year, which you are allowed to deduct.

In the 35% tax bracket, you'll save $1,050 (35% of $3,000) instead of *owing* $1,500.

Losses in excess of $3,000 can be carried forward to future years indefinitely to offset capital gains. That amount is in addition to the $3,000 annual net loss deduction.

Reminder: Under the wash-sale rule, when selling at a loss, wait at least 31 days to buy back the stock or fund. Before 31 days, the capital loss won't count. To avoid being out of the market, immediately buy a similar stock or fund to replace the one that you sold.

Example: When you sell one large-cap growth stock fund, purchase another one run by a different manager.

●**Don't invest in a fund before its annual distribution.** Most distributions occur at year-end. Call to check the distribution date. Invest after that date.

Opportunity: You'll get shares at a lower price, and you will not owe tax on gains that you didn't receive.

The New Tax Law— Opportunities and Costly Traps

Barbara Weltman, an attorney based in Millwood, New York, *www.barbaraweltman.com.* She is author of *J.K. Lasser's 1001 Deductions and Tax Breaks.* Wiley.

Tax legislation enacted recently creates both opportunities and traps for individuals.

Important: Many expired provisions were not addressed in this law and *may* be handled through a "trailer" bill.

BIG BREAK FOR INVESTORS

The cornerstone of the law is a two-year extension of the favorable tax rates on long-term capital gains and dividends. The rates had been scheduled to expire at the end of 2008—they now run through 2010. *For 2008 through 2010...*

●**Individuals in tax brackets above the bottom two brackets** pay only 15% on dividends and long-term capital gains.

●**Low-bracket taxpayers,** those in the 10% and 15% brackets, pay *nothing* on long-term gains or dividends. They can receive this type of income entirely tax free.

Strategy: Shift assets to low-bracket family members who will pay no tax on dividends and long-term gains. An easy way to do this is to make use of the $13,000 annual gift tax exclusion.

AMT RELIEF

Some middle-income taxpayers, increasingly blasted by the alternative minimum tax (AMT), can breathe a sigh of relief, at least this year. The new law creates a temporary "patch" for the AMT that will free more than 25 million middle-income taxpayers who would have paid the tax in 2008.

Catch: The patch is only for 2008. Congress will have to revisit the AMT issue. *How the patch works...*

●**The AMT exemption amounts are increased for 2008 to $69,950** on a joint return and $46,200 for single taxpayers. In 2007, the exemptions were $66,250 (joint) and $44,350 (single). Without the new patch, this year's exemption amounts would have declined to just $45,000 on a joint return and $33,750 for singles.

●**Nonrefundable personal credits,** such as the education credit and the dependent care credit, can now be used to offset AMT liability. Without this change, the only personal credits that could offset AMT liability starting in 2009 would have been the adoption credit, the child tax credit, and the retirement saver's credit.

Planning strategies: Because this fix is only temporary, individuals must continue to be proactive in minimizing or avoiding the AMT. This includes carefully timing the exercise of incentive stock options and payment (or prepayment) of state and local taxes. They are not deductible under the AMT.

MORE ROTH IRA CONVERSIONS

Currently, an individual can convert a traditional IRA to a Roth IRA only if his/her modified adjusted gross income for the year of conversion does not exceed $100,000. This limit applies to an individual taxpayer as well as a couple filing jointly. (A married person filing separately in most cases cannot convert regardless of his income.)

The new law waives this income limit, allowing anyone to convert a traditional IRA to a Roth IRA, starting in 2010.

Bonus: When the conversion is made, the reporting of any resulting income is deferred from 2010. Income is reported 50% in 2011 and 50% in 2012.

Option: Individuals can elect to report all the income in 2010.

Strategy: With a Roth conversion, you're choosing to accept a current tax bill on IRA withdrawals in exchange for future tax-free earnings from the proceeds.

As long as funds remain in the Roth account at least five years after the conversion and are not withdrawn prior to age 59½ (or for certain other permissible reasons), all money comes out tax free.

So, taxpayers who anticipate being in a higher tax bracket when they take distributions from their retirement accounts should consider conversion. Higher tax rates in general are not at all unlikely given the fact that many of the current tax rules are scheduled to expire after 2010.

Key: Use separate funds to pay the tax on a Roth IRA conversion so the account is not diminished.

BAD NEWS, TOO

While most of the new rules are favorable to taxpayers, there are some revenue raisers that many won't like.

The kiddie tax subjects a child's investment income over a threshold amount ($1,800 in 2008 and $15,000 in 2009) to tax at the parent's highest bracket. The definition of "child" changed from 2007 to 2008.

Limit starting in 2008: The kiddie tax age increases again. It now covers not only children under age 18, but also those under age 24 who are full-time students and who do not provide more than half of their own support through earned income.

Examples: Have the child own non-income-producing assets, such as US savings bonds and growth stocks. Postpone sales until after the kiddie tax no longer applies to the child.

•Increase in the cost of offers in compromise. The cost to taxpayers trying to obtain an offer in compromise from the IRS, which allows them to pay less than the full amount of tax due, increases under the new law. Taxpayers are now required to pay part of the tax owed in addition to a user fee of $150 when requesting an offer in compromise.

For a lump-sum offer, this means paying 20% of the offer up front. For offers in compromise that will be paid in installments, all proposed installments must be made while the IRS is considering the offer.

One bright spot for taxpayers: If the IRS fails to process the offer within two years, it is deemed to have been accepted.

Dial Up this Tax Deduction

Donate your old cell phone to charity, and receive a tax write-off.

What to do: Drop off your phone, charger and accessories at a participating wireless carrier's store. The wireless industry's charitable programs are now listed at *www.recyclewirelessphones.com*, or contact your wireless provider.

When possible, the phones are restored and money from the sale is earmarked for charities. Even if your cell phone is not in good enough condition to restore, you still will receive the

write-off. Consult your tax adviser to determine the value of your phone for tax purposes.

David Diggs, executive director, Wireless Foundation, which initiates and oversees philanthropic programs using wireless technology, Washington, DC. The organization's Web site is *www.wirelessfoundation.org*.

Determining the Value of Donated Goods

When used goods are donated to charity, you can deduct their value—but you may not know how to determine that number.

Helpful: Check The Salvation Army's online donation valuation guide. Go to *www.salvationarmyusa.org*, then in the search box enter "valuation guide." This will produce a link to a valuation guide that covers men's, women's and children's products, appliances, dry goods and furniture.

How to Beat The IRS!

Frederick W. Daily, Esq., a tax attorney based in Incline Village, Nevada, and author of *Stand Up to the IRS* and *Tax Savvy for Small Business*. Both from Nolo.com.

The "small case" division of Tax Court is a resource that every taxpayer facing a fight with the IRS should know about.

Don't be fooled by the name—the great majority of tax disputes involving individuals and small businesses can be appealed to the small case division. This is a way to obtain an independent review of the IRS's actions at very little cost. *How it works...*

SECOND CHANCES

Taxpayers can use the small case division to contest a tax bill or other IRS action under simplified court rules, without a lawyer. The only cost is a $60 filing fee.

When you file a case in Tax Court, the IRS is stopped from taking any further collection action. At the very least, your case will be reviewed by a "fresh pair of eyes," giving you a new chance to reach a compromise settlement.

You do not have to pay the disputed tax until the court gives its judgment—and then, of course, only if you lose.

The only requirement to qualify as a small case is that the disputed tax not exceed $50,000 per year, not counting interest and penalties. But because the IRS often assesses tax for more than a year at a time, the total amount at issue may be much higher than that.

Example: If the IRS assesses tax for three years, the tax can be as much as $150,000. Interest and penalties may push the total contested amount significantly higher. Therefore, "small cases" may not be so small.

Tactic: If a disputed tax exceeds the $50,000 limit, you can concede the excess to qualify the case to be heard as a small case.

Example: The disputed tax is $53,000. You concede $3,000 and contest the remaining $50,000 in a small case—and probably save more than $3,000 in legal expenses compared with fighting the full tax bill in a regular Tax Court case.

Types of cases: Recent law changes have expanded the jurisdiction of the Tax Court, and the small case division now hears four different kinds of tax disputes…

●**Tax deficiencies,** such as those that result from the closing of an audit in which the IRS determines additional tax is due.

●**Collection actions.** If the IRS sends a notice saying that it intends to issue a lien or levy, seize property, or take another collection action that you believe is unjustified or improper, you can file in Tax Court to suspend the action and have it reviewed.

●**Worker classification disputes.** One of the hottest areas of dispute between taxpayers and the IRS involves the classification of workers as either employees or independent contractors and the imposition of resulting employment tax liability. The Tax Court now can decide these disputes.

●**"Innocent spouse" determinations.** When one spouse believes that he/she should not be held liable on a joint tax return for taxes attributable to the other spouse (or ex-spouse) or that the tax should be allocated between the two spouses, the court can review the issue.

Warning: The only real drawback to filing in the small case division is that you can't appeal the result—the judge's decision is final. The IRS can't appeal either. Since few persons who bring small cases have the resources to appeal a regular Tax Court decision to the US Court of Appeals, giving up the right to appeal in practice usually costs nothing.

Moreover, most small cases don't go to a final decision at trial at all, but are voluntarily settled by the parties beforehand.

SETTLEMENT STRATEGY

The biggest benefit of filing a "small case" may be the extra chance it gives to settle a case. Statistics show that more than 50% of those who file in Tax Court attain some tax benefit, and thus come out ahead by doing so.

Key: When a case is filed in Tax Court, it is reviewed by IRS attorneys who weren't involved in imposing the tax bill. Unlike auditors, their concern is not to collect tax on every item that might be questioned on a return, but to dispose of cases efficiently.

When a credible case is presented to them, they have two strong incentives to settle it and avoid a trial. First, they don't want to risk losing. Second, they simply don't have the resources to litigate every case filed—they must settle many cases due to the limited number they can try.

Result: If you present your case with a credible argument to the IRS's attorneys before trial, you will have an excellent chance of getting "something" from them in a settlement.

Exactly how much depends on the strength of your case—from a modest waiver of penalties to full concession. With the only cost being a $60 filing fee, you don't need to get much from the IRS to come out ahead.

So today there's little reason not to appeal a tax bill to Tax Court if you feel you have grounds for doing so.

FIGHTING THE AUDITOR

Moreover, knowing about the small case division can help you deal with an IRS auditor from the day an audit notice arrives—and help you get a more acceptable audit result, so you don't have to go to the Tax Court.

You will be relieved of the fear that you are at the auditor's mercy because you can't fight the IRS in court.

Reality: You can!

And you can play the Tax Court "card" during an audit to negotiate a better result.

Why: The job performance of IRS auditors is measured by the number of cases they close. But when a case is filed in Tax Court, it remains open—so auditors don't want you to file in Tax Court.

Diplomatically saying to an auditor or to the auditor's manager, "I think that I may have to appeal this to Tax Court," may well get him/her to concede some gray-area or disputed items, so you may not have to appeal at all.

FILING

After receiving an IRS "deficiency notice" that states you owe a tax bill, you have 90 days in which to file a Tax Court petition.

Filing a small case petition is very simple. Just fill out the form, and mail it in with a $60 check.

You can obtain a small case petition as well as other information about the Tax Court from its Web site, *www.ustaxcourt.gov.*

Or you can write to the Clerk of the Court at 400 Second St. NW, Washington, DC 20217, or call 202-521-0700.

Read about your appeal rights in IRS Publication 5, *Your Appeal Rights and How to Prepare a Protest If You Don't Agree*, regarding tax assessments, and Publication 1660, *Collection Appeal Rights*, regarding tax collection actions. Both publications are available at *www.irs.gov.* Enter "Appeal Rights" into the search site box.

How to Get the IRS to Waive Penalty Fees

Sidney Kess, attorney and CPA, 10 Rockefeller Plaza, New York City 10020, coauthor/consulting editor of *Financial and Estate Planning* and coauthor of *1040 Preparation and Planning Guide.* (Both are from CCH.) Over the years, he has taught tax law to more than 710,000 tax professionals.

If you don't take certain required actions—such as filing returns or paying taxes—by the deadline fixed by law, you will be subject to penalties. *Fortunately, these penalties can be waived if you furnish the right excuse for your lateness...*

●**You filed a return late.** Returns that are not filed on time are subject to a penalty of 5% of the amount of tax shown on the return per year, but no more than 25% in total. The penalty can be waived if the lateness is due to *reasonable cause* and not to willful neglect.

Note: Obtaining a waiver of the penalty for late filing does not eliminate the interest and penalties for late payment of taxes.

Examples of reasonable cause...

●Death of a loved one, such as a spouse or dependent.

●Debilitating illness of yourself, your spouse, or a dependent.

●You relied on the advice of an accountant or other tax adviser (e.g., you were told you didn't have to file a tax return).

●You relied on the advice of the IRS.

Invalid excuses...

●Health problems that do not prevent you from working full time.

●Forgetfulness.

●Death or illness of your accountant.

●Busy on the job.

●**You applied for a tax refund late.** Generally, a claim for a refund of overpaid taxes must be filed within three years of the due date of the return. Refund claims filed after the expiration of this limitation period are automatically denied regardless of the validity of the claims.

The statute of limitations can be suspended for long-term financial disability—i.e., inability to manage your financial affairs because of a physical or mental condition. The impairment must be expected to result in death or to last for not less than 12 months.

Caution: This excuse does not apply if someone is legally authorized to handle your affairs.

PAYING TAXES

●**Estimated taxes.** If estimated taxes do not cover the amount required to be paid, there is an underpayment penalty. *It can be waived at the discretion of the IRS in two situations...*

●When the underpayment is due to casualty, disaster, or other unusual circumstance and it would be inequitable and against good conscience to impose the penalty.

●For reasonable cause when the taxpayer retired at age 62 or older, or became disabled in the year for which the estimated tax payment is required or in the prior year.

●**Innocent spouse relief.** On joint returns, each spouse is liable for all the tax, interest, and penalties on the return. However, one spouse may be excused from this liability under the innocent spouse rules. For this excuse to be effective, you must file a claim for innocent spouse relief. This gets you off the hook for penalties (along with taxes and interest). See IRS Publication 971, *Innocent Spouse Relief*, at *www.irs.gov*, or call 800-829-3676, for details.

RETIREMENT PLANS

●**Required minimum distributions (RMDs) at age 70½.** These must be taken from qualified retirement plans and IRAs no later than December 31 each year (April 1 of the following year can be used as the deadline only for the first RMD). However, if the failure to take the RMD on time is due to reasonable error and you have taken, or are taking, steps to remedy the insufficient distribution, you can request that the penalty be excused.

What to do: You must file Form 5329, *Additional Taxes on Qualified Plans (Including IRAs) and Other Tax-Favored Accounts*, with your return for the year, pay any excess accumulation penalty, and attach a letter of explanation. If the IRS approves of your excuse, it will automatically refund any penalty payment.

●**IRA rollovers.** Generally a rollover must be completed within 60 days of a distribution. Failure to complete the rollover in a timely manner causes the distribution to become taxable, and if under age 59½, subject to the 10% early distribution penalty. However, the IRS has been very lenient in granting extensions on equitable grounds (fairness) when the failure

to act within 60 days is beyond the taxpayer's control. *Examples...*

●Funds were stolen by the taxpayer's investment adviser.

●The taxpayer was hospitalized, disabled, suffers from mental illness, Alzheimer's disease, or substance abuse.

●There was a natural disaster, such as a blizzard.

●The bank or other financial institution failed to follow instructions to complete the rollover.

Caution: Additional time will not be given if you cash the rollover check and use the funds.

Important: The IRS has provided guidance that grants an automatic waiver for late rollovers in some situations, such as when a financial institution receives funds within the 60-day rollover period but erroneously fails to complete the rollover per the taxpayer's instructions. IRS approval is required in others. For details, see Revenue Procedure 2003-16.

●**Early distributions.** Generally, a 10% penalty applies to distributions from qualified retirement plans and IRAs before the account owner attains age 59½. However, the Tax Code provides some exceptions that can be relied upon to avoid this penalty.

Examples: Disability and taking distributions in a series of substantially equal periodic payments.

Note: In some cases, different exceptions apply to company retirement plans versus IRAs. For example, distributions from a company plan in or after the year in which you turn 55 are not penalized. This exception does not apply to IRAs.

Distributions from IRAs to pay qualified higher education costs before age 59½ are not penalized, but this exception does not apply to early distributions from qualified retirement plans.

IRS Publications 575, *Pension and Annuity Income*, and 590, *Individual Retirement Arrangements* (IRAs), offer more details.

Money Saving Tax Moves You Should Do Today

Bob D. Scharin, Esq., editor, Warren, Gorham & Lamont/RIA's *Practical Tax Strategies*, journal for tax professionals, published by Thomson/RIA, New York City. *ria.thomson.com*. He has written for and/or edited leading tax publications for more than 20 years.

D o not wait until the end of the year to start planning your taxes. *By taking all these steps, you can easily cut your tax bill...*

●**Max out your retirement plan.** Contribute the maximum to your 401(k) plan or other employer-sponsored retirement plan this year. For 2009, you can defer tax on up to $16,500 in contributions to a 401(k), 403(b), 457 or similar defined-contribution plan. If you'll be at least 50 years old by year-end, you can contribute another $5,500. Contributions to 401(k)s must be made by the end of the year for a 2009 tax benefit.

●**Create a Savings Incentive Match Plan for Employees (SIMPLE) account** if you're self-employed or run a sideline business. You can make SIMPLE as well as 401(k) contributions. SIMPLE plans are desirable if you'll have a small amount of self-employment income this year. You can contribute (and deduct) up to 100% to a maximum of $11,500. People of age 50 or older can contribute an additional $2,500. Other small-business retirement plans usually permit no more than a 25% contribution. To get SIMPLE write-offs for 2009, you must set up a plan by September 30. They can be established at most financial institutions.

●**Evaluate estimated tax payments.** If you file estimated taxes, your fourth payment for 2009 is due January 15, 2010. By then, you should know your total 2009 income.

Safe harbor: If your payments are at least 100% of your 2009 tax liability, you are protected from a penalty by a "safe harbor" rule, even if you end up owing more tax because your income increases. If your adjusted gross income (AGI) was more than $150,000 in 2009, the requirement rises to 110%.

Example: Filing jointly, you and your spouse had a total AGI of $180,000 in 2009 and owed $30,000 in taxes. To reach the safe harbor, your estimated tax payments must be at least $33,000—110% of $30,000.

If you don't have enough withheld from your paychecks, you must send the balance to the IRS in quarterly estimated payments to qualify for the safe harbor.

Trap: If you make larger tax payments during the year's last two quarters, you could owe a penalty for underpayments in earlier quarters. To avoid this, have more tax withheld from paychecks near year-end. Income tax withholding is treated as if it were paid evenly throughout the year.

Loophole: If taxes owed for 2009 will be lower than they were in 2008, you can pay less withholding and estimated tax this year and avoid a penalty if total payments are at least 90% of your 2009 obligation.

●**Profit from losses.** Stocks are struggling, and with interest rates rising, bonds sold before maturity may have lost their value. If you have losses, consider selling securities or funds to take tax deductions.

Loophole: You can deduct up to $3,000 of capital losses in excess of capital gains from your wages, pension, interest and other higher-taxed income. Additional losses then can be carried forward to future years.

Example: You end the year with $20,000 in losses in excess of capital gains (not paper losses). You can take a $3,000 deduction in 2009 and carry forward the other $17,000. The excess losses can offset future gains—up to $3,000 per year—effectively making those gains tax free.

Trap: If you sell a security and buy it back within 30 days, the loss won't count. This is known as the "wash-sale rule." To avoid it, wait at least 31 days to buy back the same security. *If you want to remain invested throughout the whole process...*

●Purchase a similar but not identical security. For example, take a loss on one large-cap growth fund, and immediately buy another large-cap growth fund.

●Buy new shares of the stock you wish to sell. Then wait more than 30 days, and sell the original lot. To use this strategy this year, you must purchase the duplicate lot before November 30.

●**Fund an Education Savings Account (ESA).** While 529 savings plans are worthwhile for funding higher education, unless your state happens to provide a tax deduction, it is better to first fund a Coverdell Education Savings Account (ESA). The limit is $2,000 per year per student. There are income limits for ESAs. Married couples with incomes over $190,000 can't make a full contribution.

If you're over the limit, you can give money to children, grandchildren, etc., who can contribute to their own ESAs.

Benefits: Like 529s, ESAs permit income to accumulate tax free. Withdrawals are tax free if the money is used for certain education-related expenses. *But ESAs have advantages over 529s…*

●Withdrawals may be used for a range of education expenses, such as tuition, room and board, uniforms and computer equipment, beginning in kindergarten. 529s must be used for college costs.

●You have complete control over how the money is invested. 529 investment options are selected by their sponsors.

●There is no time limit for tax-free withdrawals.

●**Pay a parent's expenses.** If you support a parent—even though he/she lives elsewhere—you might be able to claim him/her as a dependent. In 2008, you can deduct $3,500 ($3,650 in 2009) for each dependent, whether or not you itemize. In the 25% federal tax bracket for 2008 ($65,100 to $131,450 in taxable income on a joint return), a $3,500 deduction saves you $875. There may be big state tax savings as well.

To claim a dependency exemption for a parent, several tests must be met but these are the two toughest…

You must provide more than half of your parent's support, and…

Your parent's gross income must be less than $3,500. Gross income does not include untaxed Social Security benefits or the interest on tax-exempt investments.

Strategy: Track all your parent's expenses carefully—food, medical care, etc.—and make sure that you pay more than 50% of them during the year. If your parent lives in your home, put a value on the housing you supply.

●**Ward off the AMT.*** Increasingly, middle-income taxpayers are encountering the alternative minimum tax (AMT). If you are subject to the AMT this year, you will lose federal deductions on state and local taxes as well as miscellaneous itemized deductions.

Strategy: Postpone AMT income. For example, defer the exercise of certain types of stock options or don't make early payments of real estate and state income tax around year-end, since they are not deductible for AMT purposes. AMT planning is complex. So, arrange a midyear meeting with your tax preparer to discuss strategies that will work for you.

Free Tax Help From the IRS

James Glass, tax attorney based in New York City and contributing writer to *Bottom Line/Wealth*.

During the return-preparation season, the IRS offers several types of free assistance to taxpayers in addition to that offered on its Web site.

●**Telephone help.** To hear prerecorded messages covering a wide variety of subjects and frequently asked questions, call IRS Tele-Tax at 800-829-4477. TeleTax topics are listed on pages eight and nine of the Form 1040 instruction booklet. Taxpayers with questions

*AMT is a tax that an increasing number of Americans must pay instead of regular tax. You must calculate your tax with and without AMT and pay the higher amount. Especially vulnerable are people with many dependents, high state income tax or high miscellaneous deductions.

not covered by TeleTax can call the IRS customer service line at 800-829-1040.

●**In-person assistance.** Taxpayers who have complex issues, need to resolve a tax problem, or are more comfortable talking with someone in person can visit a local Taxpayer Assistance Center. IRS representatives in these offices can help with inquiries or adjustments to tax accounts and many other problems.

Phone numbers for local Taxpayer Assistance Centers are in telephone directories and on the IRS Web site—at *www.irs.gov* click on "Individuals" and then "Contact My Local Office."

●**Volunteer assistance with tax returns.** Free tax preparation is available through the Volunteer Income Tax Assistance (VITA) and Tax Counseling for the Elderly (TCE) programs in many communities. Volunteers help prepare basic returns for taxpayers with limited incomes.

To find the VITA or TCE site nearest you, call 800-829-1040. You may also call AARP—the largest TCE participant—to inquire about it at 888-227-7669. They have recently updated their site locator.

Surprising Small Business Saver

Kenneth Weissenberg, Esq., CPA, partner in charge of real estate services, Eisner LLP, 750 Third Ave., New York City 10017. He is a frequent lecturer and contributor to real estate publications.

Eight out of 10 companies in the US lease some or all of their equipment, according to the Equipment Leasing Association. But here's a twist and an opportunity—if you own a business, you can arrange to collect the lease payments *yourself* rather than pay them to a third party for the use of its equipment or real estate.

ADVANTAGES OF SELF-LEASING

Let's say that you own a medical practice that requires expensive equipment. When you follow the most common path, the practice will either purchase the equipment directly from a seller or lease it from a third party. But

there's another way—you can form a second company to buy the equipment and then lease it to your practice. *Advantages...*

●**Asset protection.** Owning equipment in a second company, separate and apart from a professional practice or other business, provides additional protection from the claims of creditors. The equipment is insulated and cannot be used to satisfy creditors' claims of your primary business.

●**Estate planning.** You can use self-leasing to advance your estate-planning goals. To do this, instead of owning the company that leases the equipment to your practice, you would form a limited liability company (LLC) or trust to share ownership with family members—your spouse, your children, or even your grandchildren. You can transfer interests to them at no or reduced gift tax cost, removing the assets from your estate.

The entity can obtain financing to purchase the equipment. Commonly leased equipment includes telecommunication systems, heavy machinery for factories, and medical equipment for professional practices.

Then, the net rental income (lease payments in excess of deductible expenses) becomes payable to LLC members or beneficiaries of the trust. This income splitting with your family members can lower the tax rate on rental income when they are in lower tax brackets than you.

●**Attractive financing arrangement for your main business.** Leasing is primarily a financing arrangement—a way to obtain needed equipment for a business without paying the full purchase price. Your main business does not have to come up with a down payment if it leases equipment from you, as would be the case for an asset purchase.

●**Tax deductions for your main business.** Your main business can deduct the lease payments—matching the deduction with the expense (in contrast to depreciation write-offs for purchased equipment that may occur in years after the year of purchase).

Note: There are no annual dollar or other limits on how much can be deducted for leasing any kind of property.

●**Self-leasing avoids double tax on real estate for C corporations.** If your main business is a C corporation, having it own the real estate from which the business operates can create a double taxation problem. When the corporation sells the property, it pays corporate-level tax and then you, as a shareholder, pay tax on proceeds distributed to you by the corporation. In contrast, if the realty is owned by an LLC and later sold, there is no double tax threat—all of the profits pass through to owners and are reported on the owner's personal returns.

TERMS OF THE LEASE

●**For real estate.** When purchasing real estate that you plan to lease to your business, it's a good idea to form a limited liability company to own the property.

Reason: From a tax perspective, refinancing a mortgage on the property when its value has appreciated enables owners to take out cash without triggering a taxable event. (If the property is owned by an S corporation, refinancing would result in taxable gain.) With the LLC, you achieve the same personal liability protection for yourself and your co-owners as you do with a corporation.

●**For equipment leasing,** use a trust or LLC, as mentioned above.

Make sure that it is clear in the lease which company bears the costs associated with using the property—your main business or the leasing company.

For example, in the case of real estate, is your main business or your leasing business responsible for real estate taxes? (It is common to impose this obligation on the lessee.)

When leasing equipment to your company, make sure that the company carries adequate insurance in case of damage or destruction. In most commercial leasing arrangements, the company (lessee) is liable for loss.

Strategy: In the case of equipment, try to obtain replacement value coverage for optimum protection. The cost of this insurance is deductible by the lessee.

TAX TRAPS

While there are many advantages to self-leasing equipment and real estate to your company, such as asset protection and estate-planning benefits, there are some potential tax problems. *These include...*

●**PAL rules.** For tax purposes, income from the real estate or equipment leased to yourself (which includes a business you own) generally is treated as trade or business income. It is not passive-activity income that can be used to offset losses from other passive activities in which you may have an interest.

What's more, losses resulting from the rental of property to yourself are viewed as passive-activity losses. You cannot deduct them in excess of passive-activity income.

Exception: If you actively participate in a rental activity, you may be able to deduct losses of up to $25,000 annually. This full write-off cannot be claimed if your adjusted gross income (AGI) exceeds $100,000 (the deduction limit phases out for AGI between $100,000 and $150,000).

In effect, self-leasing usually cannot be used to generate income to offset passive losses from other activities. And self-leasing cannot create deductible losses.

●**Reallocation rules.** The terms of the lease must be set at arm's length. The IRS has the authority under Code Section 482 to reallocate income between you and your business if, for example, rentals are set unrealistically high merely to generate big write-offs for your main business.

●**Purchase agreement.** The lease can be called a purchase agreement, with deductions for lease payments subject to restriction, if the arrangement effectively transfers ownership to the lessee. *For example...*

●There is only a token buyout at the end of the lease.

●Total payments, exclusive of sales taxes and financing charges, are more than 90% of the fair market value of the equipment.

Note: Rental income you receive through ownership in an LLC or trust is not treated as net earnings from self-employment. You do not owe self-employment tax on this income.

Important: Self-leasing arrangements are complex, so be sure to work with a knowledgeable tax adviser to structure your agreement and achieve your objectives.

Special Tax Breaks For Teachers, Caregivers, The Military...and More

Bob D. Scharin, Esq., editor, Warren, Gorham & Lamont/RIA's *Practical Tax Strategies*, journal for tax professionals, published by Thomson/RIA, New York City. *ria.thomson.com*. He has written for and/or edited leading tax publications for more than 20 years.

Under the tax code, some occupations are treated more favorably than others. Information is available by calling 800-829-1040 or at *www.irs.gov. Special breaks...*

●**Teachers.** They can take a $250 above-the-line deduction* for unreimbursed expenses for books and classroom supplies purchased in 2008 and 2009. Principals, aides and other "educators" also are eligible for this deduction. The educator must work at least 900 hours during the school year. You can take this write-off even if you claim the standard deduction. If you itemize, any excess can go on Schedule A. This above-the-line deduction is scheduled to expire at the end of 2009.

Example: A teacher who spends $1,000 on supplies this year can take a $250 above-the-line deduction. The other $750 can be used as a miscellaneous itemized deduction on Schedule A. These are deductible to the extent that they exceed 2% of AGI.

See IRS publication 17, *Your Federal Income Tax.*

●**Professors.** Colleges, universities and private schools offer reduced or free tuition to dependent children of faculty members—that can be worth $30,000 or more. This benefit is not taxable to the parent or the student. See IRS Publication 970, *Tax Benefits for Education.*

●**Caregivers.** If you're paid to watch children or elderly or disabled individuals in your

---

*Above-the-line deductions are taken to arrive at adjusted gross income (AGI). Below-the-line (itemized) deductions are subtracted from AGI.

---

home, deductions may offset some or all of your taxable wages.

Example: You live in a 2,500-square-foot house. You use three rooms measuring 1,000 square feet (40% of the total) for day care. You estimate that the rooms are used for day care 30% of the year. If you multiply 30% by 40%, you get 12%—the percentage you can deduct from your electricity and heating bills, etc. for business use.

See IRS publication 587, *Business Use of Your Home.*

●**Clergy.** No income tax is paid on housing that is part of compensation. Also, an allowance to rent a house or cover home ownership costs is tax-free. The tax-free allowance cannot exceed the home's fair market rental value plus utilities. See IRS Publication 517, *Social Security and Other Information for Members of the Clergy and Religious Workers.*

●**Farmers and fishermen.** If you have income from farming or fishing, you're eligible for "income averaging." You must "materially participate" in the farming or fishing business.

How it works: You figure your tax in a prosperous year as though some of the income was earned in each of the prior three years, when you were in a lower tax bracket. Schedule J must be attached to your tax return. See IRS publication 225, *Farmer's Tax Guide.*

●**National Guard members and reservists.** Some travel expenses are above-the-line deductions even if you don't itemize. You must travel at least 100 miles from home and stay overnight. See IRS publication 3, *Armed Forces' Tax Guide.*

●**Military.** "Combat pay" is free of federal income tax. One day is enough to earn the tax benefit for the month.

Example: John Smith is a sailor on an extended deployment. His ship enters a combat zone on May 31 and leaves on July 1. Three months of John's pay (May, June, July) are tax-free.

Strategy: Enlisted personnel who receive a "signing bonus" for reenlisting should do so when they're in a combat zone, if possible, so that the entire lump sum will be tax-free. However, a person can opt to treat combat pay as taxable earned income to qualify for the earned income tax credit. See IRS publication 3, *Armed Forces' Tax Guide*.

How to Shelter Your Social Security Benefits

Social Security benefits are taxable if you receive enough income from other sources. Distributions from traditional IRAs and 401(k) plans are counted toward the income limits. Distributions from Roth IRAs and Roth 401(k)s are not.

Michael J. Francis, president and CEO, Francis Investment Counsel LLC, registered investment adviser, Pewaukee, Wisconsin.

You May Qualify for an Estate Tax Refund

Some heirs may have paid too much tax in recent years if their state's death tax was tied to the federal estate tax.

Reason: The federal estate tax credit for state death taxes has been phased out, but some states failed to alter their tax structure to reflect this change. Instead, they continued to erroneously collect tax based on the old rules. Courts in such states, including Ohio, Pennsylvania and Washington, have been sympathetic to heirs and awarded refunds.

Also: A retroactive estate tax increase by New Jersey was disallowed.

What to do: If a loved one died after 2000, when the phaseout of the federal estate tax credit began, consult an estate tax expert to determine if you can file for a refund.

Sanford J. Schlesinger, Esq., is a founding partner and head of the wills and estates departments of Schlesinger Gannon & Lazetera LLP, a law firm in New York City.

Clean Up and Cash In

Most home owners have stored all kinds of things in the attic, closets and garage —furniture, old magazines, clothes, etc.

Opportunity: Take what you don't need and sell it for extra cash for the holidays— Internet auction sites make this easier than ever. Or donate it to charity to get a tax deduction this year.

Note: Deductions for clothing and household items are allowed only if the items are in good used condition or better.

Mary Hunt, editor, *Debt-Proof Living*, Box 2135, Paramount, California 90723, *www.debtproofliving.com*.

When Support Is Deductible

Edward Mendlowitz, CPA, partner, WithumSmith+ Brown, 1 Spring St., New Brunswick, New Jersey 08901. He is author of *Estate Planning*. Practical Programs.

When you pay more than 50% of the support for an individual, tax benefits can result…

●**When the individual's income doesn't exceed $3,500 in 2008** ($3,650 in 2009) (excluding tax-exempt income, such as from municipal bonds and the tax-free portion of Social Security), you may be able to claim him/her as a dependent to obtain a tax exemption of $3,500 in 2008 ($3,650 in 2009).

●**Even if the individual has income exceeding the limit, you may be able to deduct medical expenses** you pay on his behalf if the individual is a relative. (A "relative" is a parent, grandparent, sibling, child, grandchild, aunt, uncle, niece, nephew or in-law.)

Mistake: Many people fail to claim these tax breaks because they provide less than half of the individual's income—and so mistakenly assume that they provide less than half of the individual's support.

Key: "Support" includes only amounts that are actually spent on items of support, such as housing, food, clothing and medical care. It does not include income that is saved.

Example: A retired parent has a pension and Social Security income, while you pay medical bills for him. By having the parent save enough income in the bank (by putting money in the bank, he isn't using the money to pay for support) so that you pay more than 50% of his support in the form of medical payments and other items, you can obtain a deduction for the medical bills.

Tactic: When several people together provide most of an individual's support with no one person paying more than 50%, they can file a multiple support agreement, IRS Form 2120, *Multiple Support Declaration*, to obtain a dependency exemption and assign it to one member of the group (which can change from year to year), provided he pays more than 10% of support. This also enables that person to deduct medical bills paid on the dependent's behalf.

How to See if The IRS Owes You Money

Check to see if the IRS owes you money at the National Taxpayers Union (NTU) Web site, *www.ntu.org*. Click on "Find Out if the IRS Owes You Money," then enter your name and state to find out if you are owed any federal tax refunds.

Year-End Tax-Savers For Seniors

Laurence I. Foster, CPA/PFS, consultant and former partner at Eisner LLP, 750 Third Ave., New York City 10017. Mr. Foster was chairman of The Personal Financial Specialist Credential Committee at the American Institute of CPAs.

Plan your tax-saving moves before the end of the year. You'll face a steeper tax bill if you wait until after December 31 to take action. *Tax savers to consider now…*

PERSONAL TAX-SAVING TACTICS

●**Use "catch-up" wage withholding to avoid underpayment of penalties.** Check whether your taxes to date are underpaid for the year—this is most likely to be the case if you had nonwage income (such as from your investments) on which you have not paid estimated tax.

If so, make up the shortfall by increasing tax withheld from your last paychecks before year-end comes around.

Why: Withheld taxes are treated by the IRS as having been paid evenly over the year. By increasing withholding near year-end, you can retroactively avoid an underpayment penalty for an earlier estimated tax quarter that you would incur if you paid the same tax with a catch-up estimated tax payment.

●**Double up on deductions subject to AGI "floors."** Some items are deductible only to the extent that they exceed a percentage of adjusted gross income (AGI).

Examples: Medical expenses to the extent that they exceed 7.5% of AGI…miscellaneous expenses (including employee business expenses, investment and legal expenses, etc.) to the extent that they exceed 2% of AGI.

Strategy: If expenses for these items are large enough to take the deductions this year, accelerate additional expenses into this year by scheduling and paying for last-minute medical and dental appointments, subscribing to business publications, etc., before year-end. If they are not, postpone paying for such items until after December 31 to help get you over the limit next year.

●**Prepay state and local taxes.** Final state and local income tax payments for 2008 may not be due until April 15, 2009—but if you pay them by year-end, they are deductible on your 2008 federal tax return. The same rule applies to state and local property taxes.

Caution: If you are subject to the alternative minimum tax (AMT), you may not want to prepay state and local taxes and you also may not want to double up on deductions as described previously.

•Make contributions to a charity. To be deductible this year, the charitable gift must be made by year-end. For donations in 2008, gifts of any amount must be substantiated by a bank statement or written acknowledgment from the charity.

Strategy: If you own appreciated stocks or mutual fund shares that you have held for more than a year, donate them instead of cash. You'll get a full deduction for your contribution and avoid ever having to pay capital gains tax on the donated securities.

•Use credit cards to pay deductible expenses. Charges are deductible when made even if not paid off until a later year.

Note: The card must be a general-use one, such as Visa or American Express, not a store charge card.

•Convert a traditional IRA to a Roth if your AGI isn't more than $100,000. Roths can pay tax-free income, while payments from traditional IRAs are taxed at top rates as ordinary income. Roths are not subject to minimum annual distribution requirements beyond age 70½, making them more flexible for saving and funding tax-favored bequests.

Catch: Whenever a conversion is made, the value of the traditional IRA (minus any nondeductible contributions to it) is included in taxable income.

Opportunity: Making a conversion by year-end is a "can't lose" move. If the stock market goes up the next year so that the IRA's value increases, a conversion now will be less costly tax wise than one made later. If, after making a conversion this year, the market goes down and the IRA's value decreases, you can undo the conversion as late as October 15, 2008, to make another conversion later on better terms. If you don't make a conversion this year, you may never again have the chance to do so at such low tax cost.

Note: Starting in 2010, there will be no AGI limit; anyone can opt to make a Roth IRA conversion.

•Go on a gambling holiday if you have winnings to date. If you have net gambling winnings and will file an itemized return, additional gambling until year-end will be subsidized by the IRS—since any losses you incur will be deductible up to the amount of your winnings. So, if you gamble more and win, you'll win, while if you lose, you'll get a deduction.

•Use your annual gift tax exclusion. This enables you to make gifts of up to $13,000 each to as many recipients as desired, free of gift tax in 2009. The limit is $26,000 when gifts are made jointly by a married couple. Such gifts can reduce future estate taxes, as well as future income taxes when used to shift income-generating assets to a person in a lower tax bracket.

If a gift is made by check, be sure it's early enough so the check clears the bank—completing the gift—by year-end. Check with your tax adviser to find the best course of action for your particular situation.

LAST-MINUTE MOVES FOR INVESTORS

•Take tax-saving losses. If you've realized net capital gains to date this year but you have losses in your portfolio, realizing some losses by year-end can save tax dollars at no economic cost other than, possibly, trading commissions.

Best: End with a net capital loss of $3,000, the most that can be deducted against ordinary income. *How...*

•Make "bond swaps," selling a bond that has declined in value and buying another different but similar one.

•Sell the shares of a mutual fund that have declined in value, then buy back shares of a different but similar fund—or wait 31 days and buy back the same ones.

•Protect tax-favored dividends. "Qualified dividends" are subject to a top tax rate of only 15% through 2010. But to be "qualified," dividends must be paid on stock that you have held for more than 61 days during a 121-day period beginning 60 days from the ex-dividend date. So always beware of making year-end sales of stock too soon and forfeiting the lower rate on the dividends.

•Defer interest into next year. If you are receiving taxable interest on savings, invest it in a CD that will mature after year-end. You will defer the tax due on the interest from this year into next year.

More from Laurence I. Foster, CPA/PFS...

How to Get New Tax Savings From Old Tax Returns

You may be able to reduce your taxes for prior years by filing IRS Form 1040X, *Amended Tax Return.*

You can do this not only to correct errors but to get tax refunds for past years by changing filing strategies, claiming overlooked deductions and using retroactive tax breaks created by Congress and the IRS.

BASIC RULES

Amending a tax return is easy. You simply file the short 1040X form and state the change you are making on it. You do not have to refile your entire return, though you may need to attach a copy of the page or schedule you are changing.

You can amend a return up to three years after you originally filed it. *Tax-saving reasons for amending returns...*

●**Incorrect 1099s.** Upon examining all your 1099 information returns after you file, you may find that one or more overstated your income.

Alert: A survey found that almost 10% of all information returns filed by investment houses for 2003 contained mistakes—so double-check yours for this year and past years.

●**Changing filing status.** A single filer may not realize until after filing that he/she qualifies for tax-saving head of household status.

Also, married couples who file separately may save taxes by switching to joint status.

Common: Spouses who separate on hostile terms often file separately to protect themselves from each other's potential liabilities. But separate filing almost always increases their combined tax bill in such cases. If they can agree to work together, they can later file an amended return to claim joint status, get a refund and split the tax savings.

Note: It's not possible to switch from joint to separate status on an amended return.

●**Multiple support agreements.** When a number of family members contribute to pay most of the support of a retired parent or other relative but no one person pays more than half the support, they might qualify as a group to claim a dependency exemption for the relative and assign it to one person among them.

How: File IRS Form 2120, *Multiple Support Declaration.*

If this tactic is overlooked, amended returns can be used to file multiple support agreements for up to three years back, claiming dependency exemptions to get refunds.

●**Worthless securities and bad debts.** These are deductible only in the year they become worthless—but that often is not known until a later year, especially when litigation is involved.

Note: These items can be deducted up to seven years back on an amended return, instead of the normal three years.

Review your portfolio and if you find any securities or debts that went bad in the past seven years, deduct them now for a refund.

●**State tax refunds.** It's a common error to report these in income when they should be tax free or partially tax free.

A state tax refund is included in federal taxable income only if, and to the extent that, the original state tax payment was deducted on a previous year's federal return.

If you switched from claiming the standard deduction to itemizing deductions in the past three years, check to be sure you didn't pay tax on a refunded state payment that you didn't originally deduct.

Snag: The alternative minimum tax may eliminate the deduction for state taxes even if you filed an itemized return. Also, high-income individuals have their itemized deduction phased out as income rises. If you were in either situation and later received a state refund you paid tax on, double-check its taxability.

●**Casualty losses.** When a casualty loss occurs in a presidentially declared disaster, a deduction can be claimed either on that year's tax return or the prior year's return.

Filing an amended return for the prior year often results in a quicker refund—and maybe a larger one, too, depending on your tax bracket and other items on the return that impact the deduction.

•**Errors and omissions.** If you do discover that you made an error on a past year's return, or failed to report an item of income, filing an amended return to correct the mistake will minimize taxes by stopping interest from running on the liability, and increasing the chance that the IRS will waive any penalties it can apply.

AUDIT RISK

Filing an amended return will probably not result in extra audit risk.

Amending a tax return does not extend the statute of limitations for the original tax return to give the IRS any more time to audit it. And in the typical case, the IRS looks only at the particular item being amended on the return.

An amended return will draw an extra look from the IRS only if the item being amended is unusual or has a big effect on the tax bill—and even then, if the amendment and the rest of the return are proper, file it to assure you pay no more tax than you owe.

Adopting Tax Breaks Most Families Miss...

Sidney Kess, attorney and CPA, 10 Rockefeller Plaza, New York City 10020, coauthor/consulting editor of *Financial and Estate Planning* and coauthor of *1040 Preparation and Planning Guide.* (Both are from CCH). Over the years, he has taught tax law to more than 710,000 tax professionals.

Each year, about 127,000 children are adopted in this country. The adoption process is costly and lengthy and can have a major impact on a family's finances. The tax law, fortunately, provides tax breaks for adoption costs at just about every stage of the process. Knowing them can make the experience far less trying—and might even be the difference, for some families, in deciding that adopting a child is financially feasible.

THE ADOPTION CREDIT

According to the National Adoption Information Clearinghouse (NAIC), a service of the US Department of Health and Human Services, the cost of adoption can run as high as $40,000.

To encourage individuals to adopt, the tax law provides a personal tax credit. The amount of the credit is 100% of "qualifying expenses" (see below) up to $11,650 in 2008 ($12,150 in 2009).

If you adopt a child with "special needs," you can claim this credit amount regardless of the amount of expenses you incur. Even if your costs are only $2,000, you can claim the full credit. A special-needs child is defined as a US citizen or resident who, as determined by the government, because of a physical, mental, or emotional condition, is less likely to be adopted without special tax-credit assistance to the adoptive parents. *Qualifying expenses...*

•**Adoption agency fees.**

•**Attorney's fees.**

•**Court costs.**

•**Your travel expenses,** such as those incurred in picking up the child.

Expenses that don't qualify: You cannot claim the credit for government adoption assistance fees, fees to a surrogate mother, or any expenses that violate the law.

Credit limits: The full credit (including for adopting a special-needs child) can be claimed only by those with modified adjusted gross income (MAGI) up to a set amount—$174,730 in 2008 ($182,180 in 2009). (In this case, MAGI is adjusted gross income increased by certain foreign income exclusions.) The same limit applies for singles as well as joint filers. The credit phases out for MAGI between $174,730 and $214,730 in 2008 ($182,180 and $222,180 in 2009)—no credit can be claimed once MAGI reaches $214,730 in 2008 ($222,180 in 2009). A married person filing separately can claim the credit only if he/she meets the MAGI test and lived apart from his/her spouse for the last six months of the year for which the credit is being claimed.

The credit is limited to your tax liability for the year—it cannot be used to generate a tax refund. However, if the credit exceeds your liability, the excess can be carried forward for up to five years.

Important: The adoption tax credit *can* be used to offset the alternative minimum tax.

TIMING OF THE CREDIT

The adoption process often spans more than one calendar year. *When the credit is claimed depends on whether you are adopting a child who is a US citizen or resident or a foreign child…*

● **Domestic adoption.** If the adoption is not yet final by the end of the first calendar year in which qualifying expenses are paid, the credit for that year and any second-year expenses must be claimed in the second year—even if the adoption does not become final in the second year. For every year after that, qualifying expenses are claimed in the year they are paid—including for years after the adoption becomes final. For a special-needs child for whom expenses are not paid by the taxpayer, the credit is claimed in the year the adoption becomes final.

● **International adoption.** Any expenses incurred in a year prior to the year of the final adoption cannot give rise to a credit until the adoption year. Include any expenses in the adoption year when figuring the credit. As with domestic adoptions, subsequent-year expenses are claimed in the subsequent year.

EMPLOYER ASSISTANCE

According to a recent survey, about 39% of US employers offer adoption assistance—with an average maximum reimbursement of just under $4,000. If a company has an adoption plan providing assistance to employees on a nondiscriminatory basis, an employee who receives adoption benefits—direct reimbursements or payments from the plan directly to the adoption agency or other providers—is not taxed on the benefits. The amount of the exclusion is the same as the credit—$11,650 in 2008 ($12,150 in 2009). But, you can't claim the credit and exclusion for the same expenses that are covered by employer assistance.

The same MAGI limits, with phaseouts, apply for employer-paid expenses. If you receive employer-provided adoption assistance but your MAGI exceeds the limit, you must report at least some part of this benefit as additional compensation. The employer is not required to withhold taxes on this amount, so take this extra income into account in figuring your total withholding and/or estimated tax payments for the year.

RELOCATION EXCLUSION

In today's housing market—slowing down, but still robust—the value of a home can increase greatly in a short period. In general, the tax law allows home owners who have owned and used their homes for at least two of the five years before a sale to exclude gain on the sale up to $250,000 ($500,000 on a joint return).

If a home owner relocates without meeting the above time test, the exclusion amount can be prorated if the move is motivated by an *unforeseen circumstance.*

New opportunity: The IRS ruled that a couple who was required by an adoption agency to provide a separate sizable bedroom for a child being placed with them, and who had to move to meet this requirement, could count the need to move as an unforeseen circumstance and therefore prorate their exclusion (*Letter Ruling* 200613009).

ASSISTANCE FROM CHARITIES

To encourage less-affluent people to adopt, some exempt organizations, such as the Jewish Child Care Association and others, offer money to defray adoption costs.

New: The IRS has ruled recently that these payments are treated as tax-free gifts, not income, if made by a charity to an individual in response to the individual's needs. The payments may not proceed from any moral or legal duty and must be motivated by detached and disinterested generosity. To find assistance resources, visit the Child Welfare Information Gateway at *www.childwelfare.gov.*

MORE TAX BREAKS

In addition to the direct benefit for the adoption, here are some other tax breaks available for adopting a child…

● **The dependency exemption.** You can claim a dependency exemption—$3,400 in 2007 ($3,500 in 2008)—for an adopted child as long as the child is legally adopted or was placed with you for adoption by an authorized placement agency (a person or court authorized by state law to place children for legal adoption). If a child is not placed by such an agency, an exemption can be claimed only if the child is a member of your household for the entire year.

•**Medical expenses for an adopted child.** If you pay medical expenses for the child, you can include them with your deductible medical costs. The child must qualify as your dependent when the medical services are provided or when the expenses are paid.

•**Child tax credit.** In addition to the adoption credit, you may claim the child tax credit (up to $1,000), even if the adoption has not become final. These are subject to phaseouts based on income.

Key: If the adoption isn't final, the child must have been placed with you by an authorized placement agency.

TIME OFF FROM WORK

Under the federal *Family and Medical Leave Act of 1993*, companies that regularly employ 50 or more workers must provide up to 12 weeks of unpaid leave time, without penalizing the employee, for an employee who adopts a child. For more details, see "Family and Medical Leave Act (FMLA)" at the US Department of Labor Web site, *www.dol.gov.*

State law may include more liberal FMLA rules.

Example: California requires partial wage payments for adoption leave time. Contact your state department of labor for details.

Best Tax-Saving Baby Gifts

Edward Mendlowitz, CPA, partner, WithumSmith+ Brown, 1 Spring St., New Brunswick, New Jersey 08901. He is author of *Estate Planning*. Practical Programs.

When you shop for a baby gift, consider a custodial account, a tuition savings plan, a trust, or other gifting strategy designed to help newborns and their families minimize their tax bills…

Loophole: **Open a custodial account for the baby.** Accounts covered by your state's *Uniform Gifts to Minors Act* or the *Uniform Transfers to Minors Act* will be owned by the baby. Any income the account generates will be taxed at the baby's low tax rate instead of yours.

These accounts are opened in a custodian's name on behalf of a minor, who must be given complete access to the money by age 18 or 21, depending on state law. The assets belong to the child and are counted as such for financial aid purposes when going to college. The custodian—the person who looks after the money—generally is an adult family member.

Limitation: Children under the age of 18 can earn $900 in 2008 ($950 in 2009) of investment income free of tax. An additional $900 in 2008 ($950 in 2009) of investment income will be taxed at 10%. Investment earnings of more than $1,800 in 2008 ($1,900 in 2009), however, will be taxed at the parents' higher tax rate.

Trap: Grandparents who make gifts to custodial accounts for their grandchildren should not act as custodians. When they do, any money left in the account when the grandparent dies will be included in his/her taxable estate.

Read the next two loopholes to learn how to avoid this problem…

Loophole: **Have one grandparent make a gift of the money to the other grandparent.** That grandparent then gives the money to the grandchild. The other grandparent can, therefore, act as custodian without adverse estate tax consequences.

Loophole: **Open a Section 529 qualified tuition savings plan.** Annual contributions up to $13,000 ($24,000 with a consenting spouse) are gift tax free. There is a special rule for contributions to 529 plans that allows you to elect to spread a one-time transfer over five years for gift tax purposes. When the funds are used for college tuition, the income is completely tax free.

Donors can be plan trustees, controlling the funds until distributed. However, investment choices are limited by each state. Some states will give you a tax deduction for contributions—check with your accountant.

Withdrawals not used to pay college tuition are subject to income tax and a 10% penalty.

Strategy: If the designated child beneficiary does not attend college, you can switch the beneficiary to someone who would use the money to pay tuition.

Loophole: **Report US savings bond interest annually.** When your child receives US savings bonds as gifts, elect on his first tax return to report the bond's interest annually rather than let it accumulate. (File a tax return for the child right away, even though you are not required to do so.)

Reason: The baby will owe no tax as long as the interest accrued on the bond does not exceed $900 in 2008 ($950 in 2009) a year, including any other unearned income the child might have. That way, when the child ages out of kiddie tax and cashes in the bonds, no tax will be due.

Loophole: **Set up a trust for the baby.** A trust will give you more control over the funds than a custodial account. You can keep the money in the account long after the child turns age 21, or you can make distributions contingent upon certain events, such as attending college or a summer vacation trip overseas.

Loophole: **Buy additional insurance on your life.** Have the policy put into a trust for the benefit of the child, not your spouse. This prevents the proceeds from being included in either parent's taxable estate if both parents die in one accident.

Strategy: Set up a life insurance trust with principal going to the child and income to the surviving spouse. This provides income during the parent's lifetime but keeps the proceeds out of his estate.

Loophole: **Shift future income to the child.** While shifting of current income is not a good idea because most of a young child's income is taxed at the parent's bracket, consider shifting assets that will grow in value or produce income in the future.

Example: Put S corporation stock or your interest in a limited liability company that produces little current income but has future growth potential into a trust for the baby. The appreciation will be taxed at the child's lower rates when he is no longer subject to the kiddie tax.

Loophole: **Buy tax-favored investments in the baby's name.** You can reduce taxes owed on a baby's investments by putting the money into zero-coupon or regular municipal bonds or bond funds, which pay tax exempt interest. These investments are suitable until the child is no longer subject to the kiddie tax.

Another good alternative: Growth stocks that pay little or no dividends, such as start-ups, technology, or biotech stocks.

General caution: Before putting anything in a child's name, think about the impact this would have on financial aid for education.

More from Edward Mendlowitz, CPA...

All Kinds of Business Loopholes

Unique loopholes are available to tax-payers who operate certain kinds of businesses...

SERVICE BUSINESSES

Loophole: **Owners of small businesses can save taxes by using the cash method of accounting.**

How it works: Under the accrual method, businesses report income when they have a right to receive payment and deduct expenses when they become liable for them. Under the cash method, businesses report income and deduct expenses for monies actually received and paid. Businesses that have money owed to them do not have to pay tax on money they have not yet received.

Generally, companies with inventory must use the accrual basis, unless they meet certain small-business exemptions. A small business (one with less than $1 million in average sales) can use cash basis accounting even if it has inventory.

Note: C corporations with average sales of more than $5 million must use the accrual basis.

Service businesses that have no inventory and are not C corporations can use the cash method. This method is especially helpful to service businesses selling related products, for example, plumbers who also sell plumbing supplies.

DIRECT MARKETING FIRMS

Loophole: **Mailing-list development costs are immediately deductible** even though a mailing list has an extended life. Similarly, catalogs, brochures, and other advertising literature are deductible as advertising expenses, even though they will be distributed by the company and used by customers in future years.

Note: Several federal circuit courts disagree with the IRS on the tax treatment of catalog costs, contending that these costs must be capitalized and deducted over the expected benefit periods. If you publish catalogs, check with your tax adviser.

CONSTRUCTION CONTRACTORS

Loophole: **Use special tax reporting methods to save taxes on construction contracts in process.** As a rule, contractors must use the "percentage-of-completion" method of tax reporting, which means that they report taxable income throughout the project. However, small contractors (average annual gross receipts for previous three years do not exceed $10 million) can use a "completed-contract" method, delaying reporting profit until a job is completed.

STATUTORY EMPLOYEES

Loophole: **Statutory employees can fully deduct job expenses.** Certain employees, such as performing artists, models, and life insurance agents, are considered statutory employees, that is, workers deemed employees by statute. They can deduct full job-related expenses, including the costs of printing and mailing résumés and travel expenses, on Schedule C of their tax returns.

RESTAURANTS

Loophole: **Restaurants can save accounting and bookkeeping costs** by using a 52/53 week fiscal year to coordinate tax reporting with internal reporting. A 52/53 week fiscal year is designed so that the fiscal year ends on the same day of the week, such as the last Sunday of the year. The business's books are maintained by calendar week, not by calendar month. Thus, each calendar quarter includes two four-week months and one five-week month.

269

13

Investing: Money Makers, Money Savers

Warren Buffett's Secrets For Protecting Your Money in a Scary Market

Over the past few years, I spent thousands of hours with legendary Nebraskan investor Warren Buffett, chairman and CEO of the conglomerate Berkshire Hathaway. While I was writing his biography, he gave me unprecedented access to his work, opinions, struggles, triumphs, follies and wisdom. Buffett's success on Wall Street has made him the richest man in the world. But in many ways, he's closer to Main Street than Wall Street, a careful investor like you and me who still lives in the house he bought in 1958 for $31,500.

Many Americans watch Buffett very carefully when the stock market plunges and the economy teeters on the edge of disaster. In these kinds of grim markets, he has been at his most brilliant and visionary. No one has a better record of protecting assets, making shrewd purchases—and inspiring the confidence we need to survive financial turmoil. *Advice from Buffett...*

●**Invest in what you understand.** In the years 1998 to 2000, Buffett famously avoided buying Internet stocks because he didn't see how the companies could make enough money to justify their valuations. In 2002, he started warning against complicated "derivatives," including the subprime mortgage deals that have devastated such giants as the investment firm Lehman Brothers and insurer AIG—deals that are at the core of the current financial crisis.

If you want an understandable business, Buffett points to Coca-Cola, of which he owns a little more than 8%. After 122 years, the Coca-Cola Company still sells more than a billion beverage servings a day. He also is partial to Gillette, a division of Procter & Gamble. P&G makes up nearly 11% of his portfolio. Gillette

Alice Schroeder, a former Wall Street analyst and former managing director at Morgan Stanley, New York City. She is author of *The Snowball: Warren Buffett and the Business of Life*. Bantam.

dominates US razor blade sales and will never run out of customers as it expands worldwide.

●**Decide on your investing values and criteria**—then maintain them no matter how good or bad the market is. When investors get in trouble, it's usually because fear or greed has made them ignore commonsense rules.

Buffett has strategies that he follows in bull and bear markets. He looks for quality companies with ethical, highly committed management teams in essential but often unexciting industries. Most important, he waits for a time when he can acquire these companies at a large discount, often 40% below what he considers their "fair values."

In fact, Buffett's relentless focus on bargains extends to every aspect of his life. As an example, he related the following anecdote to me. He had a friend who went to stay in a house owned by Buffett's business associate Katharine Graham, the late chairman of *The Washington Post*. Afterward, the shocked friend called Buffett to tell him that Graham kept an authentic Picasso painting in the guest bathroom. Buffett said that he had used that bathroom many times over the years but never noticed the painting. What he did appreciate was that the bathroom was well-stocked with shampoos and toiletries. Buffett loves freebies.

●**Have cash on hand.** Many investors feel that they need to be fully invested and that holding cash in a portfolio is a drag on returns. Cash, however, has its advantages when markets plunge. For several years, Buffett sat on more than $44 billion of cash in Berkshire Hathaway accounts. This allowed him in September to brilliantly and carefully pick up shares of preferred stocks from General Electric and Goldman Sachs in specially negotiated deals with hefty dividends and at nearly half off the price they had been selling for a few months earlier.

●**Don't try to catch a falling knife until you have a handle on the risk.** Many investors get into trouble because they see opportunity but don't think about risk fully enough. Asking yourself, "And then what?" over and over can help you see all the possible consequences.

Let me give you an example from Buffett's life. In spring 2008, Buffett was approached about investing in, or perhaps even buying,

Bear Stearns. Until it was badly damaged by the recent subprime mortgage debacle, Bear Sterns was one of the world's largest global investment banks and brokerage firms. Buffett could have practically named his terms, but he passed on the deal. He worried that the company had at least 750,000 derivative investments. He said that even if he cloned Albert Einstein and worked 12-hour days with him, they could never properly analyze the risk of that many investments. Rebuffed by Buffett, Bear Stearns raised billions in capital from sovereign wealth funds in China and the Middle East. Those funds lost most of their money as Bear Stearns unraveled and was eventually taken over by JPMorgan Chase.

●**Don't bet the ranch.** As an investor, leave yourself a margin of safety in case something goes very wrong. Buffet says that in the past 50 years, he never permanently lost more than 2% of his own personal worth on any investment position. He has suffered heavy losses at times, but only on paper, which is why he warns against using leverage (borrowing money to increase your bet on a stock pick).

●**You can't be just a little bit smart.** Buffett feels that if you try to be just a little bit smart, you're liable to be really dumb, especially in a treacherous market such as this one. Few people have the time or inclination to study enough to beat the market. Diversification is probably your best route. Choose a low-cost index fund, and put your money into it slowly and steadily over time. That way you don't buy everything at the wrong price or the wrong time.

●**Never sell into a panic, such as the recent one.** Buffett isn't very worried about the big picture for America. He believes that the stock market does some very crazy things in the short run, but in the long run, it behaves quite rationally. Buffett's underlying belief now is that the American economy will do very well and so will people who own a piece of it. He knows that the economy might get worse for a while and even endure a long, hard recession. There are a lot of factors gumming up its potential now. But 10 years from now, he says, we'll look back and see that, as investors, we could have made some extraordinary buys.

You Have a Good Income But You're Still in Debt— What to Do

Elizabeth Warren and Amelia Warren Tyagi, coauthors of *The Two-Income Trap: Why Middle-Class Mothers & Fathers Are Going Broke* (Basic) and *All Your Worth* (Free Press). Warren is the Leo Gottlieb Professor of Law at Harvard Law School in Cambridge, Massachusetts, and an expert on bankruptcy. Her daughter, Amelia Warren Tyagi, is a financial consultant and cofounder of The Business Talent Group, Glendale, California.

You might have expected that the two-income families of today would have a higher standard of living and greater financial security than the single-earner households of past generations. The fact is, most families are buried in debt. In 1981, the average family owed just 4% of personal income in credit card and other unsecured debt. Today, that figure has tripled to 12%.

The standard advice for getting out of debt and living within a budget often fails to yield results, because it's based on an outdated 1950s model—one wage earner per household and limited sources of credit.

If you have a good income and you're still struggling with debt, try these new strategies...

SMARTER SPENDING

Old advice: Cut back on small luxuries... brown-bag your lunch...clip coupons.

New advice: Focus on big, recurring expenses. Most middle-class Americans today are sensible people who aren't blowing their paychecks on frills. The real issues are their exorbitant fixed costs—mortgage payments, premiums for health and other insurance, college tuition and car payments. Reassess those big expenses—checks you write month after month without thinking about them—to determine whether you are getting the most for your dollar.

Examples: Payments for a second car you might be able to do without...private college tuition when a less expensive public university might be fine...high-cost health insurance instead of a lower-cost HMO.

MONTHLY SERVICES

Old advice: Negotiate the best deal you can for services you pay for each month, even if it means taking out a long-term contract.

New advice: Avoid long-term contracts whenever possible. What you need in the event of a financial crisis is flexibility. In the long run, multiyear contracts for such things as satellite television service, cell-phone plans and gym memberships may cost you more in termination fees and regrets than higher-priced, short-term contracts.

MORTGAGE PAYMENTS

Old advice: Buy as much house as you can afford by borrowing the maximum amount of money your lender will allow.

New advice: Don't trust your mortgage lender or bank to tell you how much you can afford. Forty years ago, home buyers couldn't get interest-only loans or loans with "no money down." Lending standards have since been relaxed as competition has increased. *Result?* Many people are house-poor because banks have awarded them mortgages that are beyond their means.

If the only way you can meet the payments for your home is to commit to a risky mortgage that totals more than 28% of your combined incomes, don't do it. Find a house you can afford—or consider renting a house or an apartment until you can truly afford to buy.

DEBT CONTROL

Old advice: Pay off your highest-interest debt first. Then move on to the next highest, etc.

New advice: Pay off debts that bother you the most first. Being in debt is not only about dollars and cents. It's about peace of mind, too.

Is there a bill that makes your blood boil every time it appears in the mail or frequently sparks a quarrel with your spouse? Paying these bills first may not technically be the most efficient way to use your money, but it can have a significant and immediate impact on your sense of well-being.

BETTER BUDGETING

Old advice: Agree that only one spouse will handle the finances, so that the other spouse is free of the responsibility.

New advice: Each spouse should accept 100% of the responsibility for the finances. Both spouses need to create ground rules for spending and paying debts, even if only one spouse actually handles the paperwork. Otherwise, the more financially responsible spouse winds up nagging, thereby increasing the conflict and tension in the marriage.

The money and bills legally belong to both of you, even if you find it more convenient to manage them from separate checking accounts.

Make it easy for your partner to be truthful. Spouses may tell white lies about money because they don't want to justify their purchases. Promise your partner that you'll never question his/her spending as long as he stays within the household's budget for discretionary or "fun" money.

The Best Financial Advice On the Internet

Ryan M. Fleming, principal, Armstrong, Fleming & Moore, Inc., a financial planning firm in Washington, DC.

Eric Jacobson, senior analyst and fixed-income editor, Morningstar, Inc., Chicago.

Layne Aurand, statistician for the *No-Load Fund Investor*, Ardsley, New York.

Gary Schatsky, Esq., president of The ObjectiveAdvice Group, a financial advisory firm based in New York City and Florida, *www.objectiveadvice.com.*

Sam Stovall, chief investment strategist for Standard & Poor's Corp., New York City.

There's a wealth of financial information on the Internet. But how do you find the best Web sites? We asked five top financial experts to point us to the sites they find most useful and tell us why. All the sites listed below are free, although many have a charge for extra features.

RYAN M. FLEMING

●**www.fool.com.** This site is well known for teaching people how to be their own personal financial managers. It encourages and empowers them to do the necessary research. The site has links to every financial Web site

imaginable and some wonderful guides for improving your financial well-being.

The additional charge for a one-year subscription to *The Motley Fool "Stock Advisor"* newsletter is $149*, two years for $289. With this you can get personalized objective advice and a financial helpline.

Best feature: "60-Second Guides" on topics such as opening an IRA and choosing a broker.

●**www.morningstar.com.** The fund-rating service Morningstar is a great place to start your research on investments—stocks, mutual funds, closed-end funds and annuities. It has an excellent "College Savings Center" with special reports, including information about 529 plans.

Additional charge for premium membership that includes analysts' reports on 1,000 stocks and 2,000 funds, plus exclusive alert services, is $159/year.

Best feature: Ratings for more than 2,000 funds to help you compare one fund against another.

●**www.kiplinger.com.** The Kiplinger site is particularly rich with information on financial-planning topics related to its newsletters, such as *Tax Letter, Retirement Report* and *Agriculture Letter.* It contains a number of financial calculators and other helpful tools.

Best feature: "KiplingerForecasts.com," which is updated several times per day. News about gross domestic product, interest rates, unemployment, housing and retail sales. The cost is $117/year.

ERIC JACOBSON RECOMMENDS

●**www.smartmoney.com.** This is a useful site with lots of good information and tools.

Highlights: Breaking financial updates and analysis and commentary on the trendsetting stocks and tax matters as well as articles covering mutual funds and personal finance.

An additional charge for the service "Smart Money Select" is $58 per year. You receive real-time price quotes, market analysis and "Fund Map 1000," where you can see which fund categories, fund families and individual funds are ahead of the pack, based on 18 different criteria.

*All prices are subject to change.

Best feature: "This Week From Barron's," which comes out the same time as Barron's.

● **www.sec.gov.** At this site, you'll be able to look up a variety of reports and filings from companies. For stocks, you can get access to 10K (annual) and 10Q (quarterly) reports. For mutual funds, you can do prospectus research, obtain annual and semiannual reports, and 13D reports that show who owns more than 5% of a fund.

Best feature: Company filings and forms.

● **www.investinginbonds.com.** Sponsored by The Bond Market Association, this site covers Treasuries and municipal, corporate and mortgage-backed securities. There are investors' guides and a bond glossary, plus links to more than 400 sites with market and price information for all segments of the bond market.

Best feature: Seven simple steps to learn about investing in bonds.

● **www.economist.com.** Learn more about the role of the world in the marketplace. Special sections on science and technology, finance and economics, and business, together with data on world markets.

The charge for premium content is $116.79*/ year to get full access to the content of *The Economist* before it hits the newsstands.

Best feature: Financial news from Asia, Europe, the Middle East and Africa.

LAYNE AURAND SINGLES OUT

● **http://finance.yahoo.com.** On this site you'll get more than basic information about the vast majority of funds. You'll also receive many analytical tools allowing you to compare and contrast performance, cost, etc.—without any annoying registration.

The charge for "Real-Time Quotes," which provides streaming real-time quotes and market coverage including upgrades and downgrades, is $13.95/month.

Best feature: "Investing Ideas" from TradingMarkets.com, Morningstar.com and others.

● **www.schwab.com.** You don't need an account to access much of the information targeted for customers of this discount brokerage. Its mutual fund screener lets you search

*All prices are subject to change.

for specific funds based on criteria such as performance, expense ratio and investment category. (However, the "Schwab Equity Ratings," which give you an objective way to evaluate more than 3,000 stocks, is restricted to customers.)

Best feature: "Market Insight" button connecting you to "Workshops," which features investing workshops and self-paced courses.

GARY SCHATSKY, ESQ.

● **www.marketwatch.com.** This site offers the latest financial news, personal portfolio tracking (including allocation analysis, company financials, charting and relevant news to help you track your portfolio), stock quotes, expert commentary and personal financial features on topics such as mutual funds, life and money, retirement, real estate and taxes.

Best feature: Commentary from the daily-featured columnists.

● **http://moneycentral.msn.com/home. asp.** The features of this comprehensive investment site include "My Money," a customized snapshot of your finances, stocks and related news. Another section called "Investing" includes a portfolio manager that tracks investments, market reports, breaking news, stock quotes and ratings and a mutual fund screener and directory.

Best feature: A link to CNBC TV providing market news and stock picks.

● **http://money.cnn.com.** This site, from CNN and *Money* magazine, covers markets and stocks, company news, the economy, world business, technology, mutual funds, personal finances and more. "Money 101" is an interactive course in managing your finances, and "Calculators" has a mortgage refinance calculator.

Best feature: Commentary from Lou Dobbs.

SAM STOVALL

● **www.fidelity.com.** This site, which is not restricted to Fidelity mutual fund shareholders, has stocks and mutual fund recommendations from Standard & Poor's and Lehman Brothers, an archive of articles, portfolio tracking and asset allocation.

Best feature: Under "Research" find links to "Market News," "Mutual Funds" and interactive tools that enable you to compare stocks, track the Dow and more.

●**www.bloomberg.com.** This provides a quick stop to get world, financial and earnings news as well as news archives and stocks on the move. At Bloomberg University, you can register for their free on-line investing classes.

Best feature: News and commentary.

●**www.businessweek.com.** This extremely comprehensive site has S&P investment outlooks (picks and pans), and a free S&P stock report every day. The site has market outlooks, sector outlooks and economic analysis. "Special Reports" and "Video Views" give timely investment advice. There is an archive of articles and the BW 50 (which are the S&P's 500 best performers).

Best feature: "Market Snapshot," "Market Movers" and "S&P Stock Picks & Pans," under "Investing."

Are Mutual Funds Robbing You Blind?

Mutual fund expenses, currently the focus of criticism by regulators, are actually the one factor that investors can control. Simply refuse to keep pouring money into high-cost funds that can rob you of thousands of dollars in returns over the years. The average expense ratio of 1.58% for both load and no-load stock funds does not include transaction and commission costs, which can easily increase your annual expenses by 3% or more. In a year when the stock market achieves a total return of 9%, a 3% fee would reduce your annual gain by one-third. That's not chicken feed!

Fund families with the lowest expense ratios: Vanguard, TIAA-CREF, Dodge & Cox and Schwab.

Sheldon Jacobs, founder and consultant, *The No-Load Fund Investor*, Box 3029, Brentwood, Tennessee 37024.

Finding a Better Broker

Martin D. Weiss, PhD, chairman, The Weiss Group, Inc., a financial-services ratings firm, Jupiter, Florida.

Be sure to check out a brokerage's financial security and legal history before opening an account, and periodically monitor the company's condition.

Free resources to check on a brokerage's legal past: Call the Financial Industry Regulatory Authority at 800-289-9999 or use the BrokerCheck program at its Web site, *www.finra.org*, which provides information about criminal regulatory actions, complaints, etc.

Note: The Securities Protection Investors Corporation insures brokerage accounts for up to $500,000 and up to $100,000 for cash claims in the event that a brokerage fails. Most firms carry additional private insurance to cover any losses beyond that.

Mutual Fund Tax Saver

Many funds have tax loss carryforwards that can be used to offset their future capital gains, reports fund tracker Don Philips. Ordinarily, investors must pay tax on these gains each year, even if they don't sell their shares. If your fund has losses carried forward, you might not have to pay tax on net gains for years. To check a fund's tax losses, go to *www.morningstar.com*, search for the fund by the ticker symbol, then click "Tax Analysis." A minus symbol denotes a loss.

Don Philips, managing director of fund tracker, Morningstar, Inc., Chicago, *www.morningstar.com*.

Investment Salespeople Can Fool You

Beware of investment salespeople who label themselves "senior specialists" at seminars in hotels and restaurants. These people, who may also call themselves "retirement counselors" or "senior counselors," may have little or no investment training. They may urge attendees to sell off their investments and put the proceeds into other products, including some that have high commissions and early withdrawal penalties. Before giving money to anyone claiming special expertise in investments for seniors, read the SEC article *Check Out Brokers and Investment Advisers*, available at *www.sec.gov/investor/brokers.htm.*

Kristi Kaepplein, director, Office of Investor Education and Advocacy, Securities and Exchange Commission, Washington, DC.

Check Out Your Stockbroker

Stockbrokers can't have complaints expunged from their records even if customers agree to it. An appeals court reversed a ruling allowing a complaint to be removed from a broker's record, saying that customers must be able to find out about all actions against brokers. To check out a broker, go to the free database of the Financial Industry Regulatory Authority at *http://broker check.finra.org*. Also check with your state's securities regulator by going to *www.nasaa.org.*

The Washington Post.

Beware of Stocks that Offer One-Time Dividend Payouts

Lower tax rates on dividends have prompted more companies to make these special payments. Such stocks are not suitable for investors seeking dependable income streams.

Better: Stocks of high-quality companies that are steady dividend payers with yields of 3% or more and favorable investment ratings from S&P analysts.

Sam Stovall, chief investment strategist at Standard & Poor's Corp., New York City.

The Simplest System for Picking Money-Making Stocks

Pat Dorsey, CFA, director of stock analysis for Morningstar, Inc., an independent stock and mutual fund analysis company in Chicago, *www.morningstar.com*. He is also the author of *The Five Rules for Successful Stock Investing*. Wiley.

With about 6,000 major publicly traded companies in the US alone, you can't possibly research all the stocks—but you can use these simple guidelines to quickly weed out ones that don't merit further examination, saving time and money.

You can find the data you'll need on company financial statements or at free financial Web sites, like *www.morningstar.com* or *http://finance.yahoo.com. Here's what to look for…*

•**Operating income.** Many firms have exciting ideas—but if they have never achieved operating income, they have not turned those ideas into profits.

Where to find it: Income statement.

Example: Sticking with profitable companies might have helped investors steer clear of the Internet bubble. Very few dot-com stocks posted positive operating income in the late 1990s..

•**Cash flow from operations.** Companies can exaggerate profit numbers, but if cash flow from operations—the amount of cash a business is generating—is positive, you can rest assured that the firm truly is making money. At the least, this figure should have been positive for two out of the past three years.

Where to find it: Cash flow statement.

●**Free cash flow.** This is the money that a company generates beyond what it requires to operate. Free cash flow is equal to cash flow from operations minus capital expenditures (the cost of upgrading buildings and equipment).

Rule out any company that is not generating free cash flow. Divide free cash flow by sales to compare companies of different sizes—a small operation won't generate the same free cash flow as a conglomerate.

Exception: You might want to buy stock of a company that isn't generating free cash flow because it is pouring its money into profitable research or expansion. There's no guarantee that such efforts will be profitable—but if the company has quality ideas, this would be a productive use of its cash.

Where to find it: Cash flow statement.

●**Return on equity (ROE) of 10% or more.** ROE is calculated by dividing net income by shareholders' equity. If a company has not generated at least 10% ROE for four out of the past five years, it's not worth your trouble.

Where to find it: Net income is listed on the income statement. Shareholders' equity appears on the balance sheet.

Caution: In the financial sector, look for at least 12% ROE. Most financials have heavy debt, which can inflate ROE.

●**Consistent earnings growth.** Some variation from year to year is to be expected—but if earnings growth is huge one year and negative or nonexistent the next, it means one of two things…

●The stock is in a cyclical industry, such as semiconductors or agricultural machinery. Cyclicals are not appropriate for buy-and-hold investors.

●The stock carries big risks. The company might be locked in a fight with formidable competitors or dependent on just one or two products for too much of its revenue. Neither is an appealing prospect for an investor.

Where to find it: Income statement.

●**Low debt.** Be wary of any company that has a debt-to-equity ratio above 1.

Where to find it: Balance sheet, which lists liabilities and shareholders' equity.

Exception: Contemplate investing in such a stock only if it is in the financial sector, where higher debt is typical, or if both of the following are true…

●It is a proven firm in a stable industry.

●Its debt is decreasing as a percentage of assets. If a company is heading out of debt, it might not be a problem.

Example: Food company General Mills (NYSE:GIS) has a debt-to-equity ratio of about 1.4—but it also has a long-term record of success in an industry that's known for stability. If General Mills made computer chips instead of breakfast cereal, its debt would be a red flag.

WHAT TO AVOID

●**Tiny, untested companies with market capitalizations below $100 million.** Do not buy any stock that doesn't trade on the New York Stock Exchange (NYSE), American Stock Exchange (AMEX) or NASDAQ. Shares traded on smaller exchanges are more likely to be disappointments than opportunities. Look for firms that have been public companies for at least five years. Avoid initial public offerings—they're too speculative for most portfolios.

●**Foreign companies that do not have shares traded in the US.** You will be better off sticking with American depositary receipts (ADRs)—receipts for shares of foreign corporations that trade on US stock exchanges. These companies are subject to US reporting requirements.

●**Frequent "other" charges in the financial statements.** These usually reflect one-time expenses, such as the cost of a restructuring effort. Practically every firm has the occasional "other" expense, but stay away if there are big negative numbers listed for successive years. The company might be trying to disguise an ongoing problem as a one-shot cost.

Where to find it: A line labeled "Other" on the income statement.

●**Rising number of outstanding shares.** If this number is increasing by more than 2% a year, the company is making significant acquisitions or employees are being given lots of stock options. Since so many acquisitions fail, it's generally best to avoid acquisitive companies. Excessive options also dilute the value of existing shares—bad news for investors.

Where to find it: Balance sheet.

Helpful: It's a plus if the number of outstanding shares is shrinking—for instance, through buybacks. Buybacks signal that management is optimistic about the company's future—plus a reduction in outstanding shares boosts share price by increasing per-share earnings.

Avoid New Fees for Dividend Reinvestment Plans (DRIPs)

About 1,000 companies allow investors to directly purchase shares and/or reinvest dividends. Some plans, however, have started charging fees.

Charles B. Carlson, CFA, is editor of *DRIP Investor*, 7412 Calumet Ave., Hammond, Indiana 46324. *www.dripinvestor. com.*

Tax Savings for Bond Investors

Now that Uncle Sam isn't issuing Series HH bonds, investors can't roll over Series E/EE bonds into Series HH bonds to postpone paying tax on interest.

What to do: If you bought Series EE bonds after 1989, the proceeds might be income tax-free when they mature if used to pay higher-education expenses for yourself, your spouse or a dependent child. See IRS Publication 970, *Tax Benefits for Education* (800-TAX-FORM, *www.irs.gov*).

Alternative: Offset interest income by recognizing net capital losses on other assets—up to $3,000 of ordinary income.

Caution: If you collect Social Security, your income might reach a level that causes benefits to be taxable.

Daniel J. Pederson, president of The Savings Bond Informer, a savings bond consulting service, Detroit.

The Sleaziest Investment Scams Today

Chuck Whitlock, chairman of Whitlock Training Group Corporation, a company that offers on-line fraud identification and prevention training to police departments, West Linn, Oregon. He is also a journalist whose work exposing scams has been featured on TV programs including *Inside Edition* and *Extra*. A member of the *Bottom Line/Wealth* Panel of Experts, Whitlock is author of several books about scams, including *Age Without Rage*. R-W International. *www.chuckwhitlock.com.*

The rocky markets are bringing con artists out of the woodwork—and they are promoting investment scams that promise huge returns but deliver only misery. *Watch out for...*

•**Gold in the vault.** You are told that an investment broker will buy gold for you for a small fee and store it in a bank vault.

The scam: The supposed broker never buys the gold and disappears with your money.

What to do: Invest in precious metals only through a broker at a well-known investment company, or buy mining company stocks or shares of a mutual fund focused on precious metals.

•**High-yield bank paper.** You are told that you have a rare opportunity to invest in safe, high-yield financial instruments, such as debt or letters of credit, that are from established European banks and that usually are available only to governments or other banks.

The scam: These bank securities, often touted as "prime bank" instruments, do not exist. The con artist will disappear with your money.

What to do: Be wary of anyone who promises huge returns at low risk...or who suggests that you invest in anything that you have never heard of.

•**Old bonds.** You are told that you have a chance to buy—for a very low price—a bond that was issued by a well-known company decades ago when interest rates were much higher.

The scam: The matured bond has been cashed in and no longer has any investment value. Scammers buy old bond certificates traded as collectibles and sell them to investors looking for high yields.

What to do: Be wary of any corporate bonds that are offered by anyone other than a well-known brokerage firm. Call investor relations at the company that issued the bond. And be aware that a bond with a rate higher than current market rates would normally have a premium price that erases all or much of the advantage.

Your Money— Wise Ways to Boost Profit and Cut Risk

Harold Evensky, CFP, chairman of Evensky & Katz, fee-only investment consultants at 2333 Ponce de Leon Blvd., Coral Gables, Florida 33134. He lectures on investments and retirement planning internationally.

An average investor buying and selling individual stocks makes about as much sense as a novice golfer trying to beat Tiger Woods.

Problem: It's easier for average investors to determine what is a good company than what is a good stock. Think of how much money investment institutions spend on researching stocks to buy—talking with companies' customers, competitors, trade experts, etc.—and they still don't make their money on trading stocks. They make most of it charging you for investment advice.

Smartest approach for individuals: Indexing—buying the same stocks that make up a particular market index, such as the S&P 500. Low-cost index funds, which require no active stock selection or market-timing management, outperform most active managers over time.

Why indexing pays: Indexing isn't foolproof, because when the whole stock market, or the part of it that your index is following, goes down, you'll go down, too. But over a full market cycle, index funds will usually produce above-average returns because their trading expenses are much lower than those of actively managed funds and they remain fully invested at all times.

Some people resist indexing because they want to get better than "average" results. Well,

think of it instead as "par" investing (what would be normal for an *expert*). It's guaranteed to be better than average because expenses are lower. If you put together a portfolio of par-performing funds, you'll do pretty well in a market in which very few active managers actually beat par.

MARKET OUTLOOK

We believe that in the next five to 10 years, returns from stocks are going to be only modest—substantially lower than in the last 20 years and even lower than the long-term historical average of about 10% per year. We expect the S&P 500 returns to be in the 8% or 9% range and intermediate-term domestic bonds to be in the 6% range, which is historically average.

Because of these lower projected returns, we believe that index funds offer the best way to improve results by at least controlling management and trading expenses as well as taxes. If you're earning only 8% to begin with, after subtracting for expenses, taxes and inflation, you would earn only about 2.5% net in real return. That doesn't leave much wiggle room to take a chance on picking the best-performing funds.

We also like exchange-traded funds (ETFs)—baskets of securities mimicking an index—that trade all day like stocks (mutual funds can only be bought at close of market each day). ETFs are often less expensive to buy and maintain than mutual funds, but they do entail a broker's commission, so they are suitable mainly for big, one-time investments. Mutual funds are more appropriate for those who invest monthly.

ASSET ALLOCATION

Long-term performance mainly depends on how your money is allocated among a variety of stocks (large-cap, small-cap, growth, value, international, etc.), bonds and cash.

That decision is unique to an individual. It shouldn't be simply a function of your age or of how much money you have. It should also take into consideration other personal factors, such as risk tolerance.

We often advise clients to start out with the conservative allocation of 40% fixed income (bonds, etc.) and 60% stocks. If they need more income and can live with the day-to-day volatility of stocks, then they can increase the stock allocation. If they have enough of a financial cushion that they don't need so many stocks to protect against inflation and they want to decrease volatility, they can then increase fixed-income investments.

CORE VS. SATELLITE INVESTMENTS

For their stock portfolios, we recommend that clients think in terms of 80% core investments, such as conservative index funds and ETFs...and 20% satellite investments, which can be almost anything—commodities funds, utilities, emerging markets—that will hopefully do at least two percentage points better than the market each year.

Core candidates: Put 50% of your stock portfolio into one or a combination of broad market index funds.

Consider putting 10% *each* into mid-cap and small-cap value funds for stronger representation in those sectors.

Finally, for the last 10%, consider diversifying with an international fund.

Satellite holdings: These should be 20% of your stock portfolio.

BOND FUNDS

For the typical 40% bond portfolio, we like several funds that concentrate on Treasury inflation-protected securities (TIPS). For high-income investors, we like tax-free municipal bond funds of various maturities. We also include a taxable international bond fund that could offer protection against a falling dollar.

Beware—High Cost Of Dividend Reinvestment Plans

Automatic dividend reinvestment plans (DRIPs) provide a convenient way to build up investments in corporations that offer them. But check the fees involved. If a plan charges, say, a $3 fee to reinvest $25 in dividends, that's 12%—far too much.

Recommended: The plan fee should not exceed 2% of the reinvested amount. Check the terms of the reinvestment plan to learn its fee structure. In some plans, it is cheaper to buy shares through an "optional cash investment" feature than by reinvesting dividends. In that case, you may do better by taking dividends in cash, then using the cash to buy more shares.

Charles B. Carlson, CFA, editor, *DRIP Investor*, 7412 Calumet Ave., Hammond, Indiana 46324.

Better Ways to Build Your Nest Egg

Laurence J. Kotlikoff, PhD, professor of economics at Boston University and president of Economic Security Planning, Inc., which produces personal financial planning software programs, Lexington, Massachusetts (*www. esplanner.com*). As a leading expert on saving, insurance and public policy, he has served on the Council of Economic Advisers and consulted for The World Bank, Merrill Lynch, Fidelity Investments and many others. He is author or coauthor of 13 books, including his latest, coauthored with Scott Burns, *Spend 'Til the End: The Revolutionary Guide to Raising Your Living Standard—Today and When You Retire.* Simon & Schuster.

A great deal of financial planning is based on myths. Especially common are myths about the best ways to save, spend, invest and draw on various sources of income. To dispel some of these myths, we spoke with one of the nation's leading experts on personal finance and retirement planning, economics professor Laurence J. Kotlikoff, PhD, of Boston University. *His myth-busting strategies for all stages of your adult life...*

LOWER YOUR LIFE INSURANCE

Myth: Buy life insurance equal to seven times your annual wages if you are the big earner in the household.

Fact: Many people don't need that much. Remember, the goal of insurance is to equalize your living standard across good and bad times, not to pay high premiums and deprive yourself and your family of spending money so that they can have a better lifestyle when you die. In fact, if your spouse is several years younger than you or expects to retire much later than you, he/she may have more remaining lifetime earnings to protect than you do— even if you earn more in a given year. In this case, you may want greater life insurance coverage for your spouse. After all, your family's living standard is being financed not just by current earnings, but by *all* future earnings.

RIDE A STOCK ROLLER-COASTER

Myth: The older you get, the more you need to increase your investment portfolio's allocation to relatively safe bonds and decrease the allocation to relatively risky stocks.

Fact: You might be better off putting your stock holdings on a "roller-coaster."

Reason: To reduce risk and maintain a more consistent lifestyle from year to year. Instead of diversifying just your investment portfolio, to balance safety and risk you need to focus more on how that portfolio fits in with your *total* resources. That includes job earnings and other income or benefits, such as inheritances, Social Security and Medicare.

How to adjust your allocations…

●**When you're young,** start with a relatively small stock allocation, perhaps under 20%, and put the bulk of your money in safer investments that you can more easily draw on, such as bonds, bank certificates of deposit and money market funds.

Reason: You may have relatively little in assets and earnings to draw on, weak borrowing capacity and high expenses for such things as a mortgage and kids' educations.

●**Through middle age,** increase your stock allocation dramatically, perhaps to 80%, because rising job earnings help to support your lifestyle and to diversify your overall resources. This is especially wise if you are approaching a time when the last tuition bill will be paid.

●**As you approach retirement,** reduce your stock allocation, perhaps to under 40%. That's because at this point, a sharp, prolonged drop in the stock market or the unexpected loss of your job could have a bigger impact if you have not started getting Social Security checks yet or begun drawing on other sources of retirement income, such as pensions.

●**In early retirement,** increase your stock allocation to at least 50% as you start drawing on such reliable income sources as Social Security.

●**Finally, in late retirement** (after age 75), reduce stocks to 20% of your investment portfolio as the risk for rising health expenses mounts.

POSTPONE SOCIAL SECURITY

Myth: If you retire early, you would be wise to start collecting Social Security benefits as soon as you reach age 62.

Fact: Retirees are often better off postponing the start of these benefits, possibly to age 70, especially as life spans grow longer on average.

Say that 66 is the age that the government calls your "full," or "normal," retirement age, and that you could start collecting $1,000 a month at that age. If, instead, you retire early at age 62 and start taking payments, your monthly check would be $750, or 25% lower (excluding cost-of-living adjustments).

If you wait until age 70, when the benefit you are eligible for would "top out" (except for cost-of-living increases), your monthly check would be $1,320. That means you would collect a total of $30,600 extra if you live to age 85, compared with the total you would receive if you started collecting at age 62.

Waiting until age 70 to start collecting is the right choice for most people, even if that means drawing more from your retirement accounts before age 70. This, of course, assumes that you have good reason to believe that you will live beyond your mid-70s, such as a history of parents and/or grandparents living long lives, and being in good health yourself.

For an estimate of your life expectancy, go to the "Living to 100 Life Expectancy Calculator" (*www.calculator.livingto100.com*).

An even better way: In many instances, you can choose to start collecting benefits at your full retirement age—which allows your spouse to start collecting benefits of up to 50% of yours—and then you can immediately "suspend" your benefits while your spouse keeps collecting his/hers. That way, you allow the size of your future checks to grow as you wait until age 70 to start collecting again.

Caution: If you are more concerned with leaving a bequest to your children and you have concerns about whether you will live much past 70, you may want to start collecting benefits earlier so that the money can help build up your assets sooner.

Broker Checkup

Is your brokerage paying high enough interest on your cash? For many investors, the answer is *no*. At the end of each trading day, "sweep accounts" receive the proceeds from customer trades or cash deposits that aren't yet invested. More firms—especially those with their own banks—now pay savings deposit rates instead of the higher money market rates on these accounts. Some have made this change without the customer's consent.

Self-defense: Ask your stockbroker which accounts are available and about the long-term interest rate—not just the introductory rate.

Grace Vogel, executive vice president of member-firm regulation, New York Stock Exchange, New York City.

Listen in on Conference Calls—It's Legal and Free!

Listen to management conference calls for free over the Internet at the same time that institutional investors do. The Web sites such as *www.bestcalls.com* and *www.vcall.com* list times when conference calls are made—or check out a firm's own Web site. Listen especially closely when expert analysts repeatedly question management regarding a specific issue, such as a planned acquisition. This means the issue could affect the stock price.

John E. Deysher, CFA, portfolio manager, Pinnacle Value Fund, New York City, *www.pinnaclevaluefund.com*.

Dividend Powerhouses— Stocks that Pay in Any Market

Joseph Lisanti, former editor in chief of *The Outlook*, Standard & Poor's weekly investment advisory newsletter at *www.spoutlookonline.com*. Its risk-adjusted performance ranks seventh among all of the financial newsletters tracked by *The Hulbert Financial Digest* since June 1980. He is coauthor of *The Dividend Rich Investor*. McGraw-Hill.

When the stock market is struggling, investors should pay special attention to dividend-paying stocks, which provide income in any market environment.

Bonus: In market downturns, dividend-paying stocks are resilient. Income-oriented investors are reluctant to dump a stock as long as the dividend checks keep coming.

HELP FROM UNCLE SAM

In the past, taxes on dividend income were higher than on capital gains. Rather than provide shareholders with rising dividends, many companies chose to boost their stock prices by investing cash in the business or buying back their stock.

A buyback increases earnings per share— and also raises a company's share price—by lowering the number of outstanding shares.

Dividend income now is taxed at the same rate as capital gains. In 2003, the top tax rate on most dividend income was slashed to just 15%, down from an ordinary income tax rate of as high as 38.6%. That makes dividends more valuable to shareholders.

FINDING DIVIDEND DYNAMOS

More companies are using their cash to increase dividends. Look for the companies that have increased their dividends every year for the past decade. Unlike quarterly earnings, dividends can't be fudged. Companies that consistently pay generous dividends must have solid businesses.

If a company has a long record of raising dividends, it is going to do everything in its power not to break that habit. Investors would view any cut in a stock's dividend as a sign of serious trouble.

Mutual Funds You Can Trust

To find a mutual fund you can trust, look for a high-quality firm that leads the way in corporate governance.

Key measures we look at: How investors have done with the firm's funds…whether the firm launches new funds responsibly…the experience, skill and integrity of management… clarity of communication with shareholders… internal regulatory compliance and risk controls.

For more information, you can research funds on the Morningstar database at many public libraries or at *www.morningstar.com.*

Russel Kinnel, director of mutual fund research, Morningstar, Inc., Chicago. He edits *Morningstar FundInvestor.*

Exchange-Traded Funds Are Popular but Beware Of Hidden Traps…

Jim Wiandt, editor of IndexUniverse.com, which provides information and data on a wide range of ETFs and index funds, New York City. He is author of *Exchange Traded Funds.* Wiley.

Millions of investors have been racing to buy shares from a rapidly expanding universe of exchange-traded funds (ETFs). *For many, ETFs can represent good values, offering cost and tax savings and precisely defined industry or country sectors—but they also come with hidden traps…*

Trap: Focusing on narrow funds. With more than 1,000 ETFs now available to investors, investment companies have been introducing increasingly specialized versions to stand out from the crowd. You can focus on such specific areas as natural gas, medical devices or Malaysia.

What to do: Sophisticated investors may have reason to own such narrowly defined investments, but these ETFs can be extremely volatile. Most investors would be better off buying and holding funds that cover a broad spectrum of stocks.

Trap: Paying too much. Many ETFs charge low annual expense ratios—ranging up to 0.1% to 0.5%. That looks like a bargain, compared with the average actively managed domestic stock fund, which charges about 1.4%. But each time you buy ETF shares, you must pay a brokerage commission—the same fee charged for any stock trade. Commissions can be particularly burdensome for small investors. Say your commission is $10 per trade and you want to put $200 a month into a Standard & Poor's 500 stock index ETF. The commission could erode most of your profits. In contrast, most no-load mutual funds charge nothing to trade.

What to do: If you plan to buy and/or sell shares often and in small amounts, favor mutual funds. If you do decide to buy an ETF, seek low brokerage fees.

Trap: Ignoring mutual fund discounts. While ETFs charge all investors the same annual expense ratios, many conventional mutual funds give discounts to big investors. Say you want to track the S&P 500. You could buy an ETF, such as SPDR Trust, Series 1 (SPY), which charges an expense ratio of 0.09%. That appears to be a bargain compared with the Vanguard 500 Index Fund (VFINX), which charges 0.18%. But if you invest $100,000, you are eligible for the "Admiral Shares" version of that index fund (VFIAX), which charges only 0.09%.

What to do: When all the trading costs and expenses are considered, investors who want to put less than $5,000 at a time into the S&P 500 should use the Vanguard 500 Index Fund. Those investing from $5,000 to $99,999 would likely do better with the ETF. But those seeking to invest $100,000 or more should consider the Vanguard Admiral Shares. Although Vanguard charges the same expense ratio as the SPDR Trust ETF, the no-load mutual fund is free of commissions.

ETFs vs. MUTUAL FUNDS

Like an "index" mutual fund, an ETF…

●**Tracks a "basket" of stocks or bonds** reflecting a specific index or market segment.

●**Tends not to alter its list of holdings,** which saves on trading costs.

Unlike a mutual fund, an ETF…

- **Rarely distributes capital gains,** so shareholders usually don't incur taxable capital gains until the ETF is sold.

- **Is bought and sold like a stock,** at prices that change as long as markets are open.

- **Tends to have lower management fees.**

- **Requires buyers and sellers to pay brokerage commissions.**

- **Requires no minimum investment.**

Five Investing "Rules" to Follow

Gene Marcial, *Business Week's* "Inside Wall Street" columnist since 1981. For the period since 1997, when the magazine started tracking the performance of his picks, the average annual returns of his stock recommendations have bested the Standard & Poor's 500 stock index, the Dow Jones Industrial Average and the Russell 2000. He is author of *7 Commandments of Stock Investing.* FT Press.

Sometimes it seems that the stock market's ups and downs don't follow any logic. But influential Wall Street columnist Gene Marcial tells us that a few unconventional "commandments" can help you make sense of it all even in a turbulent market like the one we are in today. *His commandments and the stock opportunities they reveal now…*

BE PREPARED

Markets and particular stocks often tumble without much warning. That's why you should have a clear strategy in mind beforehand so that you can react while others are hesitating or are frozen in place…

- **Hold at least 10% of your portfolio in cash.** The enormous profits you can make from picking up a bargain once every few years is worth the low interest rates you may have to endure to keep cash on hand. For most people, the best form of "cash" is shares in a money-market mutual fund.

- **Write down a list of core stocks you want to buy** for the long haul, and buy them when they become cheap. This kind of company usually carries a high price tag but occasionally pulls back and becomes a bargain.

BUY ON PANIC

Investors can grow so fearful or disenchanted with the prospects of certain sectors of the market that they just want out. When this phenomenon occurs, they tend to dump all the stocks in that sector indiscriminately. This happened in 2007 with home builders, when the real estate market collapsed, and again this year as financial stocks reported multibillion-dollar losses from real estate loans and investments. I'm cherry-picking the best stocks in these hated and abandoned sectors now. Even if the sectors continue to tank after I buy, my stocks will be the first ones to rebound.

LOOK FOR FALLEN ANGELS

Occasionally, I notice a different kind of panic. A particular company experiences a temporary setback that the investing herd simply overreacts to, ignoring strengths that make that company ripe for recovery. Unlike "core" stocks, these are not necessarily among the most successful firms in their industries.

FOLLOW THE INSIDERS

Even in tricky times, you should consider buying stock in a company if insiders are scooping up shares.

Reason: A company's top executives and owners have the most useful information about how it will do in the future.

Resource: Track insider buying and selling at *www.vickers-stock.com.* Accounts start at $99 per month with a three-day trial period.

DON'T FEAR THE UNKNOWN

In down markets, many investors, seeking to play defense, try to stick with familiar, low-risk stocks, including brand-name American companies, such as Johnson & Johnson and Procter & Gamble, whose stock prices tend to be relatively stable. But the most potential often lies in areas that seem riskier than they really are. For example, I'm finding great buys among companies that operate in emerging economies, such as Brazil, China, India and Russia, but that are listed on major US stock exchanges. That way, I take advantage of the tremendous growth that globalization has unleashed, yet remain confident that the company complies with all US accounting regulations.

Too Many Mutual Funds Can Lower Returns

Ric Edelman, chairman of Edelman Financial Services Inc., Fairfax, Virginia, which manages $2.4 billion in assets for clients throughout the country. He is author of *Discover the Wealth Within You*. HarperCollins. *www. ricedelman.com*.

Owning shares in too many mutual funds can hurt returns. If you have more than 10 mutual funds, your paperwork, including tax record-keeping, becomes onerous…fees may be higher than necessary because some fund families charge fees for transfers among funds and tax-preparation fees increase with each holding…and fund holdings may overlap, reducing diversification.

Best: Choose one fund in each of these categories—large-cap stock, mid-cap stock, small-cap stock (a growth and value for each) as well as international stock, natural resources stock, bonds and real estate investment trusts (REITs).

Avoid narrowly focused funds, such as single-industry or single-region funds. If you have too many funds, sell ones with similar objectives—even if you have to pay capital gains tax.

Investing in Rental Properties—Just Avoid These Traps

Robert Shemin, a real estate investor in Miami Beach who has purchased more than 300 properties in the past year alone. He is author of *Secrets of a Millionaire Landlord* (Kaplan) and *Successful Real Estate Investing: How to Avoid the 75 Most Costly Mistakes That Every Investor Makes* (Wiley). *www.sheminrealestate.com*.

Many real estate books and seminars promise quick millions from buying and selling rental properties. In reality, the gains tend to be slow and steady. *Investing in rental properties can generate monthly cash flow and an average total return of about 8% a year—but to be successful, avoid these traps…*

Trap: Going it alone. Local real estate associations are of enormous value to new and seasoned investors. You can learn from attorneys, mortgage brokers, contractors and investors. Members receive discounts on home-improvement products, such as paint and carpeting, and have access to a lending library of books and how-to kits.

What to do: Contact the National Real Estate Investors Association (888-762-7342, *www.nationalreia.com*) to find an affiliated group in your area. Membership typically costs $100 to $200 a year. Take a successful member of your local real estate club to lunch, and ask him/her to share his insights. See if he is willing to give you feedback on any opportunities that you are considering. To be successful, you probably will need to review many properties before you find the right one.

Trap: Starting to buy and sell properties right away. Investing in real estate is tricky because it requires you to be an expert in many areas—finding properties…valuing them…obtaining financing…overseeing repairs…handling tenants…following the law…keeping appropriate financial and tax records.

What to do: Learn the business—and keep your risk and capital expenditures low—by wholesaling or "flipping" properties as your first venture. For the best variety of listings, stick with single-family homes, at least at first. Look for motivated sellers—foreclosures, estate sales, couples going through a divorce and for-sale-by-owner offers.

Example: I found one of my very first deals when I saw a property for sale in Nashville. I estimated that it had a market value of $100,000. Because the seller was strapped for cash, I was able to convince him to put the house under contract to me for $92,000. I told the seller that I was an investor who might find another buyer immediately or keep the home myself. The contract language gave me 60 days to find a buyer for the house. I advertised it for $100,000 in the local newspaper and at my real estate association. Within a few weeks, I negotiated a deal with a buyer at my asking price and collected a profit of $8,000, less attorney's fees. I closed on both deals simultaneously.

If I had failed to find a buyer, I would have just backed out of the original contract with no liability due to the contingency clause. My only cost would have been the attorney's fees.

What to do: Have your real estate attorney prepare a document that allows the buyer to purchase your contract with the original seller. Your fee (the purchase rights) is the difference between what you offered the seller for the house and what the buyer was willing to pay. This is much easier than having to buy a property yourself and then immediately resell it.

Important: Wholesaling is common and legal in every state. Fully disclose (in writing) your intentions to both the buyer and the seller so you won't be accused of fraud.

Trap: Underestimating carrying costs. When you start buying investment real estate, limit your risk by conservatively estimating costs. The fact that the monthly rent you'll receive is more than your mortgage payment on the property doesn't necessarily mean you'll have positive cash flow as you wait for the property value to appreciate. It can easily cost an additional 50% a month for other expenses, known in the real estate trade as "TUMMI" (taxes, utilities, maintenance, management and insurance).

What to do…

• **Ask the current owner for copies of the property's tax records** going back three to five years so you can see his/her expenses. If costs were low, that could be a sign that the property was neglected. Talk to the tenants about how the building was maintained, and do a walk-through with your own inspector. As a rule of thumb, maintenance costs should average 10% of the annual rent.

Helpful resource: *www.goodmortgage. com* (click on the calculator, then "Investment/ Rental Property") provides a calculator that analyzes cash flow and expenses on potential rental property purchases.

• **Factor in vacancies.** Check with local real estate associations to figure out vacancy rates for your community.

• **Get two or three bids for repairs from licensed contractors.** Expect to spend 20% more than the highest bid.

Reason: Underestimating the cost of projects, especially in older homes with lots of hidden problems, is the top reason new real estate investors lose money.

Trap: Buying cute. Many first-time investors look for upscale, tasteful properties they would be happy to live in themselves. That's not necessary, and it might not even be helpful.

What to do: Make sure the numbers work. I always get my best deals and highest returns in low-to-moderate income areas on ugly-duckling properties with peeling paint, broken gutters and unkempt yards. Investing in less desirable areas also may allow you to qualify for government-subsidized loan programs. You can inquire about loan programs and special funding at your local bank and real estate association.

Example: I purchased a few buildings in a lower-middle-class neighborhood in Tennessee and got a $60,000 economic development grant from the US Department of Energy to insulate the buildings and install new doors and windows.

Trap: Spending too much on "cosmetics." Fix up the property appropriately for the market, not your taste. You don't need to install granite countertops and wool carpeting if comparable rentals in the area don't have them.

What to do: The most cost-effective improvements are a nice mailbox, brass outdoor lamps and attractive landscaping. First impressions are key—most renters and buyers make their decision within the first minute of seeing a property.

Trap: Relying on bank financing. The rate for a mortgage on investment real estate is at least half a percentage point higher than for a house you plan to live in. What's more, the minimum down payment is usually 25% instead of the 10% you generally need for a primary residence.

What to do: Ask the seller if he is willing to finance the mortgage himself. This often appeals to motivated sellers who want to close a deal quickly and not wait for you to qualify for a mortgage. A seller's attorney has you sign a promissory note agreeing to make mortgage payments directly to the seller. The property is the collateral. While the interest rate is comparable to a bank's rate, you usually can negotiate a much smaller down payment.

Trap: Paying too much. If you have to get into a bidding war to purchase a property, it is probably overpriced.

What to do: Restrict purchases to bargain properties to prevent costly mistakes.

Example: One of my early purchases was a three-bedroom house in Florida. A typical home in that area could fetch $95,000, but I got it for $18,000 because it needed a roof and other repairs. My contractor estimated that it would cost $20,000 to renovate it. I figured I would be able to start renting the house within eight weeks and get a positive cash flow of a few hundred dollars a month.

Reality: The repairs cost me more than I expected—a total of $30,000. I had no rental income and was shelling out $800 a month for taxes, mortgage payments, etc. Fortunately, I had bought the house for so little that I still ended up making a profit of $40,000 within six months, including the proceeds on the sale of the home.

The Latest Financial Rip-Offs

Michael J. Byrne, chief counsel of the Pennsylvania Securities Commission in Harrisburg, Pennsylvania and head of the Enforcement Trends Project at the North American Securities Administrators Association. NASAA. *www. nasaa.org.*

The boom in oil prices and equities is reviving the popularity of many shoddy investments. *Here, ones to be wary of now...*

SELF-DIRECTED IRAs

How they work: People who leave jobs and convert large employer-sponsored retirement accounts into IRAs are urged to set up "self-directed IRAs."

Self-directed IRAs are legal, but in the hands of scammers, they are used to divert funds from sound investments, such as mutual funds and bank CDs, into risky investments that might ultimately become worthless—such as fraudulent business ventures.

Self-defense: If you want to establish a self-directed IRA, work with an adviser who is familiar with the tax complexities. Make sure both the investment and the person selling it are registered with the SEC.

OIL AND GAS LIMITED PARTNERSHIPS

How they work: Deals are promoted over the Internet or by phone.

Common ploys: A new drilling technology has been invented that can recover millions of gallons of oil left in old lines...the company pitching the partnership is operating on leased property next to a large reputable oil firm.

You buy $2,000 to $50,000 worth of shares of a limited partnership that promises attractive tax advantages. Once you invest, poor returns are blamed on equipment malfunctions and inclement weather. In some cases, the investment is a total sham—there is *no* well.

Self-defense: While some partnerships are reputable and offer big tax breaks, shady ones pop up when energy prices soar. Oil and gas exploration is so expensive that it's unlikely a little-known enterprise will strike it rich.

Check the company with your state's securities regulator. For links to state regulators, contact the North American Securities Administrators Association (202-737-0900, *www.nasaa. org,* click on "Contact Your Regulator").

EQUITY-INDEXED CDs

How they work: These CDs are sold by banks. Returns are tied to the average performance of a market index, such as the S&P 500, over a period of time, typically five years. The principal is FDIC-insured up to $100,000.

However, the CDs don't pay interest until maturity and carry penalties for early withdrawal. In rising stock markets, you don't get 100% of the gain of the index. In falling markets, you won't lose money, but you won't earn a return.

Self-defense: Don't invest in an equity-indexed CD unless you are willing to tie up your money for several years. You can compare equity-indexed CDs at *www.personalyze. org,* a Web site by MCP Premium, a creator of software for financial professionals.

Buying High

Buying stocks at their 52-week highs has been a smart strategy historically. These stocks often have momentum that can move them still higher, according to a study published in *Journal of Finance*. In a separate study, the *Chicago Tribune* found that of 256 firms whose shares hit 52-week highs on the New York Stock Exchange in mid-January, more than half outperformed the S&P 500 through the end of the first quarter—and one-tenth rose by more than 15%. But choosing the right stock is crucial—some stocks at their highs are poised to fall, while ones with rising earnings that exceed analysts' forecasts and strong cash flow could go still higher.

Self-defense: Look for stocks with price-to-earnings ratios (P/Es) under 15, which indicate a bargain.

Chicago Tribune.

Don't Over-Invest in Stocks with High Yields

These typically are in three sectors—financial, utilities and energy. If these are your main holdings, you will not be adequately diversified.

Strategy: Review individual securities and mutual fund holdings at least once a year. To determine sector breakdowns, you can type in the ticker symbols for free at Morningstar.com and click on the "Portfolio" tab and the "X-ray" view. If you discover that you have more than 20% in a particular industry, reallocate your portfolio.

Alternative: PowerShares Dividend Achievers Portfolio (PFM), an ETF that holds more than 300 stocks and currently yields 3.18%,* is diversified among industry groups.

Tom Lydon, president, Global Trends Investments, Newport Beach, California, and proprietor of *www.etftrends.com,* which provides news and analysis on exchange-traded funds.

*Yield is subject to change.

Bond Traps

Avoid government agency bonds that feature rising interest rates. "Step-up" bonds have coupon (interest) rates that increase at predetermined dates.

Trap: These bonds allow the issuer to call the bond back at par (the original face value) on each step-up date. If the potential future coupon rates sound too good to be true, they probably are. Interest rates are unlikely to keep rising at the current pace. If interest rates fall or stay the same, the bond will be called, so you'll never collect what you had hoped for.

Also: When you reinvest the proceeds, it likely will be at a lower interest rate. Ask your broker for comparative yields before buying step-up bonds, or check financial newspapers for yields.

Marilyn Cohen, president and chief executive officer, Envision Capital Management, Inc., Los Angeles, and author of *The Bond Bible.* Prentice Hall. *www.envisioncap.com.*

The Low-Cost, High-Return Portfolio

Jill Schlesinger, CFP, executive vice president and chief investment officer of StrategicPoint Investment Advisors, Providence, an affiliate of Focus Financial Partners that manages $550 million for clients. She cohosts the weekly radio show *Making Money* on Saturdays on stations throughout New England. *www.strategicpoint.com.*

Most investors know that index funds offer a low-cost, tax-efficient way to invest. These costs can be even lower if you use exchange-traded index funds (ETFs).

The variety of ETFs, which trade on exchanges just like stocks, is now increasing. You can buy ETFs specializing in gold, micro-cap and Chinese stocks. Altogether more than 900 choices are on the market, enough to build entire portfolios. *Here, the case for investing in ETFs, plus model portfolios...*

ADVANTAGES

●**Low costs.** ETFs, like index mutual funds, can keep costs down because they typically track market benchmarks. Actively managed mutual funds, in contrast, spend heavily on stock research.

In addition, mutual funds service thousands or even millions of clients, maintaining individual accounts and sending out statements. ETF issuers have little contact with shareholders.

Sample cost: For investors who simply want to track the Standard & Poor's 500 stock index, iShares S&P 500 Index Fund (IVV) comes with a rock-bottom annual expense ratio of 0.09%. That is less than even the lowest-cost index mutual fund. In comparison, the average domestic stock fund has annual expenses of 1.48%, according to mutual fund research firm Morningstar, Inc.

Caution: To buy an ETF, you must pay a brokerage commission. If you're investing a lump sum for several years, this isn't a problem, but commissions can be expensive for investors who dollar cost average, buying only small amounts each month. These investors are better off with index mutual funds.

● **Tax efficiency.** Actively managed mutual funds typically buy and sell frequently, generating hefty capital gains tax bills for shareholders. Taxes on these "phantom gains" must be paid even if you hold on to your mutual fund shares. As in index mutual funds, stocks in ETFs are not actively traded, so they rarely generate any taxable capital gains. You don't pay taxes until you sell your shares.

● **Clean record.** Throughout the after-hours trading scandals that troubled mutual funds in 2003, ETFs maintained their reputations. After-hours trading is not possible with ETFs, because ETF shares trade 24 hours a day in markets around the world. Prices change constantly, so speculators have no way to obtain guaranteed profits.

● **Trading flexibility.** Because ETFs are traded throughout the day, the investor is in the driver's seat. To make sure that you don't pay more than you want for shares, you can use limit orders (as you can for stocks). You simply tell a broker the price that you want to pay.

Example: Say shares of an ETF are trading at $10.50. You tell the broker that you are willing to pay $10. Then any time the price dips down to that level, your order will go through. In contrast, mutual fund investors must buy at the day's closing price.

CREATING A PORTFOLIO

You can build a low-cost ETF portfolio regardless of your risk appetite.

● **Balanced-growth investors** might consider an allocation of 54% equities, 28% bonds, 13% cash and 5% commodities.

● **Conservative investors** should allocate more money to bonds and cash and avoid riskier asset classes, such as commodities and emerging-market stocks.

● **Aggressive investors** should shift more of their money into stocks and/or commodities.

Helpful: Morningstar (*www.morningstar. com*) has begun rating ETFs.

Other Web sites with ETF information: *www.etfconnect.com…www.amex.com.*

Load Fund Savings

If you invest in load funds, choose the lowest-cost share class using the Financial Industry Regulatory Authority's enhanced "Mutual Fund Expense Analyzer" and "Mutual Fund Breakpoint Search Tool" at *www.finra.org.* Expense Analyzer calculates sales charges, operating expenses and other information for particular share classes. The Breakpoint Search Tool shows at what investment levels your sales charges drop. Both tools are free.

Mary Schapiro, CEO, FINRA, Washington, DC.

The Real Way to Look at Funds

Avoid the mistake that many small-cap fund investors are making right now, thinking that their fund managers are brilliant because they're beating the S&P 500. The S&P 500 is a "weighted" index dominated by the very largest companies, so it is a poor benchmark for funds that invest in small- and mid-cap firms.

Better: Gauge the performance of small-company funds against indexes such as the S&P SmallCap 600, Dow Jones Wilshire Small-Cap 1750 or the Morningstar Indexes for different investment styles.

Russel Kinnel, director of mutual fund research, Morningstar, Inc., Chicago. He edits *Morningstar FundInvestor*.

Smart Ways to Invest in Bonds

Marilyn Cohen, president and chief executive officer, Envision Capital Management, Inc., Los Angeles, and author of *The Bond Bible*. Prentice Hall. *www.envisioncap.com*.

Among my clients, especially those who are older and more affluent, there are some who own no investments other than dividend-paying, blue chip stocks. These clients are doing fine without ever having bought a bond in their lives. That's fine, if you can handle the market's ups and downs. But most baby boomers are not invested like that. They want more profit and greater opportunity than boring blue chips can provide. So they take more risk.

Example: Lots of regular investors were hammered by the tech-wreck stock market bust of 2000–2002. But what happened in 2003? The minute the market improved, these investors went right back into stocks, and many are again being whipsawed by the volatility of the markets today.

Recently, there's been some move by investors to reduce risk exposure, but for those who are nearing retirement or already in retirement, my sense is that many people's nest eggs are still much too exposed to volatile stocks.

FIXED INCOME AS A RUDDER

Bonds are a kind of rudder to one's investment ship. Fixed-income investments reduce the volatility of your overall portfolio and keep the ship on course.

If you're not incredibly wealthy, the older you are, the more fixed-income investments

you ought to have as a force for stability. This is especially true if you can't count on secure pension or annuity payments in retirement. I would say that retirees and near retirees with between $200,000 and $2 million in retirement accounts are most in need of the stability that fixed-income investments provide.

Guideline: If you're over 50, stop dreaming about making a big killing in the stock market, plant your feet on the ground and plan for the actual cash income you will need to live on in retirement. If you're age 55, for example, rearrange your holdings so that about 55% of your total portfolio is in fixed-income investments. There isn't a direct correlation between your age and the amount of bonds you hold. Much depends on your asset base and other factors. But most retirees will want to have at least 50% to 65% in fixed income.

But, as we're all living longer, that means you need an equity growth component to your portfolio. So, no matter what your age, you will never want 100% bonds.

HOW THE BOND MARKET WORKS

Unlike the stock market, the bond market actually works on a class system—the more money you have to invest, the better price and yield you can command. Trading is dominated by giant pension funds, mutual funds and other institutional investors with whom you, the small investor, can't compete.

Strategy: You don't have to be a millionaire to buy individual bonds of corporations or municipalities, but you need upwards of $100,000 to invest. Anything less, and you are probably better off buying into a mutual fund or an exchange-traded fund (ETF). The problem with bond mutual funds is that they don't have a maturity date as individual bonds do. If you have to sell shares when bond prices are down in the market, you could lose some of the principal you originally invested. Still, the stabilizing effect of bonds outweighs such problems.

Caution: Even if you have the wherewithal and the help of a professional adviser and you want to buy some individual corporate bonds right now, I would warn, do so at your peril. It's probably OK to invest in the very highest credit quality companies, such as General Electric or Johnson & Johnson, but far too many companies today are issuing bonds for purposes that are extremely deleterious to bondholders, such as mergers and acquisitions, stock buybacks, excessive compensation to top executives, etc.

Don't be intimidated shopping for bonds, but, at the same time, never let yourself be talked into buying a bond whose structure you don't fully understand. Stick with investments that can be easily described.

FIXED-INCOME CHOICES

Starting with your bank, you can buy certificates of deposit (CDs) of various maturities. As a general rule, the further out in time you're willing to go, the higher interest you'll earn. Right now, however, since interest rates are rising, it's best to keep maturities relatively short, such as nine to 12 months. Then, when the CD matures, you can probably reinvest the funds at a higher rate.

Next, there are riskless US Treasury bills, which are currently paying about 5¼% for six-month maturities. You can buy these from a bank, a broker or from the Treasury directly (800-722-2678, *www.treasurydirect.gov*). Buying direct is the best way to buy Treasuries because there is no charge (banks and brokers charge at least $25 to $50 per transaction).

MUNICIPAL BONDS

Investors in the 35% tax bracket will want to look at tax-free municipal bonds, especially if they live in a high-tax state such as California or New York. Start with bonds issued by the state in which you live because they should provide the best deal. All the major mutual fund com-

panies offer tax-exempt funds for various states. There are even a few national funds.

If you're buying individual bonds through a broker or a money manager, specify high-quality AA or AAA issues because the yield difference between investment grade and junk is not worth the risk. And stick with maturities of no more than five to 10 years. You also want to buy new issues, which you will get at the same price as big investors such as Fidelity. The secondary market in municipals is very difficult for individual investors to navigate because they never know if they're getting a fair price.

General obligation municipal bonds, backed by the state's full taxing power, are the safest, but those for essential purposes, such as water or sewer, are usually also good quality. Plan on holding muni bonds until maturity.

ETFs

ETFs are a category of index funds that are giving mutual funds a run for their money. Sponsoring companies create baskets of stocks or bonds tracking a specific index. Investors get a diversified portfolio at a reasonable cost (plus brokerage commission).

INFLATION PROTECTION

Recently, investors have enthusiastically embraced Treasury Inflation-Protected Securities (TIPS), in which the principal is adjusted for inflation every six months. The interest on these bonds is taxable when earned, that is, before the bond actually matures, so you pay taxes "as you go." You can purchase TIPS directly from the Treasury as individual bonds.

One of the attractions of ETFs is that they have very low expense ratios. But mutual funds are fighting back with equally low expenses.

14

Money Savers for Your Retirement

Stop Uncle Sam from Stealing Your Retirement Dollars

From the moment you make your first deposit in a traditional IRA or 401(k), you are building up a savings account *—for the IRS.*

Uncle Sam eventually gets a big chunk of your money. All withdrawals are taxable and at ordinary income tax rates of as high as 35%, not at the lower capital gains rate. If your retirement accounts and other assets grow to more than $3.5 million in 2009, your heirs will owe estate tax on traditional and Roth IRAs upon your death. *Five ways to protect your nest egg...*

USE ROTH IRAs

This is Uncle Sam's greatest gift to retirement savings. Yet six years after the Roth's debut, relatively few people have taken advantage of it. Roth IRAs give no up-front tax deduction, but your

money grows tax free. And, Roth IRA beneficiaries do not owe income tax on the distributions. A beneficiary can "stretch" the benefit, leaving the money to continue growing tax free over his/her life.

What to do...

● **If you're planning to open a new IRA, make it a Roth.** For a full contribution your adjusted gross income (AGI) must be less than $101,000 if single, or $159,000 on a joint return in 2008 ($105,000 if single, or $166,000 on a joint return in 2009).

● **Convert a traditional IRA to a Roth.** Until 2010, your AGI must not exceed $100,000, whether you are single or married filing jointly. You will have to pay tax on gains on the traditional IRA. Ask the financial institution that handles your IRA what your tax liability will be. If bear market losses have reduced the value of your IRA, you will owe less tax.

You can't roll over money from a 401(k) directly to a Roth. You must first roll it into a

Ed Slott, CPA, a nationally recognized IRA expert, 100 Merrick Rd., Rockville Centre, New York 11570. He is editor of *Ed Slott's IRA Advisor.* His Web site is *www.irahelp.com.*

traditional IRA and then convert that to a Roth. Ask your tax adviser for instructions on rollovers and conversions.

Loophole: Your AGI only has to fall below $100,000 for one year to qualify for conversion. If your income is a few thousand dollars more than $100,000, shift some income to the following year and/or sell stocks to take capital losses in taxable accounts. Losses also might put you in a lower bracket and reduce tax on the conversion.

Trap: Anyone who is married but files a separate return cannot convert a traditional IRA to a Roth regardless of income.

HELP FUTURE GENERATIONS DODGE TAXES

When your 401(k) or IRA assets pass to heirs, they in turn can stretch the tax shelter over their lives. *Examples...*

Example 1: A husband leaves an IRA to his wife. She names their children as her beneficiaries. After her death, her children can then get tax-free compounding on the amount that's remaining. In this manner, tax deferral could go on for generations.

Example 2: Your daughter is 40 when she inherits your traditional IRA. According to IRS tables, a 40-year-old has a life expectancy of another 43.6 years, but she must begin taking required minimum distributions (RMDs) in the year after the year of the IRA owner's death.

WATCH OUT FOR WITHDRAWAL PENALTIES

Uncle Sam's 10% early withdrawal penalty applies to both Roth and traditional IRA withdrawals made before age 59½.

There is a 50% penalty when you neglect to take RMDs on traditional IRAs. If your RMD is $20,000 and you miss the deadline, your penalty is $10,000. *What to do...*

●**Traditional IRAs.** Start taking RMDs by April 1 of the year after you turn 70½. The percentage you must withdraw each year is determined by the IRS from life expectancy tables. For more information, call 800-829-1040, or go to *www.irs.gov* or *www.irahelp.com.*

●**Roth IRAs.** There are no required distributions for Roth IRA owners.

Loophole: You can withdraw money without penalty from any IRA before age 59½ using one of three IRS formulas. But watch out—if you start spending your nest egg early, you might not have enough savings for retirement.

LET LIFE INSURANCE PAY YOUR TAXES

Employer-sponsored retirement plans, such as 401(k)s, and traditional and Roth IRAs count toward your estate, so purchase insurance to pay the estate tax. Estate tax in 2009 is as high as 45% for estates of more than $3.5 million. The income tax on distributions from traditional IRAs can be as high as 35%.

While the estate tax is supposed to vanish in 2010, it is scheduled to come back in 2011. Base your planning on the tax as it is today, affecting estates that are bigger than $3.5 million. If there is no estate tax, your heirs will get to keep the payout.

What to do: Assume that estate tax will be 50% of the value of assets—cars, homes, retirement plans, other investments, etc. Purchase enough life insurance to allow for this potential tax. At your death, insurance proceeds are free from income tax.

Important: Create a life insurance trust to own the policy so that the value is kept out of your estate. You can name beneficiaries—your spouse or children—as trustees. Make annual gifts to beneficiaries, which they should use to pay the insurance premiums. You will not owe any gift tax if the payments are no more than $13,000 per recipient in 2009 ($26,000 if given by a couple). For information, consult with an experienced trust attorney.

PROVIDE FOR BENEFICIARIES NOW

Whether you have a traditional or Roth IRA, you must name your beneficiary on a retirement plan beneficiary form, which takes legal precedence over your will.

If you don't take the right steps, a lengthy and expensive probate court process will determine who inherits your IRA.

Update beneficiary forms whenever there is a marriage or divorce, new child or grandchild or other change that would affect your beneficiary choice. Keep beneficiary forms filed with other important papers as well as with your attorney and tax adviser. Then they can be located readily by family members and the executor of your will upon your death.

Four Ways to Refeather Your Retirement Nest Egg

Jonathan Clements, former personal-finance columnist for *The Wall Street Journal*. Based in Metuchen, New Jersey, he is author of *You've Lost It, Now What? How to Beat the Bear Market and Still Retire on Time*. Portfolio.

Low interest rates and the long bear market have left many retirees strapped for cash. *Here are four strategies that can help bolster your finances...*

●**Work part-time.** If you work just part-time during retirement and earn $10,000 a year, it's like having an extra $200,000 in your retirement nest egg. Why? For every $100,000 in savings, you can expect to receive $5,000 per year in income. You also are giving your nest egg extra time to grow.

True, those extra earnings may make 50% to 85% of your Social Security retirement benefits taxable. Even after taxes, however, you still will have more money in your pocket.

●**Move to a less expensive home,** perhaps in a more affordable part of the country. You will slash property tax, homeowner's insurance and home-maintenance expenses, thus freeing up money for everyday expenses. Looking to relocate? Be sure to check out *www.bestplaces. net* or *www.retirementliving.com.*

Caution: Buying and selling homes is expensive. Purchase a place that you expect to live in for the rest of your life.

●**Consider a reverse mortgage.** This allows people age 62 or older who own their homes outright to tap into the equity without actually selling. Provided you don't move or sell your home, the mortgage doesn't have to be repaid until after your death, at which time the amount owed can't exceed your home's value.

You can receive the money as monthly income, a lump sum or a line of credit.

Get a free guide to reverse mortgages from AARP (888-687-2277, *www.aarp.org/revmort*).

●**Cut taxes.** Time withdrawals from retirement accounts and sales of taxable investments strategically. Attempt to generate just enough income each year to get to the top of the 15% federal income tax bracket, but no higher. That means income of $32,550 in 2008 ($33,950 in 2009) if you are single and $65,100 in 2008 ($67,900 in 2009) if you are married and filing jointly. These figures, which assume you take the standard deduction, will be slightly higher if you are age 65 or older or if you itemize your deductions.

Generate surplus taxable income now—for example, by selling stocks—if you expect to be in a higher tax bracket in the future. Legally required retirement-plan withdrawals at age 70 could nudge you up into the 25% income tax bracket and possibly higher.

Consumer Protection for Everyone 50+

The new Seniors section of the federal government's FirstGov.gov Web site at *www. usa.gov/Topics/Seniors.shtml* is a center for reliable information on consumer protection, health, retirement, taxes, travel, education, legal rights, etc., of special concern to persons age 50-plus.

FDA Consumer, 5600 Fishers Lane, Rockville, Maryland 20857.

Health Savings Accounts— Now Better for Companies ...For Employees, Too

As the cost of traditional health coverage escalates, more and more companies are turning to health savings accounts (HSAs) to help provide for employees' medical care. According to one report, 43% of large employers and 11% of small employers will be offering HSAs by then end of 2008. *Why there's so much interest...*

●**Low cost.** High-deductible health policies (HDHPs), which are the foundation of HSAs, are relatively cheap for companies to provide. Even when companies pay both the HDHP premiums and the HSA contributions (as explained below), it has been estimated that they can save up to 40% compared with traditional health coverage.

●**Low maintenance.** Employers are not responsible for investing HSA funds and administering the accounts. The accounts are also "portable"—account holders who leave an employer take the accounts with them, since the money in the account is theirs to keep.

●**Coverage for uninsured employees.** Employees who are otherwise uninsured are happy to get medical coverage they otherwise couldn't afford.

●**New law advantages.** The accounts are more attractive than before—more on this follows.

HOW THEY WORK

The company obtains a high-deductible health insurance policy from its insurer and pays some or all of the premiums. Then it sets up an HSA (an IRA-like savings account) for each employee with its bank or broker- age firm. The company and/or its employees each contribute to the HSA account for each employee on a tax-deductible basis.

Contributions are invested for the employee by the HSA custodian. The employee may also have the option to pick his/her own invest- ments, including certain mutual funds. Earn- ings on the contributions are tax deferred. Withdrawals to pay medical costs not covered by the insurance are fully tax free. Withdrawals for any other purpose are allowed, but subject to income tax and, if taken when the account holder is under age 65, a 10% penalty.

Meaning of HDHP: A high-deductible health policy is one with a deductible above the minimum fixed annually by the IRS. For 2009, the minimum deductible for self-only coverage is $1,150 ($2,300 for family coverage).

Maximum out-of-pocket expenses (including deductibles, copayments, and other amounts, but not premiums) can't be more than $5,950 for self-only coverage or $11,600 for family coverage.

Limitation: The account holder cannot be covered by any other health insurance policy, including Medicare. *Exceptions:* Dental and vision-care policies are permitted as are long- term-care policies, disability, per diem hospi- talization, insurance for a specific disease (e.g., cancer), and workers' compensation.

NEW CONTRIBUTION RULES

The *Tax Relief and Health Care Act of 2006,* which passed Congress in December 2006, makes a number of favorable changes to HSA rules.

Annual contributions: The maximum annual contribution to an HSA is limited to a dollar amount fixed by the IRS. For 2009, it is $3,000 for self-only coverage and $5,950 for family coverage. In the past, the annual con- tribution had to be prorated for the period of HDHP coverage for the year, so that if, say, coverage began on July 1, only half of the dol- lar limit could be contributed and deducted for the year. Now, proration is no longer required. Also, where previously the annual contribution could not exceed the policy deductible, this restriction no longer applies.

Note: Cost-of-living adjustments for the con- tribution limit will be based on the Consumer Price Index in March of each year, rather than in August.

Comparable contribution rules: In the past, the law required any employer who made HSA contributions to do so on a nondis- criminatory basis. Now, employers can make larger contributions for non-highly compen- sated employees (those who do not own 5% of the company or receive wages above an amount adjusted annually for inflation)—mean- ing that the companies can benefit rank-and- file employees without having to cover highly compensated employees.

NEW FUNDING OPTIONS

One of the criticisms of HSAs has been the difficulty for employees to come up with the money to cover deductibles and out-of-pocket costs and to make contributions. *To address this, the new law allows two types of tax-free rollovers...*

●**A rollover from an employer-sponsored flexible spending account (FSA)** or health reimbursement account (HRA). The rollover is limited to the lesser of the account balance on the date of transfer or on September 21, 2006, and must be made before January 1, 2012. A transfer may be advisable from an FSA when contributions for the year couldn't otherwise be used up and would be lost forever.

●**A rollover from an IRA, up to the HSA contribution limits for the year.** There is no deadline. Be aware that HSA eligibility must be maintained for 12 months or the IRA rollover becomes taxable.

Note: Each of these is a once-in-a-lifetime rollover opportunity. While they are not wise financial moves for everyone, they can be of some help in obtaining health coverage for certain people.

COMPANY PERSPECTIVE

A 2006 survey showed that 62% of companies covering HSAs made employer contributions.

Added break: The cost of the HDHP premiums as well as the HSA contributions when made by the employer are exempt from FICA, so companies save on payroll taxes.

Administration: Companies that want to adopt HSAs must implement payroll system changes to accommodate employee contributions.

Companies have no administrative responsibility to see when and how funds are being used in the accounts. It is up to the account holder to keep track of medical receipts proving that withdrawals are used for permissible purposes if the IRS questions the individual's return. So have the receipts handy.

INDIVIDUAL PERSPECTIVE

HSAs enable those without other employer-paid medical insurance to obtain more affordable health coverage.

Advantages...

●**For healthy individuals, HSAs help pay for health-care needs** and provide a way to save for future costs, including retirement. If funds are not used for medical expenses, they can be tapped penalty free after age 65 to provide retirement income.

●**Financial institutions are starting to offer a wider array of investment options for HSAs,** which will enable greater accumulations in these savings accounts.

Disadvantages...

●**Individuals must cover the substantial deductible each year** before insurance kicks in. This can mean serious depletion of the account.

●**Because the first dollars of medical care come out of pocket,** individuals may avoid or delay needed care. For example, traditional health policies usually provide well-baby care, something a person with an HDHP-HSA would have to pay for out of pocket.

MORE INFORMATION

For details on tax rules relating to HSAs, see IRS Publication 969, *Health Savings Accounts and Other Tax-Favored Medical Plans,* at *www.irs.gov.* To find HSA custodians, go to HSAinsider (*www.hsainsider.com*), eHealth (*www.ehealth.com*), and HSAfinder (*www.hsafinder.com*).

Avery E. Neumark, Esq., CPA, partner in charge of employee benefits and executive compensation at the accounting firm of Rosen Seymour Shapss Martin & Company LLP, 757 Third Ave., New York City 10017.

Protect Retirement Accounts from Medicaid

Protect all retirement accounts from Medicaid claims if you lack long-term-care insurance.

Most Americans still don't have such insurance. The uninsured who cannot afford long-term care can obtain it through Medicaid—but Medicaid will take their "available assets," which may include IRAs, 401(k)s and other retirement accounts, to recover the cost.

Key: The state rules will have a big impact on your planning.

Example: In some states, once an IRA's required annual distributions begin at age 70½, the IRA balance is no longer an available asset, and only a portion of each distribution can be diverted to Medicaid. So converting a regular IRA to a Roth IRA—which has no required distributions—can be a costly mistake.

Consult with a local Medicaid expert to protect assets under your state's law.

Vincent Russo, Esq., Vincent J. Russo & Associates, PC, 1600 Stewart Ave., Westbury, New York 11590. His Web site is at *www.russoelderlaw.com.*

Free Legal Help for AARP Members

Lawyers in AARP's* Legal Services Network (LSN) offer a free initial consultation, during which many concerns of people over age 50 can be handled. For more extensive work, lawyers accept special rates negotiated by AARP.

Examples: $75** for a simple will...$35 for a financial power of attorney.

Information: 888-687-2277 for a free list of participating attorneys...search in the *Yellow Pages* under "Attorneys" or "Lawyers" and then under the heading "AARP-Legal Services Network"...or search on the Web at *www.aarp. org/families/legal_issues*.

Jim Miller, editor of "Savvy Senior," a syndicated newspaper question-and-answer column for senior citizens, Norman, Oklahoma, *www.savvysenior.org*. He is also author of the book *Savvy Senior*. Hyperion.

Your 401(k) May No Longer Be a Great Investment

Contributions to 401(k) accounts and other employer retirement plans are no longer the automatic good deal that they almost always were in the past—so consider the contribution levels you will set for 2009 carefully.

Snag: If you save for retirement through stocks and equity mutual funds, employer plans now can increase the tax you owe on them, since plan payouts are taxed at ordinary income rates instead of at the low tax-favored rates (15% top) for dividends and capital gains. On the other hand, employer plan accounts are still good for interest-paying investments, and they foster regular saving.

Better way: Take advantage of a Roth 401(k) option, if available. This option lets after-tax

*Formerly known as the American Association of Retired Persons.

**All prices are subject to change.

contributions and the earnings on them grow to become fully tax free.

Randy Bruce Blaustein, Esq., senior tax partner, R.B. Blaustein & Co., 155 E. 31 St., New York City 10016.

Good Gift for a Child—a Roth IRA

Seymour Goldberg, Esq., CPA, Goldberg & Goldberg, PC, 100 Jericho Quadrangle, Jericho, New York 11753, *www.goldbergira.com*. One of the country's foremost authorities on IRA distributions, Mr. Goldberg is author of *Practical Application of the Retirement Distribution Rules* (IRG Publications), available at *www.goldbergreports.com*.

The best gift you can make to a child or grandchild may be the funds to finance annual contributions to a Roth IRA.

Many minors earn income from summer jobs, after-school work, work done for a family business, etc. These children are eligible to make Roth IRA contributions of up to 100% of their earned income, subject to the limits outlined below. If they don't have the money to do so, you can give it to them.

Big payoff: Distributions from Roth IRAs can be totally tax free, unlike those from traditional IRAs and other kinds of retirement plans. And due to the power of compound earnings over the many future years of a young child's life, the final tax-free payout may be huge.

Example: Roth IRA contribution limits are $5,000 in 2008 and 2009. Starting this year, a child age 15 makes these maximum contributions for seven years, through age 21. If the average return in the IRA is 7%—the long-term average after inflation for stocks—then at age 21, the child will have approximately $42,000 in the IRA.

Without investing another dollar, the IRA will grow to more than $750,000 by the time the child reaches age 65—all tax free, making it worth much more than the same amount of money in any other kind of retirement account.

At age 21, the child will have accumulated some future retirement security without having to save any more for retirement during his/her working life.

297

Even better: Roth contributions can be withdrawn any time tax free. Earnings withdrawals are subject to other restrictions. So during the child's life, he will have access to the funds you provided, tax free.

Make Retirement Wealth Last Longer

The order in which funds are withdrawn from different investment accounts affects how long your wealth will last. It's generally best to take funds from taxable accounts before taking them from tax-favored retirement accounts, such as IRAs and 401(k)s. *Why...*

●**Amounts in tax-favored accounts compound before taxes,** so they grow faster, and it's best to maximize such growth.

●**Smaller amounts taken from taxable accounts may be enough to meet your needs.**

Withdrawals from regular IRAs and 401(k)s are taxed as ordinary income at top rates. But capital gains are taxed at no more than 15%, and investments that haven't gained can be withdrawn tax free.

Bob Carlson, editor, *Bob Carlson's Retirement Watch*, Box 970, Oxon Hill, Maryland 20750.

Your Social Security Protection

Stephen Richardson, regional public affairs specialist, Social Security Administration, Boston.

If someone steals your Social Security number and opens fraudulent credit card accounts, they can't also steal your Social Security retirement or disability income.

There are many defenses in place to make sure your Social Security benefits go to you—and only you. Many have been strengthened since the September 11 terrorist attacks.

Anyone trying to switch your Social Security payment to a new address or to direct deposit at a bank would be asked for extensive documentation. In the case of direct deposit, the individual also would have to establish his/her identity to an official at the bank.

When you apply for benefits, you have to provide more than your Social Security number. You have to prove your identity and eligibility through such documents as a birth certificate, marriage or divorce record, driver's license and employment records.

More information: SSA Publication No. 05-10002, *Your Number and Card*, available from the Social Security Administration (800-772-1213, *www.socialsecurity.gov/pubs/10002.html*).

The 10 Best Places To Retire in America

Kenneth A. Stern, CFP, author of *50 Fabulous Places to Retire in America.* Career Press.

Your choice of where to live may be the *most important* decision you make affecting your future quality and cost of life. You can't start researching too soon.

Here's what to look for...and some of the best locations in America to consider.

WHAT TO SEEK...

What to consider in a retirement community...

●**Cost of living.** Regional differences in cost of living within the US are a lot *bigger* than many people realize.

Moving from an area with a high cost of living, such as New York or San Diego, to an area with a below-average cost of living may increase your money's purchasing power by 30% or more.

●**Taxes.** By moving from a high-tax state to a low-tax state, you can further increase your spendable income. But be sure to consider more than just income taxes. *Also consider...*

●Sales taxes. If high, they may offset the benefit of a low income tax.

•Tax treatment of capital gains, dividends and interest. If you plan to live on investment income, these taxes may be more important than income taxes.

•Property taxes. They should be a factor in any decision to buy or rent in a new community.

•Inheritance taxes. Ask yourself, *Will the move enhance or compromise my ability to leave assets to my heirs?*

•**Climate.** You'll want to move to an area with a climate you enjoy. But don't judge climate just from what you experience during a vacation-season trip. Check out the off-season climate too.

•**Recreation.** It's important to look for an area with a *wide* range of opportunities.

Be wary of moving to an area to take advantage of just one activity that it offers—you may grow tired of it or become unable to enjoy it.

Example: You move to an area that offers fabulous golf, then hurt your back so you can't play. Are there *other* activities you'll be able to enjoy?

•**Education and work.** These should be a consideration if you want to continue your education or start a new career.

•**Transportation.** You may want to "get away" when you retire—but do you want to get *so far away* that you can't easily visit family and friends, or have them visit you?

•**Health support and services.** Health care will become more important as the years pass, so investigate carefully.

10 CANDIDATES...

Summing up all the traits listed above, here are my top ten places to retire to in the US...

•**Asheville, North Carolina.** Offers sophisticated city living with a million-acre wilderness at your doorstep. Has remarkable cultural resources and small-town friendliness.

Drawbacks: Hot days during summer. Tight rental market—plan visits well in advance.

•**Clayton, Georgia.** Located on the edge of the Blue Ridge mountains, it has superb outdoor recreational opportunities. Four mild seasons and a small-town atmosphere with no hustle and bustle. Low crime.

Drawbacks: Small-town limitations on shopping and cultural opportunities.

•**Columbia, Missouri.** The best area for health care—there are more doctors per capita here than anywhere else in the US except Rochester, Minnesota (home of the Mayo Clinic). Ample cultural, educational and outdoor resources in a rural setting. Excellent overall services.

Drawback: Difficult area to reach by air.

•**Eugene, Oregon.** Located 110 miles from Portland, it's an hour from the Pacific coast to the west and the Cascade Mountains to the east. Skiing, rafting, hiking and fishing, plus the educational resources of local colleges. Laid-back lifestyle.

Drawbacks: Rains more than some might like. Air quality sometimes poor. Above average living costs.

•**Fayetteville, Arkansas.** Fantastic trout fishing and outdoor recreation on the edge of the Ozark Mountains. There are also many cultural and educational opportunities, as it is the home of the University of Arkansas.

Drawback: Property costs, while still low, are rising as big companies move into the area.

•**Fort Collins, Colorado.** The friendliest of cities, planned so you can walk rather than drive to residential, shopping and recreational areas. Hiking, biking, mountain climbing and skiing. Home of Colorado State University and a plethora of cultural events. Dry air year-round, 300 days of sunshine with little rain—but 56 inches of snow in winter.

Drawback: Local doctors are reluctant to accept Medicare without supplemental private health insurance.

•**Ocala, Florida.** This is one of four places in the world where thoroughbred race horses are raised. Beautiful rolling terrain with more than 200 spring-fed lakes and rivers, and 430,000 acres of national forests nearby. Mild climate. Low property costs. Charming Victorian architecture. Orlando is nearby—great for entertaining visiting grandchildren.

Drawbacks: Very high amount of nonviolent crime—such as larceny, gasoline drive-offs and bicycle theft. No public transportation. Limited shopping. Many tourists.

●**Prescott, Arizona.** Four mild seasons, seemingly always sunny. On the edge of the world's largest stand of ponderosa pines. Excellent golf, tennis and retirement amenities... many seniors enrolled in the local college.

Drawback: The 5,000-foot elevation may be hard on some.

●**Sarasota, Florida.** Sophisticated community with gourmet dining, symphony, ballet and many other cultural resources. Excellent beaches and parks. Low humidity for Florida. A big-city feel for a small community.

Drawbacks: The summer season is hot, tourists flock in during the winter and the cost of living is average for the ·nation but high for Florida.

●**Savannah, Georgia.** Beautiful, historic city with great food, excellent medical care. Seniors can attend college free.

Drawback: Summers are hot and humid.

Get a Free Loan From Uncle Sam

Start taking reduced Social Security benefits at age 62 and still get full benefits when you reach normal retirement age, by which time you will have to repay the money.

How: Simply withdraw your application for early benefits at least 60 days before you reach full retirement age...pay back the accrued benefits...and refile for full benefits.

Downside: This strategy can affect taxes and Medicare benefits—consult a financial adviser. Also you might not have the money to pay back.

Also: If the recipient dies before repaying the money, the surviving spouse collects reduced benefits.

Karyl Richson, spokesperson for the Social Security Administration, Baltimore, *www.ssa.gov.*

How to Live in Luxury After You Retire

Mary Hunt, editor of *Debt-Proof Living,* Box 2135, Paramount, California 90723, *www.debtproofliving.com.*

Most retirement planning focuses on the amount of annual income required to maintain your current lifestyle, but many retirees want to spend more, indulging in luxuries—particularly, frequent vacations.

To balance those ambitions with the realities of a fixed income, trim expenses before you retire. *Here's how...*

●**Stop your budget leaks.** It's easy to waste money when you feel richer. Preretirees often have ample disposable income since their kids are out of school and on their own. The most significant leakage comes from eating out, gifts to adult children (money to start a business, a down payment on a house or car, etc.), entertainment and charities.

Smart: Once you've covered essential expenses for the month—including putting at least 10% of income in savings—limit nonessential spending to half the remaining amount.

●**Pay off your house.** Having a mortgage in retirement eats up much of your monthly income...and there's little tax benefit near the end of a fixed-rate mortgage, when most of your payments go toward the principal rather than tax-deductible interest.

Smart: Divide your mortgage balance by the number of months until retirement. Then add that amount to your monthly mortgage payment. If you can't afford to do this, consider selling the house and downsizing.

●**Restructure other debt.**

Example: Pay off high-interest credit card debt with a low-rate home-equity loan. Negotiating terms is easier when you are employed rather than when you are retired and living largely off of savings.

●**Sell your second car.** This is a huge money saver if your lifestyle allows it.

Example: Mary and her husband work in the same office, so after 35 years of being a two-car family, they cut back to one car. Initial savings totaled $800 a month—$9,600 per year—on car payments, fuel, insurance, repairs, etc. They also save at least $100 a month from a secondary effect—they make far fewer unnecessary trips to stores just because of the limitations of sharing a car.

You're never too young to plan for retirement. Don't wait to save.

Little-Known Retirement Plan Loophole

Dallas L. Salisbury, president/CEO, Employee Benefit Research Institute (EBRI), a nonprofit organization focused on employee benefits, Washington, DC, *www.ebri.org.*

Employees of schools and nonprofit organizations can transfer from an employer's 403(b) retirement plan—similar to a 401(k)—to a self-directed 403(b) plan tax-free under an obscure IRS ruling (Revenue Ruling 90-24). Many employer 403(b) plans offer limited investment choices (usually fixed or variable annuities), high fees and mediocre performance. In 1990, the IRS ruled that the transfer of all or part of a 403(b) to a self-directed 403(b) would not be treated as a taxable distribution even for those under age 59½.

Important: Check plan documents to see if transfers while you are employed are permitted—the fact that the IRS allows this doesn't mean that your plan will. If you can make the transfer, set up a self-directed 403(b) plan at a brokerage firm and have your money transferred directly to it to avoid paying tax on the transfer.

Warning: If your account holds annuities, wait until surrender charges—typically for cashing out before a five- to seven-year period—have expired before transferring money. Ongoing contributions still will be made to your employer's 403(b) plan, so you'll need to transfer additional assets periodically, subject to plan rules.

Best Ways to Live Off Your Retirement Savings

Ted Saneholtz, CPA/PFS, CFP, ChFC, president, Summit Financial Strategies, 110 Northwoods Blvd., Columbus, Ohio 43235. He has been listed among America's top financial advisers by *Medical Economics, Bloomberg Wealth Manager* and *Worth* magazines.

As people live longer, their retirement can last 30, 40, even 50 years. *Two main requirements for a secure retirement...*

●**Your retirement fund must be tapped regularly** to support a comfortable lifestyle.

●**If you withdraw too much too soon, you and/or your spouse might run low** on spending money.

How to withdraw from your retirement fund each year without running out of money one day in the future...

FINDING THE MAGIC NUMBER

Withdraw a reasonable amount the first year of retirement. Then increase your withdrawal each year to keep pace with inflation.

Example: You take $50,000 from your IRA the first full year of retirement. If inflation is 4% that year, you increase your withdrawal by 4% the next year, to $52,000, and so on, each year. This will maintain your purchasing power. The challenge is to arrive at a "reasonable amount" for the Year One withdrawal. If too large, your retirement fund will be depleted quickly.

Much research has gone into determining a prudent Year One withdrawal.

Bottom line: Drawing down your retirement fund by about 5% in Year One is a feasible plan for many retirees.

You'll be on safer ground with a 4% withdrawal. Beware—starting out at the 6% level will just increase the risk that you will outlive your money.

If you have other retirement resources (such as a pension or a second home that you can sell), you might consider taking on more risk, within the range of 4% to 6%, with a higher initial payout.

PICKING THE RIGHT POCKET

Deciding how much to withdraw is only the first step.

Next: Decide which account to tap.

Example: Should your $50,000 per year come from a tax-deferred plan, such as an IRA, or from money held in a taxable account?

Often, drawing down the taxable account first—until it's depleted—makes sense.

Reason: Keeping money in your IRA permits a longer period of tax deferral. Also, you'll pay a 10% penalty if you take money from your IRA before age 59½. There are some exceptions to this penalty, such as disability. Check with your tax professional.

The situation changes after you reach age 70½. Then you're *required* to take minimum distributions from your IRA. You'll face a penalty of 50% of the money you should have taken out but didn't.

Calculating the minimum withdrawal can be complicated, so be sure to work with a knowledgeable adviser.

Strategy: At age 70½, plan your withdrawals around your required distributions.

Example: At age 72, you need to tap your retirement funds for $60,000. Your required IRA distribution for the year is $35,000. You might take $35,000 from your IRA, as required, and the other $25,000 from a taxable account.

Be aware that money coming from your IRA will be reduced by income tax, and adjust your spending plans accordingly.

Strategy: If you find yourself in a low tax bracket in any given year, convert a portion of your regular IRA to a Roth IRA. A Roth IRA can grow tax free during your lifetime and continue tax-free accumulation for your beneficiaries.

Trap: Delaying all IRA withdrawals until after age 70½ will increase your balance and your required distributions. This can push you into a higher tax bracket.

INCOME OR GAINS?

Another concern about converting a retirement fund to cash flow is working out the mechanics of tapping your portfolio.

With savings yields and stock dividends at low levels today, it's unlikely you can meet your cash flow needs from interest and dividends alone. You'll probably have to liquidate some securities or bank deposits. A "bucket to bucket" approach can provide discipline, helping to keep your cash flowing.

How it works: Maintain 12 to 18 months' worth of spending money in a cash reserve, such as a money market fund.

Example: You'd like to spend $60,000 over the next 12 months, in addition to what you will get from Social Security. Thus, keep $60,000 to $90,000 in a money market fund for ready access.

For bill paying, money can be transferred from this cash "bucket" to a checking account. Alternatively, you can arrange for regular transfers, simulating a paycheck deposit into your checking account.

Having an ample amount in a money market fund will enable you to respond to emergencies. You won't have to make hurried portfolio decisions during times of stress.

Next step: Gradually, your cash bucket will be drained. Each quarter, you must decide how to replenish it. *Options…*

● **Use current income.** Even in today's low-yield environment, you're bound to have some investment income from interest and dividends. If you want to withdraw, say, 5% of your portfolio this year, get halfway there by pulling out 2.5% worth of current yield.

Key: The investment income in your taxable account will be taxed anyway, so it might as well be moved to the cash bucket.

If you're withdrawing money from your IRA, it may make sense to tap its income, too. This will allow the stocks and bonds in your IRA to stay in place longer.

● **Rebalance your portfolio.** Cash in what's up rather than what's down.

Example: At this point in your life, you might want an asset allocation that's equally divided between stocks and bonds. Suppose, though, that recent market strength has pushed stocks up toward 60% of your portfolio. In this scenario, you would sell some stocks to raise cash and then head back toward your desired stock-bond split. On the other hand, if bonds have pulled ahead of stocks, you might sell bond fund shares or use the cash from maturing bonds.

Caution: Recognizing significant capital gains might lead to the taxation of additional Social Security benefits.

Strategy: Take gains every other year, thus subjecting Social Security benefits to taxation only in alternating years.

Example: If your modified adjusted gross income (MAGI) is normally less than $32,000 (or $25,000 for singles) except for the capital gains income you recognize each tax year as you create cash from your portfolio, then you would be better off recognizing your capital gains in every other tax year. Result: 85% of your Social Security benefits will be taxed in Year One and 0% in Year Two.

Recognizing half the gains in Year One and again in Year Two will cause 85% of your Social Security benefits to be taxed in both years!

● **Sell the losers.** If your portfolio doesn't need rebalancing, sell the securities on which you have paper losses in a taxable account. This provides immediate tax losses while deferring taxable gains.

● **Sell the bonds.** If neither rebalancing your portfolio nor harvesting tax losses is enough to refill your cash bucket, lighten up on the bonds. Hold on to stocks, which can be expected to do best over the long term.

No matter what, though, your investment portfolio should be managed to balance stocks, which can provide good returns, and bonds, which can lower your risk. Cash requirements are important but they should not push you into imprudent investment moves.

Keys to a Debt-Free Retirement

Jean Chatzky, the financial editor for *Today* on NBC and editor-at-large for *Money* magazine. She is also the author of *Pay It Down!* Portfolio. Her Internet site is *www. jeanchatzky.com.*

It's very easy for seniors to accumulate debt, but it's especially difficult for seniors to pay debt off.

Income usually falls in later years while preretirement spending habits linger. There are gifts to children and grandchildren. Grandparents may be asked to help with school bills or finance a child's new home or business—and it's hard to say *no.* Medical bills increase with age—unforeseen medical expenses are the leading cause of personal bankruptcies.

Even refinancing a mortgage at a lower rate, if you borrowed additional cash in the process, adds to your debt and risk.

But you can reduce debt...even eliminate it altogether. *How...*

● **Tally what you owe.** Sit down with your spouse or partner and look at how much you owe...and how much that debt is costing you.

It's easy to measure the cost of your debt when you're talking about a home or car loan. Payments and interest charges don't change from month to month.

It's harder to calculate credit card debt. For one thing, the outstanding balance and interest charges will fluctuate from month to month. Because you're only required to make a modest minimum payment each month, your credit card debt can seem less of a burden than it really is. Focus on the outstanding balance, not that minimum monthly payment.

You'll stay in debt for a very long time if you keep using credit cards and make only the minimum monthly payments. Set a goal to pay off all the debt within three years and make your monthly payments large enough to meet that goal. Every payment should cover that month's interest and enough principal to make a noticeable dent in your outstanding balance.

Important goal: Get your debt low enough so that your monthly payments are far less than your total monthly income. The more you have left after paying off debt, the more you have to invest so that you will be able to live better in later years.

● **Reduce debt by $10 a day.** Freeing up $10 a day to pay off debts is an attainable and effective goal—this will allow a family owing $8,000 (the average credit card debt) to get out of debt in three years.

Start by cutting the amount of your monthly payment that is wasted on interest. Lay all your credit cards on the table and list the annual percentage rate (APR) for each.

Gather all the preapproved offers for credit cards with lower interest rates that you have received recently. Then call your current card issuers and use those offers to bargain for lower rates. Card issuers reduce the interest rate more than half the time.

Next, look at all your spending to see where else you can trim.

Helpful: Create a "money map"—a list of everything you spend your money on. Track spending by writing these items down in a pocket notebook for a month or so. You can use software such as *Quicken* to track spending (*www.quicken.com*). My book also offers a guide to help you total up spending.

Realizing how much you spend on gourmet coffee, meals out and other everyday expenses can help you cut back.

Challenge: There are two areas where most people spend quite a bit more than they need to…

- Gifts. You'll be amazed at all the birthday, holiday and just-for-fun gifts you give children, grandchildren and other family members in a year's time. Your family would gladly settle for fewer and less costly gifts today if that minimizes the risk that they'll have to support you someday.

- Technology. High-speed Internet connections can cost twice as much as regular dial-up service. *Also:* Do you really need 200 cable channels and 2,000 minutes a month on your cell phone plan? Calculate how much you're paying for technology each month—and how much you would save with a slower Internet connection and cheaper TV and cell phone service.

- **Sell what you don't use—and apply the money to paying down debt.** You can sell anything from jewelry to books to extra china to old LP records, maybe even some nice furniture in the attic or basement, at a garage sale, consignment shop or on-line through eBay. If you don't know how to use eBay, do an Internet search under "eBay sales tools" to find products that will help you. Or there are specialists who will sell your things in return for a percentage of the proceeds—generally about 30%. You'll find them by doing a search for "eBay sales consultants."

Also: You may have really needed a second car when you were working and children still were living at home—but now, you might do fine with one car.

The hardest choice—but the one with the biggest savings potential—involves selling your home and using part of the proceeds to pay down debt. Parents rarely hang on to the old family home for themselves—they may keep it because they think that their kids will want it someday. In fact, kids almost never want to move back to Mom and Dad's house.

- **Institute safeguards.** Put some safeguards in place to keep from piling up more debt…

- Get rid of all but one low-rate credit card. Also, think about reducing the credit line.

- Use that card sparingly. When possible, use a debit card rather than the credit card. Each use of a debit card immediately reduces your bank balance. That limits spending to what you have in your account rather than the full amount of your credit limit.

- Get a debt buddy—a friend that you can call to consult with if you're on the verge of making a major purchase. Enlist other friends to help, too. If your inner circle knows what you are up to, they're less likely to invite you along for a day of shopping.

- **Get help when you're falling short.** See a credit counselor to set up a repayment plan. You'll be required to make a monthly payment to the counselor, who then will use the money to pay off your creditors. A debt-management program from a credit counselor can take four to five years to complete.

Don't file for bankruptcy unless an expert in the field concludes that it is the only way out for you, as it will affect your credit rating for years to come, and you could be forced to sell assets for whatever they'll bring to satisfy your creditors.

A good credit counselor will review all your finances and then determine if debt management will work for you. Only in the most dire of circumstances is he/she likely to recommend bankruptcy as the best solution to your debt problems.

Warning: Not every credit counselor is on the up-and-up. You want to work with an organization that is not-for-profit and is also a member of the Better Business Bureau (703-276-0100, *www.bbb.com*) as well as the National Foundation for Credit Counseling (800-388-2227, *www.nfcc.org*).

How to Calculate Your Retirement "Salary"

Expect to need a total of 10 times your final salary during retirement. Calculate what your salary will be at retirement...multiply that by 10...and make that your savings goal.

Breakdown: About seven times your projected final salary should be enough to pay for a lifetime annuity. When added to Social Security, the annuity will give you at least 100% of your final pay after you retire. The remaining three times your final salary can be used for investments and as a financial reserve for emergencies that come up.

David L. Wray, president, Profit Sharing/401(k) Council of America, Chicago, and the author of *Take Control with Your 401(k)*. Dearborn.

Wise Ways to Make Withdrawals from Retirement Accounts

Ed Slott, CPA, a nationally recognized IRA expert, 100 Merrick Rd., Rockville Centre, New York 11570. He is editor of *Ed Slott's IRA Advisor*. His Web site is *www.irahelp.com*.

If you participate in a 401(k) or another type of employer-sponsored retirement plan, you will have to decide what to do with your account when you leave the company. Many people roll the balance into an IRA.

Benefits: If this is done properly, not only do you maintain tax deferral, but you also control how your money will be invested.

However, an IRA rollover is not your only choice. *Other options...*

●**Take the cash.** If you do this, you'll owe income tax on the full amount right away.

●**Keep the money in your former employer's plan.** Many companies will permit you to do this.

●**Transfer money to a new employer's plan.** Even if you're not immediately eligible to participate, you can hold cash in the new plan until you can make other investments.

●**Crack your nest egg.** You can withdraw *some* of your retirement funds, pay tax on the withdrawal and then roll the balance into a tax-deferred IRA.

WHEN NOT TO ROLL OVER

Why choose one of these alternatives rather than a rollover into an IRA? *Possible reasons...*

●**You're in a cash crunch.** If you need to spend some or all of the money in your plan, you might as well withdraw it from the plan right away. That's especially true if you were born before 1936.

Loophole: People in that age group qualify for a special tax benefit. They can utilize tax-favored 10-year averaging if they take all of their money out of the plan. This could cut their taxes to a relatively low rate. (See instructions for IRS Form 4972, *Tax on Lump-Sum Distributions*.)

Trap: You don't get this tax break if you do an IRA rollover.

Key: Even if you can't utilize 10-year averaging, the current low income tax rates may make withdrawals appealing.

●**You need a helping hand.** If you don't want to manage your own retirement fund, you may prefer to leave the money with your former employer or transfer it to a new one. Inside an employer's plan, professionals may manage the investment options.

●**You want to extend tax-free growth.** Under the Tax Code, you can put off taking the required withdrawals from your company plan, even after you reach age 70½ as long as you're still working. With an IRA, you must start taking distributions after you reach age 70½.

Caveat: To postpone withdrawals beyond age 70½, you can't own more than 5% of the company that you still work for.

●**You need to keep creditors at bay.** Money in an employer-sponsored retirement plan is generally protected from creditors, judgments, divorce settlements, etc., under federal law.

Trap: Under the bankruptcy law, assets in qualified retirement plans and rollover IRAs are fully protected, but assets in traditional and Roth IRAs enjoy protection only up to $1 million.

●**You want to keep a borrowing option.** Many of the employer-sponsored plans, including 401(k)s, permit you to borrow half of your account balance, up to $50,000, even after you leave the company. This depends on your company's plan.

Plan loans may be easier to get than bank loans, with less paperwork. Also, repayments (plus interest) go to your retirement account rather than to a bank.

Problems with an IRA rollover: You can't borrow from an IRA. Furthermore, any outstanding 401(k) loans must be repaid before a rollover, reducing the amount you will have in your IRA.

Therefore, if you have outstanding loans, or think you might want to borrow in the future, keeping money in an employer's plan may be the best choice.

●**You hold appreciated employer stock** in your plan. An IRA rollover can cost you a substantial tax break.

Example: Your retirement plan account now includes $50,000 of your employer's stock, which was worth $10,000 when it was contributed to your account. If you roll over your entire account, that $50,000 eventually will be taxed at ordinary income rates, now as high as 35%, upon withdrawal.

A good strategy is to withdraw the employer shares while rolling your plan balance into an IRA. You will owe tax, but only on the value of the shares when contributed to the plan, not on their current value.

In this example, you will immediately be taxed on $10,000, but the $40,000 in net unrealized appreciation remains untaxed until your shares are sold. When you sell those shares, you will owe tax at a 15% capital gains rate, assuming current law remains in effect.

THE PENALTY BOX

Between ages 55 and 59½, you're better off keeping your money in the company plan, if

you expect to take distributions. If you need to tap your retirement plan, withdrawing money from an IRA before age 59½ may expose you to a 10% penalty.

Loophole: You can take money from your employer-sponsored plan, penalty free, if you were at least age 55 in the year you left your job.

LIFE INSURANCE

If your account in an employer-sponsored plan includes life insurance, you might want to keep your money in that plan to keep the policy in force.

Key: You may find it costly to continue your life insurance after you have left the company plan. If you are in poor health, you might not be able to buy needed coverage at a reasonable price.

WHEN IRAs ARE IDEAL

If none of the above reasons apply to you, you're probably better off with a rollover IRA. In some situations, IRAs are especially appealing.

Example: You're interested in a Roth IRA conversion. After five years and age 59½, all withdrawals from a Roth may be tax free.

Required: Only traditional IRAs may be converted to a Roth IRA. Therefore, you must first roll over a company plan distribution to an IRA, then convert the account into a Roth IRA.

Keep in mind that Roth IRA conversions are permitted only if your adjusted gross income in the year of the conversion is not more than $100,000. You'll owe tax on all the deferred income built up in the IRA when you convert an IRA to a Roth IRA.

Key: No matter what your reason, always ask for a "trustee-to-trustee transfer" when you execute an IRA rollover. Keep your hands off the money being rolled over.

Trap: If you handle the funds, you'll face mandatory 20% withholding on the rollover. You will have to make up the difference from your own pocket to avoid owing income tax.

When Can You Afford to Retire?

Jonathan D. Pond, president, Financial Planning Information, Inc., Newton, Massachusetts. He has hosted 16 prime-time TV specials for PBS, winning several awards, including one Emmy. He is author of *You Can Do It! The Boomer's Guide to a Great Retirement* and, most recently, *Grow Your Money! 101 Easy Tips to Plan, Save, and Invest* (both from Collins). *www.jonathanpond.com.*

Even though many Americans are working past age 65 to bolster their savings and investments or just to remain active, others are retiring early—either by choice or circumstance. The number of retirees is expected to mount now that baby boomers have started turning 62. But many are not prepared for the challenges or realistic about the financial considerations and assumptions that will determine how comfortable their retirement will be.

Critical factors you must consider to prepare for your retirement…

●**Life expectancy and portfolio performance.** Many retirees underestimate how long they will live and overestimate how much their investments will return annually. A Fidelity Research Institute study found that a 65-year-old man has as much chance of living to age 95 as dying before age 70.

What to do: To be financially safe, I tell my clients to expect to live to age 95—and to expect a 6% annualized return on investments, based on a mix of 60% stocks and 40% bonds and other interest-earning securities.

●**Inflation.** Based on historical inflation trends, people who retire at age 60 are likely to experience an 80% rise in living expenses by age 80. Those who retire at 65 will probably experience a 60% increase.

What to do: To calculate your income needs, figure inflation could average 3% annually. Then withdraw an annual amount in the early years of retirement—say, 4% of savings—that is enough to meet your income needs but is below the assumed growth rate of investments. That way you won't drain your assets too quickly.

●**Taxes.** Don't expect your tax bite to decline sharply in retirement—it probably won't. Keep in mind that you will pay income tax on withdrawals from traditional 401(k) accounts and IRAs.

What to do: Expect your taxes to drop by no more than 10%—and realize that they even may increase.

●**Expenses.** My retired clients find that each year, they spend 75% as much as they did in their final working years. Will your investments generate enough income to fund that spending?

What to do: Assume that you will spend at least that much, and shape a financial plan that provides enough income to support that spending.

Important: Don't leave out big-ticket expenses that still will pop up, including replacing your car, large-scale home repairs and dental work.

●**Health insurance.** Unless you get an early retirement package that extends your company's health insurance coverage until you become eligible for Medicare, you will need to factor in premiums for an individually purchased policy if you retire before age 65.

What to do: Consider obtaining temporary insurance through the stop-gap federal program COBRA…check with state programs…or look for private individual coverage with high deductibles to lower premiums.

●**Part-time work.** Finding satisfying work to supplement your income can be challenging, once you fall out of the loop in your life-long profession. And if you do find work, the extra income may mean reduced benefits from Social Security and/or higher income taxes.

What to do: I tell my clients who are considering retirement to assume that they won't find part-time work to bolster their income and to map a financial plan that doesn't count on extra income.

●**Retirement savings.** The longer you put off drawing on investment accounts—assuming that they gain value—the more income you will eventually be able to draw each year. And because of compounding, the longer you wait, the more this effect accelerates.

Examples: Assuming an annual rate of return of 6%, if you work an extra two years before starting withdrawals, you can increase the amount of income you draw annually by 10%...if you wait an extra three years, by 25%...and if you wait an extra five years, by 40%. This assumes that you would use up all of your money by age 92.

What to do: Put off retirement until your accounts are big enough to support your spending needs.

•**Social Security.** The earlier you start taking Social Security payments before you qualify for the full monthly base amount—which could be as late as age 67, depending on when you were born—the lower your monthly checks will be. They could be as much as 30% lower. Any future cost-of-living increases to Social Security checks also will be lower, because they will be calculated from a lower initial benefit amount.

What to do: Unless you really need the money or are in poor health, it's often better to delay starting benefits until you reach full retirement age.

•**Early retirement incentive package.** Your pension usually is based on the average of what you earned in the last few years of your employment. Even if your employer's early retirement incentive plan adds bonus years of employment and bonus years of age to your pension formula, it usually won't make up the difference between your average salary for your last five years and the presumably higher average salary you would have earned for your last five years if you had continued working.

What to do: Be careful not to overestimate the value of an early retirement package. You may want to consult a financial adviser for help analyzing the package.

RETIREMENT CALCULATOR

My favorite Web-based retirement calculator is free at *www.analyzenow.com.* What you will find: Free on-line information that helps you determine when to begin taking Social Security payments, how much to allocate to different investment categories, how much you need to save for retirement and how withdrawals from your retirement accounts will affect your taxes. It was created and is run by Henry K. Hebeler, a former chief economic forecaster for Boeing Company.

It May Not Pay to Work Past Age 65

The tax rate on working increases at older ages, approaching 50% for some people by age 70. Also, by age 65, people typically can receive nearly as much income and benefits in retirement as by working.

Barbara A. Butrica, PhD, senior research associate at Urban Institute, Washington, DC, and coauthor of a working paper on older workers for the Center for Retirement Research at Boston College, www.bc.edu/centers/crr.

A New Kind of Retirement Fund

Burton J. Greenwald, managing director of B.J. Greenwald Associates, Philadelphia, a financial services industry consultant specializing in strategies for mutual funds. He is former president of two major mutual fund groups and has served as a governor of the Investment Company Institute.

Several major investment companies have come up with a new way to help you plan a comfortable and enjoyable retirement.

The challenge: Figuring out how to draw cash from your investments in a way that prevents the money from running out too soon and without losing access to your principal.

One solution: A new type of mutual fund that is structured to automatically send you sizable checks regularly—typically every month. The companies have come up with a variety of names for this type of fund, including "income-replacement" and "managed-payout."

We asked mutual fund consultant Burton J. Greenwald to explain how these funds work, including their benefits and drawbacks…

HOW THEY WORK

The automatic payouts—currently ranging from an annual rate of 3% to more than 12%—are drawn from various combinations of sources. They include gains and dividends that the funds' investments generate and, in some cases, the investment principal.

The companies providing the new type of fund so far include the giants Charles Schwab & Co., Fidelity Investments, Russell Investments (a unit of Northwestern Mutual Life Insurance Co.) and Vanguard. Many others, including American Century, John Hancock, OppenheimerFunds and T. Rowe Price, are developing variations.

With some of the funds, including Fidelity's, your entire investment is depleted by a specified date. This allows the fund, which returns parts of your principal to you as a portion of the payouts, to maximize payouts until that date is reached. Other versions, including Vanguard's, seek to provide a sizable amount of annual income indefinitely without digging into your principal.

All of these new offerings are designed to be alternatives to fixed and variable annuities offered by insurance companies. Annuities provide a stream of regular income in exchange for a lump sum that you pay up-front.

PROS AND CONS

The new funds have some advantages over annuities, as well as some possible drawbacks.

Advantages of managed-payout funds…

They allow you to cash out, or add to, your investment at any time without penalty. Many annuities restrict your access to the principal.

When you die, you can pass on whatever assets remain to your heirs. That is not always true with an annuity.

The funds' annual fees and expenses (typically under 1%) tend to be much cheaper than for annuities, which often charge 2% or more.

There is potential for significant growth of your assets and/or your monthly payouts, depending on the fund's investment performance. That is not true for many annuities.

Drawbacks of managed-payout funds…

There are no guarantees that the monthly payouts will remain stable or that your investment will last. Annuities generally guarantee a minimum monthly payout.

Payouts that are not part of your original principal may trigger taxes, while sales of stocks by the fund may result in capital gains or losses that affect your tax bill. With annuities, nonretirement account payouts that are part of your original principal will not trigger income taxes, although other payouts will, and there are no capital gains or losses.

BEST STRATEGIES

Because income is not guaranteed, the new breed of managed-payout funds is best used as part of a larger strategy, in conjunction with some other types of investments, rather than as a way to invest all or even most of your nest egg. *Best possible uses…*

●**For discretionary spending.** Invest enough money in one of these funds to generate income that you expect to cover your annual discretionary spending in retirement, such as eating out and traveling. If the fund performs below your expectations, you can cut back on this discretionary spending. At the same time, you can use a traditional annuity—with its payouts guaranteed by the financial strength of the insurance company—to cover fixed expenses, such as housing and utilities costs.

●**Early in retirement.** By taking automatic payouts from one of these funds early in retirement, you can postpone tapping into other sources of retirement income, including Social Security benefits and tax-deferred investment accounts, such as IRAs. Monthly Social Security payments generally grow bigger the longer you wait (up to age 70) to start collecting them.

HOW TO CHOOSE THE RIGHT FUND

There are two approaches to managed-payout funds, typified by the following no-load (no sales commission) examples. *All offer monthly income…*

●**Fund Type 1: Asset depletion.** This works best for people who want monthly income over a specific period, such as those seeking to delay Social Security payments and those not concerned with passing assets to heirs. *Example...*

Fidelity Income Replacement Funds currently come in 14 versions. Each has a different maturity date from 2016 to 2042. In the final year, your investment is completely depleted. The shorter the time horizon, the higher the payouts for a given investment amount, because the assets are meant to be depleted more quickly. Current annual payouts range from 4.75% of your investment for the Fidelity Income Replacement 2042 Fund to 12.2% for the 2016 Fund.

Annual expenses: 0.54% to 0.67%, depending on which of the funds you choose.

Minimum investment: $25,000. 800-544-9797, *www.fidelity.com.*

●**Fund Type 2: Asset preservation.** *If you want to grow, or at least maintain, your original investment and possibly pass on the assets to heirs, consider...*

Vanguard Managed Payout Funds. You can select from three versions, each with a different annual payout target level. The funds are designed in a way that the assets are supposed to last, but the funds can dip into principal to provide payouts if performance falters, as it has this year. Annual payouts are currently 3% for the Growth Focus Fund (VPGFX)...5% for the Growth and Distribution Fund (VPGDX)...and 7% for the Distribution Focus Fund (VPDFX). The lower the payout target, the more growth the fund seeks for your investment by focusing more heavily on aggressive investments, such as stocks rather than bonds. The percentage payouts are adjusted each year, based on fund

performance over the previous three years (or shorter periods during the start-up phase), to minimize the impact of market volatility.

Annual expenses: 0.57% to 0.58%.

Minimum investment: $25,000. 800-523-7731, *www.vanguard.com.*

Funds similar to Vanguard's: Charles Schwab Monthly Income Funds come in three versions—moderate, which is paying 3% to 4% annually...enhanced, 4% to 5% annually...and maximum, 5% to 6% annually.

Expense ratio: 0.61% to 0.76%. Minimum investment: $100. 866-855-9102, *www.schwab.com.*

Trying to Find a Lost Pension?

Contact the Social Security Administration to get your earnings record. Your former employer's federal employer identification number (EIN) will be on record. Then use the EIN to search for the company at *www.freeerisa.com.* Also, check with the Pension Benefit Guaranty Corporation (*www.pbgc.gov*), the federal agency that insures corporate defined-benefit plans. Another place to check is the nonprofit Pension Rights Center at *www.pensionrights.org*, which helps employees and retirees understand and enforce their legal rights.

AARP Bulletin, 601 E St. NW, Washington, DC 20049.

15

Estate Planning Helpers

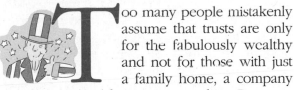

The Ultimate Tax-Free Estate Plan

Too many people mistakenly assume that trusts are only for the fabulously wealthy and not for those with just a family home, a company pension and a life insurance policy. But even these people can benefit substantially from trusts.

Reason: Trusts save thousands of dollars in gift and estate taxes and provide a way to manage assets when the original owners are no longer available. They also can protect assets from creditors and malpractice suits.

Trusts need to be set up properly if they are to be effective, so be sure to consult a knowledgeable attorney. Here are five basic types of trusts and what they can do for you.

1. LIFE INSURANCE TRUST

Let's say you own your home and have some modest investments, a pension and a

$500,000 life insurance policy. If your children are the beneficiaries of the insurance policy, your family could owe the government hundreds of thousands of dollars in additional estate taxes.

Reason: Life insurance proceeds, while not subject to federal income tax, are considered part of your taxable estate and are subject to federal estate tax—up to 45% in 2009.

Solution: Create an irrevocable life insurance trust which will own the policy and receive the cash payout upon the policy owner's death. *There are several benefits to doing this...*

●**Income for the beneficiaries.** The irrevocable life insurance trust can be structured so that your survivors receive some or all of the annual income generated by the trust. The survivors can even receive the principal—subject to certain restrictions.

Martin Shenkman, CPA and attorney who specializes in estate and tax planning and asset protection, Tenafly, New Jersey, and the author of more than 30 books, including *Inherit More: Protect Your Inheritance from Taxes, Creditors, Claimants, Medicaid and More.* Wiley. His Web site, at *www.laweasy.com,* offers free sample forms and documents.

311

●**Avoidance of estate taxes.** If it's properly structured, such a trust ensures that insurance proceeds escape taxation in your estate as well as the estate of your surviving spouse. In addition, because the proceeds are not included in your taxable estate or your spouse's taxable estate, they are not part of the public record and escape publicity. They also are not affected by probate costs.

●**Protection of assets.** The trust protects insurance proceeds from creditors and malpractice actions.

●**Reliable management.** By naming a family member and an outsider, such as a bank or accountant, to manage the trust assets, you eliminate the problem of relying on inexperienced or incapable beneficiaries to handle the trust's money.

2. CREDIT SHELTER TRUST

Even though the estate tax is repealed in 2010 no one can predict one's date of death. In the meantime, take advantage of tax-free exemption amounts.

The primary purpose of a credit shelter trust is to preserve the applicable estate-tax exemption that all individuals get in their estates.

Under the law, everyone can give away $13,000 to individuals in 2009, and a certain amount during his or her lifetime ($1 million), or upon death tax free ($3.5 million in 2009). Most couples own all of their property jointly and have wills in which the husband leaves everything to the wife and the wife leaves everything to the husband. This may not be the best arrangement.

Reason: Let's assume that a couple jointly owns an estate worth $7 million. When one of the spouses dies in 2009, there will be no estate tax because of the unlimited marital deduction. But when the second spouse dies a year later, the estate will owe nearly three quarters of a million or roughly one quarter of the estate in estate taxes.

Solution: When your joint estate exceeds twice the applicable exemption amount, divide all joint property equally between you and your spouse. For example, transform a joint brokerage account into two separate accounts with half the assets in each. Then create a credit shelter trust under each spouse's will. The trust will allow the estate of each spouse to escape tax by taking maximum advantage of the applicable exemption amount assuming there are sufficient assets to fund the trust.

Example: When the first spouse dies, the assets valued up to the applicable exemption amount go into a credit shelter trust for the benefit of the second spouse. (When the second spouse dies, those assets pass directly to the children or other heirs, with no estate tax.)

Whichever spouse survives can have the right to receive all the income produced by the trust. That spouse also has the right to take principal from the trust to maintain his or her standard of living. It's almost like having the assets in your own name.

Important: It's not enough to just create the trust. Retitle your joint property in separate names so that, upon your death, the property can be transferred to the trust in order for it to save your family additional estate taxes.

3. QTIP TRUST

A Qualified Terminable Interest Property (QTIP) trust defers taxes and helps families attain personal goals. Its aim is to ensure that, after a spouse's death, assets exceeding the applicable exemption amount pass first to the surviving spouse tax free and then to the individuals for whom they are ultimately intended.

Benefit: The trust is often used in second marriages to provide lifelong support for a current spouse. Then, after the second spouse's death, the QTIP funnels assets to the children from the first marriage.

Under this arrangement, your current spouse receives all of the income annually from the trust for life. Even though your spouse's interest in the trust property terminates upon death, the initial transfer of property to the trust still qualifies for the unlimited marital deduction.

4. CHILDREN'S TRUST

This trust is formulated to provide for your children and addresses a problem that occurs with gifts to children under the Uniform Gifts to Minors Act (UGMA) and Uniform Transfers to Minors Act (UTMA).

Problem: Under UGMA and UTMA, once children reach age 18 or 21 (depending on the state in which they reside), they can do whatever they wish with the money in their custodial accounts. If they want to use it to support a commune or buy a sports car instead of finishing college, there's nothing you can do about it.

Solution: By transferring assets to a children's trust, such as a Crummey trust, the trustee can determine how the money in the trust is to be used and how much the child can receive.

5. GRANDPARENTS' TRUST

This trust is similar to the children's trust, except that the grandparents establish it to help pay for their grandchildren's college expenses.

A separate trust can be created for each grandchild. There is a $13,000 per grandparent limit on the amount that can be placed gift-tax-free in each trust in 2009.

As with a children's trust, the trust document and the trustee define how much money can be used for which purposes.

Important: Avoid setting up a single trust that names more than one grandchild as a beneficiary. Otherwise, you will run into the expensive generation-skipping transfer (GST) tax, which, in many instances, applies to transfers of more than $3.5 million in 2009.

Note: There have been sweeping changes to the GST so consult a tax expert.

Don't Let Your Pension Die With You

Robert S. Keebler, CPA, MST, partner, Virchow, Krause & Co., LLP, 2201 E. Enterprise Ave., Appleton, Wisconsin 54913. Mr. Keebler is the author of *A CPA's Guide to Making the Most of the New IRA.* American Institute of CPAs.

Most pension plans will offer the participants two payment alternatives when they retire—either a monthly check or a lump-sum payout. The choice that you make depends on your need for retirement income...and your concerns for your heirs.

DILEMMA FOR SINGLES

The law requires the pension plan to offer married employees a "joint and survivor option" so that some monthly benefit will go to a participant's spouse subsequent to his or her death. But, a spouse can waive this right, allowing the participant to receive a larger monthly benefit or take a lump sum.

Unmarried participants have the same choice, either a monthly benefit or lump sum. But the joint and survivor option does *not* apply to unmarried employees.

On the death of an unmarried participant who has opted for monthly benefits, no further payments will be made to any of the participant's beneficiaries. The pension dies with the participant. This is the case no matter how much he has accumulated in the plan.

LUMP-SUM SOLUTION

Unmarried participants—and in many cases married participants—should opt for the lump-sum payout.

Why? Because a lump-sum payment can be rolled into an IRA. *Impact...*

●**The participant can still collect monthly benefits**—from the IRA. Basing monthly benefits on life expectancy and the rate of return on investments will ensure that the funds in the IRA last as long as the IRA owner lives.

●**Whatever remains in the IRA goes to his beneficiaries,** when the participant dies.

LUMP-SUM LIMITATIONS

Before opting for a lump sum in lieu of the monthly payments, consider the following...

●**Pension plans are insured** by the federal Pension Benefit Guaranty Corporation. Monthly payments, if you choose them, are guaranteed up to a set limit.

In contrast, IRAs are only as safe as the investments they are in. Stocks and bonds can decline in value, reducing funds available for retirement income as well as for an inheritance for heirs.

●**Pensions are professionally managed.** With IRAs, you're responsible for making the investment decisions.

Helpful: If you're intimidated by the thought of managing investments for a sizable account, think about retaining a professional money manager to handle your IRA.

● **Pensions are fully protected against the claims of creditors.** Rollover IRAs may receive similar protection, although bankruptcy protection for contributory IRAs (deductible and Roth) is limited to $1 million.

If there is any concern about creditor claims, be sure to check state law to find out if IRAs are protected.

Important: Check out the rules for both the state in which you live now as well as the state to which you may retire.

Suppose that you decide against a lump sum because you have serious concerns about creditor protection. But you still want to provide for someone other than a spouse after your death. In this case, you should consider life insurance. The amount of coverage you take can be tied to the funds your beneficiary would have received from your retirement money had you rolled the pension into an IRA.

Pass on Your Values and Wisdom

Also known as a legacy statement, an ethical will passes on your values, beliefs and wisdom. Around for more than 3,000 years, they have become more popular since the terrorist attacks of September 11, 2001. An ethical will is a nonlegal, personal letter that expresses your innermost thoughts. It can be given to a child or grandchild anytime, on any occasion.

Barry K. Baines, MD, CEO, The Legacy Center, a group that helps to preserve individuals' stories and wisdom, Minneapolis, *www.ethicalwill.com*, and author of *Ethical Wills: Putting Your Values on Paper*. Perseus.

Give to Charity Even If You Don't Have a Lot of Cash

To make a large charitable donation without a lot of cash, consider naming a charity as the owner and beneficiary of a life insurance policy. You also can use life insurance to guarantee that regular contributions to a favorite charity will continue after your death.

Example: You donate $1,000 each year. The charity uses the donation to purchase a $40,000 insurance policy on you, naming the charity as the beneficiary. Upon your death, the charity will have $40,000 to invest. If the investment earns 2.5% per year, then the charity will effectively continue to receive the same $1,000 long after you're gone.

Key: You get a tax deduction, which helps reduce your cost burden.

Martin Shenkman, CPA and attorney who specializes in estate and tax planning and asset protection, Tenafly, New Jersey, and the author of more than 30 books, including *Inherit More: Protect Your Inheritance from Taxes, Creditors, Claimants, Medicaid and More*. Wiley. His Web site, at *www.laweasy.com*, offers free sample forms and documents.

Is a Do-It-Yourself Will for You?

Nancy Dunnan, a financial adviser and author in New York City. Ms. Dunnan's latest book is titled *How to Invest $50–$5,000*. HarperCollins.

Do-it-yourself wills, using programs published by Nolo Press at *www.nolo.com* or some other software program, are recommended only if your situation is not complicated and you know exactly what you want to do. Have your attorney review whatever you put together. *I urge you to consult a lawyer if…*

● **Your will might be contested,** for instance, if there is family discord.

● **You have a child who is disabled** or other dependents.

● **You want to disinherit a spouse** or other close relative.

● **Your estate is in excess of $2 million** and therefore subject to federal estate tax.

● **You operate your own business.**

● **You gave up a child for adoption.**

● **You own many pieces of real estate** in more than one state.

● **Some of your income is derived from royalties.**

How to Keep Your Family from Fighting Over Your Money

Adam R. Gaslowitz, Esq., a nationally recognized expert in estate litigation, and a partner in the law firm Gaslowitz Frankel, LLC in Atlanta. He is also the chairman of the estate planning section of the Atlanta Bar Association. His cases have been featured on CNN and in *The New York Times.*

The more money you hope to pass along to loved ones, the greater the chance that your children will fight over it. Even close-knit families aren't immune to these problems.

Contesting a will can hold up the distribution of assets for many years. Even worse, it never resolves the emotional issues that underlie most inheritance fights, such as which of the children was loved most.

To reduce the likelihood of bitter legal disputes in your family after you are gone…

●**Treat each heir equally.** Many parents leave the largest share of their estate to the child who makes the least money. Or they put the inheritance of a free-spending child in a trust with stipulations but leave assets to his/her siblings free and clear.

Problem: Grown children often equate their inheritances with the depth of their parents' love. Children who feel they were shortchanged might sue because they believe that their siblings must have manipulated the parent.

Exception: Wills that involve family businesses. It's difficult to treat children equally if they don't all have an active interest in operating the company. If you have a family business, meet with your accountant and estate attorney to discuss business succession planning as well as distribution of nonbusiness assets among your family members. If the business is the only family asset, look into life insurance trusts or the sale of the business to provide for nonparticipating family members.

●**Reveal any big surprises before you put them in your will.** Discussions about inheritances are taboo in most families. While it's not necessary to tell your children exactly what you're planning to leave to them, make them aware of out-of-the-ordinary decisions, such as unexpected large gifts to charity or to one child.

If you don't disclose the gifts in advance, it is easier for one of your children to contest the will. Courts often agree to hear a will contest if one child appears to be unusually favored over another. In addition, explain your motivation in the will itself.

You might write—*Son, I have left your sister the summer house because she will use it more. This may seem unfair, but it doesn't mean that I love you any less. It gives me great pleasure to know that she and the children will get to enjoy it. Since you and Helen work such long hours, you would hardly spend any time there anyway. I appreciate your understanding of my wishes.*

Don't go into extensive detail. You risk slandering one of your heirs, which can give him an excuse to challenge your will.

Helpful: A well-drafted "no-contest" clause in your will—which will automatically disinherit any recipient who challenges the document—is worth including, but it is no panacea. Beneficiaries might contest the will anyway, and many probate courts will refuse to honor no-contest clauses.

●**Give away sentimental objects now.** I tried a case in which a woman wanted her $30 million estate split up equally between her son and daughter. The brother and sister wound up litigating this case for years over a single piece of jewelry—a ring that was worth only a few thousand dollars that had been passed down in their family for generations.

You can sidestep such controversy by giving your beloved personal items to family members while you are alive, especially heirlooms that you do not use or wear regularly. (Discuss tax ramifications with an adviser if you think beneficiaries will sell these items down the road.)

To avoid unhappy surprises, let each of your heirs know what you are giving the others.

●**Don't unintentionally disinherit a child.**

Common scenario: Your will divides your estate equally among your children. When you fall ill and need help with such daily chores as

315

cooking, shopping and paying bills, you rely on the child who lives closest to you. For convenience, you put the caregiver child's name jointly on your bank accounts. By law, these joint assets automatically pass to the caregiver child when you die, overriding your will—and your other children are then shortchanged.

Better: Establish power-of-attorney accounts with banks and brokerage firms so that individuals you designate—your child, a trusted friend, an accountant—can write checks and make decisions about your money on your behalf without being a joint owner of your assets.

Also remember to change your will or include flexible language that allows for tragic occurrences such as the death of a child.

SPECIAL SITUATION: SECOND MARRIAGE

A second marriage can create inheritance-planning challenges. *Smart strategies…*

● **Provide directly for children from your first marriage.** Often, a father leaves everything to his second wife with the understanding that the second wife will provide for his children from his first marriage—but taking this shortcut almost guarantees a will contest.

Better: Use marital trusts, such as a qualified terminal interest property (QTIP) trust, to earmark assets for your children upon your second spouse's death.

● **Choose a nonbiased executor.** Men often try to promote family harmony by making a second wife and one of the children from the first marriage coexecutors of their estates or cotrustees of marital trusts. This just pits the second wife against the child over such issues as how to invest assets or manage the estate.

Better: Use a bank as executor or trustee, if the will has trust provisions. Most of the large regional banks offer this service to customers.

Cost: About 1% to 2% of the estate's value on a sliding scale, based on the size of the estate.

Can You Avoid Estate Tax by Relocating?

Sanford J. Schlesinger, Esq., a founding partner and head of the wills and estates department of Schlesinger Gannon & Lazetera LLP, a law firm in New York City.

Some observers are speculating that the federal estate tax will be permanently repealed or greatly scaled back. That may come to pass, but planning to reduce postmortem taxation is still vital because of the 2001 tax law. This legislation reduced revenues for individual states, many of which are taking actions to raise their own estate taxes.

TOUGH TRANSITION

Before the 2001 tax act went into effect, federal law included a credit for state estate taxes based on a formula.

Upper limits: This tax credit went up to 16% while the highest federal estate tax rate was as much as 55%.

How it worked: When a decedent's estate was in the 55% tax bracket, the executor would pay the state an amount equal to the 16% credit and the other 39% would go to the federal government. Similar splits were made for estates in lower federal estate tax brackets.

As of 2005, this credit has been eliminated. The old system is scheduled to come back in 2011, but that may not happen if another tax law is passed in the interim, as many people anticipate.

Bottom line: The loss of this credit has cost many states significant amounts of money.

STATES STRIKE BACK

Some states have responded to this revenue shortfall by "decoupling" from the federal government's estate tax system. Rules differ greatly from state to state, however.

Favorite strategy: In several states, new laws call for the collection of the amount a state would have received if the old credit had remained in place.

For example, Alan Johnson lives in a state which has passed such a law. He dies in 2008 with a large estate.

Suppose, under pre-2002 law, Alan's estate would have paid $2 million to his state. The new law, passed by his state, calls for the same $2 million tax payment.

Trap: While Alan's estate pays the same $2 million to his state as it would have paid in 2001, there is no federal tax credit to reduce the federal estate tax obligation. Alan's estate winds up paying more, counting both federal and state estate taxes.

Loophole: Beginning in 2005, an estate can claim a federal estate tax deduction for state taxes paid. This deduction is scheduled to remain in effect through 2009.

Trap: A deduction from federal estate tax saves no more than 45 cents on the dollar in 2009. That's much less of a benefit than the old tax credit, which provided full shelter at 100 cents on the dollar.

Even after this deduction, the net state tax cost can be quite high. If the federal government picks up 45%, which is the top estate tax rate in 2009, a large estate would pay 55% (100 minus 45).

Result: The net cost could be as high as 8.8% (55% of 16%), from a 16% tax rate (the top estate tax rate in many states).

SQUEEZE PLAY

Some states set another tax trap. They have lower estate tax exemptions than the federal government.

Examples: In 2009, the federal estate tax exemption is $3.5 million. But, Massachusetts has a $1 million exemption, while in New Jersey, assets more than $675,000 are subject to estate tax.

Result: Some estates will end up owing tax to their states even when they owe no federal estate tax.

Examples: Suppose Marjorie Russell dies in New Jersey in 2009 with a $3.5 million estate. Her estate would owe no federal estate tax but it would owe New Jersey estate tax of $99,600.

This example assumes that Marjorie was unmarried, left nothing to charity and had not made taxable gifts during her lifetime.

TRIMMING THE TAX

What kind of planning might ease this state tax bite?

●**Gifting.** Giving away assets has long been a way to reduce federal estate tax, and this tactic might be especially valuable when dealing with state taxes. In some states, the taxable estate is not adjusted for lifetime gifts, as is the case under federal law.

Example: If John Green has given away $1 million and dies with $4 million, he is treated as having a $5 million estate by the IRS. Some states, though, do not follow the same add-back procedure, so John's estate is taxed for state and estate tax purposes on a smaller amount.

Key: Only three states currently have a gift tax—Louisiana, North Carolina and Tennessee.

Tactic: Execute a durable power of attorney to allow someone to make such gifts if you're no longer capable. Even deathbed gifts might produce tax savings.

While you are still capable, consider making estate-reduction gifts with borrowed money secured by your assets.

Don't give away the low-basis assets, which could provide a tax advantage if inherited at your death. Moreover, giving away appreciated assets is undesirable because the recipient will owe capital gains tax on all the appreciation if those assets are sold.

●**Balancing.** Regardless of whether you give lifetime gifts, some basic tax planning may be necessary.

Classic strategy: The first spouse to die leaves some assets to the spouse and other assets to their children. Often, these bequests are made in trust.

Given the concern over state taxes, the children's bequest might be the largest amount that won't create a federal or state estate tax—$675,000 in New Jersey, for example. The balance of the estate can be left to the surviving spouse, tax free, outright or in trust.

●**Disclaiming.** In the above scenario, you might provide for your surviving spouse to be able to "disclaim" (waive) most or all of the inheritance. The survivor can then weigh his/

317

her health, other assets, the current tax law, etc., and decide if it makes sense to disclaim some assets to the children.

Even if that means paying some state estate tax at the first death, the federal tax savings might make a disclaimer worthwhile.

●**Moving.** Rather than going through the time and expense of extensive estate tax planning, it may be simpler to move to another state. Florida, for example, does not impose estate tax and is unlikely to do so in the future.

Relocating is particularly appealing if you already have two homes, including one in a state where estate tax is not a major concern.

Trap: Changing your "domicile" may require more than simply living in Florida for seven months a year.

Strategy: You might consider filing a declaration of domicile in your new state, registering to vote there, relocating your brokerage and bank accounts, changing your driver's license, getting new plates for your car and so on. You also might sell your house in your old state and replace it with a smaller home or apartment.

In other words, make a real move. Such a change of scenery can lead to a substantial tax savings for your loved ones.

Protect Your Inheritance from Good Samaritans

Elderly people may rely on their neighbors, friends and health-care workers, but some caregivers manipulate these vulnerable individuals into putting them in their wills.

Self-defense: Look for any signs of undue influence. Do these caregivers speak poorly of family members or play on your parent's fears? Or, has your parent told you that he/she has changed his will to include gifts to religious institutions or charities? If so, consult an estate planning attorney about establishing a guardianship or irrevocable trust.

Generally, you can contest the will only after your parent has died. Then hire an attorney who specializes in inheritance litigation. Ask your estate planning attorney for a recommendation.

Adam R. Gaslowitz, Esq., a nationally recognized expert in estate litigation, and a partner in the law firm Gaslowitz Frankel, LLC in Atlanta. He is also the chairman of the estate planning section of the Atlanta Bar Association. His cases have been featured on CNN and in The New York Times.

How Life Insurance Could Kill Your Estate

Irving L. Blackman, CPA, founding partner, Blackman Kallick, LLP at 10 S. Riverside Plaza, Chicago 60606.

You may need to use life insurance to protect assets that are substantial—such as a family's business or investments—from estate tax.

Trap: If you own the insurance policy personally, the proceeds will be included in your taxable estate. Up to half of it could go to the IRS as estate tax.

Much better: Have an irrevocable life insurance trust own the insurance policy. Insurance proceeds paid to the trust will escape both estate tax and income tax and be available for use as the trust directs.

You could finance the policy's premiums by making tax-free gifts to the trust (up to $13,000 annually, $26,000 if married, for each trust beneficiary in 2009) and/or by advancing loans to the trust that will be repaid to your estate from the life insurance proceeds.

Caution: You must not retain any "incidents of ownership" in the insurance policy once it is in the trust or the IRS can tax the policy's proceeds back into your estate. Incidents of ownership include such powers as the authority to change the policy beneficiary, cancel the policy, pledge the policy as security for a loan or borrow against it.

However, the IRS has ruled that retaining the right to be repaid from the policy proceeds for loans advanced to the trust to pay the policy premiums is not considered an incident of ownership (*IRS Letter Ruling* 9809032).

Technical rules apply, so consult an expert.

Estate Planning Pitfalls

Owning assets jointly with a spouse can create estate planning pitfalls. Such property passes automatically to the surviving spouse outside the will. But, because provisions made in a will to distribute property or reduce estate taxes are bypassed, intended bequests may be invalid and tax bills increased, as the directions in a will fail to take effect.

Important: When drafting a will and estate plan, ask your attorney about the effect of *all* your jointly owned property. You may wish to change ownership to another form.

Bob Carlson, editor of *Bob Carlson's Retirement Watch*, Box 970, Oxon Hill, Maryland 20750.

Give to Charities Through Your IRA...and Leave More to Your Heirs

Jere Doyle, senior vice president, BNY Mellon's Private Wealth Management, one of the nation's leading private wealth managers, One Boston Place, Boston 02108.

A little-known way to include charitable intentions in your estate planning is to make bequests from your IRA or another tax-deferred retirement account. For tax purposes, this technique will probably yield the best overall result.

Payoff: Deferred income tax can be entirely avoided. Moreover, you may be able to pass appreciated assets to other heirs, who will inherit with a tax-saving step-up in basis.

SPLIT SHIFT

Suppose, for example, that Joan Wilson is a widow with a total estate of $4 million, half in an IRA and half in highly appreciated securities and real estate. Joan wants to leave $2 million to her children and $2 million to various charities. If the appreciated assets are left to charity while the IRA goes to the children, no federal estate tax will be due, under current law.

Trap: With this plan, the children eventually will have to pay income tax on the IRA money as it is withdrawn. At a 35% rate, the ultimate federal income tax charge could be more than $700,000.

Better approach: Bequeath the IRA to charity and the appreciated assets to your children. Again, there will be no estate tax, but the children will inherit the appreciated assets with a step-up in basis, under current law.

The children would never owe any capital gains tax on the appreciation that occurred during Joan's lifetime.

Bottom line: The latter approach passes on the estate completely tax free, saving hundreds of thousands of dollars in taxes.

Caution: Planning for charitable bequests is the opposite of planning for lifetime donations. While you are alive, it generally makes a lot of sense to give away appreciated assets and let your tax-deferred retirement plans continue to compound.

SOONER OR LATER

There are four methods you can use to make charitable bequests from your retirement plan...

●**Leave your IRA directly to charity.**

●**Leave your IRA to your spouse,** who will leave it to charity at his/her death.

●**Leave your IRA to a marital trust** with all distributions going to your surviving spouse. At his death, whatever remains goes to charity.

●**Leave your IRA to a charitable remainder trust (CRT),** which can pay income to any individual you want to name, with the charity as the recipient of the remainder interest. (Ask the charity or your tax adviser to explain how a CRT works.)

Outright bequests are most suitable if you are not married or if the bequest is relatively small in relation to your entire estate. If you're married, your spouse may not want to give up the IRA to charity.

What about the other methods? If you are confident that your spouse always will be able to handle the IRA wisely and make the appropriate charitable bequest, simply leave the IRA to your spouse.

Reality check: In many situations, you'll be better off using a trust, which can provide control and protection.

TRUST TACTICS

The Tax Code permits you to create a trust where the surviving spouse gets all the income while the first spouse to die gets to name the ultimate beneficiary, which can be a charity.

Benefits: No federal estate tax will be due at the first death. In case of need, the trustee can distribute more funds to the surviving spouse.

At the survivor's death, whatever remains in the IRA goes to the charity that you've named, tax free.

Alternative: If you want to limit the survivor's income to provide more to charity, a CRT may be appropriate. With a CRT, the spouse's income will be a fixed amount or a fixed percentage of CRT assets.

If you want to name children or grandchildren to also receive income from the trust, a CRT would be more suitable.

Caution: A present value will be placed on the projected future income to younger generations, and that amount may be subject to estate taxation.

Trap: A CRT also may result in speedier distributions from an inherited IRA, so some tax deferral may be lost.

Work with a knowledgeable tax pro who can crunch the numbers and suggest the type of trust most suitable for your family and charitable goals. This is especially important whenever an IRA is left to a trust and the trust ultimately goes to charity.

Reason: It becomes more complicated to obtain an income tax deduction and extend tax deferral.

DIVIDE AND CONQUER

The above strategies may make sense if you have $2 million in an IRA and want to leave $2 million to charity. But what if you want to leave only $100,000 to charity? Or $50,000?

You can make a specific charitable bequest from an IRA or qualified plan, but the tax treatment is unclear.

Danger: If you specify, say, an $80,000 bequest, the IRS might treat that as an $80,000 withdrawal from the IRA and assess income tax on the amount. *Strategies...*

● **Name co-beneficiaries.**

Example: You might say that 4% of the IRA goes to charity while 96% goes to a family member. With a $2 million IRA, that would mean an $80,000 charitable bequest.

Note: Satisfying a fractional bequest with the right to receive an IRA is not a taxable event.

● **Split your IRA.** Break off a smaller IRA, as destined for charity.

Example: From an IRA of $2 million, you could roll over $80,000 to a new IRA tax free. The charity could be named as beneficiary of the new IRA while a family member remains beneficiary of the old IRA, which is now worth $1,922,000.

Subsequent withdrawals from the new IRA could keep the balance at $80,000, if that's the amount you intend to bequeath to charity.

Tactic: When minimum required distributions (MRD) begin after age 70½, take some of the amount from your charitable IRA, leaving more in your family IRA.

Example: You split your IRA, as above. After some years of growth, you have $2.1 million in your family IRA (going to your spouse) and $90,000 in the IRA that will go to charity.

Say your MRD for the year is $85,000. Distributions need not be pro rata, thus you can take $10,000 from the charitable IRA.

This reduces the charitable IRA to $80,000, the amount you intend to donate. Only $75,000 (the $85,000 MRD minus the $10,000 withdrawn from the charitable IRA) need be taken from your family IRA, increasing the amount that can compound, tax deferred, for yourself and your beneficiary. The same process can continue, year after year.

By remaining vigilant, you can fulfill philanthropic goals while providing for your loved ones, too.

The Overlooked Trillion Dollar+ Income Tax Deduction

Seymour Goldberg, Esq., CPA, Goldberg & Goldberg, PC, 100 Jericho Quadrangle, Jericho, New York 11753, *www.goldbergira.com.* One of the country's foremost authorities on IRA distributions, Mr. Goldberg is author of *Practical Application of the Retirement Distribution Rules* (IRG Publications), available at *www.goldbergreports.com.*

The least understood and most complicated of income tax deductions is also the one that is most often missed—even though it could be worth a trillion dollars or more to taxpayers who are failing to claim it.

If you have deferred-income–type assets in your taxable estate—or inherit them from one—you must learn about this. *Here's the story…*

DOUBLE DANGER

When deferred-income–type assets are in your taxable estate, they can be subject to taxation at near confiscatory rates—80% or more. *Assets that face this danger include…*

●**Balances in IRAs,** 401(k)s and other tax-deferred retirement accounts.

●**Pension payments owed** to designated beneficiaries.

●**Survivor annuities** issued by insurance companies.

●**Proceeds due on installment sales.**

●**Royalty rights.**

●**Untaxed deferred interest on Series E,** EE and I savings bonds.

●**Deferred compensation coming from employers.**

●**Damage awards from lawsuits.**

●**Other income-producing items.**

The income from such items, when later paid to heirs, is called income in respect of a decedent (IRD).

Trap if you don't know the rules: The income-producing item's value is first subject to estate tax at rates up to 45% in 2009. Then the income later paid by the item—the IRD—is subject to income tax at rates up to 35%. The total tax due from adding these tax rates can be as much as 80%—leaving as little as 20% for heirs!

Example: An individual leaves $1 million in an IRA that is subject to 45% federal estate tax (this article does not consider state estate tax). The IRA's beneficiary is in the 35% tax bracket. The estate must first pay $450,000 tax on the IRA (his estate provides funds to pay this tax). Then the beneficiary must pay $350,000 of income tax payable on the distribution of the IRA balance—if he/she doesn't know the IRD rules. The total tax bill comes to $800,000 for the IRS.

TAX RELIEF FROM CONGRESS

Congress believed this full double taxation to be unfair. As a remedy, it created partial relief in the form of an income tax deduction for federal estate tax (but not for state estate tax) previously paid on an asset that creates IRD. This is often called the "deduction for IRD." It can be claimed as the IRD is paid out.

For example, an individual dies leaving $1 million in an IRA subject to 45% federal estate tax. The tax of $450,000 is paid as in the example above. The IRA's beneficiary is in the 35% tax bracket. *If he…*

●**Takes a full distribution of the $1 million,** the deduction for IRD lets him deduct $450,000 against it. As a result, he pays income tax on only $550,000—and the deduction for IRD saves him $154,000—plus state income tax savings on the deduction.

●**Takes distributions from the IRA over time,** the deduction for IRD is taken proportionately. If the IRA is distributed at a rate of $100,000 per year, the deduction for IRD is $45,000 per year until the entire $450,000 is consumed. This saves $15,400 of income tax per year plus state income tax savings on the $45,000 deduction. Any additional distributions from the IRA in excess of $1 million (due to investment returns) would be fully taxed.

OVERLOOKED DEDUCTION

The biggest mistake made with the deduction for IRD is that many people—perhaps most—*do not claim it at all.* It is the most overlooked of all income tax deductions. *Reasons why…*

●**Most individual taxpayers do not even know it exists.**

●**Professionals who deal with an estate often don't talk to each other about it,** so it falls through the cracks.

Example: Neither the executor nor the adviser who prepares an estate's tax return has responsibility for the personal tax returns of heirs who would claim the IRD deduction, and doesn't even think about it—unless there is a formal agreement stipulating that he *will* take responsibility. At the same time, the tax advisers of those heirs do not know if any estate tax was paid. Or the heirs prepare their own tax returns and are ignorant of the whole issue. So the deduction is simply missed.

●**There is no "information reporting" for the tax deduction.** No form, such as a W-2, 1099 or K-1, is filed by anyone to report the deductible amount to a taxpayer who doesn't know about it.

●**Records for past years are lost.** The IRD deduction may be spread out over numerous years—in the case of an IRA distributed over the beneficiary's life expectancy, 20 years or more. And a balance of the available deduction must be carried forward from year to year—if past records weren't prepared or were lost, the deduction is lost.

●**It's very hard to learn about the deduction.** There is no single IRS publication dedicated to explaining its application in detail—information about it is spread around different IRS publications and rulings.

Result: The deduction is routinely missed by taxpayers, often for year after year.

TRILLION-DOLLAR ERROR

The dollar volume of overlooked deductions for IRD already missed as well as what might be missed in the future stands to be huge—perhaps a trillion dollars or more.

Government data show tax-deferred retirement accounts that can produce IRD now hold $11 trillion dollars. Of this, $3 trillion is owned by persons in the highest tax brackets who are expected to owe estate tax—and both of these numbers are growing rapidly.

These retirement accounts are just one of several kinds of assets that produce IRD.

Not all of these assets will be subject to estate tax. But, if out of this more than $11 trillion, only a little more than $2 trillion eventually becomes subject to estate tax, the total deduction for IRD will be $1 trillion. As of now, most of these deductions are probably being missed!

WHAT TO DO

To save the deduction for IRD, it's essential that the tax professional responsible for an estate's tax return works together with the tax advisers of the heirs of the estate and beneficiaries of assets included in the estate, such as IRAs and pensions.

The estate's tax professional should inform each heir in writing of the amount of estate tax that was paid on each item of IRD and should spell out how the rules work. Then each heir's tax adviser must use this information to create a schedule of available deductions that may be claimed against IRD in the future.

Important: The information and schedule may have to be used for many years, long after the professionals who prepared it are gone from the scene. So it must be completely self-explanatory to be able to survive a future IRS audit and be safely stored with other vital "permanent" documents.

●**If your estate is large enough to be subject to estate tax,** discuss planning for IRD with your advisers now.

●**If you inherit an IRA or other item of IRD,** contact the executor of the deceased to learn if any estate tax was paid and obtain needed information to manage the deduction for IRD.

The technical rules for deductions for IRD are complex, so be sure you are advised by a tax professional who is very experienced in dealing with them.

Estate Tax Trap

Don't assume that you are safe from estate tax because the amount exempt from federal estate tax—$3.5 million in 2009—is more than you own.

Trap: You may owe state-level estate tax. Some states now have a lesser exempt amount than the federal amount, such as $675,000 in New Jersey and $1 million in Massachusetts and New York. Moreover, state estate tax used to be credited against the federal tax and so didn't really cost anything extra. But this credit on the *federal* return was eliminated in 2005, so the state tax now is truly an extra tax. However, the state death tax is deductible on the federal estate tax return. At this time, it is not clear if the state estate tax is deductible on the state estate tax return.

Safety: Check your state's estate tax rules to see if your estate might owe a surprise tax. If your estate is large enough to owe tax at both levels, but state rules differ from federal rules, you may need to adopt separate strategies to minimize both taxes.

Best Place to Keep Vital Documents

Lisa S. Hunter, Esq., partner, Certilman, Balin, Adler & Hyman, LLP, attorneys, East Meadow, New York.

Sudden disability or death of the head of a family can leave relatives scrambling to find vital documents.

Trap: If your documents are kept in a safe-deposit box, they may be impossible to obtain when needed.

Safety: Keep vital documents—such as your will, power of attorney and health-care proxy—in a safe but accessible location, such as your lawyer's office. Keep copies in your files at home—and include passwords that might be needed.

Other documents to have...

●**Contact list.** For all professionals involved with your assets—attorney, accountant, insurance agent, broker, banker and so on.

●**List of assets and investment accounts.** Insurance policies, bank and stock brokerage accounts, etc.—with account numbers.

●**List of outstanding debts and obligations.** Loans, credit card accounts, etc.

●**Titles and deeds.** To real estate, vehicles, a burial plot and other properties—all collected together at a safe location.

●**Copies of beneficiary designations.** For all IRAs, pension accounts and insurance policies, in case originals at a financial institution are misplaced.

●**Safe-deposit box records.** Location and the keys to it so it can be opened.

Useful: If these lists aren't in one location, keep a master list that tells where they can be found along with your vital documents.

Helpful Advice on Living Wills and Health-Care Proxies...You Really Must Have Both

Martin Shenkman, CPA and attorney who specializes in estate and tax planning and asset protection, Tenafly, New Jersey, and the author of more than 30 books, including *Inherit More: Protect Your Inheritance from Taxes, Creditors, Claimants, Medicaid and More.* Wiley. His Web site, at *www.laweasy.com,* offers free sample forms and documents.

Whenever a television news program broadcasts stories of terminally ill patients on life support, with families feuding over whether to continue treatment, many people say, "I hope something like that never happens to me. I would rather be dead."

Life-or-death decisions ought to be very well thought over—and not made alone. Everyone needs to take steps to ensure that his/her own end-of-life decisions are respected as well as to avert misunderstandings and quarrels among family members.

VITAL STEPS

First, discuss the issue with family members and loved ones, a spiritual adviser or clergyperson, a physician and a lawyer. If that sounds like a lot of people, it is. But each has important insights to contribute. Take the steps now to be sure that, should you be in a life-threatening situation and unable to speak for yourself, the decisions made for you will be the ones you would want. These discussions also help the loved ones who will be charged with making a decision understand your feelings.

When the discussions are finished, ask your lawyer to prepare a health-care proxy and living will for you. It is essential that you have both documents.

●**Health-care proxy.** Obtain a health-care proxy or health-care power of attorney—terminology varies from state to state—designating an "agent" (a person who will act on your behalf) to make medical decisions if you cannot do so. It should specify whether the agent has the authority to sign a "do not resuscitate" order to the hospital. In addition, name a successor agent to serve if the first agent cannot. They should not be a team. One person must be responsible. The proxy should include the right to move you to another hospital—even to one in another state, if differing state laws make the move necessary to carry out your wishes.

●**Living will.** Sign a personalized statement detailing your health-care wishes. Do you want life support continued if you are in a persistent vegetative state? Should religious restrictions prevail? What type of funeral do you want?

These two documents should be prepared to ensure that your personal preferences are followed. Living will and proxy forms are available on the Internet, and many people assume that filling one out will take care of the matter. In fact, very serious problems can ensue because Internet documents may not address such concerns as nutrition, hydration, funeral arrangements and religious observances.

TOUGH DECISIONS

A health-care proxy is the medical counterpart of a power of attorney. If you are responsible for your own or your family's finances, you also need a "durable" power of attorney, one that would become effective should you be incapacitated. But do not automatically ask the person who serves as your financial agent to hold your health-care proxy as well. If you name different people in the two documents, direct that health-care decisions be made by the health-care agent and that the person holding the power of attorney provide the funding to pay for those decisions.

Unlike those tragic situations that make the nightly newscasts, most cases are not clear-cut from a medical standpoint.

Two examples: Let's consider two elderly people who are hospitalized with pneumonia. One has always been strong and healthy, perhaps even recently ran in a marathon. If put on a respirator, he may well make a full recovery.

The other patient was suffering from congestive heart failure, end-stage cervical cancer, osteoporosis and chronic obstructive pulmonary disease before being stricken with pneumonia. Her prognosis is not good. But neither is it certain that she has no chance of recovering from the pneumonia. Unless she has signed a living will and health-care proxy making clear she does not want heroic measures under these circumstances, health-care providers are bound to do all they can to save her. Pneumonia, after all, is reversible.

If you hold her health-care proxy, her physicians can give you their best judgment and advise you, but there is no certainty of what lies ahead for her.

Will a life of pain simply be prolonged—possibly even made worse—if the patient is kept alive via a respirator or by inserting a feeding tube, or even by calling in a resuscitation team should her heart fail in the hospital? Does she want to live as long as possible, despite the pain and suffering? Some people do. Suppose she recovers from pneumonia but cannot live at home any longer. Would she want to go to a nursing home, if necessary, or does she prefer a quiet death at home or in a hospice? Does it make sense to try so-called heroic measures for a period to see if the patient improves and discontinue them if the patient makes no progress? Medical caretakers must try, unless the person holding the health-care proxy says no heroic measures are to be used.

The person holding the health-care proxy has the legal right to make such decisions. Nevertheless, other family members often disagree strongly. Maybe they feel guilty and want to keep Mom alive as long as possible without knowing what Mom herself wants. Or having seen news broadcasts about year-long family battles, they shudder and say, "Pull the plug."

FAMILY SQUABBLES

The Terry Schiavo case in Florida is an extreme example. Mrs. Schiavo was kept alive in a persistent vegetative state for 14 years. Her husband insisted she would not want to live that way. In an interview, he said she had made such a remark when seeing a broadcast about a similar case. Her parents insisted she be kept alive. The Florida legislature and Governor Jeb Bush sided with the parents.

It is impossible to know what Mrs. Schiavo's own views would have been. But if she would have had a health-care proxy and living will, the tragic quarrel could probably have been prevented.

The Schiavo case also illustrates why your health-care proxy should specifically authorize the person who is your agent to make decisions on your health care, including the use of a feeding tube. Again, as I said above, consider authorizing your agent to move you to another state, if necessary. The state laws vary significantly on this subject, so it is important to consult with an attorney in your own state who specializes in estate planning.

Families often quarrel over funeral arrangements, even though they may share a religion. One member interprets religious beliefs liberally, while another has a strict letter-of-the-law perspective. Or one wants to have an elaborate funeral with an expensive coffin, flowers and music, while another insists on a quiet, dignified service. A living will that specifically spells out what you want can avert such divisions among your survivors.

More from Martin Shenkman, CPA...

Why Loaning Money Makes More Sense than Giving Gifts

Seniors with wealth often make gifts to children and grandchildren. But the ups and downs of the stock market show that wealth can be lost unexpectedly. If such a thing happens after giving away too much, a generous family head may be left with too little to meet his/her own needs.

Safety: Help the younger generation by making loans to them, instead of gifts, to finance investments such as a new home, new business or higher education.

If the funds are wisely invested, the recipient will be able to repay the loan later, after profiting from it. So, if you should ever unexpectedly need the funds, you will be able to get them back, after having helped the recipient.

And if you don't need the funds in the future, you can make a gift of them at a future date.

Important: To satisfy the IRS that a loan to a family member is genuine, follow all the formalities—have a written note, set a market interest rate, have a payment schedule and see that payments actually are made on time. The note also may protect the money if the heir divorces.

Better Gifting

There's no need for most people to restrict tax-free gifts to only $13,000. Many people who learn that the annual gift tax exclusion in 2009 is $13,000 per recipient ($26,000 for gifts made jointly by a married couple) needlessly restrict gifts to that amount when they could make much larger gifts tax free.

Important: In addition to annual "exclusion amount" gifts, you can make a further $1 million of lifetime gifts free of gift tax.

These additional gifts reduce the amount of your estate that will be exempt from estate

325

tax—but with that at $3.5 million by 2009, most gift makers will not be affected anyway. Moreover, gifts of appreciating property may reduce the future estate tax by removing appreciation from an estate.

Randy Bruce Blaustein, Esq., senior tax partner at R. B. Blaustein & Co., 155 E. 31 St., New York City 10016.

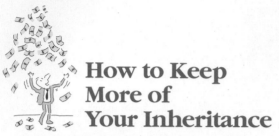

How to Keep More of Your Inheritance

Edward Mendlowitz, CPA, partner, WithumSmith +Brown, 1 Spring St., New Brunswick, New Jersey 08901. He is author of *Estate Planning*. Practical Programs.

With some tax planning, recipients of an inheritance can keep more money for themselves, not give it to the IRS. *Consider these strategies...*

Loophole: **No capital gains tax on inherited assets.** Most beneficiaries pay little or no capital gains tax when they sell inherited assets because of a tax break known as stepped-up basis. The recipient's tax cost (basis) for figuring capital gains is the value on the estate tax return, not the property's cost to the decedent.

Example: You inherit a house that cost the decedent $20,000 and is now worth $150,000. You pay no tax when you receive the house and, if you immediately sell it for $150,000, you pay no capital gains tax.

Reason: Your basis is equal to the property's value at the date of death (or six months later if the estate chose that date). Since the house was sold for the same price at which you inherited it, you pay no capital gains tax. If you sell the house for more than $150,000, the excess is taxable gain.

Loophole: **Deduct capital losses on inherited assets.** If you sell inherited property at a loss, you can deduct the loss. If you sell the house in the above example for $120,000, your tax deductible loss is $30,000, subject to annual deduction limits. Capital losses are deductible

dollar for dollar against capital gains and up to $3,000 of ordinary income each year. Excess losses can be carried forward into subsequent tax years.

Loophole: **Pay executors' fees to sole beneficiaries.** Consider paying executors' fees to beneficiaries, depending on their tax picture. Estates can deduct executors' commissions. So when the executor is also the sole beneficiary, it makes sense to pay the fees if the estate is in the 50% tax bracket (including state taxes) and the executor in the 40% tax bracket (including state taxes).

Loophole: **Disclaim inheritances.** In some situations, a great deal of estate tax can be saved when a beneficiary disclaims (gives up) an inheritance.

Example: A wife leaves $500,000 to her husband, who has a $5 million estate. No estate tax is due on the wife's death because of the unlimited marital deduction. But on the husband's death, the extra $500,000 would be taxed to his estate at the top rate (about 50% including state taxes). The tax would be $250,000.

That tax could be saved if, on the wife's death, the husband disclaims the $500,000 inheritance and lets it pass to the couple's children or other beneficiaries. The gift would not be taxed in the wife's estate because of her exemption amount—her right to bequeath up to $2 million estate tax free to beneficiaries other than her husband.

Smart move: Use disclaimers with designated beneficiaries of IRAs or pension accounts. When a surviving spouse disclaims an IRA in favor of children and grandchildren as contingent beneficiaries, post-death planning can create dynasty-type extended withdrawals over the life expectancies of the children and/or grandchildren.

Caution: To be valid, disclaimers must be made within nine months of the death and meet other strict criteria—check with an estate tax adviser.

Loophole: **Redeem business stock.** If the decedent owned stock in a C corporation with high retained earnings, the stock can then be redeemed income tax free by the estate. The redemption is treated as a capital gain. There would be no income tax payable because the value of the stock is stepped up to its value on the date of the decedent's death.

Loophole: **Don't overlook the income tax deduction for estate tax paid.** Federal estate tax paid on income in respect of a decedent is deductible as an itemized deduction on your personal tax return when you report the income. Generally, when you inherit assets, your tax cost is stepped up to the asset's date-of-death value. However, this does not apply to income earned by the decedent but paid after death, including distributions from pension, 401(k), 403(b) and IRA funds.

Note: Post-death income may be subject to both estate tax and income tax. The income tax deduction mitigates some of this double tax.

Caution: The deduction is only for the federal estate tax and not state estate or inheritance tax.

Opportunity: A surviving spouse can elect to roll over a pension distribution into an IRA and defer the payment of income tax.

Loophole: **Delay the payment of the estate tax.** Estate tax can be paid in installments, with interest, over 14 years. The decision to pay estate tax on the due date or to elect installment payments is made after the death, although it is usually considered and planned for—or against—during the estate planning process.

Caution: When you elect installment payments, the IRS files a lien on the estate's assets.

How to Audit-Proof Your Gift and Estate Tax Plan

Randi A. Schuster, Esq., principal in charge of the trust and estate group, Holtz Rubenstein Reminick LLP, a professional services firm that provides assurance, tax, financial advisory, and consulting services to businesses, 1430 Broadway, New York City 10018.

Every estate large enough to potentially owe estate tax will almost certainly be audited and must be prepared to deal with the IRS. Smaller estates may face this challenge, too.

Risk: The audit may examine not only the estate's tax return, but also gifts and trusts used to reduce the size of the estate—even if they were utilized many years earlier. *How to audit-proof gift and estate tax strategies…*

GIFT TAX TRAPS

Gifts of property, such as an ownership interest in real estate or a private business, made to the younger generation are a common means of reducing the size of a taxable estate.

Surprise danger: Due to the statute of limitations, gifts become protected from audit with the passage of time *only* if disclosed to the IRS when made on a properly filed gift tax return.

When no gift tax return is filed, the IRS has forever to audit gifts, reassess their value, and assess tax.

Trap: When gifts are made using the annual gift tax exclusion (up to $13,000 per giver per recipient in 2009), they are tax free and no gift tax return need be filed—so people usually don't file them.

But when the gift is made of property or securities that don't have a market price, such as shares in a private corporation, the IRS may come back later and say it really was worth *more* than $13,000 and so was taxable. Since no gift tax return was filed, it can do this even decades later.

Example: The owner of a private business uses the gift tax exclusion to make tax-free gifts of shares in his business to his children, doing so annually for many years. To value the gifts, he uses an appraisal of the shares, then applies discounts for their lack of marketability and minority holding status. The resulting gifts are valued below the annual exclusion amount, so he never files gift tax returns.

When the owner dies, the IRS audits his estate and discovers the series of gifts. If it then determines that the share valuations were too low and the discounts too large, it can retroactively hold the gifts to be taxable going back any number of years. The result could be an expensive audit defense at best and a huge new tax bill at worst.

Audit deterrence: File gift tax returns for all gifts—even those valued below the annual exclusion amount—unless they are of cash or traded securities with a market value that can't be disputed. Filing a proper gift tax return limits the IRS to only three years to challenge the value of the gift.

Important: Be sure the gift tax return properly discloses the gift by…

●**Obtaining necessary appraisals of all gift property.**

●**Attaching required supporting documents to the return**—such as copies of appraisals and trust documents when the gift is made to a trust.

For details regarding required appraisals and attachments, see IRS Publication 526, *Charitable Contributions.*

LIFE INSURANCE TRUSTS

Life insurance is commonly kept out of a taxable estate by placing it in an irrevocable life insurance trust (ILIT) for a family's benefit. But there are audit traps to be wary of.

How an ILIT works: A trust is created with one or more beneficiaries (such as children) to hold an insurance policy and receive policy proceeds on their behalf. The trust then will use the proceeds in the beneficiaries' interest according to its terms. *Keys…*

●**The original owner or purchaser of the policy** must not retain any "incidents of ownership" in it after it is transferred to the trust.

Examples: The legal right to borrow against the policy, change the beneficiary, or cancel it.

Audit trap: If an IRS auditor finds that the individual continued to hold one or more incidents of ownership in the policy—even if they were never exercised—the IRS can include the policy proceeds back in the individual's taxable estate.

●**Premiums for a policy held in an ILIT** are financed with funds transferred to the ILIT as gifts—legally, gifts to the trust's beneficiaries.

Snag: The $13,000 gift tax exclusion is available only for gifts of a "present interest"—that is, gifts that recipients can use right away. But a gift to be held in a trust is not a present interest—so

the funds provided to an ILIT to pay insurance premiums risk being subject to gift tax.

Solution: Whenever a gift of funds is made to the ILIT, a "right of withdrawal" is provided to each beneficiary giving a limited time (such as 30 days) in which the beneficiary can withdraw the funds from the trust. This makes the gift a present interest. The beneficiaries then choose not to take the funds—because they want to preserve the insurance benefit—and the funds are used to pay the premiums.

Audit trap: The IRS auditor will check to see if the trust beneficiaries actually received notice of their right to withdraw. If not, the IRS can hold the transfers to the ILIT to be taxable gifts. So, it's vital to be scrupulous with ILIT paperwork and records.

Another trap: If one makes a $13,000 gift to an ILIT using the gift tax exclusion, one can't make *another* gift in the same year directly to the person who is the trust beneficiary using the exclusion.

People often mistakenly think of an ILIT as different from its beneficiary for gift tax purposes, and therefore assume that a full $13,000 excluded gift can be made to both. But if you use the exclusion on one you can't use it on the other.

An IRS estate tax auditor will look for these "doubled" gifts.

WILL AND ESTATE TRAPS

Key will and estate audit issues…

●**Omitted assets.** An estate must report on its tax return everything owned by the decedent at his/her death—for instance, not just a home, but its contents, too.

Auditor's tactic: If the estate includes a home, the IRS auditor will want to see the homeowner's insurance policy to see if riders reveal ownership of items such as jewelry, furs, collectibles, and other valuable personal belongings.

The estate also includes nonprobate assets that pass outside the will—such as IRAs and retirement accounts, insurance policies, and funds held in joint bank accounts and in living trusts.

If you act as executor for an estate and fail to include all such assets in it, you may become *personally* liable for tax assessed if an

IRS auditor later discovers omitted assets after the estate is closed.

● **Document availability.** To meet the needs of an estate tax auditor, an executor may need many documents—copies of old gift tax returns, past years' income tax returns, appraisals of assets, title documents, trust documents, and more. *Traps...*

● A safe-deposit box is not necessarily the best place to keep these documents, as it may be sealed upon the owner's death. (The length of time depends on the particular circumstances.)

● A will may be best kept in a lawyer's office, because if it is kept in an individual's possession and is accidentally written upon or damaged, it may be deemed invalid or open to challenge under state law.

Consult with your executor, estate's advisers and family members about where the best place is to keep the documents they'll need.

● **Deathbed transfers.** Estate-reducing gifts can be made by an individual, or an agent authorized by power of attorney, as long as the individual is alive.

However, gift checks must be *cashed* before the gift maker dies—expect an IRS auditor to look for this.

16

Small Business, Big Savings

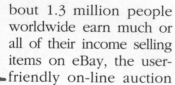

Make a Fortune As an eBay Entrepreneur

About 1.3 million people worldwide earn much or all of their income selling items on eBay, the user-friendly on-line auction site. These sellers have advantages over other retailers—they don't have to rent retail space, hire sales clerks or keep regular hours.

Still, the eBay entrepreneurs work long and hard. The process of listing a single item can take 15 minutes or more for less-experienced sellers—but eBay's elite class of power sellers whittle this down to a minute or two.

An established full-time eBay business generates an average annual gross income of $60,000, though incomes can run much higher. I know one seller who has an annual gross income of $250,000 and has hired employees.

To run a successful eBay business…

TARGET A NICHE

When you focus on a field, you build expertise in that area. You know what's in demand, the prices items are likely to fetch and how to write product descriptions that lure buyers.

Example: One seller can gross between $10,000 and $20,000 every month by selling comic books. It's not a field that just anyone could step into and be successful in. He devotes 20 to 50 hours a week to it.

Another advantage to narrowing your focus is that once buyers have purchased from you, you're likely to sell to them again.

Example: When your specialty is antique kitchen items, collectors of old toasters soon will learn that you can be trusted and will seek out your auctions.

To decide what to focus on…

Dennis L. Prince, Rocklin, California-based author of several books about eBay, including *Starting Your Online Auction Business* (Prima-Tech/Premier) and *How to Sell Anything on eBay and Make a Fortune!* (McGraw-Hill). On-line, he buys and sells movie memorabilia and vintage toys and games.

●**Make a list of the product categories** you know well and those for which you have an avenue to obtain merchandise inexpensively.

●**Do eBay market research on those categories.** The preceding 30 days of eBay sales are archived on the site under "Completed Listings." Determine prices and the percentage that goes unsold. Track a minimum of three months of data before investing heavily in inventory —longer, if the category is seasonal.

●**Proceed only if you can sell items for at least 40% above your purchase price.** A narrower margin won't provide a reasonable profit with eBay fees, the cost of lost and damaged shipments and other expenses.

●**Avoid fads.** Prices on trendy items, such as Beanie Babies and Cabbage Patch dolls, invariably tumble. You could be stuck with a pile of inventory that is worth significantly less than what you originally paid for it.

●**Don't just assume that an underserved niche is an opportunity.** If no one is selling a particular item on eBay, it may be because no one's buying. Don't stock up on inventory until you're sure that there's enough interest to support a business.

BUILD INVENTORY

To find merchandise…

●**Buy off-season,** when there are great deals on clothes, sports equipment, decorations and other seasonal items. Store merchandise until the following year.

●**Look for liquidations.** Check under "Liquidators," "Importers" or "Wholesalers" in the *Yellow Pages*, or use these terms in a search engine. If you can get good deals on products in large quantities, you should be able to auction individual units profitably.

Example: Chris P. grosses close to $2,000 a month selling clothing overstocks. He sticks with brand names, such as Levi's, and popular goods, such as blue jeans. He devotes about 15 hours a month to the business.

Important: Be selective. Items usually don't reach the liquidators unless they already have failed to sell at retail prices. Stay away from outdated technology, such as computers and cell phones. Avoid goods that aren't brand names—these may be of inferior quality.

●**Make products yourself**—saleable handmade products, including quilts, novelty T-shirts with catchy slogans or distinctive designs, even paintings and sculpture.

CREATE CUSTOMER LOYALTY

●**Be honest.** Descriptions and photos need to depict the product accurately and disclose problems. If a buyer isn't satisfied, allow a return or provide a replacement without argument.

●**Send a follow-up e-mail after shipping the merchandise** to make sure the buyer is satisfied. Ask if he/she would like to receive periodic e-mails listing current inventory. If you have a Web site featuring similar products, include the URL.

Example: A movie memorabilia dealer I know has built traffic at his *posterpalace.com* site through eBay customers.

●**Strive for positive feedback.** When a buyer or a seller has a positive experience with a transaction on eBay, he rewards the other person with a short, positive comment posted on the site. Tell buyers that you're giving them positive feedback. This reminds them to do the same for you.

MORE SMART MOVES

●**Give buyers a credit card option.** Sign up for a business account with the third-party online transaction firm PayPal (instructions are on eBay). eBay now requires sellers to accept only electronic payments (no personal checks). You'll also lose fewer sales. Buyers sometimes back out after they sleep on their purchases. PayPal bills immediately, leaving customers little time for second thoughts. PayPal fees are 30 cents* per transaction, plus 2.9% of the sale price.

●**Trim packaging expenses.** Order free co-branded express and priority mail cartons on-line from the US Postal Service at *http://shop.eBaysup plies.com*. They will be delivered right to your door.

●**Track competitors.** You might learn about a product subsector that's more popular

*All prices are subject to change.

than you imagined…or notice something in an item's description that you hadn't thought to include.

●**Keep scrupulous records of all your expenses and income.** The IRS is becoming increasingly interested in eBay sellers.

What to Do With Unused Vacation Pay

An employer's vacation policy says unused vacation may not be carried forward into the following year. However, an employee may elect to have the employer contribute the value of unused vacation time to his/her account in the employer's profit-sharing retirement plan.

IRS ruling: Amounts contributed to the retirement plan under this arrangement are free from income tax and FICA employment taxes.

IRS Letter Ruling 200311043.

How to Buy a Business with No Money Down

Edward Mendlowitz, CPA, partner, WithumSmith+Brown, 1 Spring St., New Brunswick, New Jersey 08901. He is author of *Estate Planning*. Practical Programs.

Today, buying a business with no money down is easier than ever. The competition for bank loans and venture capital is way down due to a weaker economy. The cost to borrow money is the lowest it has been in more than 40 years. Better still, as companies cut back to their core operations, thousands of high-quality businesses are being sold.

HOW LBOS WORK

Often in a leveraged buyout (LBO), a company is sold to one or more of its senior managers, who put up little or none of their own money. Instead, they use the company's assets as collateral. The lender is then repaid—typically over a period of five years—from the company's after-tax profits.

The process is similar to taking out a home mortgage. Most of the purchase price comes from the mortgage lender, and the home is used as collateral.

Just as with a mortgage, your financiers can foreclose and take over your business if you fail to pay them back.

FINDING A BUSINESS

If you enjoy your job and like your industry, consider buying your employer's company. You know the business, and its owners know you. You may be able to get financing from the owner, especially if he/she is eager to unload a unit that is performing poorly or doesn't fit in with his long-term goals.

If your employer isn't willing to sell, look at a competing company or one in an industry with which you are familiar.

Don't assume that a business is too big. If a lender likes your plan, it will finance a deal of almost any size.

Since the loan will be backed by collateral, choose a business that has physical assets, such as machinery and inventory, instead of a service business, such as a consulting firm.

Best LBO candidates: The manufacturing and distribution companies.

STUDY THE NUMBERS

There is a core to every business. Before you even look at the financial statements, get down to that core and see if buying that business makes sense.

●**Find an accountant**—preferably one with experience in LBOs.

●**Review the financial statements** of every acquisition candidate. As a potential buyer, you have the right to demand all of the company's financial records. If the company won't produce the documents you need, walk away from the deal. To be sure you're getting a good deal, review more than one business possibility, even if your first choice is to buy your employer's company.

●**Project future profits.** To obtain financing, you will need to establish why the business will become a profitable entity under your stewardship. The business does not have to be profitable today. *Examples...*

●A division may be burdened with overhead costs associated with its parent company's home office. Once the division becomes a separate entity, that overhead will be eliminated.

●Corporate managers earn salaries above the industry norm. Once the sale has been completed, you can cut salaries and give valued employees a share of the profits.

●The business may be weak as a stand-alone but strong when combined with a company you already own. A client who owned a manufacturing company purchased a competitor that had a relationship with a big corporate customer. By buying the competitor, he secured this important account.

FINDING A LENDER

To obtain financing, prepare a written plan demonstrating that you know the business very well and can steer it through the initial stages following the acquisition—when debt is high. Show that you will be able to assemble a team that can handle all areas of the business. Once the lender likes your plan, it will review your credit history before approving the deal.

Example: One of my clients runs a trucking company that distributes food products to 500 supermarkets. He purchased a company that manufactures ice cream. Under the former management, the ice cream company was losing both market share and money. The client got financing by showing that under his ownership, the ice cream company would immediately "inherit" 500 new customers—pushing sales to as much as the business could handle.

STRUCTURING THE DEAL

Unless the business's former owner provides financing, you will need to borrow from banks and/or venture capital groups.

Helpful: Consult with a banker who knows both you and the company. If the bank isn't interested in the deal or it wants another party to put up capital as well, it will point you to a venture capital firm. Very likely, the bank has its own venture capital group.

In return for a share of the business, the venture capital firm will put up 10% to 80% of the capital, and the rest comes from the bank.

At the end of the investment period, you will need to cash out the venture capital firm.

Possible "exit strategies"...

●**Use profits from the business** to buy out the venture capital firm's equity interest.

●**Do a new LBO.**

●**Sell the company,** and use the proceeds to repay your backers.

●**Take your company public.** In the initial public offering (IPO), the venture capital firm sells its shares to cash out its stake. You also may be able to sell off a small portion of your stake in the company.

MISTAKES TO AVOID

Mistake #1: Not realizing how much borrowed money is really costing you. If you buy a business and finance 80% of the purchase price at 10% interest, your average yearly cost of capital is 8% (80% of 10%). Business profits must grow by at least 8% a year to cover interest payments.

Mistake #2: Buying a business that requires heavy capital spending. Because the deal is being financed with borrowed money, avoid businesses with high up-front costs. If a business requires expensive new machinery to become competitive, pass it by.

Mistake #3: Not doing enough due diligence before you buy. Don't look only at reported sales and profits. Dig deeper. Find out how items were sold. Maybe the seller temporarily raised prices to make the income statement look more attractive to a buyer. Result? Dollar sales may be up, but unit sales are flat or down.

Making Bigger Home-Office Deductions

Generally you would deduct a percentage of your rent, insurance and other costs that relate to your entire home that corresponds to the percentage of it that is used as an office. So if you used 20% of your home for the office, you would deduct 20% of these costs.

But if a particular expense is incurred disproportionately in your office, you may be able to deduct the larger amount.

Example: If your office is 20% of your home, but you incur 40% of your home's electrical cost in it—due to electrical equipment, an air conditioner, etc.—you could deduct the 40%.

Remember, though, you have to be able to prove the larger amount.

Barbara Weltman, an attorney based in Millwood, New York, *www.barbaraweltman.com*. She is author of *The Complete Idiot's Guide to Starting a Home-Based Business*, Third Edition. Alpha.

Making a Mint From Your Home-Based Business

Jay Conrad Levinson, creator of Guerrilla Marketing International, based in San Rafael, California, *www.gmarketing.com*. Mr. Levinson is author of *Guerrilla Marketing for Free: Dozens of No-Cost Tactics to Promote Your Business and Energize Your Profits*. Mariner.

Owning a home business can be lucrative and fun. But numerous start-ups fail simply because the owners don't market their product or service effectively. *You can do better...*

CONTACTS ARE A GOLD MINE

Nearly everyone over age 50 has a large pool of friends and contacts. You may never have thought of them as people who could assist your business, yet many of them will be eager to do just that.

Make a list of the people with whom you have regular contact, as well as those you know only casually. Call them and explain briefly the type of business you want to start or are already running, and tell them what advantage your business has.

Example: You offer personalized service that a large company could never afford.

Ask if they're interested in your product or service or if they can refer you to people who would be. If the contact is unsure, ask what type of additional information he/she needs. Make notes of the information your contact asked for, and include it in your brochure and other marketing materials.

Most business owners are surprised at the positive responses. If a friend isn't interested in, say, your home repair service, he may know of someone who is. Or he just might know of a new realtor in town who is looking around for someone with your specialty.

CLUBS ARE A STRONG SUIT

Civic and community organizations will often invite small-business owners to speak on topics of interest to their members.

Examples: Investment consultants are always in huge demand. Or if you tutor children, some organizations will be eager to hear your ideas on how kids can improve their grades.

As a rule, clubs invite older people to speak because they're more likely to have the experience that members value.

When you speak to a club, *don't* make a direct sales pitch. Hand out company information afterward, and collect names of people who seem interested.

Exception: Some organizations will hold networking sessions for the purpose of letting small-business owners pitch their products.

Local chambers of commerce are usually good sources of information about organizations that invite owners of home businesses to speak to their members.

FREE NEWSPAPER ADVERTISING

In addition to speaking to local groups, write articles or columns for local papers on the same types of subjects you would speak about to local clubs. Offer to write articles free of charge. Include your name, phone number and Web site address at the end of the articles.

Essentially, that's free advertising. And once the article is published, you can get even more mileage by reprinting it and using reprints in mailings to prospective customers.

In addition to the big daily newspapers in your area, be sure to approach the growing number of neighborhood papers and even the "alternative" publications that are often aimed at younger audiences. Many civic and social organizations have newsletters that welcome articles on topics of interest to their readers.

LOCAL BULLETIN BOARDS

Community bulletin boards are another free—and overlooked—way to disseminate your company's message. They can be particularly effective if you select bulletin boards in locations frequented by likely prospects.

Example: Notices for a home-decorating service posted on bulletin boards in areas with a high concentration of new home owners.

STRATEGIC ALLIANCES

It often pays to team up with other home-business owners or even with owners of larger, established businesses for the purpose of swapping names of prospective customers.

Examples: A photographer or tutor could team up with a children's bookstore whose customers are parents...or a home-based insurance broker could form an alliance with a real estate agent who targets similar customers.

The best strategy is to start an alliance on a trial basis, say, for just six months. If it works, extend it. But there's no point in maintaining an alliance in which you give to your partner the names of many prospective customers but receive few in return.

VALUE AND LOYALTY

The big advantage of a home-based business is its ability to provide a personal touch and, through it, develop loyalty. *How to do it...*

● **Use your customers' names when contacting them.**

● **Offer free services,** such as consultations, seminars and demonstrations.

● **Respond personally by phone** whenever possible.

● **Write customers within a month after purchase.** Ask if they're happy with it or have any questions. Don't try to sell them anything at that time.

● **Use questionnaires to collect data** about customers. Ask about other places they shop, the products they like and what their ideal is in the type of service or product you're offering. Use their answers to custom-tailor your marketing message.

● **Maintain contact with your customers** by sending interesting information to them.

Example: If you know a customer hopes to vacation in Florida, send him an article you run across about a new hotel in Boca Raton.

USING THE INTERNET

The Internet has become all but indispensable in marketing a home business—if only because you can lose credibility by not having a Web site.

The cost of setting up and maintaining a Web site has plummeted. Today, many Internet service providers (ISPs) maintain modest sites for customers for only a small fee. Some do it free.

Don't let someone sell you a costly Web site. All that most home-based businesses need is four or five Web pages that explain clearly what the business does, why it does it better than competitors and how you can be contacted.

Web sites save you money in other marketing areas.

Example: Instead of printing an elaborate brochure or putting large ads in publications to explain your business, you can now buy smaller ads that ask readers to visit your Web site for more information.

Of course, when you speak to groups or write articles, mention your Web address. In this way, you save money on advertising and gain the advantage of learning the names—or at least the e-mail addresses—of prospective customers when they access your Web site.

How it works: On your Web site, offer to send additional information or a free special report to Web browsers who reply by e-mail. Someone running a home pet-care business, for example, might provide information on feline nutrition.

Depending on how much time you have, you can even offer a monthly e-letter to people who register for it on your Web site.

Once you obtain all the names and e-mail addresses of people who request this type of information, you can periodically send them other reports, as well as specific information about your products or services, especially special offers.

Cost saver: If you need any help with your Web site, phone a local high school or college and ask to talk with a student or teacher in the computer area. Students usually charge a small fraction of the fee that commercial computer service firms charge—and they frequently do a better job.

Better Ways to Work At Home

Robert Spiegel, Albuquerque, New Mexico-based author of the syndicated column *eBiz* and *The Shoestring Entrepreneur's Guide to the Best Home-Based Businesses.* Truman Talley.

Working from home poses its own set of challenges. *Here are some tips on how to make it work…*

●**Set up your office in a place where you can close the door for privacy,** be it in a spare bedroom, garage or sunroom.

●**Hold meetings and meet with clients somewhere other than your home.**

Examples: A restaurant or the seldom-used conference room of a nearby business.

●**Plan brainstorming sessions** by bringing together a number of interesting or experienced people who are willing to toss around ideas with you.

●**Take regular breaks,** which will help to recharge your batteries.

Examples: 10-minute breaks to read… lunch away from home…or a late afternoon workout at the gym.

Nine Steps to Protect Your Home-Based Business from the IRS

Sandy Botkin, Esq., CPA, president of the Tax Reduction Institute, 13200 Executive Park Terrace, Germantown, Maryland 20874. He is a former IRS attorney as well as a senior tax law specialist and author of the best-selling *Lower Your Taxes Big Time!* McGraw-Hill.

Having a home-based business can produce big tax savings. Not only will it provide many new deductions, but any losses it incurs can be deducted against other income, such as salary—providing a tax subsidy that can help you get the business through a period of start-up losses or later hard times.

You get this tax break even if your business is only a part-time sideline, such as consulting in your regular line of work, or a hobby that you've decided to turn into a business.

How a home-based business can pay off tax-wise—and how to protect its tax subsidy from the IRS…

●**Low- and zero-tax income.** By legitimately hiring your children and other family members who are in lower tax brackets and deducting their pay, you can move family income into lower tax brackets.

●**Home-office deduction.** You may be able to deduct previously nondeductible expenses of home ownership, such as a portion of utility, repair and insurance costs.

●**Travel expenses.** You can legally deduct pleasurable travel.

Examples: Travel expenses to business seminars in places like Las Vegas…business trips to cities in which you have friends or relatives.

Key: The primary purpose of the trip must be for business. Any incidental fun, however, is permitted.

●**Tax-favored benefits.** You may become able to deduct larger retirement contributions, more medical costs and other benefits.

●**Meals and entertainment.** Business owners have many more deduction opportunities in this area than employees.

●**Driving deductions.** When home is a workplace, previously nondeductible commuting can become deductible driving between two places of work.

Examples: Driving between home and another office or to a restaurant for a business-related meal.

BIGGEST SAVER

The biggest tax benefit from a home-based business may be an operating loss that these deductions, plus other business costs, combine to provide.

Business losses incurred in self-employment or through a pass-through entity, such as a partnership or S corporation, are fully deductible against other income—such as salary from a regular job and investment income. So these losses will effectively turn the business into a tax shelter.

Even better, you can carry business losses back two years to get refunds of taxes you've already paid.

You can also carry losses forward for up to 20 years—so even if losses exceed the income now available for them to be deducted against, no valid business deduction will ever be lost as long as you run your business with the appropriate "profit motive."

THE IRS CHALLENGE

When you own a home-based business that is unincorporated and is producing deductible losses, expect the IRS to question it. The critical IRS claim that you must be ready to meet is that your business is not a business at all, and, therefore, cannot produce deductible losses.

If the IRS succeeds with this claim, it won't need to bother examining your deductions on an item-by-item basis. All of them in excess of the amount of income your activity has generated will be disallowed in one fell swoop.

Key: The determining factor as to whether or not your activity qualifies as a business is whether you have a genuine *profit motive.* You do not have to actually make a profit—but you must be able to show a reasonable *intention* to make a profit.

Myth: Many people believe that to qualify as having a business, one must make a profit in three out of five years.

Reality: If you make a profit in three out of the first five years, the IRS assumes you have a profit motive. But even if you never make a profit, you can still show that you have a profit motive.

In fact, the courts have found businesses to be profit motivated after losing money for periods as long as 12 or more years in a row—making all their losses deductible.

HOW TO PROTECT YOURSELF

By taking the right steps, you can virtually ensure that your business will be safe from IRS challenge. *Nine steps that will help to prove profit-making intent…*

●**Run your business like a business.** This is first and foremost. To show that you have a real business, you must run it in a businesslike manner.

How: Keep full business books and records. Obtain local business licenses. Have a listing in the business pages of the phone book and print business cards. Consult with established experts about how to make the business succeed. Keep a business-expense diary and so on.

●**Have a written business plan**—and keep it up to date. Draw up a plan for how your business will generate money in the future. Include projections of income and expenses into future years. Describe your marketing plans and other strategies. Then *update* the plan as you go along in light of the results you get. If you lose money, change the plan to improve results in the future.

Critical: Many court decisions have turned on whether a business plan was kept updated or not. When real businesses lose money, they change the way they operate—so be sure to keep improving your written business plan, too.

●**Conduct research.** Examine the opportunities that exist in the line of work you choose before starting the business. Keep records of the research to show the IRS. If you have personal experience in the field, such as from a former job, note that, too.

●**Work regularly in the business.** If a business is a part-time activity, it's better to work at it for 45 minutes every day than one full day once every two weeks. Record all time worked in your business diary.

337

●**Keep business and personal funds separate.** Have separate bank accounts, and do not pay for personal expenses from your business account.

●**Keep your expenses proportionate to income.** If you have $5,000 of income from a sideline business, do not then spend $15,000 on travel to a business convention. Expenses must be reasonable in light of your income.

●**Be careful what you say.** Don't tell anyone your business is a "tax shelter" or make any other statements that may indicate that you run it with a tax-saving, rather than profit-making, motive.

●**Change the way you market your business** if you aren't making money.

●**Consult with experts** and be sure to follow their advice.

STRATEGY

You can keep the IRS from questioning the profit motive behind your business for five years after you start it.

How: By filing IRS Form 5213 within three years after starting the business. By the time the five years are done, you may be running profitably and so be safe from an audit—after having deducted years of losses without audit risk in the meantime. But be careful, filing this form may be risky.

Why: Filing the form puts the IRS on notice that you have a loss-making business to examine—so by filing it you may be asking for an audit. Also, if your activity is still losing money after the five years, the form authorizes the IRS to disallow *all* five years' worth of your loss deductions. Otherwise it can generally go back only three years.

Therefore, the best strategy may be to not file the form, operate with a real profit motive and follow the nine steps mentioned here to prove it.

If you do so, you may be overlooked by the IRS entirely. However, if you do end up facing an audit, you will be reasonably sure of proving your profit motive and protecting your business's status.

Beyond Cost-Cutting— Better Ways To Boost Business

To increase business, don't automatically cut prices. Many business owners are tempted to boost sales by reducing the price of products or services.

Problem: Slashing your prices will significantly reduce profit margin and may encourage your competition to start a price war.

Alternatives: Extend the time that the customer has to pay. Rather than decrease the price, give your customers something extra. Offer a "free" initial period in exchange for a longer-term agreement.

Paul Lemberg, CEO and chief business accelerator, Axcelus, a business consulting firm, Rancho Sante Fe, California. His Web site is *www.lemberg.com.*

Today's Top Franchises— Great Way to Start Your Own Business

Robert Bond, a franchising consultant in Oakland, California, and the author of *Bond's Franchise Guide* and *How Much Can I Make?* (both from Source Books).

Even with the economy gaining strength, starting a business is tricky. But, franchising decreases this risk by giving you experienced partners to lead the way. Choose carefully though. Of the 2,500 franchises available in the US, only about 500 are proven growth-oriented investments.

If you want to blaze your own trail, franchising may not be for you. You have to play by the home office's rules. Franchisors may inspect your operation to ensure that you are following their procedures. A Whopper in Boston should taste the same as one in San Diego.

Here's how to get started—and the hottest opportunities now…

FINDING A FRANCHISE

Less than 20% of franchises supply earnings statements to prospective buyers. To narrow your search and reduce risk, choose a business with at least 35 operating units. *Also focus on...*

●**Price range.** Janitorial services start at less than $15,000.* Motels can cost about $2 million or more. In the mid-range are the food-service franchises, which will require an investment of between $100,000 and $1 million. McDonald's franchises cost between $466,000 and $955,500, and availability is limited. *Other costs...*

●Franchise fee. The purchase price may or may not include a onetime franchise fee. In exchange for this fee—which ranges from $15,000 to $50,000—the franchisor generally is obligated to train you, help you select a location, negotiate a lease, obtain financing and, in some cases, build and equip the site. Ask about follow-up training.

●Supplies. You might have to buy supplies from the franchisor.

●Royalties. These range from 4% to 8% of gross sales per month.

●Advertising. You might have to pay fees for national or regional advertising.

●**Industry.** There are more than 600 franchises devoted to food service, 126 companies in cleaning/maintenance and 153 in automotive products/services. There are opportunities in pet products, athletic wear, lawn care, art, photography and printing. My free Web site, *www.worldfranchising.com*, lists more than 1,000 of the largest franchises. Contact these companies for their marketing materials.

DOING YOUR HOMEWORK

Before you sign a contract, research the business by talking with...

●**Franchisees.** Ask owners how much they earn, about their experiences with the franchisor and whether they would make the same investment decision today.

●**An experienced attorney who belongs to the Forum on Franchising of the American Bar Association (ABA).** You can locate one through the ABA's referral service (*www.abanet.org*) or contact your state bar association. Ask the attorney to review the offering circular. *He/she should pay attention to...*

*All prices are subject to change.

●Policy on franchise terminations.

●Litigation against the franchisor.

●Your territory. Appropriate size varies by local population, type of franchise and a variety of other factors.

BEST OPPORTUNITIES NOW

My favorite firms offer exceptional products and treat franchisees fairly...

●**Cleaning services**

●Jani-King International. Commercial cleaning. *Total investment:* $11,000 to $34,000.* 800-526-4546, *www.janiking.com.*

●Merry Maids. Home cleaning service. *Total investment:* $23,350 to $54,450. 800-798-8000, *www.merrymaids.com.*

●ServiceMaster Clean. Both commercial and residential cleanup. *Total investment:* $28,200 to $99,900. 800-255-9687, *www.ownafranchise.com.*

●**Food**

●Blimpie Subs & Salads. Quick sandwiches. *Total investment:* $72,800 to $338,200. 800-447-6256, *www.blimpie.com.*

●Burger King. Fast-food chain. *Average investment:* $400,000. 305-378-7579, *www.burgerking.com.*

●Carvel Corporation. Ice cream shops. *Average investment:* $300,000. 800-227-8353, *www.carvel.com.*

●Wing Zone. Takeout/delivery chicken wings. *Total investment:* $179,500 to $229,500. 877-333-9464, *www.wingzone.com.*

●**Lodging**

●Accor North America. Motel chains, including Motel 6 and Red Roof Inns. *Total investment:* Varies by each chain. *Examples:* Red Roof Inns, $2.6 million to $2.9 million...Motel 6, $1.9 million to $2.3 million. *www.accor-na.com.*

●**Other services**

●Express Personnel Services. Placement of personnel. *Total investment:* $130,000 to $160,000. 877-652-6400, *www.expressfranchising.com.*

●Money Mailer. Direct-mail advertising services. *Average investment:* $55,000. 888-446-4648, *www.moneymailer.net.*

UP-AND-COMING FRANCHISES

Franchisors are becoming much more niche-oriented. *Specialties worth watching...*

*All prices are subject to change.

339

●Animal care

Pet owners need a variety of services. *Promising franchises...*

●Aussie Pet Mobile. Grooming service. 949-234-0680, *www.aussiepetmobile.com.*

●Banfield—The Pet Hospital. 800-838-6929, *www.banfield.net.*

●Bark Busters. Home dog training. 877-500-2275, *www.barkbusters.com.*

●Auction consignment

Many people want to sell items on eBay but prefer someone else to do all the legwork. Customers keep about 40% of net proceeds. *Promising franchises now...*

●Snappy Auctions. 888-490-1820, *www.snappyauctions.com.*

●Bad backs/feet

Aging baby boomers want fast pain relief. *Promising franchises...*

●Relax the Back. 866-933-4330, *www.relaxtheback.com.*

●Foot Solutions. 866-338-2597, *www.footsolutions.com.*

Business Advisers

Take your business to the next level with a "mastermind group." The four to eight advisers on this board—each of whom has his/her own business—act as a combination cheering section and accountability tool for one another. Create a mastermind group by inviting people you meet at networking organizations, etc. The members should have similar goals, such as locally focused or global business ambitions. The group should meet for two to three hours each month. At each meeting, discuss any accomplishments and successes in the past month...current problems and concerns...and goals for the next month. Members must be willing to let others in on their business plans. Have a confidentiality agreement—a verbal one is fine.

Jane Pollak, professional speaker specializing in entrepreneurship...a coach for creative professionals, Westport, Connecticut...and author of Soul Proprietor. *Crossing.*

Protect Your Business From Thieves, Corporate Spies, More

Jason Paroff, Esq., director of computer forensics, Kroll Inc., a premier security firm, New York City.

Too many business owners view protecting their assets as a cost that has no revenue-producing benefit. In fact, taking the right preventive steps can save your company big money. *What to do...*

●**Develop a corporate security policy.** Make it clear that employees don't have the right to privacy with respect to what they store on your systems—all equipment and data are company property. Employees can be restricted from going to certain Internet sites or disseminating information outside the company.

●**Get employees to read and sign off on company policy** at least once a year.

SOFTWARE SECURITY

In addition to installing firewalls, which act as Internet security guards that monitor traffic between your company's internal network and the outside world...

●**Implement controls with passwords.** Any employee who does not possess a company-approved password is denied access to all or part of a computer network.

Example: Only you and your human resources personnel would have access to any salary and benefits information.

●**Prohibit downloading of sensitive information.** Software can automatically flag or disable downloads of confidential information by employees.

PROTECT PHYSICAL ASSETS

Depending on the size and location of your business, you will require different physical security systems...

●**Small companies in relatively secure** areas may do fine with just an office safe and an alarm system.

●**Larger companies with many entrances,** or firms that are located in high-crime areas, may require security guards and/or video cameras as well.

Many technology-related thefts involve small, expensive equipment that is easy to conceal, such as laptop computers. *Preventive steps...*

●**Install tracking software and motion alarms in laptop computers.** Software products such as Computrace (800-220-0733, *www. absolute.com*) cost less than $200* and will alert the police to the laptop's location as soon as the thief logs on to the Internet. Motion alarms, such as the Kensington SonicLock, cost about $15 and are available at most computer and electronics stores. When an equipped machine is moved, an alarm will sound.

●**Chain down equipment** that isn't frequently moved.

●**Make a trusted employee responsible for tracking** the firm's portable equipment and supplies.

Protect Your Business From Legal Woes

Andrew Josephson, area copresident of the insurance brokerage Arthur J. Gallagher & Company, Glendale, California, *www.ajg.com.*

One lawsuit can wipe out your business. And, doctors aren't the only professionals who are targeted. Architects, consultants and even travel agents may be sued by angry customers.

To safeguard your firm when apologies aren't enough...

GET PROPER LIABILITY INSURANCE

The cost depends on...

●**Your state.** California, Florida, New York and Texas have the highest rates.

●**Previous claims.** If you have faced liability lawsuits in the past, coverage will be more expensive.

●**Your industry.** Jury awards are higher in some fields. Real estate agents require more coverage than travel agents.

*All prices are subject to change.

●**The company's assets and revenues.** The higher they are, the more insurance coverage you will need.

●**Experience.** The more experience you possess, the lower your premium.

CUT COSTS

To get the best insurance rates...

●**Ask industry organizations if they offer a group rate.**

●**Ask your peers to provide independent agent referrals.**

●**Increase your deductible.**

●**Practice prudent business management.** Have contracts reviewed by a lawyer and provide a written set of policies for employees.

How to Get Top-Quality Legal Advice at Bargain Rates

John Toothman, Esq., president of The Devil's Advocate, a legal consulting firm at Box 8, Great Falls, Virginia 22066, *www.devilsadvocate.com.*

Businesses today face a dizzyingly complex maze of laws, litigation and regulation. But few have the in-house legal talent to prevent charges of wrongdoing—or defend against them.

Result: Businesses that have not planned ahead can pile up huge fees for legal advice that can be downright scary.

Better: Set up your legal management strategy *before* your business is sued or charged with a regulatory violation. Doing so requires knowing where you are most vulnerable to legal action and knowing whom to turn to if trouble does strike.

With a plan like this in place, you are prepared to get the best advice for your money.

WHERE TO START

Hiring an in-house attorney will only make sense if you're spending $1 million or more a year on legal fees. Even then, no single attorney is expert in all legal specialties. You would still have to rely on outsiders for some needs.

341

The in-house attorney for a high-tech company might know something about patents and deal making, for example, but could be completely clueless about defending against an age-discrimination suit.

Strategy: You probably already have a local attorney who helped you set up the business and provides occasional tax advice as well as a little advice on how to comply with local laws. That's the person to go to first if a legal problem arises. He/she can handle the first steps in a legal challenge and help you find the specialized service that will carry you the rest of the way.

If you don't have such a "utility" lawyer, shop for one among local attorneys who have done work for businesses similar to yours.

IDENTIFY YOUR EXPOSURE

The best strategy by far for keeping down legal bills is not getting sued. And—the best way to do that is to protect yourself where you are most vulnerable.

The most treacherous legal area for businesses today is workplace discrimination—age, disability, race, sex—and sexual harassment.

Each law governing discrimination in the workplace has its own threshold for applicability. Some apply only to businesses with more than 15 employees. Others kick in only when the business has 20 employees.

But since these thresholds are based on a moving average of how many employees you had in the last calendar year, whether you are subject to any of them could depend on what week it is.

Caution: Even if you are immune from federal law because your company is too small, state law can come into play.

Have your utility attorney refer you to local lawyers who specialize in each of the major workplace litigation areas.

Look *now* for attorneys who specialize in discrimination cases in your jurisdiction and who are active enough to keep current on all developments. Then—get briefed on the law as it applies to your business.

IF YOU ARE SUED

As soon as your attorney is fully briefed on the case against you, ask him: "How much will this cost me a month? How much will this cost me altogether? Can we work out a budget that keeps the costs down?"

Beware: A firm that refuses to lay out a budget for you either doesn't know what it is doing or has a history of piling up huge bills for other clients. Either way, that's not a firm you want working for you.

Once you have agreed to the budget, don't just assume it will be continuously met.

Monitor fees each month. If a bill is higher than you expected, phone the lawyer immediately to ask for an explanation.

If you don't complain, the lawyer will assume you can live with the bill…and the high charges will most likely continue.

SEEK A SETTLEMENT

The longer a case runs, the higher your legal fees. In numerous business litigation cases, it makes financial sense to settle quickly.

If there is no convincing reason for a failure to settle the case in a timely manner, request a face-to-face meeting with the other party.

There's no restriction on the two sides meeting in a negotiating session outside the courtroom. See if you can resolve the matter without further costly litigation.

Alternative: If the case is dragging on much too long and your attorney's explanation for the delay does not satisfy you, consider consulting another attorney.

Brief the second attorney on the highlights of the case with the basic documents and perhaps a letter from your original attorney advising a particular course of action. That should be enough for him to say, "This looks about right," or, "Hey, this just doesn't seem right."

The cost of obtaining a second opinion could be more than made up by resolving a case that otherwise could have accumulated huge legal fees or even wrecked your business.

Deductions the IRS Looks at Every Time

Martin S. Kaplan, CPA, 11 Penn Plaza in New York City, *www.irsmaven.com*. He is a frequent speaker at insurance, banking and financial planning seminars and is the author of *What the IRS Doesn't Want You to Know*. Wiley.

Those tax deductions that straddle the border between business and personal pose the greatest audit risk for small-business owners.

Examples: Travel, meals and entertainment, driving, home offices, insurance, phone expenses.

These are all examined by the IRS on *every audit*, since it always suspects that business owners are deducting personal costs.

TURNABOUT

The key to protecting these deductions is to look at special record-keeping requirements as an opportunity for making your return audit-proof—even for items well into the gray area between business and personal.

When the Tax Code or IRS rules set specific paperwork requirements for a deduction and you meet them, an IRS auditor normally has little incentive to inquire any further—and a real incentive not to, since auditors are under increasing pressure to close cases.

Example: If your records for meal deductions show, as required, who you entertained, when, where, the business purpose and the amount, an auditor is very unlikely to insist on verification that you really discussed business at the meal. It would not be cost-effective to do so and would add to the backlog of cases, so you can expect the deduction to be allowed—virtually audit-proof.

Moreover, there's a carryover benefit when the auditor moves on to items that are less well documented. If an auditor starts by examining records that are full and complete, then moves on to records for another item that are less than perfect but still professionally presented, he/she is likely to view the latter in a manner that still leads to a satisfactory audit result. *Reasons...*

- **The overall quality of the records** indicates that you aren't trying to "get away with something," so suspicions are not aroused.

- **High-quality records** will increase your chance of winning at IRS Appeals or in the small case division of Tax Court, should you go there. The auditor knows it and so has a practical reason to give enough to avoid an appeal.

- **When you present tax records in good order,** you are being considerate, helping the auditor do his job—and it is human nature for consideration to be returned.

Strategy: If called for an audit, try to direct the auditor to your best-documented deductions first.

PITFALLS

Two easy ways to lose the audit-proofing benefit that good records can give to gray area deductions...

- **The "pig rule."** The courts know that they often approve business deductions for items that are really of a personal nature when all of the required legal forms are followed—but the courts also warn what happens when people try to push these rules too far. *As one Court of Appeals has stated...*

"Perhaps in recognition of human nature, the courts have been liberal in the cases of shareholder[s]...channeling particular types of personal transactions through corporations. They have even approved payment of personal living expenses...but there is a principle of too much; phrased colloquially, when a pig becomes a hog it is slaughtered." [*Dolese*, CA-10, 605 F.2d 1146, 1154.]

Real-life examples of the "pig rule"...

- A professional deducted six personal telephone lines. That piqued the IRS auditor's interest, so he looked up the phone numbers—and found that most were those of the professional's relatives. The professional not only lost a deduction for one or two business lines he could easily have had, but had his entire return scrutinized.

- One consultant took deductions for multiple trips to distant cities that offset almost all her income. She had records for the trips—but the auditor asked why the trips hadn't produced any

343

consulting income. She said she had been seeking jobs that she didn't get—but couldn't produce any evidence, such as "turndown" letters from prospective clients, to support her claim.

The auditor might have believed she took one such trip—but not that she had spent all her income on such trips. She lost her deductions.

●In other cases, people have deducted three meals a day, business driving costs for seven days a week and work expenses for 52 weeks a year.

But no matter how "complete" records are, an IRS auditor is going to have a hard time believing such deductions. They only invite questions about your honesty that good records are meant to prevent.

●**False records.** Another way to have "excellent" records become worthless is to show the IRS they are false.

Example: One client called me after giving the IRS meticulous records for his meal expenses in town for a period during which his travel records showed he was out of town.

Automobile records also often snag those who exaggerate driving deductions. The simplest way to deduct business driving expenses is the cents-per-mile method (50.5 cents per mile during 2008), which I recommend because it is nearly audit-proof with an adequate driving log.

But larger deductions may be available using the "actual cost" method that entails recording all costs of car ownership and allocating a portion to business driving.

Trap: People who produce driving diaries that exaggerate deductions claimed under this method often are tripped up by inconsistencies between their diaries and their auto maintenance records, which the IRS can examine if this method of deduction is used.

PROTECTING BIG DEDUCTIONS

You may be entitled to deductions that look very large to the IRS and serve as an audit red flag. In that case, you should still take them—but be prepared to show that your records are honest and that you are not an example of the "pig rule" in action.

Example: The standard home-office tax deduction is not by itself much of an audit red flag these days. Technical rules do apply to the deduction—such as that the office must be used exclusively for business—but auditors do not

actually visit homes to see that they are being followed. Thus, if you genuinely use a home office as the principal place of conducting a business, you can expect reasonable deductions for it to pass without much problem.

One client of mine deducts 80% of his home as a home office—legitimately, as the home space holds his business inventory. But such a large deduction is asking for an audit—so it should be backed up with floor plans for the home and photographs that show how it is used, to stand up to an audit that may arise.

Prepare similar records in advance to prove the honesty of any other apparently "extraordinary" deduction that may be an audit red flag.

Hot New Jobs And Where to Find Them

Sophia Koropeckyj, managing director at Moody's Economy.com, an economic research firm in West Chester, Pennsylvania. The firm's clients include some of the country's largest banks, insurance companies and financial-services firms.

The growing economic recovery should create approximately 2 million jobs per year through the end of the decade, but not every economic sector will benefit.

Don't expect lost factory or information technology jobs to come back. They will continue to move overseas at a rate of about 300,000 per year. Many jobless people will need to switch careers. *What you need to know about the new job market…*

HOT INDUSTRIES

Data from the US Bureau of Labor Statistics show two trends—our aging population is demanding more health services and home-based care…and every business must upgrade its software and technology systems continually in order to stay competitive.

The fastest-growing sectors for jobs are health care (currently 14 million employees) and non-Internet technology industries (currently 5.8 million employees). Both of these hot sectors will nearly double in size by the end of the decade.

HOT PROFESSIONS

Top health-care jobs: Physicians' assistants… medical billing and health information technicians…occupational therapists…fitness trainers/aerobics instructors…veterinary assistants/laboratory animal caretakers…mental health/substance-abuse social workers…technicians in pharmacies…hospital managers.

Note: Most of the new health-care jobs created through year 2010 will not require medical degrees. For example, if you're an unemployed middle manager, consider switching to health-care administration. Hospitals will need 123,000 more managers by the end of this decade—which is an increase of approximately 30% from current levels.

Top technology jobs: Software engineers… network administrators…desktop publishers… database administrators.

WHERE THE JOBS ARE

Within the next three years, many new jobs will be in smaller cities. According to a Milken Institute survey, locations with the fastest job growth include Fayetteville, Arkansas (near the headquarters of still-fast-growing Wal-Mart)… San Diego and San Luis Obispo, California, and Fort Myers and West Palm Beach, Florida (cities that have upscale retirees and brisk tourism).

States with greatest job growth projections until 2010: Nevada anticipates a 50% increase in jobs…Colorado, 38%…Arizona, 34% …Idaho, 31%.

The Bureau of Labor Statistics projects growth by occupation and education level at *www.bls. gov/emp.*

The Five Most Common Networking Mistakes

Andrea R. Nierenberg, president of The Nierenberg Group in New York City, which provides training in sales, customer service, presentation skills and networking to businesses worldwide. She is the author of *Nonstop Networking.* Capital.

Y ou know that networking is the key to finding a great job—but there's a fine line between getting someone's respectful attention and turning someone off.

The five most common networking blunders and how to avoid them…

Mistake #1: **Asking instead of giving.** People who always ask for favors come off as selfish opportunists. Instead, find ways to help people before asking something of them. This can be as simple as passing along articles you think they might be interested in…writing letters of reference…or recommending them to headhunters.

People that you have helped will remember —and will be more likely to help you.

Mistake #2: **Hit-and-run networking.** People who move quickly from person to person at events, never having a real conversation, are not networking. They inadvertently are giving the message that other people don't matter.

Example: A woman at a party abruptly interrupted a conversation I was having, handed me her business card and said, "Call me. I'm a photographer." Then she walked away and did the same thing to someone else. She made a terrible impression because it was obvious that she was only interested in getting something for herself.

Give your complete attention to the person with whom you are speaking. And, get to know him/her. Inquire about hobbies or families. Discuss your common interests. Phone or e-mail on occasion. Networking means developing relationships, not merely "contacts."

Mistake #3: **Blatant selling.** Be subtle in your approach. Suppose you are interested in finding a marketing job and happen to meet the CEO of a local company at a party. Don't come right out and say that you're looking for a job. Ask questions to learn more about the company's marketing campaigns, philosophy, etc. Then say something like, "It sounds like a fascinating place to work. How did you get your start?"

You'll gain valuable information. The CEO will remember you more favorably than if you had moved in like a shark. Afterward, send the CEO a handwritten note on good stationery. Say, "I really enjoyed meeting you and learning about your company. Down the road, I hope we will have another opportunity to meet."

***Mistake #4:* Ignoring people who don't "count."** You never can tell who might be able to help you in some way. The wider you cast your net, the greater the opportunities. And yet many people will totally turn off their energy to people they think can't help them. They look around the room or give one-word answers.

Instead, view everyone as an important contact. Someone in the mail room might know about openings in other divisions of the company before you do—or eventually may work his way up to a high-level position and have the opportunity to recommend you for a job.

***Mistake #5:* Not following up.** Neglecting to follow up when people meet with you or help in some way makes them feel used—and guarantees that they won't help you again in the future. Let people know that you value them and care enough to cultivate the relationship.

Example: Send a thank-you note or even a bouquet to a person who arranges a meeting for you with a company executive.

How to Deduct More Business Start-Up Costs

Sandy Soltis, CPA, tax partner, Blackman Kallick, LLP, 10 S. Riverside Plaza, Chicago 60606.

Before your business is operating, your expenses aren't tax deductible. Therefore, when you start a new business, don't hesitate. Go into operation as quickly as possible.

Expenses you incur before you are actually in business ("start-up costs") are deductible up to $5,000 in the year you commence business. Amounts more than $5,000 can be amortized over 15 years. No expensing is allowed if start-up costs exceed $55,000; they must all be amortized.

BEGINNER'S COURSE

Start-up expenses, according to the Tax Code, include costs that you incur before your business actually begins.

Money spent on the following activities might be considered start-up costs...

- **The investigation into creating a business** or buying one.
- **Preliminary market research.**
- **Search for office space.**
- **Rental expenses.**
- **Supplies purchased** before business operations begin.
- **Advertising and promotional expenses.**
- **Salaries and wages** paid before the business starts.
- **Other expenses** that would be deductible if the business were operating.

Flip side: Expenses incurred while you're still trying to decide what business to go into are personal and nondeductible.

Example: Outlays for trips to evaluate potential investments or businesses won't qualify as start-up costs, so there's no tax recovery.

UP AND RUNNING

Once your company is open for business, outlays aren't considered start-up costs. Instead, they are operating costs, which might be deductible expenses.

Opportunity: You can be in business before you have any revenues. Take action so that your company is in business as soon as possible. Don't wait until you have paying customers.

Example: You decide to create a system that makes it easier for doctors to track patient histories. Chances are, you won't receive any revenues for years.

Fortunately, you can be in business long before you sell your system to hospitals or to medical groups.

How to do it: Advertise in industry publications and send out press releases. Have business cards printed. Actively solicit future sales. Hire employees.

These and other steps will show that you are truly operating a business.

Example: You have created a waterproof "thigh holster" for campers' snacks, to be sold through sporting-goods stores. When you have the displays prepared and visit sporting-goods stores asking them to carry your displays, you're in business. That's true even though it may take months before sales start coming in.

Strategy: If you incorporate your business, hold a directors' meeting right away and keep minutes. Those minutes should state for the record that you're in business and list all the steps already taken to generate revenues.

Similarly, if you form an LLC, hold a meeting of the members or elected managers.

Key: For all business structures, keep careful records of all your efforts to bring a product or service to market. Such records may be vital in showing that you actually were in business as of the date certain expenses were incurred.

RAPID WRITE-OFFS

When your company is in business, many of your outlays will be fully deductible.

Moreover, the purchase of otherwise depreciable business equipment can be deducted ("expensed") under Section 179 of the Tax Code—up to $128,000 in 2008 ($133,000 in 2009). This break applies if your total purchases for the year don't exceed $510,000 in 2008 ($530,000 in 2009). It phases out, dollar-for-dollar, above the threshold.

Strategy: A Section 179 election can be made only for the year equipment is placed in service, not necessarily when payments are made.

Thus, you can buy equipment at year-end on a credit card or installment sales agreement and take a full deduction, with no cash outlay.

Opportunity: These expensing deductions can't exceed your taxable income from business. However, you can deduct these expenses against taxable income from the active conduct of any trade or business, including wages. If you're married, you can deduct them against income reported on a joint return, including your spouse's earnings.

Strategy: Many new businesses are short on capital. In this situation, you can lease equipment and deduct the leasing costs.

You may be able to lease with the option to buy at the end of the lease. This option often makes sense, but only if the equipment has a useful life that is significantly longer than the lease term.

Strategy: Lease your business car rather than buy it. The deduction of the lease cost will generally exceed the depreciation allowance that could be claimed if the car were purchased. The more expensive the car, the greater the tax advantage of leasing.

LOSS LEADERS

In the first year of your new business, deductible expenses might exceed taxable revenues. With some business structures, you can report a loss and deduct it against other income.

Example: You go into a Web site design business in late 2008, taking in $25,000 in revenues. However, you spend $60,000 on utilities, rent, etc. Thus, your business, which you run as a sole proprietorship, reports a loss of $35,000 for the year.

However, you were ready to design Web sites for customers the first day you moved into your office and placed your equipment into service. Therefore, your outlays are largely deductible in 2008.

Caution: The IRS will look closely at such losses, especially if (1) they go on for several years, and (2) the activity involved is one that might be an enjoyable hobby, such as travel photography.

Strategy: Retain records showing that you have acted in a businesslike manner and had the goal of making a profit.

CUTTING YOUR LOSSES

What should you do in the event that your start-up business fails?

Loophole: When you put money into a specific business (not a mere search for a business opportunity), you can then deduct the expenses incurred as a capital loss or an ordinary loss, depending upon the facts and circumstances of your investment.

Trap I: Expenses incurred to generally investigate the possibilities of going into business or to purchase a nonspecific existing business are considered personal costs, and they are not deductible.

Examples: Costs included as a capital loss might include any professional fees incurred to establish a corporation as well as ordinary operating expenses of the corporation.

Trap II: While capital losses can be used to offset capital gains, only $3,000 worth of net capital losses may be deducted in a single year. Any unused losses can be carried forward to future years.

However, the costs of equipment purchased for a failed business cannot be used to figure your capital loss. Instead, your taxable gain or loss on such assets will be determined when you sell or otherwise dispose of them.

Keeping thorough records will help you maximize your tax benefits, as always.

How to Make Great Decisions in Less Time

Barry Schwartz, PhD, Dorwin Cartwright Professor of Social Theory and Social Action, department of psychology, Swarthmore College, Swarthmore, Pennsylvania. He is author of *The Paradox of Choice: Why More Is Less.* Ecco.

At work and home, we make hundreds of decisions every day, some trivial, some important—which soap to buy, which political candidate to vote for, how to plan for retirement. These days, high-tech communications only add to the difficulty. We need to make decisions even more quickly when we respond to e-mail or answer our cell phones.

The result? We choose haphazardly or, worse, we become paralyzed by information overload and end up making no decision.

Example: Employees complain that their 401(k) plans offer too few investment options, but research indicates that the more mutual funds an employer makes available, the less likely employees are to participate in the plan at all, even if it means passing up thousands of dollars in employer-matching contributions.

Here are strategies I have learned from my own and other social scientists' studies on decision making...

● **Learn to accept "good enough."** We all sometimes misuse our time and energy by trying to make the best choice. For instance, we might devote an hour or more to relatively frivolous decisions, such as choosing a restaurant, but spend just a few minutes picking a lawyer or doctor, often depending on just one friend's recommendation.

Better: Ask yourself how significantly one choice will affect your life. The more minor and short-term the impact, the less time you should spend making the decision.

The concept of "good enough" is difficult to embrace because it feels like you're settling for mediocrity—but "settling" often increases overall satisfaction.

Examples: You decide to write a heartfelt letter to your spouse on your anniversary. You want to choose just the right words—but after several drafts, you give up in frustration and just buy a card at a store. Yet even an imperfect letter would have been much more meaningful to your spouse.

Or you find a movie that you're interested in at the video store. Instead of taking it home and just enjoying it, you think there must be another that would better suit your mood. You spend 45 minutes scouring the aisles without success. By the time you leave—with your original selection in hand—you have wasted a good chunk of your precious leisure time.

● **Deliberately reduce the options when a decision is not critical.** Base your decision criteria on your past experience.

Examples: You have to hire a summer intern at work. If you have been able to find someone suitable in previous years by interviewing four candidates, set that as your limit.

You can apply the same technique to choosing a hairdresser, dog groomer or dry cleaner. Spend enough time to find someone who is adequate, then get on with your life.

● **Spend a lot of time and energy on a decision only if the extra effort can yield significantly better results.** Say that you have a choice of three long-distance phone-service providers, any of which will meet your needs. You're tempted to figure out which company's plan gives you a slight advantage, but the time-consuming and confusing process will save you no more than a few dollars a month.

You shouldn't choose blindly, but give yourself only a specific amount of time to review the plans or a deadline to make a choice.

Even spending enormous amounts of time on critical decisions, such as buying a home or helping your child choose a college, may not be worth the effort. Decisions such as these often involve more uncertainty than you ever can resolve in advance.

●**Don't let marketers play you.** Companies today are brilliant at seeding dissatisfaction in consumers to get them to buy more expensive products. This applies to everything from laundry detergent to such big-ticket items as cars. Computer software makers are notorious for this, pushing Acme Software version 7 or 8 when version 6 still is adequate for your needs. Most "enhancements" are minimal or tangential to a product's main purpose.

Smart: Stick with an older product or service until you experience shortcomings that really compromise your satisfaction. You'll save money and gain time.

●**Don't keep researching products and services after you have made a decision.** Have you ever bought a new car or computer, then scanned the newspapers each week to check the current price? This behavior just creates postpurchase misgivings.

If the car's price drops below what you paid, you will feel as if you were ripped off. If the car's price increases, you will wonder what was wrong with your particular vehicle that allowed you to get such a good deal.

People derive only modest pleasure from confirming that they got a good deal and substantial dissatisfaction from finding out that they could have done better.

●**Make most decisions irreversible.** It makes sense to want to know about a return policy when you make a purchase, but being allowed to change your mind only increases the chance that you will.

On the other hand, when a decision is final, you engage in a variety of powerful psychological processes that enhance your satisfaction about your choice relative to the alternatives.

Example: Today's proliferation of no-fault divorces and prenuptial agreements has influenced many people to stop treating their selection of a partner for life as a sacred decision. During the course of a marriage, you are likely to encounter many people who might seem better looking, smarter or more understanding than your spouse.

Always wondering whether you could have done better is a prescription for misery. You're better off thinking, *I've made my decision, so this other person's qualities have nothing to do with me. I'm not in the market.*

Drive Freight Costs Down

Purchasing World, Barrington, Illinois.

Ideas to put a lid on industrial freight costs, which are rising a lot faster than the general price level…

●**Standardize shipping instructions based on urgency.** When the lack of an item threatens a production shutdown, specify small-package or priority airfreight. When the lack could cause a stock outage, specify nonpriority (two to three days) airfreight or LTL (less-than-full-truckload). Specify a truckload or rail shipment for items for regular stock resupply or normal reorder.

●**Consolidate inbound freight.** Have the carrier consolidate two or more shipments from a single vendor (or even from several vendors) into one. Advantages are weight breaks and minimal delivery charges.

●**Think total cost.** Direct shipping charges (rates, packing, crating, insurance) aren't all. The final cost decision on mode must include indirect shipping costs such as capital that is invested in inventories, carrying charges, warehousing, cost of damage, theft, pilferage, etc. In addition, there are intangible considerations, such as system flexibility, competitive advantage, and customer goodwill.

How to Get Your Product On National TV for Next to Nothing

Allen E. Barkus, president, Ted Barkus Advertising Co., Inc., 8017 Anderson St., Philadelphia 19118.

Giving away your product as a TV game or talk show prize gives it exposure to a national audience at a cost that's a small fraction of the cost of buying a comparable amount of TV advertising time. Any nationally sold consumer product or service is a candidate for this exciting form of promotion.

How it works: Through an advertising agency that handles these promotions, your company offers its product for use as a prize to the producers of a show you think will give it the best audience (your ad agency will be able to tell you which shows have the kind of audience you're trying to target). The agency writes promotional copy to be used on the air and creates any visual material, including videos, you want to accompany the product on the show. *There are two categories of prizes...*

●**Major prizes.** They include merchandise valued at $500 or more. Manufacturers pay nominal placement fees—about $200 per broadcast—for acceptance of these products by the producers.

●**Minor prizes.** Merchandise worth $25 or more. Placement fees for these prizes are much higher...often in excess of $4,000 per broadcast.

The placement fees also vary from show to show. Products offered as prizes on *Wheel of Fortune*, for example, carry the highest placement fees. The fee for a minor prize on a single broadcast of *Wheel of Fortune* is over $4,500 (about $200 for a major prize). On *The Price Is Right*, the placement fee for a minor prize is only about $1,000, and about $200 for a major prize.

THE PAYOFF

For this fee, plus modest ad agency charges for writing the promotion copy and marketing services, your product gets national TV exposure of eight to 20 seconds (the average for most prize mentions is 10 seconds). With *Wheel of Fortune*, this exposure covers more than 30 million American homes.

Typical campaign: A $1,000 video camera given away to *Wheel of Fortune* contestants on, say, 40–50 broadcasts and to contestants on 40–50 broadcasts of *The Price Is Right* in the same period would cost a total of about $25,000 in placement fees, costs for media agencies, creative work, etc.

Payoff: The product can be seen about one billion times by consumers.

●**Comparable cost for 80–100 prime time 10-second network TV spots:** Over $550,000.

Added bonus: Some TV shows now allow manufacturers to air toll-free phone numbers when their products are being mentioned. Measuring consumer telephone response can provide valuable information about the effectiveness of your campaign.

Cost-Reduction Reminders

There are many ways to reduce costs...here are four to get you started...

●**Materials.** Look for materials that are cheaper to buy, easier to fabricate, offer a product improvement.

●**Specifications.** Consider eliminating manufacturing operations, cutting scrap, reducing rework, widening tolerances.

●**Purchasing.** Investigate quantity buys, market fluctuations, open contracts, any financing concessions from suppliers.

●**Packaging.** Costs may be reduced through redesign, new materials, different sizes, different quantities.

Purchasing Factomatic, Prentice-Hall, Englewood Cliffs, New Jersey.

Ways to Fight a Price Hike

Dr. Chester L. Karrass, *Purchasing*, Boston.

Below are four ways to fight a price hike and keep more money in your company's pocket…

●**Send the supplier a substantial purchase order,** but specify the old price, as if the announced hike had been overlooked. The implied threat—accept these terms or risk losing the whole order, perhaps even the whole account.

●**Ask for a reduction in price,** without any reference to the proposed increase. This may lead to an eventual compromise at or near the old level.

●**Acknowledge the hike,** but claim an inability to pay more than the former price for this current order. The vendor will probably agree to continue with the old price, at least for a time.

●**Turn the raise down,** out-of-hand. Say that the company will go elsewhere unless the increase is rescinded. This is risky, even if the vendor feels forced to go along, because of the resentment stirred by the take-it-or-leave-it ultimatum. Then what? Someday, when the vendor holds the bargaining leverage, expect a move to get even.

17

School and Family Money Savers

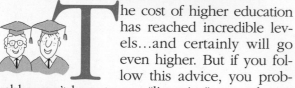

Financial Aid for Your Kids...No Matter How Much Money You Make

The cost of higher education has reached incredible levels...and certainly will go even higher. But if you follow this advice, you probably won't have to pay "list price" to send your kids to college.

There are two ways to make college more affordable...

●**Tax savings.** The Internal Revenue Code is studded with a variety of tax incentives for college education.

●**Financial aid.** Colleges arrange for loans, jobs and outright grants to help students and their parents manage all the bills.

Key: Know the trade-offs between the Tax Code and financial-aid formulas so you have the lowest net cost possible.

TYPES OF AID

The biggest mistake made by families during the college application process is not filling out standard financial-aid forms because they believe they won't qualify.

Reality: Not all of college aid is based on financial need. Most colleges also offer "merit-based aid."

Merit aid often takes the form of tuition discounts. It should be applied for.

Example: College ABC lists $15,000 as its annual tuition. Your son (who is a good student) applies to ABC, which decides to compete for his enrollment.

He might be offered a $7,500 "scholarship," effectively a 50% cut in tuition, if he chooses ABC. This scholarship is offered regardless of his family's financial circumstances.

Rick Darvis, president of College Funding, Inc., 121 N. Main St., Plentywood, Montana 59254. Cofounder and director of the National Institute of Certified College Planners, he is the author of *College Financial Aid—The Best Kept Secret in America*. College Funding, Inc. His Web site is *www.solutionsforcollege.net.*

Note: Even though merit aid isn't based on a family's finances, many colleges won't offer it to students who haven't applied for financial aid.

Bottom line: Most students wind up paying much less than the posted tuition price.

SHIFTING ASSETS

A few elite colleges do not offer merit aid; those schools offer only need-based aid.

Even if you're determined that your child will attend such a university, you should not give up on financial aid.

Families that apply for financial aid at these institutions are assigned "expected family contributions" (EFCs) based on income and assets. For parent and student, the income that you report is based on a special worksheet. Assets held by parents enjoy more protection, while the assets held by children are expected to be used for college costs.

Example: Working through the financial-aid forms, your EFC is set at $25,000 this year. If your child is accepted at a college where total costs are $20,000, no need-based aid will be offered. However, if your child goes to a college where costs are $30,000, you would be eligible for $5,000 worth of aid.

Key: The more expensive the college chosen, the more likely you will qualify for need-based aid. That's especially true for years when you'll have two or three kids in college.

Strategy: If you believe you will qualify for need-based aid, keep financial assets in your own name. And, load up on investments that won't be counted, such as life insurance, annuities and tax-deferred retirement plans. Also, be aware that home equity and farm equity are not counted at most schools.

Impact of 529 plans: These plans allow tax-free buildup and tax-free withdrawals for higher education. Depending on the type of plan, it may be counted as a parental asset for determining an EFC, or distributions may reduce the student's need-based aid.

Strategy: If you think you'll qualify for financial aid, transfer a 529 account to a non-parent (such as an aunt or a grandmother) before filling out the financial-aid form.

Caution: Beware of prepaid tuition plans, which reduce financial aid dollar for dollar.

REDUCING INCOME

Besides reducing your assets, to get need-based financial aid, you should also legally trim your reported income.

Timing: For each academic year, the prior year's income is counted. So, for the 2009–2010 school year, for example, your 2008 income will be used to determine financial aid.

Holding down your adjusted gross income (AGI) will not only reduce your tax bill, it will also drop your EFC by as much as 47%.

Example: You run a business as an S corporation. You're allowed a $250,000 business equipment write-off for 2008 ($133,000 for 2009). You bought $250,000 worth of equipment that you were planning to buy anyway, which then reduces your AGI in 2008 by $250,000 ($133,000 for 2009).

Payoff: Depending on your income level, you might save 30% in tax by reducing your AGI. In addition, the AGI reduction will increase your family's eligibility for need-based aid by as much as 47% under the financial-aid formula depending on your family's financial and household situation. Your total benefit (tax savings plus increased college aid) could be 30% plus 47%, or 77%.

Another way to reduce your AGI and enjoy a double benefit is to maximize contributions to a retirement plan. If you are in business, you can contribute (and can deduct) up to $46,000 to a profit-sharing plan in 2008 ($49,000 in 2009) and even more to a defined-benefit plan. Individual taxpayers can reduce AGI by deferring income or accelerating expenses.

Considering an MBA?

On-line programs, designed to accommodate busy schedules, are offered by 152 schools, including Duke University, University of Massachusetts and Indiana University. Choose a program that is regionally accredited and recognized by the Association to Advance Collegiate Schools of Business (*www.aacsb.edu*). On-line MBA programs require 12 to 15 courses, and costs average from $6,000 to $21,000. (Comparable campus-based degrees often cost more than $100,000.) Programs require participation in on-line discussions, and 40% of programs require some on-campus time. On-line programs have the same admissions standards as the schools' regular admissions.

Vicky Phillips, CEO, GetEducated.com, which surveys the top programs across the US every two years and offers a free report of the "Top 25 Best Buys" according to cost at its Web site, *www.geteducated.com/index.asp.*

Find Millions Of Dollars in FREE Money for College On the Web

Paul J. Krupin, president, Direct Contact PR, Kennewick, Washington, *www.directcontactpr.com.* He is also author of the *Magic Search Words* series of books, including *Magic Search Words: Scholarships.* Direct Contact. He started the series to help people use the Internet search engines more effectively.

Every year, millions of dollars of free money for college is left unclaimed because students just aren't aware of it. The Internet is a storehouse of information on scholarships and grants for students of all ages—but you have to know the best ways to find it.

Most of the scholarships are for either $500 or $1,000, though some offer as much as $10,000 per year. Some students are awarded several different scholarships. Nearly every college or university offers full scholarships that cover tuition and living expenses.

WHAT TO DO

Start your search at *www.google.com.* This popular search engine constantly updates its listings on scholarships, grants, paid fellowships, etc.

•**Plug in "money words."** Start with *scholarship.* Then search related money words, such as *grant...fellowship...assistantship,* etc. These will lead you to more revenue sources.

•**Search with word strings.** When you type more than one word in the search field, the listings will be more specific to your particular needs. Just enter the search words with a space between each word—you don't need to include "and" or a plus sign.

Example: Scholarship graphic design San Francisco 2008. The location you include can be either where you live or where you want to go to school.

Change one word at a time after your initial search. In the previous example, replace the word *scholarship* with *grant* or *graphic design* with *art.*

Helpful: Make a list of key words and their synonyms to include in your scholarship search.

•**Bypass commercial sites.** Typing *–.com* in the search field streamlines your search by eliminating paid-for scholarship search services.

•**Search your interests.** No matter what you like to do—play tennis, skydive, act, quilt—there are probably scholarships available. Pair your interests with the word *scholarship* in your search engine.

•**Search the sites of major foundations,** associations and companies. Many provide scholarships. *Some examples to search under...*

•Acting...
  ☐ Donna Reed Performing Arts scholarships
  ☐ Irene Ryan Acting Competition

•Athletics...
  ☐ National Collegiate Athletic Association or NCAA scholarships

•Business...
  ☐ IBM scholarships
  ☐ Rotary International scholarships

•Conservation...
  ☐ Soil and Water Conservation Society scholarships and awards
  ☐ World Wildlife Fund

•Science and technology...
  ☐ DuPont Challenge Science Essay Awards Program
  ☐ Intel scholarships
  ☐ Microsoft scholarships
  ☐ Military science scholarships
  ☐ National science scholarships

How to Cut Dormitory Costs

Invest in near-campus housing for your child to avoid the high cost of college dormitories. Find a house or condo within a few miles of campus in a safe neighborhood. It should be large enough for at least four tenants—one of whom will be your child. After picking a property, estimate potential rent and expenses, then make a bid that would enable you to cover your costs and have some cash left over. Do basic landscaping and repairs, then furnish the property with inexpensive, durable furniture. Charge reasonable rents, appropriate for the area, and insist on formal leases. You can pay your child a management fee to collect rents and maintain the property. Plan to sell the property when he/she finishes college.

Vita Nelson, comanager, MP63 Fund, which invests in the stocks of 63 companies that have dividend-reinvestment plans, Rye, New York.

Home-Schooled Students Outperform Others

More than 1.5 million US children are now home-schooled—and that figure is increasing by 15% a year. Home-schooled students do better on standardized tests than public- and private-school students.

Information: National Home Education Network (*www.nhen.org*)...American Homeschool Association (800-236-3278, *www.americanhome schoolassociation.org*).

Laura Derrick, president, National Home Education Network, Box 1652, Hobe Sound, Florida 33475.

Learn Anything You Want to Know On-Line

Janet Moore, chief learning officer, The Sloan Consortium, based in Needham, Massachusetts, and Angela Lovett, CEO and founder, World Wide Learn, based in Calgary, Canada.

People who want to take classes on anything from Chinese cuisine to advanced mathematics are no longer limited to the courses at nearby colleges or other institutions. The Internet makes it possible to learn from expert instructors the world over.

Even better: You can usually access your course at any time of day you choose from the comfort of your home.

All you need is basic computer knowledge and access to the Internet. If you don't have the equipment, it may well be available at your local library. Many libraries offer quick courses in using a computer.

Cost: Many courses are free. This is especially true for those leisure-time activities and courses that are offered by social and professional organizations to their members.

Classes in business management or Web-site design often cost less than $1,000, while top vocational schools charge $1,500 to $2,500 a course. Courses leading to a degree at a well-known university typically cost $900 to $3,600.

Be aware that there are pitfalls...

• **Unsuitability.** On-line learning may not suit you. Learning via a computer can be frustrating for anyone who enjoys the camaraderie of a classroom.

• **Rip-off peril.** Many less-than-reputable organizations are selling second-rate courses that are taught by unqualified instructors.

HOW TO BEGIN

The majority of American colleges and universities provide on-line programs for academic credit. Many other types of institutions also provide noncredit courses, including technical, business and vocational schools.

Example: Herkimer County Community College (315-866-0300, *www.hccc.ntcnet.com*) offers an on-line degree in travel and tourism.

In addition, colleges and other organizations also offer courses in hobbies and fine arts.

Examples: The University of Hawaii (808-956-8111, *www.hawaii.edu*) offers extensive on-line instruction in music.

When you sign up for a course, you pay a fee and receive a password that allows you to access the course's Web site. You might also receive written material or textbooks, but most of the information you're expected to learn is accessed via the Internet.

These courses differ widely, but most of them require you to read or listen to a certain amount of material and then check what you've learned either by self-testing or by submitting answers to the instructor via e-mail.

Because students are linked to the Internet, teachers can illustrate points in spectacular ways.

Examples: Courses in art can show you close-ups of some of the world's finest paintings. Music courses let you listen to a chamber orchestra in Paris.

And if you want to see or hear something again, it's easy to replay it on your computer.

Tests: In most nondegree courses, students open an e-mail containing the test, take it and send it to the instructor for grading. Teachers follow up by asking students to solve problems that are difficult for anyone who hasn't thoroughly absorbed the material.

Tests for degree courses, especially those at prestigious universities, are rarely held on-line. Instead, students go to a nearby location—usually a local university—where the test is supervised in a traditional classroom setting.

There is no camaraderie in the traditional sense, but many courses include an on-line bulletin board or chat room. These let students discuss the subject matter among themselves or ask the instructor questions that have not been adequately covered during class.

CHOOSING A SCHOOL

Several Web sites list courses offered by legitimate institutions.

Examples: The Sloan Consortium, a group of more than 500 leading US colleges and universities at *www.sloan-c.org*, and World Wide Learn, a site that lists hundreds of on-line learning centers, *www.worldwidelearn.com.*

The on-line learning department at a local university can also provide advice. Or you can contact the trade organization associated with the field in which you want to take a course.

Examples: For interior design organizations, check the Council for Interior Design Accredidation (*www.accredit-id.org*)...or for theater, art, music and dance schools, try *www. arts-accredit.org.*

For a general listing, enter a course description in an Internet search engine, such as *www.google.com.* By entering "on-line course in real estate," for example, you'll find dozens of organizations that offer instruction. Check to see if the professor/instructor is certified by a state board that licenses professionals in that field, such as a state licensed real estate broker, or check to see if the school is certified by a regional accreditor.

Important: If you plan to use the course toward a degree or to further your career, take courses only at an institution that is accredited by one of the following six regional academic associations...

●Middle States Commission on Higher Education (267-284-5000, *www.msche.org*).

●New England Association of Schools and Colleges (781-271-0022, *www.neasc.org*).

●The Higher Learning Commission of the North Central Association of Colleges and Schools (312-263-0456, *www.ncahigherlearning commission.org*).

●Northwest Commission on Colleges and Universities (425-558-4224, *www.nwccu.org*).

●Southern Association of Colleges and Schools (404-679-4500, *www.sacs.org*).

●Western Association of Schools and Colleges (415-506-0234, *www.accjc.org*).

Helpful: The Council for Higher Education Accreditation (202-955-6126, *www.chea.org*) lists institutions approved by other accrediting groups at its Web site.

If you are not using the on-line course to get a degree or to advance your career, accredited institutions are still a useful way to ensure that you pay for a quality course. Many well-known organizations and companies, including AARP at *www.aarp.org/about_aarp/nrta* or Barnes & Noble "Book Clubs" at *http://bookclubs.barnes andnoble.com*, also offer quality programs.

Many individuals offer courses on the Web as well, including experts in areas such as gardening and screenwriting. Be careful.

Example: Before taking an on-line course in screenwriting, ask whether the instructor is a member of the Screenwriters Guild of America and what films he/she has written. Then check out the answers by going to The Internet Movie Database at *www.imdb. com*, which lists films and detailed information about them.

Rule of thumb: Stay away from an on-line course if the institution's Web site is filled with ads for products and services—they may indicate that the organization is not as concerned with education as it is with quick profits.

Financial Aid for Military Families

For students who served or currently serve in the US military, college scholarships and financial aid are listed at *www.military.com* (click on "Education"). Some special college financing plans are available for children and spouses of current and former armed services members. Offers include interest-free loans, grants, the American Patriot Scholarship and aid plans from the Department of Veterans Affairs.

Raymond D. Loewe, CLU, ChFC, president, College Money, Marlton, New Jersey. *www.collegemoney.com.*

More from Raymond D. Loewe, CLU, ChFC...

Student Loans for Postgraduate Degrees

Students seeking MBAs and medical and law degrees can apply for federal funds, such as Stafford and Perkins loans, but these may

not cover the entire cost. Sallie Mae is offering additional loans.

●**Graduate business students** can apply for an MBA Stafford or MBA Private Loan, both sponsored by the Graduate Management Admissions Council.

●**Law students** may be eligible for a Law-Loans Stafford or LawLoans Private Loan. Students studying for the bar may apply for a LawLoans Bar Study Loan.

●**Medical students** may be eligible for a MedLoans Stafford Loan.

Information: Sallie Mae, 800-891-4599, *www.salliemae.com.*

How Out-of-State Students Can Pay In-State Tuition

David Wright, former senior research analyst for State Higher Education Executive Officers, a Boulder-based association of postsecondary education institutions, *www. sheeo.org.*

Typically, students who attend public colleges outside their home states will pay about four times the tuition rate that residents pay.

Good news: There is a way to go out of state and pay in-state tuition rates.

Opportunity: Most states quietly provide reduced-tuition degree programs for students from certain neighboring states. A student generally can qualify only when the program he/she wants to major in isn't available at the public college or university in his home state.

Example: He wants to specialize in marine biology, but his state's school only offers degrees in general biology.

If his state's school offers a similar program but he still prefers the out-of-state school, he may be able to shade this requirement by crafting a course of study in his chosen field that isn't quite like the one his home state offers. He should just make sure that less than half the course work overlaps what's available in his state.

The student should apply to the school first. After he is accepted, he can apply for tuition reduction.

Two types of programs provide lower tuition for out-of-state residents...

TUITION RECIPROCITY AGREEMENTS

There are four regional programs. Some also offer reciprocity at graduate, medical and professional levels. In the Southern program, out-of-staters pay the in-state rate. In New England and the Midwest, they typically pay about 150% of the in-state rate—but sometimes less, and still well below what out-of-staters normally pay.

Example: Under the New England Regional Student Program for 2008–2009, a student from Connecticut (or another New England state) could attend the University of Maine for $10,755—a savings of $9,825 over the out-of-state tuition rate and $3,605 more than the in-state tuition of $7,170.

The four programs...

●**New England Regional Student Program** (NERSP) covers Connecticut, Maine, Massachusetts, New Hampshire, Rhode Island and Vermont. 617-357-9620 or *www.nebhe.org/ explain.html.*

●**Midwestern Higher Education Compact** (MHEC) for Illinois, Indiana, Iowa, Kansas, Michigan, Minnesota, Missouri, Nebraska, North Dakota, Ohio, South Dakota and Wisconsin. 612-626-8288 or *www.mhec.org.*

●**The Southern Regional Education Board** (SREB) for Alabama, Arkansas, Delaware, Florida, Georgia, Kentucky, Louisiana, Maryland, Mississippi, North Carolina, Oklahoma, South Carolina, Tennessee, Texas, Virginia and West Virginia. 404-875-9211 or *www. sreb.org.*

●**The Western Interstate Commission for Higher Education** (WICHE). Alaska, Arizona, California, Colorado, Hawaii, Idaho, Montana, Nevada, New Mexico, North Dakota (also a member of the MHEC), Oregon, South Dakota, Utah, Washington and Wyoming. 303-541-0270 or *www.wiche.edu/SEP/WUE.*

GOOD-NEIGHBOR POLICIES

These bilateral agreements give students in one state reduced tuition at an adjacent state's colleges. Good-neighbor policies always involve two contiguous states—and usually have some limitations.

For instance, the student may have to live within 150 miles of the adjoining state's school. In some cases, reciprocity is limited to students in just one or two counties in the adjacent state.

A recent survey of interstate good-neighbor policies showed 30 states offering such policies. Download this report from *www.sheeo. org/finance/t&f_web/Section%20B-7.pdf.*

Get Money to Go Back to School

Nancy Dunnan, a financial adviser and author in New York City. Ms. Dunnan's latest book is titled *How to Invest $50–$5,000*. HarperCollins.

There are a variety of ways older people can obtain financing if they wish to return to or start college. *See below...*

●**Contact college admissions offices about special loans or scholarships.** Because of the growing number of nontraditional students, colleges hold evening classes, weekend courses and even offer child-care facilities and access to babysitting pools—all designed to make it easier for adults to crack the books.

●**Set up a 529 plan right away.** Your contributions and earnings grow free of federal tax. And, when you withdraw money, it, too, is federal tax free—as long as you use it for tuition, fees, books or supplies. It can be for a part-time, full-time or distance learning program. You control the account and can change the beneficiary to another family member at any time. So if you decide not to go to school, the money can be used to pay for the education of a relative—your child, spouse, siblings, cousin, niece, nephew, parent or grandparent.

Caution: If you take the money out for any non-college expenses, you must pay income tax plus a 10% penalty.

●**Check with your employer.** Many will foot some or all of the bill if the course work is related to your job. In some cases, you may be required to earn a B in the course in order to be reimbursed for your tuition.

●**Check your own state plan.** There are a number of advantages to opening a 529 plan in your state. Many allow residents to deduct a portion or all of their contributions from state taxes. A number of states also reduce fees for residents.

For more information: The College Savings Plan Network at *www.collegesavings.org* has a wealth of information.

Save Thousands and Grab a Degree in Just Three Years

You can save thousands in college costs with advanced placement. There are 33 Advanced Placement (AP) tests, in 19 subjects, given in mid-May every year. Course work is not required to take AP tests—a student can study on his/her own. Students scoring at least four out of a possible five get college credit for their knowledge.

Surprising: You need answer only 50% to 60% of questions correctly for a score of four.

Savings on college costs can be significant—one-third of the latest Harvard entering class had enough AP credits to start as sophomores or above…saving at least one year of tuition.

Adam Robinson, education consultant based in New York City, cofounder of The Princeton Review and author of *What Smart Students Know.* Crown.

An Insider's Secrets to Getting More Money For College

Ben Kaplan, Oregon-based founder of Scholarship-Coach.com, which provides information on obtaining college financing. He graduated from Harvard University debt-free in 1999 by using $90,000 in scholarships and is author of 12 books and CDs on paying for college, including *How to Go to College Almost for Free: 10 Days to Scholarship Success. www.scholarshipcoach.com.*

Now is the time to think about how to pay for college. Many families fail to take full advantage of the financial aid available to them and lose out on tens of thousands of dollars in grants, scholarships and subsidized loans. Even households with considerable incomes and assets can qualify. (Merit scholarships are available regardless of income.) *Here's how to get the most financial aid you can…*

●**Defer your income in the calendar year before your child graduates from high school.** The financial aid eligibility clock starts ticking sooner than most parents expect.

Example: If your student graduates high school in 2009, your income in 2008 will serve as the basis for freshman-year financial aid calculations.

Strategy: Ask employers to pay year-end bonuses early 2009 rather than during 2008. If you're self-employed, accelerate or postpone customer billing to minimize 2008 income. Avoid selling assets, such as stocks, bonds and rental property, in 2008 if proceeds will be taxed as income. (Delaying income from 2008 to 2009 might cause your aid to drop in the student's sophomore year, but you'll come out ahead, since the freshman "base" year sets the precedent for financial aid allocations.)

●**To reduce cash reserves, make major expenditures**—on home renovations, cars,

computers, entertainment systems, etc.—before applying for aid.

Reason: Colleges take most financial assets into account when they determine your need for aid but not other personal assets, such as cars or home electronics.

If your child has significant savings, urge him/her to spend his own money first—as opposed to yours—on big-ticket items.

Reason: When figuring out aid packages according to the federal methodology, colleges now expect students to contribute 20% of their assets to college costs. Parents are expected to pitch in only about 5% of their assets. (You can, of course, pay the child back later without incurring gift tax as long as you don't exceed the maximum annual gift limit of $12,000 per recipient—$24,000 for couples.)

●**Apply for aid as soon as possible.** Many colleges distribute financial aid on a first-come, first-served basis, so money might be substantially depleted long before the official end of the application period. Submit the federal government's Free Application for Federal Student Aid (FAFSA) form—as well as any additional forms required by private colleges—by January or early February of your child's senior year in high school to ensure the biggest share possible.

To gather the necessary information, you'll need to complete your tax forms well before April. If you can't, use estimates on your college aid forms (identifying them as estimates) and follow up with actual figures as soon as possible.

●**If a school's aid offer is lower than you expected,** explain special circumstances that are not covered by the aid formulas—hefty medical bills...private-school tuition for your other grade-school children...graduate school costs for your older kids, if you pay some of their bills...or an unusually high income year that is not representative of your typical earnings. Follow up with evidence, such as invoices, establishing that, for example, you're paying Grandma's hospital bills, or the last five years' tax returns to show that your income last year was much higher than normal.

●**Apply for merit-based scholarships** from corporations, foundations, associations, unions and community groups. Links to award databases can be found at my Web site, ScholarshipCoach.com.

Note: These scholarships may affect other financial aid.

●**Leverage offers from other schools.** If your top choice is X University, but Y offers more aid, call X and ask to speak to the financial aid officer responsible for your file. Explain that your child really wants to attend, but Y's aid package makes going there more financially feasible. X might increase its offer. This works best when the schools involved are rivals or the student is particularly appealing to the college because of special credentials or talents.

Working for A Low-Cost Education

The federal government and the armed forces offer a variety of programs in which college students work or provide military service in exchange for financial aid.

FEDERAL WORK-STUDY PROGRAMS

Federal work-study (FWS) programs provide part-time jobs for undergraduate and graduate students who demonstrate financial need. These programs encourage community service and work related to a student's course of study.

Most FWS jobs are on campus in one of the school's service departments. For example, students may work in the cafeteria, financial aid office or research library. FWS payment is dependent upon individual school policy, and is either paid to students or applied directly to their college cost. For information on how to apply, call the Free Application for Federal Students Aid (FAFSA) at 800-433-3243, *www.fafsa. ed.gov.*

AMERICORPS

AmeriCorps is a federal work-study service organization with more than 450 different national service programs around the country. Workers earn education vouchers in exchange for one to two years of national service.

The awards: One-year full-time service (1,700 hours) $4,725; one-year part-time service (900 hours) $2,362.50. Money may be used to help pay back student loans or finance college, graduate school or vocational school tuition.

Warning: Your child may be able to make more money for college working at a regular job.

AmeriCorps members receive a modest living allowance of approximately $150 a week—it varies by location. Members must cover their own housing and meal expenses using this allowance. Health insurance is also provided, and some members may receive child-care assistance.

Service opportunities are available in the areas of education, public safety, human needs and the environment. *Contact...*

●**AmeriCorps** at 800-942-2677, *www.ameri corps.org.*

●**The Corporation for National & Community Service** (AmeriCorps National Civilian Community Corps) at 202-606-5000, *www. americorps.org/nccc.*

The National Civilian Community Corps is AmeriCorps' residential national service program for 18- to 24-year-olds. The program is full time only and runs for 10 months. Members receive a modest biweekly allowance, and live in dormitory-style housing and receive meals. Five campuses participate in this program.

The award: After the full 10 months are completed, members receive $4,725 to help pay off their student loans or to pay for future educational expenses. Health insurance is part of their membership.

Contact: 800-942-2677.

ROTC

The US Armed Forces sponsors the Reserve Officers Training Corps (ROTC), a federal, merit-based scholarship program available at many colleges and universities.

Note: ROTC programs are highly competitive and preference is sometimes given to students studying nursing, engineering, science or business. Scholarships pay up to $16,000 a year of college tuition, plus money toward textbooks and a small yearly stipend.

In addition to their regular classes, ROTC students must attend special classes sponsored by the US Armed Forces. Upon graduation, they are committed to serve as active-duty officers for four years in the branch of service that sponsored their ROTC program.

For information about available programs, contact military recruiters, look in your college catalogs or call 800-USA-ROTC, *www.army rotc.com.* The Navy ROTC program also offers a special two-year program for college juniors and seniors. For information, call 800-USA-NAVY, *www.nrotc.navy.com/.*

How to Cut The Cost of College Extras

Tuition is not the only cost involved in going to college. You'll also need to take into account the cost of school fees, books, room and board, travel expenses and general costs of living. But there are ways to save on these add-ons.

ROOM AND BOARD

Many colleges and universities require students to live on campus during their freshman year and require freshmen to have a meal plan as well. *Other students may have these options...*

●**Campus Dormitories.** They usually come with a five- to 21-meal plan (sometimes optional) and on-site security.

●**Campus Apartments.** They usually include a kitchenette and may have some campus security.

●**Off-Campus Housing or Apartments.** They often have a kitchenette but offer no campus security. Depending on the college or university's location, even a 12-month lease may be more cost-efficient than on-campus housing. If your child wants to stay in the apartment over the summer (he/she may be working or attending summer school), one-year leases are appropriate. If not, look into nine-month leases or subletting the apartment during the summer.

COMPUTERS

On-campus computer stores frequently offer students discounts of around 10% on new computers, but check to be sure you're getting the best price.

Warning: Don't choose a model until you have checked with the college's computer center and found out which system the school uses.

Consider investing in a laptop—it costs more but can be brought along to lectures or the library.

BOOKS AND TEXTBOOKS

Most campus bookstores sell used books and they are always sold at a reduced price.

Caution: Be sure to flip through the book to make sure the text can be clearly read. Some students highlight and heavily mark their books. Students can save even more money by selling books back to the bookstore when they are no longer needed.

Don't depend solely on the campus bookstore. Most college towns have more than one bookstore, so it's a good idea to shop around and compare prices.

Another source: Enterprising students sometimes purchase bulk orders of their school's most popular textbooks and sell them to fellow students at better prices than the campus bookstore. Check out bulletin boards around campus or ask upperclassmen to find out about any available deals.

Financial-aid offices are frequently willing to make adjustments to student budgets if students can document that their books and supplies cost more than average. Save your book receipts and don't be afraid to ask the financial-aid department for help if you think your book costs are excessive.

Get Paid for Your Child to Live Off-Campus

Save on boarding costs and even make a profit! Look into purchasing an apartment or small house near campus for your child to live in. Then hire your child as the building manager in exchange for free rent, and rent out the extra bedrooms.

Rental income should offset your maintenance costs. Plus, your mortgage payments will give you equity in an asset of value while payments for a dorm or apartment would not. You can then sell the house after your child graduates and get back some or all of your original investment, or possibly even make a profit.

Managing a house is not always an easy thing to do, however, so this option works best with mature, responsible students.

Summer School Saves Time and Money

Students who want to save money should consider taking summer classes at their local community college.

Taking summer classes at a less expensive school will not only reduce your costs but may also allow your child to graduate sooner. Summer classes are also a great way to alleviate some of the pressure of an overloaded semester. They tend to be a little more lenient academically and smaller in size, which means that the professor is more accessible for one-on-one discussions and questions.

Students should always make sure that any course credits are transferable to their primary school before they enroll in a summer class.

Secrets to Repairing and Replacing Household Items

Donna S. Morris has more than 30 years of experience in the antiques and furniture repair business, La Verne, California. She is author of several books on furniture, including *Furniture Repairs from A to Z: A Quick Reference Guide of Tips and Techniques*. Phoenix.

The late Ralph and Terry Kovel, Cleveland-based authors of 90 books on antiques, including *Kovels' Antiques and Collectibles Price List 2009*. Random House Reference.

Marijo Rymer is president of Marijo Rymer Custom Clothing in Denver. She is former vice president of public relations for the Professional Association of Custom Clothiers. *www.paccprofessionals.org*.

Gray LaFortune is director of Ceramic Tile Institute of America, a tile trade organization, in Culver City, California (*www.ctioa.org*). He has been in the tile industry for 25 years.

Karen O'Brien is editor of *Toys & Prices* (Krause), an annual price guide for toy collectors, Iola, Wisconsin.

Your dining room table needs a new leg…your expensive coat is missing a button…the antique toy truck you bought on eBay is short one wheel. *Here's how to find replacement parts for these and other items…*

FURNITURE

Mass-market retailers, such as IKEA (800-434-4532, *www.ikea.com*)…Crate & Barrel (800-606-6387, *www.crateandbarrel.com*)…and Pottery Barn (888-779-5176, *www.potterybarn.com*), often can supply parts at reasonable prices, assuming that the products still are in production.

Helpful: Keep a log of purchases with retailer names and numbers, in case parts get lost or broken down the line.

●**Wooden furniture pieces.** If the retailer or manufacturer can't help, a professional woodworker could replace a broken table leg or chair back, but the bill likely would be in the hundreds. For an affordable repair, find a local woodworking hobbyist willing to take on the job for the cost of materials, plus perhaps $50 or so for his trouble. Local lumberyards might know of woodworking clubs or hobbyists in your area. Ask to see a sample of his/her work to be sure he has the necessary skills.

●**Metal table or chair legs.** Try Internet retailer Table Legs Online (877-220-3800, *www.tablelegsonline.com*).

●**Hardware,** such as knobs and handles, often go missing. A number of firms make nice reproductions, including Horton Brasses Inc. (800-754-9127, *www.horton-brasses.com*)…Ball & Ball (610-363-7330, *www.ballandball.com*)… Crown City Hardware (626-794-0234, *www.crowncityhardware.com*)…and Muff's Hardware (714-997-0243, *www.muffshardware.com*). You can e-mail a digital photo or a link to a page with the photo. Prices range from a few dollars for simple off-the-shelf parts to a few hundred for custom-made pieces.

●**Fabric.** Damaged furniture fabric is particularly difficult to replace. Even if you can find the right material, it won't match perfectly, because the new cloth won't be as faded or worn. You might have to have the whole piece reupholstered with new fabric.

Exception: If the damage is to the skirt hanging down from a couch or chair, swap it with the piece of the skirt from the back of the chair. If it's pushed up against a wall, no one will see that the back is damaged.

SILVER, CHINA AND GLASSWARE

There are dozens of "matching service" companies that sell individual pieces of china, silver or glassware to fill out collections. Among the largest is Replacements, Ltd. (800-737-5223, *www.replacements.com*). Or you may need to find a smaller firm that specializes in the particular item you're looking for. Head to our Web site, *www.kovels.com*, click "Directory," select "Matching Services," then the category you're interested in. You will have to register on our site to do this, but registration is free.

If you don't know the pattern's name, ask the matching service if you can send in a picture of one of the pieces in your set so the match can be made. Most will search for a match for free.

If your pattern is still in production, you also might be able to order individual pieces through the manufacturer. Some companies allow this only during a designated period each year. Contact the manufacturer for details.

Prices vary widely depending on the rarity and desirability of the item. Matching services tend to be cheaper than companies where you order individual pieces through manufacturers.

BUTTONS

If a garment didn't come with spare buttons or you can't locate them, the simplest solution is to remove all the buttons and sew on a new matching set.

If you love the current buttons too much to replace them, search local sewing stores for a match. *If that fails, try these merchants, each of which has thousands of buttons in stock...*

● **Allyn's Fabric & Bridal Supplies Inc.** in Denver, 303-377-4969.

● **Britex Fabrics** in San Francisco, 415-392-2910, *www.britexfabrics.com.* It even has hard-to-find, old Bakelite buttons.

● **Tender Buttons** in New York (212-758-7004) and Chicago (312-337-7033).

If you don't live in one of the above cities, you might be able to mail in a sample of the button you're trying to match. Call first, and be sure to use a padded envelope.

Many other suppliers sell buttons only in large quantities. *If you find the button you need in one of their on-line catalogs, they might be able to direct you to a retailer who has it in stock...*

● **Atlanta Thread and Supply Company,** 800-847-1001, *store.atlantathread.com.*

● **Banasch's,** 800-543-0355, *www.banaschs. com.*

● **JHB International,** 800-525-9007, *www. buttons.com.*

CERAMIC TILES

The easiest way to replace a missing or broken tile is to plan ahead. Buy 10% more tile than you need, and store the extra. If it's too late to do this, then your missing tiles will be extremely difficult to replace. Even if the tile maker is still producing the style, tiles produced at different times tend to have small but noticeable color differences.

Often the only solution is to remove tiles from inconspicuous locations, such as behind appliances or under rugs or furniture, and use them to fill in more prominent gaps. Then the new gaps can be filled with imperfectly matched tiles, since they're out of view.

Caution: Ceramic tiles break easily, so be extremely careful. Pull out surrounding grout and/or caulk first (a heat gun or hair dryer can loosen stubborn caulk), then try to gently tap the tiles free with a broad chisel and hammer.

If several rooms in your home have the same tile and many pieces are damaged or missing, combine the remaining tiles into one room and choose a new tile for the others.

TOY AND GAME PARTS

Most toy makers do not sell replacement parts, even for toys still in production. There are exceptions, however, so check the manufacturer's Web site or call its customer service number.

Example: Hasbro's Web site includes downloadable replacement-part order forms for many of the company's products, such as Tinkertoys and Clue. Go to *www.hasbro.com,* select "Customer Service," then "Replacement Parts."

A number of small companies make reproduction parts for collectible toys. Replacement parts for vintage pressed-steel trucks, such as those made by Tonka and Buddy "L," are not uncommon. Look for ads in toy magazines, such as *Antique Toy World* (available at some libraries).

Examples: Thomas Toys makes reproduction parts for a range of metal toys (810-629-8707). Dakotah Toys (605-256-6676) specializes in parts for farm toys.

Or go on-line and enter the name of the toy and the words "parts" or "replacement parts" into the Google search engine. You might turn up collectors or dealers who have the parts you need. If the toy was made in large quantities within the past 30 years, you might even be able to find an inexpensive one on eBay that could be used for parts.

Summer Camp Savings

Save on kids' summer camp by booking a year in advance. A typical sleepaway camp costs from $1,500 to $6,000 for four weeks, and prices are rising by 5% to 10% a year. Many camps offer early-bird signups at the end of the summer—you can lock in the current year's rate for the following year. A few camps allow you to lock in a lifetime rate. If the camp does not advertise an early-bird rate, ask for one.

Jeff Solomon, executive director, National Camp Association, New York City. *www.summercamp.org.*

Bigger Social Security Income for Wife Who Never Worked

Making your wife a partner in your business could boost her ultimate Social Security retirement benefits. As a partner, the wife now has self-employment income. When she reaches retirement, her benefits will be based on that income. This could far exceed the 50% of her husband's retirement benefits that she would get if she had no earnings of her own on which to compute her Social Security entitlement.

John J. Tuozzolo, associated with the firm, Collins, Hannafin, Garamella, Jaber & Tuozzolo, PC, 148 Deer Hill Ave., Danbury, Connecticut 06810. He is the author of the *Encyclopedia of Estate Planning*. Bottom Line Books.

Easy Ways to Make Planning a Family Reunion Fun for All

Unplug the Christmas Machine: A Complete Guide to Putting Love and Joy Back in the Season by Jo Robinson and Jean Staeheli. Quill.

Are you hosting a large family gathering? Because a reunion brings together people of all ages, it presents special challenges. *Ideas to make your party more enjoyable for everyone...*

●**Infants and toddlers.** Parents will appreciate a place to change diapers and a quiet room for naps and nursing. Let them know if you can provide high chairs, cribs, safety gates or playpens.

Toys: A box of safe kitchen equipment.

Food suggestions: Mild cheese, bananas, crackers, fresh bread or rolls.

●**Preschool children.** Set aside a playroom.

Best toys: Balloons, bubbles and crayons. Pay an older cousin or a neighborhood teen to baby-sit.

●**School-aged children.** A den or basement room and board games, felt pens and coloring books will keep them happy. Put them in charge of setting and decorating a children's dining table.

●**Teenagers.** Most teenagers find family reunions boring. For those who have to come, provide a room with a television, VCR/DVD player and a CD player. Teenagers may be shy around relatives they don't know. When they come out of hiding, give them tasks that encourage their involvement with others, such as helping out grandparents.

●**Older folks.** They need comfortable chairs where they can hear and see what's going on without being in the way. Some may also need easy access to a bathroom and a place to rest or to go to bed early.

Food considerations: Ask if anyone needs a low-salt, low-cholesterol or special diabetic diet. Spicy foods are probably out. Make travel arrangements for those who can't drive so they don't have to worry about inconveniencing others.

Now that you've seen to individual needs, how do you bring everyone together?

Common denominator: Family ties. Make an updated family tree and display it in a prominent place. If you have an instant camera, take pictures as people arrive and mount them on the appropriate branch of the tree.

Special: Ask everyone to bring contributions to a family museum.

Suitable objects: Old photographs, family letters, heirlooms, written family histories, old family recipes. After dinner, gather around the fire and exchange family anecdotes. You may wish to record them.

Best Family Camping Tents

A tent for camping should allow about 25 square feet of floor space for each adult and half that for each child.

For a family of four: At least 80 square feet.

Best: An umbrella tent. It folds up neatly to fit into a car trunk. And it weighs only 24 to 40 pounds.

Best material: Nylon.

Features to look for: Good cross-ventilation...openings with sturdy mesh to keep out insects...windows that close during a storm...

seams double-stitched with eight to 10 stitches per inch.

Also: Seams should be lap-felled (the material folded back on itself for extra strength and waterproofing).

Good tents have extra stitching at points of stress. Before taking the tent on a trip, set it up in the yard and douse it with a hose. Check for leaks (particularly at the seams).

Great Gifts for Kids—On-Line

With a little quick searching, it's easy to find fun stuff on the Internet for all the kids in your life. *For example...*

Custom jigsaw puzzles: Puzzles are made from your favorite photos...can have pieces in animal shapes or other unusual forms. *www. jigsawpuzzle.com.*

Kids' products: Independent reviews of award-winning, age-appropriate books, videos, software, toys, etc. Includes toll-free numbers for ordering. *www.toyportfolio.com.*

18

Money Savers for Safety and Security

Surprising Ways You Can Hurt Your Credit Score

Many would-be borrowers are discovering that their good credit scores are no longer good enough. That's because lenders and credit card issuers have become increasingly cautious as more borrowers default on their loans and fall behind on credit card payments.

Just two years ago, most of the best mortgage and credit card deals were available to anyone with a credit score of 700 (out of a maximum of 850).* Today, borrowers must have scores of at least 720—and often as high as 750—to qualify for the most appealing mortgage and credit card rates. Terms on auto loans also become less attractive for people with scores below 750.

Surprisingly, only about one-third of the formula that makes up your credit score reflects

*To obtain your credit scores, go to *www.myfico.com.*

whether you pay bills on time. The often-overlooked details that affect the remaining two-thirds could make or break your next credit application.

How to avoid hurting your score…

●**Use only a small percentage of your available credit.** The percentage of available credit that a cardholder uses determines roughly one-third of his/her credit score, making it just as important as paying bills on time.

Example: If you have just two credit cards, each with a $2,000 credit limit, and a total balance of $3,000 on these cards, your credit utilization percentage is $3,000 divided by $4,000, or 75% of your limit. (Only credit cards are included in this calculation, not home-equity lines of credit.)

John Ulzheimer, president of consumer education for Credit.com, a credit information Web site. Previously, he worked at the credit-rating organizations Fair Isaac Corporation (FICO) and Equifax. Based in Atlanta, he is author of *You're Nothing But a Number: Why Achieving Great Credit Scores Should Be on Your List of Wealth Building Strategies.* Credit.com.

A credit utilization percentage below 10% will earn you the maximum number of points in this component of your credit score. Above 10%, there is a sliding scale, and your credit score will suffer greatly if you come anywhere close to maxing out your cards. In determining this portion of the score, credit bureaus do not take into consideration whether you pay off balances in full every month or carry rotating balances.

What to do: Pay off your credit cards completely, and don't use them during the 60 days prior to submitting a loan or credit card application. Ask your credit card issuers to increase your credit limits, but do so only if you have the discipline to avoid using this extra credit.

●**Limit credit applications.** Just applying for any type of credit can damage your credit score. Approximately 10% of your overall score is based on the number of credit applications you have made during the past 12 months. (Credit applications include everything from credit card and store card applications to auto and mortgage loan applications.) If you have a limited or troubled credit history, even two or three credit applications make a significant difference. If you have a solid credit history, a few credit applications over the course of one year will not have a substantial impact, but a large number might.

What to do: If your credit history is less than stellar, do not apply for credit cards that you don't really need, including cards at retail stores that you get mainly because they offer a 10% or 15% discount on your purchases for a limited period of time. This is particularly important if you are about to submit a loan application, such as for a car loan or a mortgage. Ask your current card issuers to match competitors' terms, rather than jump from one credit card to another in search of more attractive rates. Postpone filling out applications for anything that triggers a credit check—say, for a lease on a new apartment or a new cell-phone plan—until after you have received approval on an important loan.

●**Diversify your credit.** As much as 10% of your total credit score is determined by how many different types of credit you have now and have had in the past—the more types, the better. Types of credit include credit cards,

retail cards, gas cards, auto loans, home loans, student loans and personal loans. It is particularly important to have had both major bank credit cards (or retail or gas cards) and installment debt, such as auto loans or mortgages, on your credit history, even if these accounts are unused or have been paid off.

What to do: It does not make sense to take out a loan or open a credit card account just to earn these credit score diversity points. However, if you already are considering establishing credit of a type that you never used before (such as an auto loan) instead of paying cash, realize that it may help your credit score.

●**Hang on to old cards.** Approximately 15% of your credit score is determined by the age of your oldest credit accounts—the older, the better.

What to do: Do not close your oldest credit card accounts, even if you don't use them much now. If you do not have any long-term credit accounts, ask a parent, spouse, sibling or someone else close to you to add you to his/her longest-standing credit card account as an "authorized user." You will be given points for this account's age.

Important: The Fair Isaac Corporation, which sets guidelines for the widely used FICO credit scores, is attempting to close this loophole. It might be a few years before this change takes effect, however, so you may still benefit from being an authorized user for a while. Spouses who are listed as authorized users on their partner's credit cards should either switch their status from authorized user to joint account holder…or open their own accounts and start building their own credit histories to avoid credit problems when this change finally does occur.

YOUR CREDIT SCORE

What makes up your credit score?.

●**Payment history: 35%**

●**Available credit used: 30%**

●**Length of credit history: 15%**

●**Types of credit used: 10%**

●**New credit applications: 10%**

Source: Fair Issac Corporation.

20% of All Accidents Occur in Parking Lots

William Van Tassel, PhD, manager of driver training operations at the American Automobile Association's national office in Heathrow, Florida. *www.aaa.com.*

One of every five auto accidents occurs in a parking lot, according to the Independent Insurance Agents Association. That total does not include all the small nicks and dents that usually go unreported.

Parking lot crashes often occur at low speeds, but they still can lead to expensive repairs and higher insurance premiums. Worse, sometimes pedestrians and drivers are injured.

To minimize your parking lot risks...

DRIVERS

• **Park away from busy areas.** Most drivers crowd into the spaces closest to store entrances, leaving other sections of parking lots virtually empty. Your vehicle is much less likely to be bumped or dinged—and you will have better visibility when you pull out—if you take a spot in a little-used section.

Parking away from other vehicles is particularly important in post office, convenience store and dry cleaner parking lots. Vehicle turnover is very rapid in these lots, and all that activity increases the odds of an accident.

• **Look where you are going.** Distracted driving is responsible for many parking lot accidents. We think we see an open spot in the next row or someone we know walking by. This momentary distraction is all it takes for someone to step or pull in front of us in a crowded parking lot. If your car is moving forward, your eyes must be looking forward. Use your peripheral vision to locate open parking spaces.

• **Completely clear fogged or snow-covered windows and windshields.** There is a tendency to rush out of parking lots, but driving with partially blocked windows and/or windshields greatly increases the odds of having a collision.

• **Put on your seat belt before pulling out, not while driving.** Drivers often think they are "safe" in parking lots, so they delay putting on seat belts. That's a mistake for two reasons—you could get into an accident with no seat belt on before you leave the parking lot...and fumbling with a seat belt while you are driving makes it more likely that you will have an accident.

Also, complete any cell-phone calls, put on your sunglasses if you need them, adjust your CD player or radio and enter data into your navigation system before you pull out of your parking spot.

• **Do not trust your mirrors.** Rearview mirrors do not provide a full picture of what's happening behind your car. Today's high-tech backup sensors and rear-mounted cameras do not spot all obstacles, either. To back out of a parking spot safely, rotate your body to the right, looking over your shoulder so that you face backward, leaving your left hand on the wheel.

• **Look for two empty parking spaces,** one behind the other, and pull through to the one in front so that you do not have to back up when it is time to pull out. But make sure nobody is pulling into the front spot from the other end.

• **Avoid danger zones.** Skip spots next to big vans or SUVs if you are in a smaller vehicle—you will have a hard time seeing past these vehicles when it is time to pull out. Also, try to avoid spots next to cart-collection areas—the odds of dings and dents are greatest here.

• **Turn on your headlights, even in daylight.** Headlights warn pedestrians and other drivers that your vehicle will soon pull out.

• **Don't feel hurried by other drivers.** Hurrying leads to accidents. The driver eager to have your space can wait a few more seconds as you take the time to pull out carefully.

PEDESTRIANS

• **Look for signs of movement.** Before you step out into the parking lot, pause for a moment and check for signs that a car may be pulling out of a parking spot. *Cars are so quiet that you may not even hear the engine starting. Look and listen for...*

- A puff of exhaust.

- Reverse lights coming on.

- A car door being closed—which could signal that a driver has entered the car and will soon back out.

- Movement in the driver's seat. *Examples:* The driver reaching for his seat belt or turning around to back out of a spot.

- **Don't get distracted.** Stay alert at all times. Don't make cell-phone calls, use an iPod or rummage through your purse or wallet to find your coupons. Be aware of what's going on behind you by quickly checking over your shoulder from time to time as you walk through the lot.

- **Watch out for big vehicles.** Parked SUVs and vans can block your view of cars backing out. As you pass by a big vehicle, pause a moment to check that a car isn't coming.

- **Be extra cautious at night.** It's extremely difficult for drivers to see pedestrians at night, especially if they're wearing dark clothing. Assume that even though you can see the driver, the driver cannot see you.

Financial Aid for the Mugging Victim

Lucy N. Friedman, PhD, former executive director, Victim Services, a domestic-violence prevention agency, New York City.

Financial compensation programs for mugging victims are available throughout the US. This compensation can cover both medical expenses and lost earnings. However, most of these programs utilize a means test that eliminates all but lower income victims from compensation. In addition, the victim's own medical unemployment insurance must be fully depleted before state compensation is granted.

- **Workers' compensation may cover you** (up to two-thirds of your gross earnings in New York State) if you were mugged on the job or on your way to or from company business during your workday. It will not cover you while traveling from home to work and back.

- **Homeowner's policies may cover financial losses suffered during a mugging.**

- **Mugging insurance is an idea whose time has come.** This insurance is available in New York. It covers property loss, medical care and mental anguish. If successful, this type of coverage may become available in other states.

- **A lawsuit may be successful if it can be proved that the mugging was the result of negligence.**

Example: The celebrity Connie Francis was attacked in her room at a major motel chain. She won $2 million in damages by proving that the motel's security system was inadequate.

- **The Office for Victims of Crime (OVC) provides resources.** A division of the US Department of Justice in Washington, DC, this federal agency is a national clearinghouse for emerging victim issues and resources, which are available around the clock. Crime victims have access to a criminal justice library, information specialists to answer questions, products and on-line services. Contact 800-851-3420 or go to *www.ojp.usdoj.gov/ovc/ovcres/welcome.html.*

How to Drive Safely in Summer Storms

William Van Tassel, PhD, manager of driver-training operations at the AAA's national office in Heathrow, Florida. *www.aaa.com.* He is a member of the Transportation Board's Committee on Operative Regulation and Education and a sports car racer with the Sports Car Club of America.

The best advice for driving in bad weather—don't. Postpone your trip if roads look bad or news reports warn of treacherous conditions. Unfortunately, bad weather sometimes takes us by surprise, and some trips cannot be delayed. *How to drive safely...*

THICK FOG

Turn on your fog lights if you have them—or your headlights if you don't—but not your high beams, which might cause glare. Reduce your speed enough that you could stop safely if something appears out of the fog in front of you, even if this means slowing to a crawl. Tap your brakes to flash your brake lights as you decelerate, warning drivers behind you that you are slowing. It's illegal in some states to drive with your hazard lights on, but that can increase visibility.

If you cannot see more than a few car lengths ahead, pull over and wait for the fog to lift. Pull over as far as possible so that you don't have to park on the shoulder and there is some distance between you and the road. Poor visibility could cause another vehicle to stray from its lane, creating danger for cars parked on the shoulder. Drive past the shoulder only if you are certain that the ground is level and solid enough to safely support your vehicle.

Turn on your hazard lights when you pull over, and remain inside your vehicle with your seat belt on.

Safest roadside waiting spot in a limited-visibility situation: Tucked behind a guardrail. Watch for the end of a stretch of guardrail, pull off the road, then back in behind the guardrail so that the metal barrier is between your vehicle and passing traffic.

DOWNPOUR RAIN

Downpours can severely limit visibility. See directions for driving in fog at left. In addition, wet roads reduce traction by about 30%, so reduce your speed by one-third even if visibility is good.

The first few minutes of a downpour are particularly dangerous if the region has not had rain in many days. The rain will cause oil that has collected on the road to float to the surface, creating a slick surface that further reduces traction. Drive with extreme caution, or pull over and wait 10 minutes for the oil to wash away.

Heavy rain also creates the potential for hydroplaning, in which a vehicle's tires slide across the surface of a thin film of water, robbing the driver of both traction and steering. Replace worn tires with new ones to reduce the odds of hydroplaning. Apply the brakes very gently if your vehicle does hydroplane. This shifts the weight of the car forward onto its front tires, helping to return your traction and steering.

Important: Resist the urge to slam on the brakes, which could unbalance the car and make it even more difficult to control.

FLOODING

Do not attempt to drive on a flooded road unless you are certain that the water is no more than a few inches deep. Water depth can be very difficult to gauge, and misjudgments are dangerous—so always err on the side of caution.

Turn around and find a different route, or pull over and wait for the flooding to subside. Do not wait right at the edge of the floodwater—it could rise quickly.

If other vehicles attempt to cross, watch their progress to determine water depth. If the floodwater is only a few inches deep, then it should be relatively safe to cross. Be extremely gentle on the gas pedal, and ease your vehicle through the flood area carefully.

After leaving the flood area, gently apply your brakes, using slight pedal pressure for three to four seconds several times. This helps to "sweep" the water off the brake system surfaces so that they are dry (or at least less wet) for the next application.

If your car becomes stuck on a flooded road, remain in the vehicle with your seat belt on unless there is imminent danger that water could fill the passenger compartment. If you have a cell phone, call 911. If not, yell or signal to other drivers that you need help.

STRONG CROSSWINDS

Keep your eyes far ahead on the road when driving in crosswinds. This gives you the visual cues that you need to most easily correct your course and remain in your lane.

Avoid driving next to other vehicles when there are strong crosswinds. Side-by-side driving increases the odds that you will have a collision if the wind pushes one of you out of your lane.

On windy days, ready yourself for gusts—for example, you can grip the steering wheel and prepare to make a slight correction—when your vehicle leaves protected locations and enters open spaces. These include driving out from under an overpass...entering a cleared area after driving through a densely wooded area...driving onto an exposed bridge...or accelerating past a large truck.

Self-Defense for The Latest Scams And Rip-Offs

Kelly Rote, national spokesperson for Money Management International, provider of nationwide consumer credit counseling located in Houston, Texas. Her site on the Web is *www.moneymanagement.org.*

Dan Brecher, Esq., a New York City attorney specializing in claims against brokerage firms.

Matt Brisch, communications specialist at the National Association of Insurance Commissioners (NAIC) in Kansas City, Missouri.

Michael Brown, operating revenue officer, CardCops, an on-line watchdog based in Malibu, California, that helps make selling and shopping on-line safer, *www.cardcops.com.*

Overzealous debt collectors, phony insurance salespeople and greedy stockbrokers urging customers to put their homes at risk are among the latest rip-offs to watch out for…

"ZOMBIE" DEBT
Kelly Rote, Money Management International

●**Beware of collection agencies trying to collect on "zombie" debt**—unpaid consumer bills that creditors already have written off as losses. Debt collectors will buy this charged-off debt for just pennies on the dollar and then aggressively squeeze consumers to pay it.

Self-defense: If a debt collector contacts you about a debt that you do not recognize, don't provide any information. Insist on proof of the debt—the original credit agreement and billing statements.

If you are convinced that you do owe the money and your state's statute of limitations on the debt has not expired, consider settling with the agency for a percentage of the amount that is owed. State statutes of limitations are listed at *www.creditinfocenter.com* (at the Web site click on "Credit Repair").

Also review your credit reports from Experian (888-397-3742, *www.experian.com*), Equifax (800-685-1111, *www.equifax.com*) and TransUnion (877-322-8228, *www.transunion. com*). If a zombie collector has reported the debt delinquency to the credit bureaus after it has ignored your request for proof, it is in violation of the *Fair Debt Collection Practices Act.*

File a complaint with the Federal Trade Commission, and notify each credit bureau.

BROKER MISDEEDS
Dan Brecher, Esq.

●**More stockbrokers are urging their customers to tap home equity to buy securities.** In many cases, they're pitching the chance to borrow at today's relatively low mortgage rates to fund the purchase of high-yielding junk bonds. While junk bonds do sport hefty yields, junk bonds and stocks are risky by nature—and not something you would want to pledge a good chunk of your home against.

Self-defense: Don't refinance your mortgage or use home equity to buy stocks or bonds. If you have done so on the advice of your broker and think this advice was inappropriate, you might have reason to seek restitution.

Reason: All brokers have a fiduciary duty to keep customers' interests and financial strength in mind when recommending investments.

●**Brokerages also are not reporting customer complaints,** regulatory actions and criminal convictions in a timely fashion. They are supposed to inform the Financial Industry Regulatory Authority (FINRA) of broker wrongdoings and complaints against them within a month of their occurrence—but this often does not happen. This has prompted FINRA to censure and fine 29 securities firms for making late disclosure.

Investors now will be able to find more up-to-date information on complaints and action against brokers on the FINRA's Web site, *www. finra.com.*

Self-defense: If your brokerage has consistently failed to disclose problems in a timely fashion and you believe that you lost money as a result, you might be able to bring a claim against it. FINRA's monthly disciplinary actions are reported in major newspapers and on its Web site.

FAKE INSURANCE
Matt Brisch, NAIC

●**Unlicensed insurance companies**—those that do not have a state's insurance department's approval—take your money and issue "policies," but then don't pay when you file a claim. Fake health insurance was sold to more than

200,000 people between 2000 and 2002, according to the most recent data available.

Fake insurance looks attractive because it is less expensive than the legitimate policies. The main targets of these fake policies are older adults and small businesses looking to reduce health insurance costs. Scams also are common in life and property/casualty insurance.

Self-defense: Be on the lookout for signs that an insurance policy is fake—high-pressure sales tactics, premiums that are at least 15% lower than those from familiar carriers and/or very liberal coverage rules.

Before you purchase any policy, contact your state insurance department to confirm that the company is licensed in your state. Web sites for all state insurance departments are available at *www.naic.org/state_web_map.htm.* This site also maintains a database of complaints and financial information about insurers nationwide. Go to *www.naic.org* and click on "Consumers," then on "Company Information & Complaints."

BUSINESS ID THEFT
Michael Brown, CardCops

●**Credit card thieves are ripping off small-business owners** by using a combination of fake Web sites and stolen credit card numbers.

The victims are businesses that *don't* accept credit cards. The crooks pose as the business and set up a bogus Web site. They establish an account in the business's name with a merchant processing provider—also commonly called an independent sales organization (ISO)—which transfers funds between the retailers and the credit card companies. The crooks then use the stolen credit card numbers to ring up "sales."

When the owners of the stolen credit cards see bogus charges on their bills, they complain to the credit card issuers, which will reimburse them. The card issuers then demand reimbursement from the real merchants, who actually are the victims.

If your business becomes a target of this version of identity theft, it should not be held liable for phony sales.

Self-defense: Contact the ISO that approved the establishment of the bogus account. It is an ISO's responsibility to verify a merchant's identity, and the ISO should be liable for the fraudulent charges.

Also: Sign your business up for the SelfMonitor credit-reporting service, available from Dun & Bradstreet (877-753-1444 or *www.dnb.com*). The service will alert you if a merchant account is opened in the name of your business.

Identity Theft Update —Much Better Ways to Protect Yourself

Linda Foley, founder of the nonprofit Identity Theft Resource Center in San Diego, which provides information and counseling to victims of identity theft, *www.idtheftcenter.org.* Ms. Foley, a victim herself, has provided resources and guidance to law enforcement as well as hundreds of victims throughout the country. She has testified before the Federal Trade Commission, the Social Security Administration and the US House and Senate.

Identity theft is the number-one concern of US consumers. In just the past year, it has cost shoppers and merchants about $300 billion and hit almost 10 million new victims.

What does it mean to your personal and financial security? *National expert Linda Foley answers this question and more below...*

●**How do victims discover that their identity has been stolen?** You might get a call from a debt collector...a bill for merchandise that you never bought...or have your credit card blocked because it has been charged to the limit. Victims often find out when they are denied credit or a loan or when money disappears from their checking or savings accounts. In all cases, someone has obtained your personal financial information and is stealing from you...or stealing in your name.

Seventy percent of identity thieves are unknown to their victims. Many cases occur after your information is stolen from a database that has your personal information on file.

●**Why is identity theft so common?** It is a high-profit, low-risk crime. An average thief can bring in from several hundred to several thousand dollars with a stolen identity. For instance, he/she might open up a new credit card account illegally, buy several laptop computers and then pawn them. Or he could get a second mortgage in another person's name and walk away with cash.

Less than 5% of these thieves are convicted, according to law-enforcement records. Cases cross multiple jurisdictions and are too time-consuming to devote many resources to. Credit card companies are reluctant to report fraud to authorities, fearing negative publicity.

●**How can I protect myself?** *There are four key safeguards…*

●Guard your Social Security number (SSN). It is the most widely accepted piece of identification for obtaining new credit cards, credit reports, federal benefits, etc. Don't carry your Social Security card or any other card that uses that number, such as an employee or student ID. For vital items that you need to carry, such as your health insurance card, make a photocopy and cut off the last four digits of your SSN. Hospitals will accept this if you come in with a life-threatening emergency.

Never allow a merchant to put your SSN on any check that you write. Legally, merchants are not allowed to ask for it. If one insists, threaten to complain to the Better Business Bureau.

●Don't give personal information to anyone unless you initiate the inquiry. Identity thieves routinely trick people into giving them confidential information by claiming to represent legitimate companies or government agencies.

●Pay attention to bank-account statements and credit card bills. If there is a discrepancy on a bill or a bill doesn't arrive, contact the financial institution immediately. Federal and state laws limit your losses to $50 per card if you're victimized, but you must prove that you didn't make the charges.

In addition, don't carry a bank debit card that doubles as a credit card. Money is removed from your account immediately, and you have no legal protection if a thief uses the card.

●Review your credit reports at least once a year. Make sure that no unauthorized accounts have been opened and that no changes have been made to existing accounts. You can obtain one free credit report per year from each of the agencies.

The three reporting agencies are Equifax, 800-685-1111, *www.equifax.com*; Experian, 888-397-3742, *www.experian.com*; and TransUnion, 877-322-8228, *www.transunion.com*.

Helpful: Evaluate your risk of identity theft at my organization's Web site, *www.idtheftcenter.org*.

●**What should I do if I become a victim of identity theft?**

●Close accounts that you believe have been tampered with or opened fraudulently. You may have to provide affidavits to the companies saying you didn't open the accounts. A generic ID theft affidavit is available from the Federal Trade Commission (FTC) at 877-ID-THEFT, *www.consumer.gov/idtheft*.

●Contact the fraud departments at the three major credit bureaus, and place a "fraud alert" on your name. A fraud alert requests that the credit issuers contact you by telephone before allowing a new account to be opened or an existing account to be altered. Although some credit issuers ignore these alerts, it is the best defense against fraud at this time.

●File a criminal report with local police if you have evidence of fraud—such as a suspicious charge on your credit card bill. Many creditors do require a police report before they will resolve a dispute. If the local authorities will not handle this crime, contact the county or state police.

●Call the FTC at 877-ID-THEFT. A counselor will take your complaint and advise you on how to deal with any resulting credit-related problems.

●Review *Identity Crisis: What to Do If Your Identity Is Stolen*, available from the FTC (877-ID-THEFT, *www.consumer.gov/idtheft*).

●**What is the government doing to protect me?** In December of 2003, *The Fair and Accurate Credit Transactions Act* was signed into law. It enables consumers to obtain a free copy of their credit report every year from each credit-reporting agency…forces the agencies to share consumer calls on identity theft with one another so that victims have "one-call-for-all" protection…and also prohibits companies from printing more than the last five digits of a credit card number on electronic receipts. However, in practical terms, it may take the government a long time to implement these reforms.

●**If my SSN is stolen, will the government provide me with a new one?** The Social Security Administration will assign new numbers to victims of ID theft only under extreme circumstances, such as someone stalking you or threatening your life.

●**Do I need identity theft insurance?** Some insurance and credit card companies are charging from $25 to $100 for ID theft insurance. Most people don't need it, but if you would like the extra protection, make sure the policy will cover time that's lost from work, out-of-pocket expenses and legal fees.

Best Way to Track Down Friends (or Foes)

Steven K. Brown, a former FBI agent and current owner of Millennial Investigative Agency, a private investigation company in St. Augustine, Florida, *www.stevenkbrown. com*. He is author of *The Complete Idiot's Guide to Private Investigating*. Alpha.

Looking for an old love or maybe a long-lost friend? Suspicious about a potential employee? Want to check up on your doctor or lawyer?

I have been tracking down people for 31 years—first as an FBI agent and then as a private investigator. *Here are the most effective ways to find people, largely using the Internet...*

CHASE DOWN CLASSMATES

●**Classmates.com** compiles contact information on graduates. Its database currently contains information on about 60 million people from more than 200,000 elementary schools, high schools and colleges. Their database goes back more than 50 years.

Cost: Free to browse names...$39* annually if you want to contact classmates directly.

Alternative: Locate your school's Web site to get the alumni relations officer's e-mail address or phone number. He/she usually will forward messages to former classmates at your request.

*All prices are subject to change.

Or you can use the site's link to your school's alumni magazine, which lists contact information for your class's secretary, who can often help.

FIND A LOST FRIEND

●**Internet search engines offer tremendous power to locate people.** Conduct an advanced search on several search engines using the person's full name and any unique details. For example, try including a middle initial...city of residence...or occupation. The engines will search through millions of sites for any references to that person.

Important: For best results, use more than one search engine. *Below I've listed some of my favorites...*

- *www.google.com*
- *www.looksmart.com*
- *www.lycos.com*
- *www.webcrawler.com*

●**National white-page phone directories** help you locate a person's name, address and phone number. *My favorite free sites...*

- *http://find.person.superpages.com*
- *www.whitepages.com*
- *www.canada411.com* (for Canadian directories only)
- *www.freeality.com/findet.htm*

Information on free sites tends to be a year old. If you think the person has moved, try a paid site—they are updated more frequently.

My favorite: *http://555-1212.com*

Cost: $11.99* for 100 searches.

Unpublished versus unlisted numbers: An unpublished number is not printed in phone directories, but it is available from an operator if you request it. If a number is *unlisted*, operators don't have access to it. However, most operators will verify the address of a person who has an unlisted telephone number, so that you can write to him.

●**Dig up someone's e-mail address.** *My favorite free sites...*

- *www.theultimates.com/email*
- *www.iaf.net*

●**Search publications.** *www.findarticles. com*, owned by the search engine Look Smart,

*All prices are subject to change.

allows you to search 3.5 million articles in 700 newspapers and magazines. Type the person's name into the search box, and click "Look."

●**Verify a death.** The Social Security Administration's Master Death Index contains more than 75 million names and records on the deceased. *http://ssdi.genealogy.rootsweb.com.*

CHECK UP ON YOUR DOCTOR

Disciplinary records often are available by calling your state's department of health and asking for the division that deals with medical disciplinary proceedings. Generally, you will be given a list of the actions and malpractice claims against the doctor. If you want more details, you have to request them in writing.

All the state licensing boards usually can be located through the American Medical Association (AMA) at *www.ama-assn.org/ama/pub/category/2645.html.* However, the AMA's main Web site, *www.ama-assn.org,* also provides a wealth of information about individual doctors, including their training and specialties.

●**Federation of State Medical Boards** is a convenient nonprofit clearinghouse that allows you to find out about disciplinary actions taken against a doctor by medical boards. *www.docinfo.org.* Just go to "Order Options," and click on "Get Immediate Results" or "Mail in Request."

Cost: $9.95* per report.

EXAMINE YOUR LAWYER

Backgrounds of as well as disciplinary actions against lawyers are available from...

●**American Bar Association (ABA),** which publishes a Web link to the disciplinary agency in each state. Here you also can verify that your attorney has been appropriately licensed. Some state ABA Web sites will list disciplinary actions taken against lawyers. Others do not list these actions on their Web sites, but they will make the information available when you request it in writing. *www.abanet.org/cpr/regulation/directory.pdf.* Free.

●**Martindale-Hubbell,** a service providing biographies of practicing lawyers. They include explanations of their experience, specialties, education and major clients. Each attorney is rated by his peers for legal ability and ethics.

*All prices are subject to change.

www.martindale.com. Click on "Lawyer Locator." Free.

RUN A CRIMINAL-RECORDS CHECK

There is no single comprehensive government database of criminals that is accessible to the public. *However, you still can investigate prospective employees, business partners and household help...*

●**The Federal Bureau of Prisons** provides information on all current and former federal prisoners since 1982. *www.bop.gov.* Click on "Inmate Locator" to search. Free.

●**The Federal Bureau of Investigation** provides links to databases with the names and addresses of convicted sex offenders in each state. *www.fbi.gov/hq/cid/cac/states.htm.* Free.

●**Criminal information.** Most states will provide you with some criminal records, but you must request them in writing. They usually cost less than $20. The amount and detail of information vary by state. For example, Florida offers a database of any current and past criminal online. And, Utah discloses only information about sex offenders. Even when a state does not make information available on-line, you often can get Web access to county courthouse records to learn about convictions. Do a search for the county government.

●**Background Check Gateway.** This company provides telephone numbers and Web sites, where you can learn each state's policy for making information available. *www.backgroundcheckgateway.com.* Click on "Step 3: Start Your Investigation," then "Criminal History: Does He Have a Criminal Record?" Free.

CATCH UP WITH VETERANS

●**The US Department of Veterans Affairs** will forward a letter to any veteran registered with them. Contact your local office. Free.

●**The US Department of Defense** will supply the mailing addresses for servicemen and -women on active duty in the US Armed Forces. Free to immediate family members and government officials. For all others, $3.50* per inquiry. At *www.defenselink.mil/faq,* type in "Locating Service Members" in the "Search Text" box.

*All prices are subject to change.

● **VetFriends.com**—a national military membership organization—helps both past and present servicemen and -women find one another. Enroll on its Web site, and receive e-mail when someone from your unit becomes a member. Click on "Start Here." Free. For an annual fee of $47,* you can search the organization's registry and contact others.

● **The National Archives and Records Administration** provides much information, like dates of service...decorations...date and location of death...place of burial, on deceased servicemen and -women. This information generally is free but may incur a charge depending on the search. *www.archives.gov/veterans.*

LEARN ABOUT YOUR NEIGHBORS

Public records kept by your town and county can tell you how much your neighbor paid for his home. And, thanks to the Internet, you can search those records confidentially.

Available: Date and amount of the last sale ...who sold it...address where the property tax bill is sent. In some states, you also can get tax and property assessment information.

● **Links to county tax assessors records** from around the country are available at *http://publicrecords.netronline.com.* Just click on your state, then your county. They also are available at *www.blackbookonline.info* (click on "State/Local Public Records," then your state, then "Real Estate Ownership"). Costs vary.

How to Keep Personal Info Private

Beth Givens, director, Privacy Rights Clearinghouse, San Diego, California 92103. *www.privacyrights.org.*

Earlier this year, 1,800 New York University students received an e-mail message telling them that their Social Security numbers had been posted on the Internet. This highly publicized privacy violation—which stemmed from flawed internal security measures that have since been tightened—surprised and troubled students and nonstudents alike.

*All prices are subject to change.

The NYU episode didn't surprise privacy consultant John Featherman. According to John, people only have to "Google" their names—that is, enter them in the popular search engine—to see the extent to which their privacy is compromised on the Internet. *When I looked up myself and members of my extended family, I readily found...*

● **Information on volunteer work, charitable gifts and religious affiliations.**

● **Real estate transaction amounts.**

● **Signatures on political petitions.**

● **Postings to news groups.**

● **Even the birthdays of some of our children.**

According to John, my search only scratched the surface. He notes that many types of sensitive personal information now are available over the Internet—especially to people who are willing to pay for it. Such fee-based services as Informus, Infotel and Lexis-Nexis extract information from driver's licenses, court proceedings, voter registrations and public documents. Even crime victims' and witnesses' statements may end up on the Internet.

Legislation and public pressure may limit the availability of personal data. But John says that the Internet is a haven for identity thieves and other predators.

First step in protecting yourself: Try to get information about yourself pulled from the Internet. John advises consistently and aggressively searching your name and asking the offending Web sites to have it removed. (Many will do so upon request.) Do the same with online phone directories, such as *www.switchboard.com* and *www.411.com* and sites of organizations to which you belong.

Smarter searching: Look up all the variations of your name—nicknames, with/without middle initials, maiden name, etc. Put each variation in quotes to get an exact match. If your name is a common one, try it with and without your state.

More strategies from Beth Givens, director of Privacy Rights Clearinghouse...

Be stingy about information you give out over the Internet. Don't trust sites that promise prizes or rewards in exchange for personal information.

Be aware that any message posted to a public news group or forum is available to anyone —including nonmembers. People may be able to retrieve your name and e-mail address. Use a pseudonym and a separate e-mail address to mask your identity.

Another problem with postings: Most public postings are archived in searchable files. Before you post a message, ask yourself whether you want potential employers or other people to be able to read it in years to come.

Use encryption software to keep on-line communications private. You can download the program Pretty Good Privacy free at *www.pgpi.org.*

Raise a fuss if your Social Security number is used for identification purposes. Many institutions still do this routinely. Request that they use your driver's license number instead.

Do not use computers in cybercafés or other public places to access bank accounts, pay bills or handle sensitive information.

Things may be bad in the cyber-privacy arena —but perhaps not as bad as they could be. I heard about an on-line database that purports to contain more than 220 million US driver's licenses, photos and all. Curious, I looked myself up in the database—which turned out to be a "prank" Web site. It contained no real information and showed a photo of a monkey face. Score one for privacy—for now.

Top Five Ways to Burglar-Proof Your Home

Simon Hakim, PhD, economics professor, and George F. Rengert, PhD, professor of criminal justice, both at Temple University, Philadelphia, and Yochanan Shachmurove, PhD, professor of economics, The City College of The City University of New York and The University of Pennsylvania, Philadelphia.

In a recent study, the following factors were found to be most effective against risk of home burglary…

●**A burglar alarm is the factor that reduces risk of burglary the most.** It cuts the risk by about 12%.

●**Having neighbors pick up the mail and newspapers when you're not at home** is next most important, reducing risk by about 8%.

●**An automatic time switch and/or motion detector** to turn exterior lights on and off reduces risk about 7%.

●**Having a car in the driveway** when no one is home reduces risk about 4%.

●**Having a dog in the household,** installing dead-bolt locks and having a radio or television timer to turn them on and off when nobody is home, each reduce risk by less than 3%.

Altogether, taking these steps can reduce risk of burglary by about one-third.

Should You Install A Fire Sprinkler in Your Home?

A home fire-sprinkler system can give your family extra time to escape and limit fire damage. It is activated by a fire's high temperature, and only the sprinklers closest to the fire open. Because the sprinklers react while a fire still is small, water damage is minimized. Sprinklers do not respond to minor kitchen mishaps, such as burned toast.

Cost: About $1.50 to $2 per square foot for new home construction and $3 to $5 per square foot for an existing home.

Information: Home Fire Sprinkler Coalition, 888-635-7222, *www.homefiresprinkler.org.*

Meri-K Appy, president, Home Safety Council, Washington, DC, *www.homesafetycouncil.org.*

Best Door Locks for Every Budget

Any of the following locks provides more security than the standard key-in-knob entry set found on most home doors.

- **High-security dead-bolt** has hardened cylinders and unique pin configurations to better thwart burglars.

  Cost: About $200.

- **Double-cylinder dead-bolt** has inside and outside keys and is easy to install.

  Cost: About $60.

- **Single-cylinder dead-bolt** has a metal collar outside and thumb-turn handle inside. It is inexpensive (about $25) and easy to install but not a good choice for doors with glass that a burglar could break.

- **Surface-mount interlocking dead-bolt** is hard to break by hammering or sawing but looks bulky and can be difficult to install.

  Cost: About $20.

Consumer Reports, 101 Truman Ave., Yonkers, New York 10703.

Home Safe Home—Simple Ways to Protect Your Home While You're Away

When you are away, let mail, package and newspaper deliveries continue—have a neighbor collect things for you. This is much safer than stopping the services—because stopping them means you must tell several people just how long you will be away from home. Cancel deliveries only if there is no neighbor you can trust to pick up things for you.

Ira Lipman, president of Guardsmark, Inc., one of the world's largest security services companies, Memphis. He is author of *How to Protect Yourself from Crime*. Reader's Digest Books.

"Key" Advice

As vulnerable as they are, keys are the most cost-effective security device. *Ways to make those keys significantly more secure:*

- **Stamp "Do Not Duplicate" on keys.** It's not foolproof, but it helps to hinder unauthorized key copying.

- **Use locks that require very hard-to-get key blanks.** Some blanks are secure; that is, licensed key makers don't stock the blanks; they must be acquired from the lock maker. There is a delay—not long, and worthwhile.

- **Many lock combinations** (those that can be adjusted) are set to the user's birthday, Social Security number, phone number or some other obvious set of digits. And crooks know that. In "casing" a potential burglary site, sophisticated thieves gather all the obvious numbers and usually open the safe quite easily.

  If none of the numbers work, the burglar looks in the "obvious" places for hiding the number: In the executive's diary or calendar, under the desk pad.

  Recommendation: Don't use a related number. Memorize the digits, and don't put them in "safe" places.

- **Signatures.** For important papers, sign your name in ink and with an *italic* pen. It's very hard to forge.

Safest Safes

Most home safes on the market today are designed to protect against either fire or theft, but not both. So, the best solution is to buy one of each type. Manufacturers suggest welding the theft safe inside the fire safe, then bolting the whole thing to a concrete wall or floor. *What to look for...*

- **Burglar-resistant safes.** You generally get what you pay for.

  Minimum advisable specifications: A half-inch-thick solid steel door and quarter-inch-thick solid steel walls.

Aim: To prevent a thief from peeling away the walls with a crowbar.

Make sure the safe has a relocking device in addition to a good-quality lock. If the lock is tampered with, the device automatically relocks the bolts.

●**Fire-resistant safes.**

Recommended for most homes: A safe that can withstand a temperature of 1,850°F for two hours.

Prices depend on the size, the specifications of the materials or the rating of the model. And for burglar-resistant safes, the complexity of locks and relocking devices adds to the cost.

Money saver: A used safe. The cost is 20% to 40% lower than comparable new safes.

Beware of Phishing

If you are a victim of phishing—you provided personal information at a phony Web page that claimed to come from a bank or company with which you do business—call the *real* firm immediately using the phone number on your credit card or account statement. If you change your password and account number fast enough, the scammers may not have time to misuse your account or gain access to more confidential data.

John Featherman, personal privacy consultant firm, Philadelphia.

Stop the Bills

To stop an automatic bill-payment agreement in which you grant a company permission to debit your bank account, notify the company that is debiting your account in writing. It can take 10 days to process the change. Keep records in case there is a problem. If you switch banks and want to continue automatic debits, ask your new bank if it has a kit to simplify the process of notifying all companies on your automatic-debit list.

Gerri Detweiler, president, Ultimate Credit Solutions, Inc., Sarasota, Forida, *www.ultimatecredit.com.* She is author of *Reduce Debt, Reduce Stress.* Good Advice Press 2009.

E-Mail Alert

When you are on vacation, don't set up an automatic e-mail response that mentions your vacation.

Problem: Thieves who send an e-mail to your account and receive the automatic response may use your e-mail address to figure out where you live and then rob your home while you are away.

Best: Set up a generic auto-response e-mail that simply says you will respond shortly. The same is true for telephone answering machines.

MastermindLounge.com, on-line information and discussion site for marketing professionals.

Is it Dangerous to Use a Cell Phone in a Thunderstorm?

Ronald L. Holle, a former meteorologist with the National Severe Storms Laboratory, part of the National Oceanic and Atmospheric Administration. He currently is a meteorologist and consultant with Vaisala, Inc., the world's largest manufacturer of meteorological instruments. Based in Tucson, Arizona, the company owns and operates the National Lightning Detection Network.

Lightning is far more dangerous than most people realize. It kills 50 to 75 people annually in the US and injures between 500 and 750.

Lightning also is a lot more common than most people realize. Every year in the US, between 25 and 30 million lightning strikes hit the ground. Around the world, approximately 2,000 thunderstorms (where there's thunder, there's lightning) are occurring at any given time, with as many as 100 lightning strikes every second. About two-thirds of all thunderstorms in the US occur in June, July and August.

At least 95% of lightning deaths occur outdoors. If you see lightning, get inside your home or a large building immediately.

To learn more about lightning, we talked to Ronald L. Holle, a weather consultant and former meteorologist with the National Severe Storms Laboratory...

● **Is it dangerous to talk on a phone during a thunderstorm?** Corded phones are extremely dangerous during a storm. Home phone lines are protected with surge devices, but these defenses can be overwhelmed should lightning hit a nearby power pole. Someone dies every few years while talking on a phone during a lightning strike.

Caution: Homes in isolated areas are more vulnerable because they don't share power poles with as many neighbors. In areas with multiple homes, the electricity is more likely to be "diluted" because it splits in different directions.

Portable (cordless) and cell phones are safe to use during a thunderstorm.

● **Should I unplug my computer and TV during a storm?** No, not during a storm. Electronic devices should be unplugged before a storm arrives. A few years ago, a man in Phoenix unplugged a device at the precise moment when lightning struck. He was thrown across the room.

Every year, the insurance industry pays out about a third of a million dollars in claims for losses due to lightning. Many of these losses involve electronics that are blown out by power surges.

It's a good idea to protect electronic equipment—stereos, TVs, computers, etc.—with surge protectors. Good-quality ones typically cost between $50 and $100. Like the surge protection built into houses, however, they don't offer 100% protection. Unplugging devices before a storm is the best approach.

● **Can I get electrocuted in the shower or bath?** There was a report a few years ago of someone who was killed by lightning when taking a shower. Faucets, knobs and other metal fixtures are natural conductors of electricity. So is water. A lightning strike that hits your house—or even comes close—could potentially carry enough electricity indoors through these natural conductors to cause injury or death.

● **How safe am I in a car during a thunderstorm?** A fully enclosed metal-topped vehicle is generally safe. (A convertible with a vinyl or cloth top is not safe.) The metal-topped vehicle may protect you for the same reason that buildings do—the lightning travels through the framework and to the ground. Even if you happened to be touching a metal component, such as a door handle, most of the electricity would flow around (not through) you.

There have been cases in which a lightning strike vaporized a car antenna and broke the car's windows, but the people inside were unharmed.

Some people think that it's the rubber tires that make a car safe. Not true. A few inches of rubber can't possibly "ground" a car.

● **Is it really that dangerous to be under a tree during a thunderstorm?** It's one of the most dangerous places you can be. Lightning tends to hit the tallest objects in an area. Trees are a natural target, but the lightning doesn't stop there. Electricity always seeks the easiest path to the ground. Since people conduct electricity better than trees, the lightning may jump sideways (a "side flash") if you're within three to six feet of the trunk.

● **Is it true that golfers often get hit by lightning?** Fewer than 5% of direct lightning strikes have involved golfers. However, golfers do share with other outdoor enthusiasts the two main risk factors for lightning strikes—they're out in the open, and they're often higher than the surrounding terrain.

Water activities—boating, swimming, etc.—also are risky. The current from lightning hitting water or a boat travels across the surface of the water for tens of yards and can be deadly within that distance. Check weather reports, and stay off the water if there is a chance of a storm.

● **How can I tell if lightning is close enough to be dangerous?** A thunderstorm doesn't have to be overhead to be dangerous. When you see a lightning flash, count the seconds until you hear thunder. If the interval between lightning and thunder is 30 seconds or less, get inside a substantial building or a metal-topped vehicle. Wait 30 minutes after the last flash before going back outside.

● **Does lightning ever hit the same place twice?** It happens all the time. The Empire State Building gets hit an average of 23 times a year.

● **Should I close house windows during a thunderstorm?** Most people do close windows, if only to keep out the wind and rain. However, lightning is no more likely to strike through an open window than a closed one.

381

Caution: Always close windows if there's a tree nearby. You also might want to close blinds or curtains. A lightning strike can cause the bark to explode off the trunk, and the bark can travel about 50 feet. People have been killed by flying bark. A window might offer some protection.

●**Does it make sense to get a lightning rod for my home?** Several hundred thousand homes and small businesses are hit by lightning each year in the US. But because of grounded electrical and plumbing systems, electricity from a lightning strike flows around you—through walls, plumbing and wiring—and dissipates into the ground. (Small sheds, picnic pavilions and the like are not safe from lightning.)

These days, lightning rods are usually used to protect hospitals, schools, police stations and similar structures. When lightning hits, a lightning rod and its attached thick cable take the surge in current safely to the ground.

A lightning rod on your home is not necessary, but it can offer some peace of mind. The rod is more likely to take the hit than the roof or another part of the house. Having the rod take the hit means that the massive current surge has a preferred path to follow. Otherwise, the current rips through the house and looks for something to carry it, usually the wiring or plumbing. But if the current doesn't find these paths very quickly in a short distance, then fire and other damage can occur.

A rod costs about $1,000 or more installed. Installation must be done by a licensed professional who specializes in lightning protection (check the yellow pages, or search under "lightning rod installation" on the Internet).

Dangers in Your Own Backyard

Richard O'Brien, MD, spokesman for the American College of Emergency Physicians. *www.acep.org*. He is clinical instructor at Temple University School of Medicine and an emergency physician at Moses Taylor Hospital, both in Scranton, Pennsylvania.

The combination of warm weather and outdoor activities sends millions of Americans to emergency rooms each summer.

Most of their injuries could have been prevented. *Here, an emergency room physician reveals the biggest dangers and how to avoid them...*

LAWN MOWERS

The lawn mower is probably the most dangerous tool around the house. A nine-year study published in *Annals of Emergency Medicine* reports an annual average of 74,000 emergency room visits due to lawn mower injuries. Most injuries are caused by debris flying into the bodies or eyes of lawn mower operators and bystanders. About one-third of lawn mower–related hospitalizations are due to injuries from the blades, including the loss of toes and/or fingers.

Self-defense: Remove twigs, sticks and rocks before mowing. Keep bystanders, especially children, away from the mower. Wear shoes—not sandals—long pants and safety goggles while mowing. Don't depend on glasses or sunglasses to protect eyes—they won't prevent debris from entering at the sides.

Also, wear hearing protection (ear plugs, ear mufflers, etc.). Don't use an iPod or similar portable music device—you really have to crank up the volume to hear the music, which can result in permanent hearing damage.

ELECTRIC HEDGE TRIMMERS

I see at least one patient a month who has been hurt by a hedge trimmer. It can cut off a finger instantly or cause a nasty injury—crushing tissue and bone—that is very difficult to repair.

Self-defense: Wear heavy leather or canvas gloves, sturdy shoes and long pants when using a trimmer. Don't overreach—you may lose your balance. Turn off the trimmer and unplug it before trying to clear it of stuck debris.

GARAGE DOORS

Some manual and electric garage doors have large, heavy springs on each side. A spring that suddenly loosens can hit your head with the force of a swinging baseball bat. A spring also can take off a finger.

Self-defense: Never attempt to repair or replace a garage door yourself. Hire an experienced professional to do it.

TICK BITES

Lyme disease gets most of the headlines, but ticks carry many other diseases, including ehrlichiosis and Rocky Mountain spotted fever, both bacterial infections that can cause fatigue, fever, severe muscle pain and headaches—and also can be life-threatening.

Self-defense: Removing a tick from your skin within 12 to 24 hours almost guarantees that you won't get sick. Grip the tick close to the skin with tweezers and pull it out. If part of the tick remains in the skin, try your best to remove it. If you're not able to remove it all, see a doctor. Wash the area well, and apply an antibiotic ointment to prevent infection.

If you're spending time in grassy or wooded areas, you can prevent most tick bites by using an insect repellent that contains DEET. Apply the repellent to exposed skin and clothing. A non-DEET repellent, Picaridin, is useful for people whose skin is sensitive to DEET. Also wear closed shoes rather than sandals…tuck long pants into socks…and wear a long-sleeved shirt, tucked in.

POISON IVY, OAK AND SUMAC

All of these plants contain *urushiol,* an oily substance that can cause an itchy rash in people who are sensitive to it. (To view the plants so you can identify them, go to *www.poisonivy.aesir.com.*) As little as one-billionth of a gram of urushiol can cause the rash—so even brushing against one of these plants is a problem. The oil also can get on tools, gloves and clothing and stays active indefinitely, so it must be washed off.

Self-defense: If your skin comes into contact with one of the "poisons," wash the area immediately with soap and water. If you're outside and don't have access to soap or water, splash the area with any liquid—soda, beer, etc. If a rash develops, apply *hydrocortisone* ointment, available at drugstores. If the rash worsens, see a doctor.

CYCLING

Each year, bicycle accidents result in more than half a million visits to emergency rooms. More than 800 bicyclists die annually, many from head injuries.

Self-defense: Always wear a helmet, even if you (or your children) are riding close to home. Studies indicate that helmets are up to 85% effective in preventing head injuries. Helmets with visors are helpful for preventing facial lacerations. Be sure the helmet fits properly and is buckled snugly.

Warning: Most cycling deaths occur between 6 pm and 9 pm, when visibility is diminished. Wear reflective clothing to make yourself more visible.

SWIMMING

Drowning is a leading cause of accidental death in the US.

Reasons: People overestimate their swimming ability…panic in deep water or fast currents…or consume large amounts of alcohol before entering the water.

Self-defense: Enter unfamiliar water feet-first to prevent head and neck injuries. Don't depend on flotation devices—they can fail and sink. Never drink alcohol before or while swimming.

Danger for women: The bacteria that cause urinary tract infections thrive in moist environments. Women who sit around in wet swimsuits give these organisms an opportunity to proliferate and migrate into the urethra—and possibly up into the kidneys, resulting in a potentially life-threatening infection. Change into dry clothing after you're done swimming. Also, drink lots of water—it increases urination, which helps flush bacteria from the urethra.

Crime Season Alerts

Marjory Abrams, publisher, newsletters, Boardroom, Inc., 281 Tresser Blvd., Stamford, Connecticut 06901.

Knock on wood—I have never been pickpocketed, and my family hasn't experienced much in the way of theft. According to the FBI, July and August are the worst months of the year for property crime.

Personal safety expert Captain Robert Snow, commander of the Indianapolis Police Department's organized crime branch and author of *The Complete Guide to Personal and Home Safety,* offers this advice for the home…

●**Watch your back door.** Though many homes have sturdy front doors, other doors often are not made of solid material and may shatter easily. (That's why police SWAT teams typically try the back door first when they need to break into a building.) Avoid doors with windows. Outside doors should be made of metal or solid wood. Sliding glass doors should have bar locks (metal bars that prevent anyone from sliding open the door).

●**Watch your windows, too.** The ubiquitous turn locks are no good for windows. They can be opened easily from the outside using only a butter knife. Get locks that require pressing a button to lock into rails on both sides (you can add these to existing windows)—or drill a hole in the window casing and insert a dowel so that the window can't be opened.

●**Consider replacing basement windows** —prime targets for thieves—with glass bricks, which are hard to break.

●**Install bright lights with motion detectors outdoors.** Beware of solar-powered lights, which may not illuminate when you need them most.

There are plenty of precautions to take when you're away from home as well. I was surprised to learn from Captain Snow that 30% of vehicle thefts involve keys left in the car—either accidentally or when running into a store for a quick errand. Car thieves also do quite well at beaches, pilfering purses or loose car keys from lounge chairs and using the keys' panic alarms to locate vehicles in the parking lot.

I asked Kevin Coffey, author of *Traveler Beware! An Undercover Cop's Guide to Avoiding Pickpockets, Luggage Theft, and Travel Scams,* for strategies to deter theft while traveling. He says that thieves just love carry-on bags (other people's, that is). Why? That's where travelers keep their valuables. Always rest your luggage in front of you—never to your side, in back of you or in a cart.

Be cautious when strangers strike up unprovoked conversations. Often, an accomplice may be waiting for you to be distracted. Coffey says that the best crooks are superb actors and will stage entirely believable fistfights or other dramas. While you help the "victim," someone else steals your wallet.

Be especially alert when strangers seem to require your help or offer to help you. Safeguard your property before you offer assistance—or bring the situation to the attention of a police officer or security guard.

Thieves have been known to squirt their targets with mayonnaise and then tell them that they are covered with bird poop or some other objectionable substance. The crook is kind enough to help wash the stuff off—while the accomplice does his work.

For other thief-thwarting strategies, go to *www.kevincoffey.com* and click on "Safety Tips." Stay safe!

Scammed! What We All Can Learn from These Real-Life Victims

Audri Lanford, PhD, cofounder and coeditor of ScamBusters.org, a Web site devoted to informing the public about scams and cons, based in Boone, North Carolina. For a free subscription to the ScamBusters E-letter, go to *www.scambusters.org.*

Con artists are experts at talking people out of their money. In one study conducted by AARP, 26% of those surveyed had been the victim of a scam. *Here are the stories* of five people targeted by con artists and the lessons we can learn from them...*

CREDIT CARD TRICK

Carrie, an executive and frequent business traveler, was awakened in her hotel room one night by a call from the front desk. The clerk apologized for the hour and said that the day shift had gone home without completing her registration and he needed to confirm some information. Could he have the last four digits of her credit card number?

Carrie, groggy from sleep, provided the numbers, and the clerk became perplexed. "Those aren't the numbers I have here," he said. "You had better give me the whole card number so I can reenter it." He apologized once more for the inconvenience.

Only Carrie didn't give him the number— by this time, she correctly suspected that she wasn't speaking to the front desk at all. Carrie

*These stories are based on actual cases reported to ScamBusters.org. The names have been changed to protect privacy.

told the "clerk" that she would deal with the problem in the morning and then hung up.

Lesson: Always be wary about giving out your credit card number. Also, con men like to throw you off-balance. Waking you in the middle of the night is one such tactic. Other common tactics include saying that a family member is in the hospital or that you have just won a big prize.

OVERPAYMENT

When Dana's purebred bulldog gave birth to puppies, she put them up for sale on the Internet for $2,000 each. A check arrived from a buyer for $2,200—$200 too much. Dana contacted the buyer, who said that the extra was to cover shipping. The buyer had made arrangements with an animal-transport company and asked Dana to send the company a check for $200. Dana complied, and the puppy was picked up. Only later did her bank tell her that the buyer's $2,200 check had bounced. By then, it was too late to get back the puppy and stop payment on her check, which had gone to a scam artist.

Lesson: It can take weeks for your bank to determine that a check is bad—sometimes more than a month, in the case of foreign or cashier's checks. Even if your bank has made the funds available to you, that's no guarantee that the check has cleared and the funds won't be recalled. If you must accept a large check, call your bank and ask when it will know for sure that the check is good.

Scam variation: An American is "hired" by a foreign company looking for local representatives to process payments. When the company's "customers" send payments, the American deposits the checks in his/her own account, then writes a check for 90% of the total amount to the foreign company's headquarters and pockets the difference. By the time the American discovers that the checks he received have bounced, he already has sent several checks, which have been cashed. One man lost $8,400 this way.

FOREIGN INHERITANCE

Sarah, a woman with strong religious beliefs, was contacted via e-mail by a person who said that she was an elderly widow living overseas. The widow was looking for someone to help her use her late husband's money to spread the word

of God. She said she was dying of cancer and had no children or other family. The two women traded e-mails about religion and the Bible, and eventually Sarah agreed to help. A short time later, the plan hit a snag—there were unexpected taxes and fees involved in transferring the widow's money, and with most of her funds tied up by this snafu, the widow couldn't afford to pay the charges. Sarah agreed to send a check for several hundred dollars. A week later, the widow reported another snag and more fees. Sarah grew suspicious and ended the relationship.

Lesson: Sarah responded to the e-mail because of her desire to help others. It could have been much worse—many people who fall for this scam lose thousands of dollars, not just a few hundred. Sarah got off cheap, in part because she was willing to admit to herself that she had been had. Many victims send numerous checks for ever-larger amounts before they concede that something is wrong. It's easier to write another check than admit to themselves that they have been fooled.

"YOU'RE BEING SCAMMED"

Andy received an e-mail from what seemed like the Internet transaction company PayPal. The e-mail said that the company's security programs had registered attempts to log into his account from an overseas address. Had he tried to use PayPal while traveling internationally? If not, he should click the link in the e-mail to report fraud.

Andy hadn't left the country, so he clicked the link. In truth, no one had tried to log into his account—yet. The e-mail warning of the fraud came from a scammer, not from PayPal, and the link directed Andy to a sham site that only appeared to be a PayPal site. He was prompted to provide his account number and password when reporting the fraud, and the scammer used this information to steal the $450 that was in his real PayPal account.

Lesson: Links in e-mail messages can't be trusted. Andy could have made sure he was dealing with the real PayPal by typing *www. paypal.com* into his Web browser and accessing his account independently. This scam also shows how clever con artists can be in throwing us off guard—the scammer panicked Andy by telling him that he was being scammed.

JURY DUTY

Thelma, a single mother, received a call from the county clerk. She had failed to report for jury duty, so a warrant had been issued for her arrest. Thelma argued that she had never received a jury duty notice, but the clerk was skeptical. Finally, he consented to check out her story. What was Thelma's Social Security number so he could make sure he had the right person? Thelma wisely refused to provide it.

Lesson: The phrase "Social Security number" should always put you on high alert—even if you've been thrown off-balance by a con man's tale of a warrant issued for your arrest. To verify whether a caller is legitimate, hang up, look up the phone number of the office or organization that seems to be calling and call that number.

How to Survive a Disaster

Amanda Ripley, a senior writer for *Time* magazine, based in Washington, DC, who covers homeland security and risk for the publication. She covered the 9/11 terrorist attacks in New York City and Hurricanes Katrina and Rita from New Orleans, helping *Time* win two *National Magazine Awards*. She has traveled the world studying disasters, natural and man-made, and is author of *The Unthinkable: Who Survives When Disaster Strikes—and Why*. Crown. *www.theunthinkable.com*.

Most people assume that they have little control over whether they live or die in a disaster. In reality, we have more control over our fate than we realize. We interviewed Amanda Ripley, author of *The Unthinkable: Who Survives When Disaster Strikes—and Why*, about what we can do to improve our odds.

PREPARING WELL IN ADVANCE

Eight ways you can prepare for the unknown…

●**Understand the freeze response.** People worry that they will panic in a disaster, but a far greater danger is that they will freeze up and do nothing. This reaction is rooted in survival instincts from deep in humanity's past—predators sometimes abort their attacks when their prey fails to fight back—but it can be deadly in modern disasters.

Example: Survivors of the 1994 MV Estonia ferry disaster in the Baltic Sea reported that some passengers stood around doing nothing as the ship sank.

If traumas and shocks have caused you to temporarily freeze up in the past, remind yourself that your urge to delay (or gather unnecessary items before fleeing) is not productive, though it might feel very natural in the heat of the moment.

Also, so you can help others, be aware that loud shouting tends to snap people out of a trance. Flight attendants on some airlines are trained to scream, "Get out!" at passengers on planes that are on fire, rather than speak to them politely.

●**Put less faith in your experience.** Our past experiences play a major role in shaping our responses to future events. If local authorities have warned you to evacuate your home during five previous storms, but each warning turned out to be unnecessary, your experience might tell you that there's no need to evacuate for future storms.

Unfortunately, experience does a poor job of preparing us for exceptional situations. The fact that your home has survived five previous hurricanes does not guarantee that it will survive a direct hit or a more powerful storm. Older people are particularly likely to put too much faith in past experiences during a disaster because they are most likely to have survived previous ones.

Example: Almost three-quarters of those killed by Hurricane Katrina in 2005 were over age 60, old enough to remember similar warnings about Hurricane Betsy in 1965 and Hurricane Camille in 1969. Many of them may have concluded that there was no need to evacuate.

●**Know your surroundings, wherever you are.** Knowing the location of a building's fire escape routes or a town's storm evacuation route not only makes it easier to find these emergency routes, it also increases the odds that your brain will continue to function productively during a disaster.

In high-stress disaster situations, our brains rapidly sort through our relevant knowledge in search of useful information and an appropriate response. If we have no relevant information in our mental files, it greatly increases the odds that our brain will shut down or that it will come up with a solution that isn't helpful, such as waiting for an elevator rather than taking the stairs to get out of a burning building.

A piece of information as simple as "this is the evacuation route" can be enough to keep us thinking straight and get us moving in the right direction, particularly if this information is familiar enough that it is second nature.

Example: Many people think that nearly all passengers in airline accidents die. In fact, between 1983 and 2000, 56% of passengers aboard planes that suffered serious accidents survived. Passengers who review the airline safety information card before every flight are more likely to have evacuation routes and basic safety procedures ingrained in their minds and are more likely to survive an accident, according to the National Transportation Safety Board.

The safest seat on an airplane…is the one you can get out of fastest. So the aisle seat near an exit row is slightly safer than other seats on a plane, on average, according to a study from University of Greenwich in London, England.

●**Get to know your neighbors.** Professional rescue teams might be slow to reach you in a disaster. Your neighbors are much closer—and they are your best chance for survival if you are trapped or injured during a disaster. The better your neighbors know you, the more likely they are to check on your safety.

●**Take control of your life.** People who chronically see themselves as victims of events are likely to respond poorly to disasters. If you are prone to a victim mentality, pick some element of your life and prove to yourself that you can take control of it. Change something about yourself that you have always wanted to change…or gain knowledge that helps you control your fears.

Example: If you fear flying, read about airplane design. Understanding the basics of aeronautics can help you feel that you have a measure of control even in a plane, increasing the odds that you will remain calm and react well if you are involved in a crash.

●**Honestly assess your blind spots.** Do you consider fire drills foolish? Do you walk brazenly through open areas during lightning storms? Would you drive your car across a flooded road? Lightning, fire and flood are the most consistently underestimated dangers in the US and cause many avoidable deaths. Start treating these risks with greater caution.

Men, in particular, are more likely to die in fires, floods, lightning storms and hurricanes, partly because men are more likely than women to be overconfident in their abilities. This overconfidence leads some men to downplay or ignore impending dangers and evacuation warnings, sometimes until it's too late to escape. Overconfidence also causes men to attempt to drive or swim across flooded areas or walk across open areas during lightning storms.

●**Meditate.** A 2005 study led by Harvard Medical School instructor Sara Lazar found that meditating on a regular basis expands the portion of the brain, the prefrontal cortex, that handles decision making under extreme stress.

●**Shed excess pounds.** Overweight people are more likely than fit people to die in disasters. They cannot flee danger as quickly and are at greater risk for secondary injuries, such as heart attacks triggered by the stress.

DURING A DISASTER

Things to do during a disaster…

●**Breathe deeply.** Breathe in for four counts, hold for four counts, then breathe out for four counts—and repeat until the fear abates. Some police departments now train officers to use deep-breathing techniques to tamp down the natural fear response during high-speed pursuits.

●**Think of your family.** Many disaster survivors report that thoughts of loved ones helped them continue fighting for life when they were on the verge of giving up.

●**Think like a soldier.** Anecdotal evidence suggests that former soldiers are more likely to survive disasters than the rest of us. They know to assess the situation…consider the options… select what seems to be the best one…then take action. This regimented system leaves little room for the worry and confusion that prevents many disaster victims from acting promptly.

Example: When former Navy pilot Joe Stiley was trapped in a crashed airliner sinking to the bottom of the frozen Potomac River in 1982, he calmly implemented a plan of action—free his trapped left leg…remove his seat belt…free his trapped colleague…swim out of the plane. Having this step-by-step plan kept him focused on his task so that his mind did not become overwhelmed by the situation.

387

Only five of the 79 people aboard survived, but Stiley and his colleague were among them.

Cell-Phone Dangers

Rebecca Shannonhouse, editor, *Bottom Line/Health*, 281 Tresser Blvd., Stamford, Connecticut 06901.

There are more than 208 million cell-phone users in the US—and researchers are now beginning to identify some of the associated risks.

While studies have shown that there appears to be no increase in the risk for brain cancer among cell-phone users, these devices may not be safe in all circumstances.

Driving while talking on a cell phone is dangerous—even if you're using a "hands-free" model. A new study indicates that motorists who talk on *any* type of cell phone show the same kind and degree of impairment—such as slowed reaction times—as drunken drivers.

People engaged in cell-phone conversations experience "inattention blindness"—even though they're looking at the road and traffic, their ability to process information drops by as much as 50%, explains Frank Drews, PhD, professor of psychology at the University of Utah in Salt Lake City and coauthor of the study.

Some people argue that other distractions, such as putting on makeup or talking to a passenger, are equally risky, but Drews doesn't buy it. "I've never seen a driver putting on makeup in the car—but at least every fourth or fifth driver is on a cell phone."

Meanwhile, in London, a 15-year-old girl recently suffered severe injuries after being struck by lightning while talking on her cell phone. People struck by lightning are often not critically injured, but holding a cell phone to the ear during a storm can provide a conduit that allows electricity—more than 100 million volts, in some cases—to flow into the body.

These recent developments show that it pays to think before you pick up a cell phone.

Terror Alert—Our Food Is in Danger

Marion Nestle, PhD, MPH, Paulette Goddard Professor of nutrition, food studies and public health at New York University in New York City. She is also the author of *Safe Food: Bacteria, Biotechnology and Bioterrorism*. University of California.

Virtually all Americans feel threatened by terrorism. But there's relatively little discussion of one of the most frightening scenarios—deliberate food poisoning by our enemies. How safe is our food supply? What can we do to protect ourselves?

Marion Nestle, PhD, MPH, a leading expert in food safety, gives some answers below…

●**Is our food actually vulnerable to terrorism?** Our food is vulnerable, period. According to the Centers for Disease Control and Prevention, there are an estimated 76 million cases of food poisoning yearly in the US, which cause 325,000 hospitalizations and 5,000 deaths.

These are presumably the result of accidental contamination. And if our food-safety system can't prevent them, it certainly can't protect us against intentional food-borne illness.

No one can say for sure just how serious the threat of food terrorism is. Uncertainty is one of the things that makes terrorism so frightening —by nature, it's unpredictable.

●**What are the possible scenarios?** The one known case of politically motivated food terrorism in the US happened in 1984 and involved a domestic group. The members of a religious cult had established a commune in a small town in Oregon, and a dispute arose with their neighbors over use of land. To disrupt a county election, members of the cult sprinkled toxic Salmonella bacterium on salad bars and in cream pitchers in 10 restaurants—750 people got sick, 45 severely enough to be hospitalized.

Other instances of deliberate food contamination both here and abroad include the case of an angry employee at a large medical center in Dallas who gave his coworkers doughnuts and muffins tainted with *Shigella* bacterium, causing severe gastrointestinal illness…citrus fruits harvested in Israel that were laced with mercury…and grapes from Chile that were poisoned with cyanide.

Cases of accidental food poisoning demonstrate the wider vulnerability of our food supply. One outbreak of Salmonella poisoning in 1994 affected more than 220,000 people in 41 states. The source was discovered to be a premixed ice cream base (a mixture of eggs and cream). It was shipped to a processing plant in a tanker truck that had previously carried unpasteurized liquid eggs and hadn't been properly cleaned.

A terrorist who wanted to make hundreds of thousands of people sick could introduce a handful of *Salmonella* or *Listeria* bacterium into a truck, and if no one is checking, it could have far-reaching consequences.

●**Isn't our government checking?** If people assume that everything they eat has passed some sort of government inspection, they're wrong. The current system is riddled with holes.

For one thing, oversight is fragmented. The US Department of Agriculture is responsible for the safety of meat, eggs and poultry, while fruits, vegetables and most other foods fall under the jurisdiction of the Food and Drug Administration.

Other agencies—the US Department of Commerce, which has a hand in seafood inspection, the Environmental Protection Agency and the Customs Department, among others—play lesser roles. However, their efforts are not coordinated with one another.

Big problem: Government inspections aren't routine. Measures to prevent contamination through proper food handling and bacteria control rely on voluntary compliance by food companies and random sampling. Full-scale inspections don't happen unless people start getting sick.

Imported food—an obvious concern when terrorism is the issue—is a case in point. We bring in approximately $50 billion worth of fresh and processed foods yearly, and food imports have been involved in a number of food-poisoning outbreaks.

A few years ago, more than 550 people were unintentionally infected with hepatitis A from green onions that were imported from Mexico. Three of the victims ended up dying.

●**How can we protect ourselves?** By following the same basic household safety procedures

that we all should be taking to minimize the risk for accidental contamination. These steps offer some protection against food terrorism by killing bacteria that may be intentionally added to food.

To make sure that meat, poultry, egg dishes, casseroles and other types of foods are fully cooked, always use a clean food thermometer to determine the internal temperature of the food you are cooking.

Cook ground beef, pork roasts and chops to at least 160°F, beef roasts and steaks to 145°F for medium rare, or to 160°F for medium. Cook whole poultry to 180°F and chicken breasts to 170°F. Cook eggs until the yolks and whites are firm. Don't use recipes in which eggs remain raw or only partially cooked.

When reheating leftovers, heat them thoroughly to at least 165°F. When cooking in a microwave oven, make sure there are no cold spots in food where bacteria can survive. Cover food and stir for even cooking. Rotate the dish once or twice during cooking if your microwave does not have a turntable.

Cold foods should be kept at 40°F or colder. Defrost food in the refrigerator. Never thaw food on the counter. Refrigerate or freeze perishables, prepared foods and leftovers within two hours or less.

●**How effective are these practices?** The most effective way to prevent food contamination—either accidental or deliberate—is a coordinated program that's called Hazard Analysis and Critical Control Point (HACCP). This means identifying all the places where contamination can occur and having procedures in place to make sure it doesn't happen.

There are HACCP programs in various food industries, including meat and poultry, eggs and fruit juices, but, by and large, these aren't as effective as they could be because of flaws in design and sloppiness in carrying them out. If we want to prevent intentional contamination, more careful monitoring is essential.

For more information on keeping food free from bacteria, go to the Partnership for Food Safety Education's Web site, *www.fightbac.org* or call the FDA's Food Safety Information Hotline at 888-723-3366.

Dangerous Things That Don't Seem Dangerous at All

Laura Lee, a researcher located in Rochester, Michigan, and the author of eight books, including *100 Most Dangerous Things in Everyday Life and What You Can Do About Them.* Broadway.

Most of us tend to worry about the wrong things. We worry about safety each time we board an airplane, though we are far more likely to die in a car accident.

Some seemingly harmless products pose significant risks that most Americans have never considered. *Here, four of the surprising dangers that most of us encounter regularly...*

DISHWASHERS

Each year, an average of about 7,500 Americans suffer dishwasher-related injuries. Most of these are cuts or punctures caused by upturned knives or forks.

Steam burns from opening up the door and leaning over the dishwasher—or reaching in immediately after the cycle is finished—also are common dishwasher injuries.

Young children and pets can be poisoned if they ingest the soap residue in the dispensing compartment. According to research by the Royal Children's Hospital of Australia, far more children are poisoned this way than by eating dishwashing detergent out of the box.

Self-defense: Always load knives and forks into your dishwasher with their pointy ends down. And, stand clear when opening the door immediately after the cycle ends. If children or pets are around, remove any residue from the compartment as soon as the door is opened.

BAGELS

Their hard crusts require a sharp knife and significant force. The result can be a serious hand injury. How great is the danger? No definitive statistics are available, but American emergency rooms report that palms sliced open by kitchen knives, often with serious ligament or tendon damage, are among the most common accidents they treat. Emergency medics even have a phrase for this type of injury—they call it "bagel hand."

A bagel's hard crust also can damage the esophagus if too large a piece is swallowed.

Self-defense: Buy a bagel slicer. For $10 to $20, your hands will be safe. If you use a cutting board, slice the bagel away from your body with a good-quality serrated bread knife. If no cutting board is available, use your palm to hold the bagel flat on a counter, being careful not to curl your fingers around it. Slice parallel to the counter and away from your body.

COTTON SWABS

Cotton swabs carry warnings on their packaging that caution against putting them in ears—yet that is exactly how most people use them. In 1999 alone, 6,500 people in Britain went to the hospital for cotton-swab accidents—more than twice the number that hurt themselves with razors, the seemingly more dangerous grooming item.

Figures on total injuries aren't kept in the US, but there were at least 100 documented cases of "serious" eardrum injuries caused by cotton swabs in this country between 1992 and 1997.

Self-defense: Never insert a cotton swab in your ear. Even if you don't pierce your eardrum, you may push earwax further in, which can do serious damage to the lining of your ear canal and eardrum. Earwax generally will work its way out on its own through the actions of the jawbone.

CRUTCHES AND WHEELCHAIRS

These devices, designed to help us cope with injuries, can lead to new ones. Crutches are involved in some 74,000 injuries in the US each year and wheelchairs account for about 95,000. Many of these injuries occur when the crutches or wheelchairs are used on slick or uneven surfaces. Stairs are particularly challenging.

Self-defense: Learn to handle these rehabilitation aids properly before you use them in challenging conditions. Using crutches can be tiring, so rest often. Even if you don't feel tired, prolonged crutch use can cause nerve damage in the armpits and numbness in the hands, leading to falls. Crutches become even more hazardous when set to the incorrect height—the proper height is two inches below your armpit while standing.

Don't let anyone carry your wheelchair up or down a flight of stairs while you are in it unless there are no other options and you trust the carriers' strength and coordination.

Index

A

AAA travel discounts, 165–66
Abdominal exercise, 235
AB-rated generic drugs, 184–85
Accidents
  checking used cars for, 158
  occurrence of, in parking
    lots, 369–70
Account, delays in crediting
  your, 33
Accountant, finding, 332
Acetyl-L-carnitine in protecting
  ears, 225
Acne
  natural remedies
    for, 210–11, 224
  saving money on creams
    for, 204
Adoptions
  employer assistance for, 266
  tax breaks for, 265–67
Advertising, getting free
  newspaper, 334–35
Affordable travel club, 106–7
Airlines
  checking flight status, 130

complaining to, 129–30
frequent-flier program
  in, 115, 131
getting best seats on, 114–15
getting discounts on
  charter, 118
getting free day trip on, 115
getting refund on fare, 115
inside information on, 118
Registered Traveler program
  and, 126
saving on round-trip, 118
senior discounts for, 6
timing in booking seats on, 123
Airports
  check-in lines at, 114
  free parking at, 114
  rental cars away from, 115
  rights in searching at, 114
Alarm discount on home
  insurance, 62
Alcoholic beverages, saving on, 16
Allergies, supplements in
  relieving, 209–10
Allergy tests, uses of, 210
Almonds for weight loss, 237

Aloe vera natural remedies
  for psoriasis, 224
  for wounds/burns, 224
Alpha-lipoic acid in protecting
  ears, 225
Alternative minimum tax (AMT),
  248–49
  relief from, 251
  warding off, 257
Alternative treatments,
  investigating, 190
Alzheimer's disease
  aspirin for, 196
  curry for, 226
America Dog & Cat Hotel, 111
American Association of Retired
  Persons (AARP)
  discounts, 5
  free legal help for
    members, 297
American Bar Association
  (ABA), 376
Forum on Franchising of
  the, 339
American Volkssport
  Association, 242